Introduction to Business Analytics Using Simulation

Jonathan P. Pinder
Wake Forest University
School of Business
Winston-Salem, NC, United States

ELSEVIER

ACADEMIC PRESS
An imprint of Elsevier

Introduction to Business Analytics Using Simulation

Academic Press is an imprint of Elsevier
125 London Wall, London EC2Y 5AS, United Kingdom
525 B Street, Suite 1800, San Diego, CA 92101, United States
50 Hampshire Street, 5th Floor, Cambridge, MA 02139, United States
The Boulevard, Langford Lane, Kidlington, Oxford OX5 1GB, United Kingdom

Notices

Knowledge and best practice in this field are constantly changing. As new research and experience broaden our understanding, changes in research methods, professional practices, or medical treatment may become necessary.

Practitioners and researchers must always rely on their own experience and knowledge in evaluating and using any information, methods, compounds, or experiments described herein. In using such information or methods they should be mindful of their own safety and the safety of others, including parties for whom they have a professional responsibility.

To the fullest extent of the law, neither the Publisher nor the authors, contributors, or editors, assume any liability for any injury and/or damage to persons or property as a matter of products liability, negligence or otherwise, or from any use or operation of any methods, products, instructions, or ideas contained in the material herein.

Library of Congress Cataloging-in-Publication Data
A catalog record for this book is available from the Library of Congress

British Library Cataloguing-in-Publication Data
A catalogue record for this book is available from the British Library

ISBN: 978-0-323-91717-9

For information on all Academic Press publications
visit our website at https://www.elsevier.com/

Publisher: Katey Birtcher
Editorial Project Manager: Naomi Robertson
Production Project Manager: Nadhiya Sekar
Designer: Ryan Cook

Printed by King Printing Co., Inc.

Printed in the United States of America
Last digit is the print number: 9 8 7 6 5 4 3 2

Preface

The primary objective of business analytics is using information to make optimum rational business decisions. As managers do not know what will happen in the future, uncertainty is an essential element in real decision making. *Introduction to Business Analytics Using Simulation Models* introduces students to the reality of managerial decision making under uncertainty in the context of business analytics. In the current parlance of business analytics, this book presents the foundations for *prescriptive analytics*.

Simulation is integrated throughout the book as a mechanism to introduce and link the business analytics topics of descriptive, predictive, and prescriptive modeling for undergraduate and masters-level business students. This book is innovative because it integrates simulation and decision making from the very first chapter and continues it throughout the entire book. As this book demonstrates the true uncertainty and variability found in business practice, it provides a better foundation for business analytics for business majors than do standard introductory business statistics books.

Concomitant with accounting, the course this textbook is designed for is often business students' first encounter with how businesses operate. Students at this juncture of their education require exposure to the uncertainty engrained in the applications found in the functional areas of accounting, finance, human resource management, marketing, and operations management. This book uses simulation applications from each functional area, as well as other risk management applications, throughout the entire book.

The forward-thinking pedagogical view is that introductory probability and statistics courses should be simulation based to provide inexperienced students with a firsthand understanding, through experiential learning, of the true, messy, and ambiguous nature of the unknowable (uncertain) future that inextricable links probability to data analysis and decision making. As an example, will one ad campaign work better than another ad campaign? If so, how much should be budgeted? These decisions require an analysis of past data (if it exists), understanding of the uncertain future, and an optimization process to select the best decision. Simulation is better suited pedagogically for the descriptive, predictive, and prescriptive phases of business analytics than conventional methods are because:

1. Students can see how the data were generated. This allows students to experience the true variation in data rather than relying on descriptive statistics that students believe are completely perfect (accurate) in the manner of traditional math classes.
2. When students can understand how data are generated, they become better at analyzing data.
3. Choosing the optimum decisions makes the students quickly realize why they need probability. They are not calculating probabilities simply for the sake of calculating probabilities; the probabilities are embedded in the simulations and decision-making applications. In this manner, they experience why they need probability to make decisions.

Excel is used for all the examples and exercises in the book because Excel is used ubiquitously in business and in business school courses that follow the introductory course. Furthermore, several very useful analytics templates (regression, probability distributions, hypothesis testing, etc.) are available to facilitate the data analyses and simulations.

In teaching preliminary versions of this book, it has become obvious that simulation is essential for solving complex probability problems and to convey statistical and probabilistic topics that students have extreme difficulty grasping. Consider these two examples. First, a simulation demonstrating that ordering to meet demand on average will never meet demand on average, connects students in a real world management fallacy and they get a managerial insight often missed by practicing managers. Second, a simulation of a sample of 43 stores' revenues clearly demonstrates to the students the concepts of standard error versus standard deviation—a concept that is exceedingly difficult for most students to grasp through mathematical notation.

Thus, this book uniquely integrates the standard topics found in introductory business statistics and business analytics courses by using simulation as a pedagogical vehicle and as managerial decision-making tool. As such, students exit the course with practical Excel skills, an introductory proficiency with probability and fundamental statistical procedures, managerial decision-making skills, a deeper understanding of the role of probability in decision making, and an understanding of managerial issues encountered in various functional areas.

Acknowledgments

Love and thanks to my wonderful wife Julie—I won the matrimonial lottery; and my wonderful family, Alexander, Margaret, Matthew, Thomas, and Elizabeth—always with love.

Many thanks to the students of Wake Forest University—you make getting up and coming to work each day a joy. It is a privilege, pleasure, and honor to be in class with you.

Finally, a special thank you to Katey Birtcher for giving me the chance, Naomi Robertson for guiding me, and Nadhiya Sekar for the meticulous detail work. You three have made the book come true.

Contents

Contents

Business analytics is making decisions

If a man will begin with certainties, he shall end in doubts; but if he will be content to begin with doubts, he shall end in certainties.
Francis Bacon (1605)

Chapter outline

Introduction

This chapter introduces the topics within business analytics and the analytic process of using probability to make business decisions that have a high degree of uncertainty. Decision analysis and Monte Carlo simulation are introduced as methods of understanding, structuring, and making managerial decisions.

1.1 Business analytics is making decisions subject to uncertainty

Decisions are made in every area of directing a business (Fig. 1.1). What is the long-term strategy of the company? Does the firm need to hire? How are cash flow problems handled? Under what conditions does the company obtain financial backing for capital development? How should the company's products and services be marketed? How should the company conduct research and development? Will customer demand continue? What is the lost opportunity if the company fails to meet customer demand?

Introduction to Business Analytics Using Simulation. https://doi.org/10.1016/B978-0-323-91717-9.00001-2

1

FIGURE 1.1 Drawing of a Gargoyle at Oxford University.

How is capacity to be managed? Does the company build, lease, subcontract, expand its present facility, relocate, and automate? Will competitors also increase capacity? Thus managers must continuously make decisions about investments, products, resources, suppliers, financing, and marketing methods, among other items.

Suppose you are a brand manager in your company's snack foods division. After a number of successful years in the market, your snack product has matured and sales have begun to decline. A brand extension has been proposed. How do you decide if this is the right course of action? Or perhaps you work for an electronics superstore chain that wants to expand. You've been assigned the task of choosing where to locate new stores. Your team is generating lots of ideas for sites. How do you know when to call a halt to the research and select from among the various alternatives?

These and many other decisions are determined every day in offices around the globe. The difficulty in making such decisions arises from uncertainty of the consequences of the decisions. Risk, the likelihood of incurring negative consequences, such as a loss, is inevitably involved in undertaking these decisions. Thus risk assessment and risk management are critical to effective management.

This book provides a foundation for managerial economic decision making and for subsequent topics such as risk management and real options. Furthermore, there is the added benefit that such decision-making skills can be applied to decisions in your personal life, such as how much to offer (bid) when buying a house, and many other decisions.

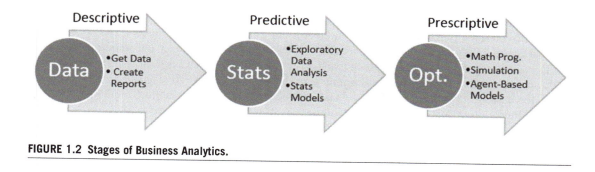

FIGURE 1.2 Stages of Business Analytics.

Stephen Jay Gould said, "Misunderstanding of probability may be the greatest of all impediments to scientific literacy." The aim of this book is to give students—through simulation—a better understanding of probability and how to make decisions in the face of the pervasive uncertainty we all face.

1.2 Components of business analytics

Business analytics is using data to build analytic models to manage decisions in the face of the unknown (uncertain) future. To accomplish the optimum decisions, business analytics is the synthesis and integration of the fields of statistical analysis, management science, and information technology to solve business problems faced by managers (without exaggeration) millions of times a day.

While there is quite a bit of open discussion about what specifically constitutes business analytics, for the introductory purpose of this book, the subject is divided into three broad topics:

Descriptive analytics uses data to report and understand past and current business performance. These reports involve using statistics to summarize and report data to keep managers informed about business metrics such as sales, revenue, profit, budgets, expenses, inventory, and customer status. Such descriptive statistical reports are used to measure trends and levels over time in much the same manner as a driver uses the instruments on a dashboard to measure driving toward a destination.

Predictive analytics uses construct predictive models from data to forecast future behavior of the business environment and the enterprise. An example of a predictive model would take pricing, advertising, promotions, and holidays into account to forecast demand.

Prescriptive analytics uses predictive models to decide on the best (optimum) choices. The term *decision making* is synonymous with the predictive stage of business analytics. Examples of predictive (decision-making) models include pricing, capacity, advertising and promotions, hiring, location, and supply chain decisions (Fig. 1.2).

As an example, retailers manage seasonal inventory of products by the quantity they order and pricing decisions during the season. One key aspect of these decisions is how many units to order and when to manage markdowns through the season to maximize profits. For example, consider an online retailer who wants to sell outdoor furniture beginning in March. The retailer will need to decide how much to order, when and how much to reorder, how to adjust prices during the season, and when to stop reordering and discount the remaining inventory to clear it out to make room for winter merchandise. For a national chain, with thousands of products, this can result in millions of decisions required of managers. Descriptive analytics are used to keep managers informed about past sales (demand)—that is, units sold each day, week, month, over similar time periods in the past. Predictive analytics is used to construct forecasting (predictive models) to take pricing, advertising, promotions, and holidays into account. Prescriptive analytics is then used to decide, based on the predictive models, the best (optimum) decisions to make about pricing, ordering, advertising, and promotions.

1.3 Uncertainty = probability = stochastic

The consequences of managerial decisions occur in the future and as such are nearly always uncertain. Uncertainty is measured by probability. Thus the core knowledge of business analytics is the study of applied probability, probability that is measured and estimated using data. In the world of mathematics, a situation that is measured by probability is often referred to as a stochastic (pronounced stuh-KA-stik) process. The opposite of stochastic is deterministic; deterministic models have no uncertain (random) elements. Factors in the business world, such as interest rates, energy prices, and currency exchange rates, are uncertain. Thus most business decisions are stochastic optimization problems. To make the best decisions when faced with uncertainty, the emphasis of this book is on creating and using probability models (including simulation) for stochastic optimization.

The following three fundamental sets of business analytics tools are presented in this book:

1. Structuring a decision problem:	DECISION ANALYSIS
2. Measuring uncertainty: descriptive and predictive analytics:	PROBABILITY and STATISTICAL ANALYSIS
3. Determining the optimum decision: prescriptive analytics:	SIMULATION and OPTIMIZATION

These topics are discussed and integrated with the components of business analytics throughout the book. Thus this book presents a unique, applied combination of topics. These topics are often presented in separate texts and courses, which minimizes their power to solve real managerial problems. The combination of these topics provides you with strong fundamental managerial decision-making skills that can be applied to a wide variety of situations.

1.4 Example of decision making and the three stages of analytics

Example 1.1 Deciding upon a medical treatment
Consider an individual patient with Graves disease. This is an immune system disorder that results in the overproduction of thyroid hormones (hyperthyroidism). The patient is presented with three possible treatments: (1) do nothing because the patient is not required to have a medical treatment,

(2) radiation therapy, or (3) surgery. Obviously, we would like to know with certainty (100%) that the outcome will be that the patient is made well. For various medical reasons, however, that cannot be perfectly (100%) predicted. Whether the patient will be well or not well therefore is considered to be random. The patient might then ask which treatment has the highest likelihood of achieving an outcome of being well. Ascertaining those probabilities is the result of collecting data from clinical trials. Consider a medical study with approximately 3000 participants, 1000 in each of three groups: The first group is comprised of individuals given a placebo. Individuals in the second group were given radiation therapy, and the remaining individuals in the third group were treated with surgery. Next, data regarding the level of the hormone in question are measured and individuals thus diagnosed as either well or not well. Suppose the data are as presented in Table 1.1.

The left-hand column heading (Obs) stands for *observation,* meaning an observed and measured data point. In this case, an observation represents one person in the study, and there are 1000 observations (people) in each treatment group and 3000 total observations. Next, as part of the descriptive stage of analysis, the data would be tabulated in a frequency count and reported as in Table 1.2.

Reporting the results as percentages, which are the empirical probabilities, would also be part of the descriptive stage of the analytics process. Determining whether the probabilities of being well for the

Table 1.1 Hypothetical data from hyperthyroid study

Obs	Group	Outcome
1	1	well
2	1	well
.	.	.
.	.	.
.	.	.
999	1	not well
1000	1	not well
1001	2	well
1002	2	well
.	.	.
.	.	.
.	.	.
1999	2	not well
2000	2	not well
2001	3	well
2002	3	well
.	.	.
.	.	.
.	.	.
2999	3	not well
3000	3	not well

Table 1.2 Hypothetical tabulated results from hyperthyroid study

	Placebo	Radiation	Surgery
Well	508	996	994
Not well	492	4	6
Total	1000	1000	100

three treatments are statistically and significantly different would be a task associated with the predictive stage. Finally, deciding on a specific treatment would be the decision-making task associated with the prescriptive stage.

1.5 Introduction to decision analysis

Decision analysis is the field of economic scientific analysis devoted to scientific methods to make decisions using accepted, structured processes. Decision analysis includes tools to identify, represent, and formally assess important aspects of decision making. Decision analysis also provides methods for prescribing a recommended course of action for the decision maker. Thus decision analysis provides the foundation for business analytics.

A decision tree is a diagram that represents the possible choices and outcomes that confront a decision maker. Because the decision tree shows all possible choices and their associated outcomes, it is a fundamental tool for prescriptive decision making. The decision tree for the Graves disease treatment decision is shown in Fig. 1.3.

Decisions are events the decision maker can control (shown as squares in Fig. 1.3). Random events are outcomes that the decision maker cannot control (shown as circles in Fig. 1.3). One of the most important aspects of decision making is recognizing what can truly be controlled (decisions) versus what cannot be controlled (random). In practice, people are often delusional about what they can "make happen" (control); this is called a wish rather than a decision. In a marketing example, reducing the price cannot make customers buy the company's product, but it may influence the probability that demand will increase.

Decision makers are often interested in long-run outcomes, such as the long-run return of an investment choice. Example 1.2 provides an illustration of a simple decision tree and the associated long-run outcomes.

Example 1.2 A simple decision tree
Which choice should be selected: Option A, consisting of $100 "for sure" (absolutely certain) or Option B, consisting of a 50% chance of $300? The decision tree in Fig. 1.4 represents the decision between Options A and B.

The long-run outcome of choosing Option A is obviously $100. The long-run consequence of choosing Option B is 50%*$300 + 50%*$0 = $150. The $150 long-run outcome is referred to as the expected value and is the weighted average of the uncertain outcomes of Option B. The concept of expected value will be discussed in further detail in the next chapter.

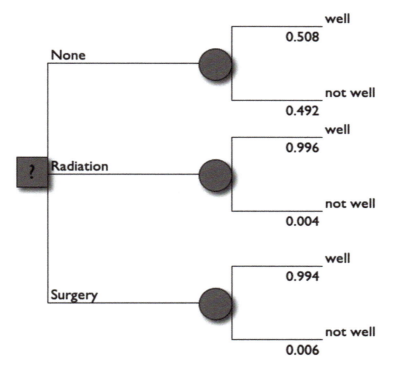

FIGURE 1.3 Decision Tree for Graves Disease Treatment.

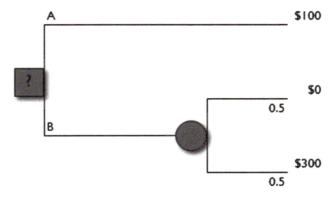

FIGURE 1.4 Fundamental Decision Tree With Expected Value.

1.6 What is simulation?

A simulation is a mathematical model that attempts to emulate the behavior and operation of a real-world process over time. Simulation is a process of creating a model of what could happen in an uncertain world and using that model to decide which course of action to take in the real world. Thus simulation is used for decision analysis problems that have uncertainty (probability) where a theoretical solution method would be either difficult or impossible. Simulation is an extremely flexible methodology especially suited to making decision under uncertainty. Simulation is a process of creating a model of what could happen in an uncertain world and using that model to decide which course of action to take in the real world.

A simulation model of the Graves disease example would be used to study the potential variations away from the data in the study that could happen. Such a model would be useful to determine if one treatment is statistically and significantly different than the others and what operational consequences might occur, such as costs, staffing, capacity, and individual health outcomes.

1.6.1 Why use simulation?

Three reasons for using simulation as in business analytics are as follows:

1. Most people cannot deeply understand how probability models the uncertainty of future events, and how forecasts are never exact or perfect. Simulation provides a clear demonstration of the effects of uncertainty and probability on decision making. Thus simulation provides an excellent foundation for understanding the true nature of uncertainty and probability.
2. Making decisions in the face of uncertainty is a core business analytics activity. There are many decisions in which the complexities of the uncertainties become too unwieldy and mathematically complex for traditional probability analysis to be employed. These decisions require a more robust solution methodology; simulation provides a solution methodology that is more easily understood and able to be implemented.
3. A major portion of business analytics involves data analysis. As data analysis consists of scrutiny of the variation of data and the causes for that variation, analysts cannot properly analyze data without an understanding of how the variation in the data was generated. By creating simulations, analysts learn how real data could have been generated. Creating simulations requires analysts to understand what factors can cause the data to behave in various ways and to what extent randomness will be present in the data.

Simulation is featured in this book to teach the counterintuitive nature of probability and how that counterintuitive quality impacts managerial decision making. When an analyst constructs a simulation model, the analyst creates a dynamic model of how the business situation could evolve and, at the same time, discovers a deeper understanding of how and why the situation behaves as it does.

Unlike traditional mathematical models that only measure expected value (average), simulation models can measure many other attributes of a system or process. For example, a simulation can be used to estimate the likelihood (i.e., the risk) of an investment losing money. As a result, simulation models provide better measurement and understanding of risk and return trade-offs. This will be demonstrated in some of the subsequent examples.

Trygve Haavelmo of Norway, winner of the 1989 Nobel Memorial Prize in Economic Sciences, reasoned that quantitative economic models must necessarily be probability models (by which today would mean stochastic). Deterministic models are obviously inconsistent with observed economic quantities, and it is illogical to apply deterministic models to nondeterministic situations. Thus economic models should be explicitly designed to incorporate randomness. It follows, then, that simulation is an appropriate method to quantify, estimate, and conduct inferences about the economic models with uncertainty.

1.6.2 Simulation applications

Simulation is used extensively in the areas of operations and finance. Currently, marketing is underusing simulation—but that means there are plenty of opportunities to bring simulation to bear in marketing decisions.

Some examples of applications of simulation are AT&T Internet network design and analysis, Weather Channel weather models, Google searches and mapping of directions, Expedia system for online reservations, and HP's new production facility. Cummins Engine, Merck, P&G, Kodak, United Airlines, and others use simulation financial models to determine which investment projects to choose.

There is more than one way to get to Charlotte.

1.7 Monte Carlo simulation

There are many forms of simulation, such as agent-based modeling, discrete event simulation, deterministic simulation, and Monte Carlo simulation. For the purposes of this book, the term *simulation* will refer to a form of simulation called Monte Carlo simulation.

A Monte Carlo simulation repeatedly, and randomly, samples from a probability distribution to simulate possible outcomes. The results of these outcomes are measured to study and observe the long-run behavior of the process being modeled. In the context of decision making, the process can then be optimized by altering various model parameters.

Monte Carlo simulation was invented by scientists working on the atomic bomb in the 1940s, who named it for the city in Monaco famed for its casinos and games of chance. The central idea of Monte Carlo simulation is to use random numbers to model the behavior of a complex system or process. Monte Carlo simulations have been applied to a wide range of problems in science, engineering, sociology, economics, and business—with business applications in virtually every industry.

Monte Carlo simulation is an effective modeling tool whenever managers must make an estimate, forecast, or decision in which there is significant uncertainty. If you do not use simulation, your estimates or forecasts could be extremely erroneous, with adverse consequences for your decisions. Often, when managers are faced with an uncertainty, they fall into the temptation of replacing the uncertain number in question with a single average value. Typically, managers fall into the peril of subconsciously and erroneously using the law of large numbers. The principle of this law states that as sample size (n) increases, probabilities converge to their true values. Dr. Sam Savage refers to this as "the flaw of averages," and it is a fundamental fallacy in decision making.

Most business activities, plans, and processes are too complex for an analytical solution. But you can build a spreadsheet model that lets you evaluate your plan numerically—that is, you can change numbers and consider the results of what-if scenarios.

Example 1.3 A warranty decision

A cell phone manufacturer offers an extended warranty for $100 for a cell phone that costs $400. The rate of claims is approximately 1 claim per 500 warranty purchases; that is, of 500 people who buy the extended warranty only about 1 person files a claim and has the phone replaced. In general, should people buy the warranty? Why or why not? Should you purchase the warranty? What is the difference between those two questions? Fig. 1.5 shows a portion of a spreadsheet simulation of this example decision.

Examining the Claim column shows there were 22 claims; this is slightly different and more realistic than the predicted 20 (1/500 * 10,000 = 20). Pressing the F9 key will cause the number of claims to change—varying around 20. Chapter 7 will explain and demonstrate the estimation of how many claims around the 20 could reasonably occur. That is, how many claims above or below (±) 20 could happen. In this example, the average number of claims away from 20 is about 4.5. More will be explained about this number (i.e., standard deviation) later.

C10		✕ ✓	*fx*	=(RAND()<Rate_of_Incidence)*1		
	A	B	C	D	E	
1	Price	$100				
2	Insured Value	$400				
3	Rate of Incidence	0.002	= 1/500 = 2/1000			
4	Expected	20				
5						
6			0.9976			
7	Total =	$1,000,000	22	$9,600	$990,400	
8	Avg =	$100.00	0.0024	$0.96	$99.04	
9		Customer	Revenue	Claim	Cost	Profit
10		1	$100	0	$0	$100
11		2	$100	0	$0	$100
12		3	$100	0	$0	$100
13		4	$100	0	$0	$100
14		5	$100	0	$0	$100
15		6	$100	1	$400	($300)
16		7	$100	0	$0	$100
17		8	$100	0	$0	$100
18		9	$100	0	$0	$100
19		10	$100	0	$0	$100
10005		9,996	$100	0	$0	$100
10006		9,997	$100	0	$0	$100
10007		9,998	$100	0	$0	$100
10008		9,999	$100	0	$0	$100
10009		10,000	$100	0	$0	$100

FIGURE 1.5 Simulation of the Cell Phone Warranty Problem.

Also note that the average cost of a warranty to the phone manufacturer is about $0.80 per warranty, and the company is making an average of $99.20 of profit per warranty:

Average revenue = $100
Average cost = 1/500 × $400 = $400/500 = 4/5 = 8/10 = $0.80
Average profit = $100 − $0.80 = $99.20

The simulation demonstrates again that the average is not compelled to happen, even in 10,000 trials. Thus simulation demonstrates how the practice of business will vary from the theory of business.

Based on the average rate of incidence, you should not buy the warranty—unless you are significantly more prone to breaking things and thus have a much higher rate of breaking things. You would need to have at least a 25% chance of breaking your cell phone before the warranty would be a good idea; you would have to have a breaking rate 125 times higher [(1/4)/(1/500) = 500/4 = 125] than the average person (i.e., you would have to be 125 times more accident prone than average).

Example 1.4　A further look at the warranty decision

Consider again the $100 warranty for a $400 cell phone. How might the rate of incidence of 1 claim per 500 vary? How might that affect the company's forecasts of profit? How does this situation apply to banks?

The graph in Fig. 1.6 shows the results of another set of 10,000 trials of the simulation from Example 1.3. Each trial is a single customer and whether that customer's cell phone breaks and the customer makes a claim. Each vertical jump in the graph represents a claim.

There are 18 total claims in the 10,000 trials, with 5 claims within the first 1000 customers (trials). That is a rate of 0.005 (5/1000), significantly more than the 2 per 1000 one might expect for those 1000 customers. This again illustrates the necessity of studying simulation to see that rare events, such as 5 claims within 1000, will happen (i.e., the corollary to the law of large numbers). Furthermore, in the case of rare events, accidents, and illness, for example, most people expect rare events to happen later—not now. But independence tells us differently.

The graph in Fig. 1.7 shows another set of 10,000 trials of the same simulation in which there were 31 claims. There were 6 claims in the first 231 trials, thus causing the rate of incidence to be almost 2.6%, a very significant deviation from the expected rate of 0.2%. Even with the 10,000 trials the rate of the sample of 10,000 is 0.31% (31/10,000), nearly 50% larger than an analyst would expect.

These two examples demonstrate how simulation provides evidence about how a system will not necessarily conform to the average behavior so often assumed by managers lacking fundamental understanding of probability. Thus simulation is a powerful tool for decision makers. The graphs in Figs. 1.8, 1.9, 1.10, 1.11, and 1.12 provide more results of 10,000 trials and demonstrate the how simulation can give analysts better understanding of the true variation in the behavior of a system.

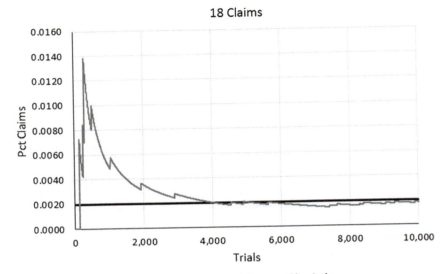

FIGURE 1.6 Results of a Set of 10,000 Trials of Cell Phone Warranty Simulation.

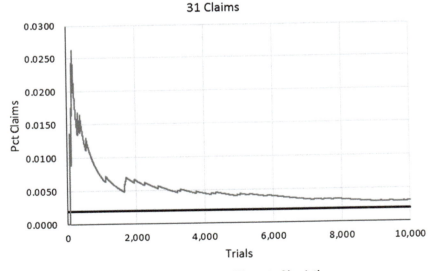

FIGURE 1.7 Results of a Set of 10,000 Trials of Cell Phone Warranty Simulation.

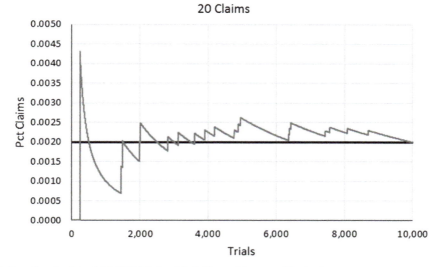

FIGURE 1.8 Results of a Set of 10,000 Trials of Cell Phone Warranty Simulation.

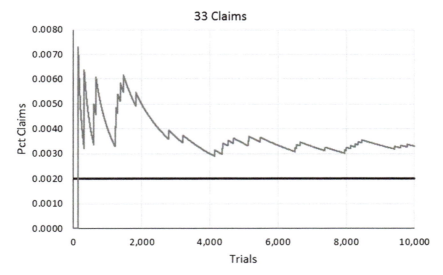

FIGURE 1.9 Results of a Set of 10,000 Trials of Cell Phone Warranty Simulation.

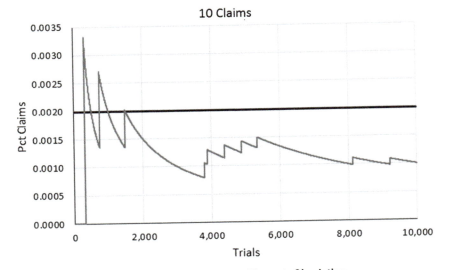

FIGURE 1.10 Results of a Set of 10,000 Trials of Cell Phone Warranty Simulation.

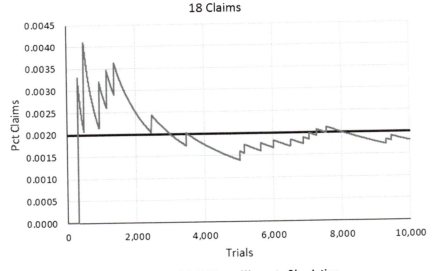

FIGURE 1.11 Results of a Set of 10,000 Trials of Cell Phone Warranty Simulation.

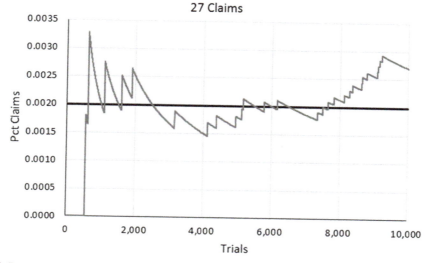

FIGURE 1.12 **Results of a Set of 10,000 Trials of Cell Phone Warranty Simulation.**

Anything that can happen will happen—variation of the law of large numbers.

Exercise Set 1: Introduction to Decision Making

1. As you place an item in your shopping cart online, the online retailer automatically offers an extended warranty for $10 for a tablet that costs $65. The rate of claims is approximately 6 claims per 1000 warranty purchases—that is, of 500 people who buy the extended warranty about 3 people file a claim and have the tablet replaced.
   a. Should people, in general, buy the warranty?
   b. Should you buy the warranty?
   c. How did the manufacturer decide to charge $10?
   d. How much should the manufacturer charge?
   e. How is this situation similar to bank loans?

2. Piedmont Natural Gas (PNG) is offering a plan to cover hot water heater failures. For a customer enrolling in the plan for a year at $7 per month, PNG will pay up to $1000 in repairs or replacement for the customer's hot water heater. Suppose that for the targeted customers hot water heaters can fail equally likely throughout the year and that the customers will remain on the plan even after their hot water heaters fail. Thus you can assume that PNG will collect an entire year of payments for a customer who enrolls in the plan. PNG has the choice of either enrolling a customer in

the plan or not enrolling the customer. If PNG does not enroll the customer in the plan, then PNG collects $0.

   a. Draw the decision tree for this problem.
   b. Calculate the probability of hot water heater failure that is required for PNG to break even. That is, at what probability is $EV_{Not\ Enroll} = EV_{Enroll}$?
   c. Given a 5% probability of hot water heater failure, calculate the expected value of perfect information.

3. Assume deaths from motor vehicle accidents occurred at a rate of 15.5 per 100,000 people (such information is available from the *Statistical Abstract of the United States* or from actuarial data). Furthermore, suppose the insurance company sells policies that offer to pay $100,000 if an insured person dies in a motor vehicle accident.

   a. How much should you charge for these policies?
   b. How is this situation similar to bank loans?

4. An insurance company has two classes of car insurance customers. The first class has a rate of incidence of one car totaled (beyond repair) per 100,000 customers; the second class has a rate of one car totaled per 1000 customers. The current rate for the low-risk class for insuring a $25,000 car is $350 per year. What should the rate (annual premium) be for the high-risk class so that the insurance company receives the same average profit per customer? The difference in the two rates is called the risk premium.

Case 1.1

Wilson Food Company

The Wilson Food Company has been a nationally recognized producer of family foods for 65 years. Over these years it has been fortunate to be participating in a growing market. But this will probably not be true in the future.

Recently, sales have been falling along with the drop in birth rate. In fact, most long-term predictions foresee this lower birth rate as a permanent phenomenon.

Two months ago, at a corporate long-range planning session, it was agreed that the company should consider the expansion of its product line beyond family foods. It was unanimously decided that the first move should be to change the name to the Wilson Company.

Shortly after the meeting a proposal was made to produce and market a line of geriatric foods. These prepared foods would be aimed at the 65-and-over age bracket. Preliminary analysis indicated that this market had above-average growth potential over the next 30 years, and at present few firms competed in this market.

In addition, this analysis showed that if sales were high, an average profit of $12 million per year could be realized over the first 5 years of the project's life. If, on the other hand, sales were low, the company could incur an average loss of $3 million per year over the same time period.

Based on historical experience, the management of the Wilson Company thought that the likelihood of high sales from any project was 0.30 and the likelihood of low sales was 0.70.

The manager of marketing, Janet Collins, was unclear as to what she should do next. She felt she had two alternatives. The first would be to undertake a market survey, which would yield additional information to better reach a decision. The second alternative would be to omit a survey and base the decision on current information.

Case—cont'd

If a survey were undertaken, the results would predict either success for the product (high sales), inconclusive results, or product failure (low sales).

Survey results are by no means perfect. Ms. Collins has conducted countless surveys in the past and has some information that may be helpful in reaching a decision alternative. First, if one considers all those products that have achieved a high level of sales in the marketplace, the results indicate that in 60% of the cases the survey forecasts success, in 30% of the cases the result was inconclusive, and in 10% of the cases the survey forecasts failure. Next, if one considers all those products that have achieved a low level of sales, these surveys showed that in 20% of the cases the survey forecasts success, in 30% the result was inconclusive, and in 50% the survey forecasts failure.

Decision trees

Knowledge comes by taking things apart: analysis. But wisdom comes by putting things together.
—John A. Morrison

Chapter outline

Introduction

This chapter provides extensive confirmation of the need for using probability in managerial decision making. To accomplish this, a general decision-making process is defined along with the essential concepts of how to construct and use a decision tree to map out decisions and uncertainty. Because decision trees require measuring uncertainty, fundamental elements of probability are defined. Examples are used to explain the role of probability in managerial decision making. Properties of decision trees and probability are presented along with examples that demonstrate the use of probability and expected value of perfect and imperfect information.

2.1 Introduction to decision making

Decision making is a critical problem-solving skill for managers. To create effective tools for business analytics decision making, it is necessary to analyze the decision-making process itself. What follows is a general model of decision making, adapted from *Judgment in Managerial Decision Making* by Max Bazerman of Harvard University and Don Moore of Carnegie Mellon University. It is a prescriptive model that outlines an optimal approach to making decisions in a rational manner. Of course, real-world decision making regularly falls short of this purely rational ideal. Nobel prize winners Amos Tversky and Daniel Kahneman have published extensive research on erroneous judgments made in decision making (e.g., see *Judgment Under Uncertainty: Heuristics and Biases* in the journal *Science*). But given the clinically proven errors of judgment that can cloud critical thinking and problem solving in the workplace, an introduction to some ideal problem-solving methods is useful.

2.1.1 Define the problem

Defining, or framing, the problem is perhaps the most important step and is where managers often make mistakes. There are obvious mistakes that can be identified—for example, defining the problem in terms of a proposed solution. In the snack food example from Chapter 1, focusing too quickly on the proposed brand extension can interfere with a more fundamental and broad-based analysis of the factors contributing to the brand's current health. Another problem is diagnosing the problem in terms of its symptoms. Prematurely addressing the symptom of low current sales can lead to a misguided attempt to launch a new ad campaign. If the symptom is actually caused by distribution snarls, those advertising dollars will be wasted. Managers often respond to the problems as they come to us when they are not the right problems to address. Do not let the symptoms or the proposed solution inhibit your effort to uncover the underlying problem.

2.1.2 Identify and weight the criteria

Managers often need to accomplish more than one objective when making a decision. In the electronics superstore situation, the choice of new store locations will depend upon such factors as inexpensive commercial rental space, the existence of an adequately trained labor pool, proximity to existing distribution centers, ease of access for customers, and market research about sales potential in a specific city or neighborhood. The relevant criteria will vary in importance; once they have all been identified, they should be weighted according to their relative importance. In the electronics superstore example, if demand and rental costs are deemed significantly more important than proximity to an existing distribution center, these differentials should be quantified by the numerical criterion assigned to each outcome. When making individual, rather than enterprise, decisions, the economics concept of utility must be considered. Utility provides a more complete measurement of a decisions' outcome, although accounting for individual utility can seem nebulous and challenging.

To make a decision, a decision maker must select an objective. Common objectives are to minimize cost, maximize profit, maximize utility, minimize work, and maximize efficiency. A mathematical function that expresses such an objective is called an *objective function*. An optimization problem must have an objective function.

An example of an objective function is an equation to calculate profit using parameters for fixed cost, variable cost, price, and quantity sold. These parameters, as well as others depending on the situation, constitute a *cost structure*. Because many cost structures are idiosyncratic to the situation, it is very important to consider the cost structure of the specific contextual situation when constructing an objective function.

2.1.3 Generate alternatives

In many situations, this is the most creative and challenging aspect of making decisions because this is the point at which many options for potential solutions and their associated outcomes should be generated. Many creative solutions are prematurely judged and abandoned at this point. Decision makers should put in as many alternatives as possible; the decision tree will do the work to help determine the best (optimal) solution.

2.1.4 Evaluate each alternative

The cost structure should determine how well each alternative solution satisfies each of the criteria. This involves forecasting uncertain future conditions. But in this rational model, the potential consequences of choosing each possible alternative are assessed and assigned a numerical value. Be sure to look at the values of each outcome and assess if they adequately represent the rank order of preferences. For example, suppose two alternatives' outcomes each result in $1000. The decision maker should reflect on whether there is truly indifference between the two outcomes.

2.1.5 Compute the optimal decision

If these steps have been followed correctly, then the last step is a straightforward matter. The alternative with the best "score" is the rational choice. For this book, this is determined by computing the expected value for each random event and choosing the option with the best expected value.

In summary, stochastic optimization decision problems, such as Example 1.2 from Chapter 1 of $100 for sure or a 50% chance of $300, have three key elements:

1. A DECISION (or set of decisions)
2. An OBJECTIVE to be optimized
3. UNCERTAINTY (probability)

Although these are broad decision-making steps, this book will present a more specific set of steps for developing prescriptive models for decision making. The first component of these models is the decision tree.

2.2 Decision trees and expected value

Many complex business situations have significant uncertainties (probabilities); thus, **decision trees** are an essential tool to ascertain the structure of decisions (choices) and uncertain outcomes (random events) faced by business analysts. Furthermore, defining the decision trees is often a necessary tool required to design, analyze, and present simulations.

One objective of a decision tree is to calculate the *expected value* of each decision (each option). For most of this book, the objective function is to *maximize* the expected value. To further consider the concept of expected value, consider the question raised in Example 1.2:

Which choice should be selected: option **A**, consisting of $100 "for sure" (absolutely certain), or option **B**, consisting of a 50% chance of $300? The decision tree in Fig. 2.1 represents the decision between options **A** and **B**.

Expected value (EV) is a weighted average and is another phrase for long-run average. An expected value is equal to the sum of the probabilities times their respective outcomes:

$$EV_e = \sum_i (p_i v_i),$$

where e is a specific random *event*, i is the set of outcomes, p_i is the probability of outcome i, and v_i is the value associated with outcome i. v_i is referred to as an *end value*. When an expected value is a monetary value, it is often called an *expected monetary value* (EMV).

In this example, the expected values are computed:

$$EV_A = 1.00\,(\$100) = \$100$$

$$EV_B = 0.50\,(\$100) + 0.50\,(\$0) = \$150$$

The decision maker must ascertain whether the worst possible outcome ($0 in this example) is *cata-strophic* or not. For most enterprise decisions, if an outcome is not *catastrophic* (resulting in death or other ruinous results), then the decision maker should choose the decision with the best expected value.

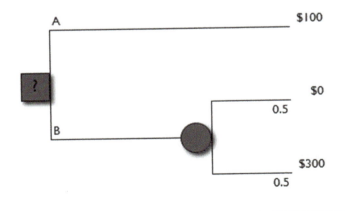

FIGURE 2.1

Fundamental Decision Tree With Expected Value

Initially, many people are opposed to choosing the option with the highest expected value (option **B**) because of their concern regarding the worst-case scenario—a very reasonable concern. People who choose such an option are *risk averse*. One way to understand why maximizing expected value is considered risk neutral, and is thus the preferred objective, is to suppose you manage 10 salespeople who make one call per hour and each call yields $100 profit. Thus, they make $1000 profit per hour.

In contrast, a colleague manages 10 salespeople who make one call per hour, but half of their calls result in $0 profit and the other half yield $300 profit. On average, your colleague's salespeople will make $1500 profit per hour. Who will get the bigger raise at the end of the year—you or your colleague? So, "long-run" does not have to be sequential (serial)—it can be simultaneous (parallel). The simulation of this example, shown in Fig. 2.2 shows the long-run effect of choosing the option with the lower expected value. Furthermore, the decisions do not have to be identical—just consistent with and not have catastrophic (series ending) consequences.

The graph in Fig. 2.3 shows the expected value (average) for each of the options during the first 4000 trials of the simulation. The graph also shows both the significant difference between the two choices on average and the long-run convergence, as a result of the *law of large numbers*, to the *expected value* of $150. Many risk-averse people will choose the sure thing ($100) over the apparently risky (possible $0) choice.

E8			f_x	=IF(RAND()<ProbB1,Outcome_B1,Outcome_B2)				
	A	B	C	D	E	F	G	H
1		End Value	Probability					
2	Outcome A	$100	100%					
3	Outcome B1	$0	50%					
4	Outcome B2	$300	50%					
5								
6								
7		Trial	Outcome A	Total A	Avg A	Outcome B	Total B	Avg B
8		1	100	100	100	300	300	300
9		2	100	200	100	0	300	150
10		3	100	300	100	300	600	200
11		4	100	400	100	0	600	150
12		5	100	500	100	300	900	180
13		6	100	600	100	300	1200	200
14		7	100	700	100	0	1200	171
15		8	100	800	100	0	1200	150
16		9	100	900	100	0	1200	133
17		10	100	1000	100	0	1200	120
10002		9,995	100	999500	100	0	1475400	148
10003		9,996	100	999600	100	300	1475700	148
10004		9,997	100	999700	100	0	1475700	148
10005		9,998	100	999800	100	300	1476000	148
10006		9,999	100	999900	100	0	1476000	148
10007		10,000	100	1000000	100	300	1476300	148

FIGURE 2.2

Simulation of 10,000 Trials of $100 Versus 50% Chance of $300

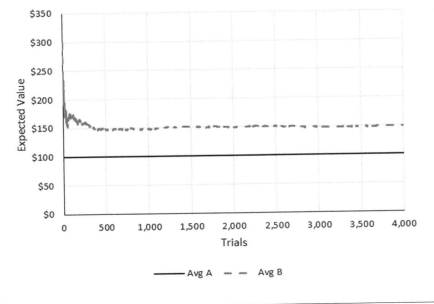

FIGURE 2.3

Convergence of the Expected Value

The two lines in the graph in Fig. 2.4 show the long-run difference between the two decisions. This difference reflects the cumulative consequences due to such risk aversion.

This example demonstrates why companies should be *risk neutral*—that is, neither risk averse (overly conservative) nor risk seeking (overly optimistic)—and should tend to *maximize the expected value* of profit rather than being concerned about short-run variations (volatility). Individuals must often be concerned with both short-run (I must eat today) and long-run (I need enough money to retire someday) issues. Thus, individuals need to be aware of the extreme variation that can happen in the short run.

If an outcome is NOT CATASTROPHIC, then EXPECTED VALUE can be used.
(Why?)
If an outcome is catastrophic, then the only way to win is to NOT PLAY!

2.3 Overview of the decision-making process

A *decision-making process* requires a stochastic optimization solution, such as that of a decision tree or a simulation. A typical decision-making process is summarized by these steps:

1. List all the events.
   DECISIONS are *choices*, events that the manager *can* control.
   RANDOM EVENTS are *events* that are *uncertain* (unknown) as to their outcome. They have probabilities associated with them and are events that the manager *cannot* control. Random does not necessarily imply for no reason.

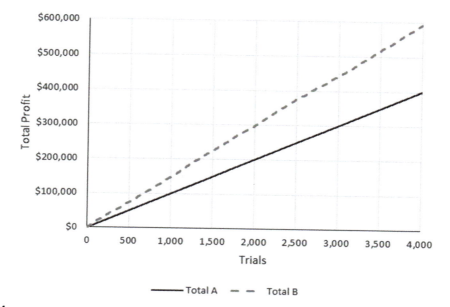

FIGURE 2.4

Cumulative Results of 4000 Trials of $100 Versus 50% Chance of $300

Fig. 2.5 illustrates how Robert Frost might have used a decision tree with probabilities to decide which road to take.

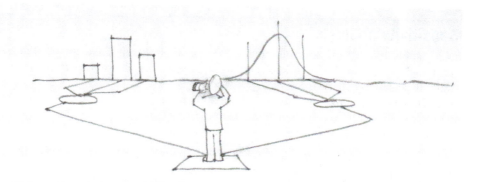

FIGURE 2.5

Robert Frost Using Probability in a Decision Tree to Decide the Road Not Chosen

2. **Use the list to draw the DECISION TREE.**
   Time proceeds from left to right →.
   - Squares represent decisions.
   - Circles represent random events.
   Be sure to include ALL POSSIBILITIES. Extra branches cannot create incorrect decisions.
3. **Compute the END VALUES.**
   Analyze the COST STRUCTURE of the decisions and outcomes. Consider all costs and monetary benefits. Nonmonetary benefits can be considered using utility and sensitivity analysis.
   Compute the specific monetary outcomes for each outcome—a common mistake is to omit part of the monetary amount to be accumulated after expected values have been calculated.
   Be sure that the rankings of the end values accurately represent the decision maker's true priorities—consider whether any of the outcomes are catastrophic for the decision maker. If so, then that outcome should have a large penalty.
   When the timing of costs and benefits are important, then NET PRESENT VALUES are used.
4. **Assign probabilities to each outcome (branch) of each RANDOM EVENT (circle).**
   These probabilities must add up to 1.00 (100%) for each RANDOM EVENT (circle).
5. **Compute the EXPECTED VALUES for each RANDOM EVENT (circle).**
   An EXPECTED VALUE is a weighted average computed by summing the product of the probabilities and their associated end values—that is, in Excel, use the following formula:

$$= \text{SUM (probabilities * end values)}$$

   Choose the appropriate decision based upon the objective (e.g., maximum expected profit, minimum expected cost) for each DECISION (square).

2.4 Sensitivity analysis

What could happen? Which information is critical? What are the quantitative effects of deviations from the assumptions? Answering these questions is part of the process called *sensitivity analysis*. The essential question in sensitivity analysis is:
   How much would your assumptions and information have to change before you would regret your decision? How likely is it that you are making the wrong decision?
   Think again about the decision presented in Example 1.2:

Would you rather have $100 "for sure" (absolutely certain) or a 50% chance of $300?
The part of the problem that is least certain is the probability of getting $300. Since that probability measures the certainty/uncertainty of the success of getting $300, then that piece of information should be the initial focus of sensitivity analysis. Fig. 2.7 shows which choice should be made (under the assumption of maximizing expected value) at all values of the probability of getting $300 ($p$).

To determine the critical value at which the (0,300) option should be chosen:

Example 2.1 A Warranty Decision

A cell phone manufacturer offers an extended warranty for $100 for a cell phone that costs $400. The rate of claims is approximately one claim per 500 warranty purchases—that is, of 500 people who buy the extended warranty, only about 1 person files a claim and has the phone replaced. In general, should people buy the warranty? Why, or why not? Should you purchase the warranty? What is the difference between those two questions?

Using the steps of the decision-making process as outlined, do the following:

1. List all the events.
    DECISION: To purchase, or not purchase, the warranty.
    RANDOM EVENT: Whether the cell phone breaks and a claim is filed.
2. Use the list to draw the DECISION TREE.
    Time proceeds from left to right. In this example, the decision happens before the random event:
    - A square represents the decision to purchase, or not purchase, the warranty.
    - The circles represent the random event of whether the phone breaks or not.
3. Compute the END VALUES.
    If the customer purchases the insurance, then the outcome is a cost of $100 regardless of whether the phone breaks or not.
    If the customer does not purchase the insurance, then the outcome is a cost of $400 if the phone breaks or $0 if it does not break.
4. Assign probabilities to each outcome (branch) of each RANDOM EVENT (circle).
    The probability of the phone breaking is 1/500. The probability of the phone not breaking is
    $1 - 1/500 = 499/500$.
5. Compute the EXPECTED VALUES for each RANDOM EVENT (circle).
    For the option in which the customer buys the warranty, the expected value is:

$$EVBuy = 1/500 * \$100 + 499/500 * \$100 = \$100$$

For the option in which the customer does not buy the warranty, the expected value is:

$$EVNot\ Buy = 1/500 * \$400 + 499/500 * \$0 = \$0.80$$

Choose the appropriate decision based upon the objective of minimum expected cost. Notice that the difference between the two alternatives ($100 – $0.80 = $99.20) is the profit the manufacturer makes from customers who purchase the warranty. Thus, do not buy the warranty, because none of the possible outcomes are catastrophic.

Fig. 2.6 shows the decision tree and expected values.

Because the probabilities are estimated and uncertain (yes, the uncertainties themselves are uncertain), over what range of probabilities would you get the same decision? How the probabilities are estimated will be discussed in much further detail in subsequent portions of the book. Which numbers are you most, and least, comfortable with? These questions lead to one of the most important topics in this book—sensitivity analysis.

$$\text{Set } EV_{\$}100 \equiv EV_{\$0,\$300}$$
$$100 = p*300 + (1-p)*0$$
$$p = 100/300 = 1/3,$$

where p is the probability of $300. Thus, the (0,300) option should be chosen for $p \geq 1/3$.

Thus, the question to be answered is how likely is it that p is actually less than 1/3? The answer to that problem can typically only be answered in the context of each specific problem setting.

Example 2.2 provides a demonstration of the decision-making process and sensitivity analysis when the probabilities are not perfectly known.

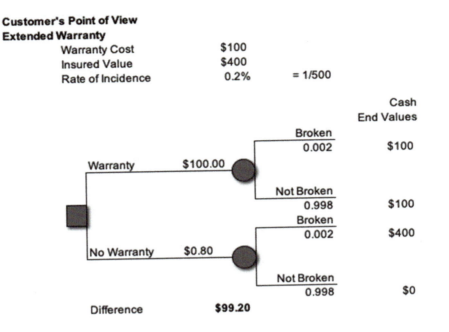

Customer's Point of View
Extended Warranty

Warranty Cost	$100	
Insured Value	$400	
Rate of Incidence	0.2%	= 1/500

Cash End Values

Warranty — $100.00

Broken 0.002 — $100
Not Broken 0.998 — $100

No Warranty — $0.80

Broken 0.002 — $400
Not Broken 0.998 — $0

Difference — $99.20

FIGURE 2.6

Decision Tree for the Cell Phone Warranty Problem

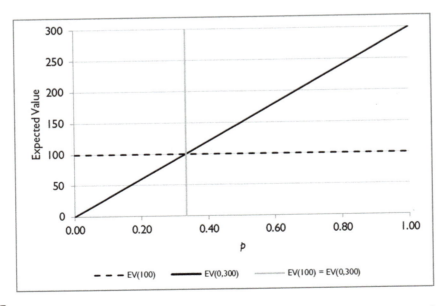

EV(100)   EV(0,300)   EV(100) = EV(0,300)

FIGURE 2.7

Breakeven Probability for the Fundamental Decision Tree

Example 2.2 Simplified Investment Decision

An investor is considering investing $20,000 in one of three alternatives: a certificate of deposit (CD), a low-risk stock fund, and a high-risk stock fund. She considers there to be three possible outcomes: a strong, moderate, or weak stock market. The CD provides a 6% annual rate of return. Table 2.1 lists the returns for the various possible outcomes from investing the $20,000.

Table 2.1 Returns for simplified investment decision.

Investment	State of the Stock Market		
	Strong	**Moderate**	**Weak**
CD	1200	1200	1200
Low-risk stock fund	4300	1200	−600
High-risk stock fund	6600	800	−1500

The investor believes that the probability of a strong stock market is 20% (denoted $P(Strong) = 20\%$), the probability of a moderate stock market is 50% (denoted $P(Moderate) = 50\%$), and the probability of a weak stock market is 30% (denoted as $P(Weak) = 30\%$). Which investment should be chosen according to the EMV criterion?

Using the steps from Section 2.3, do the following:

1. List all the events.

   DECISIONS: Which investment to choose: CD, low-risk stock fund, or high-risk stock fund.

   RANDOM EVENTS: State of the stock market: Strong, moderate, or weak.

2. Use the list to draw the DECISION TREE.

   See Fig. 2.8

3. Compute the END VALUES.

$$\text{End Value}_{CD} = 0.06\,(\$20,000) = \$1200,\text{ regardless of the state of the stock market.}$$

   The end values are shown in Fig. 2.8.

4. Assign probabilities to each outcome (branch) of each RANDOM EVENT (circle).

   The probabilities of the states of the stock market are given in the problem and are listed on the decision tree in Fig. 2.8.

5. Compute the EXPECTED VALUE for each RANDOM EVENT (circle).

$$EV_{CD} = 0.20\,(\$1200) + 0.50\,(\$1200) + 0.30\,(\$1200) = 1.0\,(\$1200) = \$1200$$
$$EV_{\text{Low-risk Stocks}} = 0.20\,(\$4300) + 0.50\,(\$1200) + 0.30\,(-\$600) = 1.0\,(\$1200) = \$1280$$
$$EV_{\text{High-risk Stocks}} = 0.20\,(\$6600) + 0.50\,(\$800) + 0.30\,(-\$1500) = 1.0\,(\$1200) = \$1270$$

Choose the low-risk stock fund because it maximizes the EMV.

Suppose the investor is comfortable with the assessment of a probability of 20% for a strong market. However, the investor is less sure of the probability assessments for the other two outcomes. Under what range of probabilities for a weak stock market does the EMV criterion result in choosing the low-risk stock fund? To answer this question, vary the values of the probability of a weak stock market until the final decision changes. Remember, the probability of a moderate stock market is:

$$P\,(\text{Moderate}) = 1 - P\,(\text{Strong}) - P\,(\text{Weak})$$

Begin with the extremes: if $P(Weak) = 0\%$, then there would be no chance of a weak market, which would lead to investing in the high-risk stock fund. Conversely, if $P(Weak) = 80\%$ (since $P(Strong) = 20\%$), then there would be a large chance of a weak market and one would likely want to invest in a CD. Varying $P(Weak)$ within this range will determine the critical values at which the investment decision answer changes.

To determine the critical value at which the CD should be chosen:

$$Set\ EV_{CD} = EV_{\text{Low-risk Stock}}$$
$$\$1200 = 0.2\,(\$4300) + (1 - 0.2 - P\,(\text{Weak}))\,(\$1200) + P\,(\text{Weak})\,(-\$600)$$
$$\$1200 = 0.2\,(\$4300) + 0.8\,(\$1200) - P\,(\text{Weak})\,(\$1200) - P\,(\text{Weak})\,(\$600)$$
$$P\,(\text{Weak}) = (0.2\,(\$4300) + 0.8\,(\$1200) - \$1200)\,/\,(\$1200 + \$600) = 34.4\%$$

Continued

Example 2.2 Simplified Investment Decision—cont'd

Thus, if the probability of a weak stock market is greater than, or equal to, roughly 34%, then the CD should be chosen. To determine the critical value at which the high-risk stock fund should be chosen:

$$Set\ EV_{\text{Low-risk Stock}} = EV_{\text{High-risk Stock}}$$
$$0.2\ (\$6600) + (1 - 0.2 - P\ (Weak))\ (\$800) + P\ (Weak)\ (-\$1,500) =$$
$$0.2\ (\$4300) + (1 - 0.2 - P\ (Weak))\ (\$1,200) + P\ (Weak)\ (-\$600)$$

$$0.2\ (\$6600) + 0.8\ (\$800) - P\ (Weak)\ (\$800) - P\ (Weak)\ (\$1500) =$$
$$0.2\ (\$4300) + 0.8\ (\$1200) - P\ (Weak)\ (\$1200) - P\ (Weak)\ (\$600)$$

$$P\ (Weak) = (0.2\ (\$6600) + 0.8\ (\$800) - 0.2\ (\$4300) - 0.8\ (\$1200))\ /$$
$$(\$800 + \$1500 - \$1200 - \$600 = 28\ \%$$

Thus, if the probability of a weak stock market is less than, or equal to, roughly 28%, then the high-risk stock fund should be chosen. Managerially, the range for P(Weak), over which the low-risk stock should be chosen is relatively small:

$$(28\% \le P(\text{Weak}) \le 34.4\%).$$

It is unlikely that this probability could be measured that accurately, and thus the decision set should be narrowed to choose between the high-risk stock fund and the CD. You must then estimate the range in which the actual probability of a weak stock market falls and then choose the high-risk stock fund if $P(Weak) \le \sim 33\%$ or the CD if $P(Weak) \ge \sim 33\%$.

The graph in Fig. 2.9 shows the expected values for each option given the assumption that $P(Strong)$ is relatively certain to be 20%.

This example illustrates the process of determining the effect of varying a piece of information with a large degree of uncertainty. An analyst must ascertain which pieces of information are the least certain (weakest) and determine what will happen as the real value diverges from the assumed value.

The lazy person works the hardest and the cheapskate pays the most.

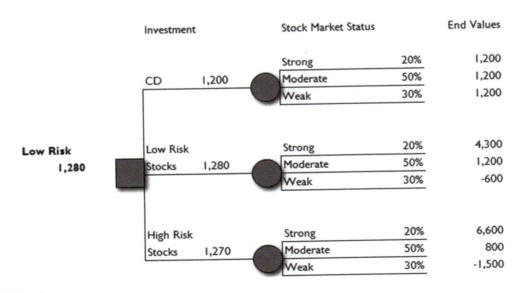

FIGURE 2.8

Simplified Investment Decision Tree

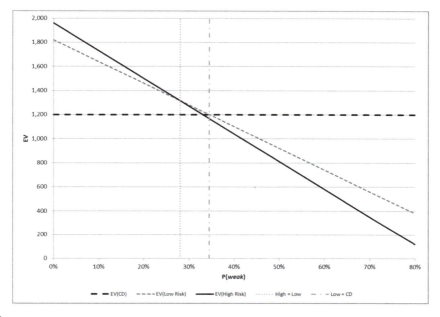

FIGURE 2.9

Sensitivity Analysis for the Simplified Investment Problem

2.5 Expected value of perfect information

The concept of *expected value of perfect information* (EVPI) is similar to sensitivity analysis. The EVPI is how much additional money could be made on average if you knew *with certainty* what would happen. Initially this may seem irrelevant, as no such certainty exists. But this concept provides the limit as to what you would pay to know the future. In more practical terms, the EVPI provides the upper bound on what you would pay for information such as a perfect forecast, perfect marketing research, perfect knowledge of stock prices in the future, credit worthiness, and perfect testing procedures. Thus, if the cost of such forecasts exceeds the EVPI, then they are not worth pursuing.

As an example, suppose that a 100% accurate marketing research forecast of demand could be obtained for $500,000. Furthermore, suppose that with this information the optimum profit for the new product is $2 million and without the marketing research the profit would be only $1.75 million. The EVPI is $250,000 and is less than the $500,000 that would have to be spent to obtain the additional $250,000. Clearly, that marketing research is not worth purchasing.

The essential concept for determining the Expected Value of Perfect Information is:

EVPI is based on omniscience, not omnipotence.

Consider the decision presented in Example 1.2:

Would you rather have $100 "for sure" (absolutely certain) or a 50% chance of $300?
Imagine that this decision is faced on a daily basis and at the beginning of each day the outcome of $0 or $300 is known (hence, *omniscient = perfect information*). With a perfect forecast, the

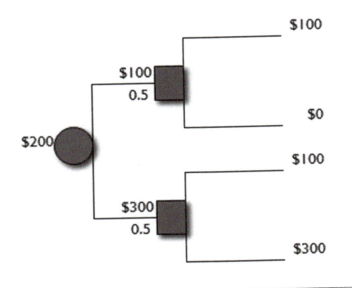

FIGURE 2.10

Decision Tree With Perfect Information

forecast is $0 for half the days and $300 for the other half. With this knowledge, the outcomes are known, but you cannot make them happen, hence *omniscient*, not *omnipotent*. Clearly on the days when $0 is the outcome, you would choose the $100 option, and on the days when $300 is the outcome, you would choose the $300 rather than the $100. As the outcomes are known (certain) before the decision is made, the decision tree becomes as shown in Fig. 2.10.

Thus, *with* perfect information, the expected value is:

$$\text{EV}_{\textbf{with Perfect Information}} = 0.50\,(\$100) + 0.50\,(\$300) = \$200$$

Without the perfect information, the expected value is:

$$\text{EV}_{\textbf{without Perfect Information}} = \max\,[\text{EVA}, \text{EVB}]$$

$$\text{EV}_{\textbf{without Perfect Information}} = \max\,[\$100, 0.50\,(\$0) + 0.50\,(\$300)]$$

$$\text{EV}_{\textbf{without Perfect Information}} = \max\,[\$100, \$150] = \$150$$

Thus, the Expected Value *of* the Perfect Information is:

$$EV_{\text{of}}\ \text{Perfect Information} = EV_{\text{with}}\ \text{Perfect Information} - EV_{\text{without}}\ \text{Perfect Information} =$$
$$\$200 - \$150 = \$50 = \text{EVPI}$$

$$\text{EV}_{\textbf{of Perfect Information}} = \text{EV}_{\textbf{with Perfect Information}} - \text{EV}_{\textbf{without Perfect Information}}$$

$$\text{EV}_{\textbf{of Perfect Information}} = \$200 - \$150 = \$50$$

2.6 Properties of decision trees

A challenging aspect of structuring decision trees is that there are many possible decision trees for the same set of decisions. *Linear transformations* (multiplying by, and/or adding, a constant) of the outcomes will not change the final answer; these will simply rescale the end values. The following examples will help you consider why this must be true from both mathematical and logical standpoints.

Similarly, often there are equivalent ways that sequential and simultaneous decisions and outcomes (branches and probabilities) can be constructed.

2.6.1 Linear transforms

Changing the end values by a linear function (e.g., $EV_{\text{transform}} = c_0 + c_1\, EV_{\text{original}}$) will not change the decision. First, consider what happens when a constant c is added to all end values.

As

$$EV = \sum_i (p_i\, v_i) = p_1\, v_1 + p_2\, v_2 + \ldots + p_i\, v_i,$$

adding a constant, c, to all the end values (v_i) yields an expected value of:

$$p_1\,(v_1 + c) + p_2\,(v_2 + c) + \ldots + p_i\,(v_i + c) = [p_1 v_1 + p_2 v_2 + \ldots + p_i v_i] + [p_1 c + p_2 c + \ldots + p_i c]$$

$$= EV + [p_1 c + p_2 c + \ldots + p_i c] = EV + c\,[p_1 + p_2 + \ldots + p_i]$$

$$= EV + c \sum_{ip_i} \left(\text{because the probabilities must sum to 1, then } \sum_{ip_i} = 1\right) = EV + c$$

Thus, if $EV_A > EV_B$, then $(EV_A + c) > (EV_B + c)$, and decision A is preferred to decision B with, or without, the constant added. This is why *sunk costs* are irrelevant to making a decision.

As an example, add $50 (a constant) to all of the end values of the $100 for sure versus 50% chance of $300 problem (Fig. 2.11).

The lower branch is still the best decision. Next, consider what happens when the *end values* are multiplied by a constant.

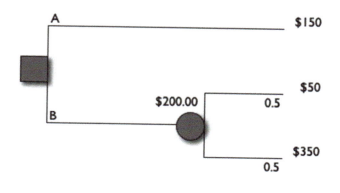

FIGURE 2.11

Adding a Constant Does Not Change the Decision

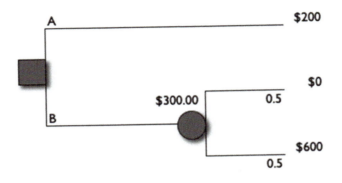

FIGURE 2.12

Multiplying by a Constant Does Not Change the Decision

Again start with:

$$EV = \sum_i (p_i v_i) = p_1 v_1 + p_2 v_2 + \dots + p_i v_i$$

Then multiplying all the end values by a constant, c, yields an expected value of:

$$p_1 \, cv_1 + p_2 \, cv_2 + \dots + p_i \, cv_i = cp_1 v_1 + cp_2 v_2 + \dots + cp_i v_i = c \, [p_1 v_1 + p_2 v_2 + \dots + p_i v_i] = c \, EV$$

If $EV_A > EV_B$, then $c \, EV_A > c \, EV_B$, and decision A is preferred to decision B with, or without, the constant multiplied.

As an example, multiply each of the end values of the $100 for sure versus 50% chance of $300 problem by 2 (Fig. 2.12).

The lower branch is still the best decision. In an applied example, converting all end values from US Dollars to Euros (multiplying by a constant) would not change the decision.

Finally, consider those three versions of the decision tree at the same time (Fig. 2. 13).

Although those three decision trees have different psychological effects associated with them, they yield the same answer: choose the lower branch: option **B**.

The TRUTH is the TRUTH, and nothing you do that is arbitrary will change the TRUTH.

2.6.2 Equivalent decision structures

Decisions or events that are in sequential order can be structured as simultaneous for the purposes of constructing a decision tree. As an example, consider a retailer who must determine both the price of an item and the quantity to order. For the sake of simplicity, consider only two price levels and two corresponding quantities for each price level. The retailer is considering selling the product for either $20 or $25. If the price is $20, then demand will be higher, and the decision will be between 5000 and 7500 units. If the price is $25, then demand will be lower, and the decision will be between 3000 and 5000 units. Fig. 2.14 shows two decision trees that represent the decision equivalently.

Similarly, sequential random events can be equivalently represented. As an example, consider a store with demand for a product that is dependent upon the weather. If the weather is sunny, then

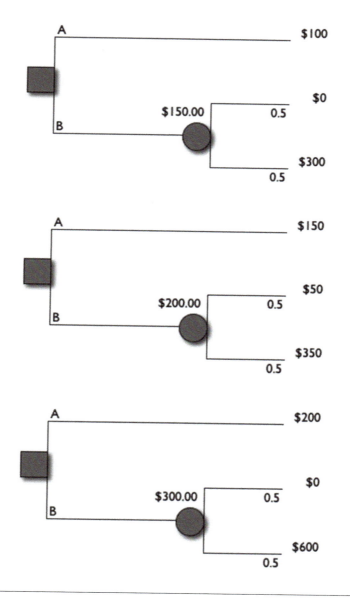

FIGURE 2.13

Three Versions of the Fundamental Decision

demand will be higher than if it is rainy. The probability of sunny weather is 80%. Table 2.2 lists the demand and probabilities of the associated demand depending upon the weather.

Fig. 2.15 shows two decision trees that represent the random events equivalently. The first tree is typically preferrable because it represents the time dependency of the two random events; however,

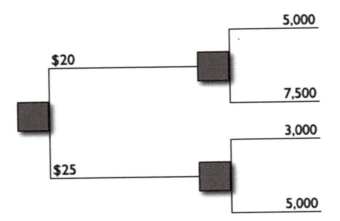

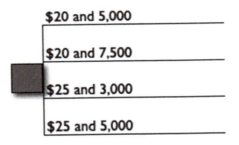

FIGURE 2.14

Decision Trees Representing Sequential Decisions

Table 2.2 Probabilities and associated demand.

Weather	Probability	Demand	Probability
Sunny	80%	50	30%
		75	70%
Rainy	20%	30	60%
		50	40%

mathematically, the two trees are equivalent. Note in the lower tree that the sums of probabilities of sunny, 24% + 56% = 80%, and rainy, 12% + 8% = 20%, just as they did in the top tree. This mathematical fact leads toward an introductory discussion of probability.

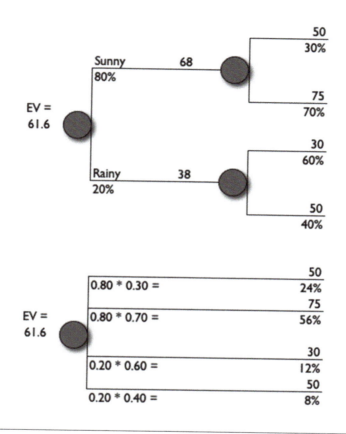

FIGURE 2.15

Decision Trees Representing Sequential Random Events

2.7 Probability: the measure of uncertainty

By using probability to account for uncertainty and risk, decision analysis provides a method for making better managerial decisions. Thus, decision analysis requires estimates of probability. Two natural next questions are as follows: Where do the probabilities come from? What do they mean? Before those questions can be answered, basic principles and terminology of probability theory must be more fully explained.

Probability is the branch of mathematics concerned with the quantification and analysis of random processes. Another term for a random process is an *uncertain process*. Reminder: another term for a *random process* is a **stochastic process**. A process is considered to be statistically random when the outcomes are not certain or perfectly predictable. The mathematical opposite of random is *deterministic*.

Statistical randomness does not necessarily imply without reason or cause. Statistically random implies that the outcomes are not deterministically foreseeable. As an example, a competitor's bid for a construction project is not known to us with certainty. Thus, although the competitor used a nonrandom process to determine their bid, from our perspective the bid is statistically random. As another example, consider weather forecasting. The physics involved in whether it rains tomorrow are sufficiently complex as to be not perfectly forecastable. Thus, even though there is a deterministic process that causes it to either rain or not rain, the process is sufficiently uncertain for it to be viewed as statistically random.

This distinction between purely random and statistically random is important to remember because it allows managers to use probability to make decisions about processes with underlying rules that are not readily apparent to the analyst, like a competitor's pricing policy. Thus, we can study phenomenon today that may have very complex rules and formulas that have yet to be discovered.

Although there are many views of probability, for this book, probability is a measure of the relative likelihood of an event happening in the future. Thus, it is an estimate of the likelihood of an event in the future based upon the relative frequency of events in the past. Thus, one mathematical definition of probability is as follows:

$$\text{Probability of an event } x = \frac{\text{No. of times the event } x \text{ happened}}{\text{No. of times the event could have happened}}$$

In notational form:

$$P(x) = n(x) / n;$$

where $n(x)$ is number of times x happened and n is the total number of outcomes (*sample size*). $n(x)$ is sometimes simplified as f, where f is used to represent the number of times (*frequency*) an outcome occurs. Often, a simplified notation of probability is used:

$$p = f / n;$$

where p is understood to be a probability of an event (outcome), f is the frequency of that outcome, and n is the sample size.

Probability tells you how many people will do a specific something—but it will not tell you who will do it; that is frustrating.

2.8 Where do the probabilities come from?

Obviously, probabilities are a critical set of information necessary for solving stochastic optimization problems. Three types of probabilities are *subjective*, *empirical*, and *theoretical* probability, each with their own source of information.

Subjective (*EXPERIENCE-based*) probabilities, sometimes called *personal* probabilities, are determined by the experience of the decision maker. Examples: risk assessment (Lloyds of London), game theory, general business strategy, and odds for sporting events.

Empirical (*DATA-based* or *evidence-based*) probabilities are determined by using historical data. In the simplest case—like the medical treatment example (Example 1.1)—the probabilities are estimated by using the relative frequencies of the outcomes. In more complex cases, statistical analysis is used to determine the appropriate probabilities. Empirical probabilities are the focus of this book. **Theoretical** (*THEORY-based*) probability, sometimes referred to as *classical* probability is determined by "theory" or concept. These probabilities are usually determined by calculating the possible number of combinations. Examples: rolling dice, flipping coins, colored balls in "urns," Bernoulli trials, and binomial and Gaussian (normal) distributions.

Summary:

- **Subjective:** EXPERIENCE BASED
- **Empirical:** EVIDENCE BASED, also DATA BASED
- **Theoretical/Classical:** THEORY BASED

2.9 Elements of probability

Many probability problems are confusing due to their wording (semantics). To reduce the difficulties and confusion due to ambiguity and interpretation of the wording situations concerning probability, it is necessary to define some common elements and terms of probability. Table 2.3 provides definitions and examples of elemental probability terms.

Table 2.3 Fundamental probability terms and concepts.

Term	Concept	Examples
Random process	A phenomenon or process with uncertain results (outcomes)	Rolling a single die Demand for milk in a single day at a specific store
Trial	Elemental unit of a random process	A single die roll A single day of milk demand at a specific store
Outcome	Elemental result of a random process	A single die roll is a 2 Demand for milk in a single day is 10 gallons
Probability space	Set of all possible outcomes	A single die roll $\in \{1, 2, 3, 4, 5, 6\}$ Demand for milk in a single day $\in \{0, 1, 2, \ldots, \infty\}$ gallons
Event	Set, or subset, of outcomes	A single die roll is even Demand for milk in a single day is 10, or fewer, gallons
Probability	Measure of the likelihood of an event	1/6 chance that a single die roll is a 2 14% chance that demand for milk in a single day is 10 gallons
Random variable	A quantity resulting from an event of a random process	The number of spots on a single die roll Demand for milk on a specific day
Discrete random variable	A random variable with separate, countable outcomes	The number of spots on a single die roll Demand for milk on a specific day
Continuous random variable	A random variable with infinite, uncountable outcomes	Inches of rain on a specific day Amount of time spent in line waiting for a bank teller

Example 2.3 Home insurance

Consider the problem of insuring a house from both the homeowner's and the insurance company's points of view (Fig. 2.16). The annual premium for this homeowner is $350; the home's insured value is $350,000, and the rate of incidence (probability) of total loss is 1 in 100,000 = 1/100,000 = 0.00001.

Furthermore, consider these questions.

1. For the homeowner, the expected value is less expensive to not buy insurance, so why do we buy insurance?

    A fire is catastrophic for most people, and *insurance is the price of certainty*.

2. How would you modify the decision tree from the homeowner's point of view to get the correct answer (buy insurance)?

    Put −$10,000,000,000 ($\cong -\infty$) as the end value for fire.

3. How does rising incidence of fire influence price?

    The insurance company must increase price to cover increased losses to maintain the same return.

4. Why do insurance companies use expected value?

    A single fire is not catastrophic for the pool of insured people, and the no-fires (nonclaimants) pay for the fires.

    Two of the most common decisions faced by companies are *how much product or capacity to have* and *what price should be charged*. Examples of these two common decisions are presented to provide a deeper understanding of how decision trees are used in business analytics to make decisions.

    The first is an example of the Newsvendor Problem. Newsvendor problems arise whenever a decision maker must decide *how much to have*, such as in supply chain and capacity decisions. The Newsvendor Problem is used in many settings, such as retail and grocery supply chain management, airline ticket sales, and hotel reservations. The Newsvendor Problem is a part of the broader management topic of *revenue management*. The next example is a simplified example to illustrate how the problem got its name.

2.10 Probability notation

Terminology and notation are used to provide a common international language to describe a field of study. Just as music has its own set of terms and notation, probability has a set of terms and notation. These terms and notation provide a consistent method for expressing elemental ideas in a common form.

The probability that the random variable X has an outcome of x is defined, or calculated, according to a probability function, $f(x)$:

$$f(x) = \text{Probability of } x = P(X = x)$$

As an example, the demand for a specific model of car next month is a random variable (unknown and uncertain quantity); using this notation, the probability of demand being five cars next month could be written as:

$$P(\text{Demand} = 5)$$

or, more simply,

$$f(5).$$

Random variables, and their associated probability distributions, are categorized as either *discrete* or *continuous*. Discrete random variables result in values that are *separately countable* and unable to be further divided into components. Two examples are demand for cars and number of passengers arriving at an airline gate for a flight. Continuous random variables result in values

House Insurance

Premium	$350
Insured Value	$350,000
Rate of Incidence	0.00001

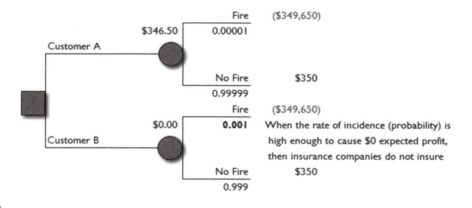

Homeowner's Point of View   End Values

Company Point of View

When the rate of incidence (probability) is high enough to cause $0 expected profit, then insurance companies do not insure

FIGURE 2.16

Expected Value for Homeowners Insurance

Example 2.4 Newsvendor problem

The Newsvendor Problem is a classic inventory/capacity decision problem that provides the foundation for many capacity and pricing problems. A newsvendor at a newspaper and magazine stand in a subway station must determine how many newspapers to stock to sell on Sunday. The newsvendor buys the paper for $0.50 and sells it for $3.50. The vendor sells excess newspapers and magazines for recycling at a rate that converts to $0.05 per Sunday paper. The various quantities of newspapers sold (assume sales = demand) the previous 100 Sundays is given in Table 2.4. As an example, 10 papers were sold on 30 of the previous 100 Sundays. What is the expected value of the number of papers demanded on a Sunday? How many Sunday newspapers should the newsvendor order?

As a first estimate, compute the *expected value* of the number of newspapers demanded by taking the sum of the products of the probabilities times their associated outcomes:

$$EV_{Demand} = 30/100 \ (10) \ + 40/100 \ (11) \ + 20/100 \ (12) \ + 10/100 \ (13) \ = 11.1 \ newspapers$$

To determine the number of newspapers to stock (order), use the steps from Section 2.3:
1. List all the events.
    DECISION: How many newspapers to order.
    RANDOM EVENTS: Number of newspapers requested (demand).
2. Use the list to draw the DECISION TREE.
    See Fig. 2.17.
3. Compute the END VALUES.

$$\text{End Value}_{order} = \text{Revenue} - \text{Cost}$$
$$\text{End Value}_{order} = \text{Units Sold} * \text{Price} - \text{Order} * \text{Variable Cost} - \text{Cost of Shortage} - \text{Cost of Extra}$$
$$\text{Units Sold} = \text{MIN}(\text{Demand}, \ \text{On Hand})$$
$$\text{Cost of Shortage} = \text{Goodwill Loss} = \ (\text{Demand} - \text{Units Sold}) * \text{Goodwill}$$
$$\text{Cost of Extra} = \text{Salvage Value} = (\text{Order} - \text{Units Sold}) * \text{Recycle Value}$$

Note that in this situation, because the vendor gets $0.05 per extra paper, the Cost of Extra is actually revenue rather than a cost. The end values are shown in Fig. 2.17.
4. Assign probabilities to each outcome (branch) of each RANDOM EVENT (circle).
    The probabilities of demand are determined by the frequencies of each demand value.
    For example, $P(Demand=10) = 30/100$.
5. Compute the EXPECTED VALUE for each RANDOM EVENT (circle).

$$EV_{order \ 10} = 0.30 \ (\$30.00) \ + 0.40 \ (\$30.00) \ + 0.20 \ (\$30.00) \ + 0.10 \ (\$30.00) \ = \$30.00$$
$$EV_{order \ 11} = 0.30 \ (\$29.55) \ + 0.40 \ (\$33.00) \ + 0.20 \ (\$33.00) \ + 0.10 \ (\$33.00) \ = \$31.97$$
$$EV_{order \ 12} = 0.30 \ (\$29.10) \ + 0.40 \ (\$32.55) \ + 0.20 \ (\$36.00) \ + 0.10 \ (\$36.00) \ = \$32.55$$
$$EV_{order \ 13} = 0.30 \ (\$28.65) \ + 0.40 \ (\$32.10) \ + 0.20 \ (\$35.55) \ + 0.10 \ (\$39.00) \ = \$32.45$$

The optimum amount to order is 12 newspapers. Why is the solution not the 11 newspapers that would meet demand on average? In addition, note that the difference between the expected values of ordering 12 or 13 newspapers ($EV_{12}-EV_{13}$) is only $0.10. Would you be willing to pay $0.10 to always have enough newspapers on hand? What would the Goodwill (Cost of Shortage) need to be to justify ordering 13 newspapers?

In this example, the decision and random event branches take a step toward continuous (numerical) values. This does not necessarily make the problem more difficult—just bigger. It is important to use a decision tree to set up and illustrate the problem, then a tabular form can be used to solve larger problems. The ability of spreadsheets to perform large numbers of similar calculations (by using either *copy* and *paste*, or the Data Table command) provides the means of solving problems involving many more choices and outcomes.

A spreadsheet solution for this example is shown in Fig. 2.18.

Example 2.5 demonstrates how the Newsvendor Problem is applied to car rentals, as is common in revenue management applications.

Table 2.4 Estimated probability distribution of demand for sunday newspapers

Demand	Sundays
10	30
11	40
12	20
13	10

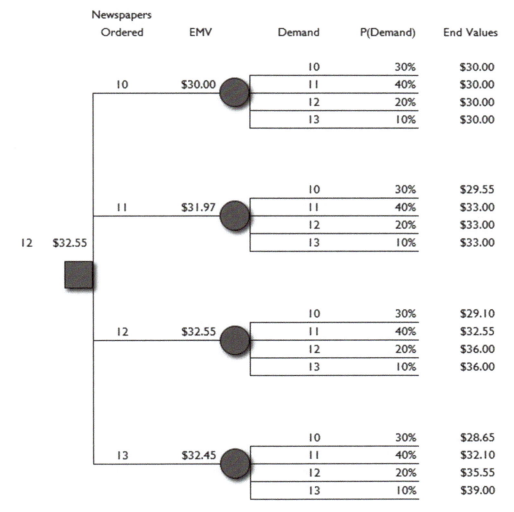

FIGURE 2.17

Decision Tree for the Newsvendor Problem

12			f_x {=SUM((I8:I20=I3)*B8:B20)}						
	A	B	C	D	E	F	G	H	I
1	Price	$3.50							
2	Variable Cost	$0.50					Order		12
3	Salvage Value	$0.05					Max EMV		$32.55
4	Goodwill	$0.00							
5									
6				Newspapers					
7	Scenario	Ordered	Demanded	Units Sold	Shortage	Extra	End Value	Probability	EMV
8	1	10	10	10	0	0	$30.00	30%	$30.00
9	2	10	11	10	1	0	$30.00	40%	
10	3	10	12	10	2	0	$30.00	20%	
11	4	10	13	10	3	0	$30.00	10%	
12	5	11	10	10	0	1	$29.55	30%	$31.97
13	6	11	11	11	0	0	$33.00	40%	
14	7	11	12	11	1	0	$33.00	20%	
15	8	11	13	11	2	0	$33.00	10%	
16	9	12	10	10	0	2	$29.10	30%	$32.55
17	10	12	11	11	0	1	$32.55	40%	
18	11	12	12	12	0	0	$36.00	20%	
19	12	12	13	12	0	1	$36.00	10%	
20	13	13	10	10	0	3	$28.65	30%	$32.45
21	14	13	11	11	0	2	$32.10	40%	
22	15	13	12	12	0	1	$35.55	20%	
23	16	13	13	13	0	0	$39.00	10%	

FIGURE 2.18

Spreadsheet Solution for the Newsvendor Problem

that are **infinitely divisible**. Two examples are the number of cubic feet of natural gas used by customers in a heating season and the amount of time required to service an aircraft between flights.

Some variables are technically discrete but so numerous as to be nearly continuous. Two examples are money and bits of information required for a digital recording. Rather than thinking of variables as dichotomously either discrete or continuous, it is useful to think of a metaphorical continuum at the seashore beginning with large rocks (discrete) transitioning to pebbles (still discrete—but quite numerous), which then give way to sand (technically discrete but practically continuous), finally ending in the ocean (continuous).

2.11 Applications of decision analysis and decision trees

Decision analysis and, more specifically, decision trees are used in many different industries. The warranty example from Example 2.1 is a starting point for considering how insurance companies use decision analysis. Example 2.3 shows how decision tree are used at a larger scale for homeowners insurance.

Example 2.5 Car Rental Problem

On Thursday evening, the manager of a small branch of a car rental agency finds that she has six cars available for rental on the following day. However, she can request delivery of additional cars, at a cost of $20 each, from the regional depot. Each car that is rented produces an expected profit of $40 (not including the $20 of delivery cost if incurred). After reviewing records for previous Fridays, the manager finds that the number of cars requested on 20 previous Fridays is 7, 9, 8, 7, 10, 8, 7, 8, 9, 10, 7, 6, 8, 9, 8, 8, 6, 7, 7, 9. How many cars should be ordered? How do "goodwill" losses affect the number of cars to be ordered? What is the EVPI?

Using the steps from Section 2.3, do the following:

1. List all the events.
   DECISION: How many cars to order
   RANDOM EVENTS: Number of cars requested (demand)
2. Use the list to draw the DECISION TREE.
   See Fig. 2.19.
3. Compute the END VALUES .

$$\text{End Value}_{order} = \text{Revenue} - \text{Cost}$$
$$\text{End Value}_{order} = \text{MIN} \, (\text{Demand}, \ \text{On Hand}) \, * \text{Profit} - \text{Order} * \text{Order Cost} - \text{Cost of Shortage}$$
$$\text{Cost of Shortage} = \text{Goodwill Loss} = \text{MAX} \ (\text{Demand} - \text{On Hand}, \ 0) \, * \text{Goodwill}$$

The end values are shown in Fig. 2.19.

4. Assign probabilities to each outcome (branch) of each RANDOM EVENT (circle).
   The probabilities of demand are determined by the frequencies of each demand value.
   For example, the probability that demand is 6 equals 2/20 (10%) because 2 of the 20 data observation are equal to 6.
5. Compute the EXPECTED VALUE for each RANDOM EVENT (circle).

$$EV_{order \ 0} = 0.1 \, (\$240) + 0.3 \, (\$240) + 0.3 \, (\$240) + 0.2 \, (\$240) + 0.1 \, (\$240) = \$240$$
$$EV_{order \ 1} = 0.1 \, (\$220) + 0.3 \, (\$260) + 0.3 \, (\$260) + 0.2 \, (\$260) + 0.1 \, (\$260) = \$256$$
$$EV_{order \ 2} = 0.1 \, (\$200) + 0.3 \, (\$240) + 0.3 \, (\$280) + 0.2 \, (\$280) + 0.1 \, (\$280) = \$260$$
$$EV_{order \ 3} = 0.1 \, (\$180) + 0.3 \, (\$220) + 0.3 \, (\$260) + 0.2 \, (\$300) + 0.1 \, (\$300) = \$252$$
$$EV_{order \ 4} = 0.1 \, (\$160) + 0.3 \, (\$200) + 0.3 \, (\$240) + 0.2 \, (\$280) + 0.1 \, (\$320) = \$236$$

Choose order 2 if Goodwill = $0 because it maximizes the expected (monetary) value.

Thus, the optimum number of cars to order is two additional (eight total) cars. The EVPI is computed in this manner:

$$EV_{with} \text{ Perfect Information} = 0.1 \, (\$240) + 0.3 \, (\$260) + 0.3 \, (\$280) + 0.2 \, (\$300) + 0.1 \, (\$320) = \$278$$

Without the perfect information, the expected value is:

$$EV_{without} \text{ Perfect Information} = \$260$$

Thus, the Expected Value *of* the Perfect Information is:

$$EV_{of} \text{ Perfect Information} = EV_{with} \text{ Perfect Information} - EV_{without} \text{ Perfect Information} = \$278 - \$260 = \$18$$

Thus, $18 is the most you would pay each week for improving the forecast of demand to be more certain. So, you would not work more than an hour (at $18/hour) to improve the forecasting accuracy.

As in the previous newsvendor example, the decision and random event branches take another step toward continuous (numerical) values. Again, it is important to use a decision tree to set up and illustrate the problem, then use the computer to solve the problem. A spreadsheet version of the solution is shown in Fig. 2.20.

In this problem, the Goodwill loss amount is the penalty for not meeting demand and is completely unknown at this point, and thus it would be the first candidate for sensitivity analysis. With a value of Goodwill at $0, the decision is to order two additional cars. At a value of Goodwill = $26.27, the decision is to order either two or three additional cars (which would you chose and why?); at a value of $160, the decision is to order four additional cars. What do you recommend and why?

Continued

Example 2.5 Car Rental Problem—cont'd

The next example illustrates the second common decision managers regularly face—what price to charge for products or services. Bidding problems are the foundation for understanding pricing problems. Prior to solving the problem, it is essential to determine whether the problem is a *high*, or *low*, *bidder wins* situation.

In bidding/pricing situations, the decision and random event branches are continuous (numerical) values. Even though all the branches are not full enumerated, a decision tree is vital to set up and illustrate the problem.

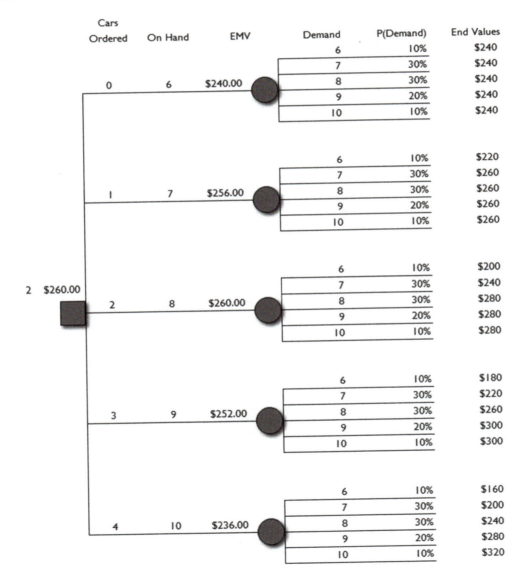

FIGURE 2.19

Decision Tree for the Car Rental Example

	A	B	C	D	E	F	G	H
1								
2								
3								
4		On Hand	6				Order	2
5		Profit	$40				Max EMV	$260.00
6		Cost	$20					
7		Good Will	$0.00					
8				Cars				
9		Scenario	Ordered	Available	Demanded	End Value	Probability	EMV
10		1	0	6	6	$240	10%	$240.00
11		2	0	6	7	$240	30%	
12		3	0	6	8	$240	30%	
13		4	0	6	9	$240	20%	
14		5	0	6	10	$240	10%	
15		6	1	7	6	$220	10%	$256.00
16		7	1	7	7	$260	30%	
17		8	1	7	8	$260	30%	
18		9	1	7	9	$260	20%	
19		10	1	7	10	$260	10%	
20		11	2	8	6	$200	10%	$260.00
21		12	2	8	7	$240	30%	
22		13	2	8	8	$280	30%	
23		14	2	8	9	$280	20%	
24		15	2	8	10	$280	10%	
25		16	3	9	6	$180	10%	$252.00
26		17	3	9	7	$220	30%	
27		18	3	9	8	$260	30%	
28		19	3	9	9	$300	20%	
29		20	3	9	10	$300	10%	
30		21	4	10	6	$160	10%	$236.00
31		22	4	10	7	$200	30%	
32		23	4	10	8	$240	30%	
33		24	4	10	9	$280	20%	
34		25	4	10	10	$320	10%	

FIGURE 2.20

Spreadsheet Solution for the Car Rental Example

2.12 Summary of the decision analysis process

1. **Decisions** and **Random Events** = Structuring the problem
2. **End Values** = Measuring the outcomes (Cost Structure)
3. **Probabilities** = Weighting the outcomes
4. **Expected Values** = Weighted averages
5. **Choosing the Optimum** = Making the best decision

Example 2.6 Bidding

A real estate developer is interested in buying a downtown property to convert office space into a commercial and residential property. The developer estimates the present value of the revenue to be $3,000,000. The developer must submit a bid to obtain the property. A bid of $1,200,000 is certain to lose the bid. At the other extreme, a bid of $2,500,000 is certain to win the bid. Furthermore, the developer estimates that a bid of $2,000,000 has a 50% chance of winning the bid.

Why is it sufficient to know the present value of the project but not the costs if the bid is won?

As the current owners hope to obtain the maximum amount of money for their property, this is a *high bid wins* situation. Because money is a continuous variable, the bidding decision is continuous as well. Rather than enumerate all possible bids, ellipses, or an arc, are used to indicate the options not shown between the decision branches. The decision tree shown in Fig. 2.21 shows the structure of the problem.

Because the bids are continuous, their associated probabilities must be interpolated as a function of the bid. See the IF statement in the Excel edit box in Fig. 2.22 for the Excel formula for the piece-wise linear function used to calculate the probabilities.

Exercise Set 2: Decision Trees

1. A real estate investor owns a small office building she has leased to a major insurance company for a rental fee based on a share of the profits. If the insurance company is successful, the present value of future rentals is estimated at $15 million. If the insurance company is not successful, the present value of the rentals will be $2 million. The insurance company has offered the investor $6 million to buy the property outright. On an EMV basis, what probability would need to be assigned to "success" for the investor to be indifferent between selling and not selling?

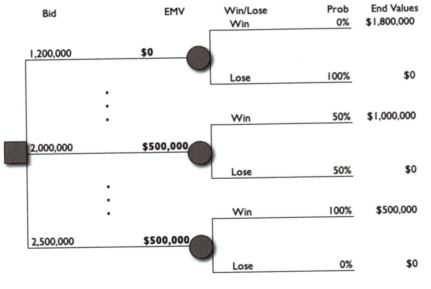

FIGURE 2.21

Decision Tree for the Bidding Example

	D14		✕ ✓	fx =IF(C14<$B$7,$D$6*C14+$E$6,IF(C14>$B$8,1,$D$7*C14+$E$7))		

	B	C	D	E	F
1					
2	Revenue	3,000,000			
3					
4					
5	Bid	P(win)	Slope	Intercept	
6	1,200,000	0%	0.000000625	-75.00%	
7	2,000,000	50%	0.000001000	-150.00%	
8	2,500,000	100%			
9					
10			Max EV Profit	$562,500 =MAX(E14:E40)	
11			Opt Bid	2,250,000 =INDEX(C14:C40,MATCH(E10,E14:E40,0))	
12					
13		Bid	P(win)	EV Profit	
14	50,000	1,200,000	0.00%	$0	
15		1,250,000	3.13%	$54,688	
16		1,300,000	6.25%	$106,250	
17		1,350,000	9.38%	$154,688	
18		1,400,000	12.50%	$200,000	
19		1,450,000	15.63%	$242,188	
20		1,500,000	18.75%	$281,250	
21		1,550,000	21.88%	$317,188	
22		1,600,000	25.00%	$350,000	
23		1,650,000	28.13%	$379,688	
24		1,700,000	31.25%	$406,250	
25		1,750,000	34.38%	$429,688	
26		1,800,000	37.50%	$450,000	
27		1,850,000	40.63%	$467,188	
28		1,900,000	43.75%	$481,250	
29		1,950,000	46.88%	$492,188	
30		2,000,000	50.00%	$500,000	
31		2,050,000	55.00%	$522,500	
32		2,100,000	60.00%	$540,000	
33		2,150,000	65.00%	$552,500	
34		2,200,000	70.00%	$560,000	
35		2,250,000	75.00%	$562,500	
36		2,300,000	80.00%	$560,000	
37		2,350,000	85.00%	$552,500	
38		2,400,000	90.00%	$540,000	
39		2,450,000	95.00%	$522,500	
40		2,500,000	100.00%	$500,000	

FIGURE 2.22

Spreadsheet Solution for the Bidding Example

2. Currently, a brand of cereal is contributing $1,000,000 of annual profits. The brand manager of the cereal is responsible for increasing this amount for the upcoming year and thinks the brand can do better with a "new and improved" cereal. She estimates that the annual profits for such a cereal are equally likely to be $500,000, $900,000, or $1,800,000. A test market could provide a forecast of

the future profitability of the improved cereal. Construct a decision tree to determine the most that should be paid for such a test market.

3. A bank is developing policies for deciding whether to accept or deny credit card applications from existing customers. For a specific class of customers, if the bank accepts the application, then there is a 95% chance the customer will remain with the bank and a 5% chance the customer will close (terminate) their account. If the customer's application is denied, then there is a 50% chance the customer will remain with the bank and a 50% chance the customer will close their account. Currently, the typical annual profit from a customer whose credit card application has been accepted is $185, whereas the typical annual profit from a customer whose credit card application has been denied is $250.

   a. Explain the cost structure and reasoning for the values.
   b. Should the bank accept or decline such applications?
   c. What typical annual profit from a customer whose credit card application has been denied is needed to reconsider accepting their application?

4. A commercial banker is considering which of two loan applications to accept. Both loans are short term (1 year) for $100,000 at an annual rate of 8.5%. With the tightening of credit, the bank is using these two customers as test cases to determine future lending practices at the bank. The first customer is a retail tire store and, based on its credit score, is representative of a specific credit risk category of customers. Based on the company's credit score and financial statements, there is a 0.5% (= 0.005) chance that this customer will default. In such a case, the bank recovers about 85% of the loan amount. The second customer is a restaurant and is representative of a higher credit risk category with a 1.5% chance of default and a recovery rate of about 60%.

   a. Which loan has the better expected value?
   b. What percentage should be added to the interest rate to make the less attractive expected value a viable loan? This percentage is often referred to as a *risk premium.*

5. A computer manufacturer is bidding to provide computers to a university. The manufacturer estimates the cost to provide the computers to be $3,250,000. Based on previous contracts, the manufacturer estimates that a bid of $5,000,000 is certain to lose the bid. At the other extreme, a bid of $3,000,000 is certain to win the bid. Furthermore, the manufacturer estimates that a bid of $3,800,000 has a 50% chance of winning the bid.

   a. Draw the decision tree for this problem.
   b. Calculate the optimum bid and its associated expected value.

6. A contractor has decided to place a bid for a project. It is estimated that a bid of $240,000 will have a 20% chance of winning the contract, a bid of $220,000 has a 60% chance of winning, and a $200,000 bid has an 80% chance of winning. It is thought that any bid under $180,000 is certain to win, whereas a bid of $260,000 or more is certain to lose.

   If the manufacturer wins the contract, she must solve a design problem in one of two possible ways. She can hire outside consultants, who can guarantee a satisfactory solution, for a price of $80,000. Alternatively, she can invest $30,000 in an attempt to solve the design problem internally; if that effort fails, then she must hire the consultants. She estimates that the probability of successfully solving the design problem in-house is 60%. Once this problem has been solved, the additional cost of fulfilling the contract is $140,000. Construct a decision tree to determine the optimum decision.

7. Piedmont Natural Gas (PNG) is offering a plan to cover hot water heater failures. For a customer enrolling in the plan for a year at $7.00 per month, PNG will pay up to $1000 in repairs

or replacement for the customer's hot water heater. Suppose that for the targeted customers hot water heaters can fail equally likely throughout the year, and that the customers will remain on the plan even after their hot water heaters fail. Thus, you can assume that PNG will collect an entire year of payments for a customer who enrolls in the plan. PNG has the choice of either enrolling a customer in the plan or not enrolling the customer. If PNG does NOT enroll the customer in the plan, then PNG collects $0.

a. Draw the decision tree for this problem.

b. Calculate the probability of hot water heater failure that is required for PNG to break even. In other words, at what probability is $EV_{Not\ Enroll} = EV_{Enroll}$.

c. Given a 5% probability of hot water heater failure, calculate the EVPI.

8. An analyst for a venture capital firm is considering two investments. Both investments are short-term (1-year) investments. One potential investment is in a telecommunications company with a forecasted profit of $2,000,000. Based on research of similar telecommunications ventures, potential market demand, and the financial statements of the telecommunications firm, there is a 60% chance of receiving the $2,000,000 profit and a 40% chance of a loss of $250,000. The second investment is in a pharmaceutical company. Based on research of similar pharmaceutical ventures, potential market demand, and the financial statements of the pharmaceutical firm, there is an 90% chance of receiving a profit of $1,500,000 and a 10% chance that this pharmaceutical venture will result in a loss of $500,000. Calculate the EVPI.

9. An investor is considering investing $15,000 in one of three alternatives: a CD, an exchange-traded fund (ETF) that is comprised of S&P 500 stocks, and a high-risk mutual fund. She considers there to be three possible outcomes: a strong, moderate, or weak stock market. The CD provides a 5% annual rate of return. Table 2.5 gives the rates of return for the various possible outcomes from investing the $15,000.

a. The investor believes that the probability of a strong stock market is 35%, the probability of a moderate stock market is 40%, and the probability of a weak stock market is 25%. Which investment should be chosen according to the EMV criterion?

b. The investor is comfortable with the assessment of a probability of 20% for a weak market. However, she is less sure of the probability assessments for the other two outcomes. Under what range of probabilities for strong stock market does the EMV criterion give the same answer as part (a)?

10. A manufacturer receives regular contracts for large consignments of parts for the automobile industry. This manufacturers' production process is such that when it is operating correctly, 90% of all parts produced meet specifications. However, the production process is prone to a particular malfunction, whose presence can be checked at the beginning of a production run.

Table 2.5 Estimated probability distribution of annual demand

Investment	State of the Stock Market (%)		
	Strong	Moderate	Weak
CD	5	5	5
S&P 500 ETF	15	10	−10
High-tech mutual fund	25	5	−20

Table 2.6 Estimated probability distribution of annual demand

Annual Demand	Probability
400,000	0.25
900,000	0.50
1,300,000	0.25

When the process is operated with this malfunction, 30% of the parts fail to meet specifications. The manufacturer supplies parts under a contract that will yield a profit of $20,000 if only 10% of the parts are defective and a profit of $12,000 if 30% of the parts are defective. The cost of checking for the malfunction is $1000, and if it turns out that repair is needed, the repairs cost a further $2000. Historically, it has been found that the production process functions correctly 80% of the time. Should the manufacturer check the process at the beginning of a production run?

a. Construct a decision tree to determine the optimum decision.

b. Suppose the proportion of occasions on which the production process operates correctly is unknown. Under what range of values for this proportion would the decision in part (a) be appropriate according to the EMV criterion?

11. A truck and automobile manufacturer is going to produce a new vehicle and wants to determine the amount of annual capacity it should build. The new vehicle will sell for $25,000 and have a variable cost of $19,000. Building a unit of annual capacity will cost $6000, and each unit of capacity will cost $1500 annually to maintain—regardless of whether the capacity is used or not. Ford is using a 10-year planning horizon and has forecasted demand over the 10-year period as low, medium, or high. Low demand would be approximately 400,000 vehicles per year for 10 years. Medium demand would be approximately 900,000 vehicles per year for 10 years. High demand would be approximately 1,300,000 vehicles per year for 10 years. The estimated probabilities are given in Table 2.6. What capacity level should the manufacturer choose?

12. After extensive forecasting and developing a production plan, a chocolate manufacturer knows it will need 10 tons of sugar 6 months from now. The purchasing manager has three options for acquiring the necessary sugar:

a. She could buy the sugar now at the current market price and inventory it until needed.

b. She could buy a futures contract now, in which she would pay a set price now for delivery in 6 months.

c. She could wait and buy the sugar in 6 months at the going market price at that time.

The current market price is $0.084 per pound. Due to lost interest and other factors, the inventory holding cost rate is 10% per year. For example, holding $100 of sugar for a year would cost $10. The price of sugar bought now, for delivery in 6 months (the futures contract), is $0.0851 per pound. The transaction costs for 5- and 10-ton futures contracts are $65 and $110, respectively.

The forecasting group has estimated the possible sugar prices in 6 months (in $/pound) and their associated probabilities (Table 2.7).

For this exercise, assume that no sugar can be bought in the intervening 6 months and that sugar can only be bought in 5-ton increments. Construct a decision tree to determine the optimum decision.

Table 2.7 Estimated probability distribution of price in 6 months

Price ($)	Probability
0.078	0.05
0.083	0.25
0.087	0.35
0.091	0.20
0.096	0.15

Table 2.8 Risk report: frame development

Activity	Cost/month (thousands)	Probability of success	Time required for effort (months)	Total cost (thousands)
3D printing development				
Material development	125	0.90	6	750
Printer modification	460	0.75	6	2760
Injection molding				
Normal basis	375	1.00	12	4500
Accelerated basis	1000	1.00	6	6000

Table 2.9 Eden Paper's costs

Bag type	No. of bundles	Bags per bundle (000)	Total bags (000)	EPC's cost (per 000)
Quart liquor bags	2190	3.0	6570	$78.30
10-pound heavy-duty grocery bags	3320	1.0	3320	$118.10
20-pound heavy-duty grocery bags	2920	0.5	1460	$170.70
1/8 barrel sacks	2500	0.5	1250	$162.20

13. A company uses natural gas in its production-processing operations. Neighboring companies in its Upstate New York area have successfully drilled for gas on their premises, and the company is considering following suit. Their initial expenditure would be drilling; this would cost $180,000. If they struck gas, they would have to spend an additional $150,000 to cap the well and provide for the necessary hardware and control equipment. At the current price of natural gas, if the well is successful, it will have a value of $850,000. However, if the price of gas rises to double its current value, a successful well will be worth $1,600,000. The company believes its chance of finding gas is 30%; it also believes that there is a 50% chance that the price of gas will double. Construct a decision tree to determine the optimum decision. Backup is cheap; heart failure is not!

Case

LMT engineering

The LMT Engineering Company has just been awarded a development contract by the US military to design, develop, and demonstrate critical components of a new drone system. The system will be part of a program that is currently receiving much attention in the industry.

An integral part of a drone is the frame. The frame is the main body of the drone. It is often in an "X"-style design, with four arms extending out from a central body. The frame is typically where all the other components are housed, including rotors, battery, boards, and camera setup. Due to the unusual specifications for this drone system, LMT is unable to produce a single-piece frame of the required specifications using the existing equipment and materials.

The engineering department has prepared two alternatives for developing the frame: either injection molding or an improved 3D printing process. LMT must decide which process it should select. The risk report prepared by the engineering department is shown in Table 2.8.

Injection Molding

This process involves joining several shorter lengths of extruded metal into a frame of sufficient length. This work will require extensive testing and reworking over a 12-month period at a cost of $150,000 per month. Although this process will definitely produce an adequate frame, it merely represents a slight modification of existing technology.

3D printing

To make the frame as a single piece, it will be necessary to modify the 3D printer at a monthly cost of $160,000 and to improve the material used at a monthly cost of $50,000. Each of these steps would require 6 months of steady work.

If successful, this process would produce a frame of superior quality at a lower overall cost. As opposed to injection molding, there is some risk that LMT will be unable to perfect the 3D printing process.

After studying the technical problems, the engineering department feels there is a 9 in 10 chance of perfecting the material. However, there is a 1 in 10 chance that at the end of the 6-month development effort, it will know that a satisfactory material cannot be developed within any reasonable time and cost framework, and it will have to rely on injection molding.

The engineers believe there is a three in four chance of successfully modifying the printer but a one in four chance that at the end of a 6-month printer development project, the 3D printing process will have to be abandoned because a printer with the necessary capabilities will be shown to be infeasible.

Other information

Development of the frame must be completed within 18 months to avoid holding up the rest of the contract. It has also been determined that, if necessary, the injection molding work could be done on an accelerated basis in a 6-month period at a monthly cost of $400,000.

The director of engineering, Dr. Denice Ellis, is most interested in the opportunity provided by this contract to explore new technology in the 3D printing process. She feels that if LMT is successful in producing the frame as a single piece, LMT's reputation in the field will be greatly enhanced. In addition, it would be able to complete development of the frame well under budget.

After a preliminary review of the problem, LMT's president, Frank Dominguez, has not yet reached a final decision. Like Dr. Ellis, he is intrigued by the possibility of successfully developing the 3D printing process. He feels that this would give LMT an excellent chance at some additional contracts. He is concerned, however, about the possibility of wasting money on unsuccessful development or of being forced to do injection molding on an accelerated basis.

LMT's contract is for a fixed total amount spread over several years. Mr. Dominguez wants to minimize the expenditures on the frame portion to free up money for technical developments on other components of the drone system, which could improve LMT's position for future defense and commercial business.

Eden paper

Fred Jackson, one of the three partners of Eden Paper Company (EPC), settled down at his desk for some planning. His bid to the State of North Carolina's Division of Purchasing and Property was due in about 2 weeks, and he had as yet made no decision as to what prices EPC would offer for the four classes of bags the state was seeking.

Case—cont'd

North Carolina permitted the sale of hard liquor only in its state-owned liquor stores. The state required bids every 6 months for the contract to supply its stores with four sizes of paper bags: the quart liquor size, 4-1/2 x 16-1/4 inches, with a 2-1/2-inch tuck; 10-pound heavy-duty grocery bags, 6-1/2 x 13-5/16 inches, with a 4-1/6-inch tuck; 20-pound heavy-duty grocery bags, 8-3/16 x 16 inches, with a 5-1/4-inch tuck; and 1/8 barrel sacks, 10-1/4 x 14 inches, with a 6-1/4-inch tuck. EPC and its competitor had to provide a price per thousand for each of the four bag sizes. The North Carolina Division of Purchasing and Property indicated in its request for bids just how many bundles of each type of bag would be required and how many of each size bag were to be packaged in a bundle. The division determined its supplier by adding up the full cost of the contract as a bid by each potential supplier and awarding the full contract to the overall low bidder.

The division required that bidders submit samples of their products. Prices were F.O.B. locations listed in the proposal, namely the nearly 100 liquor stores situated throughout the state. The vendor was obligated to meet a monthly shipping schedule that reached them at the beginning of each month. The date of delivery was on about the 15th of the month, and following each delivery, the vendor would invoice the State Liquor Commission.

Eden Paper Company

EPC was one of North Carolina's largest distributors of paper and plastic packaging materials, custodial supplies, and maintenance equipment. The company bought materials from more than 40 manufacturers and made them available to factories, businesses, hospitals, and government facilities. Packaging and wrapping materials, including tapes, accounted for about half of a typical year's business, whereas office products represented another 10%. Materials and tools for cleaning and maintenance accounted for a further 10%, and another 20% of EPC's business was food related: paper plates, cups, napkins, and the like.

Last year, about 11% of EPC's sales came from contracts, like the one for the North Carolina liquor stores, which were awarded on the basis of competitive bids.

Eden Paper's Costs

Mr. Jackson began his deliberations about the size of the bid by determining how much it would cost EPC to provide the required bags. The table below shows the number of bundles of each type of bag specified in the contract, the number of bags per bundle, the total bags, and EPC's cost per thousand bags.

From Table 2.9, Mr. Jackson determined that EPC's cost for the full contract would be $1,358,495.

Additional costs, beyond the cost of goods sold, had to be considered. To meet the specifications of the contract, EPC would have to maintain a substantial inventory of all four types of bags. Mr. Jackson estimated that EPC would have to keep an additional $250,000 worth of inventory during the 6 months of the contract. There would be no significant increase in labor, administrative, or clerical costs. However, there would be some minor additional trucking costs: in a few instances, EPC would have to send its fleet to areas of the state where it currently had no need to travel. Mr. Jackson estimated that the route extensions would cost EPC a total of about $6000.

Mr. Jackson decided that he should apply a 12% discount rate to the cash flows associated with this contract. Currently, EPC faced a tax rate of 42%.

Assessing the distribution for the competitor's bid

Mr. Jackson next thought about the possible bids his competitor could make. He compared his estimated costs with the size of the winning bid for several previous contracts similar in type to this one. As a result of this analysis, Mr. Jackson decided that his competitor's bid was as likely to be above $1,600,000 as below. Having determined the median of the distribution for his competitor's bid, Mr. Jackson proceeded to evaluate other bids against that median.

There was only a .25 probability, he thought, that the competitor's bid would be lower than 97% of the median. On the other side, he felt there was a .75 probability that the competitor's bid would be less than 103% of the median. His competitor's bid was almost certain to lie between 91% and 111% of the median. Using these assessments, Mr. Jackson felt that he could choose the appropriate bid for EPC to submit.

Decision making and simulation

3

In theory there is no difference between theory and practice—In practice there is.
—Yogi Berra

Chapter outline

Introduction

The objective of this chapter is to demonstrate the construction and usage of simulation to model uncertainty in managerial, prescriptive decision making. Simulation concepts and terminology are introduced along with a general outline of how to structure simulations. Examples of simulations are used to demonstrate the role of probability in managerial decision making and to demonstrate the usefulness of simulation for resolving issues in understanding uncertainty and probability.

3.1 Simulation to model uncertainty

There are many decisions in which the complexities of the uncertainties and probabilities become too unwieldy for decision trees to be employed. These decisions require a more robust solution methodology—simulation.

As stated in Chapter 1, a simulation is a mathematical model that attempts to emulate the behavior and operation of a real-world process over time. Thus, simulation is used for decision analysis problems that have UNCERTAINTY (probability) where a theoretical solution method would be either difficult or impossible. Simulation is an extremely flexible methodology especially suited to making decisions under uncertainty.

Introduction to Business Analytics Using Simulation. https://doi.org/10.1016/B978-0-323-91717-9.00003-6

Unlike decision trees, which only measure expected value, simulation models can measure many other attributes of a system or process. For example, a simulation can be used to estimate the likelihood (i.e., the risk) of an investment losing money. As a result, simulation models provide better measurement and understanding of risk and return trade-offs.

3.2 Monte Carlo simulation and random variables

A Monte Carlo simulation repeatedly, and randomly, uses a random number generator to create samples from a distribution to simulate possible outcomes. The results of these outcomes are measured to study and observe the long-run behavior of the process being modeled. In the context of decision making, the process can then be optimized by altering various model parameters.

The RAND() function is the building block for all random number generation in Excel. The RAND() function in Excel generates random numbers equally likely between 0 and 1. More specifically, the is less than but not equal to 1; for example, from 0 to 0.9999999…:

$$0 \leq \text{RAND}() < 1$$

It is common to wonder "why is RAND() < 1 and not ≤ 1?" Consider 10 ping pong balls numbered 0 to 9 as shown in Fig. 3.1.

FIGURE 3.1

Ten Ping Pong Balls Numbered 0 to 9

Note that there are 10 ping pong balls. The range of the set of 10 ping pong balls can be represented mathematically as:

$$0 \leq \text{Ping Pong Ball} \,\# < 10$$

Using the 10 ping pong balls to simulate a 90% chance of an event, such as "Rain," you could designate ping pong ball numbers 0 through 8 as "Rain" and 9 as "No Rain." You could map the random draw with the following Excel pseudocode:

$$= \text{IF (PING PONG BALL} < 8\,9, \text{`` Rain`` , `` No Rain``)}$$

Next, consider 100 ping pong balls numbered 0 to 99 as shown in Fig. 3.2.

Note that there are 100 balls, and if you wanted to simulate a 90% chance of an event, such as "Rain," you could designate balls 0 through 89 as "Rain" and 90 through 99 as "No Rain." You could map the random draw with the following Excel pseudocode:

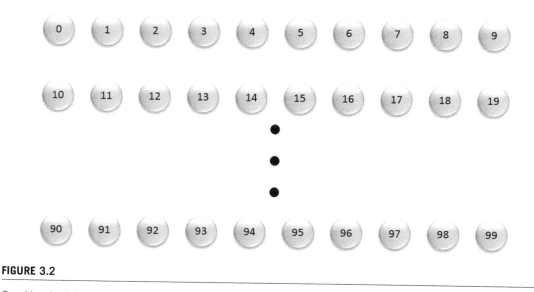

FIGURE 3.2

One Hundred Ping Pong Balls Numbered 0 to 99

There are several methods to simulate a 90% chance of rain using Excel. A common method is to use an IF statement:

$$= \text{IF} (\text{RAND} () < 0.90, \text{`` Rain``} , \text{`` No Rain``})$$

One more direct method is to simply use the conditional portion of the IF statement and then convert the TRUE or FALSE to a 1 or 0 (respectively) by multiplying by 1:

$$= (\text{RAND} () < 0.90) \times 1$$

This formula will yield a 1 when the RAND() is less than 0.90 (remember the 0 counts as a possibility, just like the 0 ping pong ball) and will yield a 0 when the RAND() is greater than or equal to 0.90.

A *random variable* is a set of uncertain outcomes, resulting from a random process. The set of probabilities (likelihoods) of all outcomes of the random variable is called a *probability distribution*. As an example, consider the Rain/No Rain example given earlier. *Weather* would be considered the random variable. The two outcomes of the *Weather* random variable are Rain and No Rain. As the weather is uncertain, it is a random variable and the probabilities (90% and 10%, respectively) associated with each outcome constitute the *probability distribution*. Probability distributions are often represented graphically by a histogram, such as the one shown in Fig. 3.3.

The notation for this probability distribution is:

$$P (Weather) = \begin{cases} P (Rain) = 0.90 \\ P (No\ Rain) = 0.10 \end{cases},$$

where $P(X)$ is the mathematical notation for the statement *the probability of the random variable X*. Note that the total probability distribution must add up to 100%.

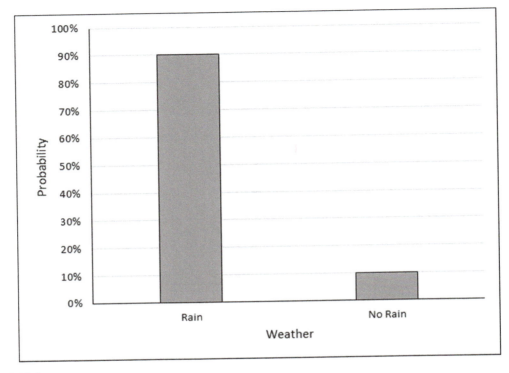

FIGURE 3.3

Probability Distribution for the Rain/No Rain Example

Random variables, and their associated probability distributions, are categorized as either **_discrete_** or **_continuous_**. For discrete random variables, the probability function that details the probability distribution is called the _probability mass function_ (**_pmf_**). For continuous random variables, the probability function is called the _probability density function_ (**_pdf_**). Thus, for a discrete random variable, the **_pmf_** is a single bar of the probability distribution (histogram).

It is common to use $f(x)$ to represent a **_pdf_** or a **_pmf_**. Thus, another common method of notation for the weather random variable **_pmf_** is:

$$f(Weather) = \begin{cases} f(Rain) = 0.90 \\ f(No\ Rain) = 0.10; \end{cases}$$

The random variable _Weather_ has two distinctly separate outcomes, and it is a discrete random variable. Thus, the probability distribution (histogram) shown in Fig. 3.3 is the **_pmf_** of the _weather_ random

---

Example 3.1 RAND() is a continuous uniform distribution

Construct a simulation to determine the probability distribution of the RAND() function.

The spreadsheet in Fig. 3.4 shows a portion of the 10,000 random variable values generated by the RAND() function. Pressing the F9 key will generate 10,000 more random numbers.

B2 | fx =RAND()

	A	B	C	D	E
1	Obs	Data			
2	1	0.2519			
3	2	0.3779			
4	3	0.8417			
5	4	0.0344			
6	5	0.4812			
7	6	0.1913			
8	7	0.3197			
9	8	0.6732			
10	9	0.9221			
11	10	0.4811			
9995	9,994	0.7058			
9996	9,995	0.4756			
9997	9,996	0.0313			
9998	9,997	0.8407			
9999	9,998	0.3856			
10000	9,999	0.7663			
10001	10,000	0.6195			

FIGURE 3.4

Ten Thousand Randomly Generated Values of RAND()

variable. If the random variable *Rain* was measured in inches of rain (rather than as a *yes/no* binary variable), then the random variable would be a *continuous* random variable and would be described mathematically with a ***pdf***.

The histogram in Fig. 3.5 illustrates the distribution of the RAND() function. The fact that the RAND() function is equally likely is what makes it *uniformly distributed*. Further discussion of the uniform distribution is presented in Chapter 7.

3.3 Simulation terminology

As with probability, to work with other analysts, it is important to know the terminology associated with simulation. Some common simulation terms are as follows:

***Trial*:** One simulated scenario that results in an outcome. Trials may or may not be independent.
***Run*:** A set of trials.
***Random number*:** A number generated (usually by computer) according to a specified probability distribution. For example, in a simulation of a manufacturing system, the processing time of a specific machine would be a random number and would usually be from an exponential distribution. Reminder: the RAND() function in Excel generates random numbers equally likely between 0 and 1 (actually, less than but not equal to 1; e.g., from 0 to 0.9999999…); this is the building block for all random number generation in Excel.
***Policy*:** A decision carried out and measured by the simulation model. For example, in the Monte Hall Three Door Problem, one policy is to always switch doors after being shown an empty door, another policy is to not switch, and a third policy is to randomly choose between the two remaining doors. In an application of supply chain management, an example of a policy would be to simulate ordering 500 units of inventory each month for a year.

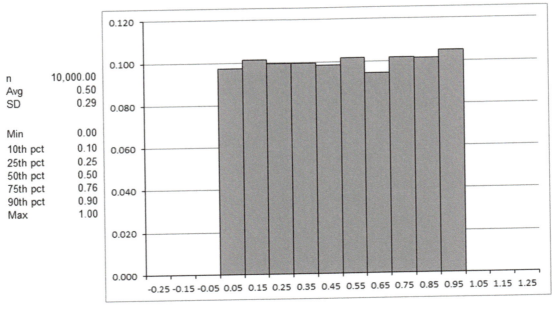

n   10,000.00
Avg   0.50
SD   0.29

Min   0.00
10th pct   0.10
25th pct   0.25
50th pct   0.50
75th pct   0.76
90th pct   0.90
Max   1.00

FIGURE 3.5

Histogram and Descriptive Statistics for 10,000 Values of RAND()

3.4 Overview of the simulation process

The construction of a simulation typically follows these steps:

1. Identify the problem—what decisions are to be made?
2. What factors are given (data)?
3. Which factors are uncertain (random)? What distribution does each factor look like—is it normal, uniform, historical, and so forth?
4. What is the timing/precedence of events? Draw a decision tree if necessary!
5. How is "success" measured; how is the best policy going to be measured?
6. Construct one trial—based on a given policy. Proceed from left to right for each event in the correct time order.
7. Once you have one trial correct, repeat the trials a sufficient number of times (usually at least 1000 trials) to create a single run that will give you a good idea of how the system is operating. The number of trials required depends on the complexity of the situation. If the average of the set of trials is not stable, then more trials are needed. More trials are typically required if the situation has:
   a. several random variables
   b. several decisions
   c. large variance in a random variable
8. Create several runs of your trials to determine the optimal policy. Using the DATA TABLE command in Excel is a good method to use 1 set of many trials to create several runs; for example, a set of 10 runs is 10 sets of trials.

Table 3.1 Excel formulas for common random variable generators

Distribution	Parameters	Examples	Sim Result	Formula
Binomial	*prob*	0.05	0	$= (\text{RAND}() < prob) \times 1$
Uniform	*lower*	100	136.20	$= lower + \text{RAND}() \times range$
Continuous	*upper*	200		
	range	100		
Uniform	*lower*	1	2	$= \text{TRUNC}(lower + \text{RAND}() \times (range + 1))$
Discrete	*upper*	6		
	range	5		
Triangular	*lower*	100	154.09	$= lower + (\text{RAND}() + \text{RAND}()) \times (range)/2$
	upper	200		
	range	100		
Normal	average	100	92.82	$= average + \text{NORM.S.INV}(\text{RAND}()) \times sd$
	standard deviation (*sd*)	20		$= \text{NORM.INV}(\text{RAND}(), average, sd)$

A more detailed description of how to generate random variables from various probability distributions is provided in Appendix 1.

3.5 Random number generation in Excel

Excel has some built-in methods of generating random numbers using the DATA ANALYSIS tools. There are often problems with using that method. First, those tools frequently contain programming errors that vary from version to version of Excel. Second, the random numbers that are generated are static, not dynamic. Thus, you only get one sample, and pressing to recalculate will not generate new samples of random numbers (Table 3.1).

3.6 Examples of simulation and decision making

Simulation models are used to demonstrate probability and statistical concepts and to build probability models in many different industries. Example 3.2 is a demonstration of a simulation that portrays the mathematical aspects of the *law of large numbers* (LLN).

Example 3.2 The law of large numbers

Consider a simulation of flipping a "fair" (each side equally likely) coin—that is, each side has a 50% chance of occurrence.

The spreadsheet in Fig. 3.6 shows a portion of 10,000 simulated coin flips.

Examining the Heads (1) and # of Heads columns shows that the simulated coin behaves in the unpredictable manner that a real coin would. In fact, you should flip a coin 20 times and make a similar record. Although flipping four tails in a row might be considered unusual for someone unfamiliar with probability, the simulation shows that flipping four tails in a row can be very natural. The term *independence* is also demonstrated—a real coin has no *memory* of previous flips. Just because tails have

| B2 | | ▼ | : | ✕ | ✓ | f_x | =(RAND()<0.5)*1 | |

	A	B	C	D	E
1	Trial	Heads (1)	# of Heads	Pct Heads	
2	1	1	1	1.00	
3	2	0	1	0.50	
4	3	1	2	0.67	
5	4	0	2	0.50	
6	5	0	2	0.40	
7	6	1	3	0.50	
8	7	1	4	0.57	
9	8	1	5	0.63	
10	9	0	5	0.56	
11	10	0	5	0.50	
12	11	0	5	0.45	
13	12	0	5	0.42	
14	13	1	6	0.46	
15	14	0	6	0.43	
16	15	1	7	0.47	
9996	9,995	1	5023	0.50	
9997	9,996	1	5024	0.50	
9998	9,997	0	5024	0.50	
9999	9,998	0	5024	0.50	
10000	9,999	0	5024	0.50	
10001	10,000	0	5024	0.50	

FIGURE 3.6

Simulation of 10,000 Coin Flips

happened four times in a row does not mean that the coin is "due" for an outcome of heads. Thus, the outcome of the next flip is not influenced by the previous flip—this is *independence* in the probability sense of the word. The coin flips are sequentially *uncorrelated* to each other.

One form of the LLN states that the probability of an outcome converges to its true value as the sample size increases. This is stated mathematically as:

$$f/n \to p \text{ as } n \to \infty;$$

where "→" is the symbol for *goes to* or *approaches*.

Thus, the spreadsheet in Fig. 3.6 shows that as the number of trials, n (*sample size*), increases, the true probability of flipping heads converges to the true value of 50%.

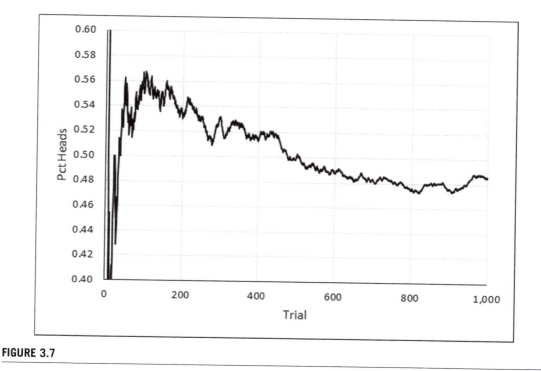

FIGURE 3.7

Average Percentage of Heads in First 1000 of 10,000 Simulated Coin Flips

The graph in Fig. 3.7 shows the results of the first 1000 trials of the coin flipping simulation. Note how the value of p, the percentage (probability) of heads, diverges from 50% at about 100 trials, and that even at 1000 trials, the value of p diverges from 50% by about 2% (p at a sample size of 1000 $\geq$ 48%). This demonstrates that even 1000 trials (or data points) may not be sufficient to accurately estimate a specific value. More importantly, it shows how real life truly varies from theory. This idea is best stated by Yogi Berra as follows:

In theory there is no difference between theory and practice—In practice there is.

The graph in Fig. 3.8 shows the results of 10,000 trials of the coin flipping simulation. Note how the value of p, the percentage (probability) of heads, diverges from 50% at about 3000 trials, and that even at 10,000 trials, the value of p diverges from 50%. This again demonstrates how real data will deviate from theory.

The LLN states that $f/n \rightarrow p$, then $f \rightarrow np$. Thus, anything that can happen ($p > 0$) will happen ($f > 0$) and, due to independence, could happen the very next time.

Anything that can happen will happen.

In contrast to Example 3.2, Examples 3.3, 3.4, 3.5, and 3.6 demonstrate how simulation is used to create **prescriptive** decision-making models for common situations found in business analytics.

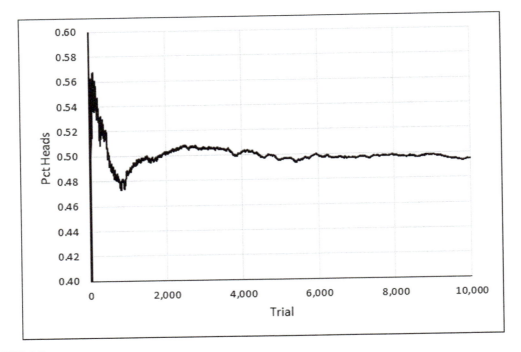

FIGURE 3.8

Average Number of Heads in 10,000 Simulated Coin Flips

Example 3.3 Service level for delivery trucks

A package delivery company owns 15 trucks in this region. Five of the trucks are relatively new, and each of these trucks has a 5% chance of not being in service on any day. The other 10 trucks are older and have a 10% chance of being in service on any day. The contractor needs 14 trucks to deliver packages tomorrow. What is the probability that the contractor will have enough trucks? How many new trucks should you have to have a 98% chance of having at least 14 trucks to make deliveries?

In this model, a single simulation trial consists of a single day in which 5 new and 10 old trucks are either in or out of service. The RAND() function in Excel simulates whether each truck is in service (1) or out of service (0). A simple Excel formula to simulate whether a new truck is in service (95% probability of being in service) is:

$$= (\text{RAND ()} < 0.95) \times 1$$

The (RAND() < .95) portion of the formula is a conditional test that results in TRUE for random numbers: $0 \leq \text{Rand()}$ ≤ 0.95. The $\times 1$ portion of the formula converts the TRUE or FALSE conditional result into a numeric value: 1 or 0 corresponding to TRUE or FALSE. In this manner, it is simple to construct a simulated binomial random variable. Similarly, the formula to simulate whether an old truck is in service (90% probability of being in service) is:

$$= (\text{RAND ()} < 0.90) \times 1$$

An abridged view of the simulation with 10,000 repetitions (trials) of the 15 trucks is shown in Fig. 3.9.

	New trucks					Old trucks										Avg 13.760 SD 1.069
Trial	1	2	3	4	5	1	2	3	4	5	6	7	8	9	10	Total
1	1	1	1	1	1	1	1	1	1	1	1	1	0	1	0	13
2	1	1	1	1	1	1	1	1	1	1	0	1	1	1	1	14
3	1	1	1	1	1	0	1	1	1	1	0	1	1	1	1	13
4	1	1	1	1	1	1	1	1	1	1	1	1	1	1	1	15
5	1	1	1	1	1	1	1	1	1	1	1	1	1	1	1	15
6	1	1	1	1	1	1	1	1	1	1	1	1	1	0	1	14
7	1	1	1	1	1	1	1	1	1	1	1	1	1	1	1	15
8	1	1	1	1	1	1	1	1	1	1	1	1	1	0	1	14
9	1	1	1	1	1	1	1	0	1	1	1	0	1	1	1	13
10	1	1	1	1	0	1	1	1	1	1	0	1	1	1	1	13
·																·
·																·
·																·
10,000	1	1	1	1	1	1	1	1	0	1	1	1	1	1	1	14

FIGURE 3.9

Simulation of Availability of 5 New and 10 Old Trucks

The total number of trucks available (Total) can be used to determine the likelihood of the number of trucks available and is shown in the probability distribution presented in Fig. 3.10.

The probability of being able to meet demand is called the *service level*. If 14 or 15 trucks are available on a specific day, then there will be sufficient delivery capacity for that specific day. Thus, the service level in this example is the probability of 14 or 15 trucks working on the specific day. The service level provided by the 15 trucks is $f(14) + f(15)$. According to the simulation, these 15 trucks provide a service level of $f(14) + f(15) = 0.3708 + 0.2698 = $ **64.06%**. Note that the expected number of trucks available is:

$$95 \times 5 + 0.90 \times 10 = 13.75 \cong \mathbf{14}$$

Many managers, and analysts, would be surprised that the expected number of trucks available ($\cong 14$) being equal to the amount required provides only a 64% service level. As such, providing the average number of trucks needed would result in a shortage of trucks for more than 1 day in 3 days.

Additional trucks can be added to determine the number of trucks needed to achieve a 98% service level. Cost structure information is required to ascertain whether a 98% service level merits the cost of additional trucks. Thus, the appropriate service level depends upon the cost structure. Such information would involve obtaining a daily lease rate to supply the shortage of trucks and daily cost of idle trucks (an opportunity cost). Simulating additional new trucks yields the service levels shown in Table 3.2.

Thus, a simulation model can be used to determine various operating characteristics of this delivery system, such as service level (probability of having enough delivery trucks) and the optimum number of trucks. This situation would be mathematically difficult to solve using standard probability formulas such as combinatorics.

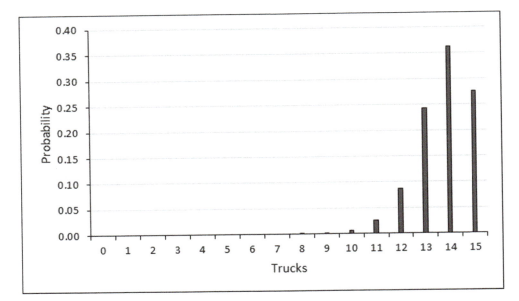

FIGURE 3.10

Probability Distribution of Availability of 5 New and 10 Old Trucks

Table 3.2 Service level as a function of new trucks			
New Trucks	**Total Trucks**	**Expected No. of Trucks**	**Service Level (%)**
5	15	13.75	64
6	16	14.70	87
7	17	15.65	96
8	18	16.60	99

As shown in Chapter 2, two of the most common decisions faced by companies are *how much product or capacity* **to have** and **what price** *should be charged.* The next example is the Newsvendor Problem. The Newsvendor Problem arises whenever a decision maker must decide *how much to have*, and it is the basis for *revenue management.* It is used in many settings, such as retail and grocery supply chain management, airline ticket sales, and hotel reservations. The next example is similar to Example 2.4 and is presented to illustrate how simulations can solve and enhance a deeper understanding of supply chain and capacity decisions.

Example 3.4 Optimization: The Newsvendor Problem

The Newsvendor Problem is a classic inventory/capacity decision problem that provides the foundation for many capacity and pricing problems. A newsvendor at a newspaper and magazine stand in a subway station must determine how many newspapers to stock to sell on Sunday. The newsvendor buys the paper for $0.50 and sells it for $3.50. The vendor sells excess newspapers and magazines for recycling at a rate that converts to $0.05 per Sunday paper. The various quantities of newspapers sold (assume sales = demand) the previous 100 Sundays is given in Table 3.3. As an example, 10 papers were sold on 50 of the previous 100 Sundays. How many Sunday newspapers should the newsvendor order?

Table 3.3 Probability Distribution of Demand

Demand	Sundays	Probability
9	25	0.25
10	50	0.50
11	25	0.25

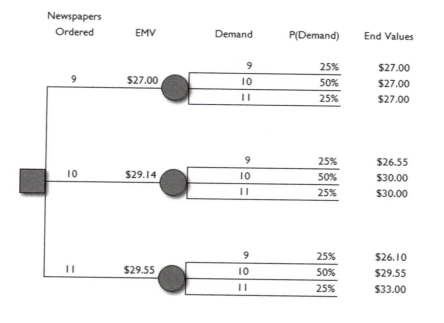

FIGURE 3.11

Decision Tree for the Newsvendor Problem

Prior to building a simulation, it is useful to construct a decision tree to view the decisions and random events to be included in the simulation model. The decision tree for this example, along with the expected monetary value for each choice, is shown in Fig. 3.11.

Often, deciding how to generate the random numbers is one of the most difficult tasks in creating the simulation. There are many methods by which demand could be simulated. For the moment, a *nested IF* formula is used:

$$= IF\,(RAND\,() < 0.50,\ 10,\ IF\,(RAND\,() < 0.50,\ 9,\ 11))$$

A better method, using the VLOOKUP function, will be presented in Chapters 5 and 6. The various components of the simulation are shown in Fig. 3.12.

Note that the *Order* of 10 is only a starting point—not necessarily the final answer; that number is initially used to create the simulation.

| F13 | ▼ | : | × | ✓ | f_x | =1.96*STDEV.S(F15:F1014)/A1014^0.5 | | | | | |

	A	B	C	D	E	F	G	H	I	J	K
1	COST STRUCTURE				SIMULATION PROBABILITIES AND VALIDATION						
2	Price	$3.50			Theory			Simulation			
3	Variable Cost	$0.50		Demand	Frequency	Prob	Frequency	Prob			
4	Salvage Value	$0.05		9	25	25.0%	262	0.262			
5	Goodwill	$0.00		10	50	50.0%	495	0.495			
6				11	25	25.0%	243	0.243			
7	Ordered	10			100	100.0%	1000	1.000			
8	TVC	$5.00			10 = Expected Demand						
9											
10									OPTIMIZATION		
11	SIMULATION										
12	Averages:		9.98		0.24	0.26	$29.10		Max Profit	$29.48	
13					Margin of Error =		$0.09		Opt Order	11	
14		Trial	Demand	Units Sold	Shortage	Extra	Profit				
15		1	9	9	0	1	$26.55			Order	Avg Profit	Margin of Error
16		2	9	9	0	1	$26.55		Current	10	29.10	0.09
17		3	11	10	1	0	$30.00			9	27.00	0.00
18		4	9	9	0	1	$26.55			10	29.16	0.09
19		5	10	10	0	0	$30.00			11	29.48	0.15
20		6	10	10	0	0	$30.00				
21		7	10	10	0	0	$30.00				
22		8	9	9	0	1	$26.55				
23		9	11	10	1	0	$30.00				
24		10	9	9	0	1	$26.55				
1009		995	9	9	0	1	$26.55				
1010		996	9	9	0	1	$26.55				
1011		997	10	10	0	0	$30.00				
1012		998	11	10	1	0	$30.00				
1013		999	10	10	0	0	$30.00				
1014		1000	9	9	0	1	$26.55				

FIGURE 3.12

Simulation with Optimization of the Newsvendor Problem

Note that the optimum amount to order, 11, is not equal to the average demand of 10. Ordering to meet average demand is an extremely common mistake made by many companies. The optimization of the simulation was performed using Excel's *One-Way Data Table* command.

Also notice that the average profit for ordering nine is exactly equal to the corresponding expected monetary value (EMF) from the decision tree shown earlier (Why? Is this a coincidence?). In contrast, the average profit for ordering 10 is not exactly equal to the corresponding EMF from the decision tree shown earlier (Why not?). Finally, the average profit for ordering 11 is also not exactly equal to the corresponding EMF from the decision tree shown earlier (Why not?).

The *margin of error* is a statistic that is calculated to determine the answers to those questions. The margin of error is a measure of the accuracy of a sample average. In probability terms, there is approximately a 95% chance that the true average is within the range of the sample average ± margin of error.

For example, there is a 95% chance that the true average profit associated with ordering 11 is within $0.09 of the simulation value of $29.10. In this context, the appropriate formula for margin of error is

$$= 1.96 \times sd / \sqrt{n},$$

where *sd* is *standard deviation* and *n* is the sample size (number of trials in this example). Briefly, the standard deviation is a measure of how much, on average, the data varies from the average. Conceptually (not mathematically), it is the average amount away from average.

The appropriate Excel formula for margin of error, in the simulation spreadsheet shown in Fig. 3.12, is:

$$= 1.96 \times STDEV. S (F15 : F1014) / A10140.5$$

The margin of error and statistical sampling will be discussed in further detail in Chapter 8.

Next is a more detailed example of a typical Newsvendor Problem—how much to order to maximize profit. In this example, **Order** is the decision variable. The simulation allows the decision variable (**Order**) to be changed until the **Average Profit** is maximized.

Example 3.5 A retail newsvendor decision

An online/catalog retailer will sell Adirondack chairs this season. The retailer purchases the chairs from a supplier at a cost of $175 and will sell them for $250. Demand has been forecasted to be 2000 chairs this season but is not known for certain and could range anywhere from 1000 to 3000 chairs. At the end of the season, the company will have a "half-off" sale to clear out any remaining inventory. Determine the optimum number of chairs to order.

The spreadsheet in Fig. 3.13 demonstrates a typical managerial simulation that could be used to determine the number of chairs to order. This simulation consists of 1000 trials, each trial having demand randomly occuring equally likely between 1000 and 3000 and the associated profit resulting from that randomly generated demand. Note that 2000 chairs (the average) shown in the spreadsheet is *not* necessarily the optimum quantity of chairs to order. Also notice that ordering the average demand will result in sales that are **less than the average demand** and will have the managerial effect of not meeting sales goals (budgets). The optimum number depends upon the cost structure and is determined by changing the decision variable (**Order**) to be changed until the **Average Profit** is maximized.

Although the decision (**Order**) is the number of chairs in this example, similar decisions of capacity (how much to have) are found in finance, human resources, marketing, and operations contexts. This example shows how critical decision making and problem solving is to managers. Yet as basic as this task is, many organizations do not solve problems using processes that result in optimal solutions.

The next example is a *bidding problem*. Bidding problems arise in retail pricing and purchasing decisions. Bidding problems occur whenever a decision maker must decide *what price*. Frequently, the pricing and order quantity (Newsvendor) decisions must be solved simultaneously; that *two-variable* problem is addressed in Chapter 10 with the use of regression. Managers do not initially think of pricing items, such as soft drinks, gasoline, books, cars, and airline tickets, as bidding. However, with the advent of eBay, it is easier to see that all pricing is fundamentally a bidding process.

B11	▼	⋮	✕	✓	*fx*	=ROUND($B$4+RAND()*($C$4-$B$4),0)

	A	B	C	D	E	F
1	Price	250				
2	Sale Price	125				
3	VC	175				
4	Demand	1000	3000			
5	Order	**2000**				
6	TVC	$350,000				
7						
8	Average	2,002	1,747		253	**$118,376**
9					Pr(Loss)	0.0%
10	Trial	Demand	Sales	Shortage	Extra	Profit/Loss
11	1	1,794	1,794	0	206	$124,250
12	2	2,902	2,000	902	0	$150,000
13	3	2,844	2,000	844	0	$150,000
14	4	2,678	2,000	678	0	$150,000
15	5	2,466	2,000	466	0	$150,000
16	6	1,511	1,511	0	489	$88,875
17	7	2,964	2,000	964	0	$150,000
18	8	1,760	1,760	0	240	$120,000
19	9	2,733	2,000	733	0	$150,000
20	10	2,566	2,000	566	0	$150,000
1005	995	2,562	2,000	562	0	$150,000
1006	996	1,079	1,079	0	921	$34,875
1007	997	1,637	1,637	0	363	$104,625
1008	998	2,972	2,000	972	0	$150,000
1009	999	1,054	1,054	0	946	$31,750
1010	1000	1,895	1,895	0	105	$136,875

FIGURE 3.13

Simulation of Order Quantity

> ## Example 3.6 Bidding: Introduction to pricing decisions
>
> A company is bidding to supply cardboard boxes to an online retailer. The competitors' bids are equally likely to be above or below $250,000. The competitors' bids are nearly certain to be between $200,000 and $300,000. The analyst has no further information regarding the likelihood of the competitors' bids, so it must be assumed (for the moment) that all bids between $200,000 and $300,000 are equally likely. If the bid is won, the total cost of completing the order is $185,000. Determine the optimum bid.
>
> One important difference between the Newsvendor Problem example and the bidding problem is that the decision in the Newsvendor Problem is a *discrete* integer decision, whereas the decision in the bidding problem is *continuous*. Thus, the decision tree can only show some of the nearly infinite number of branches.
>
> In each bidding problem, it is extremely important to determine whether the highest bidder wins or loses. This depends upon the context (situation) and determines the portion of the probability distribution that represents the probability of winning or losing.
>
> This is a **low bidder wins** situation because the online retailer wants the least expensive boxes (hence why they are having suppliers bid against each other). First, a decision tree is constructed to depict the decisions and random events. The decision tree, along with the expected monetary value for each choice, is shown in Fig. 3.14.

In this example, the probability of winning or losing is a bit less obvious than in the previous example. As low bid wins, if you bid the lowest ($200,000), then you would have a 100% chance of winning. In contrast, if you bid the highest ($300,000), then you would have no chance (0%) of winning. As there is no information regarding any of the likelihoods, then a *uniform distribution* can be assumed.

Fortunately, once the random bids are generated according to a uniform distribution, the probabilities are a result of the simulation.

Use the information from Table 3.1 to generate a continuous *uniformly distributed* random bid. This can be accomplished using a form of the following formula:

$$= 200,000 + \text{RAND}() \times 100,000$$

Note in the simulation, shown in Fig. 3.15, that the **Bid** of $250,000 is only a starting point—not necessarily the final answer. That number is used to initialize the simulation.

Two optimization tables were created using Excel's *One-Way Data Table* command. *Optimization 1* covers the wide range of bids to determine the optimum region. *Optimization 2* covers a smaller range of bids to determine the optimum bid more specifically. The margin of error is used to determine the degree to which the bids can be accurately optimized. Examine the *Avg Profit* in *Optimization 2*. Note that $33,825 − $1,660 ($32,165) is greater than $30,420; thus, bidding $240,000 is significantly better than bidding $230,000. Also note that $32,165 is *not* greater than the average profit of $32,305 associated with the bid of $250,000. Thus, bidding $240,000 will have approximately the same results as bidding $250,000. Thus, pressing the recalculation button, F9, will cause the optimum to change between $250,000 and $240,000. Thus, there is no need to be more accurate than $10,000 in the bid. The graph in Fig. 3.16 shows the results of the two optimizations.

You could move the starting point from $220,000 to $225,000 to ascertain the performance of bidding $245,000. Then you can enter $245,000 as the bid and study the results of bidding $245,000 in the simulation (Fig. 3.17).

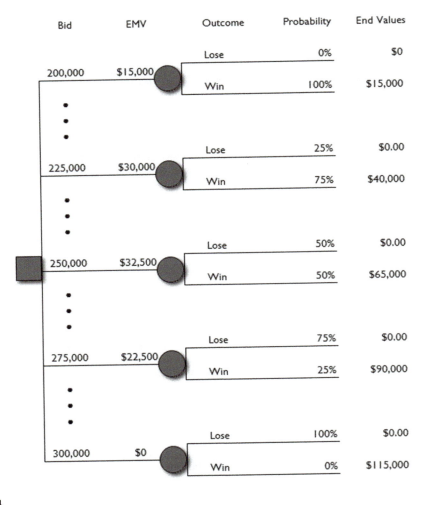

Bid	EMV	Outcome	Probability	End Values
200,000	$15,000	Lose	0%	$0
		Win	100%	$15,000
225,000	$30,000	Lose	25%	$0.00
		Win	75%	$40,000
250,000	$32,500	Lose	50%	$0.00
		Win	50%	$65,000
275,000	$22,500	Lose	75%	$0.00
		Win	25%	$90,000
300,000	$0	Lose	100%	$0.00
		Win	0%	$115,000

FIGURE 3.14

Decision Tree for the Bidding Problem

Another compelling benefit of using simulation as an analysis tool is that you can measure a variety of aspects of the situation. In this example, we can not only determine the optimum bid and estimate the results average profit but also estimate the probability of winning (~60%) and learn that it is not optimal to try to win the bid all the time. That would lead to a phenomenon known as the *winner's curse*—in which the bidder pays too much on average, thereby reducing the profit in the long run. This phenomenon is readily observed in eBay auctions in which bidder's emotions and remorse at losing can cause them to overpay for items.

| B16 | ▼ | : | ✕ | ✓ | *fx* | =$F$4+RAND()*Bid_Range |

	A	B	C	D	E	F	G	H	I	J
1	**COST STRUCTURE**					**SIMULATION PROBABILITIES**				
2	Cost	$185,000					**Theory**			
3	Bid Range	$100,000				Bid	Prob(Win)	Prob(Lose)		
4	Bid	**$250,000**				200,000	100%	0.0%		
5						225,000	75%	25.0%		
6						250,000	50%	50.0%		
7						275,000	25%	75.0%		
8						300,000	0%	100.0%		
9							2.5	250.0%		
10						250,000	= Expected Bid			
11										
12	**SIMULATION**									
13	Averages:	249,765.46	49.1%	$31,915.00		**OPTIMIZATION I**				
14	Margin of Error	$1,798.13	3.1%	$2,015.05			Max Profit	**$31,590.00**		
15		Trial	Comp. Bid	Win	Profit		Opt Bid	**250,000**		
16		1	$231,523.37	0	$0.00					
17		2	$271,735.50	1	$65,000.00		Bid	P(Win)	Avg Profit	Margin of Error
18		3	$200,562.43	0	$0.00		Current	250,000	49%	31,915	2,015
19		4	$294,154.98	1	$65,000.00			200,000	100%	15,000	0
20		5	$210,978.09	0	$0.00			225,000	76%	30,360	1,061
21		6	$236,238.45	0	$0.00			**250,000**	49%	**31,590**	2,015
22		7	$208,026.46	0	$0.00			275,000	25%	22,230	2,407
23		8	$286,376.85	1	$65,000.00			300,000	0%	0	0
24		9	$204,757.71	0	$0.00						
25		10	$205,391.69	0	$0.00		**OPTIMIZATION 2**				
26		11	$232,110.15	0	$0.00			Max Profit	**$33,825.00**		
27		12	$226,814.36	0	$0.00			Opt Bid	**240,000**		
28		13	$295,623.49	1	$65,000.00						
29		14	$200,934.04	0	$0.00			Bid	P(Win)	Avg Profit	Margin of Error
30		15	$256,378.79	1	$65,000.00		Current	250,000	49%	31,915	2,015
31		16	$207,600.91	0	$0.00		10,000	220,000	80%	28,070	865
32		17	$212,257.81	0	$0.00			230,000	68%	30,420	1,306
33		18	$289,495.52	1	$65,000.00			**240,000**	62%	**33,825**	1,660
34		19	$297,691.05	1	$65,000.00			250,000	50%	32,305	2,015
35		20	$291,951.61	1	$65,000.00			260,000	38%	28,500	2,257
1010		995	$257,237.45	1	$65,000.00						
1011		996	$243,919.01	0	$0.00						
1012		997	$204,527.16	0	$0.00						
1013		998	$216,105.81	0	$0.00						
1014		999	$221,131.16	0	$0.00						
1015		1000	$206,896.89	0	$0.00						

FIGURE 3.15

Simulation of the Bidding Problem

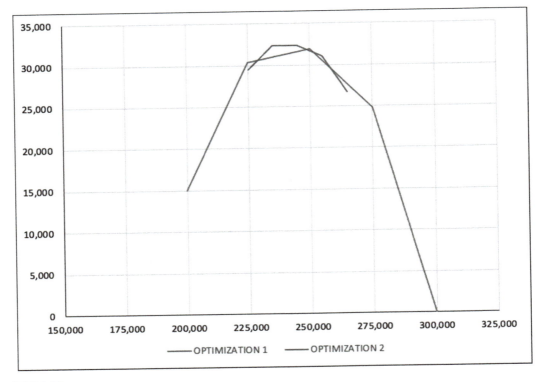

FIGURE 3.16

Simulation Results of the Bidding Problem

Exercise Set 3: Simulation and Decision Making

1. Create a random number generator for a uniform distribution [0, 0.999) using 10 ping pong balls numbered from 0 to 9. Create a random number generator for a uniform distribution [0, 0.999) using 10-sided dice (with 10 faces numbered 1 through 10, commonly known as a D-10).

2. Create a simulation of flipping 100 pennies.
   a. Show the probability distribution (histogram) for the number of heads and the number of tails.
   b. Describe the appearance of the distribution.
   c. What is the most likely outcome?
   d. Give the range of the number of heads that happens two out of three times. In other words, find x such that two out of three times (67%), the number of heads will be within x of 50 heads.

3. Suppose you roll a single six-sided die (D-6) and then flip that number of pennies. Construct a simulation to estimate the probability of each outcome.

| B16 | ▾ | : | ✕ ✓ | fx | =$F$4+RAND()*Bid_Range |

	A	B	C	D	E	F	G	H	I	J
1	**COST STRUCTURE**					**SIMULATION PROBABILITIES**				
2	Cost	$185,000					**Theory**			
3	Bid Range	$100,000				Bid	Prob(Win)	Prob(Lose)		
4	Bid	**$240,000**				200,000	100%	0.0%		
5						225,000	75%	25.0%		
6						250,000	50%	50.0%		
7						275,000	25%	75.0%		
8						300,000	0%	100.0%		
9							2.5	250.0%		
10						250,000 = Expected Bid				
11										
12	**SIMULATION**									
13	Averages:	250,837.56	60.7%	$33,385.00		**OPTIMIZATION I**				
14	Margin of Error	$1,813.52	3.0%	$1,665.81		Max Profit	$32,045.00			
15	Trial	Comp. Bid	Win	Profit		Opt Bid	250,000			
16	1	$214,869.25	0	$0.00						
17	2	$237,657.47	0	$0.00		Bid	P(Win)	Avg Profit	Margin of Error	
18	3	$269,905.46	1	$55,000.00		Current	240,000	61%	33,385	1,666
19	4	$253,373.22	1	$55,000.00		25,000	200,000	100%	15,000	0
20	5	$290,504.14	1	$55,000.00			225,000	75%	30,040	1,073
21	6	$279,567.25	1	$55,000.00			250,000	49%	32,045	2,015
22	7	$277,294.55	1	$55,000.00			275,000	25%	22,770	2,426
23	8	$258,660.34	1	$55,000.00			300,000	0%	0	0
24	9	$288,917.82	1	$55,000.00						
25	10	$277,802.70	1	$55,000.00		**OPTIMIZATION 2**				
26	11	$249,160.77	1	$55,000.00		Max Profit	$33,110.00			
27	12	$274,337.28	1	$55,000.00		Opt Bid	240,000			
28	13	$297,475.88	1	$55,000.00						
29	14	$210,244.51	0	$0.00		Bid	P(Win)	Avg Profit	Margin of Error	
30	15	$270,600.04	1	$55,000.00		Current	240,000	61%	33,385	1,666
31	16	$279,866.50	1	$55,000.00		5,000	230,000	70%	31,545	1,278
32	17	$255,778.94	1	$55,000.00			235,000	64%	32,150	1,486
33	18	$221,189.70	0	$0.00			240,000	60%	33,110	1,669
34	19	$225,051.87	0	$0.00			245,000	55%	32,760	1,852
35	20	$201,078.52	0	$0.00			250,000	51%	33,020	2,015
1010	995	$260,821.54	1	$55,000.00						
1011	996	$224,379.76	0	$0.00						
1012	997	$282,257.86	1	$55,000.00						
1013	998	$242,295.78	1	$55,000.00						
1014	999	$225,501.17	0	$0.00						
1015	1000	$283,565.58	1	$55,000.00						

FIGURE 3.17

Simulation of the Bidding Problem at the Optimum Bid

4. A FedEx contractor owns 50 trucks in a region. Ten of the trucks are relatively new, and each of these trucks has a 95% chance of being in service on any day. Twenty trucks are older and only have a 90% chance of being in service on any day. Twenty trucks are much older and have an 80% chance of not being in service on any day. The contractor needs 44 trucks to deliver packages tomorrow. What is the probability that the contractor will have enough trucks?

5. A soft drink distributor currently owns 20 trucks that have a 90% chance of being in service on any day. New trucks have a 2% chance of not being in service on any day. Demand for delivery is forecasted to be normal with an average of 30 truckloads per day and a standard deviation of 5 truckloads per day. If there is a shortage of trucks, the contractor must lease a truck for the day at a cost of $125 per day. New trucks cost $50,000, and as such, the cost of an idle truck is a function of opportunity cost and other similar factors and can be estimated using an 18% APR. Determine the number of new trucks the distributor should purchase.

6. A contractor has to decide how much to bid for a construction project. It will cost $4000 to prepare the bid. This cost would be incurred whether or not the bid was accepted. The previous winning bids for similar projects have been (in thousands): 80, 60, 70, 60, 60, 80, 80, 60, 80, 80, 50, 50, 60, 60, 70, 70, 50, 80, 60, 70, 50, 80, 70, 60, 80, 80, 80, 90. If the contractor wins the bid, the cost of completing the project will be $50,000. What is the optimum bid?

7. A paper company is bidding to supply paper bags to the North Carolina ABC stores. The cost of the contract is estimated to be $136,000. The competitors' bids are estimated to be normally distributed with an average bid of $166,000 and a standard deviation of $20,000. What is the optimum bid? Why is a fixed markup an inappropriate pricing strategy? Is "we match anyone's price" an appropriate pricing strategy?

8. A dairy supplies 15 local restaurants with ice cream for their desserts each week. Each week, on average, 30% of the restaurants order a gallon of vanilla ice cream. The ice cream is produced once a week before orders are taken and cannot be stored for longer than a week (unsold must be discarded). How much ice cream should be produced each week if the selling price to restaurants is $15 per gallon and the cost to the dairy is $9 per gallon?

9. A dairy distribution center supplies 25 grocery stores with milk each week. Each week, on average, 60% of the grocery stores order a delivery of a pallet of milk containing 100 gallons of milk. The milk is delivered once a week to the distribution center before orders from the grocery stores are received and cannot be stored for longer than a week (unsold milk must be discarded).
   a. Use simulation to graph the distribution of demand.
   b. Compute the average demand for milk from the distribution center.
   c. How much milk should be produced each week if the price to grocery stores is $2.00 per gallon and the cost to the dairy is $1.50 per gallon?
   d. How much milk should be produced each week if the price to grocery stores is $3 per gallon and the cost to the dairy is $1.00 per gallon?
   e. How much milk should be produced each week if the price to grocery stores is $2.00 per gallon and the cost to the dairy is $1.00 per gallon?

10. A dairy manufactures ice cream as part of its operations. It supplies ice cream to 75 local restaurants. The dairy makes a 5-gallon size of ice cream for these restaurants. Fifteen of these restaurants are frequent customers and order ice cream about 60% of the time (about 6 out of 10 days). Thirty of the 75 restaurants are less frequent customers and order ice cream about 35% of

the time. The remaining 30 restaurants are infrequent customers and order ice cream about 10% of the time. It costs the dairy $6.25 to make the 5 gallons of ice cream. In turn, they sell the 5 gallons for $25.00.

a. What does the distribution of demand look like?

b. What is the average demand?

c. Calculate the optimum expected value resulting from the optimum production.

d. Calculate the optimum number of 5-gallon units to produce. Is it the average demand?

e. Calculate the optimum service level.

f. How would changes in price affect demand?

11. On Thursday evening, the manager of a small branch of a car rental agency finds that she has six cars available for rental on the following day. However, she is able to request delivery of additional cars, at a cost of $20 each, from the regional depot. Each car that is rented produces an expected profit of $40 (not including the $20 of delivery cost if incurred). After reviewing records for previous Fridays, the manager finds that the number of cars requested on 20 previous Fridays is 7, 9, 8, 7, 10, 8, 7, 8, 9, 10, 7, 6, 8, 9, 8, 8, 6, 7, 7, 9. How many cars should be ordered? How do "good will" losses affect the number of cars to be ordered?

12. Last year, a chain of consumer electronics store sold, on average, 120 large screen TV sets per week with a standard deviation of 25 sets. These sets sold for $1800 each. Use simulation to determine the average weekly, monthly, and annual revenue from sets sold and the corresponding standard deviations. Of what managerial use is standard deviation?

13. A fruit and vegetable wholesaler buys strawberries at $20 per case and resells them at $50 per case. Because the wholesaler markets primarily to "natural" grocery stores, no preservatives are added to these strawberries. Thus, any cases not sold on the first day are given to a local food bank. If grocers place an order and the wholesaler has run out of strawberries, then that unsatisfied demand is lost and grocers buy strawberries from another wholesaler. Demand data is given in the following table. As an example, there were 15 days in which 10 cases of strawberries were ordered. What is the optimum number of cases of strawberries for the wholesaler to order each day?

Sales per day	No. of days
10	15
11	20
12	40
13	25

14. An online/catalog retailer will sell Adirondack chairs this season. The retailer purchases the chairs from a supplier at a cost of $175 and will sell them for $250. Demand has been forecasted to be 2000 chairs this season, but demand is not known for certain and could range anywhere from 1000 to 3000 chairs. At the end of the season, the company will have a half-off sale to clear out the inventory. Determine the optimum number of chairs to order.

a. Why does the retailer not want to carry the chairs in inventory for the subsequent year? Assume a *uniform distribution* for demand.

  b. Construct a simulation to determine how many chairs the retailer should order. Is it the average demand? Why or why not?

  c. Graph the distribution of demand to validate the probability distribution. Assume a *triangular distribution* for demand.

  d. Construct a simulation to determine how many chairs the retailer should order.

  e. Graph the distribution of demand to validate the probability distribution. Why is it not sufficient to simply calculate the average of the simulation demand to validate the simulation?

  f. Did the change in the probability distribution of demand change the solution? If so, then how and why?

15. Colonial Developers is a commercial land developer that specializes in building shopping centers and wants to develop land near New Bern, North Carolina. Colonial expects that the Net Present Value (~ profit over time in today's dollars) without the cost of the land will be $50,000,000. In other words, after considering the time value of money without the cost of land (i.e., accounting for discounting the future cash flows except for the cost of the parcel of land), they will make $50,000,000 in pre-land cost profit. There is a parcel of land that has been appraised for $30,000,000, and several other developers are vying for the same property. Colonial has bid against several of the companies many times before and estimates the bids to range between $35,000,000 and $45,000,000. Assume a uniform distribution for the bids.

  a. Construct a simulation to determine the optimum bid. Is it the average bid? Why or why not?

  b. Graph the distribution of bids to validate the probability distribution. Assume a triangular distribution for the bids.

  c. Construct a simulation to determine the optimum bid.

  d. Graph the distribution of bids to validate the probability distribution. Why is it not sufficient to simply calculate the average of the simulation demand to validate the simulation?

  e. Did the change in the probability distribution of bid change the solution? If so, then how and why?

16. A company is bidding to provide new computers to a consulting firm. The cost to provide the computers is $650,000. The company has bid against several of the companies many times before and estimates the bids to range between $550,000 and $850,000. Assume a uniform distribution for the bids.

  a. Construct a simulation to determine the optimum bid. Is it the average bid? Why or why not?

  b. Graph the distribution of bids to validate the probability distribution. Assume a triangular distribution for the bids.

  c. Construct a simulation to determine the optimum bid.

  d. Graph the distribution of bids to validate the probability distribution. Assume a normal distribution for the bids.

  e. Construct a simulation to determine the optimum bid. Is it the average bid? Why or why not?

  f. Graph the distribution of bids to validate the probability distribution.

  g. Why is it not sufficient to simply calculate the average of the simulation demand to validate the simulation?

  h. Did the change in the probability distribution of bid change the solution? If so, then how and why?

17. Your company is bidding against three competitors to supply office furniture for a new bank headquarters. The cost to provide the furniture is estimated to be between $950,000 and $1,150,000. The company has bid against the three companies many times before. Assume triangular distributions for each random variable. The estimates of the ranges of the competitors' distributions of bids are:

	Bids	
Competitor	**Low ($)**	**High ($)**
Allied	925,000	1,250,000
Boston Group	900,000	1,300,000
Continental	1,000,000	1,400,000

   a. Compute the average bid of the competitors.
   b. Construct a simulation to determine the optimum bid. Is it the average bid? Why or why not?
   c. Graph the distribution of bids to validate the probability distribution.

18. A convention with 1200 attendees is scheduled to take place in November in Boston. At a price of $450, approximately 480 attendees will stay at the convention hotel. Based on previous demand data analysis, a $20 price change results in a 15% change in demand. Based upon the market value and opportunity cost of the square footage, the rooms have a variable cost of $260. The rooms also have a shortage cost (of turning away a booking) of $230 per guest turned away (this amount is determined by the profit of a room and the profit associated with the average profit from food and drinks per room).
   a. Calculate the optimum price and demand without consideration for the uncertainty of demand.
   b. Calculate the optimum price and demand assuming a triangular distribution of ±10%.
   c. Why is part (b) necessary? Why can you *not* just do part (a) to get the price and quantity? What does part (b) take into account that part (a) does not?

19. Demand for a specific $1000 passenger cruise booking is 1000 passengers. A $50 price change results in a 10% change in demand. Fixed cost of operating the ship is $250,000, and the variable cost for a single passenger is $375. Due to the average amount of profits for a booking due to food, drinks, gift shop items, and so forth during a cruise, the cost of not being able to book a room for a passenger (shortage cost) is approximately $1500.
   a. Calculate the optimum price and demand without consideration for the uncertainty of demand.
   b. Calculate the optimum price and demand assuming a triangular distribution of ±10%.
   c. Why is part (b) necessary? In other words, why can you *not* just do part (a) to get the price and quantity? What does part (b) consider that part (a) does not?

Extra practice

1. Construct a simulation to estimate the probability distribution for the number of heads when flipping 10 coins simultaneously. Show how this directly relates to Galton's Quincunx.

2. Gambler's Ruin. Suppose that a gambler begins a game with balance of $20 and plays a game in which on each play she wins $1 with probability p and loses $1 with probability $q = 1 - p$. This problem is an illustration of a specific random walk because the gambler's balance at any time t changes by a random amount.

   a. A Fair Game is one in which the average (Expected Value) winnings of each play is $0. Construct a simulation of the gambler's balance over time for a game of rolling a single 20-sided die (D-20). In this version, the player wins $1 if any of the 11 through 20 sides are rolled and loses $1 if 1 through 10 are rolled.

   b. Construct a simulation of the gambler's balance over time for a game of rolling a single 20-sided die (D-20). In this version, the player loses $1 if 10 through 20 are rolled and wins $1 is any of the one through nine sides are rolled.

3. Prior to the upcoming college basketball season, a college basketball coach has estimated an 80% chance of winning any specific game. Suppose the season is 30 games long and the coach believes a 20 or more-win season will get the team selected for the NCAA tournament. Create a simulation of the season.

   a. Show the probability distribution for the number of wins in a season.

   b. Determine the probability of the team getting into the NCAA tournament.

   c. Describe the appearance of the distribution.

   d. How is this similar to the flipping of the pennies? How is it different?

   e. What device could you use to simulate a season by hand?

4. The Newton–Pepys Problem is a probability problem concerning the probability of throwing sixes from a certain number of dice. In 1693, Samuel Pepys and Isaac Newton corresponded over a problem posed by Pepys in relation to a wager he planned to make. The problem was this: Which of the following three propositions has the greatest chance of success?

   a. Six fair dice are tossed independently, and at least one six appears.

   b. Twelve fair dice are tossed independently, and at least two sixes appear.

   c. Eighteen fair dice are tossed independently, and at least three sixes appear.

   Pepys initially thought that outcome (c) had the highest probability.

5. You have a coin that you know is biased; one side has a higher probability of turning up than the other side. Create a simulation that shows a process by which you can use this coin to make fair decisions (decisions with equal likelihood).

6. An investment magazine assessed the performance of 277 mutual funds over the previous 10 years. For each of the 10 years, they determined which funds performed better than the S&P 500. The research showed that 5 of the 277 funds performed better than the S&P 500 for 8 or more of the 10 years. Given that investment portfolios constructed by blindfolded monkeys throwing darts at the *Wall Street Journal* have a 50% probability of performing better than the S&P 500, determine the number of funds (out of 277) that would be expected to perform better than the S&P 500 for 8 or more of the 10 years.

Case

Swannanoa snowboards

The Swannanoa Snowboard Company, located near Asheville, North Carolina, will sell snowboards next winter. The company's founder and president, David Wilcox, was trying to determine production for the upcoming season's sales. Swannanoa's factory and shipping schedules require that all snowboards it sells next winter must be manufactured by October of this year, before the winter season begins. As this year's production begins, Swannanoa does not have any old snowboards in inventory.

Swannanoa's cost of manufacturing is $138 per snowboard. Swannanoa's snowboards will sell for $260 this winter. If demand is less than supply, then Swannanoa will attempt to sell the unsold inventory at cost during a 1-month "SALE" at the end of the winter. Inventory remaining at that point will be held until the next season (approximately 6 months). If Swannanoa is unable to meet demand, then excess demand will be lost to other competitors.

The predictions about demand for snowboards next winter depend on the general weather patterns, which may be normal or cold. If next winter's weather is normal, then demand for Swannanoa's snowboards will have probability 1/4 of being below 60,000, probability 1/2 of being below 75,000, and probability 3/4 of being below 90,000. If next winter's weather is cold, then demand for Swannanoa's snowboards have probability 1/4 of being below 80,000, probability 1/2 of being below 100,000, and probability 3/4 of being below 125,000. It is currently estimated that the probability of cold weather next winter is 1/3, and the probability of normal weather is 2/3.

In a production planning session, a marketing manager remarked that good forecasts of the coming winter's general weather would be available in September. But the manufacturing director replied that a delay of snowboard production until September could substantially increase Swannanoa's total production costs, perhaps by $100,000 or more.

Vogel Pump Company

In June, the Vogel Pump Company received an order for 10 spare high-pressure pumps from Sierra Airlines. The special pumps were part of the hydraulic system for a particular model of aircraft in the Sierra fleet.

Vogel Pump did not carry the pump in stock but rather customized a pump that was in stock. This pump was a standard size used in many airplanes. The fittings, however, were nonstandard. When Sierra bought the airplanes in which these pumps were used, its management had decided that flying requirements peculiar to this airline necessitated a slightly different pump than standard, and Vogel Pump had designed a special pump accordingly. No other airlines used this pump, and Sierra was on the point of converting its fleet of aircraft to aircraft that would no longer use this special pump. Upon inquiry, the production manager of Vogel Pump learned that this lot of pumps would almost certainly last until Sierra's current aircraft had been entirely replaced.

The standard pumps cost Vogel Pump about $23,500 to manufacture. The first step in the customization process was disassembly process. Setup for this operation costs about $4700, whereas the variable cost was about $1220. After disassembly, each pump was individually subjected to a series of drilling, grinding, and finishing operations, the cost of which was $8650 per pump. In addition, there was a single setup cost of $4500 associated with these operations. The machined pumps were then reassembled at a cost of about $3250 per pump; after which they were subjected to a quality control test, the cost of which was negligible.

After disassembly and before the remaining operations, the pumps were subjected to a 100% inspection. In the past, an average of 6% of all the disassembled pumps failed to pass this inspection and had to be scrapped. The reassembly operation was more difficult to control. There has been considerable difficulty in meeting standards on this type of pump in the past; only 80% of the pumps had proved acceptable.

National Home Products

The National Home Products Company was a major manufacturer of brooms, brushes, mops, and other home cleaning devices. During the previous year, its sales were $244.5 million, primarily through hardware dealers and grocery chains. To achieve this sales level, the company had spent about $23.3 million on advertising and sales promotion during the previous year.

Continued

Case—cont'd

In December, the executive committee of the company was meeting to determine the advertising and sales promotion budget for the upcoming year. Of particular concern to the committee was a decision as to what to spend on a line of carpet sweepers that had encountered considerable competitive pressure during the year.

George Williams, the company sales manager, thought that a continuation of present advertising and promotional policies on the carpet sweepers would result in further decrease in sales. He therefore suggested an increase in advertising and promotion from $750,000 to $2,000,000 without any change in price.

He said he thought that unless something was done, sales during the upcoming year would amount to about 500,000 units. He was unsure of this quantity, estimating that there was a minutely small chance that sales might be as low as 325,000 units. He added that the chances were 1 in 2 that sales would be below his 500,000 unit estimate and were 1 in 4 that they might even be below 450,000 units.

When Julie Glass, the company controller, asked how high the carpet sweeper sales might go if no changes were made in advertising and promotional policies, Mr. Williams responded that there was almost no chance of exceeding 625,000 units and only a 1 in 4 chance of exceeding 550,000 units.

Mr. Williams said he believed that the proposed $1,250,000 increase in advertising and promotion was almost certain to increase sales by 10% over these estimates and perhaps by as much as 40% as an upper limit. The increase was as likely to be above 25% as below it, as likely to be between 20% and 30% as outside that range, and as likely to be above 30% as below 20%.

Ms. Glass said that she wondered how competition would react to this advertising and promotion increase. Mr. Williams replied that he really was not sure but that the increases he had just projected assumed that the competition would not change their current policies at all. He added that he thought the odds were about 3 to 1 that the competition would not respond in the upcoming year. Even if they did, he thought there would still be some increase in sales, although only about half of the increases he estimated, assuming no competitive response.

The sales price of the carpet sweeper to National's distributors was $55 per unit. The variable cost per unit was $38.50 for production levels below 500,000 units per year and $42.35 for production levels above 500,000 units per year (due to overtime costs). According to the company's production manager, Joseph Alexander, the current maximum annual production capacity is 525,000 units. At a production level above 500,000 units, the fixed production costs for the year associated with the product line would increase somewhere between 8% and 12% above the current amount of $672,000.

Probability: measuring uncertainty

The true logic of this world is the calculus of probabilities.
—James Clerk Maxwell

We may not be able to get certainty, but we can get probability, and half a loaf is better than no bread.
—C.S. Lewis

When I encounter extremely difficult problems, I go back to the beginning and study probability.
—Nobel Prize for Economics winner

Chapter outline

Introduction

The purpose of this chapter is to introduce and examine formal probability concepts and terminology. Specifically, the interpretation of probability as being a long-run relative frequency is discussed along with ideas of discrete versus continuous random variables. The probability of an event is a conditional probability when the likelihood of that event depends upon the likelihood of a precipitating event. Bayes' theorem makes use of conditional probability to determine the probability of other related conditional probabilities.

4.1 Probability: measuring likelihood

Probability is a measure of the relative likelihood of an event happening in the future. One method of estimation of the likelihood of an event in the future is to use the relative frequency of events in the past:

$$\text{Probability of an event } x = \frac{\text{No. of times the event } x \text{ happened}}{\text{No. of times the event could have happened}}$$

In notational form:

$$P(x) = n(x) / n,$$

where $n(x)$ = number of times x happened and n = total number of outcomes (*sample size*). $n(x)$ is sometimes simplified as f, where f is used to represent the number of times (*frequency*) an outcome happens:

$$p = f / n,$$

where p is agreed to be a probability of an event (outcome), f is the frequency of that outcome, and n is the number of times the event could have happened (sample size).

4.2 Probability distributions

A *random variable* is a set of uncertain outcomes, resulting from an event of a random process. The set of probabilities (likelihoods) of all outcomes of the random variable is called a *probability distribution*. As an example, consider the demand for a specific model of car next month. It is uncertain how many cars will be sold; this quantity is considered to be a random variable, and the probabilities associated with each possible quantity of demand constitute the probability distribution.

Random variables, and their associated probability distributions, are categorized as either *discrete* or *continuous*. For discrete random variables, the probability function that details the probability distribution is called the *probability mass function* (*pmf*). For continuous random variables the probability function is called the *probability density function* (*pdf*). Thus, for a discrete random variable, the *pmf* is a single bar of the probability distribution (histogram). For a continuous variable, the *pdf* is the height of the continuous probability distribution curve.

Recall that the probability that a random variable, X, has an outcome of x is defined, or calculated, according to a probability function, $f(x)$:

$$\text{Probability of } x = P(X = x) = f(x) = pmf \text{ or } pdf$$

depending on whether the random variable X is discrete or continuous, respectively.

The probability of a random variable being less than or equal to x is denoted as $F(x)$ and is referred to as the *cumulative density function* (*cdf*):

$$\text{Probability} \leq x = P(X \leq x) = F(x) = cdf$$
$$= \text{The area under the } f(x) \text{ curve to the left of } x = \text{The left tail}$$

If $f(x)$ is a continuous function, then $F(x)$ is the integral of $f(x)$ from $-\infty$ to x:

$$F(x) = \int_{-\infty}^{x} f(x)\, dx$$

Similarly, if $f(x)$ is a continuous function, then the complement, $1 - F(x)$, is the integral of $f(x)$ from x to ∞:

$$1 - F(x) = \text{Probability} \geq x = P(X \geq x)$$
$$= \text{The area under the } f(x) \text{ curve to the right of } x = \text{The right tail}$$
$$1 - F(x) = \int_{x}^{\infty} f(x)\, dx$$

These notations and the corresponding concepts are shown in Fig. 4.1.

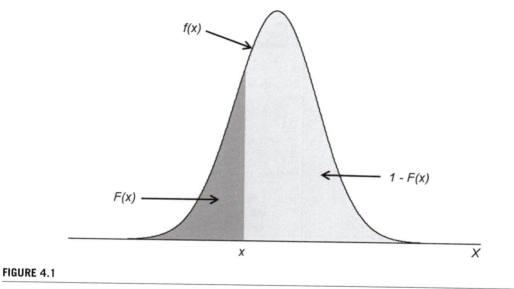

FIGURE 4.1

Notation for Probability Distribution

4.3 General probability rules

Table 4.1 presents a list of definitions and examples of elemental probability terms. The table enables discussion of the general rules of probability.

Table 4.1 Fundamental probability terms and concepts

Term	Concept	Examples
Random process	A phenomenon or process with uncertain results (outcomes)	Rolling a single die Demand for milk in a single day at a specific store
Trial	Elemental unit of a random process	A single die roll A single day of milk demand at a specific store
Outcome	Elemental result of a random process	A single die roll is a 2 Demand for milk in a single day is 10 gallons
Probability space	Set of all possible outcomes	A single die roll $\in \{1, 2, 3, 4, 5, 6\}$ Demand for milk in a single day $\in \{0, 1, 2, ..., \infty\}$ gallons
Event	Set, or subset, of outcomes	A single die roll is even Demand for milk in a single day is 10, or fewer, gallons
Probability	Measure of the likelihood of an event	1/6 chance that a single die roll is a 2 14% chance that demand for milk in a single day is 10 gallons
Random variable	A quantity resulting from an event of a random process	The number of spots on a single die roll Demand for milk on a specific day
Discrete random variable	A random variable with separate, countable outcomes	The number of spots on a single die roll Demand for milk on a specific day
Continuous random variable	A random variable with infinite, uncountable outcomes	Inches of rain on a specific day Amount of time spent in line waiting for a bank teller

The general rules of probability can now be expressed in those terms and are listed in Table 4.2.

Table 4.2 Summary of general probability rules

Event	Condition	Probability rule
A	Event A occurs	$P(A) \in [0,1]$ $0 \le P(A) \le 1$
Complement of A = not A	Event A *does not* occur	The sum of all elemental probabilities must equal 1 Thus, $P\left(A'\right) = 1 - P(A)$ $\sum P(A)_{\forall A} = 1$
A and B	Events A *and* B both occur	$P(A \cap B) = P(A)\,P(B)$ if A and B are independent $P(A \cap B) = P(A \mid B)\,P(B)$ if A and B are not independent
A given B	Event A occurs after event B has occurred	$P(A|B) = P(A \cap B)/P(B)$
A or B	Either event A *or* B occurs	$P(A \cup B = P(A) + P(B) - P(A \cap B)$ If A and B are mutually exclusive, then $P(A \cap B) = 0$ and $P(A \cup B) = P(A) + P(B)$

The probability of an event not occurring is called the *complement* and is $1 - P(A)$. Two outcomes are called ***disjoint*** or ***mutually exclusive*** if they both cannot happen. For instance, for a single die roll, the outcomes 1 and 2 are disjoint since they both cannot occur. However, the outcomes *1* and *rolling an odd number* are not disjoint, since both occur if the outcome of the roll is a 1.

Calculating the probability of disjoint outcomes is easy. When rolling a die, the outcomes 1 and 2 are disjoint, and the probability that one of these outcomes will occur can be computed by *adding* their separate probabilities as:

$$P(1 \text{ or } 2) = P(1) + P(2) = 1/6 + 1/6 = 1/3$$

What about the probability of rolling a 1, 2, 3, 4, 5, or 6? Here again, all of the outcomes are disjoint, so we add the probabilities:

$$P(1 \text{ or } 2 \text{ or } 3 \text{ or } 4 \text{ or } 5 \text{ or } 6)$$
$$= P(1) + P(2) + P(3) + P(4) + P(5) + P(6)$$
$$= 1/6 + 1/6 + 1/6 + 1/6 + 1/6 + 1/6 = 1$$

This property is known as the ***addition rule*** and guarantees the accuracy of this approach when the outcomes are disjoint. Thus, in general:

OR = Additive

Two processes are ***independent*** if knowing the outcome of one provides no information about the likelihood of the outcome of the other. For instance, flipping a coin and rolling a die are two independent processes; knowing the coin was heads does not help determine the outcome of a die roll. However, stock prices usually move up or down together, so they are not independent. Thus, in general:

AND = Multiply

Some further important probability concepts are as follows.

The ***complement*** of outcome x is all of the other outcomes that are not the outcome x. For example, the complement to P(*Heads*) is P(*Tails*) and the complement to rolling a *1* on a single die is 5/6. Typically, if the probability of the event x is $P(x) = p$, then the *complement* of the event

$$P\left(x^{'}\right) = 1 - P(x),$$

or, more compactly,

$$q = 1 - p,$$

where q is the complement of p.

Conditional probability is a probability that depends upon the occurrence of another event. Mathematically, the conditional probability of an event, *A*, is the probability that the event will occur given the knowledge that event *B* has already occurred. This probability is written P(*A*|*B*) and is stated as:

$$P(A \mid B) = \frac{P(A \cap B)}{P(B)}$$

Conditional probability is the opposite of independence. In conditional probability, the answer is "it depends" … for independence, "it does not depend."

Example 4.1 OR and AND probabilities: the probability of "some" rain

The probability of rain, as given in the newspaper, for the next 3 days is 30, 60, and 10%, respectively. What is the probability of getting some rain?

1. Solve this problem using simulation.

The spreadsheet shown in Fig. 4.2 consists of 1000 trials of 3 sequential days of rain or no rain using the probabilities associated with each day.

2. Solve this problem using theory.

There are two ways to solve this problem. The shortest way is to first compute the probability of no rain using the **AND** rule to multiply to get the joint probability as follows:

$$P(\text{No Rain}) = P(\text{No Rain 1 AND No Rain 2 AND No Rain 3})$$
$$= (1-0.30) * (1-0.60) * (1-0.10)$$
$$= 0.70 * 0.40 * 0.90 = 0.252$$

Next, compute the probability of some rain as the complement of no rain:

$$P(\text{Some Rain}) = 1 - P(\text{No Rain}) = 1 - 0.252 = 0.748 = 74.8\%$$

The second way to compute this probability is the most cumbersome way. First enumerate all of the possible 3-day events (outcomes). Then use the **AND** rule (multiply) to compute the joint probability for each possible 3-day event. For example:

$$P(\text{Rain all 3 days}) = P(\text{Rain 1 AND Rain 2 AND Rain 3})$$
$$= 0.30 * 0.60 * 0.10 = 1.8\%$$

•
•
•

$$P(\text{Rain on day 3 only}) = P(\text{No Rain 1 AND No Rain 2 AND Rain 3}) = 0.70 * 0.40 * 0.10 = 2.8\%$$

Continued

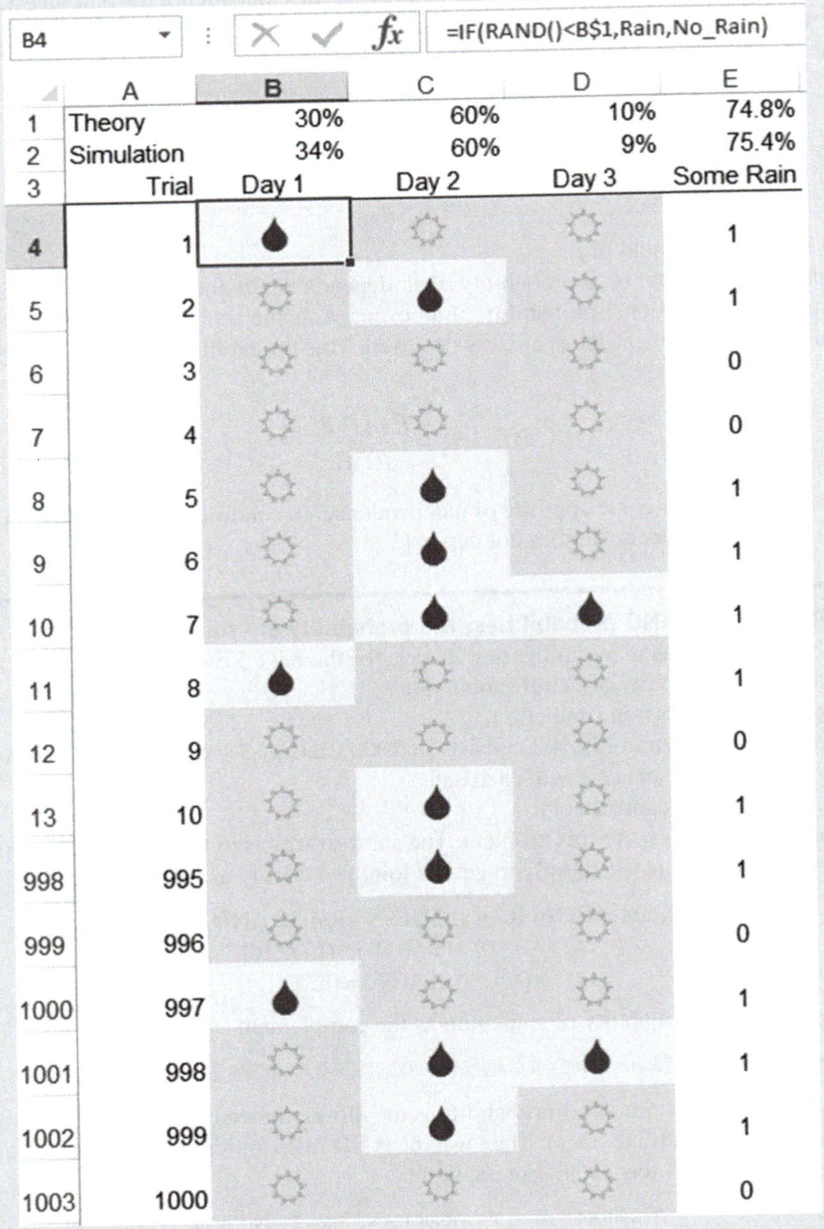

B4		⋮	✕ ✓ ƒx	=IF(RAND()<B$1,Rain,No_Rain)	

◢	A	B	C	D	E
1	Theory	30%	60%	10%	74.8%
2	Simulation	34%	60%	9%	75.4%
3		Trial	Day 1	Day 2	Day 3	Some Rain

	A	B Day 1	C Day 2	D Day 3	E Some Rain
4	1	🌧	☼	☼	1
5	2	☼	🌧	☼	1
6	3	☼	☼	☼	0
7	4	☼	☼	☼	0
8	5	☼	🌧	☼	1
9	6	☼	🌧	☼	1
10	7	☼	🌧	🌧	1
11	8	🌧	☼	☼	1
12	9	☼	☼	☼	0
13	10	☼	🌧	☼	1
998	995	☼	🌧	☼	1
999	996	☼	☼	☼	0
1000	997	🌧	☼	☼	1
1001	998	☼	🌧	🌧	1
1002	999	☼	🌧	☼	1
1003	1000	☼	☼	☼	0

FIGURE 4.2

One Thousand Trials of 3 Days of Weather

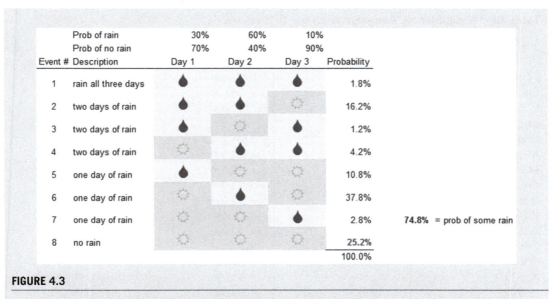

		30%	60%	10%	
Prob of rain					
Prob of no rain		70%	40%	90%	
Event # Description		Day 1	Day 2	Day 3	Probability
1	rain all three days	🌢	🌢	🌢	1.8%
2	two days of rain	🌢	🌢	☼	16.2%
3	two days of rain	🌢	☼	🌢	1.2%
4	two days of rain	☼	🌢	🌢	4.2%
5	one day of rain	🌢	☼	☼	10.8%
6	one day of rain	☼	🌢	☼	37.8%
7	one day of rain	☼	☼	🌢	2.8%
8	no rain	☼	☼	☼	25.2%
					100.0%

74.8% = prob of some rain

FIGURE 4.3

Theoretical Solution for the Probability of "Some" Rain Example

Finally, use the **OR** rule to add each 3-day outcome with rain together as in Fig. 4.3.

Problems of this sort are typically solved using probability notation and equations to provide an exact solution. The ease of solving this problem with simulation and the ability to explain the simulation to others demonstrate the power of simulation.

4.4 Conditional probability and Bayes' theorem

Conditional probability is a probability that depends upon the occurrence of another event. Mathematically, the conditional probability of an event, A, is the probability that the event will occur given the knowledge that event B has already occurred. This probability is written $P(A|B)$ and is stated as:

"The probability of A **given** B "

In the special case where events A and B are independent (where event B has no effect on the probability of event A), the conditional probability of event A given event B is simply the probability of event A—that is, $P(A)$.

Although the mathematical description and notation for conditional probability can be confusing, conditional probability is commonly used. Fundamentally, conditional probability is simply using the appropriate denominator for the probability calculation. For example, consider the information from the US Census Bureau (*Table 1: Total U.S. Resident Population by Age, Sex, and Series: April 1, 2020*) is shown in Table 4.3.

Table 4.3 US population, estimated from the 2020 census

Age (Years)	Female	Male	Total
<5	9,510,000	9,948,000	19,458,000
5 to 9	9,974,000	10,456,000	20,430,000
10 to 14	10,650,000	11,175,000	21,825,000
15 to 19	10,576,000	11,053,000	21,629,000
20 to 24	**10,556,000**	10,981,000	**21,537,000**
25 to 29	**11,309,000**	11,656,000	**22,965,000**
30 to 34	11,313,000	11,588,000	22,901,000
35 to 39	11,035,000	11,254,000	22,289,000
40 to 44	10,290,000	10,353,000	20,643,000
45 to 49	10,252,000	10,258,000	20,510,000
50 to 54	10,445,000	10,401,000	20,846,000
55 to 59	11,255,000	10,933,000	22,188,000
60 to 64	10,824,000	10,247,000	21,071,000
65 to 69	9,423,000	8,538,000	17,961,000
70 to 74	7,720,000	6,775,000	14,495,000
75 to 79	5,290,000	4,354,000	9,644,000
80 to 84	3,519,000	2,623,000	6,142,000
≥85	3,885,000	2,178,000	6,063,000
Total	**167,826,000**	164,771,000	**332,597,000**

According to Census 2020, the estimated population in the United States was 332.597 million people—of which 167.826 million were female and 164.771 million were male; in addition, 21.856 million people were females in their 20s:

- The census showed that **50.5%** of all persons are female:

$$167,826,000 / 332,597,000 = 0.505$$

Now consider the following statements based on that census data:
- The census showed that **49.1%** of those in their 20s are female:

$$21,865,000 / (21,865,000 + 22,637,000) = 0.491$$

- The census showed that **13.0%** of females are in their 20s:

$$21,865,000 / 167,826,000 = 0.130$$

- The census showed that **6.6%** of the population is females in their 20s:

$$21,856,000 / 332,597,000 = 0.066$$

In each of those statements, the base (denominator) is the referent group—the *given*. The base (denominator) is the *condition* that creates the conditional probability.

The probability statements that correspond to the previously mentioned statements are:
- The probability of a randomly selected person being female is **0.505.**
- The probability of a randomly selected person being female, given the person is 20-something, is **0.491.**

- The probability of a randomly selected person being 20-something, given the person is female, is **0.130.**
- The probability of a randomly selected person being a 20-something female is **0.066.**

These probability statements are written symbolically as follows:

$P(female) = $ **0.505**—this is a *marginal* probability.
$P(female|20\text{-}something) = $ **0.491**—this is a *conditional* probability.
$P(20\text{-}something|female) = $ **0.130**—this is a *conditional* probability.
$P(20\text{-}something \cap female) = $ **0.066**—this is a *joint* probability.

> My favorite fellow of the Royal Society is the Reverend Thomas Bayes, an obscure 18th-century Kent clergyman and a brilliant mathematician who devised a complex equation known as the Bayes theorem, which can be used to work out probability distributions. It had no practical application in his lifetime, but today, thanks to computers, is routinely used in the modelling of climate change, astrophysics and stock-market analysis.
>
> **—Bill Bryson**

Example 4.2 Joint, marginal, and conditional probabilities

Two factories, *A* and *B*, produce radios. Each radio produced in factory *A* has a 5% probability of being defective, whereas each radio produced in factory *B* has a 1% probability of being defective. Both factories produce the same number of radios.

a. If you buy a radio, what is the probability that you will get a defective radio?

b. If you get a defective radio, what is the probability that the radio came from factory *A*?

c. Suppose you purchase two radios that were produced at the same factory. If the first radio that you check is defective, what is the conditional probability that the other one is also defective?

d. Suppose that instead of the production of both factories being equal, factory *B* produces 50% more radios. If you get a defective radio, what is the probability that the radio came from factory *A*?

Although problems of this sort are typically solved using probability notation and equations, a table typically provides an easier method to solve the problem. Begin with the following information.

Because both factories produce the same number of radios, use the ***relative*** frequencies to fill out the following table:

	OK	Defective	Total
Factory A			50
Factory B			50
			100

Next, use the following statement:

Each radio produced in factory *A* has a 5% probability of being defective, whereas each radio produced in factory *B* has a 1% probability of being defective to add additional relative frequencies:

	OK	Defective	Total
Factory A		0.05*50 = **2.5**	50
Factory B		0.01*50 = **0.5**	50
			100

Continued

In probability notation, $P(Defective|A) = 5\%$ and $P(Defective|B) = 1\%$. These are *conditional* probabilities. The vertical bar "|" is the symbol for "given," and you should think of it as the division sign. For example:

$$P(Defective \mid A) = 0.05 = 2.5/50$$

Next, fill in the rest of the table using addition and subtraction:

	OK	Defective	Total
Factory A	47.5	2.5	50
Factory B	49.5	0.5	50
	97.0	3.0	100

In probability notation: $P(Defective) = 3\%$ and $P(OK) = 97\%$. These are *marginal* probabilities. Now, probability questions can be answered as follows:

a. If you buy a radio, what is the probability that you get a defective radio?

$$P(Defective) = 3/100 = 3\%$$

b. If you get a defective radio, what is the probability that the radio came from factory A? In other words, given all defective radios, what percentage came from factory A?

$$P(A \mid Defective) = 2.5/3 = 83.3\%$$

c. Suppose you purchase two radios that were produced at the same factory. If the first radio that you check is defective, what is the conditional probability that the other one is also defective? First, consider the probabilities of which factory the first defective radio came from:

$$P(A \mid Defective) = 2.5/3 = 83.3\% \text{ and } P(B \mid Defective) = 0.5/3 = 16.7\%$$

Next, weight the probability of getting a second defective radio. This will be higher than the unconditional 3% chance of getting a defective radio:

$$(2.5/3 \times 5\%) + (0.5/3 \times 1\%) = (0.8333 \times 0.05) + (0.1666 \times 0.01) = 4.3\%$$

d. Suppose that instead of the production of both factories being equal, factory B produces 50% more radios. If you get a defective radio, what is the probability that the radio came from factory A?
Redo the table with the new information:

	OK	Defective	Total
Factory A	47.5	2.5	50
Factory B	74.25	0.01*75 = 0.75	50*1.5 = 75
	121.75	3.25	125

Use the frequencies even though they are now messy:

$$P(A \mid Defective) = 2.5/3.25 = 76.9\%$$

Why is this probability less than the initial answer of 83.3%—why did the probability go down? Even in very serious decision-making situations, such as assessing the evidence of guilt or innocence during a trial, most people fail to properly evaluate objective probabilities. The psychologists Daniel Kahneman and Amos Tversky are famous for their work with probability and common mistakes people make using probability: Daniel Kahneman won a Nobel Prize for this work, and Amos Tversky would have been a co-winner with him, but the Royal Swedish Academy of Sciences does not award prizes posthumously. The following example from their research illustrates a common error in the estimation and use of probability.

Example 4.3 Kahneman and Tversky's cab problem: Bayes' theorem

A cab was involved in a hit-and-run accident at night. Two cab companies, the Green and Blue, operate in the city: 85% of the cabs in the city are Green and 15% are Blue. A witness identified the cab as Blue. The court tested the reliability of the witness under the same circumstances that existed on the night of the accident and concluded that the witness correctly identified each one of the two colors 80% of the time and failed 20% of the time. What is the probability that the cab involved in the accident was Blue rather than Green?

Again, beginning with the information given, use frequencies to fill out the following table:

1. Eighty-five percent of the cabs in the city are Green and 15% are Blue.

	SAYS Blue	SAYS Green	Total
IS Blue			15
IS Green			85
			100

2. The witness correctly identified each one of the two colors 80% of the time and failed 20% of the time.

	SAYS Blue	SAYS Green	Total
IS Blue	0.80*15=12	0.20*15=3	15
IS Green	0.20*85=17	0.80*85=68	85
			100

Alternately, the frequency for *SAYS Green* can be computed by subtracting the *SAYS Blue* frequency from the *Total* frequency: $85 - 68 = 17$.

Next, fill in the rest of the table using addition:

	SAYS Blue	SAYS Green	Total
IS Blue	12	3	15
IS Green	17	68	85
	29	71	100

Converting frequencies to percentages, notice that the forecasts' (*SAYS*) probabilities 29% and 71% are quite different from the actual (*IS*) probabilities of 15% and 85%.

Now using the table to answer the question, the probability that the cab is actually Blue (*IS Blue*) *GIVEN* that the witness states that it is Blue (*SAYS Blue*) is:

$$P(IS\ Blue \mid SAYS\ Blue) = 12/29 = 41.4\%$$

Given that this value is less than 50%, the witness *is most likely wrong* about the color of the cab!

This notion of improving probability estimates based upon updated information and conditional probabilities is known as Bayesian probability. Bayes' theorem is formally stated as:

$$P(A \mid B) = \frac{P(B \mid A)\,P(A)}{P(B)}$$

Continued

In the context of the previous example, event A is "IS Blue" and event B is "SAYS Blue." Thus:

$$P(A) = 15\%$$
$$P(B) = 29\%$$
$$P(B|A) = 80\% \quad \text{(given in the story)} = 12\%/15\%$$

Consequently, using Bayes' theorem:

$$P(A|B) = \frac{0.80\,(0.15)}{0.29} = \frac{0.12}{0.29} = \frac{12}{29} = 41.4\%$$

You don't know what you don't know . . . so you don't know how important it could be.

Exercise Set 4: General Probability Rules

1. A contractor is planning a construction project to be completed in three stages. The contractor has estimated that the chance that the first stage will be completed on time is 70%. She has also estimated that if the first stage is completed on time, the chance that the second stage will be completed on time is 80%. Finally, she has estimated that given both the first and second stages are completed on time, the chance of the third stage will be completed on time is 90%. What is the probability the project will be completed on time? Draw a probability tree to describe this problem. What can you extrapolate from this problem regarding large projects?

2. A company has 2000 employees, 800 of whom are female; 300 of the female employees earn at least $60,000 per year and 200 of the men earn at least $60,000 per year.
   a. What is the probability that a randomly selected individual earns less than $60,000 per year?
   b. What is the probability that a randomly selected male earns less than $60,000 per year?
   c. What is the probability that a randomly selected female earns less than $60,000 per year?
   d. If a randomly selected individual earns at least $60,000 per year, what is the probability that this person is female?
   e. If a randomly selected individual earns less than $60,000 per year, what is the probability that this person is male?
   f. What is the appropriate managerial conclusion?

3. As a sales promotion, a soft drink manufacturer places winning symbols under the caps of 10% of all soft drink bottles. If you buy a six-pack of soft drinks, what is the probability that you will win a prize? Create a simulation to validate your answer.

4. Stephanie is concerned about getting a job. She estimates that she has a 75% chance of getting a job offer for each job she applies for. How many jobs must she apply for to have at least a 98% chance of getting at least one offer? Create a simulation to validate your answer.

5. One percent of people at age 40 who participate in routine cancer screenings have cancer, 80% of people with cancer will get positive screenings, and 10% of people without cancer will also get positive screenings.
   a. Construct a contingency table for this problem.
   b. Draw a probability tree for this problem.

c. State relevant joint, marginal, and conditional probabilities for this problem.

d. In a routine screening, a person in this age group had a positive screening. What is the probability that the person actually has cancer? This type of question has been asked of physicians and medical students with a very small proportion of them answering correctly.

6. There are two people going to a concert that starts at 9:00 p.m. Each person will arrive at the concert independently between 8:00 and 9:00 p.m. Assume their arrival times are independently uniformly distributed over 8:00 to 9:00 p.m. Whoever arrives first will wait for the other one outside so that they can go to the event together. They also agree to two rules. First, if it is 8:50 p.m. and you are waiting, then wait no longer and go in. Second, if you have been waiting for 10 minutes, then you wait no longer and go in. What is the probability that the two people will actually meet outside before going in?

a. Solve this problem with simulation.

b. Solve this problem graphically.

c. Solve this problem analytically.

7. A soft drink company employs drivers to deliver products and stock them in grocery stores. Applicants for this position are given a preemployment test to increase the likelihood of reliability and retention. Test questions are multiple choice questions, and each has five possible answers. Assume that all guesses are equally likely.

a. If 60% of the respondents got the correct answer, what is the percentage of applicants who actually know the correct answer?

b. If 70% of the respondents got the correct answer, what is the percentage of applicants who actually know the correct answer?

c. If 68% of the respondents got the correct answer, what is the percentage of applicants who actually know the correct answer?

8. Marketing research firms often contact respondents by sampling random telephone numbers. Although interviewers currently reach about 76% of US households selected, the percentage of those contacted who agree to answer the survey has fallen. Assume that the percentage of those who agree to answer the survey is 38% and that percentage is irrespective of contact. (Why is that a reasonable assumption?)

a. What is the probability that the next household on the list will be contacted but will refuse to answer the survey?

b. What is the probability of failing to contact a household or of contacting the household but not getting them to agree to answer the survey?

c. What are the managerially appropriate marginal, joint, and conditional probabilities?

9. Automobile state inspections are required annually to register vehicles for license plates and license plate renewals. Suppose that 18% of all cars inspected have problems that need to be corrected. State inspections fail to detect these problems 12% of the time. However, an inspection never detects a problem when there is no problem. Suppose a car is inspected and passes inspection (found to be free of problems); what is the probability that there is actually something wrong that the inspection failed to uncover?

10. A customer has applied for a 1-year loan of $100,000 at an interest rate of 10%. If the bank does not approve the loan application, the $100,000 will be invested in bonds that earn a 6% annual

return. Currently, if the loan were to be approved, the bank believes there is a 4% chance that this customer will default on the loan, in which case the bank will lose the $100,000.

For $1000, the bank can examine the customer's credit record to determine a favorable or unfavorable credit score. Past data indicates that in cases where the customer did not default on the loan, the probability of receiving a favorable credit score was 80%. Furthermore, in cases where the customer defaulted on the loan, the probability of receiving a favorable credit score was 25%.

  a. Construct a contingency table for this problem.
  b. Draw the appropriate decision tree.
  c. State relevant joint, marginal, and conditional probabilities for this problem.
  d. Use the decision tree and construct a simulation to determine the best course of action for the bank to maximize expected profit.
  e. Calculate and interpret the expected value of perfect information.

11. A product manager must determine whether her company should market a new brand of toothpaste. It has been estimated that if the new product succeeds in the marketplace, then the company will earn $1,800,000 in profit from the sale of the new toothpaste. If the product fails, the company expects that it could lose $750,000. If she chooses not to market the new toothpaste, then there would be negligible effects on the profits of other products in the company's product portfolio. The brand manager has estimated that the new toothpaste brand has about a 50% chance to succeed.

Before making her recommendation regarding the toothpaste introduction, the manager can spend $75,000 on a marketing research study. Such a study of consumer preferences will yield either a positive or negative recommendation, each with a probability of 50%. Given a positive recommendation to market the new product, there is a 75% chance that the product will actually succeed. Given a negative recommendation, there is still a 25% chance the product will still actually succeed.

  a. Draw the appropriate decision tree and determine the best course of action for the manager to maximize expected profit.
  b. Calculate and interpret the expected value of perfect information.

12. A company is considering whether to market a new product. For the sake of simplicity, assume that if this product is marketed, there are only two possible outcomes: success and failure with probabilities p and $1 - p$, respectively. If the product is marketed and fails, then the company will lose $4.5 million. If the product is marketed and is a success, then the company will gain $7.5 million. The company is also considering whether to conduct marketing research among prospective buyers of this product. The results of the survey can be classified as favorable, neutral, or unfavorable. In similar cases where the proposed products proved to be market successes, the likelihoods that the survey results were favorable, neutral, and unfavorable were 60, 30, and 10%, respectively. In similar cases where the proposed products proved to be market failures, the likelihoods that the survey results were favorable, neutral, and unfavorable were 10, 20, and 70%, respectively.

  a. Construct a contingency table for this problem.
  b. Draw a probability tree for this problem.
  c. State relevant joint, marginal, and conditional probabilities for this problem.
  d. If $p = 50\%$ and the cost of the survey is $150,000, then what should the company do to maximize their expected value regarding marketing this product?
  e. If $p = 40\%$, what values (if any) of the marketing research survey would the company choose to conduct the survey?

Further Exercises: Common Interview Questions Regarding Probability

1. In a room with n people, what is the probability that two people celebrate their birthday on the same day of the year? How large should n be so that the probability of a shared birthday is greater than 50%? Assume 365 days per year. This problem is well documented as the Birthday Problem.

2. In *Catch 22*, a novel about World War II bomber pilots, Joseph Heller states that the probability of a B-17 getting shot down on any given mission is 2%. The author states that since the required number of missions was 50, there was a 100% chance of getting shot down; how do we know this is wrong, and what is the probability of surviving 50 missions?

3. You have a coin that you know is biased; one side has a higher probability of turning up than the other side. Describe a process by which you can use this coin to make fair decisions (decisions with equal likelihood).

4. The probability of rain, as given in the newspaper, for the next 3 days is 30, 20, and 30%. What is the probability of getting some rain?

5. You are one of 100 people standing in line to get onto an airplane that has 100 seats. There is a seat for every person in line, and each of you has a boarding pass for your assigned a seat. The first person to walk onto the plane drops his boarding pass and, instead of picking it up, decides, "I'm just going to sit anyplace." He takes a seat at random.

Now, every other passenger will take either their assigned seat or, if that seat is taken, that passenger will take any seat at random.

As you are such a kind, generous, and accommodating person, you decide to be the last passenger to walk onto the plane. Obviously, there is going to be one seat left because everyone else is sitting in their correct seat, or not. What are the chances that you get to sit in your assigned seat?

6. What is the probability of making everyone happy?

Case

Royal Riband

As cruise season approaches, Royal Riband must determine the pricing and quantity of different classes and types of cabins. Storms obviously play a significant role in influencing the demand for cruises. Due to the margins of error in storm prediction, although 20% of the seasons are forecasted to be stormy, only 15% of the seasons are actually stormy. Of the seasons that were actually stormy, 80% were forecasted to be stormy. The upcoming season is currently forecasted to not be stormy.

Having already determined the pricing and promotions to influence demand, Royal Riband is currently trying to determine the amount of cabin reservations to book for a specific category of 250 cabins for a specific voyage. In stormy seasons, the cancelation rate is approximately 10% compared to the 2% for nonstormy seasons. Customers in this category who cancel their reservations have 75% of their purchase price refunded (i.e., they forfeit 25% of the price for canceling their reservation).

For this particular cruise, this category of cabins is priced at $1000. If the number of booked customers exceeds capacity, then the cruise line offers volunteers $400 to rebook on a subsequent cruise. In overbooking cases such as these, due to lost sales, displacement of future sales, and other considerations, the cruise line considers the cost of one overbooking to be $1400.

Subjective probability distributions

What are the chances based on experience? Most of us think that we are "better than average" in most things. We are also "miscalibrated," meaning that our sense of the probability of events doesn't line up with reality.
—Richard Thaler (2017 Nobel Prize Winner)

Chapter outline

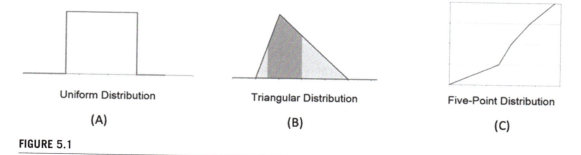

FIGURE 5.1

Three Distributions for Subjective Probability

(A) Uniform distribution, (B) triangular distribution, and (C) five-point distribution.

Introduction to Business Analytics Using Simulation. https://doi.org/10.1016/B978-0-323-91717-9.00005-X

Introduction

Lack of data is a common excuse from managers for not using probabilities in decision making. The object of this chapter is to demonstrate how to derive probability distributions from managerial experience. The use of two-, three-, and five-point estimates to create useful probability distributions is explained and demonstrated in this chapter. Fig. 5.1 shows the shapes of these three probability distributions.

5.1 Subjective probability distributions: probability from experience

Subjective probability is based upon experience of an expert but has no recorded data. There are numerous situations in which expert estimates of probability based upon experience are required. A common example is the estimation of task times in project management. Project managers must frequently use their previous experience to estimate how long it might take to do portions of a project to estimate the range of time it will take to complete the entire project.

Empirical probability is data driven and is the primary focus of this book. In the fields of medicine and business, data-driven probability is referred to as *evidence-based* probability.

Both subjective and empirical probability estimates come from data—the main difference being whether or not the data have been recorded. Clearly, empirical probability is preferred when data are available, but subjective probability estimates from experts are necessary in situations when no recorded data are available. An example from practice is in the estimation of the duration of activities for a project that has never been done before, such as the research and development of a new medical treatment.

For many people, the term *subjective* evokes negative feelings associated with the word *arbitrary*. Subjective means *using judgment*—not arbitrary. Both subjective and empirical probability estimates come from data—the main difference being whether or not the data have been recorded. Clearly, empirical probability is preferred when data are available, but subjective probability estimates from experts should not be disregarded.

A natural question is, "Why use subjective probability?" The answer is that often analysts and decision makers recognize uncertainty associated with an important aspect of a decision but lack data to explicitly determine the range and variability of the uncertain factor. Most people make the mistake of resorting to using a single number, such as the average or the *mode* (the most likely number). Using a single number obscures the risks and opportunities present due to the effect of the full probability distribution.

In a simple example, you might estimate that the time to drive to the airport is between 30 and 45 minutes. In a managerial example, a project manager might not know the exact cost of a specific activity but, based on experience, estimate the cost to be between $1500 and $2000.

Decision analysis and simulation models, which incorporate uncertainty and risk, are significant improvements over simplistic models that use a single estimate rather than a probabilistic approach. Thus, to create better analyses, subjective two-, three-, and five-point estimation of probability distributions are presented here.

There are many managerial situations in which probabilities are needed, but neither data nor theoretical probability distributions are available. In such situations, experiential information provided by an expert might be suitable—and is much better than a single-number estimate.

5.2 Two-point estimation: uniform distribution

When there is no information as to whether any particular outcome is more or less likely to occur than any other outcome, the outcomes are equally likely. The probability distribution for that situation is called a *uniform distribution*. The *uniform distribution* is an example of a theoretical distribution that can be used for subjective probability estimation. Uniform distributions can be either discrete or continuous.

5.2.1 Discrete uniform distribution

Given the minimum (a) and the maximum (b) outcomes, the number of equally likely outcomes is n and is equal to $(b - a + 1)$. The probability mass function (pmf) for the **discrete uniform distribution** is (Fig. 5.2):

$$f(x) = 1/n = 1/(b - a + 1) \quad \text{for } a \leq x \leq b$$

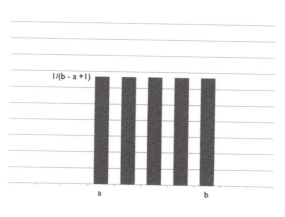

FIGURE 5.2

Probability Mass Function (pmf) for the Discrete Uniform Distribution

The cumulative distribution function (cdf) for the discrete uniform distribution is (Fig. 5.3):

$$F(x) = (x - a + 1)/(b - a + 1) \quad \text{for } a \leq x \leq b$$

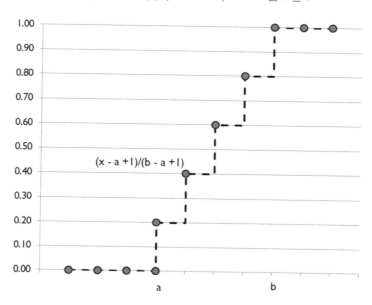

FIGURE 5.3

Cumulative Distribution Function (cdf) for the Discrete Uniform Distribution

Example 5.1 Discrete uniform probability

Demand for a particular class of hotel rooms is uniform between 10 and 20. The hotel has a capacity of 17 such rooms. What is the probability that they will have to turn customers away—that is, what is the probability of shortage?

There are 11 outcomes: {10, 11, 12, 13, 14, 15, 16, 17, 18, 19, 20}, and each outcome is equally likely. Counting from 11 to 20 and then accounting for the 10 yields $n = (20 - 10 + 1) = 11$. Thus, the probability of each outcome is $1/11 = 9.09\%$. In probability notation:

$$f(x) = 1/11, \quad \text{for} \ \ 10 \le x \le 20.$$

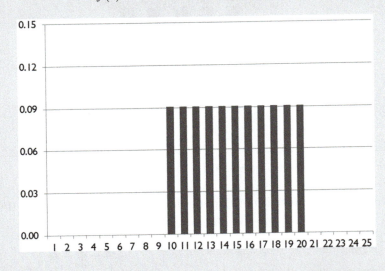

FIGURE 5.4

Probability Mass Function (*pmf*) for the Discrete Uniform Distribution [10, 20]

The probability of shortage is:

$$P(x>17) = f(18) + f(19) + f(20) = 3(1/11) = 3/11 = 0.272727 \ \ldots \ = 27.27\%$$

The formula to simulate a **discrete** uniform random variable is:

$$= \text{lowerbound} + \text{TRUNC}(\text{RAND}() * (\text{range} + 1))$$

Thus, for this problem, the formula is:

$$= 10 + \text{TRUNC}(\text{RAND}() * 11)$$

Consider that when the RAND() is 0, the random variable will be 10; when the RAND() is 0.999…, the random variable is $10 + \text{TRUNC}(10.9999\ldots) = 10 + 10 = 20$. Finally, the average of RAND() is 0.50, which results in $10 + \text{TRUNC}(0.50*11) = 10 + \text{TRUNC}(5.5) - 10 + 5 = 15$, the average and median of the distribution.

Refer to Table 5.1 for a review of random number generators for simple distributions.

The output of a simulation of 10,000 trials using $= 10 + \text{TRUNC}(\text{RAND}()*11)$ is shown in Fig. 5.5.

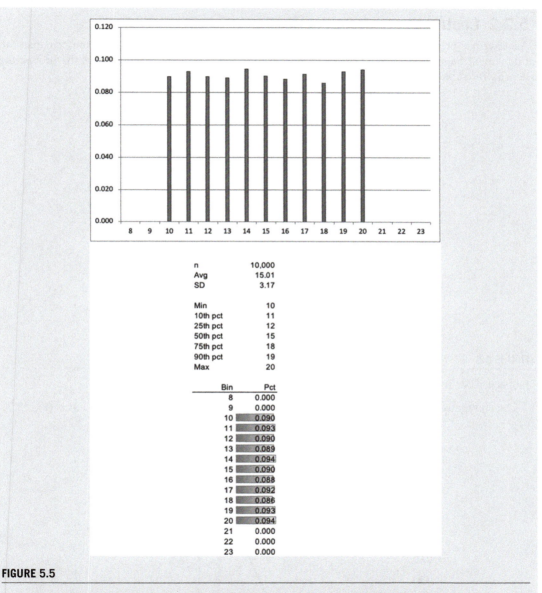

FIGURE 5.5

Distribution of 10,000 Random Observations From the Discrete Uniform Distribution [10, 20]

Again note that the theoretical *pmf* for this distribution is 1/11 (= 0.09999…). Also notice that the simulation results are close to theory, although not exactly like theory in the same way that real data will be close to theory but not exactly the same as theory.

5.2.2 **Continuous uniform distribution**

As described previously, without information as to the likelihood of outcomes, the uniform distribution should be assumed. Given the minimum (*a*) and the maximum (*b*) outcomes, the probability density function (*pdf*) for the **continuous uniform distribution** is (Fig. 5.6):

$$f(x) = 1/(b-a) \quad \text{for} \quad a<b$$

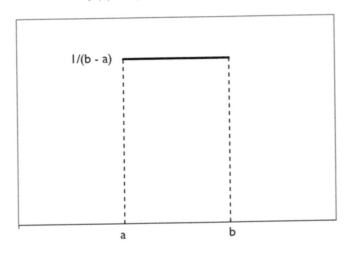

FIGURE 5.6

Probability Density Function (*pdf*) for the Continuous Uniform Distribution

The cumulative distribution function (*cdf*) for the **continuous uniform distribution** is (Fig. 5.7):

$$F(x) = (x-a)/(b-a) \quad \text{for} \quad a \le x \le b$$

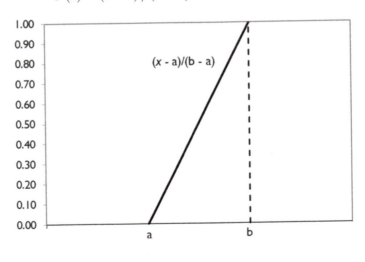

FIGURE 5.7

Cumulative Distribution Function (*cdf*) for the Discrete Uniform Distribution

Example 5.2 Continuous uniform probability

Suppose demand for T-shirts at a concert is estimated to be somewhere between 5% and 10% of ticket sales. What is the probability that demand will be less than 7% of ticket sales?

As there is no further information regarding the most, or least, likely percentage of ticket sales, all percentages are considered as equally likely—including the fractions of percentages in between 5% and 10%. For example, there could be 821 T-shirts purchased out of ticket sales of 15,000. This would equate to 821/15,000 = 0.547333(...). In probability notation:

$$f(x) = 1/(10\% - 5\%), \text{ for } 5\% < x < 10\%$$

The graph of the *pdf* of the *continuous* uniform distribution between 5 and 10 is shown in Fig. 5.8.

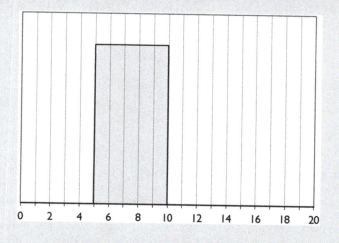

FIGURE 5.8

Continuous Uniform Distribution [5%, 10%]

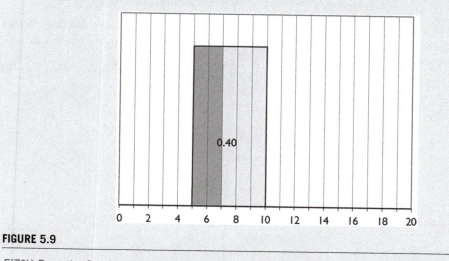

FIGURE 5.9

$F(7\%)$ From the Continuous Uniform Distribution [5%, 10%]

We want to know the probability that demand will be less than 7% of ticket sales, and this is:

$$P(X \leq 7) = F(7) = (7-5)/(10-5) = 2/5 = 40\%$$

The formula to simulate a *continuous* uniform random variable is:

$$= \text{lowerbound} + \text{RAND}()*\text{range}$$

Thus, for this problem, the formula is:

$$= 0.05 + \text{RAND}()*0.05$$

This equation is derived by inverting the graph of the *cdf* for the continuous uniform distribution—that is, use the percentile as the x variable, which will be the RAND()) and the outcome of the random variable as the y variable and then solving for y:

cdf for the *continuous* uniform distribution:

$$F(x) = (x-a)/(b-a)$$

Using words rather than symbols:

$$\textit{percentile} = (\textit{outcome} - \textit{lowerbound})/(\textit{upperbound} - \textit{lowerbound})$$

Solving for the *outcome* variable:

$$\textit{percentile} \; (\textit{upperbound} - \textit{lowerbound}) = (\textit{outcome} - \textit{lowerbound})$$
$$\textit{lowerbound} + \textit{percentile} \; (\textit{upperbound} - \textit{lowerbound}) = \textit{outcome}$$
$$\textit{outcome} = \textit{lowerbound} + \textit{percentile} \; (\textit{upperbound} - \textit{lowerbound})$$

Rather than having Excel compute (*upperbound* − *lowerbound*) many thousands of times, it is faster to calculate *range* = (*upperbound* − *lowerbound*) once and then refer to range in the simulation formulae. Thus, substituting range and RAND() yields the following formula:

$$\textit{outcome} = \textit{lowerbound} + \text{RAND}() \; (\textit{range})$$

This process of random number generation is called the *inverse transformation method* and can be used to derive the simulation formulas for many probability distributions. A list of such simulation formulas is given in Appendix A1.3.

The output of a simulation of 10,000 trials using = 0.05 + RAND()*0.05 is shown in Fig. 5.10.

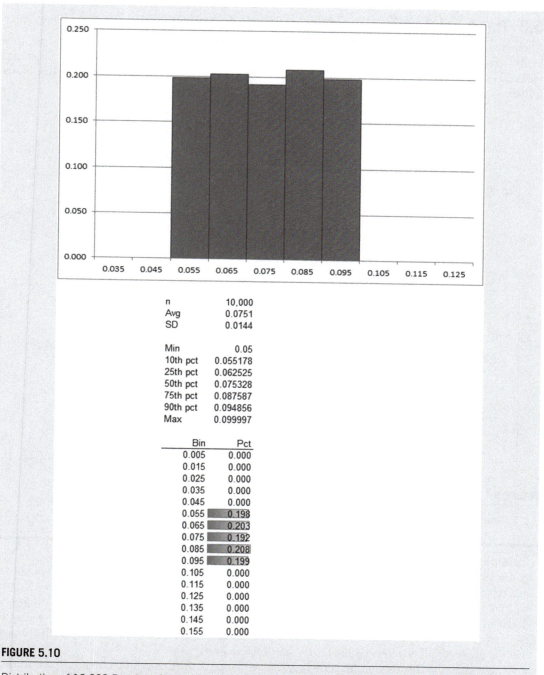

Bin	Pct
0.005	0.000
0.015	0.000
0.025	0.000
0.035	0.000
0.045	0.000
0.055	0.198
0.065	0.203
0.075	0.192
0.085	0.208
0.095	0.199
0.105	0.000
0.115	0.000
0.125	0.000
0.135	0.000
0.145	0.000
0.155	0.000

n	10,000
Avg	0.0751
SD	0.0144
Min	0.05
10th pct	0.055178
25th pct	0.062525
50th pct	0.075328
75th pct	0.087587
90th pct	0.094856
Max	0.099997

FIGURE 5.10

Distribution of 10,000 Random Observations From the Continuous Uniform Distribution [5%, 10%]

5.3 Three-point estimation: triangular distribution

Another method to construct a subjective distribution is to estimate the minimum, maximum, and "most likely" (***mode***) values (denoted as a, b, and c, respectively). This three-point subjective estimate provides an estimate for a triangular probability distribution. The *pdf* is given by the piecewise function as follows:

$$f(x) = \begin{cases} \dfrac{2(x-a)}{(b-a)(c-a)} & \text{for } a \le x \le c \\ \dfrac{2(b-x)}{(b-a)(b-c)} & \text{for } c \le x \le b \end{cases}$$

The *cdf* is given by the function as:

$$F(x) = \begin{cases} \dfrac{(x-a)^2}{(b-a)(c-a)} & \text{for } a \le x \le c \\ 1 - \dfrac{(b-x)^2}{(b-a)(b-c)} & \text{for } c \le x \le b \end{cases}$$

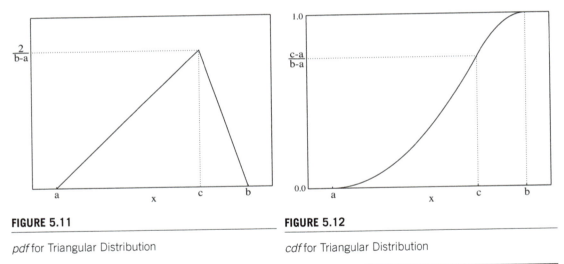

FIGURE 5.11

pdf for Triangular Distribution

FIGURE 5.12

cdf for Triangular Distribution

Example 5.3 Subjective distribution: triangular distribution

A brand manager is asked to estimate the time for a new product to be developed and brought to market. She estimates, based on past experience with similar new products and customers, that it will take at least 4 months, and at most 9 months, to get the product to market. She also estimates that it will most likely take about 6 months to get the product to market. The product is seasonal with the start of the season beginning 7 months from now and lasting for 3 months. What is the likelihood that the product will be ready by the beginning of the season?

The probability distribution function (*pdf*) and cumulative distribution function (*cdf*) are shown in Figs. 5.13 and 5.14, respectively.

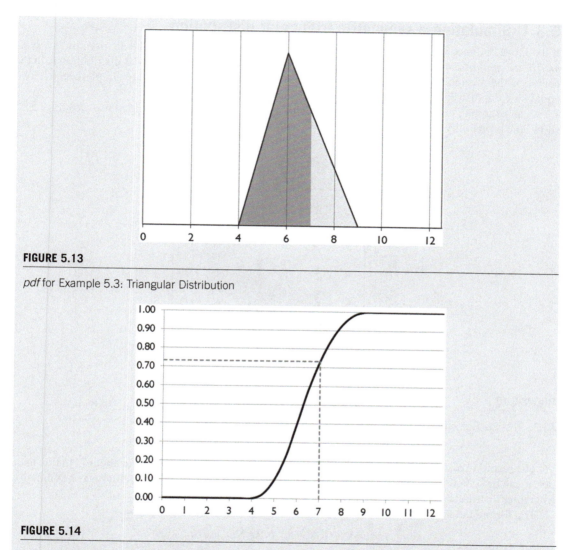

FIGURE 5.13

pdf for Example 5.3: Triangular Distribution

FIGURE 5.14

cdf for Example 5.3: Triangular Distribution

The probability that the time is less than or equal to 7 months is calculated using the *cdf* function from earlier:

$$P(Time \leq 7) = F(7) = 1 - (9-7)^2 / ((9-4)(9-6)) = 1 - 2^2 / (5(3)) = 15/15 - 4/15 = 11/15 = 73.3\overline{3}\%$$

Check using geometry:

$$F(7) = 1 - \text{area of light shaded triangle to right of 7}$$
$$F(7) = 1 - 1/2\,\text{base} \times \text{height}$$
$$F(7) = 1 - 1/2(9-7) \times [(9-7)/(9-6) \times (2/(9-4))]$$
$$F(7) = 1 - 1/2(2) \times [2/3 \times 2/5] = 1 - 4/15 = 11/15$$

5.3.1 Simulating a symmetric triangular distribution

If the mode and median are the same value for a *triangular distribution*, then the distribution is a ***symmetric** triangular distribution*. In other words, the most likely value of a triangular distribution is in the center of the triangle. Simulating symmetric triangular distribution is relatively simple because two equal uniform distributions added together create a symmetric distribution.

As an example, determine the probability distribution of two standard six-sided die (*d6*). Fig. 5.15 shows the probability space with all 36 possible outcomes.

FIGURE 5.15

All 36 Possible Outcomes From the Sum of Two Dice

The resulting distribution is a discrete triangular distribution that is symmetric about **7**. In this manner, it can be seen that the distribution of the sum of two identical uniform distributions is a symmetric triangular distribution.

The formula to simulate a ***continuous** symmetric triangular* random variable is:

$$= lowerbound + (\text{RAND}() + \text{RAND}()) * range/2$$

Consider a symmetric triangular distribution between 10 and 20, with 15 as the most likely. When both of the RAND()s are 0, the random variable will be $10 + (0+0)*(20-10)/2 = 10$. When both of the RAND()s are 0.999..., the random variable is $10 + (\sim2)*(20-10)/2 = 10 + 10 = 20$. Finally, because the average of RAND() is 0.50, the most likely number will be $10 + (0.50 + 0.50)*(20-10)/2 = 10 + 1*5 = 15$; 15 is the *maximum likelihood estimator* as well as the *average* and *median* of the distribution. The results of 10,000 simulations of

$$= 10 + (\text{RAND}() + \text{RAND}()) * 5$$

are shown in Fig. 5.16.

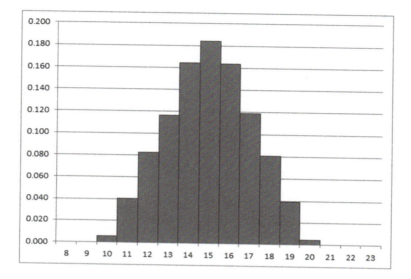

n	10,000
Avg	14.99
SD	2.04

Min	10.02711
10th pct	12.21952
25th pct	13.54065
50th pct	14.98135
75th pct	16.45702
90th pct	17.76212
Max	19.95779

Bin	Pct
8	0.000
9	0.000
10	0.005
11	0.040
12	0.082
13	0.117
14	0.164
15	0.184
16	0.164
17	0.119
18	0.081
19	0.039
20	0.005
21	0.000
22	0.000
23	0.000

FIGURE 5.16

Distribution of 10,000 Random Observations From the Continuous Symmetric Triangular Distribution [10, 20]

5.3.2 Simulating an asymmetric triangular distribution

An **asymmetric** *triangular distribution* is more difficult. The *cdf* for an asymmetric triangular distribution is:

$$F(x) = \begin{cases} \frac{(x-a)^2}{(b-a)(c-a)} & \text{for } a \le x \le c \\ 1 - \frac{(b-x)^2}{(b-a)(b-c)} & \text{for } c \le x \le b \end{cases}$$

Let the values in the *cdf* earlier be represented as:

$$a = \min$$
$$b = \max$$
$$c = mostlikelyoutcome$$
$$range = (\max - \min)$$
$$range1 = (most\ likely - \min)$$
$$range2 = (\max - most\ likely)$$
$$F(c) = range1/range$$

Using the inverse transformation method yields:

```
= IF(rand # < F(most likely), min + (range * range1 * rand #) ^ 0.5,
     max - (range * range2 * (1 - rand #)) ^ 0.5),
```

where *rand#* is a generated in a cell external to the formula cell so that specific can be accessed twice. As the specific percentile associated with the generated is not required, the formula shown later is used in practice:

$$= IF\left(rand\# < F(most\ likely) \min + range1*RAND()^\wedge 0.5, \max - range2*RAND()^\wedge 0.5\right)$$

Although the percentile generated by the second version does not specifically equate to the outcome in the same way as the outcome from the first method, the second formula has the advantages of being faster to compute and not requiring an external RAND().

Using the parameters from Example 5.3 of $a = 4$, $b = 9$, and $c = 6$ yields:

lower bound = 4
upper bound = 9
most likely = 6
range = (9 − 4) = 5
range1 = (6 − 4) = 2
range2 = (9 − 6) = 3
F(c) = 2/5 = 0.40

Fig. 5.17 shows the output of a simulation of 10,000 trials using:

$$= IF\left(RAND() < 0.40, 4 + 2*RAND()^\wedge 0.5, 9 - 3*RAND()^\wedge 0.5\right)$$

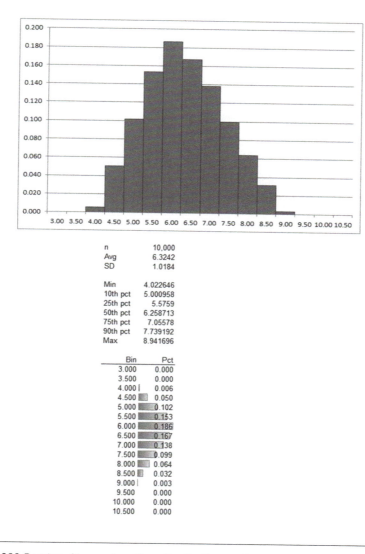

FIGURE 5.17

Distribution of 10,000 Random Observations From the Continuous Asymmetric Triangular Distribution (4, 9, 6)

5.4 **Five-point estimates for subjective probability distributions**

The *five-point estimate* is often a more effective method to construct a subjective distribution. The five-point estimate is constructed based on the 0th, 25th, 50th, 75th, and 100th percentiles. These percentiles are called the *quartiles*.

The first step in estimating the distribution is to estimate the *median* (50th percentile) by estimating the value that half of the outcomes would be below and half of the outcomes would be above. Next, the maximum and minimum outcomes are estimated. Finally, the first and third quartiles are estimated by appraising the ranges in which the outcomes are likely to occur 1 in 4 times. In other words, estimate the first and third quartiles by answering the following questions: There is a 25% chance that the outcomes will be below which value (*first quartile*)? There is a 25% chance that the outcomes will be above which value (*third quartile*)?

When working with data, the median, quartiles, and extremes (minimum, and maximum) are referred to as the *five-number summary*. The five-number summary provides a brief summary of the overall distribution of the data. The five-number summary is often used to display a *boxplot*.

A *boxplot* is graph that summarizes the distribution of data in terms of percentiles, using the median of a group as the midpoint (50th percentile). The box surrounding the median shows the 25th (lower) and 75th (higher) percentiles. The lines extending from the boundaries of the box (whiskers) denote the range of values less than 1.5 interquartile ranges (IQRs) from the boundary of the box. Any between 1.5 and 3 IQRs from the box boundary are often considered outliers; data beyond 3 IQRs from the boundary are extreme outliers.

Boxplots are often used to compare the distributions of two sets (groups) of data. Fig. 5.18 shows the boxplots for two groups (A and B) and their components.

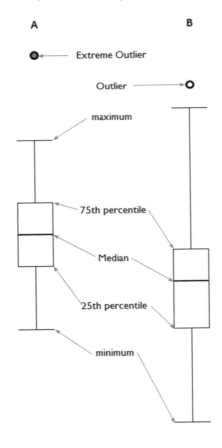

FIGURE 5.18

Components of Boxplots

Data for several factors or groups can be compared with boxplots. In the previous example, group B has a wider range of values, whereas group A has a smaller distribution with one extreme outlier. This diagram also shows that the median for group A is higher than that of group B.

Example 5.4 Subjective distribution: five-point estimate

A brand manager is asked to estimate the time for a new product to be developed and brought to market. She estimates, based on past experience with similar new products and customers, that it will take at least 4 months, and at most 9 months, to get the product to market. She also estimates that half the previous products took longer 6 months to get the product to market. Furthermore, she also estimated that three-quarters of the products took longer than 5.5 months (about 22 weeks) to reach the market and three-quarters of the products reached the market in less than 7.5 months. The product is seasonal with the start of the season beginning 7 months from now and lasting for 3 months. What is the likelihood that the product will be ready by the beginning of the season?

These estimates are tabulated to determine the cumulative distribution function (*cdf*) shown in Table 5.1.

Table 5.1 Five-point estimate of new product development time

	P(*Time* ≤ t) t	Cdf
Min	4.0	0.00
1st Quartile	5.5	0.25
Median	6.0	0.50
3rd Quartile	7.5	0.75
Max	9.0	1.00

The graph of the cumulative distribution function (*cdf*) is shown in Fig. 5.19.

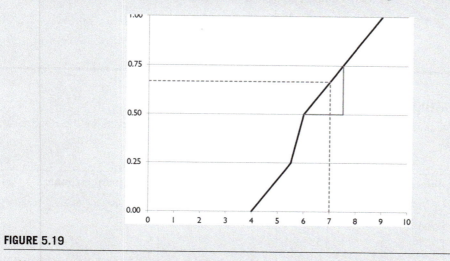

FIGURE 5.19

cdf for Example Five-Point Estimate

The probability that the time is less than or equal to 7 months is calculated using the slope-intercept parameters for the line segment of the *cdf* between 6 and 7.5 months:
Check using linear interpolation:

$$F(7) = 0.50 + (7-6)/(7.5-6) \ (0.75-0.50)$$
$$= 0.50 + 1/1.5 \ (0.25)$$
$$= 0.50 + 2/3(0.25) = 3/6 + 2/3(1/4) = 3/6 + 1/6 = 4/6 = 2/3 = \mathbf{66.\overline{66}}$$

The initial table of the *cdf* can be expanded to calculate the slopes and intercepts for each line segment by using the formulas from the previous example. Using the function, these slopes and intercepts can then be implemented in a spreadsheet to calculate the cumulative probability for any value of the random variable. Table 5.2 shows the layout for the implementation of the slope-intercept formulas in a spreadsheet.

Table 5.2 Slope-intercept table to calculate a five-point estimate of *cdf*

	t	$P(Time \le t) = cdf$	Slope = $\Delta cdf/\Delta t$	Intercept = cdf – Slope $\times t$
Min	4.0	0.00	0.166̄	−0.666̄
1st Quartile	5.5	0.25	0.5000	−2. 5000
Median	6.0	0.50	0.166̄	−0.5000
3rd Quartile	7.5	0.75	0.166̄	−0.5000
Max	9.0	1.00	0.166̄	0.5000

The slope and intercept for any range of the five-point estimate can now be obtained from Table 5.2. As an example, $F(7)$ is within the range for [6, 7.5] and yields:

$$P\,(Time \le 7) = F\,(7) = 0.166\overline{6}\,(7) - 0.50 = 7/6 - 3/6 = 4/6 = 2/3 = \mathbf{66.\overline{66}\%}$$

5.4.1 Simulating a five-point distribution

Simulating the five-point distribution first requires inverting the formula by reversing the *x* and *y* variables in Table 5.2.

Table 5.3 Slope-intercept table to simulate a random variable from a five-point estimate

	$P(Time \le t) = RAND()$	T	Slope = $\Delta t/\Delta RAND()$	Intercept = t – Slope $\times$ RAND()
Min	0.00	4.0	6	4
1st Quartile	0.25	5.5	2	5
Median	0.50	6.0	6	3
3rd Quartile	0.75	7.5	6	3
Max	1.00	9.0	0	9

As in the previous example in which the outcome of 7 was at the 67th percentile—that is, $F(7) = 0.666\overline{6}$—a RAND() of $0.666\overline{6}$ results in an outcome of 7.

Use VLOOKUP(_) to determine the slope and intercept corresponding to the percentile generated by the RAND(). A RAND() of $0.666\overline{6}$ yields an outcome of 7, as shown in Fig. 5.20:

$$= \text{Slope}_{\text{RAND()}} * \text{RAND()} + \text{Intercept}_{\text{RAND()}}$$
$$= 6*2/3 + 3 = 7$$

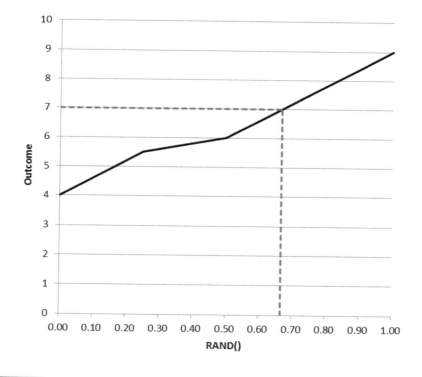

FIGURE 5.20

Simulation of a Single Observation From a Five-Point Estimate

Similarly, a RAND() of 0.837 yields an outcome of 8.02:

$$= \text{Slope}_{\text{RAND()}} * \text{RAND()} + \text{Inctercept}_{\text{RAND()}}$$
$$= 6*0.837 + 3 = 8.02$$

In addition, it is shown in Fig. 5.21.

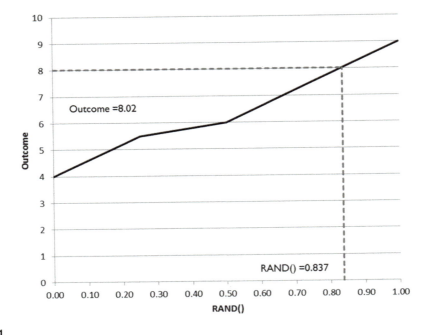

FIGURE 5.21

Simulation of a Single Observation From a Five-Point Estimate

5.4.2 Other estimates for subjective probability distributions

It is often difficult for novices to estimate the quartiles necessary for the five-point estimation method. In such circumstances, interpolation provides another method for estimating subjective distributions.

Example 5.5 Subjective distribution without quartiles
An operations manager has an opportunity to bid on a batch of components necessary to manufacture units required for the completion of a product order. A batch of the components typically costs the company $400 to manufacture. The manager estimates the probabilities of competitors' bids as shown in Table 5.4. Calculate the optimum bid.

Table 5.4 Subjective probability estimates of competitors' bids

Bid	Prob (%)
100	15
200	35
300	40
400	10

These probability estimates are used to determine the cumulative distribution function (*cdf*) shown in Fig. 5.22.

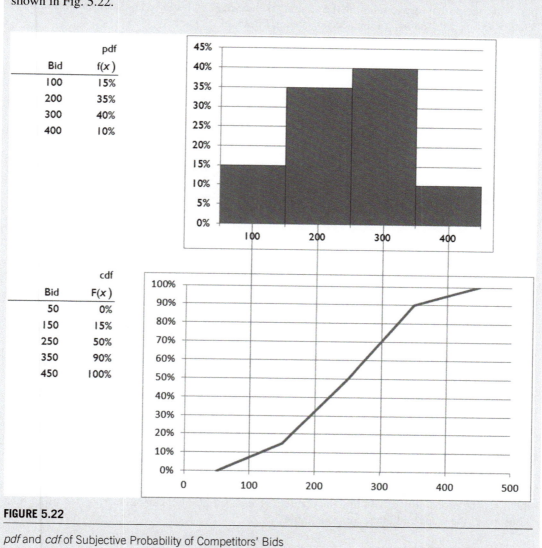

	pdf
Bid	f(x)
100	15%
200	35%
300	40%
400	10%

	cdf
Bid	F(x)
50	0%
150	15%
250	50%
350	90%
450	100%

FIGURE 5.22

pdf and *cdf* of Subjective Probability of Competitors' Bids

Given that the supplier will choose the highest bid for the parts, the *high bid wins* for this example. Thus, the probability of winning the contract is the *cdf*, $F(x)$. Initially, consider the bids of $100, $200, $300, or $400 shown in the decision tree in Fig. 5.23.

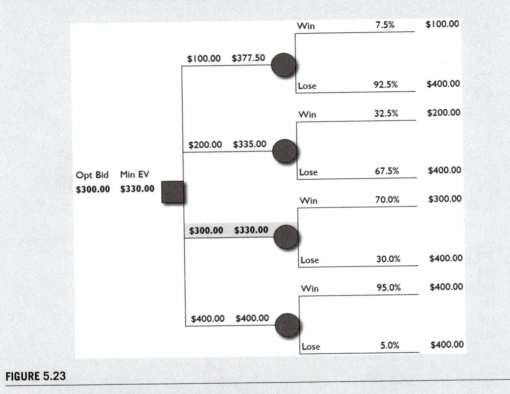

FIGURE 5.23

Initial Decision Tree to Determine the Optimum Bid

As the bids are actually a continuous variable, interpolation can be used to calculate the probability of winning the contract given a specific bid in the same manner as with the five-point estimation method. The probability of winning the contract given a specific bid can be interpolated using functions to get the slope and intercept from Table 5.5.

Table 5.5 Continuous subjective probability estimates of competitors' bids

Bid	P(Win/Bid) cdf (%)	Slope = Δcdf/ΔBid	Intercept = cdf − Slope × Bid
50	0	0.0015	−0.075
150	15	0.0035	−0.375
250	50	0.0040	−0.500
350	90	0.0010	0.550
450	100	0.0010	0.550

Thus, using interpolation allows us to refine the search by reducing the bid increments until an optimum bid as shown in Fig. 5.24.

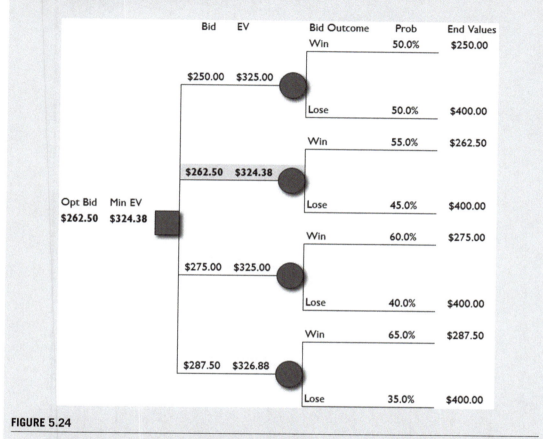

	Bid	EV	Bid Outcome	Prob	End Values
			Win	50.0%	$250.00
	$250.00	$325.00			
			Lose	50.0%	$400.00
			Win	55.0%	$262.50
	$262.50	$324.38			
			Lose	45.0%	$400.00
Opt Bid Min EV			Win	60.0%	$275.00
$262.50 $324.38	$275.00	$325.00			
			Lose	40.0%	$400.00
			Win	65.0%	$287.50
	$287.50	$326.88			
			Lose	35.0%	$400.00

FIGURE 5.24

Final Decision Tree to Determine the Optimum Bid

A simulation of this bidding process demonstrates the five-point estimation simulation method and the benefit of examining the consequences of losing that are not demonstrated in the decision tree. To construct a simulation to solve this example, the table for mapping the RAND() to the appropriate slope and intercept for interpolation must be constructed as shown in the simulation in Fig. 5.25.

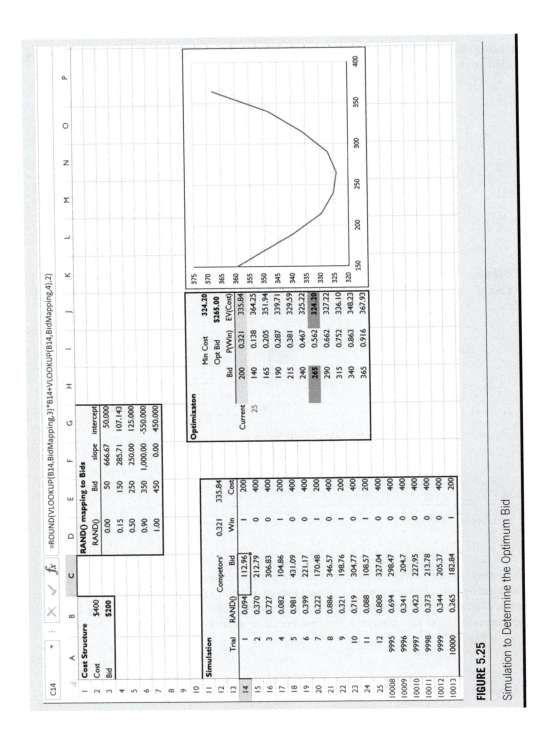

FIGURE 5.25

Simulation to Determine the Optimum Bid

Exercise Set 5: Subjective Probability Distributions

1. A shipping company has an overstock of packing material it wishes to sell via an auction. The company has 7.25 tons of the packing material and estimates that the material will sell for somewhere between $0.40 per pound and $0.60 per pound.
   a. Compute the probability that the company will receive more than $6000.
   b. Compute the probability that the company will receive less than or equal to $8000.
   c. Compute the amount that provides the company with a 90% chance of receiving at least that amount. In other words, find x for $F(x) = 90\%$, which is typically written as $x = F - 1(0.90)$ and is the inverse *cdf*.
   d. What is the managerial use of the number in part (c)?
   e. Compare and contrast the probability distribution of the unit cost to that of the revenue.
   f. Construct a simulation of the revenue.

2. An R&D project requires the scheduling and coordination of large numbers of tasks. It is important to complete the project by a specific date. When the times to complete the tasks are uncertain, the project completion time is uncertain. Consider a project with the tasks given in the following table (the times are in weeks). Create a simulation to develop the probability distribution for the estimated completion date.

Task	Precedence	Completion time estimates		
		Min	**Most likely**	**Max**
A	None	10	14	18
B	None	6	8	10
C	B	8	12	16

   a. Compute the most likely completion time.
   b. Compute the probability that the project will be done in 15 weeks or less. In other words, suppose the project due date is computed using the most likely times, and compute the probability of finishing on time.
   c. Compute the probability that the project will take more than 15 weeks to complete.
   d. Compute the due date that will provide a 95% chance of finishing on time.

3. A marketing project requires the scheduling and coordination of tasks. It is essential to complete the project by a specific date. This project has the tasks given in the following table (the times are in weeks). Create a simulation to develop the probability distribution for the estimated completion date.

Task	Precedence	Completion time estimates		
		Min	**Most likely**	**Max**
A	None	2	3	4
B	None	6	8	10
C	A	2	6	7
D	B	3	5	7
E	B	4	5	8
F	C, D	2	3	4
G	E	2	6	8

4. A company is bidding to supply cardboard boxes to an online retailer. The competitors' bids are most likely to be about $160,000. The competitors' bids are nearly certain to be between $145,000 and $190,000. If the bid is won, the most likely total cost of completing the order is $135,000. The cost is nearly certain to be between within 10% of the estimate of $135,000.
   a. Construct a cumulative distribution table and graph of the probability of winning as a function of the bid.
   b. Construct a simulation to determine the optimum bid.
   c. Construct a decision tree to determine the optimum bid.
   d. Compare and contrast the two methods.

5. A company is bidding to supply cardboard boxes to an online retailer. The competitors' bids are equally likely to be above or below $160,000. The competitors' bids are nearly certain to be between $145,000 and $190,000. It is estimated that there is a 25% chance that the bids might be below $155,000 and a 25% chance that they might be above $175,000. If the bid is won, the total cost of completing the order is $135,000.
   a. Construct a cumulative distribution table and graph of the probability of winning as a function of the bid.
   b. Construct a simulation to determine the optimum bid.
   c. What makes constructing a decision tree more difficult in this example?

6. For a batch of 50 reconditioned parts, the operations manager estimates that (a) half the time, at least 85% of the components in a batch will be usable; (b) at most 98% of the components will be usable; (c) at least 75% of the components will be usable; (d) 75% of the time, at least 80% of the components will be usable; and (e) 75% of the time, no more than 95% of the components will be usable. Construct a cumulative distribution table and graph of the probability of yield (number of usable components).

7. An online/catalog retailer will sell Adirondack chairs this season. The retailer purchases the chairs from a supplier at a cost of $175 and will sell them for $250. Demand has been forecasted to be 2000 chairs this season but is not known for certain and could range anywhere from 1000 to 3000 chairs. At the end of the season, the company will have a half-off sale to clear out the inventory. Determine the optimum number of chairs to order.
   a. Why does the retailer not want to carry the chairs in inventory for the subsequent year? Assume a **uniform** distribution for demand.
   b. Construct a simulation to determine how many chairs the retailer should order. Is it the average demand? Why or why not?
   c. Graph the distribution of demand to validate the probability distribution. Assume a **triangular** distribution for demand.
   d. Construct a simulation to determine how many chairs the retailer should order.
   e. Graph the distribution of demand to validate the probability distribution. Why is it not sufficient to simply calculate the average of the simulation demand to validate the simulation?

8. A commercial land developer specializes in building shopping centers and wants to develop some property near Hilton Head, South Carolina. To develop the land, the developer must bid to obtain the property. The developer has estimated the net present value (NPV) without the cost of the land to be $15,500,000. The developer estimates that the bids will most likely be $13,000,000 and will not be lower than $12,000,000 and not more than $14,000,000.

    a. Construct a cumulative distribution table and graph of the probability of winning the bid.
    b. Construct a decision tree to determine the optimum bid.
    c. Construct a simulation to determine the optimum bid.

9. A company is concerned about the number of usable components it receives from a supplier. For a setup cost of $800 and a variable cost of $60, the company can make their own parts. The company can buy reconditioned components in batches from a supplier, but the number of usable components varies significantly. These reconditioned parts come in batches of 50, and the company has recently been paying $2200 for these batches. Furthermore, the supplier will provide fully tested and guaranteed components for $100 each. The company needs 45 components to fulfill a new contract. For the reconditioned parts, the operations manager estimates that (a) half the time, at least 85% of the components in a batch will be usable; (b) at most 98% of the components will be usable; (c) at least 75% of the components will be usable; (d) 75% of the time, at least 80% of the components will be usable; and (e) 75% of the time, no more than 95% of the components will be usable.

    a. Construct a cumulative distribution table and graph of the probability of yield (number of usable components).
    b. Construct a simulation to determine the optimum decision.
    c. Construct a decision tree to determine the optimum decision.
    d. Compare and contrast the two methods.

10. A commercial land developer specializes in building shopping centers and wants to develop some property near Blowing Rock, North Carolina. To develop the land, the developer must bid to obtain the property. The developer has estimated the net present value (NPV) without the cost of the land to be $20,800,000. The developer estimates that the competitors' bids are nearly certain to be between $14,400,000 and 19,800,000 and equally likely to be above or below $18,000,000. It is estimated that there is a 25% chance that the bids might be below $15,300,000 and a 25% chance that they might be above $19,440,000.

    a. Construct a cumulative distribution table and graph of the probability of winning the bid.
    b. Construct a decision tree to determine the optimum bid.
    c. Construct a simulation to determine the optimum bid.

11. Two construction companies, Pine Grove Construction (PGC) and Eagle Construction, are bidding against one another to construct a new community center. PGC estimates that it will cost $1,260,000 to build the community center. Based on previous contract bidding, PGC believes that Eagle Construction will place a bid according to the following probability distribution. What should PGC bid?

Eagle Construction's Bid ($)	Probability
1,260,000	0.05
1,270,000	0.35
1,280,000	0.30
1,290,000	0.20
1,300,000	0.10

    a. Construct a decision tree to determine the optimum decision.
    b. Construct a simulation to determine the optimum decision.

12. Demand for a specific $1000 passenger cruise booking is 1000 passengers. A $50 price change results in a 10% change in demand. Fixed cost of operating the ship is $250,000, and the variable cost for a single passenger is $375. Due to the average amount of profits for a booking due to food, drinks, gift shop items, and so forth during a cruise, the cost of not being able to book a room for a passenger (shortage cost) is approximately $1500.

    a. Calculate the optimum price and demand without consideration for the uncertainty of demand.
    b. Calculate the optimum price and demand assuming a triangular distribution of ±10%.
    c. Why is part (b) necessary? In other words, why can you *not* just do part (a) to get the price and quantity? What does part (b) take into account that part (a) does not?

13. A convention with 1200 attendees is scheduled to take place in November in Boston. At a price of $450, approximately 480 attendees will stay at the convention hotel. Based on previous demand data analysis, a $20 price change results in a 15% change in demand. Based upon the market value and opportunity cost of the square footage, the rooms have a variable cost of $260. The rooms also have a shortage cost (of turning away a booking) of $230 per guest turned away (this amount is determined by the profit of a room and the profit associated with the average profit from food and drinks per room).

    a. Calculate the optimum price and demand without consideration for the uncertainty of demand.
    b. Calculate the optimum price and demand assuming a triangular distribution of ±10%.
    c. Why is part (b) necessary? In other words, why can you *not* just do part (a) to get the price and quantity? What does part (b) take into account that part (a) does not?

Cases

National Home Products

The National Home Products Company was a major manufacturer of brooms, brushes, mops, and other home cleaning devices. During the previous year, its sales were $244.5 million, primarily through hardware dealers and grocery chains. To achieve this sales level, the company had spent about $29.3 million on advertising and sales promotion during the previous year.

In December, the executive committee of the company was meeting to determine the advertising and sales promotion budget for the upcoming year. Of particular concern to the committee was a decision as to what to spend on a line of carpet sweepers that had encountered considerable competitive pressure during the year.

George Williams, the company sales manager, thought that a continuation of present advertising and promotional policies on the carpet sweepers would result in further decrease in sales. He therefore suggested an increase in advertising and promotion from $500,000 to $1,000,000 without any change in price.

He said he thought that unless something was done, sales during the upcoming year would amount to about 200,000 units. He was unsure of this quantity, estimating that there was a minutely small chance that sales might be as low as 150,000 units. He added that the chances were 1 in 2 that sales would be below his 200,000 units estimate and were 1 in 4 that they might even be below 180,000 units.

When Julie Glass, the company controller, asked how high the carpet sweeper sales might go if no changes were made in advertising and promotional policies, Mr. Williams responded that there was almost no chance of their exceeding 240,000 units and only a 1 in 4 chance of exceeding 210,000 units.

Mr. Williams said he believed that the proposed $500,000 increase in advertising and promotion was almost certain to increase sales by 10% over these estimates and perhaps by as much as 40% as an upper limit. The increase was as likely to be above 25% as below it, as likely to be between 20% and 30% as outside that range, and as likely to be above 30% as below 20%.

Case—cont'd

Ms. Glass said that she wondered how competition would react to this advertising and promotion increase. Mr. Williams replied that he really was not sure but that the increases he had just projected assumed that the competition would not change their current policies at all. He added that he thought the odds were about 3 to 1 that the competition would not respond in the upcoming year. Even if they did, he thought there would still be some increase in sales, but only about half of the increases he estimated, assuming no competitive response.

The sales price of the carpet sweeper to National's distributors was $55 per unit. The variable cost per unit was $38.50 for production levels below 220,000 units per year and $41.25 for production levels above 220,000 units per year (due to overtime costs). According to the company's production manager, Joseph Alexander, the current maximum annual production capacity is 230,000 units. At a production level above 220,000 units, the fixed production costs for the year associated with the product line would increase somewhere between 8% and 12% above the current amount of $486,000.

Crown-Zeno Boxes

Elliott Smith, a senior sales manager at the Crown-Zeno Boxes Company (CZB), settled down at his desk for some planning. His bid to Amazon.com was due in about a week, and he had as yet made no decision as to what prices CZB would offer for the four classes of corrugated cardboard boxes the online merchant was seeking. The high number of shipments by Amazon required bids every 6 months for the contract to supply its distribution centers with four sizes of corrugated cardboard boxes: $12 \times 9 \times 3$, $12 \times 9 \times 4$, $14 \times 9 \times 6$, and $16 \times 12 \times 6$ (dimensions in inches). CZB and its competitors had to provide a price per thousand for each of the four box sizes. Amazon indicated in its request for bids just how many bundles of each type of box would be required and how many of each size box were to be packaged in a bundle. Amazon determined its supplier by adding up the full cost of the contract as a bid by each potential supplier and awarding the full contract to the overall low bidder.

Amazon required that bidders submit samples of their products. Prices were FOB distribution centers listed in the proposal. The vendor was obligated to meet a monthly shipping schedule that reached them at the beginning of each month. The date of delivery was on about the 15th of the month, and following each delivery, the vendor would invoice Amazon.

Crown-Zeno Boxes Company

CZB was one of North Carolina's largest manufacturers of packaging materials. The company custom manufactured a variety of packing products, usually custom printing the packaging for the customers. Packaging and wrapping materials, including tapes, accounted for about most of a typical year's business. This contract could be the beginning of a lucrative, long-standing relationship with the growing online giant.

Most of CZB's sales came from contracts, like this one, which were awarded on the basis of competitive bids.

Crown-Zeno Boxes' Costs

Elliott Smith began his deliberations about the size of the bid by determining how much it would cost CZB to provide the required boxes. Table 5.6 shows the number of bundles of each type of box specified in the contract, the number of boxes per bundle, the total boxes, and CZB's cost per 1000 boxes.

From Table 5.6, Mr. Smith determined that CZB's cost for the full contract would be $2,935,602.

Table 5.6 Crown-Zeno Boxes' costs

Box dimensions (inches)	No. of bundles	Boxes per bundle (000)	Total boxes (000)	CZB cost (per 000)
$12 \times 9 \times 3$	1800	3.0	5400	$217.50
$12 \times 9 \times 4$	2800	1.0	2800	$277.20
$14 \times 9 \times 6$	3200	0.5	1600	$356.00
$16 \times 2 \times 6$	2400	0.5	1200	$343.30

Continued

Case—cont'd

Additional costs, beyond the cost of goods sold, then had to be considered. To meet the specifications of the contract, CZB would have to maintain a substantial inventory of all four types of boxes. Mr. Smith estimated that CZB would have to keep an additional 25% of the boxes in inventory to be available immediately during the 6 months of the contract. There would be no significant increase in labor, administrative, or clerical costs. However, there would be some minor additional trucking costs: in a few instances, CZB would have to send its fleet to areas where it currently had no need to travel. Mr. Smith estimated that the route extensions would cost CZB a total of about $3600. Mr. Smith decided that he should apply a 12% discount rate to the cash flows associated with this contract.

Assessing the distribution for the competitor's bid

Mr. Smith next thought about the possible bids his competitor could make. He compared his estimated costs with the size of the winning bid for several previous contracts similar in type to this one. As a result of this analysis, Mr. Smith decided that his competitor's bid was as likely to be above $3,400,000 as below. Having determined the median of the distribution for his competitor's bid, Mr. Smith proceeded to evaluate other bids against that median.

There was only a 0.25 probability, he thought, that the competitor's bid would be lower than 95% of the median. On the other side, he felt there was a 0.75 probability that the competitor's bid would be less than 105% of the median. His competitor's bid was almost certain to lie between 90% and 115% of the median. Using these assessments, Mr. Smith felt that he could choose the optimum bid for CZB to submit.

Empirical probability distributions

What are the chances based on past data?

Chapter outline

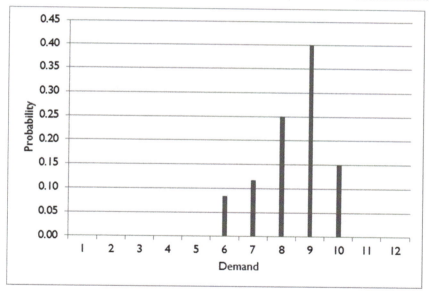

FIGURE 6.1

Example of an Empirical Probability Distribution

Introduction

The objective of this chapter is to demonstrate how to convert data into probabilities to solve managerial decisions. Real historical (empirical) data do not necessarily fit a known distribution, yet these data frequencies and rankings can be used to estimate the appropriate empirical probability distribution.

Introduction to Business Analytics Using Simulation. https://doi.org/10.1016/B978-0-323-91717-9.00006-1

Subsequently, the empirical distributions are used in decision trees and simulations to make optimum managerial decisions.

6.1 Empirical probability distributions: probability from data

The material in this chapter explains how to use probability distributions estimated from historical data.

Empirical probability is probability based upon data. That data can be either the result of a designed experiment (*experimental data*) or the result of situations that occur beyond the control of the analyst (*observational data*). In the fields of medicine and business, data-driven probability is referred to as evidence-based probability.

6.2 Discrete empirical probability distributions

Recall that $f(x)$ is the probability of a specific outcome x—that is, the probability of a specific value of a random variable. Discrete empirical probability can be calculated by counting the number of occurrences of each outcome (numeric or otherwise):

$$f(x) = P(x) = \frac{n(x)}{n}, \tag{6.1}$$

where $n(x)$ is the number of data points equal to the value x and n is the total number of data points (sample size). This follows from the notion of probability introduced in Chapter 1 as follows:

$$f(x) = \text{Probability of an event } x = \frac{\text{No. of times the event } x \text{ happened}}{\text{No. of times the event could have happened}}$$

Example 6.1 Discrete empirical probability distribution

A human resources analyst is examining the potential financial implications of employees choosing retirement plans. The company has four retirement plans: A, B, C, and D. A sample of 25 employees and the plans they have selected is shown in Table 6.1. Construct the distribution for the choice of retirement plans.

Table 6.1 Sample data for retirement plan selection

Obs	Plan	Obs	Plan	Obs	Plan
1	B	11	C	21	C
2	C	12	D	22	C
3	C	13	B	23	B
4	C	14	A	24	B
5	C	15	C	25	C
6	C	16	D		
7	D	17	C		
8	B	18	C		
9	D	19	A		
10	B	20	D		

It is useful to first sort the data. The frequencies and probabilities are readily computed after sorting as in Fig. 6.2.

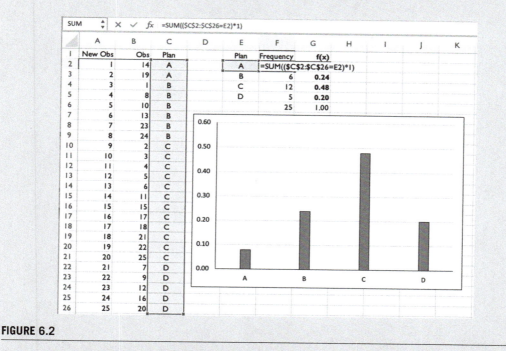

FIGURE 6.2

Example of Discrete Empirical Probability Distribution

As would be expected due to the *law of large numbers*, the accuracy of this method of determining discrete probability improves for larger samples. The degree of improvement will be discussed in Chapter 8.

Examining the previous spreadsheet reveals that there are two methods by which a set of empirical data may be used to generate random variables:

1. Using the *full list of data*: Give each element a $1/n$ probability of selection. The data can be first sorted. Sorted data provide the analyst a better understanding of the likelihoods of the various outcomes—this, in turn, provides the analyst with a much better understanding of the data.

2. Using the *data distribution*: This works well when there are not an overly cumbersome number of levels of the discrete variable.

The spreadsheet shown in Fig. 6.3 demonstrates how the discrete example could be simulated using the full list of data.

	G3		⋮	✕	✓	*fx*	=VLOOKUP(RAND(),$C$2:$D$27,2)			
	A	B	C	D	E	F	G	H	I	J
1	Obs	Plan	RAND()	Plan						
2	1	B	0.00	A		0.034544	A	=VLOOKUP(F2,$C$2:$D$27,2)		
3	2	C	0.04	A			D	=VLOOKUP(RAND(),$C$2:$D$27,2)		
4	3	C	0.08	B						
5	4	C	0.12	B						
6	5	C	0.16	B						
7	6	C	0.20	B						
8	7	D	0.24	B						
9	8	B	0.28	B						
10	9	D	0.32	C						
11	10	B	0.36	C						
12	11	C	0.40	C						
13	12	D	0.44	C						
14	13	B	0.48	C						
15	14	A	0.52	C						
16	15	C	0.56	C						
17	16	D	0.60	C						
18	17	C	0.64	C						
19	18	C	0.68	C						
20	19	A	0.72	C						
21	20	D	0.76	C						
22	21	C	0.80	D						
23	22	C	0.84	D						
24	23	B	0.88	D						
25	24	B	0.92	D						
26	25	C	0.96	D						
27			1.00	D						

FIGURE 6.3

Simulation of Discrete Data Using the Full List of Data

The spreadsheet shown in Fig. 6.4 is an example of how the discrete empirical data could be simulated using the **probability distribution** of the data computed from the previous example.

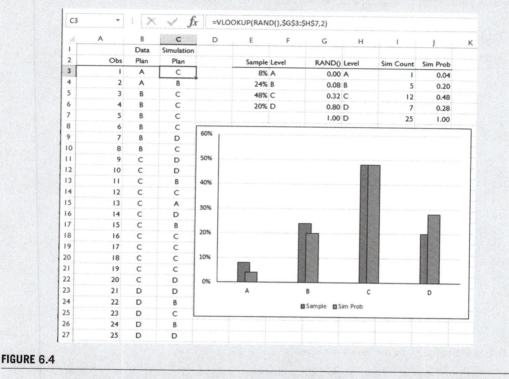

FIGURE 6.4

Simulation of Discrete Data Using the Probability Distribution of the Data

The second method is fundamentally the same as the first but takes advantage of the way VLOOKUP works when using an *approximate match* for data in which the data key (first column of the data) is sorted from smallest to largest. Compare the two methods mentioned previously to note that the data distribution method is the full list of data method with the repeated outcomes removed.

Example 6.2 Discrete empirical distribution: numeric random variable

Consider a hotel with nine rooms of a specific class available. Table 6.2 contains 60 weeks of demand. What is the likelihood that the hotel will have enough capacity? What is the probability of a shortage?

Table 6.2 Data for hotel demand

Night	Demand	Night	Demand	Night	Demand	Night	Demand
1	6	16	10	31	9	46	10
2	9	17	7	32	9	47	8
3	8	18	8	33	9	48	8
4	9	19	10	34	8	49	8
5	9	20	6	35	7	50	10
6	8	21	9	36	9	51	8
7	10	22	9	37	7	52	7
8	10	23	9	38	10	53	8
9	10	24	9	39	9	54	8
10	9	25	6	40	10	55	9
11	8	26	9	41	9	56	9
12	8	27	8	42	7	57	6
13	9	28	9	43	9	58	8
14	7	29	9	44	9	59	7
15	9	30	8	45	6	60	9

It is useful to first sort the data smallest to largest, as shown in Table 6.3.

Table 6.3 Sorted data for hotel demand

Obs	Night	Demand	Obs	Night	Demand	Obs	Night	Demand	Obs	Night	Demand
1	1	6	16	12	8	31	10	9	46	41	9
2	20	6	17	18	8	32	13	9	47	43	9
3	25	6	18	27	8	33	15	9	48	44	9
4	45	6	19	30	8	34	21	9	49	55	9
5	57	6	20	34	8	35	22	9	50	56	9
6	14	7	21	47	8	36	23	9	51	60	9
7	17	7	22	48	8	37	24	9	52	7	10
8	35	7	23	49	8	38	26	9	53	8	10
9	37	7	24	51	8	39	28	9	54	9	10
10	42	7	25	53	8	40	29	9	55	16	10
11	52	7	26	54	8	41	31	9	56	19	10
12	59	7	27	58	8	42	32	9	57	38	10
13	3	8	28	2	9	43	33	9	58	40	10
14	6	8	29	4	9	44	36	9	59	46	10
15	11	8	30	5	9	45	39	9	60	50	10

Note that *obs* is frequently used as an abbreviation for *observation*—the term for a unit of observed data. A frequency count results in the probability distribution in Table 6.4.

Table 6.4 Empirical probability distribution for hotel demand

Demand	Count (nights)	Probability	Probability
6	5	5/60	0.0833
7	7	7/60	0.1167
8	15	15/60	0.2500
9	24	24/60	0.4000
10	9	9/60	0.1500
	60	60/60	1.0000

As the discrete data are easily summarized, a five-number summary is not necessary to determine the probabilities. The probability distribution of demand is displayed in the histogram shown in Fig. 6.5.

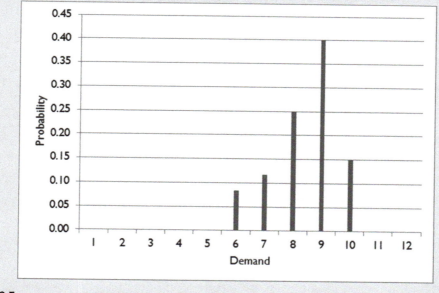

FIGURE 6.5

Discrete Probability Distribution of Hotel Demand Data

First, consider the probability of shortage. With nine rooms, the probability of shortage is: (Table 6.4)

$$P\,(demand = 10) = f(10) = 9/60 = 0.15 = 15\%$$

With nine rooms, the probability of meeting demand (no shortage) is:

$$P\,(demand \leq 9) = F\,(9) = 1 - f(10) = 1 - 0.15 = 0.85 = 85\%$$

Service level is the probability of meeting demand. Thus, the service level for nine rooms is 85%.

Example 6.3 **Empirical distribution in a decision tree: quantity decisions**

Given a daily rental rate of $150 per night, an opportunity leasing cost of $85, and the nightly demand from Example 6.2, compute the expected demand and determine the optimum block of rooms.

The decision tree used to determine the optimum block of rooms is shown in Fig. 6.6.

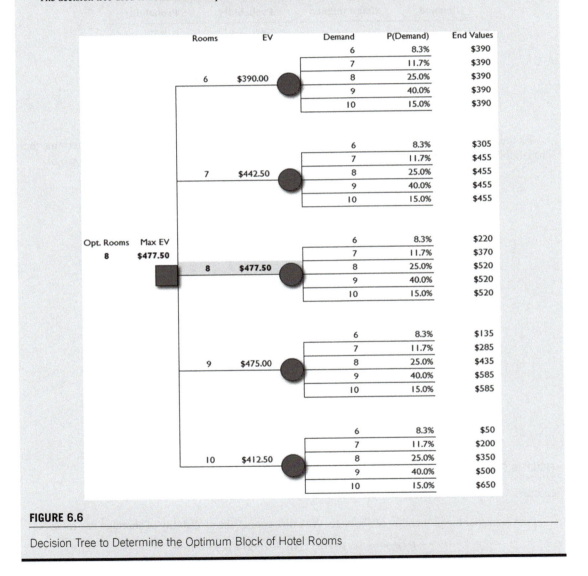

FIGURE 6.6

Decision Tree to Determine the Optimum Block of Hotel Rooms

Example 6.4 Simulation of discrete empirical distribution

Consider the hotel in Examples 6.2 and 6.3. Use a simulation to determine the optimum room block.

With a small set of outcomes, it is easier to use the data distribution method rather than the full list of data method. Thus, simulate demand for hotel rooms using the data distribution method because the data in this example are discrete with only five levels (Fig. 6.7).

B12	▾ : ✕ ✓ *fx*	=VLOOKUP(RAND(),$I$3:$J$7,2)								
	A	B	C	D	E	F	G	H	I	J
1	Cost Structure				Probability Information				VLOOKUP Table	
2	Price	$150.00			Demand	Count(nights)	Probability	Probability	Random Number	Demand
3	VC	$85.00			6	5	5/60	0.0833	0.0000	6
4	Goodwill	$65.00			7	7	7/60	0.1167	0.0833	7
5					8	15	15/60	0.2500	0.2000	8
6	Simulation				9	24	24/60	0.4000	0.4500	9
7	Rooms Blocked	9			10	9	9/60	0.1500	0.8500	10
8	TVC	$765.00				60		1.0000	1.0000	
9	Avg Demand	8.42								
10	Avg:	8.37		14%		$461.26		Optimization		
11		Trial	Demand	Rooms Rented	Shortage	Extra	Profit	Max Profit	$462	
12		1	9	9	0	0	$585.00	Opt Block	9	
13		2	9	9	0	0	$585.00	Rooms	Avg Profit	Service Level
14		3	10	9	1	0	$520.00	Current	9	$461	86%
15		4	8	8	0	1	$435.00		6	$236	0.11
16		5	6	6	0	3	$135.00		7	$341	0.18
17		6	7	7	0	2	$285.00		8	$434	0.44
18		7	7	7	0	2	$285.00		9	$462	0.87
19		8	9	9	0	0	$585.00		10	$424	1.00
20		9	8	8	0	1	$435.00				
21		10	9	9	0	0	$585.00				
1006		995	6	6	0	3	$135.00				
1007		996	8	8	0	1	$435.00				
1008		997	8	8	0	1	$435.00				
1009		998	7	7	0	2	$285.00				
1010		999	9	9	0	0	$585.00				
1011		1000	10	9	1	0	$520.00				

FIGURE 6.7

Simulation to Determine the Optimum Block of Hotel Rooms

With the table constructed in the manner shown in the previous example, a function can be used in conjunction with the RAND() function to provide discrete random variables. Note that *Goodwill* has been set at the loss of one sale (*Price* − *VC*). You should use sensitivity analysis to determine how changing *Goodwill* would change the optimum decision.

The hotel room block reservation is an example of the application of the Newsvendor Problem. Another example is presented in Example 6.5.

Example 6.5　Optimization: car rentals

On Thursday evening, the manager of a small branch of a car rental agency finds that she has six cars available for rental on the following day. However, she is able to request delivery of additional cars, at a cost of $20 each, from the regional depot. Each car that is rented produces an expected profit of $40 (not including the $20 of delivery cost if incurred). After reviewing records for 20 previous Fridays, the manager finds that the number of cars requested on those previous Fridays is 7, 9, 8, 7, 10, 8, 7, 8, 9, 10, 7, 6, 8, 9, 8, 8, 6, 7, 7, 9. How many cars should be ordered? How do "goodwill" losses affect the number of cars to be ordered?

A typical small-scale spreadsheet simulation is shown in Fig. 6.8.

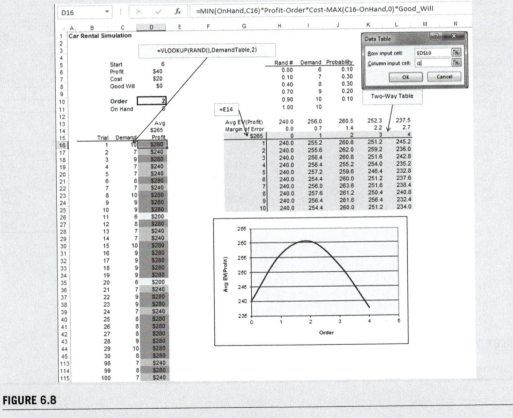

FIGURE 6.8

Simulation to Determine the Optimum Number of Rental Cars

Note that the decision variable, **Order**, was set at **2** as a starting point that serendipitously coincided with the optimum order quantity for a *Goodwill* of $0. The two-way Data Table is used to determine the optimum order quantity by running 10 sets of trials (10 *runs*) for each potential **Order** quantity. Using the two-way table to run 10 sets of 100 trials results in a smaller spreadsheet than using 1000 trials. Multiple regression (polynomial order = 2) could be used to determine the optimum **Order** quantity by regressing *AvgEV(Profit)* as the Y variable and using **Order** and **Order**^{2} as the X variables.

6.3 Continuous empirical probability distributions

With continuous empirical data, $f(x)$ can be calculated using the cumulative distribution function (*cdf*), $F(x)$. When calculating probabilities from historical data, $F(x)$ is called the *empirical cumulative distribution function* and is abbreviated as $ECDF(x)$. The $ECDF(x)$ is easily calculated by first sorting the data from smallest to largest and then using the frequency counts to determine the cumulative probability:

$$ECDF(x) = F(x) = P(X \le x)/n$$

where $n(X \le x)$ is the number of data points less than or equal to the value x and n is the total number of data points (sample size).

Example 6.6 Empirical distribution in a decision tree: pricing decisions

A company is bidding to supply parts to an electronics manufacturer. The competitors' bids for 10 previous similar contracts are shown in Table 6.5. If the bid is won, the total cost of completing the contract is $350,000. What is the optimum bid?

Table 6.5 Empirical probability distribution for the bidding example

Obs	Bid	Obs	Bid	Obs	Bid
1	369,800	5	387,300	9	401,400
2	403,200	6	404,800	10	380,300
3	401,800	7	389,700		
4	387,600	8	407,700		

Consider the abbreviated generic bidding decision tree in Fig. 6.9.

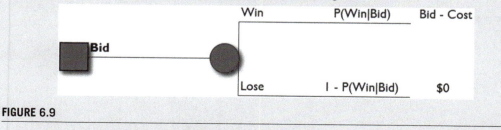

FIGURE 6.9

Abbreviated Generic Decision Tree for the Bidding Example

As the electronics manufacturer will purchase the least expensive components, *low bid wins* in this situation. Because low bid wins, the probability of winning given a specific bid is:

$$P\left(Win \mid Bid\right) = 1 - F\left(Bid\right) = 1 - ECDF$$

Based on the decision tree, the expected value for a given bid is calculated:

$$EV_{Bid} = P\left(Win \mid Bid\right)\left(Bid - \$350,000\right) + \left(1 - P\left(Win \mid Bid\right)\right)\left(\$0\right) = P\left(Win \mid Bid\right)\left(Bid - \$350,000\right)$$

To compute $P(Win|Bid)$, first calculate the $ECDF$. The $ECDF$ is computed by first sorting the data from largest to smallest, then calculating the number of data points less than or equal to each data point, and finally dividing those results by the sample size:

$$ECDF\left(x\right) = F\left(x\right) = P\left(X \leq x\right) = n\left(X \leq x\right)/n$$

The $ECDF$ is shown in Fig. 6.10.

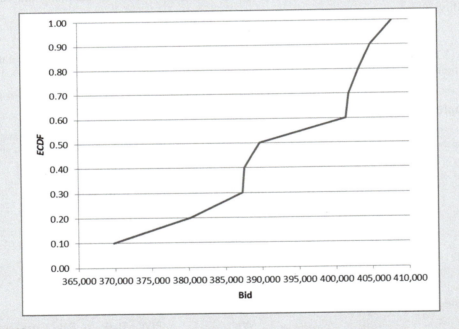

FIGURE 6.10

Empirical Cumulative Distribution Function *(ECDF)* for the Bidding Example

The probabilities of winning is then calculated as $P(Win|Bid) = 1 - ECDF$. Probabilities corresponding to specific bids can be calculated in a manner similar to the *cdf* for five-point estimates in Chapter 5. Thus, for *low bid wins* bidding, the probability of winning is $1 - cdf$. Conversely, for *high bid wins* bidding, the probability of winning is the *cdf*.

The probability of winning as a function of the bid is shown in Fig. 6.11.

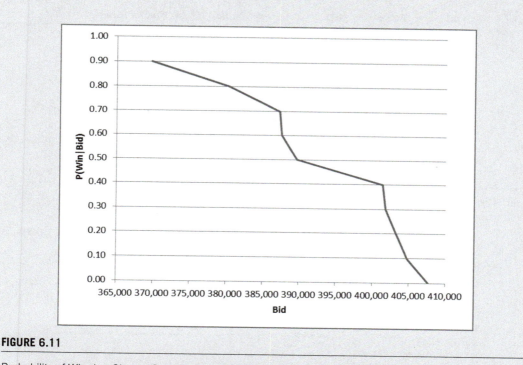

FIGURE 6.11

Probability of Winning Given a Specific Bid $(1 - ECDF)$ for the Bidding Example

From the *ECDF*, the slopes and intercepts to calculate the probability of winning given a specific bid using interpolation can be calculated using the method shown in Table 6.6.

Table 6.6 Slope-intercept table to calculate $P(Win|Bid) = 1 - ECDF$

Rank	Obs	ECDF	Bid	$P(Win|Bid)$	Slope = $\Delta P(Win|Bid)/\Delta Bid$	Intercept = ECDF − Slope × Bid
1	1	0.10	369,800	0.90	−0.0000095	4.42
2	10	0.20	380,300	0.80	−0.0000143	6.23
3	5	0.30	387,300	0.70	−0.0003333	129.80
4	4	0.40	387,600	0.60	−0.0000476	19.06
5	7	0.50	389,700	0.50	−0.0000085	3.83
6	9	0.60	401,400	0.40	−0.0002500	100.75
7	3	0.70	401,800	0.30	−0.0000714	29.00
8	2	0.80	403,200	0.20	−0.0000625	25.40
9	6	0.90	404,800	0.10	−0.0000345	14.06
10	8	1.00	407,700	0.00	−0.0000345	14.06

Using Table 6.6 and the VLOOKUP function, the expected value for a bid, EV_{Bid}, can be calculated using:

$$EV_{Bid} = P\,(Win \mid Bid)\,(Bid - \$350,000) = (Slope\,(Bid) + Intercept)\,(Bid - \$350,000)$$

The optimum bid is obtained using Excel's One-Way Data Table command (Fig. 6.12).

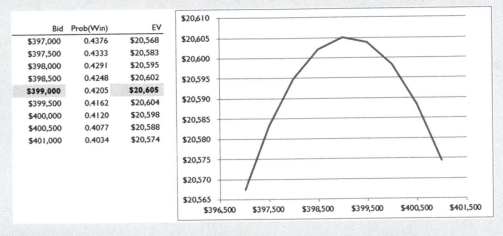

Bid	Prob(Win)	EV
$397,000	0.4376	$20,568
$397,500	0.4333	$20,583
$398,000	0.4291	$20,595
$398,500	0.4248	$20,602
$399,000	**0.4205**	**$20,605**
$399,500	0.4162	$20,604
$400,000	0.4120	$20,598
$400,500	0.4077	$20,588
$401,000	0.4034	$20,574

FIGURE 6.12

Calculation of Optimum Bid Using a One-Way Table

In a manner similar to the method used to simulate the *five-point estimate*, the *ECDF* must first be inverted (refer to Examples 5.2 and 5.4) as shown in Table 6.7 and corresponding graph shown in Fig. 6.13.

Table 6.7 Slope-intercept table to generate random bids for simulation

Rank	ECDF = Rand()	Bid	Slope = ΔBid/ ΔECDF	Intercept = Bid – Slope * ECDF
1	0.00	359,300	105,000	359,300
2	0.10	369,800	105,000	359,300
3	0.20	380,300	70,000	366,300
4	0.30	387,300	3,000	386,400
5	0.40	387,600	21,000	379,200
6	0.50	389,700	117,000	331,200
7	0.60	401,400	4,000	399,000
8	0.70	401,800	14,000	392,000
9	0.80	403,200	16,000	390,400
10	0.90	404,800	29,000	378,700
	1.00	407,700	0	407,700

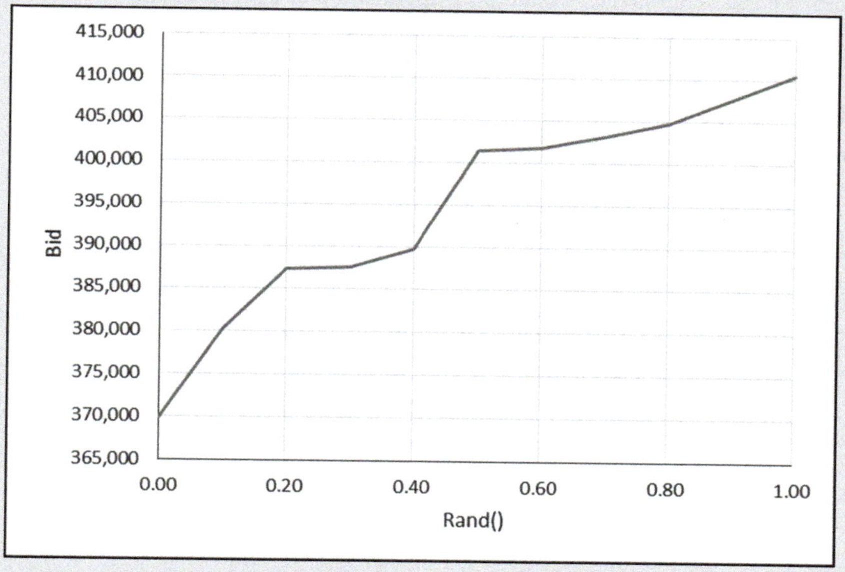

FIGURE 6.13

Inverse ECDF for Generating Random Bids for Simulation

As is the case of simulating the *five-point estimate*, the RAND() must be calculated in a cell that is external to the cell used to compute the random variable so that the slope and intercept will correspond to the appropriate percentile specified by the RAND(). Then the VLOOKUP function is used to determine the appropriate slope and intercept to calculate the random bid that would correspond to the percentile generated by the RAND().

How the competitors' bid would be simulated and then the optimum bid determined is demonstrated in the spreadsheet shown in Fig. 6.14.

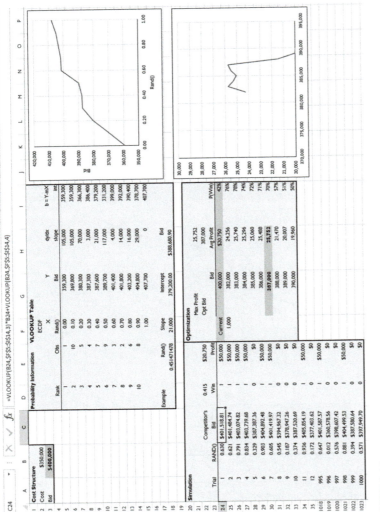

FIGURE 6.14

Simulation to Determine the Optimum Bid

Exercise Set 6: Empirical Probability Distributions

1. The following table shows some items from a Human Resources database, representing the status of five people at a particular point in time.

Obs	Gender	Salary ($)	Education	Experience (years)
1	M	48,500	HS	8
2	F	42,400	BA	2
3	M	69,800	MBA	1
4	F	88,500	MBA	8
.				
.				
.				
N	F	46,700	BA	8

a. What is the unit of observation (elementary unit) for this data set?

b. What kind of data is this—univariate, bivariate, or multivariate; longitudinal (time series) or cross-sectional; experimental or observational?

c. Which variables are discrete or continuous; qualitative or quantitative; nominal, ordinal, or interval?

2. Consider the order size of recent customers (in units).

Observation	Units ordered
1	9
2	11
3	12
4	50
5	51
6	51
7	51
8	51
9	51
10	88
11	90
12	91

a. Construct a histogram for the order size (by hand and in Excel).

b. Calculate the ECDF.

c. What is the probability that an order will be greater than 50?

d. What is the probability that an order will be less than 80?

e. What are the average and standard deviation for this distribution? Is the distribution normal (Gaussian)?

3.   Weekly demand (order size in gallons) for a dairy is given next. Assume that orders are in lot sizes of 25.

Week	Demand	Week	Demand	Week	Demand
1	75	21	75	41	125
2	25	22	50	42	75
3	50	23	150	43	75
4	150	24	125	44	50
5	125	25	50	45	150
6	50	26	100	46	50
7	75	27	75	47	25
8	75	28	100	48	175
9	100	29	50	49	25
10	50	30	25	50	50
11	150	31	25	51	100
12	75	32	50	52	200
13	50	33	100	53	50
14	150	34	175	54	50
15	50	35	175	55	100
16	75	36	75	56	125
17	75	37	100	57	100
18	50	38	50	58	125
19	50	39	75	59	100
20	50	40	50	60	125

a.   Construct a histogram for the demand (order size) by hand and in Excel.
b.   Calculate the ECDF.
c.   What is the probability that demand for a week will be greater than 100 gallons?
d.   What is the probability of shortage if you produce 125 gallons?
e.   What are the average and standard deviation for this distribution? Is the distribution normal (Gaussian)?

4.   Consider the order size (in dollars) of recent customers.

Obs	Order	Obs	Order	Obs	Order
1	21,859	16	21,464	31	22,341
2	23,996	17	27,206	32	19,434
3	22,948	18	21,163	33	18,448
4	24,913	19	23,628	34	23,574
5	19,692	20	18,114	35	24,370
6	17,088	21	25,870	36	22,209
7	25,577	22	21,228	37	19,947
8	22,853	23	22,443	38	21,123
9	22,449	24	23,821	39	23,063
10	23,683	25	21,455	40	19,510

Obs	Order	Obs	Order	Obs	Order
11	22,770	26	20,483	41	23,009
12	19,970	27	22,681	42	25,085
13	22,074	28	20,625	43	27,609
14	25,261	29	20,719	44	22,822
15	20,717	30	20,462	45	24,262

a. Construct a histogram for the order size.
b. Calculate the ECDF.
c. Calculate the probability that an order will be greater than $20,000.
d. Calculate the probability that an order will be less than $22,000.
e. Calculate orders corresponding to the 10th, 25th, 80th, and 90th percentiles.
f. What are the average and standard deviation for this distribution? Is the distribution normal (Gaussian)?

5. Use Yahoo's financial website (http://finance.yahoo.com) to obtain the past year's daily stock prices for Coca-Cola, Duke Energy, and Vanguard S&P 500 mutual fund.
   a. Construct the time series plot for each stock.
   b. Construct the histogram of daily price changes (in percentage) for each stock.
   c. OPTIONAL: What is the annual rate of return for each stock (based on stock price alone—not including dividends, although you would want to include them)?

6. The marketing managers of a consumer electronics company need to determine the effect of a competitor's television advertisements on the company's sales. Sales records for the last 120 weeks are shown in Table 6.8.

Table 6.8 Sales and competitor's advertising

Week	Competitor advertises	Sales	Week	Competitor advertises	Sales	Week	Competitor advertises	Sales
1	No	High	41	No	High	81	No	High
2	No	Low	42	No	Medium	82	Yes	Low
3	Yes	Medium	43	No	High	83	No	Medium
4	No	Low	44	No	Medium	84	No	Medium
5	No	Low	45	Yes	Low	85	No	Low
6	No	Medium	46	Yes	Low	86	Yes	High
7	No	Low	47	Yes	Medium	87	Yes	High
8	Yes	Low	48	No	Medium	88	Yes	Low
9	No	Low	49	Yes	Low	89	Yes	High
10	Yes	Medium	50	Yes	High	90	Yes	Medium
11	Yes	High	51	No	High	91	No	Low
12	No	Low	52	Yes	Low	92	No	Low
13	No	High	53	Yes	Medium	93	No	Medium
14	Yes	High	54	Yes	Medium	94	No	Low
15	Yes	High	55	Yes	Medium	95	Yes	High
16	Yes	Low	56	No	Low	96	No	Low

Continued

Table 6.8 Sales and competitor's advertising—cont'd

Week	Competitor advertises	Sales	Week	Competitor advertises	Sales	Week	Competitor advertises	Sales
17	No	Low	57	No	High	97	No	High
18	Yes	High	58	Yes	Low	98	Yes	Low
19	Yes	Low	59	Yes	Low	99	Yes	Low
20	No	Low	60	No	Low	100	No	Low
21	Yes	High	61	Yes	Low	101	No	Medium
22	No	High	62	No	Medium	102	Yes	Low
23	Yes	High	63	Yes	Low	103	Yes	Low
24	No	High	64	No	Low	104	Yes	Low
25	No	High	65	Yes	Low	105	No	High
26	Yes	High	66	No	Medium	106	No	High
27	Yes	High	67	Yes	Medium	107	No	High
28	No	High	68	No	High	108	Yes	Medium
29	No	Low	69	Yes	High	109	Yes	Low
30	Yes	Low	70	No	High	110	Yes	Low
31	Yes	Low	71	Yes	Medium	111	No	Low
32	Yes	Medium	72	Yes	High	112	No	High
33	Yes	Low	73	Yes	Low	113	Yes	Low
34	No	High	74	No	Low	114	No	High
35	Yes	High	75	Yes	Medium	115	Yes	High
36	Yes	High	76	Yes	Low	116	Yes	Low
37	No	Low	77	Yes	Low	117	No	High
38	No	Medium	78	No	High	118	Yes	Low
39	Yes	Low	79	No	Medium	119	Yes	Medium
40	Yes	Medium	80	Yes	Low	120	No	High

a. Construct a contingency (frequency) table and a probability (relative frequency) table.
b. Construct a probability tree.
c. What is the probability that the competitor *will advertise?*
d. What is the probability that sales will not be high?
e. What is the probability that sales will not be low?
f. What is the probability that either the competitor will advertise or only low sales will be achieved?
g. What is the probability that if the competitor advertises, high sales will be achieved?
h. What is the probability that if the competitor does not advertise, high sales will be achieved?
i. Construct a decision tree for a decision the company might need to make.

7. Each day the manager of a local bookstore must decide how many copies of the local newspaper to order. She must pay the publisher $0.20 for each copy, and she sells the newspapers for $0.50 each. Newspapers that are unsold at the end of the day are recycled at no gain or loss (i.e., they are considered worthless). Sixty days of demand are shown in Table 6.9.

Table 6.9 Newspaper demand

Obs	Demand	Obs	Demand	Obs	Demand
1	15	21	10	41	12
2	13	22	12	42	14
3	10	23	14	43	13
4	12	24	10	44	12
5	12	25	12	45	12
6	15	26	11	46	13
7	14	27	13	47	12
8	12	28	13	48	11
9	14	29	12	49	14
10	13	30	13	50	10
11	11	31	13	51	14
12	13	32	13	52	12
13	11	33	13	53	15
14	10	34	12	54	11
15	12	35	13	55	12
16	11	36	15	56	14
17	10	37	15	57	12
18	12	38	14	58	11
19	15	39	14	59	11
20	12	40	12	60	11

   a. What is the average number of units sold in a day?
   b. Construct a simulation to determine the optimum decision.
   c. Construct a decision tree to determine the optimum decision.
   d. Compare and contrast the two methods.

8. A contractor must decide how much to bid for a construction project. It will cost $4000 to prepare the bid. This cost would be incurred whether or not the bid was accepted. The previous winning bids for similar projects have been (in thousands): 80, 60, 70, 60, 60, 80, 80, 60, 80, 80, 50, 50, 60, 60, 70, 70, 50, 80, 60, 70, 50, 80, 70, 60, 80, 80, 80, 90. If the contractor wins the bid, the cost of completing the project will be $50,000. Construct a decision tree and a simulation to determine the optimum bid.

9. On Friday evening, the manager of a small branch of a car rental agency finds that she has four cars available for rental on the following day. However, she is able to request delivery of additional cars, at a cost of $25 each, from the regional depot. Each car that is rented produces an expected profit of $65 (not including the $25 of delivery cost if incurred). After reviewing records for previous Saturdays, the manager finds that the number of cars requested on 25 previous Fridays is 11, 11, 11, 10, 11, 13, 12, 11, 12, 10, 11, 11, 14, 10, 12, 15, 12, 11, 13, 13, 14, 11, 12, 11, 10. How many cars should be ordered? How do "goodwill" losses affect the number of cars to be ordered?

10. A small resort hotel has 10 rooms and rents them for $120 per night. The frequency of demand for rooms is given in Table 6.10; for example, there were 4 days in which only eight rooms were rented.

Table 6.10 Hotel room demand

Rooms	Days
8	4
9	8
10	12
11	24
12	32

  a. What is the average demand?
  b. What is the average number of units rented in a day?
  c. Construct a simulation to determine the optimum decision.
  d. Construct a decision tree to determine the optimum decision.
  e. Compare and contrast the two methods.
11. A buyer for a chain of department stores must place orders for athletic shoes 6 months before the shoes will be sold in the stores. At this time, the buyer must determine the order size for a particular style of running shoe for the upcoming spring season. Each pair of this style costs the department store $45. The department store sells these shoes for $70 per pair. Any shoes unsold by the end of the fall season will be sold at a closeout sale for $35. The probability distribution of demand has been determined by the analytics area and is given in Table 6.11. Assume that the department store chain must order these shoes in lots of 100 pairs. Construct a simulation and a decision tree to determine the optimum order.
12. A small resort hotel has 10 rooms and rents them for $120 per night. Demand for rooms for 80 nights is given in Table 6.12.
  a. What is the optimum size (number of rooms) for the hotel?
  b. Construct a simulation to determine the optimum decision.
  c. Construct a decision tree to determine the optimum decision.
  d. Compare and contrast the two methods.

Table 6.11 Probability distribution for demand

Demand (pairs)	Probability
100	0.025
200	0.050
300	0.075
400	0.100
500	0.150
600	0.200
700	0.175
800	0.100
900	0.075
1000	0.050

Table 6.12 Hotel room demand data

Obs	Demand	Obs	Demand	Obs	Demand	Obs	Demand
1	11	21	11	41	12	61	12
2	9	22	12	42	12	62	9
3	11	23	12	43	12	63	11
4	11	24	11	44	12	64	10
5	12	25	9	45	10	65	12
6	10	26	10	46	9	66	10
7	11	27	12	47	12	67	12
8	10	28	12	48	11	68	9
9	11	29	8	49	10	69	10
10	9	30	10	50	8	70	12
11	11	31	12	51	11	71	11
12	11	32	12	52	12	72	12
13	10	33	11	53	12	73	11
14	12	34	8	54	11	74	11
15	11	35	9	55	12	75	10
16	12	36	11	56	11	76	12
17	11	37	12	57	12	77	12
18	11	38	12	58	12	78	10
19	9	39	11	59	12	79	11
20	12	40	12	60	12	80	8

    e. What actions can the hotel do to optimize its revenues given that the hotel cannot easily change the number of rooms?

13. Two construction companies, Pine Grove Construction (PGC) and Eagle Construction, are bidding against one another to construct a new community center. PGC estimates that it will cost $1,260,000 to build the community center. Based on previous contract bidding, PGC believes that Eagle Construction will place a bid according to the probability distribution shown in Table 6.13. What should PGC bid?

    a. Construct a simulation to determine the optimum decision.

    b. Construct a decision tree to determine the optimum decision.

Table 6.13 Bidding probabilities

Eagle Construction's Bid ($)	Probability
1,260,000	0.05
1,270,000	0.35
1,280,000	0.30
1,290,000	0.20
1,300,000	0.10

Table 6.14 Milk demand data

Milk (gallons)	No. of weeks
0	0
50	3
100	7
150	22
200	18
250	0

Table 6.15 Milk demand data

Week	Demand	Week	Demand	Week	Demand
1	75	21	75	41	125
2	25	22	50	42	75
3	50	23	150	43	75
4	150	24	125	44	50
5	125	25	50	45	150
6	50	26	100	46	50
7	75	27	75	47	25
8	75	28	100	48	175
9	100	29	50	49	25
10	50	30	25	50	50
11	150	31	25	51	100
12	75	32	50	52	200
13	50	33	100	53	50
14	150	34	175	54	50
15	50	35	175	55	100
16	75	36	75	56	125
17	75	37	100	57	100
18	50	38	50	58	125
19	50	39	75	59	100
20	50	40	50	60	125

14. Costco must determine how much milk to order to meet demand for the upcoming week at a specific store. Costco buys milk for $2.00 per gallon and sells the milk for $2.35 per gallon. Demand for 50 previous weeks at that store is shown in Table 6.14. Note that orders are delivered in trays (lot sizes) of 50.
    a. What is the average number of gallons sold in a week—that is, what is your forecast for next week?
    b. Construct a decision tree to determine the optimum amount of milk to order for next week.
    c. Construct a simulation to determine the optimum amount of milk to order for next week.
    d. Service level is the probability of meeting demand; also equal to $1 - P(\text{stockout})$. What is the service level at the optimum stock level?
    e. What would goodwill loss need to be in order to stock at the next highest level?

15. Weekly demand (order size in gallons) for milk from a dairy is listed in Table 6.15. Assume that orders are in lot sizes of 25.
    a. Construct a contingency (frequency) table and a probability (relative frequency) table for demand.
    b. Construct a decision tree.
    c. How much milk should be produced each week if the selling price to grocery stores is $1.85 per gallon and the cost to the dairy is $0.65 per gallon?
16. A fruit and vegetable wholesaler buys strawberries at $20 per case and resells them at $50 per case. Because the wholesaler markets primarily to "natural" grocery stores, no preservatives are added to these strawberries. Thus, any cases not sold on the first day are given to a local food bank. If grocers place an order and the wholesaler has run out of strawberries, then that unsatisfied demand is lost and grocers buy strawberries from another wholesaler. Demand data for 100 typical days is given in Table 6.16. What is the optimum number of cases of strawberries for the wholesaler to order each day?
    a. Construct a simulation to determine the optimum decision.
    b. Construct a decision tree to determine the optimum decision.

Table 6.16 Strawberry demand data

Obs	Demand	Obs	Demand	Obs	Demand	Obs	Demand
1	391	26	393	51	369	76	377
2	459	27	355	52	391	77	315
3	322	28	433	53	387	78	310
4	412	29	255	54	429	79	264
5	323	30	393	55	400	80	467
6	430	31	385	56	267	81	299
7	310	32	373	57	323	82	351
8	405	33	383	58	373	83	375
9	444	34	319	59	395	84	362
10	353	35	326	60	355	85	375
11	384	36	385	61	334	86	361
12	332	37	363	62	351	87	399
13	268	38	334	63	314	88	287
14	436	39	408	64	402	89	332
15	384	40	320	65	365	90	302
16	434	41	362	66	469	91	335
17	295	42	323	67	243	92	345
18	324	43	391	68	367	93	310
19	405	44	439	69	306	94	331
20	402	45	339	70	326	95	394
21	351	46	364	71	383	96	331
22	336	47	390	72	349	97	296
23	257	48	348	73	378	98	294
24	384	49	360	74	391	99	357
25	415	50	372	75	371	100	341

Table 6.17 Bidding data

Obs	Bid	Obs	Bid	Obs	Bid
1	890,000	10	920,200	19	1,007,100
2	1,110,500	11	1,035,400	20	803,200
3	944,000	12	911,000	21	945,200
4	1,139,100	13	945,100	22	983,500
5	1,177,300	14	1,007,600	23	1,153,600
6	1,080,100	15	1,075,100	24	1,135,800
7	1,021,200	16	1,025,200	25	984,900
8	908,000	17	961,100		
9	1,051,300	18	1,103,900		

17. A commercial land developer specializes in building shopping centers and wants to develop some property near Hilton Head, South Carolina. To develop the land, the developer must bid to obtain the property. The developer has estimated the net present value (NPV) without the cost of the land to be $1,500,000. The developer has bid against several of the same competitors many times before and has the results of the bids as shown in Table 6.17.

  a. Construct a cumulative distribution table and graph of the probability of winning the bid.
  b. Construct a decision tree to determine the optimum bid.
  c. Construct a simulation to determine the optimum bid.

Cases

Axonne advertising

Axonne was a mature proprietary laundry detergent that had been marketed for a decade. Axonne's marketing program had undergone little change for some time when a new product manager, Elizabeth Thomas, assumed responsibility for the brand.

Ms. Thomas undertook a careful review of the brand's history and available marketing research information. There were six competing brands, three of which (including Axonne) accounted for 70% of the market and were nationally distributed and supported by media advertising. Axonne was an important, but not dominant, brand among the three, with a 15% share of market. No consumer promotion (dealing, couponing, etc.) was used to any appreciable extent, and price cutting (discounting) was negligible, but all three major brands were priced above the level of the remaining brands in the category, and all three advertised heavily.

After working on Axonne for several months, Ms. Thomas became convinced that sales could be increased by repositioning the brand. The brand's advertising agency prepared and tested some new approaches in focus group interviews. The results were quite favorable.

Encouraged, Ms. Thomas authorized the agency to produce two ad campaigns, to be aired in two different test markets using local TV stations, Internet ads, and newspaper inserts, representing two different advertising strategies: one emphasizing what was labeled an "emotional" appeal and the other a "rational" approach. Ms. Thomas also used one test market as the benchmark using the current ad campaign.

Ms. Thomas also knew that using various ad campaigns could provoke a response from the competition in which the competition would discount the price of their product to try to offset the effect of the new ad campaign. Thus, it was necessary to test a number of stores sufficient to determine the effects of competitors' price reductions.

Sales measurements were obtained based on point-of-sale information from 585 stores in the three test markets. The experiment was run for 3 months, a period known from prior investigations to be sufficient for the long-term response to advertising to become clear. Table 6.18 shows the results of the experiment.

Case—cont'd

Table 6.18 Results of the Axonne ad experiment

Store	Ad	Comp. discount	Units sold
1	Rational	No	132
2	Emotional	Yes	83
3	Emotional	Yes	81
4	Current	No	126
5	Rational	Yes	130
6	Current	No	119
7	Current	No	130
8	Rational	No	160
9	Emotional	Yes	67
10	Emotional	Yes	77
.			
.			
.			
576	Rational	No	148
577	Current	No	119
578	Rational	Yes	111
579	Emotional	Yes	72
580	Current	No	119
581	Current	No	120
582	Emotional	Yes	65
583	Current	No	123
584	Rational	Yes	103
585	Emotional	Yes	66

Piedmont Bank credit cards

Piedmont Bank is concerned about whether granting (accepting) credit cards affects whether customers are retained (keep their accounts open) or defect (close their accounts). This kind of analysis is referred to as customer retention. The first 10 out of 1246 accounts are shown in Table 6.19. The second column, Credit Card, lists whether the customer's credit card application was accepted or declined. The third column, AcctStatus, lists whether the customer's account is open or closed (retained or defected). The fourth column, Annual Profit, lists the annual profit Piedmont Bank made from that customer during the past 12 months.

1. Create the CONTINGENCY TABLE (frequencies) for Credit Card versus AcctStatus.
2. The following probabilities are of managerial concern:
   a. Calculate the probability that a customer's credit card application will be accepted—that is, $P(Accepted)$.
   b. Calculate the probability that a customer will be retained (keep their account open) if their credit card application was accepted—that is, $P(Open|Accepted)$.
   c. Calculate the probability that a customer will be retained (keep their account open) if their credit card application was declined—that is, $P(Open|Declined)$.
3. Construct a histogram of annual profit with the first bin midpoint at $150 and with bin midpoints in increments of $25.

Continued

Case—cont'd

Table 6.19 Customer retention data

Customer	Credit card	AcctStatus	Annual profit ($)
1	Accepted	Open	287.35
2	Accepted	Open	241.05
3	Accepted	Open	260.10
4	Declined	Open	324.53
5	Accepted	Open	356.43
6	Declined	Closed	270.00
7	Accepted	Open	321.07
8	Accepted	Closed	273.52
9	Accepted	Open	337.10
10	Accepted	Open	318.07
.		.	
.		.	
.		.	
1246	Accepted	Open	278.92

4. Calculate the following to answer questions that arose during the meeting:
   a. Calculate the probability that the annual profit for a customer is greater than $250—that is, $P(\text{Annual Profit} > \$250)$.
   b. Calculate the average annual profit for a customer whose credit card application was accepted and their account is open.
   c. Calculate the average annual profit for a customer whose credit card application was declined and they closed the account.
5. Draw and label the appropriate decision tree.

Camden Electronics

Camden Electronics Inc. is a small electronics firm that produces a variety of special-purpose analog-to-digital converters, which are used primarily for process control. Its business has grown to a sales level of $250,000,000 per year.

The analog-to-digital converters produced by the company are devices for converting readings of instruments measuring such things as temperature, pressure, rate of flow, and humidity into a set of signals that are fed into computers. The computers then process the data, compute a correction if needed, and transmit the correction back so that the process can be adjusted.

Most of the converters produced by Camden make use of semiconductor components of relatively common designs. The specifications of the semiconductors are, in fact, quite flexible, and it is common practice for the Camden purchasing agent, Laura Greene, to search for good buys on batches of the components. Whenever she finds a potentially good buy, she obtains a set of specifications of the circuit from the seller and passes it on to the electronics department. The engineering department examines both the electronic characteristics and the physical structure of the components to determine whether they can be used without undue modification of the converters in which they will be installed.

Quite frequently, Ms. Greene has been able to purchase batches of components that have been classified as rejects by the Components Division of Cynctron Manufacturing Company. These batches generally contain a high percentage of components that are usable by Camden Electronics. In addition to its industrial sales, Cynctron's Components Division acts as the source of silicon diodes, microprocessors, integrated components, and circuitry mounted on cards for the Products Division of Cynctron, including the Consumer Products Division, the Communication Division, and the Military and Aerospace Division. Each division produces a wide variety of products in large volume. Due to the volume, the assembly of most products is highly automated, thus requiring high accuracy in the location of contact and connection points of the components. Hence, the Components Division must make tests at regular intervals of both the electronic and physical characteristics of the parts. Should it turn out on inspection that some characteristic of the part tested lies outside the fairly

Case—cont'd

stringent tolerance required for use in one of the product divisions of Cynctron, all of the parts produced in the batch are put aside and subsequently sold outside the company. A study made at Cynctron has shown that it is not economically feasible for them to test and sort the batch in the Products Division.

Cynctron always sells these rejects in the same way. A list is kept of purchasing agents who will buy parts with specific characteristics; these purchasing agents are emailed and informed when a batch of potential interest is available. If interested, each purchasing agent makes a sealed bid and Cynctron sells the batch of components to the winner.

Ms. Greene has recently been informed of the availability of a batch of 100 components identified by Cynctron as MATS314Q. Over the past 2 years, Ms. Greene has bid on 85 previous batches of these components and has saved the winning unit bids (Table 6.20).

Table 6.20 Bidding data

Contract	Unit bid per est. good unit	Contract	Unit bid per est. good unit	Contract	Unit bid per est. good unit
1	334.10	30	317.60	59	324.30
2	282.60	31	282.70	60	267.40
3	286.80	32	326.70	61	309.60
4	263.80	33	327.30	62	286.10
5	269.00	34	270.50	63	275.40
6	323.00	35	260.20	64	317.60
7	335.00	36	328.00	65	260.80
8	281.50	37	264.40	66	305.90
9	279.00	38	334.60	67	286.90
10	281.70	39	326.70	68	310.70
11	330.00	40	268.30	69	260.10
12	270.20	41	289.30	70	309.00
13	294.10	42	318.50	71	299.40
14	270.10	43	303.20	72	294.60
15	278.70	44	321.30	73	323.10
16	261.60	45	311.80	74	313.30
17	307.40	46	300.00	75	272.40
18	273.50	47	269.80	76	270.10
19	311.30	48	299.00	77	338.70
20	316.20	49	313.20	78	264.50
21	309.60	50	306.20	79	337.20
22	301.80	51	303.80	80	318.40
23	300.20	52	332.80	81	271.80
24	296.00	53	324.50	82	273.50
25	309.70	54	332.40	83	266.20
26	275.50	55	290.40	84	335.00
27	307.10	56	278.50	85	337.70
28	331.50	57	280.50		
29	327.00	58	277.60		

Continued

Case—cont'd

The Cynctron salesman, Robert Williamson, always supplies an estimate of the yield of good parts in each batch. It is in his best interest to supply a conservative estimate since, in the long run, his ability to sell depends on providing his customers with at least as many units as he estimates. For the current batch, Mr. Williamson estimates the yield to be 90%. Based on past situations where Mr. Williamson had estimated a 90% yield and Camden had won the bid, Ms. Greene estimated that half the time the actual yields were above 93%. Furthermore, she estimated that two-thirds of the actual yields were between 91% and 95%, and thus she estimated the actual yields were approximately normal in their distribution.

With the information from Cynctron on the characteristics of item MATS314Q, the engineering department has informed Ms. Greene that Camden can use the item now. They have received a contract to supply 25 pressure sensing and control devices, each of which would require four of these components.

For Camden to manufacture the same circuit by regular methods, the cost would be $7500 for setup plus a cost of $310 per unit produced. Cynctron's price for tested and guaranteed MATS314Q's in quantities of 200 or less is $550 each. Camden does not carry these components in inventory.

With this information and the data given in Table 6.20, Ms. Greene is about to make her analysis and determine what to bid. As she looked over the data on the past bids, she remarked to her assistant, "It looks to me as if the other bidders are bidding about $300 per estimated good unit. Thus, for a batch of 100 components with an estimated yield of 90%, I would guess the competitor's bid would be about $27,000. From what I know of their use of this circuit, their yield of good items should be about the same as ours."

Brompton Medical Center NICU

Brompton Medical Center (BMC) is a medium-size general hospital with services including a neonatal intensive care unit (NICU), cancer treatment center, and center for gerontology. With continuously rising health care costs, inventory management is a significant concern. Robin Roberts, an inventory manager for BMC, was concerned about the inventory of disposable items used in the NICU.

The inventory of such items was critical both in patient care and cost management. Ms. Roberts decided to tackle one commonly used item first—disposable electrocardiogram (ECG) electrodes. She thought if she could figure out an inventory management model for this item, then other items could be modeled in a similar manner.

An ECG (or EKG, abbreviated from the German Elektrokardiogramm) is a graphic produced by an electrocardiograph, which records the electrical activity of the heart over time. Analysis of the various waves and normal vectors provides important diagnostic information for the cardiac care of premature babies. Heart and lung problems frequently accompany premature births due to the lack of complete in utero formation of vital organs.

An ECG is obtained by measuring electrical potential between various points of the body using a biomedical instrumentation amplifier. A lead records the electrical signals of the heart from a particular combination of recording electrodes that are placed at specific points on the patient's body. Thus, a sufficient supply of ECG electrodes is critical to monitoring the cardiac status of premature babies in BMC's NICU.

ECG Electrode Inventory

Ms. Robert's first consideration was to examine demand for ECG electrodes. After examining the previous 7 years of demand, she was able to statistically determine that there currently was no trend nor seasonality in the monthly demand. Based on this, she decided that the previous 86 months of ECG electrode usage, shown in Table 6.21, should be sufficient for her inventory analysis.

After obtaining the usage data, she obtained accounting information to determine the relevant inventory costs associated with stocking ECG electrodes. She tallied up various factors, such as administrative time, opportunity costs, and insurance, and decided that the cost to place an order with the medical supplier was approximately $238 and the cost of keeping a single ECG electrode for a month was approximately $0.15.

After examining these costs, Ms. Roberts examined previous purchase orders to determine the time between placing an order and receiving an order. The typical time between placing an order and receiving an order was 1 month. If the NICU ran short of ECG electrodes, then they typically rush ordered a small quantity (lot sizes of 25) at a cost that was 40% higher than the usual unit cost of $2.50, with an additional shipping cost of $45.

eOptics call center

In 1995, eOptics was born by a company formed by Dr. Robert J. Morrison and his son Jim (the current president of eOptics, not of The Doors). Dr. Morrison is the co-patent holder of the soft contact lens and the "eye doctor to royal families and

Case—cont'd

Table 6.21 Previous 86 months of ecg electrode usage

Month	Volume	Month	Volume	Month	Volume	Month	Volume
1	193	23	187	45	162	67	185
2	175	24	175	46	195	68	177
3	186	25	180	47	181	69	188
4	190	26	187	48	195	70	223
5	195	27	172	49	182	71	201
6	214	28	195	50	190	72	168
7	160	29	206	51	180	73	156
8	197	30	174	52	189	74	172
9	179	31	187	53	189	75	189
10	200	32	170	54	199	76	178
11	196	33	177	55	170	77	180
12	204	34	159	56	169	78	174
13	203	35	194	57	199	79	182
14	191	36	166	58	159	80	181
15	198	37	191	59	188	81	178
16	184	38	163	60	192	82	203
17	206	39	173	61	171	83	195
18	212	40	173	62	172	84	189
19	189	41	190	63	161	85	185
20	172	42	197	64	212	86	207
21	190	43	176	65	193		
22	186	44	185	66	197		

movie stars," as well as a professor of both ophthalmology and optometry. Jim holds five patents related to the design and manufacture of frames and lenses but is mostly obsessed with the company goal, "Good vision shouldn't cost so much!!"

eOptics was the first site on the net devoted to optics and is the recipient of many awards. Today, it is a company devoted to providing fun, hard-to-find, and low-cost optical products over the Internet.

Jim was reviewing the staffing needs for the Call Center. Although most of the orders were received via its website, a significant number of customers ordered via the phone, usually after asking technical questions about various products. The average revenue per phone call was about $195 with an average product cost of $122. This cost is eOptics' cost of the optical product only and excludes the cost of taking the order. His current problem was to evaluate a staffing and scheduling problem for the Call Center.

The Call Center

The Call Center was the heart of eOptics customer service operations. The department received and processed calls for technical information and orders for customers. Despite the practice by other online retailers of handling phone orders via subcontracted firms (usually overseas), Jim had decided to keep customer service in-house. This was found to improve and control customer service quality. Thus, staffing and scheduling were key to customer satisfaction.

The department operated from 6:00 to 12:30 a.m. every day. The volume of calls processed in the Call Center had not increased significantly in the past year. The scheduling problem in the Call Center was magnified because of the variability in the call volume. Currently, one part-time call operator and three full-time call operators were working at the Call Center.

Continued

Case—cont'd

Each operator had an average processing rate of five calls per hour. The operators' compensation package (including taxes, benefits, etc.) was currently $34.54 per hour.

Forecasting

Jim had just hired a newly minted MBA, Josh Bell, to perform various marketing functions, including marketing research. The first thing Mr. Bell had to do was analyze call volumes to determine what factors might account for the variability in the call volumes. Then he would work out a schedule for the number of staff to meet the predicted demand.

In his initial analysis of 2 years of hourly call volumes, Mr. Bell was able to determine that there currently was no trend nor seasonality in the hourly call volumes. Based on this, he took a random sample of hourly call volumes, shown in Table 6.22, to use as the basis for determining his staffing schedule. He still had to contend with the variation in call volume to determine how many hours of staffing to schedule each day. If he scheduled hours, he had to pay for them even if the operators sat idle. However, if the volume of calls was so high that the callers could not reach the Call Center, then some orders might be lost. Based on previous research, it was estimated that 80% of such calls were lost.

Table 6.22 Random sample of 100 hourly call volumes

Hour	Volume	Hour	Volume	Hour	Volume	Hour	Volume
1	33	26	33	51	36	76	26
2	17	27	22	52	28	77	25
3	21	28	15	53	20	78	30
4	19	29	15	54	27	79	28
5	35	30	25	55	27	80	28
6	32	31	30	56	29	81	23
7	25	32	18	57	20	82	24
8	28	33	25	58	22	83	27
9	31	34	25	59	27	84	27
10	29	35	40	60	16	85	16
11	27	36	26	61	23	86	24
12	20	37	27	62	26	87	28
13	24	38	29	63	24	88	35
14	25	39	23	64	23	89	22
15	31	40	22	65	19	90	20
16	19	41	24	66	33	91	30
17	29	42	33	67	25	92	23
18	20	43	20	68	23	93	37
19	31	44	22	69	32	94	21
20	33	45	30	70	27	95	28
21	23	46	33	71	32	96	16
22	19	47	26	72	26	97	23
23	15	48	23	73	27	98	27
24	34	49	16	74	27	99	25
25	28	50	21	75	30	100	36

Theoretical probability distributions

What are the chances based on theory?

Chapter outline

FIGURE 7.1

Uniform, Poisson, and Normal Probability Distributions

Introduction

An understanding of *classical* probability distributions is an essential building block for optimum managerial decision making as well as for the introduction to the study of statistics. Theoretical distributions can also be used when data is scarce or nonexistent, but the decision maker has an expert

Introduction to Business Analytics Using Simulation. https://doi.org/10.1016/B978-0-323-91717-9.00007-3

163

knowledge of the underlying random process. The uniform, Bernoulli, binomial, Poisson, and normal distributions are introduced in this chapter. Decision trees and simulation are employed to explain and demonstrate the use of these probability distributions.

7.1 Theoretical/classical probability

Theoretical (*classical*) probability is based upon formulaic theory of determining likelihood. Recall that for a given random variable, the set of likelihoods for all outcomes of a random variable is called a *probability distribution*. Although there are many theoretical distributions, this chapter provides an overview of four of the most commonly used distributions: the *uniform*, *binomial*, *Poisson*, and *normal* probability distributions.

As described earlier, random variables and their associated probability distributions are categorized as either **discrete** or **continuous** depending on whether the outcomes are separately countable (e.g., cars) or not (e.g., gallons of gasoline). The binomial and Poisson distributions are discrete distributions. There are both discrete and continuous versions of the uniform distribution. The normal distribution is a continuous distribution but can be used to approximate some discrete random variables.

7.2 Review of notation for probability distributions

As described in Section 4.2, the probability that the random variable X has a specific outcome of x is defined, or calculated, according to a probability function, $f(x)$:

$$f(x) = \text{probability of } x = P(X = x)$$

For discrete random variables, the probability function, $f(x)$, is called the *probability mass function* (*pmf*). For continuous random variables, the probability function, $f(x)$, is called the *probability density function* (*pdf*). For every theoretical probability distribution, there is a specific mathematical function that defines the probability function $f(x)$.

The probability of a random variable being less than or equal to x is denoted as $F(x)$ and referred to as the *cumulative density function* (*cdf*).

$$F(x) = \text{probability} \le x = P(X \le x)$$
$$= \text{the area under the } f(x) \text{ curve to the } \textbf{left} \text{ of } x = \text{the } \textbf{left tail}$$

If $f(x)$ is a continuous function, then $F(x)$ is the integral of $f(x)$ from $-\infty$ to x:

$$F(x) = \int_{-\infty}^{x} f(x)\, dx$$

Similarly, if $f(x)$ is a continuous function, then the compliment, $1 - F(x)$, is the integral of $f(x)$ from x to ∞:

$$1 - F(x) = \text{probability} \ge x = P(X \ge x) =$$
$$= \text{the area under the } f(x) \text{ curve to the } \textbf{right} \text{ of } x = \text{the } \textbf{right tail}$$

$$1 - F(x) = \int_{x}^{\infty} f(x)\, dx$$

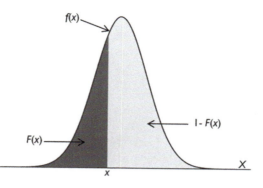

FIGURE 7.2

Notation for *cdf* and *pdf* for Continuous Probability Distributions

7.3 Discrete theoretical distributions
7.3.1 Uniform distribution

The *uniform* distribution is a probability distribution in which there is no information as to whether any particular outcome is more or less likely to occur than any other outcome. Uniform distribution is a two-parameter distribution with all values between the lower and upper bounds being equally likely. In other words, it is a distribution in which no information as to the likelihoods of the outcomes is available.

Given the minimum (a) and the maximum (b) outcomes, the number of equally likely outcomes is n and is equal to ($b - a + 1$). The probability mass function (*pmf*) for the **discrete uniform distribution** is (Fig. 7.3):

$$f(x) = 1/n = 1/(b - a + 1) \quad \text{for } a \leq x \leq b \tag{7.1}$$

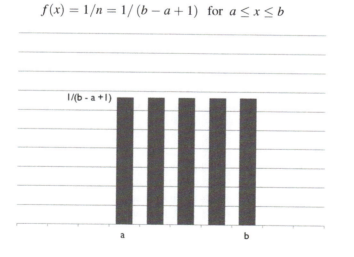

FIGURE 7.3

Probability Mass Function (*pmf*) for the Discrete Uniform Distribution

The cumulative distribution function (*cdf*) for the discrete uniform distribution is (Fig. 7.4):

$$F(x) = (x - a + 1)/(b - a + 1) \quad \text{for } a \leq x \leq b \tag{7.2}$$

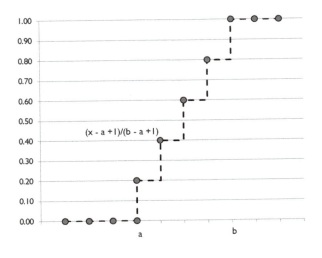

FIGURE 7.4

Cumulative Distribution Function (*cdf*) for the Discrete Uniform Distribution

7.3.2 Bernoulli distribution

The *Bernoulli* distribution is a discrete distribution having two (*dichotomous*) possible outcomes with the probabilities designated as p and its complement, $q = 1 - p$. A common mistake is to assume that, since there are two outcomes, $p = 0.50$ (as in the case of a fair coin flip). One has only to look at the daily probability of rain in the weather forecast to see that p does not always equal 50%. This distribution is the fundamental building block of many probability distributions.

7.3.3 Binomial distribution

Of considerably more use is the *binomial* distribution. Binomial distribution is a discrete probability distribution of *the number of successes* in a sequence of n independent *dichotomous* events, each with a probability, p, of *success*. The complement of p is $q = (1 - p)$. Thus, the binomial distribution is the sum of a series of *Bernoulli trials*. A trivial example is the random variable of the number of heads given five coin flips. The range of outcomes of this random variable is the set of integers from 0 to 5 = {0, 1, 2, 3, 4, 5}.

The average number of occurrences for the binomial distribution is np, and the variance (more on this later) for the binomial distribution is npq. As an example, for five coin flips, the average number of heads is 5(0.50) = 2.5. This demonstrates that the average is *not* the most likely outcome. Thinking that the average is the most likely outcome is a common mistake. Reminder: the *mode* is the term used to designate the most likely outcome. This also demonstrates that although the outcomes are discrete integers, the average does not have to be a discrete integer.

Before specifying the probability mass function (*pmf*), the ***three*** parameters of a binomial distribution (x, n, p) must be defined:

$$x = \text{number of } successes$$

Success is a relative term commonly used to indicate the one of two *dichotomous* states is of specific interest. In some situations, the outcome associated with *success* can be an undesirable state.

n = number of trials or sample size

Reminder: $n! = n\ factorial = n(n-1)(n-2)\ldots(1)$.
  For example, $5! = 5(4)(3)(2)(1) = 120$.
  Note that by definition, **$0! = 1$.**
  n−x = number of failures.
  p = probability of successes.
  q = probability of failure. Note that q = (1 − p).

Using these parameters, the probability mass function (*pmf*) for the **binomial distribution** is:

$$f(x) = \frac{n!}{x!\,(n-x)!}p^x q^{(n-x)} \tag{7.3}$$

The first term, $\dfrac{n!}{x!\,(n-x)!}$, is the number of outcomes with exactly x successes among n trials. This is the number of ways (combinations) that exactly x success can occur among the n trials. If x has occurred, then there must be x successes and (n − x) failures. Thus, for a single outcome of x successes and (n − x) failures, there would be x success at p each and (n − x) failures at q each:

$$\overbrace{(pp\ldots p)}^{x}\overbrace{(qq\ldots q)}^{n-x} = p^x q^{(n-x)}$$

Thus, the probability for a single outcome of x successes is $p^x q^{(n-x)}$. Since there are $\dfrac{n!}{x!\,(n-x)!}$ ways to get that single outcome, each at a probability of $p^x q^{(n-x)}$, the total probability for getting x successes is:

$$f(x) = \frac{n!}{x!\,(n-x)!}p^x q^{(n-x)}$$

Example 7.1 Binomial distribution: small average

A bakery owns three delivery trucks of the same age (why is that important?). Based on previous service records, the probability that a single truck will be in service on any given day is 99%. What is the probability of having only two trucks available tomorrow? What is the probability of having at least two trucks?

To fully describe the situation in this example, compute the entire probability distribution for the number of trucks in service:

$$P(X = 0\ trucks) = f(0) = \frac{3!}{0!(3-0)!}0.99^0(0.01^3)$$
$$= \frac{3!}{1(3!)}1(0.01^3)$$
$$= 1(1(0.01^3)) = 0.01^3 = 0.000001$$

$$P(X = 1\ truck) = f(1) = \frac{3!}{1!(3-1)!}0.99^1(0.01^2)$$
$$= \frac{3!}{1(2!)}0.99(0.01^2)$$
$$= 3(0.99(0.01^2)) = 0.000297$$

$$P(X = 2 \; trucks) = f(2) = \frac{3!}{2!(3-2)!} 0.99^2 (0.01^1)$$

$$= \frac{3!}{2!(1!)} 0.99^2 (0.01)$$

$$= 3(0.99^2 (0.01)) = 0.029403$$

$$P(X = 3 \; trucks) = f(3) = \frac{3!}{3!(3-3)!} 0.99^3 (0.01^0)$$

$$= \frac{3!}{3!(0!)} 0.99^3 (0.01^0)$$

$$= 1(0.99^3 (1)) = 0.99^3 = 0.970299$$

The resulting distribution is shown in Table 7.1.

Table 7.1 *CDF* and *PMF* for binomial number of trucks available

x	Combinations n!/(x!(n−x)!)	pmf = f(x)	cdf = F(x)
0	1	0.000001	0.000001
1	3	0.000297	0.000298
2	3	0.029403	0.029701
3	1	0.970299	1.000000

Thus, the probability of only two trucks is $f(2) =$ **2.94%**, and the probability of at least two trucks is $f(2) + f(3)$ or $1 - F(1) = 1 - 0.000298 =$ **99.97%**.

The graph of the *pmf* of this binomial distribution is shown in Fig. 7.5.

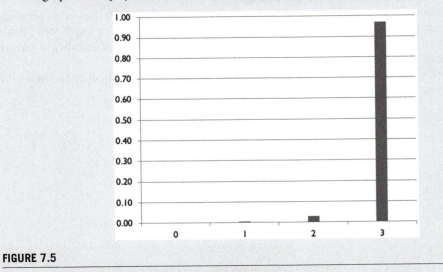

FIGURE 7.5

Binomial Probability Distribution for the Number of Trucks Available

Simulating a binomial using the RAND() function was demonstrated in Example 3.3 in Chapter 3:

$$= (RAND\,() < p)*1,$$

where p is the probability of the event x occurring. The spreadsheet shown in Fig. 7.6 displays the simulation of a *binomial* random variable, such as the binomial random number of trucks available in Example 7.1.

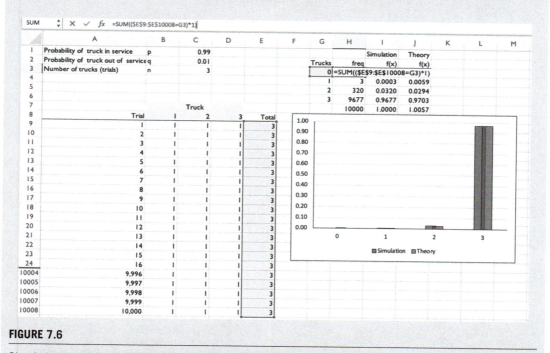

FIGURE 7.6

Simulation of a Binomial Distribution of the Number of Trucks Available

Chapter 8 will discuss how to test whether the simulation value of 97.35% for $f(3)$ is *statistically significantly different* (i.e., *not close enough*) from the theoretical value of 97.03%. In other words, the accuracy of the simulation can be calculated and will be discussed in the next chapter. Furthermore, there are statistical tests to determine if the entire simulation distribution accurately fits the theoretical distribution and vice versa. Those tests will be presented in Chapter 9.

Example 7.2 Binomial distribution: large average

A resort hotel has a 10% rate of guests with reservations who do not show up (no shows) for the rooms they reserved. If the hotel has 80 rooms and they accept 85 reservations, what is the probability of shortage?

There are two viable random variables: *arrivals* or *no shows*. In either case, the random variable will range from 0 to well beyond a number readily calculated with a simple calculator. In situations such as this in which there are numerous outcomes, compute the probability distribution using a spreadsheet. In this case, to keep the range small, the random variable was chosen to be the number of *no shows*. The distribution is shown in the spreadsheet in Fig. 7.7.

D16		✕ ✓ *fx*	=C16*($C$3)^B16*($C$4)^($C$5-B16)		
	A	B	C	D	E
1	Biniomial Distribution				
2					
3	Probability of no show	p		0.1 "success"	
4	Probability of arrival	q		0.9 "failure"	
5	Number of reservations (trials)	n		85	
6	Number of no shows (successes)	x			
7	Avg	np		8.50	
8	SD	(npq)^.5		2.77	
9					
10					
11	prob(X=x) = f(x) = n!/(x!(n-x)!) p^x q^(n-x)				
12					
13					
14				Combinations	P(X=x)	P(X<=x)
15		Arrivals x: no shows		n!/(x!(n-x)!)	pmf = f(x)	cdf = F(x)
16	85	0	1	0.000129	0.000129
17	84	1	85	0.001218	0.001347
18	83	2	3,570	0.005686	0.007033
19	82	3	98,770	0.017479	0.024512
20	81	4	2,024,785	0.039813	0.064325
21	80	5	32,801,517	0.071663	0.135988
22	79	6	437,353,560	0.106167	0.242155
23	78	7	4,935,847,320	0.133130	0.375286
24	77	8	48,124,511,370	0.144225	0.519510
25	76	9	411,731,930,610	0.137102	0.656613
26	75	10	3,129,162,672,636	0.115775	0.772388
27	74	11	21,335,200,040,700	0.087709	0.860097
28	73	12	131,567,066,917,650	0.060097	0.920193
29	72	13	738,799,683,460,649	0.037496	0.957690
30	71	14	3,799,541,229,226,200	0.021426	0.979116
31	70	15	17,984,495,151,670,700	0.011269	0.990385
32	69	16	78,682,166,288,559,200	0.005478	0.995863
33	68	17	319,357,027,877,093,000	0.002470	0.998333
34	67	18	1,206,459,883,091,240,000	0.001037	0.999370
35	66	19	4,254,358,535,111,220,000	0.000406	0.999776
36	65	20	14,039,383,165,867,000,000	0.000149	0.999925

FIGURE 7.7

Binomial Probability Distribution for the Number of Arrivals and No Shows

Note that the conditional formatting in column D creates the histogram for the *pmf*, and the conditional formatting in column E represents the *cdf*.

Since 0 *no shows* is a demand of 85 rooms, then 4 *no shows* is a demand of 81 rooms. Thus, any one of these five outcomes, 0, 1, 2, 3, 4 *no shows*, would cause demand to exceed the 80 room capacity of the hotel. Thus,

$$P\,(Shortage) = P\,(Demand \geq 81\ \ rooms) = P\,(No\ \ Shows \leq 4\ \ customers)$$

From the table in the spreadsheet in Fig. 7.7:

$$P\,(No\ \ Shows \leq 4\ \ customers) = F\,(4) = 0.0643 = 6.43\%$$

The *service level* is the complement of the probability of shortage:

$$Service\ \ Level = 1 - P\,(Shortage) = 1 - 0.0643 = 93.57\%$$

The graph of the *pmf* for Example 7.2 is displayed in Fig. 7.8. Note that as *np* goes to **8** or greater that the distribution becomes more *bell shaped* (normal).

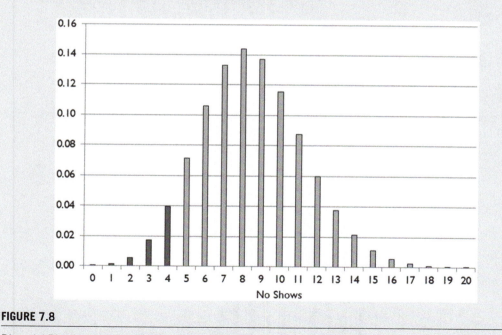

FIGURE 7.8

Binomial Distribution With $n = 85$ and $p = 0.10$

The spreadsheet shown in Fig. 7.9 demonstrates how to simulate a *binomial* random variable with $n = 85$ *Bernoulli* trials and $p = 0.10$. Note the simulation estimate of shortage is 6.21% versus the theoretical value of 6.43%. The *margin of error* is computed by the following formula:

$$= 1.96 * sd / \sqrt{n} \qquad\qquad (7.4)$$

The *margin of error* and the accuracy of simulation will be discussed in further detail in Chapter 8.

| SUM | ▾ : X ✓ *fx* | =SUM(E9:CK9) | | | | | | | | | | | | | | | | | | | |

	A	B	C	D	E	F	G	H	I	J	K	L	M	N	CF	CG	CH	CI	CJ	CK
1	Probability of no show	p		0.1 "success"																
2	Probability of arrival	q		0.9 "failure"																
3	Number of reservations (trials)	n		85																
4	Capacity			80																
5			Service Level	93.63%																
6			P(Shortage) =	6.37%																
7			Margin of Error	0.48%										Customer						
8		Trial	Arrivals	No Shows	Shortage	1	2	3	4	5	6	7	8	9	10	80	81	82	83	84	85
9		1	=SUM(E9:CK9)	9	0	1	1	1	1	1	0	1	0	1	0	1	1	1	0	1	0
10		2	78	7	0	1	1	1	1	1	1	1	1	1	1	1	1	1	1	1	1
11		3	81	4	1	1	1	1	1	1	1	1	1	1	1	0	1	1	1	1	1
12		4	74	11	0	1	1	1	1	1	0	1	1	1	1	0	1	1	1	1	1
13		5	71	14	0	1	1	1	1	1	1	1	1	1	1	0	1	1	1	1	1
14		6	76	9	0	0	1	1	1	1	1	1	1	1	1	1	1	1	1	1	1
15		7	76	9	0	1	1	1	1	0	1	1	1	1	0	1	1	1	1	1	1
16		8	75	10	0	1	1	1	1	1	1	0	1	1	1	1	1	1	1	1	0
17		9	81	4	1	1	1	1	1	1	1	1	1	1	1	1	1	1	1	1	0
10002		9,994	77	8	0	1	1	0	1	1	1	1	1	1	1	0	1	1	1	1	0
10003		9,995	75	10	0	1	1	1	1	1	1	1	1	1	1	0	1	1	1	1	1
10004		9,996	79	6	0	1	1	1	1	1	1	1	1	1	1	0	1	1	1	1	1
10005		9,997	78	7	0	1	1	1	1	1	1	1	1	1	1	1	1	1	1	0	1
10006		9,998	78	7	0	1	1	1	1	1	1	1	0	1	1	1	1	1	1	1	1
10007		9,999	80	5	0	1	1	1	1	1	1	1	1	1	1	1	1	1	1	1	1
10008		10,000	81	4	1	1	1	1	1	1	1	1	1	1	1	1	1	1	1	1	1

FIGURE 7.9

Simulation of Binomial Distribution With *n* = 85 and *p* = 0.10

The graph in Fig. 7.10 shows the probability distributions (*pmf*) of the simulation and the theoretical *binomial* (85, 0.10).

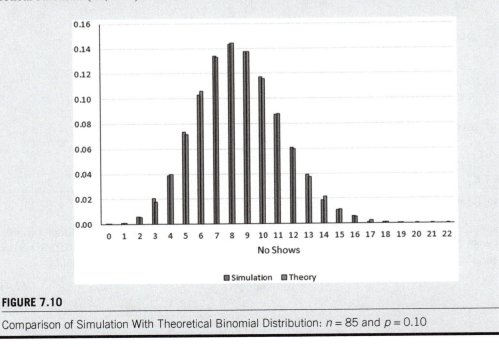

FIGURE 7.10

Comparison of Simulation With Theoretical Binomial Distribution: *n* = 85 and *p* = 0.10

7.3.4 Poisson distribution

A *Poisson* distribution is the probability of a specific number of events per time period. Some examples include arrivals per hour, demand per month, customers per minute, packages delivered per day, storms per month, and defects per batch. The *Poisson* distribution is often the distribution preferred for *rare events* such as fires, earthquakes, tsunamis, and other disasters. One characteristic of the *Poisson* distribution is that **variance is equal to the average**. By convention, the average is typically denoted using the lowercase Greek letter lambda: λ.

As with the binomial distribution, the Poisson distribution becomes more bell shaped (normal) as the average increases. When the average is approximately **8**, the Poisson and the binomial are very close to a discrete normal.

A comparison of the distribution in Fig. 7.11 and that of Fig. 7.12 demonstrates how the *Poisson* becomes more symmetric and normal as the average increases from 4 to 14. This is because no outcomes can be less than 0, and that causes the left tail to truncate at 0 for distributions with low (**<8**) averages.

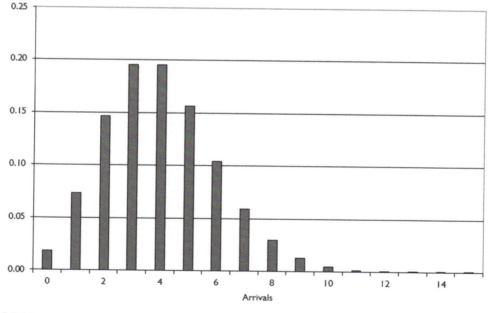

FIGURE 7.11

Probability Distribution for the Poisson Distribution With $\lambda = 4$

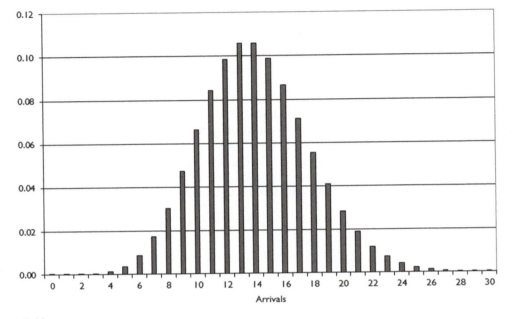

FIGURE 7.12

Probability Mass Function (*pmf*) for the Poisson Distribution With $\lambda = 14$

The *pmf* for the **Poisson distribution** is:

$$f(X) = \frac{e^{-\lambda}\lambda^x}{x!}, \tag{7.5}$$

where λ is the average number of arrivals in a constant period of time and $e = 2.71828182846....$ Like π, e is nonterminating and nonrepeating—that is, a *transcendental* number.

Example 7.3 Poisson probability: small average

Demand for a particular exclusive class of hotel rooms is Poisson with an average of two per week. Suppose the hotel has **three** such rooms. What is the probability that they will have to turn customers away—that is, what is the probability of shortage?

The probability of shortage is the upper tail (shaded portion) of the distribution. In this situation, it is easier to compute the probability of shortage using the complement:

$$P(X > 3) = 1 - F(3) = 1 - (f(0) + f(1) + f(2) + f(3))$$
$$P(X > 3) = 1 - (e^{-2}2^0/0! + e^{-2}2^1/1! + e^{-2}2^2/2! + e^{-2}2^3/3!)$$
$$P(X > 3) = 1 - (e^{-2}(1/1 + 2/1 + 2^2/(2 \times 1) + 2^3/(3 \times 2 \times 1)) = 1 - (e^{-2}(1 + 2 + 2 + 4/3))$$
$$P(X > 3) = 1 - (e^{-2}(6\,1/3)) = 1 - 0.85712346 = 0.14287654 = 14.3\%$$

Thus, there is a 14.3% chance of having to turn customers away and a service level (probability of meeting demand) of 85.7%. Fig. 7.13 shows $P(X > 3) = 1 - F(3)$ for the Poisson distribution with $\lambda = 2$.

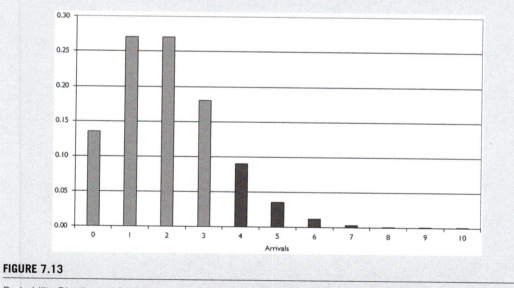

FIGURE 7.13

Probability Distribution for Poisson Arrival Process With $\lambda = 2$

One method to simulate a *Poisson* distribution is by using the **data distribution** method shown in Examples 6.1 and 6.4, and a VLOOKUP function. The spreadsheet in Fig. 7.14 shows a simulation of Example 7.3 with an average of two arrivals per week and a capacity of three:

| B28 | | f_x | =VLOOKUP(RAND(),$F$3:$G$23,2) | | | |

	A	B	C	D	E	F	G	H	I	J	K
1	**Cost Structure**			**Probability Table**		**VLOOKUP Table**			**Simulation Results**	Simulation	Theory
2	Capacity	3		Demand	f(x)	RAND()	Demand		Demand	f(x)	f(x)
3	Avg Demand	2		0	0.1353	0.0000	0		0	0.1370	0.1353
4				1	0.2707	0.1353	1		1	0.2910	0.2707
5				2	0.2707	0.4060	2		2	0.2410	0.2707
6				3	0.1804	0.6767	3		3	0.1780	0.1804
7				4	0.0902	0.8571	4		4	0.0930	0.0902
8				5	0.0361	0.9473	5		5	0.0400	0.0361
9				6	0.0120	0.9834	6		6	0.0150	0.0120
10				7	0.0034	0.9955	7		7	0.0050	0.0034
11				8	0.0009	0.9989	8		8	0.0000	0.0009
12				9	0.0002	0.9998	9		9	0.0000	0.0002
13				10	0.0000	1.0000	10		10	0.0000	0.0000
14				11	0.0000	1.0000	11		11	0.0000	0.0000
15				12	0.0000	1.0000	12		12	0.0000	0.0000
16				13	0.0000	1.0000	13				
17				14	0.0000	1.0000	14				
18				15	0.0000	1.0000	15				
19				16	0.0000	1.0000	16				
20				17	0.0000	1.0000	17				
21				18	0.0000	1.0000	18				
22				19	0.0000	1.0000	19				
23				20	0.0000	1.0000	20				
24											
25			P(Shortage)	15.3%							
26			Service Level	84.7%							
27		Trial	Arrivals	Rooms Filled	Shortage	Extra					
28		1	2	2	0	1					
29		2	2	2	0	1					
30		3	2	2	0	1					
31		4	1	1	0	2					
32		5	1	1	0	2					
33		6	2	2	0	1					
34		7	0	0	0	3					
35		8	1	1	0	2					
36		9	6	3	3	0					
37		10	1	1	0	2					
1022		995	1	1	0	2					
1023		996	1	1	0	2					
1024		997	3	3	0	0					
1025		998	2	2	0	1					
1026		999	2	2	0	1					
1027		1000	3	3	0	0					

FIGURE 7.14

Simulation of a Poisson Arrival Process With $\lambda = 2$

Example 7.4 Poisson probability: large average

A bank has an average of eight defaults per month for a particular loan portfolio in a specific region. What is the probability of more than six defaults?

The graph of the *pmf* of the Poisson distribution with $\lambda = 8$ is shown in Fig. 7.15.

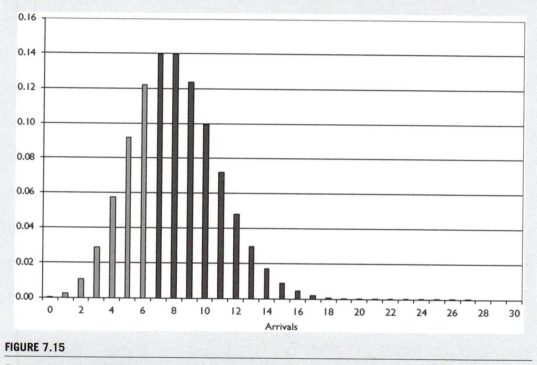

FIGURE 7.15

Poisson Probability Distribution for $\lambda = 8$

The probability of more than six defaults is the upper tail (shaded portion) of the distribution. The spreadsheet in Fig. 7.16 demonstrates how to compute the *pmf* for a *Poisson* distribution with a large number of outcomes.

| D5 | | ▾ | ⋮ | ✕ | ✓ | f_x | =POISSON.DIST(C5,$C$3,0) |

▲	A	B	C	D	E
1	Poisson Distribution Example				
2					
3		average	8		
4			x	f(x)	F(x)
5			0	0.0003	0.0003
6			1	0.0027	0.0030
7			2	0.0107	0.0138
8			3	0.0286	0.0424
9			4	0.0573	0.0996
10			5	0.0916	0.1912
11			6	0.1221	0.3134
12			7	0.1396	0.4530
13			8	0.1396	0.5925
14			9	0.1241	0.7166
15			10	0.0993	0.8159
16			11	0.0722	0.8881
17			12	0.0481	0.9362
18			13	0.0296	0.9658
19			14	0.0169	0.9827
20			15	0.0090	0.9918
21			16	0.0045	0.9963
22			17	0.0021	0.9984
23			18	0.0009	0.9993
24			19	0.0004	0.9997
25			20	0.0002	0.9999
26			21	0.0001	1.0000
27			22	0.0000	1.0000
28			23	0.0000	1.0000
29			24	0.0000	1.0000
30			25	0.0000	1.0000

FIGURE 7.16

Computation of a Poisson Probability Distribution With $\lambda = 8$

Thus, the probability of more than six defaults can be computed as:

$$P(X>6) = 1 - P(X = 6) = 1 - F(6) = 1 - 0.3134 = 0.6866 = 68.66\%$$

Thus, there is a 68.66% chance of having more than six defaults per month.

The spreadsheet in Fig. 7.17 shows a simulation of Example 7.4 with an average of eight defaults per month constructed in the same manner as the simulation in Example 7.3.

B9		:	✕	✓	*fx*	=VLOOKUP(RAND(),$G$3:$H$28,2)						

	A	B	C	D	E	F	G	H	I	J	K	L
1	**Cost Structure**				**Probability Table**		**VLOOKUP Table**			**Simulation Results**	Simulation	Theory
2	Default Level	6			Demand	f(x)	RAND()	Demand		Demand	f(x)	f(x)
3	Avg Defaults	8			0	0.0003	0.0000	0		0	0.0000	0.0003
4					1	0.0027	0.0003	1		1	0.0000	0.0027
5			Avg	P(Defaults>6)		2	0.0107	0.0030	2		2	0.0050	0.0107
6	Theory	8.00	68.66%		3	0.0286	0.0138	3		3	0.0340	0.0286
7	Simulation	8.02	68.40%		4	0.0573	0.0424	4		4	0.0800	0.0573
8	Trial	Defaults	Defaults >6		5	0.0916	0.0996	5		5	0.0880	0.0916
9	1	4	0		6	0.1221	0.1912	6		6	0.1090	0.1221
10	2	9	1		7	0.1396	0.3134	7		7	0.1270	0.1396
11	3	12	1		8	0.1396	0.4530	8		8	0.1560	0.1396
12	4	9	1		9	0.1241	0.5925	9		9	0.1070	0.1241
13	5	6	0		10	0.0993	0.7166	10		10	0.0980	0.0993
14	6	4	0		11	0.0722	0.8159	11		11	0.0770	0.0722
15	7	6	0		12	0.0481	0.8881	12		12	0.0490	0.0481
16	8	11	1		13	0.0296	0.9362	13		13	0.0340	0.0296
17	9	5	0		14	0.0169	0.9658	14		14	0.0190	0.0169
18	10	3	0		15	0.0090	0.9827	15		15	0.0090	0.0090
19	11	6	0		16	0.0045	0.9918	16		16	0.0040	0.0045
20	12	7	1		17	0.0021	0.9963	17		17	0.0030	0.0021
21	13	8	1		18	0.0009	0.9984	18		18	0.0010	0.0009
22	14	8	1		19	0.0004	0.9993	19		19	0.0000	0.0004
23	15	6	0		20	0.0002	0.9997	20		20	0.0000	0.0002
24	16	6	0		21	0.0001	0.9999	21		21	0.0000	0.0001
25	17	10	1		22	0.0000	1.0000	22		22	0.0000	0.0000
26	18	15	1		23	0.0000	1.0000	23		23	0.0000	0.0000
27	19	10	1		24	0.0000	1.0000	24		24	0.0000	0.0000
28	20	9	1		25	0.0000	1.0000	25		25	0.0000	0.0000
29	21	9	1									
30	22	5	0									
31	23	9	1									
32	24	6	0									
33	25	6	0									
1003	995	8	1									
1004	996	8	1									
1005	997	7	1									
1006	998	11	1									
1007	999	6	0									
1008	1000	8	1									

FIGURE 7.17

Simulation of a Poisson Arrival Process With $\lambda = 8$

Notice the variation in the number of defaults per month, and consider the effects of simply using the average of **eight** each month—the effects of not considering the variation that can actually occur.

It is important to note that the binomial and Poisson probability distributions are often quite close numerically. One fact that differentiates the two distributions is that the range of the binomial is finite from 0 to n, whereas the theoretical range for the Poisson is from 0 to $+\infty$.

7.4 Continuous probability distributions

Random variables that can assume any value between two other specified values are considered to be *continuous* random variables. Some examples are time, distance, weight, spatial volume, and percentages. Although technically money is discrete, it can usually be treated as continuous—in much the same manner as digital music and photography.

7.4.1 Continuous uniform distribution

As described previously, without information as to the likelihood of outcomes, the uniform distribution should be assumed. Given the minimum (a) and the maximum (b) outcomes, the probability density function (*pdf*) for the **continuous uniform distribution** is (Fig. 7.18):

$$f(x) = 1/(b-a) \quad \text{for } a \leq x \leq b \tag{7.6}$$

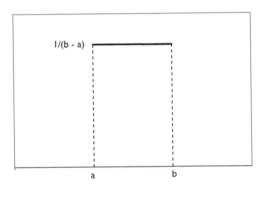

FIGURE 7.18

Probability Density Function (*pdf*) for the Continuous Uniform Distribution

The cumulative distribution function (*cdf*) for the *continuous uniform distribution* is (Fig. 7.19):

$$F(x) = (x-a)/(b-a) \quad \text{for } a \leq x \leq b \tag{7.7}$$

7.4.2 Normal distribution

One of the most widely known, and perhaps overused, of all distributions is the normal distribution. Many variables in business are normally distributed. Some examples of variables that could be normally distributed include the annual cost of household insurance and the cost per square foot of renting warehouse space, and many items produced or filled by machines are normally distributed.

Introduction of the *normal curve* is generally credited to the French mathematician Abraham DeMoivre, and widespread usage is credited to mathematician and astronomer Karl Gauss (1777–1855). Gauss recognized that the errors of repeated measurement of distances are often normally distributed. Thus, the normal distribution is sometimes referred to as the *Gaussian distribution* or the normal curve of errors. A direct modern application of Gauss's work is statistical process control (i.e.,

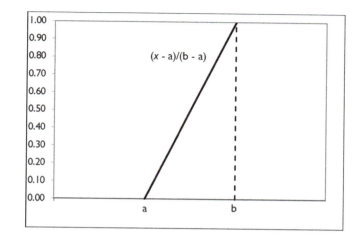

FIGURE 7.19

Cumulative Distribution Function (*cdf*) for the Continuous Uniform Distribution

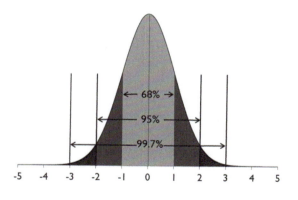

FIGURE 7.20

The Standard Normal Distribution: $N(0,1^2)$

Six-Sigma). An example is the distribution of measurements of machine-produced parts, which often yield a normal distribution of errors around a mean specification.

Due to the *central limit theorem* (to be discussed in the next chapter), the normal distribution arises mostly due to the summing of measurements. Thus, when large enough size samples are gathered, many statistics are normally distributed regardless of the shape of the underlying distribution from which they are drawn. This phenomenon will be shown in Chapter 8 as the averages for the binomial and Poisson distributions grow beyond approximately 8.

To compute probabilities with the normal distribution, the concept of *standard deviation* must be described. In broad terms, the standard deviation is the *average amount away from average*. It would not be unusual or unlikely to be 1 standard deviation away from average.

To introduce the normal distribution, consider a random variable that has an average of 0 and an average amount away from 0 of 1 unit shown in Fig. 7.20.

For all normally distributed variables:

Average ± 1 standard deviation is about 68% of the data 2 out of 3
Average ± 2 standard deviations is about 95% of the data 19 out of 20
Average ± 3 standard deviations is about 99.7% of the data 997 out of 1000

To illustrate the role of the average (represented by the Greek letter mu: μ) and the standard deviation (represented by the Greek letter sigma: σ), study the graph of the three normal distributions with the parameters shown in Fig. 7.21:

$$\mu = 0 \ \sigma = 1 \ \text{(the standard normal distribution)}$$
$$\mu = 3 \ \sigma = 2$$
$$\mu = 6 \ \sigma = 1$$

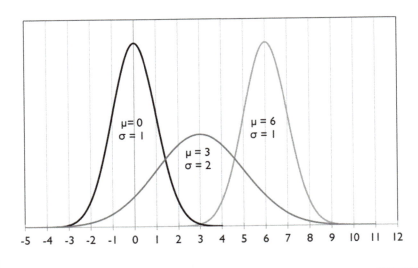

FIGURE 7.21

Comparison of Three Normal Distributions

$X \sim N(\mu, \sigma^2)$ is used as notation to indicate a random variable that follows the Gaussian (normal) distribution with a **mean** of μ and a **standard deviation** of σ. Note that:

$$\text{variance} = \sigma^2$$

The *pdf* for a **normal distribution** is given by the formula:

$$f(x) = \frac{1}{\sigma\sqrt{2\pi}} e^{-\frac{1}{2}\left(\frac{x-\mu}{\sigma}\right)^2} \tag{7.8}$$

The quantity in the parenthesis, $\left(\dfrac{x-\mu}{\sigma}\right)$, is the **number of standard deviations away from average**. This quantity is denoted by the letter z and referred to as the *z-score*, or standard score. This is a measure of how far the observed data point is away from average. The choice of the letter z is standard practice and may have originated from the German word for numbers or count: *Zählen*.

Every change in a parameter (μ and σ) determines a different normal distribution. This characteristic of the normal distribution (a family of distributions) would make analysis by the normal distribution even more tedious because of the volumes of normal distribution tables (one for each different combination of μ and σ) that would be required. Fortunately, a method was developed by which all normal distributions can be converted into a single distribution: the *standard normal* (z) distribution: $\mu = 0$, $\sigma = 1$.

A useful measure of a normal distribution is the *coefficient of variation* (CV):

$$CV = Standard\ Deviation/Average = \sigma/\mu$$

The CV is the relative, percentage measure of the variation in the data.

As an example, suppose the average amount spent on groceries in a week is $100 with a standard deviation of $10. The CV is 10/100 = 10%. Thus, spending $120 in a week would be 2 standard deviations (2 times $10) above from average and would be represented by $z = (120 - 100)/10 = 2$ standard deviations above average, which would be at approximately the 97.5th percentile (95% + the 2.5% from the left tail = 97.5%). Thus, your grocery bill will be $120 or less about 97.5% of the time. In addition, 97.7% is the more accurate probability that results from using a normal distribution table (or a statistical function in Excel or other statistical software). This example of 2 standard deviations above average in a normal distribution with an average of $100 and a standard deviation of $10 is illustrated in Fig. 7.22.

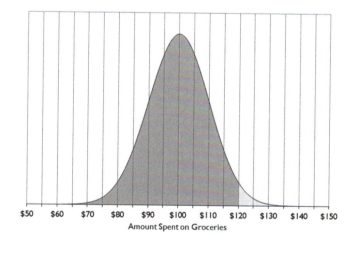

FIGURE 7.22

2 Standard Deviations Above Average in a Normal $N(100, 10^2)$ Distribution

The *cdf* for a normal distribution is given by the following formula:

$$F(x) = \int_{-\infty}^{x} f(x)\, dx = \Phi(z)$$

Thus, $F(x)$ denotes a generic cumulative probability distribution, and $\Phi(z)$ specifically denotes the cumulative normal distribution.

Example 7.5 Normal Probability

Demand for diesel fuel for a single day for a delivery truck is normally distributed and has a mean of 50 gallons and a standard deviation of 3 gallons (variance = 9). This demand can be denoted as a random variable, X, and may be notated as either $X \sim N(50, 3^2)$ or $X \sim N(50, 9)$. Find the probability that demand will be less than or equal to 56 gallons for a single day—that is, find $P(X \le 56)$.

$$P(X \le 56) = F(56) = \Phi\left(\frac{56 - 50}{3}\right) = \Phi(2) =$$

0.97725 (from a table of Standard Normal probabilities).

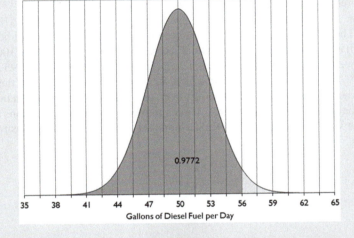

FIGURE 7.23

Two Standard Deviations Above Average in a Normal $N(50, 3^2)$ Distribution

Finding a value of a normal random variable associated with a given probability requires the use of the *inverse normal function* and is indicated by:

$$\Phi^{-1}(P(X \le x)) = Z_{P(X \le x)}$$

$$\Phi^{-1}(F(x)) = Z_{F(x)},$$

where $Z_{F(x)}$ is the number of standard deviations that corresponds to the cumulative probability (less than or equal to x). Less formally:

$$\Phi^{-1}(probability) = z_{probability}$$

For example, $\Phi^{-1}(0.975) \cong 1.96$. In managerial terms, if you want the value that would be at the 97.5th percentile, you need to add 1.96 *standard deviations* to the average. In the previous example,

$$50 + 1.96(3) = 55.88$$

would be at the 97.5th percentile.

Example 7.6 Inverse normal probability

Consider the demand for diesel fuel for a single day for a delivery truck from the previous example.

$X \sim N(50, 3^2)$. Find the value corresponding to the 90th percentile—in other words, the value that has a 90% probability that the random variable will be less than or equal to it—that is, solve for x such that $P(X \le x) = F(x) = 90\%$.

$$X = 50 + \Phi^{-1}(.90) * 3$$
$$X = 50 + z_{.90} * 3$$
$$X = 50 + 1.281552 * 3$$
$$X = 53.845,$$

where 1.281552 is *interpolated* from a table of standard normal values. Thus, there is a 90% chance that the random variable X will be less than or equal to 53.845. Fig. 7.24 shows the 90th percentile for the standard normal distribution.

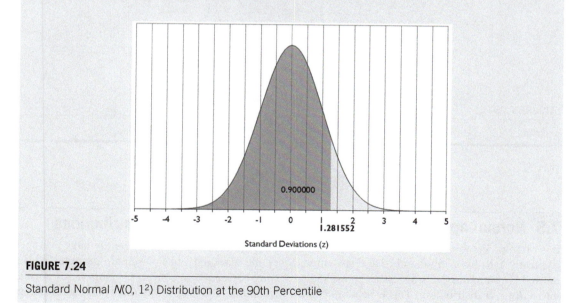

FIGURE 7.24

Standard Normal $N(0, 1^2)$ Distribution at the 90th Percentile

Fig. 7.25 shows that the 90th percentile for a $N(50, 3^2)$ normal distribution is at the same number of standard deviations (z) as the standard normal distribution.

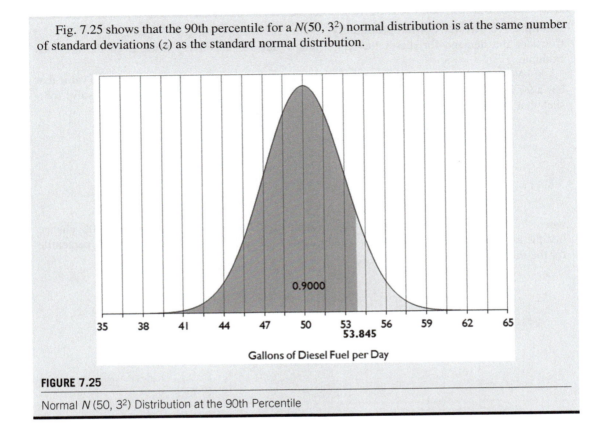

FIGURE 7.25

Normal $N(50, 3^2)$ Distribution at the 90th Percentile

7.5 Normal approximation of the binomial and Poisson distributions

It is often acceptable to estimate binomial or Poisson distributions that have sufficiently large averages (typically ≥ 8) by using the normal distribution. Since the binomial and Poisson are discrete and the normal is continuous, it is necessary to use the *continuity correction* to convert the *continuous* normal into a *discrete* distribution. This is accomplished by computing the probability (area) for each discrete value of x by computing the probability that the random variable X is between $x \pm 0.5$.

$$\begin{aligned} f(X = x) &= P(x - 0.5 \leq X \leq x + 0.5) \\ &= P(X \leq x + 0.5) - P(X \leq x - 0.5) \\ &= F(x + 0.5) - F(x - 0.5) = \Phi(Z_{x+0.5}) - \Phi(Z_{x-0.5}) \end{aligned}$$

Example 7.7 Discrete normal probability approximation of binomial and Poisson distributions

A delivery service has a fleet of 60 trucks. Each day, the probability of a truck being out of use due to factors such as breakdowns or maintenance is 10%.

a. What is the probability that seven or more trucks are out of service at any time?

b. What is the probability that exactly six trucks are out of service?

To use the normal approximation to the binomial distribution, first compute the average and standard deviation for the binomial:

$$\text{Average} = np = 60\,(0.10) = 6$$

$$\text{Standard Deviation} = (npq)^{1/2} = (60\,(0.10)\,(0.90))^{1/2} \cong 2.3238$$

a. $P\,(X \geq 7) = 1 - F\,(6.5) = 1 - \Phi\left(\dfrac{6.5 - 6}{2.3238}\right) = 1 - \Phi\,(0.2152) = 1 - 0.5852$

$\qquad = 0.4148 = \textbf{41.48}\%$ (Binomial $= 39.35\%$)

$\Phi(0.2152) = 0.5852$ is from a table of standard normal values.

Fig. 7.26 shows the probability distribution for part (a) of Example 7.7.

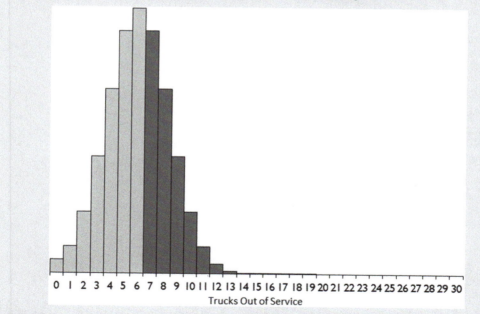

FIGURE 7.26

$(1 - F(6))$ for the Normal Approximation of the Binomial Distribution (60, 0.10)

b. $P(X = 6) = F(6.5) - F(5.5) = \Phi\left(\dfrac{6.5 - 6}{2.3238}\right) - \Phi\left(\dfrac{5.5 - 6}{2.3238}\right)$

$\qquad = \Phi(0.2152) - \Phi(-0.2152)$

$\qquad = 0.5852 - 0.4148 = 0.1704 = \textbf{17.04}\%$ (Binomial $= 16.93\%$)

Fig. 7.27 shows $f(6)$ within the probability distribution for part (b) of Example 7.7.

Note the use of both complementarity (58.52% and 41.48%) and symmetry of the normal distribution ($np = 6$ as the average) to simplify this specific computation.

The binomial distribution solutions are:

a. $P(X \geq 7) = 1 - F(6) = 1 - (f(0) + f(1) + f(2) + f(3) + f(4) + f(5) + f(6)) = 39.35\%$

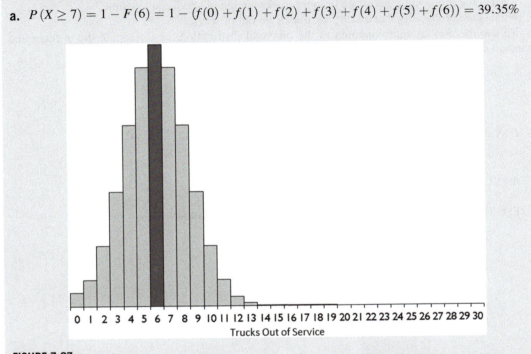

FIGURE 7.27

$f(6)$ for the Binomial Distribution (60, 0.10)

b. $P(X = 6) = f(6) = 60!/(6!((60-6)!))0.10^6 (0.90)^{(60-6)}$

$= 60!/(6!(54!))0.10^6 (0.90)^{54}$

$= (60(59)(58)(57)(56)(55))/(6(5)(4)(3)(2))0.10^6 (0.90)^{(54)}$

$= (59(58)(19)(14)(55))0.10^6 (0.90)^{54}$

$= 0.1693 = \textbf{16.93\%}$

A comparison of the normal approximation and the binomial distributions is shown in Fig. 7.28.

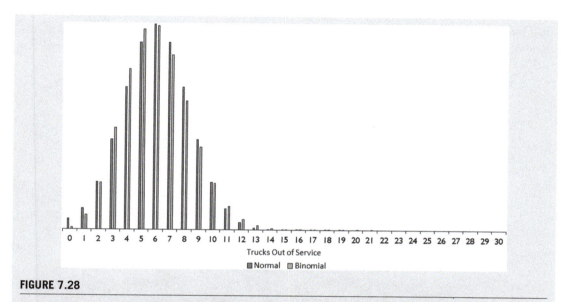

Trucks Out of Service

Normal ▢ Binomial

FIGURE 7.28

Comparison of Normal and Binomial for Example 7.7

Using the normal distribution to approximate a Poisson distribution is similar to using the normal distribution to approximate the binomial distribution, *except* that the variance is equal to the average for the Poisson. In other words, the standard deviation of a Poisson distribution is equal to the square root of the average:

$$\sigma = \sqrt{\lambda}$$

To use the normal approximation to the Poisson distribution, first compute the average and standard deviation for the Poisson:

$$\text{Average} = np = 60(0.10) = 6$$
$$\text{Standard Deviation} = (6)^{1/2} = 2.4495$$

a. $P(X \geq 7) = 1 - F(6.5) = 1 - \Phi\left(\dfrac{6.5 - 6}{2.4495}\right) = 1 - \Phi(0.2041) = 1 - 0.5809 = 0.4191$
$= \mathbf{41.91\%}$ (Poisson $= 39.37\%$)

$\Phi(0.2041) = 0.5809$ is from a table of standard normal probabilities.

b. $P(X = 6) = F(6.5) - F(5.5) = \Phi\left(\dfrac{6.5 - 6}{2.4495}\right) - \Phi\left(\dfrac{5.5 - 6}{2.4495}\right)$
$= \Phi(0.2041) - \Phi(-0.2041)$
$= 0.5809 - 0.4191 = 0.1618 = \mathbf{16.18\%}$ (Poisson $= 16.06\%$)

Note that at an average of 6, probabilities in the distributions are similar; the approximations are much better when the **average is ≥ 8**. The following table shows the discretized normal approximation to the binomial distribution alongside the true values of the comparable binomial and Poisson distributions. Specifically, Fig. 7.29 shows the discretized normal with an average of 6 and a standard deviation of 2.3238, as binomial distribution with $p = 0.10$ and $n = 60$ ($np = 6$ and $(npq)^{1/2} = 2.3238$), and a Poisson with an average of 6 ($\lambda = 6$ and $\sqrt{\lambda} = 2.4495$).

x	Normal $f(x)$	Binomial $f(x)$	Poisson $f(x)$
0	0.0090	0.0018	0.0025
1	0.0174	0.0120	0.0149
2	0.0396	0.0393	0.0446
3	0.0750	0.0844	0.0892
4	0.1183	0.1336	0.1339
5	0.1555	0.1662	0.1606
6	0.1704	0.1693	0.1606
7	0.1555	0.1451	0.1377
8	0.1183	0.1068	0.1033
9	0.0750	0.0686	0.0688
10	0.0396	0.0389	0.0413
11	0.0174	0.0196	0.0225
12	0.0064	0.0089	0.0113
13	0.0020	0.0037	0.0052
14	0.0005	0.0014	0.0022
15	0.0001	0.0005	0.0009
16	0.0000	0.0001	0.0003
17	0.0000	0.0000	0.0001
18	0.0000	0.0000	0.0000
19	0.0000	0.0000	0.0000
20	0.0000	0.0000	0.0000

FIGURE 7.29

Comparison of the Normal, Binomial, and Poisson Distributions With Average = 6

7.6 Using distributions in decision analysis

Often, using the normal distribution for decision analysis requires using discrete probabilities for each branch of a random event node. Thus, when using a normal distribution, it might be necessary to compute a discrete version of the normal distribution. This is accomplished in the same manner as the continuity correction of the normal distribution to approximate the binomial or Poisson distributions shown in the previous example. Compute the probability (area) for each discrete value of x by computing the probability that the random variable X is between $x \pm 0.5$ units of each integer:

$$f(X = x) = P(x - 0.5 \leq X \leq x + 0.5)$$
$$= P(X \leq x + 0.5) - P(X \leq x - 0.5)$$
$$= F(x + 0.5) - F(x - 0.5) = \Phi(z_{x+.05}) - \Phi(z_{x-.05})$$

Example 7.8 Decision tree with continuous normal probability: bidding

A company is bidding to supply computer servers to a large bank. The company expects the competitors' bids to be normally distributed with an average of $2,500,000 and a standard deviation of $350,000. If the company wins the bid, it will cost the company $2,165,000 to supply the servers to the bank.

Because the client (the bank) wants the least expensive computer servers, this is a *low bid wins* situation. Given a *bid*, the expected value of that bid is:

$$EV\,(bid) = P\,(\text{win} \mid bid) * (bid - cost) + (1 - P\,(\text{win} \mid bid)) *0$$
$$= P\,(\text{win} \mid bid) * (bid - cost)$$

Note that in a *low bid wins* setting, the P(win|bid) is the right (upper) tail of the distribution.

$$EV\,(bid) = (1 - \Phi(z\,(bid))) * (bid - cost)$$
$$= (1 - \Phi((bid - average)/sd) * (bid - cost)$$

Because the normal distribution is symmetric:

$$EV\,(bid) = \Phi\,(- (bid - average)/sd) * (bid - cost)$$
$$= \Phi\,((average - bid)/sd) * (bid - cost)$$

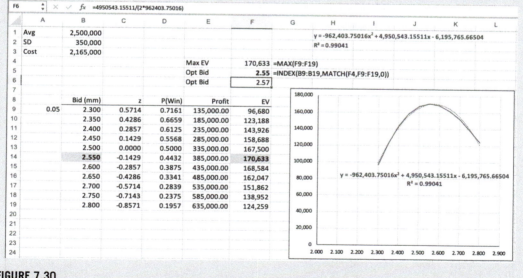

FIGURE 7.30

Expected Value Calculations for the Decision Tree for the Bidding Example

The spreadsheet with the expected value calculations is shown in Fig. 7.30.

A simulation model is enlightening to better understand the risk and rewards. In this simulation model, a single simulation trial consists of a single competitor's bid in which the bid comes is generated from a normal distribution with an average of $2500 (in thousands) and a standard deviation of $350 (also in thousands). The Excel formula to simulate the competitor's bid is:

$$= Avg\_Bid + NORM.S.INV\,(RAND\,()) * SD\_Bid \tag{7.9}$$

In this formula, *Avg_Bid* and *SD_Bid* are named ranges for the average and standard deviation, respectively, of the competitors' bids. The NORM.S.INV(RAND()) portion of the formula creates a random *z-score* corresponding to the random percentile resulting from the RAND() function. For example, if the RAND() generates a value of 0.84134, then the resulting *z-score* is 1.000 and the resulting bid is 2500 + (1)*350 (in thousands of dollars). The simulation is shown in Fig. 7.31.

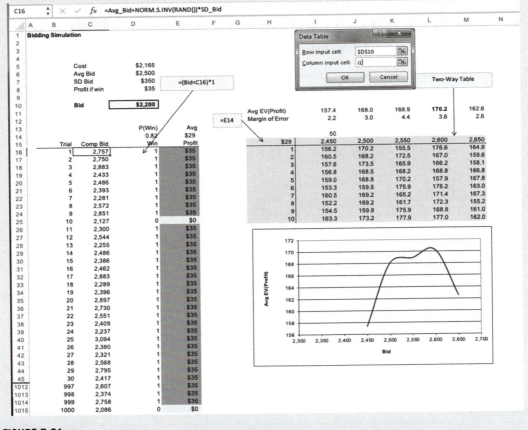

FIGURE 7.31

Spreadsheet Simulation of the Bidding Example

Because this problem is a *low bid wins* problem, the decision variable, **Bid**, was initialized at a values below average to win the bid more than 50%. Thus, **2200** (in thousands of dollars) was a starting point. The average competitors' bid of **2,500,000** would work as an initial value, but it would not indicate which tail was the appropriate winning tail of the distribution. The Two-Way Data Table is used to determine the optimum bid by running 10 sets of trials (10 *runs*) for each potential **Bid**. The initial value of

$2,200,000 can then be replaced by the optimum **Bid** to examine the simulation at that specific **Bid** ($2,600,000). As in the previous example, multiple regression could also be used to determine the optimum **Bid** by using $AvgEV(Profit)$ as the Y variable and using **Bid** and **Bid**^{2} as the X variables.

Example 7.9 Discrete normal probability for decision trees

Demand for hotel rooms of a specific day and category is approximately normally distributed with a mean of 50 and a standard deviation of 3 ($X \sim N(50, 3^2)$). The hotel has 56 rooms available.

a. Calculate the service level.

$$P(X \leq 56) = F(56.5)$$
$$= \Phi\left(\frac{56.5 - 50}{3}\right) \quad \text{(from a table of standard normal values).}$$
$$= \Phi(2.1667)$$
$$= 0.9849 = \mathbf{98.49\%}$$

b. Calculate the probability that this random variable will be equal to 56—that is, find $P(X \leq 56)$.

$$P(X = 56) = f(56)$$
$$= F(56.5) - F(55.5)$$
$$= \Phi\left(\frac{56.5 - 50}{3}\right) - \Phi\left(\frac{55.5 - 50}{3}\right)$$
$$= \Phi(2.1667) - \Phi(1.8333)$$
$$= 0.9849 - .9666 \quad \text{(from a table of standard normal values)}$$
$$= 0.0183 = \mathbf{1.83\%}$$

Thus, for a decision tree with discrete branches, each branch requires the discrete probability approximation using the continuity correction method. In other words, each bar (probability) of the distribution shown in the following graph (Fig. 7.32) would be computed in a similar manner.

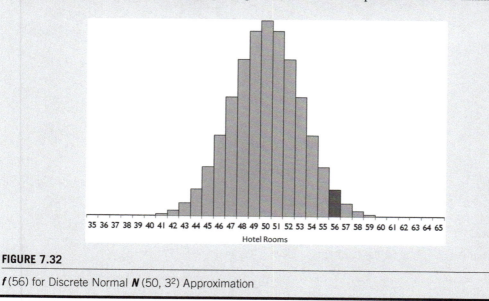

35 36 37 38 39 40 41 42 43 44 45 46 47 48 49 50 51 52 53 54 55 56 57 58 59 60 61 62 63 64 65

Hotel Rooms

FIGURE 7.32

$f(56)$ for Discrete Normal $N(50, 3^2)$ Approximation

Example 7.10 Decision tree with discrete normal probability

On Friday evening, the manager of a small branch of a car rental agency finds that she has four cars available for rental on the following day. However, she can request delivery of additional cars, at a cost of $25 each, from the regional depot. Each car that is rented produces an expected profit of $65 (not including the $25 of delivery cost if incurred). After reviewing records for previous Saturdays, the manager finds that the average number of cars requested on previous Fridays is 11 with a standard deviation of 3.32. How many cars should be ordered?

The abbreviated decision tree is shown in Fig. 7.33.

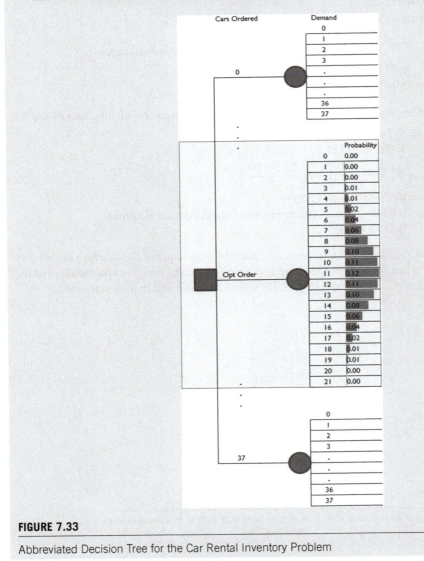

FIGURE 7.33

Abbreviated Decision Tree for the Car Rental Inventory Problem

The distribution of demand is shown in Fig. 7.34 (assuming that the demand is normally distributed).

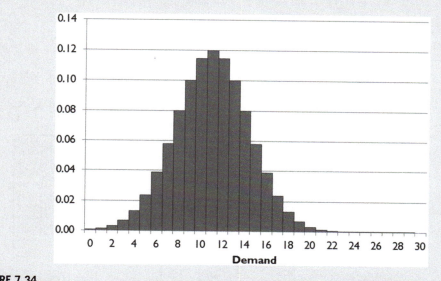

FIGURE 7.34

Normal $N(11, 3.32^2)$ Distribution of Demand

The spreadsheet shown in Fig. 7.35 is constructed to calculate one decision branch with a single random demand—representing the portion of the generalized decision tree shown in Fig. 7.33. The components of the spreadsheet are:

1. Cost structure.
2. Decision variable (how many cars to order).
3. Range of outcomes (demand) and their associated probabilities (see the previous example for calculating the probability of a single branch) and end values (monetary outcomes).
4. Expected value for the single decision branch as a result of all the outcomes.
5. One-Way Table to calculate each decision branch. This is used to determine the optimum decision—the decision corresponding to the maximum expected value. The column numbers are the number of cars to order and are plugged into the decision variable.

Fig. 7.35 shows the components of a spreadsheet used to compute the optimum order quantity for the car rental in Example 7.10.

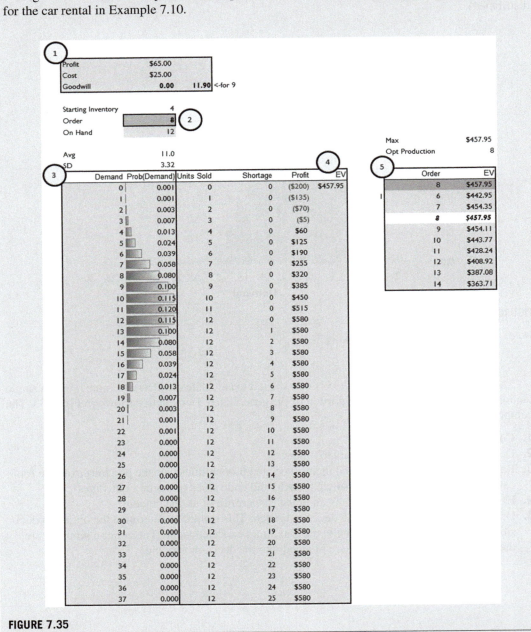

FIGURE 7.35

Spreadsheet Components for the Decision Tree of the Car Rental Inventory Problem

The spreadsheet in Fig. 7.36 shows how this decision can be estimated using simulation.

B15   fx =ROUND(Avg+NORM.S.INV(RAND())*SD,0)

COST STRUCTURE

Profit	$65.00
Cost	$25.00
Goodwill	$0.00
Beginning Inv.	4
Ordered	8
TVC	$200.00
On Hand	12

SIMULATION PROBABILITIES AND VALIDATI

	Theory	Simulation
Avg	11.00	11.02
SD	3.32	3.31

OPTIMIZATION

Max Profit	$360.27
Opt Order	12

	Order	Avg Profit	Margin of Error
	8	299.92	3.62
Current	9	323.93	4.97
	10	343.00	6.62
	11	347.25	8.18
	12	360.27	8.89
	13	350.68	10.49
	14	345.37	11.30
	15	329.80	11.94
	16	311.56	12.51
	17	282.85	13.10

SIMULATION

Averages: 11.02   3.33   0.31 $299.92

Margin of Error = $3.62

Trial	Demand	Units Sold	Shortage	Extra	Profit
1	8	8	0	0	$320.00
2	10	8	2	0	$320.00
3	14	8	6	0	$320.00
4	12	8	4	0	$320.00
5	7	7	0	1	$255.00
6	9	8	1	0	$320.00
7	18	8	10	0	$320.00
8	14	8	6	0	$320.00
9	11	8	3	0	$320.00
10	3	3	0	5	($5.00)
11	10	8	2	0	$320.00
12	8	8	0	0	$320.00
13	9	8	1	0	$320.00
14	10	8	2	0	$320.00
15	20	8	12	0	$320.00
16	12	8	4	0	$320.00
17	13	8	5	0	$320.00
18	12	8	4	0	$320.00
995	11	8	3	0	$320.00
996	13	8	5	0	$320.00
997	10	8	2	0	$320.00
998	15	8	7	0	$320.00
999	12	8	4	0	$320.00
1000	15	8	7	0	$320.00

FIGURE 7.36

Spreadsheet Simulation of the Car Rental Inventory Problem

Note that the optimum order amount of 11 is not the same thing as the average demand of 11 or the current simulation value of On Hand = 11. The order amount of 11 results in 15 cars on hand awaiting an average demand of 11.

How would the problem solution change if demand followed a Poisson distribution rather than the normal distribution? You should rerun this simulation with a *Poisson* distribution with an average of 11 and note the advantages and disadvantages of using *normal* or *Poisson* distributions.

7.7 Overview of probability distributions

Brief descriptions of the probability distributions discussed in this book are listed in Table 7.2.

Table 7.2 Properties of Common Probability Distributions

Distribution continuous/discrete (c/d)	Description	$f(x)$	Mean & SD	Distribution
1. **TRIANGULAR** c	Subjective estimate from minimum, maximum, and most likely		$(a + b + c)/3$ $((a^2 + b^2 + c^2 - ab - ac - bc)/6)^{.5}$	a c b
2. **QUARTILE** c	Subjective estimate based on Median, Min, Max, and Quartiles		n.a.	
3. **EMPIRICAL** c/d (Historical)	Collected data that doesn't fit a known distribution	$F(x) = \frac{\#x \leq X}{n}$	$\bar{X}$ sd	
4. **UNIFORM** c/d	No information—all events are equally likely	$1/(b - a)$ $1/(b - a + 1)$	$(a + b)/2$ $(b - a)/\sqrt{12}$	a b a b
5. **BINOMIAL** d	Two events—number of successes → proportion	$\frac{n!}{x!(n-x)!}p^x q^{(n-x)}$	np $\sqrt{np(1 - p)}$	
6. **POISSON** d	Number of events (occurrences) in a given amount of time	$\frac{e^{-\lambda}\lambda^x}{x!}$	λ(events/time) $\sqrt{\lambda}$	
7. **EXPONENTIAL** c	Time between events (occurrences)— frequently service/processing time	$\lambda e^{-\lambda x}$	$1/\lambda$(time/event) $1/\lambda$	
8. **NORMAL** c	Symmetric about mean—one "bump"— distribution of sums and averages	$\frac{1}{\sigma\sqrt{2\pi}}e^{-\frac{1}{2}\left(\frac{x-\mu}{\sigma}\right)}$	$\bar{x} = \mu$ sd $= \sigma$	

Run the numbers, then buy the RED one.

Exercise Set 7: Theoretical Probability Distributions

Check each exercise with simulation where possible.

Discrete theoretical distributions

1. Monthly demand for a particular model of car at a car dealership is uniformly distributed between 0 and 20.
   a. Write the probability function, $f(x)$, for this random variable. Is it a *pmf* or a *pdf*?
   b. What are the average and standard deviation? What is the managerial interpretation of these?
   c. What is the probability that demand will be 10 cars?
   d. What is the probability of a shortage if the dealer has 10 cars on the lot?
   e. What is the probability that demand will be between 10 and 15 cars?
   f. What other information would be required to determine how many cars for the dealer to order?
   g. What would happen to this distribution if the sales price for the cars changes? What will happen to the distribution if the dealer has a promotion and/or advertises?

2. What is the probability distribution for the number of heads resulting from flipping 10 pennies? What is the probability distribution for the number of heads resulting from flipping 100 pennies?

3. As a sales promotion, a soft drink manufacturer places winning symbols under the caps of 10% of all soft drink bottles. You buy a six-pack of soft drinks. What is the probability that you will win a prize?

4. Suppose you roll a single six-sided die (D-6) and then flip that number of pennies.
   a. Compute the probability of each outcome.
   b. Construct a simulation to estimate the probability of each outcome.
   c. Compare the simulation probabilities (empirical) to the theoretical probabilities.

5. Two basketball teams are playing a best-of-seven championship series. One team has a 60% chance of winning any single game. Assume that the games are independent (hmm?). What is the probability that the team with the better single-game probability wins the series?

6. Demand for a specific model of car at a car dealership is Poisson with an average of four per month.
   a. What is the probability of not selling any of this model during a month?
   b. What is the probability of selling more than three of this model during a month?

7. Assume that about 95% of the people who purchase tickets on a particular flight show up for the flight. Thus, airlines often make more reservations than the airplane will hold. A small commuter jet has a capacity of 10 seats. Twelve tickets have been sold for this flight.
   a. What is the probability of one empty seat?
   b. What is the probability that the flight is full?
   c. What is the probability that there will be ticket holders without a seat (overbooking)?
   d. How does (c) change as the number of tickets sold varies from 10 to 15 and as the probability of no show varies from 5% to 15%?

8. An analyst for a propane company has analyzed demand for tanks of propane over the previous 5 years and noted a strong rise in demand during months in which there are severe storms (hurricanes, tornados, etc.) due to people without power using propane to cook and heat with propane. Furthermore, the analyst has noted that in one region the probability of a severe storm is approximately 10% each month.
   a. Assuming a binomial distribution, what is the probability of no storms in that region in a year?
   b. Assuming a binomial distribution, what is the probability of more than one storm in that region in a year?

   c. Assuming a Poisson distribution, what is the probability of no storms in that region in a year?

   d. Assuming a Poisson distribution, what is the probability of more than one storm in that region in a year?

9. An insurance company has introduced a policy that covers manufacturing companies for a specific injury to its line workers. The probability of a worker having this injury is 1 in 1000. The company has 12 workers.

   a. Why is the normal approximation not appropriate?

   b. What is the probability that there will be an injury?

   c. What is the probability of more than two injuries?

10. An online commerce site receives an average of six orders per minute. Assume orders arrive in a Poisson manner.

   a. Use simulation to compute the following probabilities: $P(\text{Orders} = 6)$, $P(\text{Orders} > 6)$, $P(\text{Orders} < 6)$.

   b. Determine the average transaction time and average waiting time for an order assuming an exponential service time of 8 seconds per order. See Appendix A1.3 for the formula to simulate an exponential random variable.

11. A consulting firm has an average of six new contracts of a specific type of project per month.

   a. What is the probability of not obtaining any new projects of this type during a month?

   b. What is the probability of obtaining five or six projects in a month?

   c. What is the probability of obtaining more than four projects in a month?

12. A FedEx contractor owns 50 trucks in a region. Twenty of the trucks are relatively new, and each of these trucks has a 5% chance of not being in service on any day. Ten trucks are older and only have a 90% chance of being in service on any day. Twenty trucks are much older and have a 20% chance of not being in service on any day.

   a. The contractor needs 40 trucks to deliver packages tomorrow. What is the probability that the contractor will have enough trucks?

   b. Is the number of trucks in service normally distributed? Why or why not?

Continuous theoretical distributions

13. Interpolation: The marketing department of a clothing retailer produces mail order catalogs and is evaluating the effectiveness of their mailings. The following table gives the number of catalogs mailed out and the sales corresponding to those catalogs.

Catalogs (thousands)	Sales (thousands of dollars)
5	50
10	125
15	170
20	200
25	215
30	230
35	245
40	250

   a. What sales would be expected from mailing 22,500 catalogs?

   b. What sales would be expected from mailing 34,000 catalogs?

    c. How many catalogs would be needed to generate approximately $220,000?

    d. How many catalogs should be mailed?

14. A contractor regards the cost of satisfying a particular contract as having a normal probability distribution with a mean of $500,000 and a standard deviation of $50,000.

    a. There is a 95% chance that the cost will be between what two values?

    b. What is the probability that the cost will be within 5% of the expected cost?

    c. What is the probability that the cost will be greater than $450,000?

    d. There is a 75% chance that the cost will be less than what value?

15. A manager must estimate a budget for the upcoming planning period. The manager has forecast the expenditures for a particular department to be $1,250,000. Based on past data, deviations from the budget are known to follow a normal probability distribution with a mean of 0% and a standard deviation of 5%.

    a. There is a 95% chance that expenditures will be between what two values?

    b. What is the probability that expenditures will be greater than $1.32 million?

    c. What is the probability that expenditures will be greater than $1.4 million?

    d. There is a 75% chance that expenditures will be less than what value?

16. A plant that bottles propane used for grilling uses an average of 125,000 ft.^{3} of propane a day with a standard deviation of 15,000 ft.^{3}

    a. What is the probability that production for a day will exceed 135,000?

    b. What daily capacity would satisfy daily production 95% of the time?

    c. What is the probability that production for a day will be less than 120,000?

17. Demand for a particular SKU of khaki pants at an online/catalog retailer is forecasted to be normally distributed with a mean of 1200 units per month and a standard deviation of 100 units per month.

    a. What is the probability that demand will exceed 1000 units next month?

    b. What is the probability of shortage if 1050 units are produced?

    c. How many units should be produced for a 90% service level (a 10% chance of not meeting demand)?

    d. What production level would result in a 70% chance of stocking out (incurring a shortage)? Under what conditions would such a policy be useful?

18. A company is bidding to supply computer servers to a large bank. The company expects the competitors' bids to be normally distributed with an average of $2,500,000 and a standard deviation $350,000.

    a. What is the probability of winning if you bid $3,000,000?

    b. What is the probability of losing if you bid $2,000,000?

    c. What is the probability of winning if you bid $1,850,000?

    d. What is the appropriate bid to have a 75% probability of winning the bid?

    e. What is the appropriate bid to have a 95% probability of winning the bid?

19. A supplier of trees to home and garden/hardware chains claims that 90% of the supplier's dogwood trees survive the first year.

    a. What is the probability distribution for the survival of a single tree?

    b. What is the probability distribution for the number of trees surviving from a batch of 250 trees?

    c. What is the probability of at least 230 trees surviving from a batch of 250 trees?

    d. What is the probability distribution for the percentage of trees surviving from a batch of 250 trees?

20. An oil company purchases crude oil for use to manufacture gasoline by bidding in a commodities market. Currently, bids for crude oil are normally distributed with an average of $68.15 per barrel with a standard deviation of $1.75.
  a. What is the probability of winning if you bid $68.00?
  b. What is the probability of losing if you bid $67.50?
  c. What is the probability of winning if you bid $68.90?
  d. What bid will result in an 80% chance of winning the bid?

21. A manufacturer of air compressors examines the quality of the finish for blemishes that do not affect the performance (superficial blemishes). Units with such blemishes are sold at a discount. The motor housings for compressors have a 2% rate of superficial blemishes. What is the probability that 4 or more compressors in a batch of 500 compressors have superficial blemishes?

22. Assume that about 5% of the people who make airline reservations on a particular flight do not show up for the flight. Thus, airlines often make more reservations than the airplane will hold. If the airplane holds 100 passengers, how many reservations can the airline make and still be 90% sure that everyone who shows up for the flight with reservations can be accommodated?

23. An insurance company has introduced a policy that covers certain forms of personal injury with the standard payment of $100,000. The yearly premium for the policy is $25. On average 100 claims per year lead to payment. There are more than 1 million policyholders. What is the probability that more than $12 million will have to be paid out in a year?

Decision models using theoretical probability distributions

24. It is uncertain as to what a competitor will bid on an upcoming contract to supply parts to an aircraft manufacturer. The bid is almost certain to be between $250,000 and $300,000.
  a. Write the probability function, $f(x)$, for this random variable. Is it a *pmf* or a *pdf*?
  b. What are the average and standard deviation? What is the managerial interpretation of these?
  c. What is the probability that the competitor's bid will be less than $280,000?
  d. What is the probability of a winning the bid if you bid $255,000?
  e. Suppose your cost to fulfill the contract if you win is $245,000. What is the optimum bid?

25. A company is bidding to supply parts to a computer manufacturer. The competitor's bids are estimated to be normally distributed with an average of $260,000 and a standard deviation of $15,000. If the bid is won, the total cost of completing the order is $185,000.
  a. Calculate the optimum bid using a decision tree.
  b. Construct a simulation to determine the optimum bid.
  c. Why is a fixed markup an inappropriate pricing strategy? Is "we match anyone's price" an appropriate pricing strategy?

26. A company is bidding to supply computer servers to a large bank. The company expects the competitors' bids to be normally distributed with an average of $2,500,000 and a standard deviation $350,000. If the bid is won, the total cost of completing the order is $1,850,000.
  a. Calculate the optimum bid using a decision tree.
  b. Construct a simulation to determine the optimum bid.

27. Once prices and restrictions have been determined for a specific flight, it is revenue management's responsibility to determine the number of seats available in each fare category. An aircraft seat for a particular flight is a highly perishable commodity; once the plane takes off, the unsold product is lost forever. The challenge in yield management is to optimize the trade-off between the cost of an empty seat (the lost discount fare) and the cost of turning away a full-fare passenger (the difference between full and discount fare). As an example, consider the following problem. An aircraft has 100 seats, and there are two types of fares: full ($500) and discount ($320). Although there is unlimited demand for discount fares, demand for full fares is equally likely anywhere between 10 and 30.

   a. How many seats should be protected for full-fare passengers (what is the "booking" limit—the maximum number of discount tickets to be sold)?

   b. Resolve the problem with demand for full-fare seats being normally distributed with an average of 20 seats and a standard deviation of 5 seats.

   c. How would you solve this problem if you had historical data?

28. An online/catalog retailer will sell Adirondack chairs this season. The retailer purchases the chairs from a supplier at a cost of $175 and will sell them for $250. Demand has been forecasted to be 2000 chairs this season with a standard deviation of 10%. At the end of the season, the company will have a half-off sale to clear out the inventory. Determine the optimum number of chairs to order.

   a. Construct a decision tree to determine how many chairs the retailer should order. Is it the average demand? Why or why not?

   b. Construct a simulation to determine how many chairs the retailer should order.

   c. Graph the distribution of demand to validate the probability distribution.

   d. Assume a triangular distribution ± 3 standard deviations. Did the change in the probability distribution of demand change the solution? If so, then how and why?

29. Triangle Developers is a commercial land developer that specializes in building shopping centers and wants to develop land near Charleston, South Carolina. Triangle expects that the net present value (~ profit over time in today's dollars) without the cost of the land will be $65,000,000. In other words, after considering the time value of money without the cost of land (i.e., accounting for discounting the future cash flows except for the cost of the parcel of land), they will make $65,000,000 in profit—not counting the cost of the land. There is a parcel of land that has been appraised for $42,000,000, and several other developers are vying for the same property. Colonial has bid against several of the companies many times before and estimates the bids to average $42,000,000 with a standard deviation of approximately 10% of the average (i.e., CV is 10%).

   a. Calculate the optimum bid using a decision tree.

   b. Construct a simulation to determine the optimum bid.

30. Demand for a perishable product is estimated to have a normally distribution distributed with a mean of 336 units per week and a standard deviation of 48 units. The unit variable cost is $36.

   a. How many units should be ordered if price = $40?

   b. How many units should be ordered if price = $72?

   c. How many units should be ordered if price = $62?

   d. What price is needed to justify ordering 415 units? What would happen to the distribution of demand?

31. A buyer for a direct mail (catalog) merchant is trying to decide how many sweaters of a particular SKU should be purchased for the upcoming season. The cost of the sweater to the merchant is $30.00 and it sells for $58.95. Sweaters not sold during the upcoming season are sold at a 50% discount (from the selling price). The buyer's forecast for demand is 680 sweaters for the season. The forecasting errors are normally distributed with an average of 0 and a standard deviation of 85 sweaters for the season.

   a. In practical terms, what happens to the stock level (the amount to buy) as the price goes up? Why?

   b. What would the selling price have to be (keeping all other data the same) to justify ordering 680 sweaters?

32. On Friday evening, the manager of a small branch of a car rental agency finds that she has five cars available for rental on the following day. However, she is able to request delivery of additional cars, at a cost of $35 each, from the regional depot. Each car that is rented produces an expected profit of $75 (not including the $35 of delivery cost if incurred). After reviewing records for previous Saturdays, the manager finds that the average number of cars requested on previous Fridays is 25. How many cars should be ordered if demand is Poisson? How many cars should be ordered if demand is normally distributed?

33. A local dairy supplies 15 local restaurants with ice cream for their desserts each week. Each week, on average, 30% of the restaurants order a gallon of vanilla ice cream. The ice cream is produced once a week before orders are taken and cannot be stored for longer than a week (unsold ice cream must be discarded). How much ice cream should be produced each week if the selling price to restaurants is $15 per gallon and the cost to the dairy is $9 per gallon?

34. Weekly demand (order size in gallons) for milk at a dairy is normally distributed with an average demand of 1250 gallons and a standard deviation of 150 gallons. How much milk should be produced each week if the selling price to grocery stores is $1.85 per gallon and the cost to the dairy is $0.65 per gallon?

35. A tire manufacturer has a contract with a large rental fleet of cars. The manufacturer guarantees tread-life. If a tire fails before the guaranteed number of miles, the company offers a $1.25 refund for every 1000 miles less than guaranteed. The unit contribution of a tire is $0.50 per 1000 miles. The tread-life of the tire under consideration is approximately normally distributed with an average of 22,267 miles with a standard deviation of 2104 miles. What number of miles should the manufacturer guarantee?

36. A local dairy manufactures ice cream as part of its operations. It supplies ice cream to 75 local restaurants. The dairy makes a 5-gallon size of ice cream for these restaurants. Fifteen of these restaurants are frequent customers and order ice cream about 60% of the time (about 6 out of 10 days). Thirty of the 75 restaurants are less frequent customers and order ice cream about 35% of the time. The remaining 30 restaurants are infrequent customers and order ice cream about 10% of the time. It costs the dairy $6.25 to make the 5 gallons of ice cream. In turn, they sell the 5 gallons for $25.00.

   a. What does the distribution of demand look like?

   b. What is the average demand? What is the standard deviation, and what does standard deviation mean?

c. Calculate the optimum number of 5-gallon units to produce. Is it the average demand?
d. Calculate the optimum service level.
e. Calculate the optimum expected value resulting from the optimum production.
f. How would changes in price affect demand?

37. Demand for a particular model of rental car is approximately normally distributed with an average of 370 units per day and a standard deviation of 64 units per day. The rental price for these cars is $85, the variable cost is $25 per day, and the fixed cost is $8200 per day. What is the optimum number of cars for the rental company to own?

38. A soft drink distributor owns 20 trucks that have a 90% chance of being in service on any day. New trucks have a 2% chance of being out of service (not available for deliveries) on any day. Demand for deliveries is forecasted to be normal with an average of 30 truckloads per day and a standard deviation of 5 truckloads per day. If there is a shortage of trucks, the contractor must lease a truck for the day at a cost of $225 per day. New trucks cost $65,000, and as such, the cost of an idle truck is a function of opportunity cost and other similar factors and can be estimated using an 18% APR. Determine the number of new trucks the distributor should purchase.

39. A convention with 1200 attendees is scheduled to take place in November in Boston. At a price of $450, approximately 480 attendees will stay at the convention hotel. Based on previous demand data analysis, a $20 price change results in a 15% change in demand. Based upon the market value and opportunity cost of the square footage, the rooms have a variable cost of $260. The rooms also have a shortage cost (of turning away a booking) of $230 per guest turned away (this amount is determined by the profit of a room and the profit associated with the average profit from food and drinks per room).

a. Calculate the optimum price and demand without consideration for the uncertainty of demand.
b. Calculate the optimum price and demand assuming a normal with a standard deviation of 10%.
c. Why is part (b) necessary? Why can you *not* just do part (a) to get the price and quantity? What does part (b) take into account that part (a) does not?

40. Demand for a specific $1000 passenger cruise booking is 1000 passengers. A $50 price change results in a 10% change in demand. Fixed cost of operating the ship is $250,000, and the variable cost for a single passenger is $375. Due to the average amount of profits for a booking due to food, drinks, gift shop items, and so forth during a cruise, the cost of not being able to book a room for a passenger (shortage cost) is approximately $1500.

a. Calculate the optimum price and demand without consideration for the uncertainty of demand.
b. Calculate the optimum price and demand assuming a normal with a standard deviation of 10%.
c. Why is part (b) necessary? In other words, why can you *not* just do part (a) to get the price and quantity? What does part (b) take into account that part (a) does not?

Cases

Blue Eagle Propane

Blue Eagle Propane gas tanks provide portable fuel for barbecue grills, outdoor space heaters, fire pits, natural gas genera-tors, and gas lights. The company needs a fleet of 80 trucks to meet deliveries for a particular region. Due to maintenance and repair, the trucks each have an 8.5% chance of being out of service on any given day.

The current director of operations for the region is Noah Wayne Hellman. Mr. Hellman received his MBA from a mid-tier university. He has estimated that 88 trucks should be a sufficient number of trucks to meet demand. You have been getting feedback from delivery operations that the drivers are frustrated that there are often not enough trucks to meet the delivery schedule. It has been determined, based upon the cost of delayed delivery and idle trucks, that a 92.5% service for any given day is the optimum service level.

Craven Aerospace

Craven Aerospace Inc. is an electronics firm that produces a variety of electrical components, which are used as parts in the manufacture of commercial aircraft. Its business has grown to a sales level of $750,000,000 per year.

Most of the components produced by Craven make use of parts with common designs. The specifications of the parts, in fact, are quite flexible, and it is common practice for the Craven purchasing agent, Grace King, to search for good buys on batches of the components. Quite frequently, Ms. King has been able to purchase batches of components that have been classified as rejects by the Operations Division of Northern Light Manufacturing Company. These batches generally contain a high percentage of circuits that are useable by Craven. Northern Light always sells these rejects in the same way. A list is kept of purchasing agents who will buy parts with specific characteristics; these purchasing agents are e-mailed and informed when a batch of potential interest is available. If interested, each purchasing agent makes a sealed bid and Northern Light sells the batch of components to the winner.

Ms. King has recently been informed of the availability of a batch of 100 circuits identified by Northern Light as Q314R. Over the past 2 years, Ms. King has bid on 15 previous 100-unit batches of these circuits. In every case, a company called *Sonarscan* has bid on the components as well. Sonarscan makes depth-sounding gear for yachting and deep-sea fishing.

The Northern Light salesman, Robert Sonnberg, always supplies an estimate of the yield of good parts in each batch. It is in his best interest to supply a conservative estimate, since, in the long run, his ability to sell depends on providing his customers with at least as many units as he estimates. Table 7.3 shows his estimates of the yield and what the winning bid turned out to be in the 15 situations in the past when Craven made a bid. The bids that were won by Craven are marked with an asterisk.

Table 7.3 Yield estimates and winning bids

Estimate of Yield (%)	Winning Bid ($)	Estimate of Yield (%)	Winning Bid ($)
80	2425	80	2375
90	2750*	90	2750*
70	2075	80	2400
80	2350	70	2075
80	2425	70	2125
90	2775*	90	2725*
70	2100	80	2375
70	2150		

Case—cont'd

For the current batch, Mr. Sonnberg estimates the yield to be 90%. Coincidentally, in each of the past situations where Mr. Sonnberg had estimated a 90% yield, it turned out that Craven had won the bid, so the actual yields were known. Based on past situations where Mr. Sonnberg had estimated a 90% yield and Craven had won the bid, Ms. King estimated that half the time the actual yields were above 93%. Furthermore, she estimated that two-thirds of the actual yields were between 91% and 95% and that the actual yields were approximately normal in their distribution.

With the information from Northern Light on the characteristics of item MATS314Q, the engineering department has informed Ms. King that Craven can use the item now. They have received a contract to supply 25 pressure sensing and control devices, each of which would require four of these circuits.

For Craven to manufacture the same circuit by regular methods, the cost would be $750 for setup plus a cost of $31 per unit produced. Northern Light's price for tested and guaranteed MATS314Q's in quantities of 200 or less is $55 each. Craven does not carry these circuits in inventory.

With this data, Ms. King is about to make her analysis and determine what to bid. As she looks over the data on the past bid, she remarks to her assistant, "It looks to me as if the Sonarscan people are bidding about $30 per good unit. From what I know of their use of this circuit, their yield of good items should be about the same as ours."

Simulation accuracy: central limit theorem and sampling

Is the difference significant?

Chapter outline

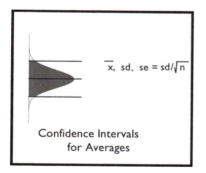

FIGURE 8.1

Confidence Intervals for Proportions

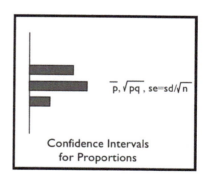

FIGURE 8.2

Confidence Intervals for Means

Introduction

By introducing the central limit theorem, this chapter marks the subtle transition from the subject of probability into that of statistics. Statistics is the science of using data to determine if probabilities are

Introduction to Business Analytics Using Simulation. https://doi.org/10.1016/B978-0-323-91717-9.00008-5

209

statistically significantly different. Stated in another way, statistics determines whether factors, such as region, price, or weather, affect probability distributions. As an example, recall the medical treatment example from Chapter 1. Statistical procedures can determine the likelihood that the medical treatments *are*—or *are not*—statistically significantly different.

Nearly all data analysis involves using the information gathered from a *sample* to ascertain conclusions about the population from which the sample was taken. The mathematical data requisites for using the central limit theorem to calculate *confidence intervals* and *hypothesis tests* are presented, along with examples, in this chapter.

8.1 Introduction to sampling and the margin of error

Undoubtedly you have witnessed the average profit vary within one of the many simulations that have been discussed so far in this book. You have probably wondered *how much could that average have varied,* or *how close is this average to the real answer.* The formula for *margin of error* was presented in Chapters 3 and 7 to provide a measure of the accuracy of the simulations' results (e.g., a probability or an average profit). The statistical tools of **sampling, hypothesis testing**, and **confidence intervals** are founded on the concept of the margin of error and are discussed and demonstrated in this chapter.

Not only are *sampling, hypothesis testing*, and *confidence intervals* essential skills simulation; they are essential for all data analysis. More specifically, these tools are required in the areas of marketing research, operations management, quality control, financial analysis, and human resource management. A deep understanding of hypothesis testing and confidence intervals begins with explanation of what happens when probability distributions are added together.

8.2 Linear properties of probability distributions

Prior to learning the mathematics of adding probability distributions, the mathematical effects of adding and/or multiplying a random variable's outcomes by a constant must be explained. These effects are necessary to distinguish the important difference between mathematically transforming a single random variable and adding random variables.

Recall from Chapter 4 that a **random variable** is a set of uncertain outcomes, resulting from an event of a random process. The set of probabilities (likelihoods) of all outcomes of the random variable is called a **probability distribution**.

Adding a constant c to all outcomes will shift all the outcomes by that constant. For example, adding 2 to the result of a single roll of a six-sided die (D-6) will shift the discrete uniform distribution up by 2: from [1, 2, 3, 4, 5, 6] to [3, 4, 5, 6, 7, 8]. Note that the shape and range of the distribution are unchanged. Thus, the average is shifted by the constant, but the standard deviation and variance are unaffected:

$$\text{Avg}_{X+c} = \text{Avg}_X + c$$

$$\text{Var}_{X+c} = \text{Var}_X$$

$$\text{SD}_{X+c} = \text{SD}_X,$$

where X is a random variable with its associated probability distribution and c is a constant.

Multiplying a random variable by a constant c will multiply each of the outcomes by c but not change the number of outcomes. For example, if you multiply the result of a single roll of a six-sided die (D-6) by 2, the outcomes of the discrete uniform distribution will *rescale proportionately* by 2: from [1, 2, 3, 4, 5, 6] to [2, 4, 6, 8, 10, 12]. Note that the shape of the distribution is unchanged, but the range has been changed. Thus, the average and the standard deviation are multiplied by the constant:

$$Avg_{cX} = c*Avg_X$$

$$SD_{cX} = c*SD_X$$

As an example, a normal probability distribution with an average of $10,000 and a standard deviation of $500 has the same probabilities as normal distribution rescaled with an average of 10 and a standard deviation of 0.50. Furthermore, these properties are the reason the *z-score* transforms normal distributions into the standard normal distribution.

The fact that multiplying by a constant does *not* change the shape of the probability distribution is an extremely important property to remember!

8.3 Adding distributions

There are many circumstances in which random variables must be either combined (aggregated) or separated (disaggregated). Although the mathematics for determining the sum or average of the resulting random variable's distribution is intuitive, determining the standard deviation of the resulting distribution is not easily understood. Most statistical procedures are built upon the concept of comparing and contrasting variation in outcomes—that is, comparing and contrasting distributions of sums and averages of random variables and their variation.

Standard deviation is the common measure of variation in outcomes and is the typical (*standard*) amount away from average (*deviation*) and is often represented by σ (the Greek letter s). Although standard deviation is the commonly used measure of variation of data, there is another measure of variation that is used to calculate standard deviation: *variance*. Variance is the square of standard deviation:

$$\text{Variance} = \sigma^2, \quad \text{and thus} \quad \sigma = \sqrt{\text{Variance}}$$

Historically, variance was an intermediate step in calculating standard deviation and has no useful managerial meaning because the units of variance are units squared rather than original units. As an example, suppose expenses are normally distributed with an average of $1000 and a standard deviation of $100. The variance is $\sigma^2 = \$100 \times \$100 = \$10,000$ squared—which has no direct managerial interpretation.

The importance of variance is that it is the intermediary calculation used to determine the appropriate standard deviation for sums and averages. As an example, the variance of a sum of two independent (uncorrelated) distributions is the sum of the variances:

$$Var_{1+2} = Var_1 + Var_2$$

IMPORTANT → The same is not true for standard deviation:

$$SD_{1+2} \neq SD_1 + SD_2$$

Thus, when combining distributions, *variance* is the measure that should be used to determine the variation of the resulting distribution. The following example demonstrates how two binomial distributions added together would create a new random variable and how the resulting average and standard deviation would be calculated (Example 8.1).

Example 8.1 Adding binomial distributions

A specific class of rooms at a resort hotel has a 15% rate of reservations in which the people do not show up (no shows). The hotel chain owns two similar hotels, one with 25 such rooms and the other with 30 rooms.

a. What is the probability that exactly 4 rooms are empty among the two hotels if all 55 rooms are reserved?

Since there is no distinction between which hotels the empty rooms are in, the two binomial distributions can be combined into a single distribution. Let X_1 = the number of empty rooms in the first hotel and X_2 = the number of empty rooms in the second hotel. Then $X_{1+2} = X_1 + X_2$ and the new random variable X_{1+2} is a binomial distribution with $n = (25 + 30)$ and $p = 0.15$.

The histogram in Fig. 8.3 shows the *probability mass function (pmf)* for the binomial distribution with $n = 55$ and $p = 0.15$, with $f(4)$ highlighted.

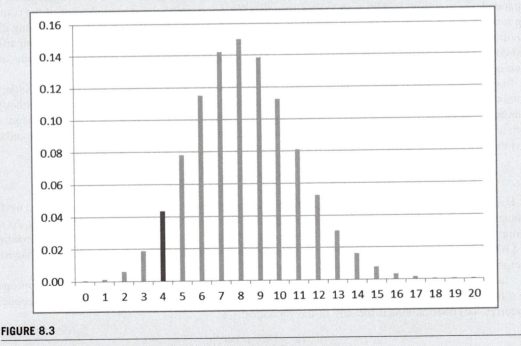

FIGURE 8.3

$f(4)$ in the Binomial Distribution With $n = 55$ and $p = 0.15$

Thus, to answer part (a):

$$P(X_{1+2} = 4 \text{ rooms}) = f(4) = \frac{(25+30)!}{4!(25+30-4)!} 0.15^4 (0.85^{(25+30-4)})$$

$$= \frac{55!}{4!(51!)} 0.15^4 (0.85^{51})$$

$$= \frac{55(54)(53)(52)}{4(3)(2)} (0.15^4 (0.85^{51}))$$

$$= (55(9)(53)(13))(0.15^4 (0.85^{51}))$$

$$\cong 0.043406 \cong \mathbf{4.34\%}$$

b. If all 55 rooms are reserved, what is the probability that less than 4 rooms are empty among the two hotels?

$$P(X_{1+2} < 4 \text{ rooms}) = F(3) = f(0) + f(1) + f(2) + f(3)$$

$$\cong 0.000131 + 0.001274 + 0.006069 + 0.018921$$

$$= F(3) \cong 0.026395 \cong \mathbf{2.64\%}$$

Notice that the normal approximation is not appropriate for either of the two distributions individually because their averages (np) are too low. But the average of the combined distribution meets the requirements for using the normal approximation. To examine the benefits and implications of combining the two distributions, the normal approximation to the combined (aggregated) binomial distribution is demonstrated.

Examine the averages of the two distributions separately:

$$Avg_1 = n_1 p_1 = 25\,(0.15) = 3.75$$
$$Avg_2 = n_2 p_2 = 30\,(0.15) = 4.50$$

Since $p_1 = p_2$, then:

$$Avg_{1+2} = (n_1 + n_2)\,p_1 = n_1 p_1 + n_2 p_1 = Avg_1 + Avg_2$$
$$Avg_{1+2} \qquad = (25+30)\,(0.15)$$
$$= (55)\,(0.15) = 8.25 \quad (= 3.75 + 4.50)$$

Thus, the aggregated average is computed as would be expected. Unfortunately, computing the appropriate *standard deviation* is not intuitive. Instead of using individual standard deviations to calculate aggregate standard deviation, *variance* must be used as an intermediary to calculate the appropriate standard deviation. Thus, the computations to calculate the appropriate standard deviations are initially computed using variance:

$$Var_1 = n_1 p_1 q_1 = 25\,(0.15)\,(0.85)$$
$$Var_2 = n_2 p_2 q_2 = 30\,(0.15)\,(0.85)$$

Since $p_1 = p_2$, then:

$$Var_{1+2} = (n_1 + n_2)\, p_1 q_1 = Var_1 + Var_2$$

Then:

$$
\begin{aligned}
SD_{1+2} &= \sqrt{Var_1 + Var_2} \\
&= (Var_1 + Var_2)^{1/2} \\
&= ((n_1 + n_2)\, p_1 q_1)^{1/2} \\
&= ((25 + 30)(0.15)(0.85))^{1/2} \\
&\cong 2.6481
\end{aligned}
$$

Note that SD_{1+2} is *not* equal to the standard deviation for each hotel added together. For example, this is the *incorrect* way to compute the aggregate SD:

$$
\begin{aligned}
SD_1 &= (n_1 p_1 q_1)^{1/2} \\
&= (25\,(0.15)\,(0.85))^{1/2} \\
&\cong 1.7854
\end{aligned}
$$

$$
\begin{aligned}
SD_2 &= (n_2 p_2 q_2)^{1/2} \\
&= (30\,(0.15)\,(0.85))^{1/2} \\
&\cong 1.9558
\end{aligned}
$$

$$SD_{1+2} \neq (n_1 p_1 q_1)^{1/2} + (n_2 p_2 q_2)^{1/2} = 3.7412$$
$$\neq 2.6481 \text{ (the correct value computed from the variances)}$$

This is because:

$$SD_{1+2} = ((n_1 + n_2)\, p_1 q_1)^{1/2} \neq (n_1 p_1 q_1)^{1/2} + (n_2 p_2 q_2)^{1/2}$$

Thus:

$$Var_{1+2} = Var_1 + Var_2$$

$$SD_{1+2} \neq SD_1 + SD_2$$

Now, because the combined average for this example *is about 8 (or greater)*, the normal approximation using the continuity correction can be used to provide an approximate solution to the problem.

Fig. 8.4 shows the histogram for the discrete normal approximation with an average of 8.25 and a standard deviation of 2.6481.

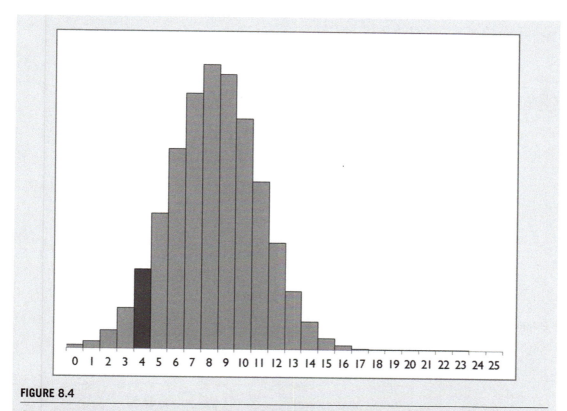

FIGURE 8.4

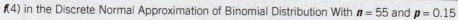

f(4) in the Discrete Normal Approximation of Binomial Distribution With $n = 55$ and $p = 0.15$

a. What is the probability that exactly four rooms are empty among the two hotels?
To answer part (a) using the normal approximation (Fig. 8.5):

$$P(X_{1+2} = 4 \text{ rooms}) = f(4)$$
$$= F(4.5) - F(3.5)$$
$$= \Phi\left(\frac{4.5 - 8.25}{2.6481}\right) - \Phi\left(\frac{3.5 - 8.25}{2.6481}\right) = \Phi(-1.4161) - \Phi(-1.7937)$$
$$\cong 0.07837 - .03642$$
$$= 0.04195 \cong \mathbf{4.20\%} \text{ (compared to } \mathbf{4.34\%} \text{ from above)}$$

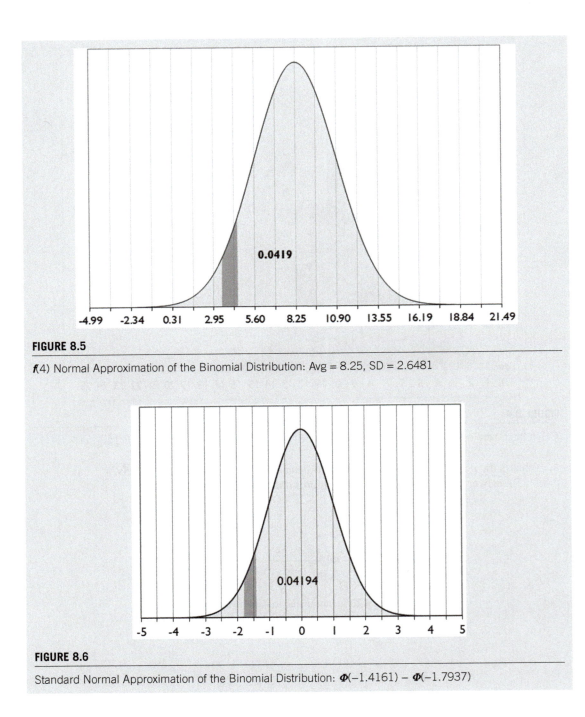

FIGURE 8.5

f(4) Normal Approximation of the Binomial Distribution: Avg = 8.25, SD = 2.6481

FIGURE 8.6

Standard Normal Approximation of the Binomial Distribution: $\Phi(-1.4161) - \Phi(-1.7937)$

b. What is the probability that less than four rooms are empty among the two hotels?

To answer part (b) using the normal approximation:

$$P(X_{1+2} < 4 \text{ rooms}) = F(3.5)$$

$$= \Phi\left(\frac{3.5 - 8.25}{2.6481}\right) = \Phi(-1.7937) \cong 0.03642 \cong 3.64\% \quad \text{(compared to 2.64\% from above)}$$

The Poisson distribution has the interesting property that the average and variance are equal. This property provides an easy mechanism to further examine the implications and applications of aggregating (combining or *conjoining*) and disaggregating (separating) distributions:

Example 8.2 Adding Poisson distributions

A car dealership sells four cars of a specific model on average each month.

a. What is the probability of selling exactly four cars in 3 months (one quarter of a year)?

Because there is no distinction between the months, it is not difficult to combine the three Poisson distributions into a single distribution. Let X_i = the number of cars sold in month i for $i = 1, 2, 3$ (i.e., X_1, X_2, X_3). Then X_{1+2+3} = $X_1 + X_2 + X_3$ and the new random variable X_{1+2+3} is a Poisson distribution with $\lambda = (4 + 4 + 4)$. The histogram in Fig. 8.7 shows the *pmf* for the Poisson distribution with $\lambda = 12$:

From the previous chapter, $f(x) = e^{-\lambda}\lambda^x/x!$, so to answer part (a):

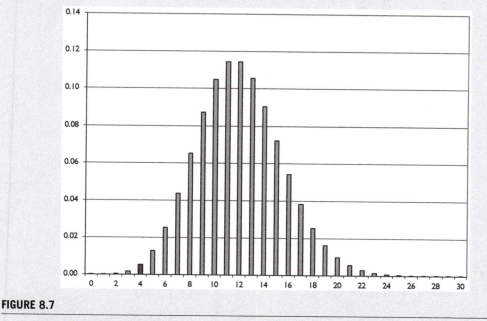

FIGURE 8.7

Poisson Distribution With $\lambda = 12$

$$P(X_{1+2+3} = 4 \text{ cars}) = f(4)$$
$$= e^{-12}(12^4)/4!$$
$$\cong 0.005309 \cong \textbf{0.531\%} \text{ (note that 0.5\% is about 1 in 200)}$$

b. The same car dealership sells 36 cars of a different model on average each year. What is the probability of selling more than 1 car of this model in a month?

Part (b) requires disaggregating an annual demand into a single month. Ignoring seasonality for the moment, the annual demand can be thought of as the aggregation of 12 monthly Poisson distributions, and thus the disaggregated parts are also Poisson distributions. In this case, $\lambda_{month} = \lambda_{year}/12 = 36/12 = 3$. Mathematical proofs of this property of the Poisson distribution are available in books on probability theory that are more mathematically detailed.

$$P(X_{one\ month} > 1 \text{ car}) = 1 - F(1)$$
$$= 1 - (f(0) + f(1))$$
$$= 1 - e^{-3}(3^0/0! + 3^1/1!)$$
$$= 1 - e^{-3}(1 + 3)$$
$$\cong 1 - 0.199148 = 0.800852 \cong \textbf{80.09\%}$$

The histogram in Fig. 8.8 shows the probability of selling more than one car for the Poisson distribution with $\lambda = 3$.

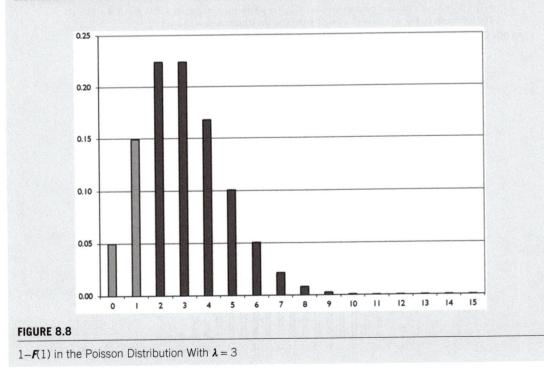

FIGURE 8.8

$1 - F(1)$ in the Poisson Distribution With $\lambda = 3$

Return to question (a) of Example 8.2 to examine the benefits and implications of adding distributions. Comparing the Poisson distribution to the normal approximation, notice that the normal approximation is not appropriate for a single month because the average ($\lambda = 4$) is too low. But the average of the combined (quarterly) distribution meets the requirements for using the normal approximation.

First, examine the averages of the two distributions separately:

$$Avg_{1+2+3} = Avg_1 + Avg_2 + Avg_3$$

Because $\lambda_1 = \lambda_2 = \lambda_3$:

$$Avg_{1+2+3} = 3(\lambda_1) = 3(4) = 12$$

Again, the aggregated average is computed as would be expected. Notice that the mathematical operations for standard deviation do not work as one might expect. Thus, the computations are done with *variance*:

(Recall that for a Poisson distribution the variance is equal to the average.)

$$Var_i = \lambda_i = 4, \quad \text{for } i = 1, 2, 3.$$

$$Var_{1+2+3} = Var_1 + Var_2 + Var_3$$

Since $\lambda_1 = \lambda_2 = \lambda_3$:

$$Var_{1+2+3} = 3(\lambda_1) = 3(4) = 12 \text{ (which is equal to } Avg_{1+2+3} \text{ since the distribution is Poisson)}$$

Then:

$$SD_{1+2+3} = (12)^{1/2} \cong \mathbf{3.4641} \neq (4^{1/2}) + (4^{1/2}) + (4^{1/2})$$

Thus, SD_{1+2+3} is not equal to the sum of the standard deviations for each month. For example, although

$$SD_1 = (4)^{1/2} = 2$$

is true, $SD_{1+2+3} \neq 6$. Specifically:

$$SD_{1+2+3} = 3.4641 \neq \left(4^{1/2}\right) + \left(4^{1/2}\right) + \left(4^{1/2}\right) = 6$$

Thus, 6 is not the correct value for SD_{1+2+3}; therefore:

$$Var_{1+2+3} = Var_1 + Var_2 + Var_3$$

$$SD_{1+2+3} \neq SD_1 + SD_2 + SD_3$$

Thus, instead of using the individual standard deviation to calculate aggregate (or disaggregate) standard deviation, *variance* should be used as an intermediary to calculate the appropriate standard deviation. Now, because the combined average is 12 (>8), the normal approximation using the continuity correction can be employed to solve the problem.

Fig. 8.9 shows the histogram for the discrete normal approximation with an average of 12 and a standard deviation of 3.4641.

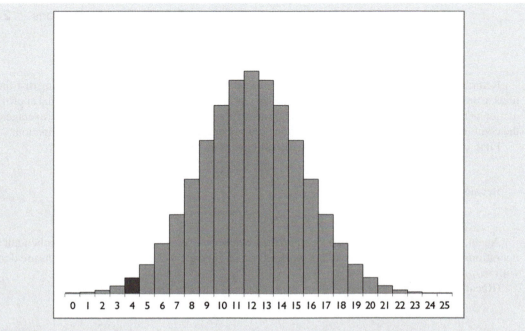

FIGURE 8.9

Normal Approximation of the Poisson Distribution With $\lambda = 12$

To answer part (a) using the normal approximation:

$$P(X_{1+2+3} = 4 \text{ cars}) = f(4)$$
$$= F(4.5) - F(3.5)$$
$$= \Phi\left(\frac{4.5 - 12}{3.4641}\right) - \Phi\left(\frac{3.5 - 12}{3.4641}\right)$$
$$= \Phi(-2.1651) - \Phi(-2.4537)$$
$$= 0.01519 - .00707 \cong 0.00812 \cong \textbf{0.812\%} \text{ (compared to } \textbf{0.531\%} \text{ from above)}$$

0.00812

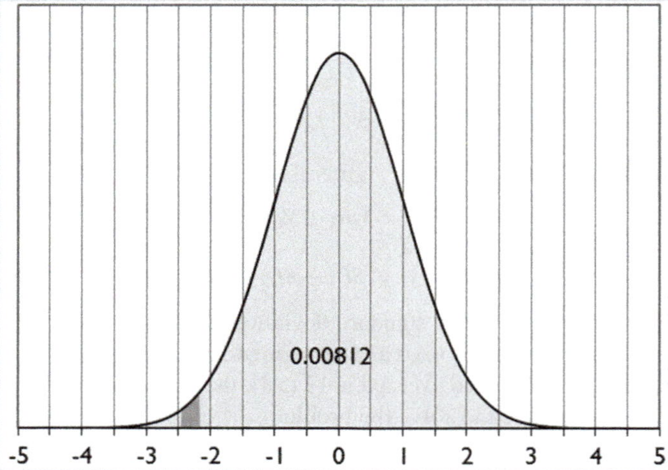

FIGURE 8.10

Standard Normal Distribution for $\Phi(-2.1651) - \Phi(-2.4537)$

The difference between the exact answer and the normal approximation is due to the fact that these probabilities are in the tails and the probabilities in the tails of distributions are sensitive to small changes because of the nonlinear nature of the normal distribution. Given a $\lambda_{month} = 3$ (<8) for part (b), it would be inappropriate to use the normal approximation to answer part (b). But it is useful to note that the standard deviation for a month would be calculated:

$$Var_{year} = \lambda_{year} = 36Var_{month} = \lambda_{month} = 36/12 = 3$$

$$SD_{month} = 3^{1/2} \cong 1.732$$

Rather than:

$$SD_{month} = SD_{year}/12 = 6/12 = 0.50 \quad \text{(incorrect)}$$

Again, illustrating that *variance* should be used as an intermediary to calculate the appropriate standard deviation.

Example 8.3 Adding normal distributions

A credit card company receives payments that average $12,600,000 per month, with a standard deviation of $2,500,000 from customers in a region. The company receives payments that average $14,400,000 per month, with a standard deviation of $3,600,000 from customers in a second region.

a. What is the probability of receiving less than $26.5 million in a single month?

To combine the two normal distributions into a single distribution, let X_1 = the payments received in the first region and X_2 = the payments received in the second region. Then $X_{1+2} = X_1 + X_2$ and the new random variable X_{1+2} is a normal distribution with an average of ($12.6 + $14.4 = $27 million). The standard deviation of X_{1+2} is computed as:

$$Var_1 = 2,500,000^2 \text{ and } Var_2 = 3,600,000^2$$

$$Var_{1+2} = \left(2,500,000^2 + 3,600,000^2\right)$$

$$SD_{1+2} = \left(2,500,000^2 + 3,600,000^2\right)^{1/2} \cong 4,382,921$$

Note that working with a *scalar* (e.g., $1,000,000) does not change the results.

$$Var_1 = 2.5^2 \text{ and } Var_2 = 3.6^2 \text{ (in millions) } Var_{1+2} = \left(2.5^2 + 3.6^2\right)$$

$$SD_{1+2} = \left(2.5^2 + 3.6^2\right)^{1/2} \cong 4.382921 \text{ million}$$

Thus, the distribution for payments received from both regions in a single month is normal with an average of $27 million and standard deviation of $4.3829.

To answer part (a):

$$P(X_{1+2} < \$26.5 \text{ million}) = F(26.5)$$
$$= \Phi((26.5 - 27)/4.3829)$$
$$= \Phi(-0.1141)$$
$$\cong 0.45459 \cong \textbf{45.46\%}$$

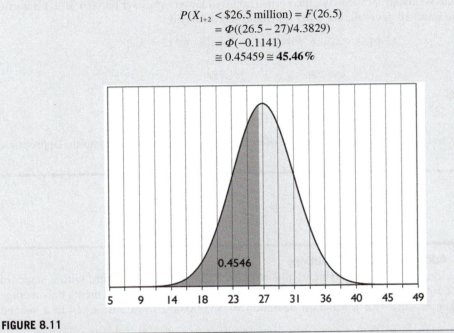

FIGURE 8.11

$F(26.5)$ in a Normal Distribution $N(27, 4.3829^2)$

To combine the two normal distributions for 3 months into a single distribution, let X_{qtr} = the payments received from both regions for 3 months. Then $X_{qtr} = X_{1+2} + X_{1+2} + X_{1+2}$ and the new random variable X_{qtr} is a normal distribution with an average of (3*$27 million = $81 million). The standard deviation of X_{qtr} is computed as:

$$Var_{1+2} = \left(2.5^2 + 3.6^2\right) \text{ (in millions)}$$

$$Var_{qtr} = Var_{1+2} + Var_{1+2} + Var_{1+2} = 3\left(2.5^2 + 3.6^2\right)$$

$$SD_{qtr} = \left(3\left(2.5^2 + 3.6^2\right)\right)^{1/2} \cong \left(3^{1/2}\right) 4.382921 \cong 7.5914 \text{ million}$$

Thus, the distribution for payments received from both regions in a quarter is normal with an average of $81 million and standard deviation of $7.5914 million.

b. There a 95% chance that the company will receive less than what amount for a single quarter (3 months) from these two regions combined?

$P(X_{qtr} < x_{qtr}) = 95\%$ occurs at roughly 1.645 standard deviations (z) above average. This is written in notation as:

$$x_{qtr} = 81 + \Phi^{-1}(0.95)\ (7.5914)\ \ x_{qtr} = 81 + z_{0.95}(7.5914)$$

$$x_{qtr} = 81 + 1.645(7.5914) \cong \$93.49 \text{ million}$$

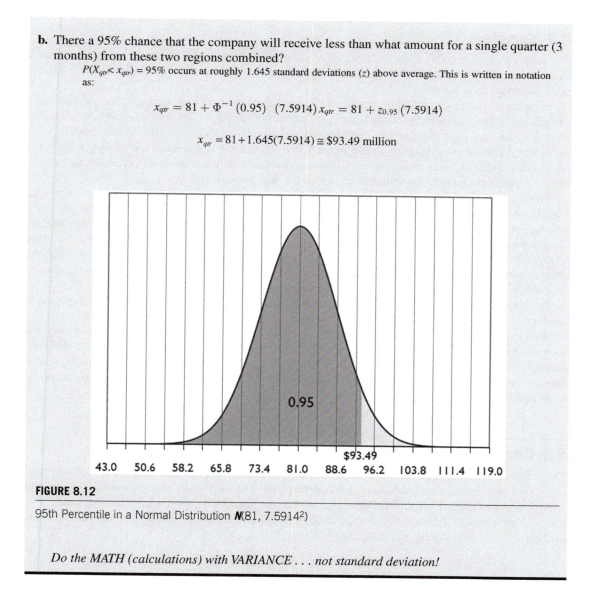

FIGURE 8.12

95th Percentile in a Normal Distribution $N(81, 7.5914^2)$

Do the MATH (calculations) with VARIANCE . . . not standard deviation!

8.4 Samples

The purpose of a sample is to use a small set of information (the *sample*) to make inferences about a larger set of data (the *population*). For the sample to accurately represent the population, the sample must be randomly selected.

Sampling is the process used to produce a subset of elements that represent the characteristics of a population without examining all the elements in that population. A random selection of individual items is necessary to produce a valid sample. When a sample is randomly selected, the items or units are selected from a population in such a manner that the sample is unbiased and closely reflects the parameters of the original population. This, in turn, provides statistical confidence and inference regarding the characteristics of a population from which the sample was drawn.

There are many random sampling methods. One common method is *simple random sampling* (SRS), which involves using a random selection method to draw a fixed number (sample size of *n* observations) of the sampling units from the frame without replacement—that is, not allowing the same sampling unit to be selected more than once. In the SRS method, each unit of observation is assigned an equally likely random number. The sample of *n* observations can then be selected by sorting the observations from smallest to largest according to their assigned random numbers and then selecting the observations associated with the *n* lowest random numbers.

By definition, a ***statistic*** is a number computed from a sample. The typical purpose of statistics is to summarize attributes and characteristics of the entire population.

As a metaphor, consider a cook making a large pot of stew. To evaluate the entire pot of stew, the cook must take a sample of the stew. Obviously, the stew must be well stirred (randomly sampled) and the spoon needs to be sufficiently large ($n \geq 30$) . . . but not so large as to consume too much of the stew. Interestingly, the spoon size (sample size) is not overly related to the size of the pot (population). In other words, you do not need a large sample size for a large population.

8.5 Central limit theorem

The central limit theorem states that the distribution of sample sums and averages are normal—provided that the individual observations are ***independent and identically distributed*** (IID)—and this provision is essential. The standard deviation of the averages (SD_{Avg}) is called *standard error*. This standard error is how the sample averages would vary *if* more than one sample were drawn. The standard error for sample averages is computed by using:

$$SD_{Avg} \;=\; SE = SD_{Sample}/n^{1/2}$$

Keeping in mind how distributions can be aggregated, think about what would occur *if* you were to repeatedly draw samples from the same population. The central limit theorem states that sample averages and the sample sums follow a normal distribution . . . regardless of the distribution of the population. This concept is illustrated in Fig. 8.13.

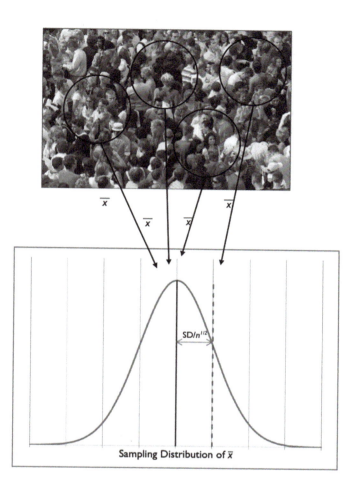

FIGURE 8.13

Sample Averages Are Normally Distributed

The Central Limit Theorem:

Averages (and sums) are NORMAL (when $n \geq 30$). The standard deviation of the sample averages is $SD/n^{1/2}$ . . . and is called the STANDARD ERROR of the average.

Remember:

Standard deviation is to **DATA** as *standard error* is to **sample averages.**

Warning: The n observations must be IID!!

In fact, any number computed from a sample (a *statistic*) will have a standard error that measures its variation from the expected value of the parameter. Thus, standard error is how any number computed from a sample (average, sum, slope, intercept, etc.) will vary away from the sample statistic.

The simulation in Example 8.4 illustrates the concept of the central limit theorem.

Example 8.4 Simulation example of the central limit theorem

Consider a random variable from a continuous uniform distribution over the range [80,120].

The graph of the *pmf* of the population with the continuous uniform distribution [80,120] is shown in Fig. 8.14.

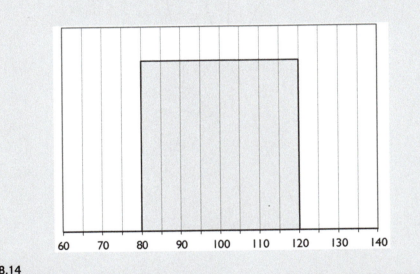

FIGURE 8.14

Continuous Uniform Distribution U[80, 120]

First, examine the simulation results of drawing two observations ($n = 2$) randomly from the uniform distribution. The sum and average for the two observations are then computed. This process is repeated for 10,000 samples. The distribution of the sample averages of 10,000 samples with sample size of 2 is shown in Fig. 8.15. Note that the distribution of the averages is a triangular distribution, *not* a *uniform* distribution, and the most likely value (*mode*) already indicates the population average.

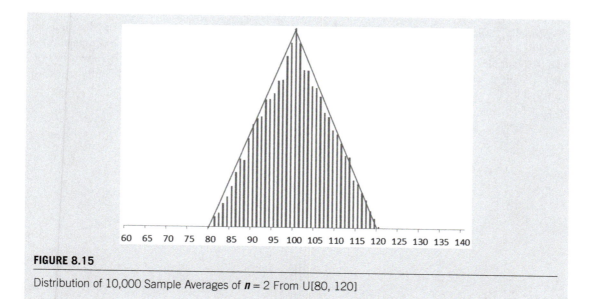

FIGURE 8.15

Distribution of 10,000 Sample Averages of **n** = 2 From U[80, 120]

Next, look at the results of drawing five observations randomly (*n* = 5) from the distribution. Again, the sum and average for the five observations are then computed. The process is repeated for 10,000 samples. The distribution for sample averages for the 10,000 samples with sample size of 5 is shown in Fig. 8.16. Note that with even a sample size of only 5, the distribution is becoming *bell shaped* (closer to normal).

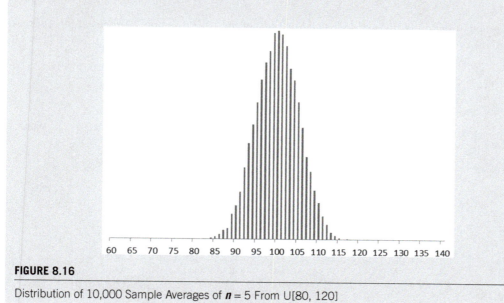

FIGURE 8.16

Distribution of 10,000 Sample Averages of **n** = 5 From U[80, 120]

Finally, look at the results of drawing 30 observations randomly ($n = 30$) from the distribution. Again, the sum and average for the 30 observations are then computed. This process is repeated for 10,000 samples. The distribution for the 10,000 samples with sample size of 30 is shown in Fig. 8.17. With a sample size of only 30, the distribution is considered to be sufficiently close to normal.

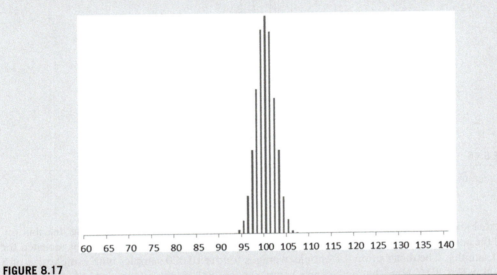

FIGURE 8.17

Distribution of 10,000 Sample Averages of **n** = 30 From U[80, 120]

The graph of the *probability density function (pdf)* of the 10,000 sample averages of 30 observations is shown in Fig. 8.18.

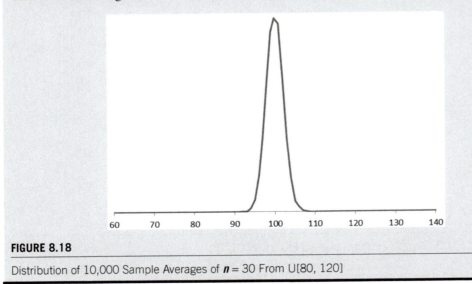

FIGURE 8.18

Distribution of 10,000 Sample Averages of **n** = 30 From U[80, 120]

Although this simulation shows what happens to the sample averages drawn from a uniform distribution, theory and experimentation have proven that the same effect occurs *regardless of the distribution of the population*.

Thus, the amazing mathematical fact is, *regardless of the distribution of the data* (population), as sample sizes get larger, the distribution of the **sample averages** gets closer and closer to a normal distribution. This fact is illustrated in the graph shown in Fig. 8.19.

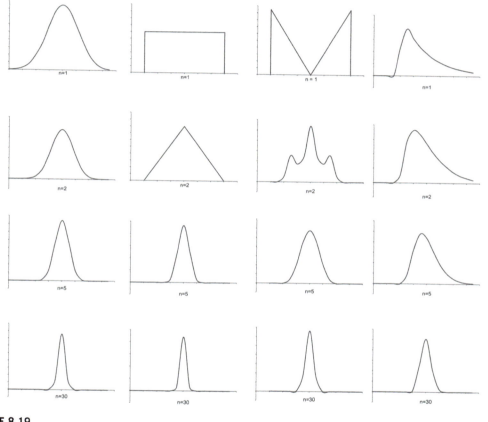

FIGURE 8.19

Central Limit Theorem: Sample Size and Population Effects

What would the graphs above look like if they were totals (sums) rather than averages?

Example 8.5 Central limit theorem applied to sampling

Monthly credit card billings for 50 randomly selected accounts have an average of $86.00 and a standard deviation of $70.71.

a. What is the probability distribution of the billing for a single account?

Without the accompanying sample data, the probability distribution for a single account is unknown. Thus, the answer to part (a) is that the distribution is *unknown*, but with the sample data, *an empirical distribution would be appropriate* to model the distribution of individual accounts.

WARNING:

Assuming the individual accounts to be normally distributed simply because a sample standard deviation was computed would be a severe mistake.

b. What is the probability distribution for the total billings of 50 accounts?

By the central limit theorem, the total (sum) will be **normal**. To answer part (b), calculate the average total and standard deviation of the total this way:

$$Avg_{Total} = 50(\$86.00) = \mathbf{\$4,300.00}$$

$$SD_{Total} = (Var_{Total})^{1/2} = (50(\$70.71)^2)^{1/2} = 50^{1/2}(\$70.71) = \mathbf{\$500.00}$$

c. What is the probability that a set of 50 accounts will have total billings of less than $5000?

Use the information from part (b) to answer part (c):

$$P(Billings_{Total} \leq \$5,000) = F(5000) = \Phi\left(\frac{5000 - 4300}{500}\right)$$
$$= \Phi(1.40) \cong 0.91924 \cong \mathbf{91.92\%}$$

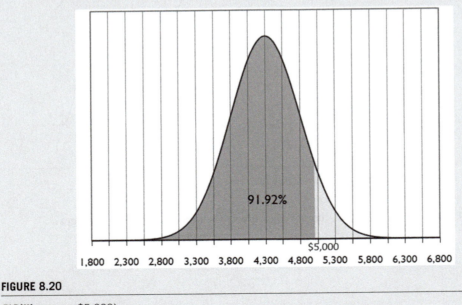

91.92%

$5,000

1,800 2,300 2,800 3,300 3,800 4,300 4,800 5,300 5,800 6,300 6,800

FIGURE 8.20

$P(Billings_{Total} \leq \$5,000)$

d. What is the distribution of the average billings of 50 accounts?

> By the central limit theorem, the sample averages will be normal. To answer part (d), calculate the average of the sample averages and the standard deviation of the averages (*standard error*) this way:

$$Avg_{SampleAvg} = \$86.00$$

$$SD_{SampleAvg} = SD_{Total}/n = \sqrt{n}SD_{data}/n = \frac{\sqrt{n}}{n}SD_{data} = \frac{\sqrt{n}}{n}\frac{\sqrt{n}}{\sqrt{n}}SD_{data} = SD_{data}/(\sqrt{n}$$

$$= \$70.71/50^{1/2} \cong \$10.00$$

e. Compute the sample average billings for 50 accounts above which there is only a 5% chance of occurrence. Alternatively stated, there is a 95% chance that sample average billings for 50 accounts will be less than what value?

> The 95% occurs at approximately 1.645 standard errors ($z_{95\%}$) above the average. Thus:

$$Billings_{Avg} = \$86.00 + 1.645(\$10.00) \cong \$102.45$$

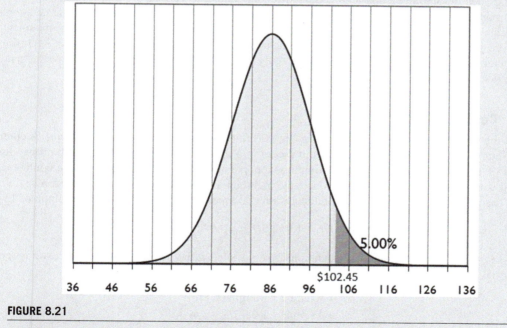

FIGURE 8.21

$P(Billings_{Avg} \le x) = 95\%$

Thus, any sample of 50 accounts with an average above $102.45 should be more closely examined. Furthermore, if the sampling was deemed to have been properly conducted, then the frame (population) from which the accounts were sampled should be examined.

8.6 Confidence intervals and hypothesis testing for proportions

The central limit theorem states that the distribution of sample averages is normal with a standard deviation of $SD_{sample}/n^{1/2}$. The standard deviation of the sample average is called the *standard error*.

Because a proportion of occurrences is the number of occurrences divided by the sample size, a sample proportion is a sample average and follows the central limit theorem. Since binomial ("yes–no") variables are sample proportions (and hence are sample averages), they follow a normal distribution with an average of p and a *standard error* of:

$$SE = SD_p = SD_{Sample}/n^{1/2} = (pq)^{1/2}/n^{1/2} = (pq/n)^{1/2}.$$

where

n = sample size
p = the number of occurrences/sample size = # "yes"/n
q = the complement of p = $(1-p)$.

The foundation for applying the central limit theorem is that one sample will show the way in which repeated samples would behave. The following example illustrates the concept of the central limit theorem as applied to sampling a binomial variable from a population. The sample proportions are normal, and the standard deviation of the normal distribution is $(pq/n)^{1/2}$. According to mathematical notational convention, a "^" (pronounced "hat") indicates the sample estimate of the corresponding parameter. Therefore, $\hat{p}$ is the estimate of the proportion of the population ($\hat{p}$) calculated from a sample. According to the central limit theorem, if you were to repeatedly sample, the sample proportions ($\hat{p}$) would have a normal distribution.

8.6.1 Confidence intervals

One of the most common applications of the central limit theorem is the *confidence interval*. A confidence interval makes use of the central limit theorem to estimate a range that has a high probability (e.g., 95% chance) of containing the true unknown population value to be estimated. The confidence interval is often specified by giving the estimate and then a *plus/minus* number called the *margin of error*. The margin of error for a 95% confidence interval *for samples greater than 30* is computed by:

$$1.96\,(SE) = 1.96\left(SD_{Sample}/n^{1/2}\right),$$

where 1.96 is the number of standard deviations (z) associated with 95% around the center (average) of the normal distribution. Thus, a 95% confidence interval is typically computed by:

$$95\%\ CI = \text{Average} \pm \text{Margin of Error}$$
$$= \text{Average} \pm 1.96(SD_{Sample}/n^{1/2})$$

Specifically for binomial (*dichotomous*) variables:

$$95\%\,CI_p = \hat{p} \pm 1.96(\hat{p}\hat{q}/n)^{1/2}$$

The concept and application of a 95% confidence interval is demonstrated in Example 8.6.

Example 8.6 Confidence intervals for proportions

A home and garden/hardware chain purchased a batch of 250 dogwood trees from a supplier. The chain sold all 250 trees, and after a year, 207 had survived. The supplier claims that 90% of the trees it sells will survive.

a. What is the probability distribution for the number of trees that will survive from a random sample of 250?

This problem consists of adding Bernoulli distributions, thus resulting in a binomial distribution. In this case, n = 250, and based on the empirical probability from the sample data,

$$p = 207/250 = 0.828 \text{ and } q = 1 - 0.828 = 0.172$$

The histogram in Fig. 8.22 shows the *pmf* for the binomial distribution with $n = 250$ and $p = 0.828$.

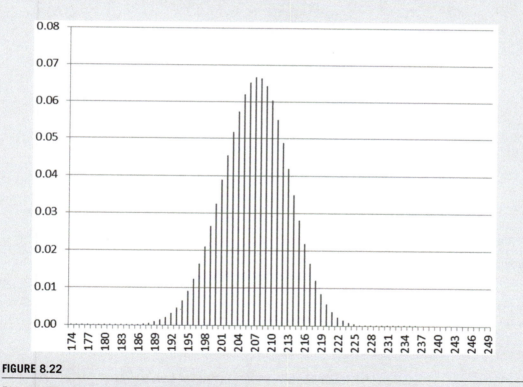

FIGURE 8.22

Binomial Distribution With $n = 250$ and $p = 0.828$

Sir Francis Galton invented a device that mechanically creates a normal distribution that occurs from the combination of a large number of independent Bernoulli random events. The device consists of a staggered array of pins mounted on a vertical board. The normal distribution occurs when a series of balls drops onto the top of the array of pins. When a ball hits a pin, it bounces to the left or right with equal probability and then falls down to the next level. When the ball reaches the last level, it falls into one of the bins at the bottom. As the balls stack up in the bins, they form a normal curve. Consider a Galton Board with 250 rows of pins and 251 bins at the bottom, numbered from 0 to 250, representing the number of trees that survived. It is easy to see that the normal approximation for the binomial distribution with $n = 250$, $p = 0.50$ is appropriate, thus illustrating the central limit theorem via the sum of 250 IID Bernoulli trials results in a binomial.

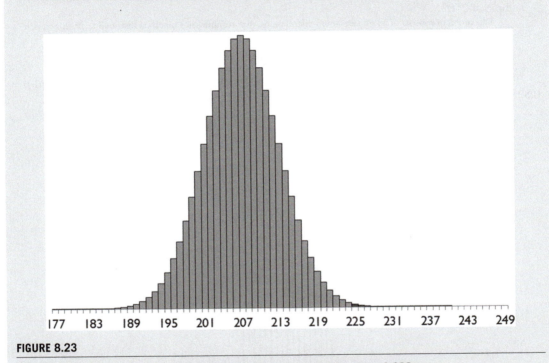

FIGURE 8.23

Normal Approximation for the Binomial Distribution With $n = 250$ and $p = 0.828$

Thus, for part (a), either the binomial distribution with $n = 250$ and $p = 0.828$ or the discrete normal distribution with the continuity correction could be used:

$$\text{Average} = np = 250(0.828) = 250(207/250) = \textbf{207}$$

$$\text{Standard Deviation} = (npq)^{1/2} = (207(0.172))^{1/2} = \textbf{5.9669} \, (\cong 6)$$

In fact, with an average this large, it is common practice to forgo the continuity correction. Thus, using the continuous normal distribution $N(207, 6^2)$ shown in Fig. 8.24 would be satisfactory.

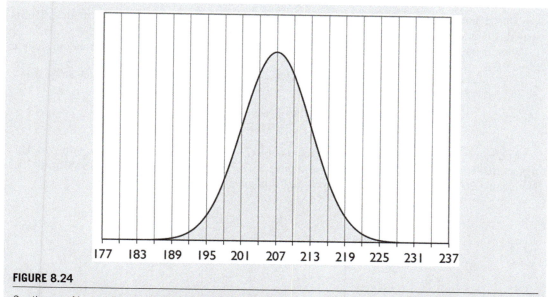

FIGURE 8.24

Continuous Normal Distribution N(207, 5.9669²)

b. Given the sample information, what is the probability that 225 or more trees (90%) survive from a random sample of 250?

Using the binomial distribution:

$$P(X \geq 225 \text{ trees}) = 1 - F(224)$$
$$= f(225) + f(226) + \ldots + f(250)$$
$$= 0.00094 = \mathbf{0.094\%}$$

Thus, there is almost no chance of 225 or more trees surviving given the sample proportion of 207/250. This would lead one to believe that a 90% survival rate is not realistic (or truthful). As $1-F(224)$ is difficult to compute without a computer, it is useful to answer part (b) using the normal distribution with the continuity correction:

$$P(X \geq 225 \text{ trees}) = 1 - F(224.5) = 1 - \Phi\left(\frac{224.5 - 207}{5.9669}\right)$$
$$= 1 - \Phi(2.9328) = 1 - 0.9983 = 0.0017 = \mathbf{0.17\%}$$

To answer part (b) using the continuous normal distribution:

$$P(X \geq 225 \text{ trees}) = 1 - F(225) = 1 - \Phi\left(\frac{225 - 207}{5.9669}\right)$$
$$= 1 - \Phi(3.0166) = 1 - 0.9987 = 0.0013 = \mathbf{0.13\%}$$

The managerial conclusion is as follows: either (1) this sample is a very unlikely sample of trees, or (2) if this random sample is typical of the supplier's quality, then it is very unlikely that a 90% survival rate (225 out of 250) could be achieved.

Thus, the normal distribution provides good approximation for the binomial distribution. This is why this method is often used to answer such questions involving sampling.

c. What is the 95% confidence interval for the **number of trees** that survive from a random sample of 250?

To answer part (c), the values that are symmetric about the mean that constitute a 95% probability are approximately 1.96 standard errors away from average:

$$95\% \text{ Confidence Interval} = 207 \pm 1.96(5.9669) \quad \text{(from part a))}$$
$$= 207 \pm 11.70 = [195.30 \ 218.70] \text{ trees} = [195 \ 219] \text{ trees}$$

The value $1.96(5.9669) \cong 11.70$ (approximately 12) is referred to as the *margin of error*. This means that it would not be unreasonable to have a difference of about 12 trees away from 207. Notice that $207 + 12 = 219$ is still relatively far from the claim of 225 trees.

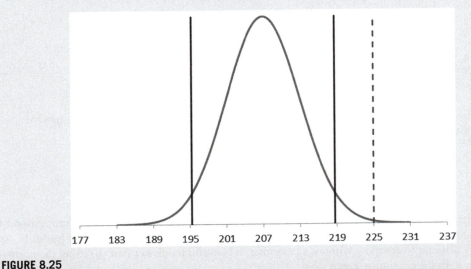

FIGURE 8.25

95% Confidence Interval for the Number of Trees Surviving From a Batch of 250 Trees

This further illustrates the following: either (1) a very bad sample of trees, or (2) if this is a random sample that is typical of the supplier's quality, then it is very unlikely that 225 surviving trees out of 250 trees could be achieved.

d. What is the probability distribution for the **proportion** of trees that survive from a random sample of 250?

Since the sample proportion of surviving trees is simply a constant (1/250) times the number of trees in part (a), the distribution for the proportion of surviving trees is still a normal distribution with an average of:

$$\hat{p} = \# \text{ survive}/n = 207/250 = 0.828$$

As we are multiplying by a constant $(1/n)$ rather than adding distributions, the standard deviation for the sample proportion is:

$$SD_{proportion} = \frac{SD_{trees}}{n}$$
$$= \frac{(n\hat{p}\hat{q})^{1/2}}{n}$$
$$= \frac{n^{1/2}(\hat{p}\hat{q})^{1/2}}{n}$$
$$= \frac{(\hat{p}\hat{q})^{1/2}}{n^{1/2}}$$
$$= \left(\frac{\hat{p}\hat{q}}{n}\right)^{1/2}$$

$$SD_{proportion} = \left(\frac{0.828(0.172)}{250}\right)^{1/2}$$
$$= \mathbf{0.023868}$$

As the proportion is a total divided by sample size, the proportion is an average and conforms to the central limit theorem for averages, and thus the *standard error* for averages (and thus proportions) is $SD/n^{1/2}$. Therefore, the answer for part (d) is $N(0.828, 0.023868^2)$, which is the correct distribution for the sample proportion.

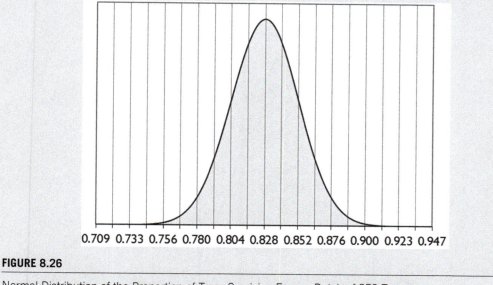

| 0.709 | 0.733 | 0.756 | 0.780 | 0.804 | 0.828 | 0.852 | 0.876 | 0.900 | 0.923 | 0.947 |

FIGURE 8.26

Normal Distribution of the Proportion of Trees Surviving From a Batch of 250 Trees

e. What is the probability the proportion of trees that will survive from a random sample of 250 will exceed 90%?

Because proportions are continuous, answer part (e) using the continuous normal distribution:

$$P(p \geq 90\%) = 1 - F(0.90)$$
$$= 1 - \Phi\left(\frac{0.900 - 0.828}{0.023868}\right)$$
$$= 1 - \Phi(3.0166)$$
$$= 1 - 0.9987$$
$$= 0.0013 = \mathbf{0.13\%}$$

As expected, this is the same answer as part (b) shown earlier.

f. What is the 95% confidence interval for the proportion of trees that survive from a random sample of 250?

Answer part (f) in the same manner as part (c):

$$95\% \text{ Confidence Interval} = 0.828 \pm 1.96(0.023868)$$
$$= 0.828 \pm 0.047 = [\mathbf{78.1\%}, \mathbf{87.5\%}] \text{ survival rate}$$

The value $1.96(.023868) \cong 4.7\%$ (approximately 5%) is the *margin of error*. This means that it would not be unreasonable to have a difference of about a 5% survival rate away from an 83% survival rate. Note that 83% + 5% = 88% does not reach the 90% claim.

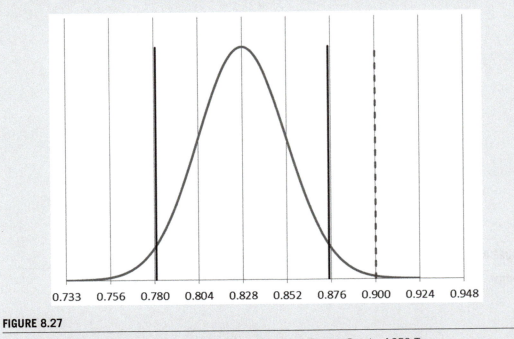

0.733   0.756   0.780   0.804   0.828   0.852   0.876   0.900   0.924   0.948

FIGURE 8.27

95% Confidence Interval for the Proportion of Trees Surviving From a Batch of 250 Trees

As a check, use the confidence intervals for the proportion from part (f) to get the confidence interval for the number of trees (part (c)). From part (f), multiplying by a constant of 250 trees does not change the shape of the distribution:

$$95\% \text{ Confidence Interval} = [\textbf{78.1\% 87.5\%}] \text{ survival rate}$$
$$\text{Lower } 95\% \text{ CI} = \textbf{0.781}(250) = 195.25 \text{ trees (the difference is due to rounding)}$$
$$\text{Upper } 95\% \text{ CI} = \textbf{0.875}(250) = 218.75 \text{ trees}$$
$$95\% \text{ CI from part (c)} = 207 \pm 11.70 = [\textbf{195.30 218.70}] \text{ trees}$$

The slight differences between the confidence intervals in parts (c) and (f) are due to rounding. As expected, multiplying by a constant ($n = 250$) did not change the probabilities or the probability distribution.

A way to answer the managerial question that is driving Example 8.6 would be to ask: How far away from 90% is the sample average? We got 82.8%. How unusual would that be? Is the difference of 7.2% a big deal or not? These questions lead to the most powerful and common application of the central limit theorem: **hypothesis testing**.

8.6.2 Hypothesis testing

The *hypothesis test* is an essential application of the central limit theorem. A hypothesis test, as the name implies, is the test of a formalized mathematical hypothesis about the population based upon the sample. The first step of the hypothesis test is to construct the *null hypothesis* (H_o) and the *alternate hypothesis* (H_a). In standard scientific practice, the null hypothesis is that there *is no effect* due to the treatment under consideration. In contrast, the alternate hypothesis is that there *is an effect* due to the treatment under consideration.

A classic example of hypothesis testing is in screening for cancer. The null hypothesis would be that you do not have cancer, and the alternate hypothesis would be that you do have cancer. A specific medical test would be conducted, and the results would indicate, but not necessarily confirm, whether or not you have cancer.

There are two types of errors associated with hypothesis testing: *type I* and *type II* errors. The type I error is a *false positive*: rejecting the null hypothesis when it should not be rejected. The type II error is a *failure to detect*: accepting the null hypothesis when it should be rejected.

The decision tree in Fig. 8.28 shows the structure of hypothesis testing and the two types of errors.

Another way of describing the two errors is to put them in a contingency table similar to the one used in the Bayesian analysis presented in Chapter 4:

	Says H_0	**Says H_A**
Is H_0	OK	Type I: False Positive
Is H_A	Type II: Failure to Detect	OK

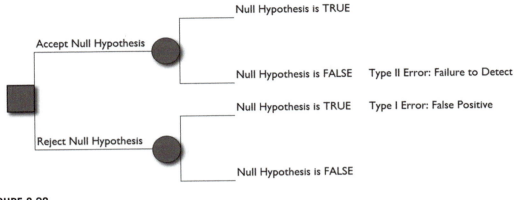

FIGURE 8.28

Decision Tree With Type I and Type II Errors

In the cancer screening example, a type I error is a *false positive*: saying you have cancer when you do not. This is rejecting the null hypothesis when you should not. A type II error is a *failure to detect*: saying you do not have cancer when you really do; in the cancer screening context, this is very serious! This is accepting the null (*failing to reject the null*) when you should reject the null in favor of the alternative hypothesis—the alternate hypothesis being that there is a significant difference.

Due to a statistician/geneticist named Sir Ronald Aylmer Fisher, it is standard practice to have a 5% or less chance of a type I error. This corresponds to a 95% confidence interval; a 1 in 20 chance of the results occurring due to chance alone.

In 1933, Fisher wrote "The Arrangement of Field Experiments" in the *Journal of the Ministry of Agriculture*, stating:

Note that this is based on what might have been expected to occur under the influence of only random variation. Fisher goes on:

[T]he evidence would have reached a point which may be called the verge of significance; for it is convenient to draw the line at about the level at which we can say "Either there is something in the treatment or a coincidence has occurred such as ***does not occur more than once in twenty trials***." This level, which we may call the 5 percent level point, would be indicated, though very roughly, by the greatest chance deviation observed in twenty successive trials.

If ***one in twenty*** does not seem high enough odds, we may, if we prefer it, draw the line at one in fifty (the 2 percent point) or one in a hundred (the 1 percent point). Personally, the writer prefers to set the low standard of significance at the 5 percent point, and ignore entirely all results which fail to reach this level.

From these statements, the level of statistical significance of 0.05 was born. There is no mathematical reason that 0.05 is the optimum type I error level—it simply became the accepted standard. The scientific community spent decades arguing about what the cutoff should be and, after some high-handed direction from Fisher, ultimately came to general agreement to accept Fisher's cutoff.

A *p-value* is the ***level of significance***. It is the probability of a type I error (*false positive*):

Thus:

p-value = **P**(REJECT the Null Hypothesis|Null Hypothesis Is TRUE) = **P(false positive)**
Mathematically, a hypothesis test is simply an algebraic rearrangement of the confidence interval.
To test a specific value (*test value*):
Starting with the general formula for a confidence interval:

$$Test\ Value = Sample\ Average \pm z\left(SD_{sample}/n^{1/2}\right)$$

$$|z| = |(Test\ Value - Sample\ Average)/\left(SD_{sample}/n^{1/2}\right)|$$

(note that |...| is the absolute value),

where z is the number of standard errors that the *sample average* is away from the *test statistic* (z in this procedure). If the test statistic $|z|$ is more than 1.96, then the null hypothesis is rejected. In such a situation, the sample average is deemed to be *statistically significantly different from* the test value.

As the hypothesis test is an algebraic rearrangement of the confidence interval, the hypothesis test does not lead to a different managerial conclusion. Thus, if the *test value* lies outside the 95% confidence interval, then the *test statistic* (z) will be greater than 1.96 and will result in a rejection of the null hypothesis.

These concepts are best illustrated through the situation presented in the previous example.

Example 8.7 Hypothesis testing of proportions

A home and garden/hardware chain purchased a batch of 250 dogwood trees. The chain sold all 250 trees, and after a year, 207 had survived. The supplier claims that 90% of the trees it sells will survive.

a. What are the null and alternative hypotheses?

For part (a), there are several equivalent *null/alternative* hypothesis pairs:

1. Using $\overline{X}$ as the average number of trees that survive:

Null Hypothesis (H_0) : $\overline{X} = 225$
Alt. Hypothesis (H_A) : $\overline{X} \neq 225$

2. By subtracting 207 from 250, $\Delta\overline{X}$ becomes the difference between the average number of trees that survive and the claim of 250:

Null Hypothesis (H_0) : $\Delta\overline{X} = 0$
Alt. Hypothesis (H_A) : $\Delta\overline{X} \neq 0$

3. Using $\overline{p}$ as the average proportion of trees that survive:

Null Hypothesis (H_0) : $\overline{p} = 0.90$
Alt. Hypothesis (H_A) : $\overline{p} \neq 0.90$

4. By subtracting 0.828 from 0.90, $\Delta\overline{p}$ becomes the difference between the average proportion of trees that survive and the claim of 90%:

Null Hypothesis (H_0) : $\Delta\overline{p} = 0$
Alt. Hypothesis (H_A) : $\Delta\overline{p} =/0$

With this type of variable, using the *proportion* variable in the third and fourth hypothesis pairs is the most common practice. The third pair is typically the easiest version for novices to learn. Thus, the example will continue by using this hypothesis pair:

$$\text{Null Hypothesis } (H_0): \quad \bar{p} = 0.90$$
$$\text{Alt. Hypothesis } (H_A): \quad \bar{p} \neq 0.90$$

b. Show four possible outcomes from a random sample, and state the statistical and managerial consequences.

There are many sampling outcomes that could occur. The graphs in Fig. 8.29 show the sample from the example ($p = 0.828$) and its relationship to that of the claimed distribution. The two distributions are visually significantly different and are statistically significantly different—and not in a good way.

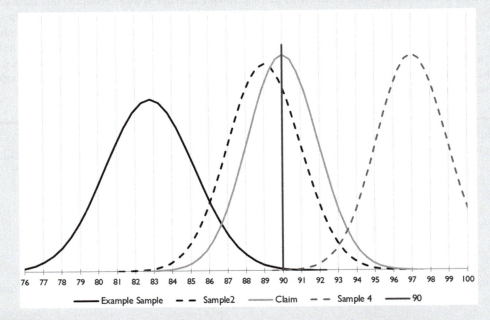

FIGURE 8.29

Four Potential Sampling Proportions

Furthermore, the graph in Fig. 8.29 shows that *Sample 2* is not statistically significantly different from the claim of 90%. This would be the most difficult case to express to people lacking a statistical education—that the lower average (89%) is close enough to 90% to not constitute a problem. *Sample 4* has a distribution that is statistically significantly different from the claim, but in a good way.

c. What is the appropriate standard error?

When computing *confidence intervals*, the proportion estimated from the sample (p) is used to estimate the sample *standard deviation* and subsequently the *standard error*. In other words, for confidence intervals:

$$SE_p = (\hat{p}(1 - \hat{p})/n)^{1/2}$$

Thus, in the previous example (Example 8.6), $\hat{p} = 0.828$ was used to compute the *standard error*. In contrast, when conducting the hypothesis, the *null hypothesis* test value is assumed to be true (*innocent until proven guilty*). Thus, the test value is used to compute the standard error (*SE*):

$$SE_p = (p\,(1-p)\,/n)^{1/2}$$

$$SE_p = \left(\frac{0.9\;(0.1)}{250}\right)^{1/2} \cong \mathbf{0.018974}$$

(compared to 0.023868 in Example 8.6).

In other words, use the proportion $\hat{p}$ estimated from the *data* (the sample) when computing the standard error for use in a *confidence interval*; use the proportion p estimated from the *test value* (*not the sample* (P)) when computing the standard error for use in a *hypothesis test*:

$$\text{Confidence Interval} \rightarrow SE_p = \left(p\left(1-p\right)\right)/n^{1/2}$$

$$\text{Hypothesis Test} \rightarrow SE_p = (p_{testvalue}\,(1 - p_{testvalue}))\,/n^{1/2}$$

d. How many standard errors way from the claim of 90% survival is the sample proportion?

$$observation = average \pm z\ SE0.828 = 0.900 - z\,(0.018974)$$

$$z = (\,0.828 - 0.900\,)\,/0.018974 = -\mathbf{3.795}\ \text{standard errors}$$

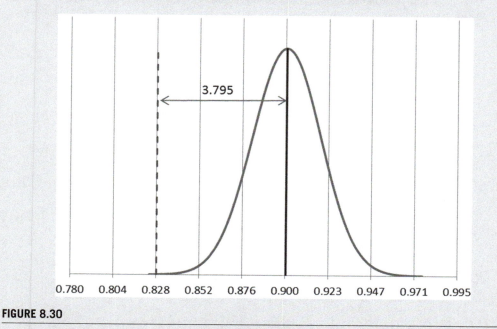

FIGURE 8.30

82.6% Is 3.795 Standard Errors Away From the ***Test Value*** of 90%

e. What are the statistical and managerial conclusions?

Statistical conclusion: Because the .828 is more than 1.96 (95%) standard errors away from the test value, the *null hypothesis* would be rejected, and we would state that the sample average *is* statistically significantly different from the test value.

In other words, the 82.8% from the sample **is** statistically significantly different from the 90% claimed by the supplier.

Managerial conclusion: Because the two values are statistically significantly different and because the sample is significantly less than the claim, we would conclude that either this sample of trees is of unacceptable quality or that the supplier's trees are of unacceptable quality. Either conclusion means that the supplier is accountable for the problem and not "chance" or "tough luck."

Example 8.8 Hypothesis testing of simulation proportions

Consider again the home and garden/hardware chain that purchased a batch of 250 dogwood trees. The chain sold all 250 trees, and after a year, 207 had survived. The supplier claims that 90% of the trees it sells will survive. Construct a simulation based upon this sample, and generate the distribution of the number of trees that survived. Generate the distribution of the percentage (proportion) of trees that survived.

a. Calculate the margin of error and 95% confidence interval for each trial of 250 trees.

b. Test whether the simulation average is significantly different from the hypothesis of 90%.

The simulation spreadsheet shown in Fig. 8.31 assumes that the data from the sample of 250 is a representative sample. Note that in 1000 trials, there were *no* samples of 250 in which 90% (225) or more of the trees lived. This indicates that either the sample of 250 trees was significantly different from the regular batches of trees or that the claim of 90% is significantly different from regular batches of trees. In other works, either this batch of 250 trees was of lower quality or the 90% claim is not true.

J13 fx =(C13<$G$7)*1

	A	B	C	D	E	F	G	H	I	J	K	L	M	N	O	P	Q	R	S	T	IU	IV	IW	IX	IY	IZ
1	n	250																								
2	p	82.8%	207																							
3	q	17.2%																								
4	p null	90.0%	225																							
5	Conf. Level	95%	1.960																							
6		Sum	Avg	SD	SE	ME																				
7	Theory	207	0.828	0.377	0.024	0.047	0.875																			
8	Simulation	206.95	0.828	0.377	0.024	0.047																				
9																										
10	# >=225	0	0																							
11	Avg	206.95	0.828	0.377	0.376	0.024	0.047			97.1%																
12	Trial	Sum	Avg	SD	SD	SE	ME	Lower CI	Upper CI	Avg<95% CI	1	2	3	4	5	6	7	8	9	10	245	246	247	248	249	250
13	1	211	0.844	0.364	0.363	0.023	0.045	0.799	0.889	1	1	1	1	1	1	1	0	1	1	1	0	1	1	1	1	1
14	2	204	0.816	0.388	0.387	0.025	0.048	0.768	0.864	1	1	1	1	1	1	1	1	1	1	1	1	1	1	1	1	1
15	3	222	0.888	0.316	0.315	0.020	0.039	0.849	0.927	0	1	1	1	1	1	0	1	1	0	1	1	1	1	1	1	1
16	4	204	0.816	0.388	0.387	0.025	0.048	0.768	0.864	1	0	1	1	1	1	1	1	1	1	1	1	1	1	1	1	1
17	5	203	0.812	0.391	0.391	0.025	0.048	0.764	0.860	1	1	1	1	1	0	1	1	0	1	1	1	1	0	1	1	1
18	6	213	0.852	0.356	0.355	0.022	0.044	0.808	0.896	1	1	1	1	0	1	0	1	0	1	1	1	1	1	1	0	1
19	7	195	0.780	0.415	0.414	0.026	0.051	0.729	0.831	1	0	1	1	0	0	1	1	1	0	0	1	1	1	1	0	1
20	8	203	0.812	0.391	0.391	0.025	0.048	0.764	0.860	1	0	1	0	1	1	0	1	0	0	1	1	1	0	1	1	1
21	9	210	0.840	0.367	0.367	0.023	0.045	0.795	0.885	1	0	1	0	0	1	1	1	1	1	1	1	1	1	1	1	1
22	10	209	0.836	0.371	0.370	0.023	0.046	0.790	0.882	1	1	1	1	1	1	1	1	1	0	1	1	1	1	0	1	1
1007	995	206	0.824	0.382	0.381	0.024	0.047	0.777	0.871	1	1	1	1	1	0	1	1	1	0	1	1	1	1	1	0	1
1008	996	211	0.844	0.364	0.363	0.023	0.045	0.799	0.889	1	1	1	1	1	1	1	1	1	1	1	1	0	1	1	1	1
1009	997	210	0.840	0.367	0.367	0.023	0.045	0.795	0.885	1	1	1	1	0	0	1	1	1	1	1	1	1	1	1	1	1
1010	998	205	0.820	0.385	0.384	0.024	0.048	0.772	0.868	1	1	1	1	1	0	1	1	0	1	0	1	0	1	1	0	0
1011	999	221	0.884	0.321	0.320	0.020	0.040	0.844	0.924	0	1	1	1	0	1	1	1	1	1	1	1	1	1	1	1	1
1012	1000	209	0.836	0.371	0.370	0.023	0.046	0.790	0.882	1	1	1	1	1	1	1	1	1	1	1	1	1	1	1	0	0

FIGURE 8.31

Simulation of 1000 Trials of 250 Trees Assuming the Sample Data Survival Rate

Fig. 8.32 shows the distribution of the number of trees (column B from the spreadsheet in Fig. 8.31) and the distribution of the percentage (proportion) of trees that survived (column C). Note that the only difference between the distributions is the product of the constant (scalar): 250.

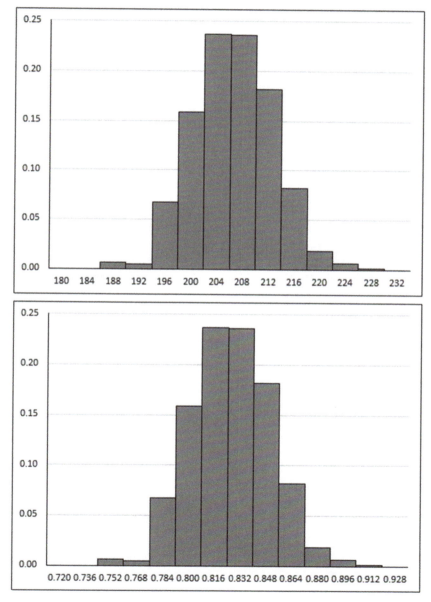

FIGURE 8.32

Probability Distribution of the Number of Trees and the Proportion of 250 Trees Assuming the Sample Data Survival Rate

The simulation shown in the spreadsheet in Fig. 8.33 assumes that the claim of 90% is true. Note that in 1000 trials, there were no samples of 250 in which 207 (82.8%) or fewer trees lived. This again indicates that either the sample of 250 trees was significantly different from the regular batches of trees or that the claim of 90% is significantly different from regular batches of trees. Also note that 95% of the samples' confidence intervals encompass the true value of 95%. Thus, when you construct a 95% confidence interval from a single sample, there is a 95% chance that the interval contains the true value of the parameter.

| J13 | | | f_x | =(H13<$B$2)*($B$2<I13) | | | | | | | | | | | | | | | | | | | | | | |

	A	B	C	D	E	F	G	H	I	J	K	L	M	N	O	P	Q	R	S	T	IU	IV	IW	IX	IY	IZ
1	n	250																								
2	p	90%	<-Assumes 90% is true																							
3	q	10%																								
4	Conf. Level	95%	1.960																							
5																										
6		Sum	Avg	SD	SE	ME																				
7	Theory	225	0.900	0.300	0.019	0.037																				
8	Simulation	224.94	0.900	0.299	0.019	0.037																				
9																										
10	# <=207	0	0.000																							
11	Avg	224.94	0.900	0.299	0.299	0.019	0.037			0.95																

	Trial	Sum	Avg	SD	SD	SE	ME	Lower CI	Upper CI	CI True	1	2	3	4	5	6	7	8	9	10	245	246	247	248	249	250
13	1	225	0.900	0.301	0.300	0.019	0.04	0.863	0.937	1	1	1	1	1	1	1	1	0	1	1	0	1	1	1	1	1
14	2	227	0.908	0.290	0.289	0.018	0.04	0.872	0.944	1	1	1	1	0	1	1	1	1	1	1	1	1	1	1	1	0
15	3	229	0.916	0.278	0.277	0.018	0.03	0.882	0.950	1	1	1	1	1	1	1	1	1	1	1	1	1	1	1	1	1
16	4	226	0.904	0.295	0.295	0.019	0.04	0.867	0.941	1	0	0	1	0	1	1	1	1	0	1	1	1	1	0	0	1
17	5	225	0.900	0.301	0.300	0.019	0.04	0.863	0.937	1	1	1	1	1	1	1	1	1	1	1	1	1	0	0	1	
18	6	226	0.904	0.295	0.295	0.019	0.04	0.867	0.941	1	1	1	1	1	1	1	1	0	1	0	1	1	1	1	1	1
19	7	224	0.896	0.306	0.305	0.019	0.04	0.858	0.934	1	1	1	1	1	1	1	1	0	1	0	1	1	1	1	1	1
20	8	233	0.932	0.252	0.252	0.016	0.03	0.901	0.963	0	1	1	1	1	1	1	1	1	1	0	1	1	1	1	1	1
21	9	234	0.936	0.245	0.245	0.015	0.03	0.906	0.966	0	1	1	1	1	1	1	1	0	1	1	1	1	1	1	1	0
22	10	228	0.912	0.284	0.283	0.018	0.04	0.877	0.947	1	1	1	1	0	1	1	1	1	1	0	1	0	1	1	1	1
1007	995	222	0.888	0.316	0.315	0.020	0.04	0.849	0.927	1	1	1	1	1	1	1	1	1	1	0	1	1	1	1	1	1
1008	996	220	0.880	0.326	0.325	0.021	0.04	0.840	0.920	1	1	1	1	1	1	1	1	0	1	0	1	0	1	1	1	0
1009	997	215	0.860	0.348	0.347	0.022	0.04	0.817	0.903	1	1	1	0	0	1	1	1	1	0	1	1	1	1	1	1	1
1010	998	229	0.916	0.278	0.277	0.018	0.03	0.882	0.950	1	1	1	1	0	1	1	1	1	1	1	1	0	1	1	1	1
1011	999	221	0.884	0.321	0.320	0.020	0.04	0.844	0.924	1	1	1	1	1	1	0	1	1	0	1	1	1	1	1	1	
1012	1000	228	0.912	0.284	0.283	0.018	0.04	0.877	0.947	1	1	1	1	1	1	1	1	1	1	1	0	1	1	

FIGURE 8.33

Simulation of 1000 Trials of 250 Trees Assuming a 90% Survival Rate

The graph in Fig. 8.34 shows the distribution for the percentage of live trees assuming the sample is representative and the distribution assuming the 90% survival rate is correct. The disparity between the two distributions clearly demonstrates that, even allowing for random chance, there is a statistically significant difference between the sample average of 82.8% and the claim of 90%.

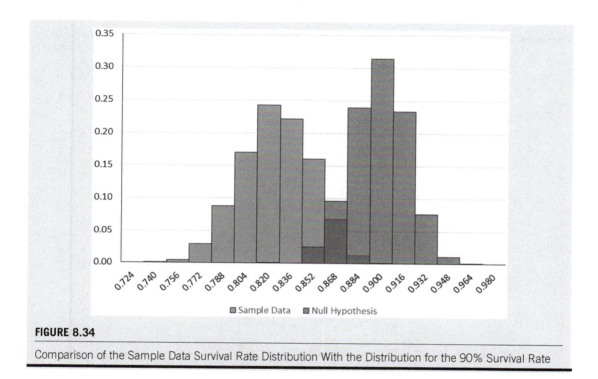

FIGURE 8.34

Comparison of the Sample Data Survival Rate Distribution With the Distribution for the 90% Survival Rate

8.7 Confidence intervals and hypothesis testing for means

As the central limit theorem shows that many sample averages would be normally distributed, ONE SAMPLE provides enough information to make inferences (*confidence intervals* and *hypothesis tests*) about the underlying population represented by the one sample. Refer to Fig. 8.13, which provides an illustration of the concept of the central limit theorem.

8.7.1 Samples with n > 30: use standard normal distribution

The size of the sample determines the computations of *confidence intervals* and *hypothesis testing* for numeric variables. The following example shows that for samples greater than 30, the calculations for numeric variables are much the same as the calculations for proportions.

Example 8.9 Confidence intervals for means: *n* > 30

An aircraft parts supplier needs to know the average age of a particular model of aircraft. One hundred aircraft are selected at random. The aircraft in the sample have an average age of 12.5 years with a standard deviation of 8.15 years. One specific type of part has a typical life of 10 years before it must be replaced.

a. What is the probability distribution for the average age from a random sample of 100 aircraft?

By the central limit theorem, the sample averages will be **normal**. To answer part (a), compute the standard deviation of the averages (*standard error*) this way:

$$Avg_{Sample\ Avg} = \mathbf{12.5}\ years$$

$$SE = SD_{Sample\ Avg} = 8.16/100^{1/2} \cong \mathbf{0.815}\ years$$

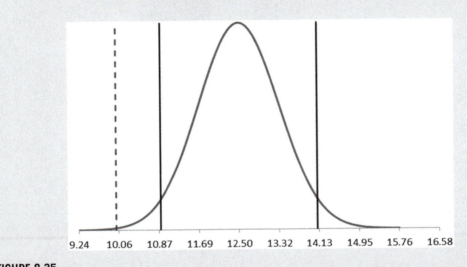

9.24   10.06   10.87   11.69   12.50   13.32   14.13   14.95   15.76   16.58

FIGURE 8.35

95% Confidence Interval for the Average Aircraft Age

b. What is the 95% confidence interval for the average age of the aircraft?

To answer part (b), the values that are symmetric about the mean that constitute a 95% probability are approximately 1.96 standard errors away from average:

$$95\%\ Confidence\ Interval = 12.5 \pm 1.96(0.815)$$
$$= 12.5 \pm 1.5974 = \mathbf{[10.9\ 14.1]\ years}$$

Note that the value $1.96(.815) \cong 1.6$ years is the *margin of error*. Based on the confidence interval, the aircraft should have already had that part replaced.

Example 8.10 Hypothesis testing of means: $n > 30$

An aircraft parts supplier needs to know the average age of a particular model of aircraft. One hundred aircraft are selected at random. The aircraft in the sample have an average age of 12.5 years with a standard deviation of 8.15 years. One specific type of part has a typical life of 10 years before it must be replaced.

a. What are the null and alternative hypotheses?

For part (a), there are two equivalent *null/alternative* hypothesis pairs:

1. Using $\overline{X}$ as the average age:

$$\text{Null Hypothesis } (H_0): \quad \overline{X} = 10$$
$$\text{Alt. Hypothesis } (H_a): \quad \overline{X} \neq 10$$

or

2. By subtracting the test value from both sides of the preceding hypotheses, $\Delta\overline{X}$ becomes the difference between the sample average and the test value:

$$\text{Null Hypothesis } (H_0): \quad \Delta\overline{X} = 0$$
$$\text{Alt. Hypothesis } (H_a): \quad \Delta\overline{X} \neq 0$$

With numeric variables, either of the two sets of hypotheses are commonly used in practice. To demonstrate the concept of *significant difference*, the example will continue by using this hypothesis pair:

$$\text{Null Hypothesis } (H_0): \quad \Delta\overline{X} = 0$$
$$\text{Alt. Hypothesis } (H_a): \quad \Delta\overline{X} \neq 0$$

b. Show four possible outcomes from a random sample, and state the statistical and managerial consequences.

Many sampling outcomes could occur. Part (b) is answered by examining the graph in Fig. 8.36, which shows the sample from the example (*sample average* = 12.5) and its relationship to that of the value in question (10 years). The sample average of 12.5 in this example is clearly statistically significantly different.

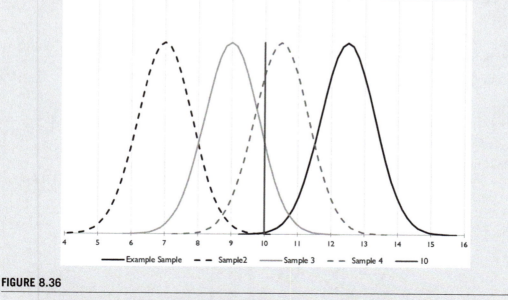

FIGURE 8.36

Comparison of Four Possible Distributions of Sample Averages

Furthermore, the graph in Fig. 8.36 shows that *Sample 2* is statistically significantly below the value of 10 years. *Sample 3* is *not* statistically significantly below the value of 10 years. *Sample 4* is *not* statistically significantly different from the value of 10 years. Finally, the sample average of 12.5 in this example is clearly statistically significantly different (higher) from the value of 10 years.

To illustrate how testing the difference is the same as testing the data values, subtracting 10 years from the sample shown in Fig. 8.36 yields Fig. 8.37.

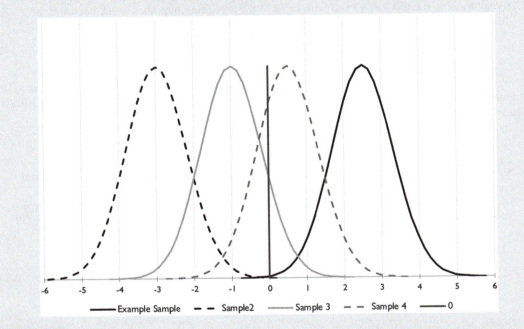

FIGURE 8.37

Comparison of Four Possible Distributions of Sample Averages' Difference From 10 Years

Notice that except for the numbers on the horizontal scale, the two graphs are identical.

REMEMBER: You cannot do anything arbitrary that will change the truth.

c. How many standard deviations way from the 10-year claim is the sample average?
Using 0 as the test value and 2.5 (= 12.5 − 10) as the sample average:

$$observation = average \pm z \; SE$$

$$0 = 2.5 - z \, (0.815)$$

$$z = (\, 0 - 2.5) \, / \, 0.815 = -3.07 \; \textbf{standard errors}$$

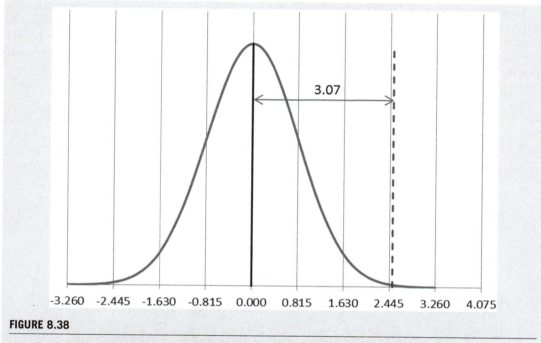

FIGURE 8.38

Hypothesis Test of 2.5 Years = 0 Years (12.5 Years = 10 Years)

d. What are the statistical and managerial consequences?

Statistical conclusion: As 2.5 is more than 1.96 (95%) standard errors away from 0, the *null hypothesis* would be rejected. Thus, 12.5 years is *statistically significantly different* from 10 years (i.e., 2.5 is not "close enough" to 0), and we would state that the sample average is statistically significantly different from the test value. Managerial conclusion: The average aircraft are significantly older than 10 years, and the part will need to be replaced if it has not been already. This is a good potential market for this company.

8.7.2 Small (n ≤ 30) samples: use Student's t-distribution

W.S. Gossett, while working for Guinness Brewery from 1906 to 1908, used slips of paper drawn from a hat to simulate and estimate *small sample corrections* to the standard normal probabilities, $f(z)$. Another researcher at Guinness had previously published a paper containing trade secrets of Guinness. To prevent further disclosure of confidential information, Guinness prohibited its employees from publishing any papers regardless of the contained information. However, after imploring the brewery and explaining that his research was of no possible practical use to competing brewers, he was allowed to publish them, but under the pseudonym *Student*. Thus, this family of distributions is now referred to as *Student's t-distribution*.

This distribution is designated at t_{df}, where *df* is the number of degrees of freedom, and for this procedure:

$$df = n - 1$$

Thus, with a sample of 20, the *t-distribution* with $df = 19$ is used to determine the appropriate probabilities and their associated number of standard deviations—or standard errors—depending upon the situation. Figure 8.39 shows how adding data to the sample size causes the distribution to become closer to normal. Notice that at $df = 30$ (a sample size of $n = 31$), the *t*-distribution is very nearly normal.

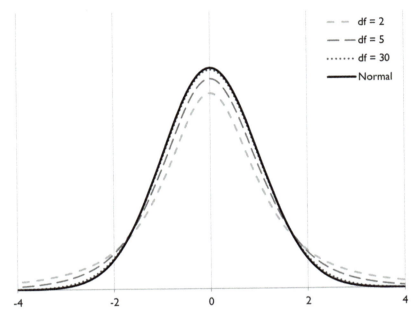

FIGURE 8.39

Comparison of t_2, t_5, and t_{30} Distributions With the Standard Normal Distribution

Rather than the 1.96 that corresponds to 95% for the normal distribution for small samples, values larger than 2 are used to compensate for the smaller sample size. The next two examples illustrate how the *t*-distribution is used to compensate for small ($n \leq 30$) samples.

Example 8.11 Confidence intervals for means: $n \leq 30$
A soft drink distributor claims that a new display, featuring a life-size picture of a well-known athlete, will increase product sales in supermarkets by an average of 50 cases in a week. A random sample of 20 supermarkets had the following increases in sales (in cases): 43, 71, 41, 40, 33, 46, 41, 30, 49, 51, 32, 55, 52, 30, 28, 48, 46, 48, 60, 38.

a. Calculate the parameters for the distribution of the sample averages.

As the sample size is 20 (<30), Student's t-distribution with 19 degrees of freedom ($df = 19$) is the appropriate distribution for the sample averages. To answer part (a), calculate the average and *standard error* (standard deviation of the averages) this way:

$$Avg_{Sample\ Avg} = SUM(Sample\ Data)/n = \textbf{44.1000 cases}$$
$$SE = SD_{Sample\ Avg} = SD_{Sample}/20^{1/2} \cong 10.9251/20^{1/2} \cong \textbf{2.4429 cases}$$

b. What is the 95% confidence interval for the average increase in sales from a random sample of 20?

To answer part (b) using Student's t-distribution with 19 degrees of freedom ($df = 19$), the appropriate value for 95% comes from the *t-table* in the appendix. The values that are symmetric about the mean that constitute a 95% probability are approximately 2.093 standard errors away from average:

$$95\% \text{ Confidence Interval} = 44.10 \pm 2.093(2.4429)$$
$$= 44.10 \pm 5.113 = \textbf{[38.99 49.21] cases}$$

Note that this interval does *not* contain the claim of 50 cases.

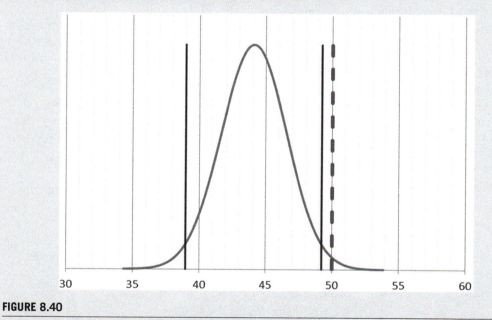

FIGURE 8.40

95% Confidence Interval for the Average Increase in Sales

c. What is the probability that the average increase in sales is 50 or more cases from a random sample of 20?

$$P(CasesIncrease_{Sample\ Avg} \geq 50) = 1 - F(50)$$
$$= 1 - T_{19}\left(\frac{50 - 44.10}{2.4429}\right)$$
$$= 1 - T_{19}(2.620) \cong 0.00843 \cong \textbf{0.843\%}$$

where $T_{df}(x)$ is the cumulative probability from a t-distribution—that is, $T_{df}(x)$ is the *cumulative density function (cdf)* for a t-distribution with $n-1$ degrees of freedom (represented by the subscript df). In other words, $T_{df}(x) = F(x)$ for the t-distribution. Note that standard tables of the t-distribution do not cover all values of x. This makes it necessary to use a computer for such calculations. But note that because 50 is outside the 95% confidence interval, 2.42 is outside the 2.093 t-value for 95%. This is the concept that hypothesis testing is built upon.

d. What are the statistical and managerial consequences?

   Statistical conclusion: Since the claim of 50 cases is outside the 95% confidence interval, the sample average is *statistically significantly different* from the claim of 50.

   Managerial conclusion: It is extremely unlikely that the distributor's claim of an average of 50 cases is valid, and thus there is a problem with the distributor's claim.

Example 8.12 Hypothesis testing of means: $n \leq 30$

A soft drink distributor claims that a new display, featuring a life-size picture of a well-known athlete, will increase product sales in supermarkets by an average of 50 cases in a week. A random sample of 20 supermarkets had the following increases in sales (in cases): 43, 71, 41, 40, 33, 46, 41, 30, 49, 51, 32, 55, 52, 30, 28, 48, 46, 48, 60, 38.

a. What are the null and alternative hypotheses?

b. Show four possible outcomes from a random sample, and state the statistical and managerial consequences.

c. How many standard deviations away from the claim of 50 cases is the sample average?

d. What are the statistical and managerial consequences?

a. There are two equivalent null/alternative hypothesis pairs:

1. Using $\bar{X}$ as the average sales:

$$\text{Null Hypothesis } (H_0): \quad \bar{X} = 50$$
$$\text{Alt. Hypothesis } (H_a): \quad \bar{X} \neq 50$$

or

2. By subtracting the test value from both sides of the preceding hypotheses, $\Delta\bar{X}$ becomes the difference between the sample average and the test value:

$$\text{Null Hypothesis } (H_0): \quad \Delta\bar{X} = 0$$
$$\text{Alt. Hypothesis } (H_a): \quad \Delta\bar{X} =/0$$

With numeric variables, either of the two sets of hypotheses are commonly used in practice. For simplicity, the example will continue by using this hypothesis pair:

$$\text{Null Hypothesis } (H_0): \quad \bar{X} = 50$$
$$\text{Alt. Hypothesis } (H_a): \quad \bar{X} \neq 50$$

b. Show four possible outcomes from a random sample, and state the statistical and managerial consequences.

Many sampling outcomes could occur. Part (b) is answered by examining the graph in Fig. 8.41, which shows the sample from the example (*sample average* = 44.10 cases) and its relationship to that of the value in question (50 cases). The sample average from the example data is obviously statistically significantly different from 50 cases—and not in a good way:

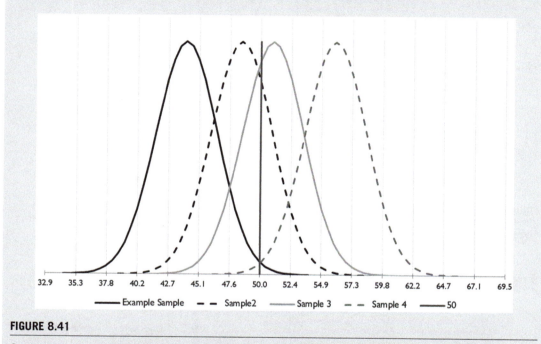

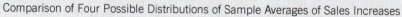

FIGURE 8.41

Comparison of Four Possible Distributions of Sample Averages of Sales Increases

Furthermore, Fig. 8.41 shows that *Sample 2 is not* statistically significantly different from the value of 50 cases. *Sample 3 is not* statistically significantly above (or different from) the value of 50 cases. *Sample 4 is* statistically significantly different from the value of 50 cases—in a good way.

c. How many standard deviations way from the claim of 50 cases is the sample average?

$$observation = average \pm t \ SE$$

$$44.1 = 50 - t(2.4429)$$

$$t = (44.10 - 50)/2.4429 = -2.42 \ \text{standard erros}$$

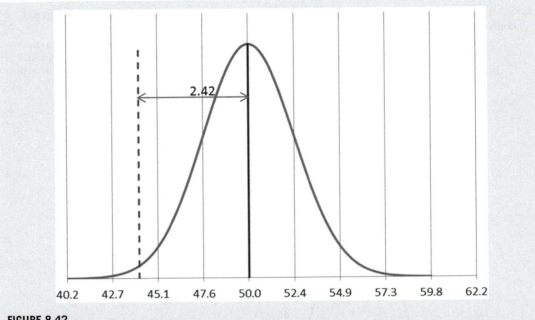

FIGURE 8.42

Hypothesis Test for Sales Increase = 50 Cases

d. What are the statistical and managerial consequences?

Since hypothesis testing uses the same information as confidence intervals, the hypothesis test is a direct mathematical transform of the confidence interval. Thus, the statistical and managerial conclusions must be the same.

Statistical conclusion: Because the claim of 50 cases is outside the 95% confidence interval, the sample average is *statistically significantly different* from the claim of 50.

Managerial conclusion: It is extremely unlikely that the distributor's claim of an average of 50 cases is valid, and thus there is a problem with the distributor's claim.

REMEMBER: You cannot do anything arbitrary that will change the truth.

The computations for confidence intervals and hypothesis testing are simple to create in a spreadsheet, as shown in Fig. 8.43.

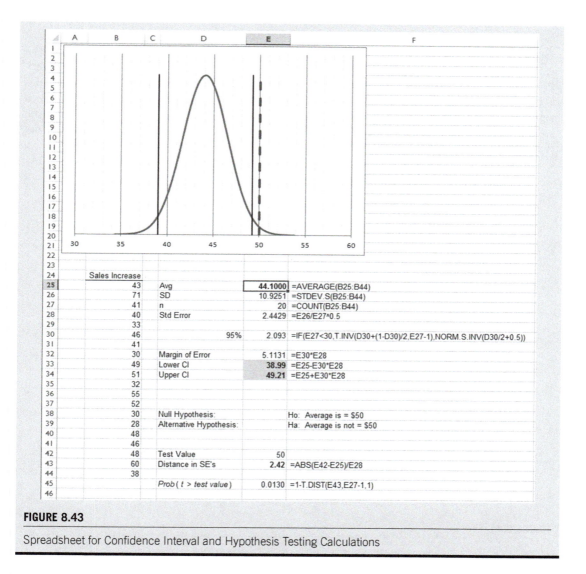

FIGURE 8.43

Spreadsheet for Confidence Interval and Hypothesis Testing Calculations

Example 8.13 Hypothesis testing of simulation means

Consider again the soft drink distributor who claims that a new display, featuring a life-size picture of a well-known athlete, will increase product sales in supermarkets by an average of 50 cases in a week. A random sample of 20 supermarkets had the following increases in sales (in cases): 43, 71, 41, 40, 33, 46, 41, 30, 49, 51, 32, 55, 52, 30, 28, 48, 46, 48, 60, 38. Create a simulation based upon the sample data and a second simulation assuming that the increase in sales of 50 cases is true.

The simulation shown in the spreadsheet in Fig. 8.44 assumes that the data from the sample of 20 stores are a representative sample and are thus representative of the results of the promotion. The simulation was created using the empirical probabilities from the sample and the VLOOKUP function. Note that in 1000 trials, there were only 7 samples (trials) in which the average increase in sales is greater than or equal to the claim of 50 cases. This indicates that either the sample of 20 stores was significantly different from typical stores or that the claim of 50 cases is significantly different from what the promotion will actually achieve. In other words, either this sample of 20 stores was not typical or the 50-case claim is not true.

D8		f_x =(B8>=$B$5)*1																										
	A	B	C	D	E F G H I	J K	L M	N O	P Q	R S	T U	V W	X Y	Z	AA	AB												
1	Theory	44.1	10.9	2.4	5.1																							
2	Simulation	44.1	10.6	2.4	5.0																							
3																												
4	Conf. Level	95%	2.09																									
5	Test Value	50																										
6		1.6%		0.007	Store																							

Trial	Avg	SD	Inc>=50	1	2	3	4	5	6	7	8	9	10	11	12	13	14	15	16	17	18	19	20	Rank	RAND()	Sales Increase
1	41.1	9.2	0	43	30	43	30	60	41	30	41	40	55	40	48	60	41	38	30	41	30	40	40	1	0.00	28
2	45.7	11.1	0	46	30	60	55	51	33	60	55	32	60	60	46	51	38	30	49	28	49	41	40	2	0.05	30
3	45.3	7.7	0	30	43	51	55	40	28	52	46	51	43	49	38	41	52	55	51	51	46	46	38	3	0.10	30
4	40.4	11.0	0	28	41	40	30	41	52	71	46	32	40	52	30	28	33	40	46	30	32	40	55	4	0.15	32
5	43.2	14.9	0	30	30	43	28	71	30	40	30	48	60	41	60	28	71	46	55	32	60	32	28	5	0.20	33
6	40.8	9.4	0	51	55	46	30	52	48	48	30	28	32	33	40	49	48	33	52	30	43	28	40	6	0.25	38
7	46.0	11.4	0	71	55	41	46	52	38	41	46	48	40	51	28	46	30	48	28	71	43	48	48	7	0.30	40
8	50.0	10.5	0	43	30	28	55	71	48	51	48	43	51	52	55	71	46	60	52	52	46	46	51	8	0.35	41
9	43.7	12.9	0	46	32	41	30	30	28	40	71	38	51	49	43	32	41	71	60	38	51	30	52	9	0.40	41
10	44.8	12.0	0	28	32	49	48	32	71	48	41	30	46	51	40	41	71	41	55	41	48	30	52	10	0.45	43
11	41.0	12.0	0	49	33	33	32	49	43	28	40	28	48	55	43	30	71	33	30	48	38	60	28	11	0.50	46
12	46.1	12.5	0	48	41	55	43	48	43	43	60	71	30	38	41	71	30	60	33	55	43	30	38	12	0.55	46
13	44.4	8.2	0	41	30	41	43	41	49	51	55	38	55	46	28	41	48	49	49	49	55	48	30	13	0.60	48
14	44.3	11.8	0	28	33	46	28	43	38	60	51	55	46	41	32	49	71	38	49	60	49	28	40	14	0.65	48
15	49.3	10.6	0	51	55	48	60	71	46	38	46	60	48	52	48	46	41	71	52	38	33	33	48	15	0.70	49
16	46.0	11.5	0	41	30	30	51	41	40	46	60	41	41	71	48	46	41	46	48	52	71	48	28	16	0.75	51
17	50.7	12.4	1	60	71	60	71	38	48	40	48	71	33	32	52	49	51	46	60	51	30	52	51	17	0.80	52
18	48.3	9.6	0	46	46	46	30	60	60	55	46	49	51	30	38	51	48	40	46	71	52	49	51	18	0.85	55
19	49.1	9.6	0	40	55	55	60	46	28	41	48	60	51	52	49	41	40	60	49	71	41	46	48	19	0.90	60
20	39.5	8.0	0	32	38	46	55	43	51	28	30	38	30	46	40	51	43	43	38	33	33	28	43	20	0.95	71
21	47.3	5.1	0	48	38	43	49	60	46	52	52	49	46	40	48	48	46	43	52	46	49	51	40		1.00	71
22	38.4	7.7	0	32	46	38	30	32	60	43	40	40	38	40	28	32	33	46	41	32	46	30	40			
995	42.1	9.5	0	49	33	52	40	43	52	30	40	55	41	38	38	43	46	49	28	48	28	60	28			
996	41.6	12.1	0	28	30	30	30	38	30	30	43	52	55	32	46	30	38	71	60	48	48	41	51			
997	45.7	10.1	0	48	51	46	46	49	46	71	49	46	32	46	28	60	55	46	41	51	33	38	32			
998	44.2	11.5	0	49	49	46	49	41	52	30	33	51	40	28	60	51	55	71	30	41	32	30	46			
999	41.2	6.9	0	40	46	38	46	30	52	28	41	46	40	46	32	46	43	43	49	46	32	33	46			
1000	44.6	10.4	0	51	43	49	43	51	28	55	48	51	38	38	71	52	28	48	38	52	32	43	33			

FIGURE 8.44

Spreadsheet for Confidence Interval and Hypothesis Testing Calculations

A distribution for the sales increase must be chosen to simulate the null hypothesis assumption that the 50-case increase is true. As the sample could have come from a wide variety of distributions, this example is unlike the null hypothesis simulation shown in Example 8.8 in which it was known that the sample distribution was a binomial distribution. In particular, for this example, there is no specific reason a normal distribution should be assumed. Thus, a brief analysis of the sample data must occur. Fig. 8.45 shows the univariate distribution of sales increases for the 20 stores in the sample.

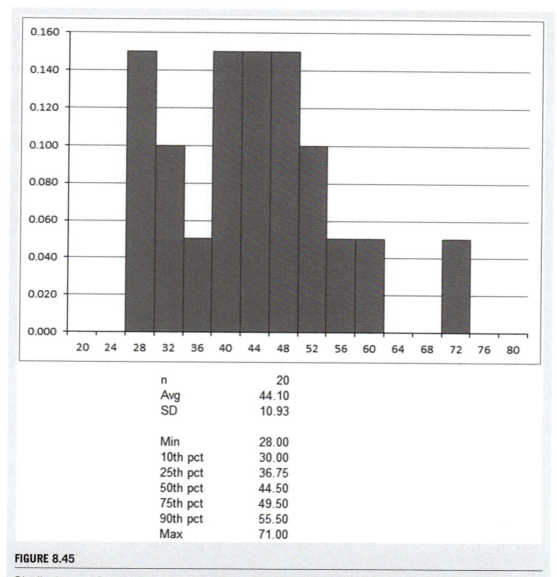

n	20
Avg	44.10
SD	10.93
Min	28.00
10th pct	30.00
25th pct	36.75
50th pct	44.50
75th pct	49.50
90th pct	55.50
Max	71.00

FIGURE 8.45

Distribution and Sample Statistics for the Sales Increases for the 20 Stores

As there was no further probability information provided, a uniform distribution (*no informa-tion*) was selected for the simulation. To verify the average, the average of the sample assuming a uniform distribution was calculated: $(28 + 71)/2 = 99/2 = 49.5 \cong 50$. Furthermore, the large variance of the uniform distribution is more in keeping with the *innocent until proven guilty* spirit of the null hypothesis than distributions that are less spread out (*tighter*) about their mean. Thus, the null hypothesis simulation was generated by sampling 20 stores' sales increases from a discrete uniform distribution [28, 71] to match the sample data.

The simulation shown in the spreadsheet in Fig. 8.46 assumes that the claim of an increase of 50 cases is true and uses a discrete uniform distribution [28, 71] for the sales increase. Note that in 1000 trials, there were 23 samples out of 1000 (2.3%) in which an increase of 44.1 or fewer cases was achieved. This again indicates that either the sample of 20 stores was significantly different from a sample of typical stores or that the claim of sales of 50 additional cases is significantly different from the actual increase due to the promotion—that the promotion will not be as effective as claimed.

| E9 | | ✕ ✓ fx | =ROUND($AA$1+RAND()*$AA$3,0) |

	A	B	C	D
1	Theory	50.0	12.4	
2	Simulation	49.5	12.3	
3				
4	Conf. Level	95%	2.09	
5	Null Value	50		
6				
7				0.023 Store
8	Trial	Avg	SD	44.1

					AA
Min					28
Max					71
Range					43
Average					44.10
SD					10.93
Lower					22.69
Upper					71.41
Obs					Sales Increase

Trial	Avg	SD	D	1	2	3	4	5	6	7	8	9	10	11	12	13	14	15	16	17	18	19	20	Obs	Sales Increase
1	52.2	13.7	0	56	44	46	71	70	47	31	65	36	64	39	40	29	48	55	41	61	67	66	67	1	43
2	48.9	14.9	0	61	29	67	54	55	38	45	69	35	33	67	51	69	28	29	36	62	39	66	45	2	71
3	46.5	11.7	0	32	62	47	37	41	44	48	60	35	43	56	35	28	55	47	42	42	70	67	39	3	41
4	51.6	11.8	0	41	61	52	35	29	43	51	61	40	46	67	51	52	54	69	48	69	40	52	70	4	40
5	52.6	13.7	0	61	69	47	41	62	46	53	57	60	33	61	29	69	55	69	69	59	50	32	29	5	33
6	49.7	12.6	0	65	35	42	66	36	71	45	65	60	46	33	30	60	41	54	38	49	42	62	54	6	46
7	47.9	13.3	0	53	34	46	34	53	58	40	60	41	54	38	64	71	28	44	34	67	29	65	45	7	41
8	48.4	14.3	0	53	38	34	32	52	66	69	60	35	66	69	61	33	36	57	42	33	38	31	62	8	30
9	58.2	10.9	0	66	49	62	53	66	55	63	40	67	60	63	70	48	64	69	64	67	63	29	45	9	49
10	47.8	11.9	0	67	48	64	58	51	48	40	55	67	42	48	32	58	31	30	32	44	40	59	42	10	51
11	51.3	13.5	0	42	59	57	51	57	67	49	66	35	61	71	29	41	66	54	35	50	38	29	68	11	32
12	50.5	13.7	0	36	30	46	45	60	64	36	28	39	57	54	37	53	66	71	67	68	50	63	39	12	55
13	48.2	11.7	0	44	70	46	65	48	47	33	53	29	58	55	59	39	54	35	29	59	40	45	56	13	52
14	47.2	10.6	0	38	61	54	62	42	46	56	36	37	58	57	54	63	55	41	41	36	32	42	32	14	30
15	53.8	13.7	0	53	65	54	70	60	59	70	43	32	55	63	36	70	50	50	29	30	51	68	67	15	28
16	48.5	11.5	0	48	53	59	45	47	53	35	67	71	46	31	37	41	60	61	40	37	51	32	56	16	48
17	46.1	10.7	0	45	28	33	44	55	38	58	55	45	38	41	51	32	60	35	58	64	39	43	59	17	46
18	42.1	8.5	1	48	43	42	37	51	41	40	33	43	31	47	38	36	52	46	33	38	68	41	34	18	48
19	45.3	11.5	0	63	53	37	40	49	42	28	38	42	45	62	32	44	33	66	42	31	65	46	48	19	60
20	48.0	11.0	0	56	39	50	50	39	58	38	48	34	47	56	63	48	28	39	56	59	69	51	32	20	38
21	51.3	12.3	0	44	49	61	45	57	34	64	47	30	69	45	32	62	67	38	56	59	60	42	65		
22	47.7	15.4	0	66	34	35	37	71	29	44	34	69	30	40	70	57	56	51	30	40	68	59	34		
995	47.5	12.6	0	61	39	70	52	62	35	32	38	64	55	39	32	55	68	50	36	37	47	43	35		
996	51.1	14.3	0	44	70	55	58	31	42	31	53	47	71	41	49	68	34	56	65	42	28	66	70		
997	52.8	11.4	0	54	45	66	52	66	42	41	62	47	39	65	48	61	66	55	53	71	38	30	54		
998	52.6	13.7	0	56	56	65	29	45	54	54	70	66	47	51	68	30	30	53	52	61	71	31	63		
999	49.4	12.6	0	53	67	48	39	30	37	58	50	70	58	29	50	56	40	62	46	71	34	43	47		
1000	50.3	12.8	0	67	47	50	39	52	43	59	62	42	53	49	36	62	64	30	43	29	39	70	70		

FIGURE 8.46

Simulation of 20 Stores' Sales Increases Using the Uniform [28, 71] Distribution

These simulations demonstrate that a single sample can provide the inference about what would happen if multiple samples were taken and how those results would compare to a specific outcome. Therefore, it is not necessary to take multiple samples; we can arrive at statistical conclusions (inferences) based on the results of a single sample—thus the high degree of utility of sampling in marketing research, medical research, quality control, financial analysis, and sports analytics.

Exercise Set 8: Central Limit Theorem and Sampling
Adding independent random variables

1. X is a random variable resulting from the roll of a single standard die (with six faces numbered 1 through 6, commonly known as a D-6).
   a. What is the probability distribution of $2X$?
   b. Calculate the probability that $2X$ will be 4.
   c. Calculate the probability that $2X$ will be less than 6.
   d. What is the probability distribution of $X + X$?
   e. Calculate the probability that $X + X$ will be 4.
   f. Calculate the probability that $X + X$ will be less than 6.
   g. Use simulation to determine the difference between $10X$ and the sum of 10 D-6 dice.

2. The average weight of a box shipped by a company is 40 pounds with a standard deviation of 5 pounds. The boxes are all the same size, and thus the same number of boxes fit in a truck. The current truck can hold 50 boxes and has a weight limit of 2000 pounds.
   a. What is the probability distribution of total weight of 50 boxes?
   b. What is the probability that 50 boxes will overload the truck?
   c. What is the probability that 48 boxes will not overload the truck?
   d. How many boxes should be loaded on the truck?
   e. How many trucks are needed to transport 10,000 pounds—and how many boxes per truck?

3. An insurance company has 10,000 automobile policyholders. The expected yearly claim per policyholder is $240 with a standard deviation of $800.
   a. State the mathematical properties that are required to make use of the central limit theorem.
   b. Calculate the probability distribution of the total claims for a year.
   c. Calculate the probability that the total claims for a year exceed $2.6 million.
   d. Calculate the total claims for a year that have a 95% probability of being exceeded.

4. A chain of restaurants has seven restaurants in the region: five in North Carolina and two in Virginia. The monthly sales at each of the restaurants in North Carolina are normally distributed with an average of $125,000 per month and a standard deviation of $20,000. The monthly sales at each of the restaurants in Virginia are normally distributed with an average of $200,000 per month and a standard deviation of $25,000.
   a. Calculate the probability distribution of total sales for the seven restaurants for a month.
   b. Calculate the probability that total monthly sales will be less than $1,000,000.
   c. Calculate the quarterly sales that have a 90% probability of being exceeded.

5. A family owns six franchises of a restaurant. Monthly revenue varies and is normally distributed. The monthly average revenue (in thousands of dollars) and standard deviation of each restaurant are listed as follows:

Restaurant	Average revenue (000)	Standard deviation (000)
1	90	9
2	130	10
3	80	10
4	120	8
5	120	10
6	110	8

    a. Calculate the total amount of revenue that will be exceeded 80% of the months. In other words, only 1 month in 5 would have revenue less than this amount.

    b. Calculate the probability of revenue exceeding $2,000,000 in a quarter from all six restaurants combined.

6. A chain of banks has six branches in the region: four in North Carolina and two in Virginia. The amount of monthly commercial loans at each of the branches in North Carolina is normally distributed with an average of $12,650,000 per month and a standard deviation of $1,750,000. The amount of monthly commercial loans at each of the branches in Virginia is normally distributed with an average of $21,320,000 per month and a standard deviation of $2,840,000.

    a. Calculate the probability distribution of total commercial loans for the six branches for a month.

    b. Calculate the probability that total loans will be less than $100,000,000.

    c. Calculate the quarterly loans that have a 95% probability of being exceeded.

7. An insurance company specializes in commercial insurance. There are six regions: three in North Carolina and three in Virginia. The number of claims each month in each of the North Carolina regions is approximately normally distributed with an average of 12 claims per month and a standard deviation of 3 claims per month. The number of claims each month in each of the Virginia regions is approximately normally distributed with an average of 16 claims per month and a standard deviation of 4 claims per month. Claims are handled by a team of adjusters, and one team can handle 2 claims.

    a. Calculate the probability of more than 235 claims in a quarter from all six regions combined.

    b. Calculate number of adjuster teams that would most closely provide a 90% service level for a month (a 90% chance of not having a shortage within a month).

8. A commercial real estate company has property listings in four cities: Raleigh, Winston-Salem, Greensboro, and Charlotte. The company has an average two sales per month in each of the larger two cities (Raleigh and Charlotte) and one sale per month in each of the two smaller cities.

    a. Use the Poisson distribution to calculate the probability of selling a total—from all four cities combined—six properties in 1 month.

    b. Calculate the probability of selling less than 15 properties for all four cities combined for one quarter of a year.

    c. Calculate the number of properties from the two larger cities combined for a year that would provide a 90% service level. In other words, what is the number of properties, for the two larger cities combined for a year, for which there is a 90% chance that demand will be less than or equal to that number of properties?

9. A regional manager of 43 small retail stores must estimate the financial performance for next month. Table 8.1 lists the 43 stores' contributions from this past month.

    a. State the mathematical properties that are required to make use of the central limit theorem.

    b. Calculate the probability distribution of total contribution for the 43 stores for a month and for a quarter.

    c. Calculate the probability that total contribution for next month will be less than $100,000,000.

    d. Calculate the quarterly contribution, which has a 95% probability of being exceeded.

    e. Create a simulation to verify the answers.

10. An auditor for a large credit card company estimates that the monthly charges for an account in a specific class of customers is $450 with a standard deviation of $56.

Table 8.1 Contribution by store			
Store	**Contribution**	**Store**	**Contribution**
1	173,720.23	23	179,705.41
2	214,644.71	24	202,953.17
3	143,558.59	25	238,971.04
4	180,965.36	26	138,972.05
5	190,847.52	27	183,703.65
6	180,938.48	28	183,035.78
7	194,397.35	29	151,735.14
8	279,154.56	30	156,352.66
9	234,975.45	31	185,226.26
10	276,825.67	32	285,616.93
11	203,635.44	33	185,775.43
12	215,280.78	34	198,758.76
13	234,587.57	35	150,444.95
14	206,890.26	36	163,673.10
15	199,427.40	37	154,901.93
16	160,968.52	38	263,732.52
17	158,389.51	39	165,236.20
18	148,519.77	40	267,523.02
19	124,143.44	41	176,191.96
20	236,283.43	42	169,872.81
21	159,610.82	43	197,929.79
22	203,037.60		

a. What is the probability distribution for the monthly charges of a single account?

b. What is the probability distribution for the total monthly charges a sample of 50 accounts?

c. From a sample of 50 such accounts, what is the probability of total monthly charges exceeding $23,000?

d. What is the probability distribution for the average monthly charges of a sample of 50 accounts?

e. Given a sample of 50 accounts, what is the probability that the average monthly charge exceeds $460?

11. The probability distribution for demand for a product is approximately normal with a mean of 240 units per week and a standard deviation of 40 units.

a. How many units should a retailer have in stock to ensure a 5% or less chance of running out during the week?

b. What is the mean and standard deviation for daily sales (consider 5 days/week)?

c. What is the mean and standard deviation for annual sales (consider 52 weeks/year)?

    d. What is the probability of annual sales exceeding 13,200 units (consider 52 weeks/year)?

    e. What is the probability of annual sales exceeding 13,000 units (consider 52 weeks/year)?

12. The business manager for a law firm monitors charges for various clients and cases. The manager estimates that the average charges for a specific category of case are $6250 with a standard deviation of $1220.

    a. What is the probability distribution for the charges of a single case?

    b. Calculate the probability distribution for the total charges for 150 cases.

    c. What is the probability distribution for the average charges for a sample of 60 cases?

    d. Create a simulation to estimate the probability distribution for the total charges for 150 cases and compare it to part (b).

13. A FedEx contractor owns 50 trucks in a region. Twenty of the trucks are relatively new, and each of these trucks has a 5% chance of not being in service on any day. Ten trucks are older and only have a 90% chance of being in service on any day. Twenty trucks are much older and have a 20% chance of not being in service on any day.

    a. The contractor needs 40 trucks to deliver packages tomorrow. What is the probability that the contractor will have enough trucks?

    b. Is the number of trucks in service normally distributed? Why or why not?

14. A specific class of rooms at a resort hotel has a 5% rate of reservations in which the people do not show up (no shows). The hotel chain owns three similar hotels, two with 20 such rooms and the other with 30 rooms.

    a. Use theoretical probability to determine the probability distribution of demand if all 70 rooms are reserved.

    b. Use theoretical probability to determine the probability that exactly 5 rooms are empty among the three hotels if all 70 rooms are reserved.

    c. Create a simulation to determine the probability distribution of demand if all 70 rooms are reserved.

    d. Create a simulation to determine the probability that exactly 5 rooms are empty among the three hotels if all 70 rooms are reserved.

15. The default rate for a specific class of loans is 2%.

    a. What is the probability distribution for the default of a single loan?

    b. What is the probability distribution for the number of loans defaulting from a portfolio of 3500 loans?

    c. What is the probability distribution for the percentage of loans defaulting from a portfolio of 3500 loans?

    d. Calculate the probability of more than 60 loans defaulting from a portfolio of 3500 loans.

    e. Calculate the probability of at least 50 loans defaulting from a portfolio of 3500 loans.

    f. Create a simulation to calculate the probability of more than 60 loans defaulting from a portfolio of 3500 loans.

    g. Create a simulation to calculate the probability of at least 50 loans defaulting from a portfolio of 3500 loans.

16. A supplier of trees to home and garden/hardware chains claims that 90% of the supplier's dogwood trees survive the first year.

    a. What is the probability distribution for the survival of a single tree?

    b. What is the probability distribution for the number of trees surviving from a batch of 250 trees given a 90% survival rate?

   c. Calculate the probability of at least 230 trees surviving from a batch of 250 trees given a 90% survival rate.

   d. Calculate the probability distribution for the percentage of trees surviving from a batch of 250 trees.

   e. Create a simulation to determine the probability of at least 230 trees surviving from a batch of 250 trees given a 90% survival rate.

   f. Create a simulation to determine the probability distribution for the percentage of trees surviving from a batch of 250 trees given a 90% survival rate.

17. The goal of your marketing campaign is for more than 25% of supermarket shoppers to recognize your brand name.

   a. If the marketing campaign has achieved the 25% target, then what is the probability distribution of an individual person recognizing your brand?

   b. If the marketing campaign has achieved the 25% target, then what is the probability distribution of the percentage of 150 people recognizing your brand?

   c. If the marketing campaign has achieved the 25% target, then what is the probability distribution of the number of people recognizing your brand from a sample of 150 people?

Sampling: estimating and testing proportions

18. Create a simulation of flipping 100 pennies. Statistically test the significance of the number of heads generated in the simulation versus the theoretical number of heads.

   For exercises 19 through 26:

   a. Draw pictures of possible results (outcomes) from such a sample and the managerial conclusion that would result from each outcome.

   b. Compute the 95% confidence interval.

   c. State the null and alternative hypotheses.

   d. State the appropriate statistical conclusion.

   e. State the appropriate managerial conclusion.

19. A poll of 809 randomly selected registered voters revealed that 426 of the voters plan to vote for a specific candidate in the coming election between two candidates.

20. In a blind taste test of a soft drink, 866 out of 1245 tasters preferred the new flavor of soft drink to the old.

21. A test of two website designs (A and B) was conducted to determine which design produced more ad click-throughs. The two website designs were tested by randomly showing the two designs to web visitors. Of the 3545 ad click-throughs, 1717 selected ads from design A.

22. A survey of 252 customers, selected at random from a large database, found that 208 are satisfied with the service they are receiving.

23. In a poll of 2336 US adults, 560 replied "yes" that the US economy was headed in a positive direction. A news organization claimed that 28% of the of US adults felt the economy was headed in a positive direction.

24. The goal of your marketing campaign is for more than 25% of supermarket shoppers to recognize your brand name. A recent survey of 150 randomly selected shoppers (random shoppers would be lots more fun) found that 21.3% recognized your brand name.

25. A credit risk analyst for the credit card issuing department of a bank has sampled 350 credit card holders. Of those sampled, 18 have defaulted in the previous year. A credit card default rate above 5% would indicate a serious concern for the collection of the credit card debt.

Sampling: estimating and testing means

26. There are eight sections of a required college course. The grades for one section are shown in the following.

    a. State the mathematical properties that are required to make use of the central limit theorem.

    b. Based upon this one section, calculate the probability distribution of the course averages for the eight sections.

    c. Calculate the 95% confidence interval.

    d. What is the practical meaning of the standard deviation in this context?

    e. What is the practical meaning of the standard error in this context?

Obs	Grade	Obs	Grade	Obs	Grade
1	85.4	13	91.3	25	85.5
2	83.3	14	85.3	26	94.6
3	88.2	15	95.4	27	91.4
4	86.0	16	89.9	28	78.2
5	84.9	17	86.9	29	89.9
6	81.3	18	83.2	30	77.5
7	91.3	19	91.3	31	79.9
8	85.7	20	86.2	32	82.2
9	94.3	21	87.0	33	84.0
10	79.8	22	80.3	34	78.8
11	82.3	23	82.4	35	81.4
12	95.5	24	96.3	36	84.5

27. A random sample of 36 home property values in one community showed an average loss in value of $11,560 with a standard deviation of $1500. The national average loss was $10,000

    a. Draw pictures of possible results (outcomes) from such a sample and the managerial conclusion that would result from each outcome.

    b. Compute the 95% confidence interval.

    c. State the null and alternative hypotheses.

    d. State the appropriate statistical conclusion.

    e. State the appropriate managerial conclusion.

28. At a recent meeting, it was decided to go ahead with the introduction of a new product if "interested consumers would be willing, on average, to pay $20.00 for the product." A study was conducted, with 315 randomly interested consumers indicating they would pay an average of $18.14 for the product. The standard deviation of the prices in the sample was $2.98.

    a. Draw pictures of possible results (outcomes) from such a sample and the managerial conclusion that would result from each outcome.

    b. Compute the 95% confidence interval.

    c. State the null and alternative hypotheses.

    d. State the appropriate statistical conclusion.

    e. State the appropriate managerial conclusion.

    f. How would the problem change if the sample size was 20 yet the average and standard deviation stayed the same? What are the implications of this question?

    g. With a sample size of 20 and a sample standard deviation of $2.98, how would the average have to change before changing the managerial decision?

29. A random sample of 50 medium-sized businesses in one state showed an average increase over the past 2 years in hiring of 260 employees with a standard deviation of 35. The national average increase for similar-sized companies was 275 employees.

    a. Draw pictures of possible results (outcomes) from such a sample and the managerial conclusion that would result from each outcome.

    b. Compute the 95% confidence interval.

    c. State the null and alternative hypotheses.

    d. State the appropriate statistical conclusion.

    e. State the appropriate managerial conclusion.

30. Your bakery produces loaves of bread with "1 pound" written on the label. Here are the weights of randomly sampled loaves from today's production: 0.993, 1.002, 1.039, 1.037, 0.953, 1.009, 1.030, 1.003, 0.958, 0.996, 0.967, 0.971, 1.026, 0.960, 1.042, 1.012, 0.962, 1.035, 1.007, 1.007, 0.962, 0.965.

    a. Draw pictures of possible results (outcomes) from such a sample and the managerial conclusion that would result from each outcome.

    b. Compute the 95% confidence interval.

    c. State the null and alternative hypotheses.

    d. State the appropriate statistical conclusion.

    e. State the appropriate managerial conclusion.

    f. Create a simulation to demonstrate whether the bakery is meeting the 1-pound specification.

31. An analyst for Medicare fraud analysis has randomly selected a sample of 30 claims. The sample claim average is $330.55 with a sample standard deviation of $90.31. The sample frame (population) has an average of $299.73 with a standard deviation of $93.79.

    a. Draw pictures of possible results (outcomes) from such a sample and the managerial conclusion that would result from each outcome.

    b. Compute the 95% confidence interval.

    c. State the null and alternative hypotheses.

    d. State the appropriate statistical conclusion.

    e. State the appropriate managerial conclusion.

32. Here are satisfaction scores for 12 randomly selected customers: 89, 98, 96, 65, 99, 81, 76, 51, 82, 90, 96, 76.

33. An ad in the newspaper purports that consumers should expect to save money by shopping at Walmart. The results of a study of randomly selected items priced at Walmart and at Target are listed in Table 8.2.

34. In a random sample, eight corporate customers were interviewed to estimate the number of laptop computers they planned to order next year: 220, 180, 240, 470, 640, 320, 450, 350.

Table 8.2 Item price by store

Obs	Product	Walmart ($)	Target ($)
1	Levi's jeans	41.65	41.99
2	Walking shoes	54.95	59.95
3	Dress shirt	26.95	24.99
4	Farberware pots & pans	39.97	44.99
5	Pod coffee maker	79.99	89.99
6	Chocolate meal replacement shake	6.50	4.79
7	Maxwell House coffee	6.59	6.25
8	Kolcraft baby stroller	87.90	69.99
9	Suave shampoo	2.94	2.99
10	Shaving cream	6.13	5.49
11	Schwinn bike	238.00	239.99
12	DVD player	70.00	79.99
13	*Friends* DVD	55.19	67.99
14	Headphones	39.99	39.99
15	Lego Friends house	56.00	59.00
16	Spalding NBA basketball	24.96	15.99

Cases

Omni Resort Villas

As vacation season approaches, Omni Resort Villas must determine the pricing and quantity of different classes and types of villas. Hotels and resorts must manage risk of lost revenues due to no shows. Storms obviously play a significant role in influencing the demand for villas.

The hurricane season is listed as proceeding from June 1 through November 30 (26 weeks). The current forecast is for the 2022 season to be an average hurricane season. According to the National Oceanic and Atmospheric Administration records, there have been 296 hurricanes in the past 48 years (seasons). The analysis, shown in Fig. 8.47, indicates that hurricanes follow a Poisson probability distribution.

Having already determined the pricing and promotions to influence demand, Omni is currently trying to determine the number of villa reservations to book for a specific category of 250 villas for a specific week in July. For a week with a storm, the cancellation rate is approximately 12%, as compared to the 4% for typical (nonstormy) week. Customers for these villas are required to pay a nonrefundable deposit of one night.

For the specific week in July, this category of villas is priced at $2975. If the number of booked customers exceeds capacity, then Omni must accommodate the customer at another property. In overbooking cases such as these, due to lost future rentals, displacement of other rentals, and other considerations (food, bike rentals, gift shop sales, etc.), Omni considers the loss (after collecting the week's rental) of one overbooking to be $5400.

Adventure Luggage 1

Adventure Luggage is a manufacturer of luggage and leather goods established in 1877 in Milwaukee, Wisconsin, by trunk maker Joseph A. Daventer, a Bavarian. In 1956, the company opened a manufacturing operation in Tennessee, and the company's headquarters and plant facilities followed in 1959. Adventure was bought by Brown Forman Corporation before being acquired by Clarion Capital Partners (a private equity firm) in 2007.

Adventure luggage has been recognized as being of fine quality. The company is known for producing distinctive collections of luggage such as Wings and Tweed, which are associated with traditional American style.

Case—cont'd

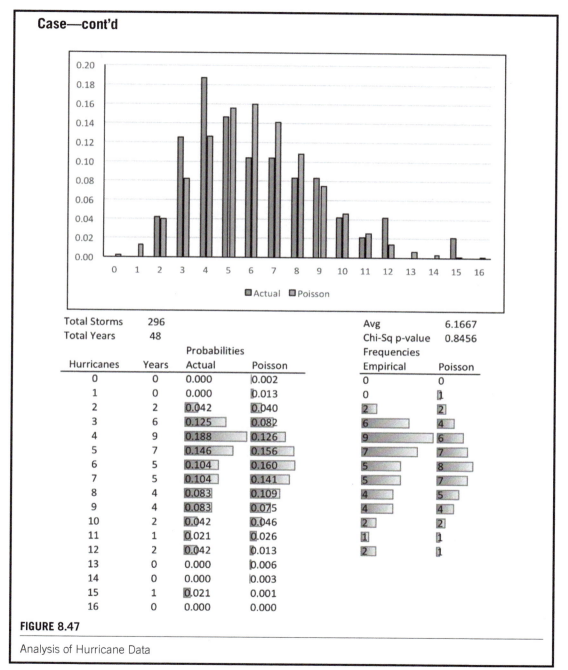

| Total Storms | 296 | | | Avg | 6.1667 |
| Total Years | 48 | | | Chi-Sq p-value | 0.8456 |

| | | Probabilities | | Frequencies | |
Hurricanes	Years	Actual	Poisson	Empirical	Poisson
0	0	0.000	0.002	0	0
1	0	0.000	0.013	0	1
2	2	0.042	0.040	2	2
3	6	0.125	0.082	6	4
4	9	0.188	0.126	9	6
5	7	0.146	0.156	7	7
6	5	0.104	0.160	5	8
7	5	0.104	0.141	5	7
8	4	0.083	0.109	4	5
9	4	0.083	0.075	4	4
10	2	0.042	0.046	2	2
11	1	0.021	0.026	1	1
12	2	0.042	0.013	2	1
13	0	0.000	0.006		
14	0	0.000	0.003		
15	1	0.021	0.001		
16	0	0.000	0.000		

FIGURE 8.47

Analysis of Hurricane Data

Continued

Case—cont'd

Adventure uses leather in the production of many of its product lines. Due to design and style considerations, the specifications of the leather are, in fact, quite flexible, and it is common practice for the Adventure purchasing agent, Jim Makins, to search for good buys on batches of leather. Whenever he finds a potentially good buy, he obtains a sample of the leather from the seller and passes it on to the production group. The production group examines both the leather characteristics and the potential cost to determine whether that batch can be used without undue modification of the luggage line in which it will be used.

Quite frequently, Mr. Makins has been able to purchase batches of leather that have been classified as rejects by seat manufacturing divisions of luxury car manufacturers such as Acura, Audi, BMW, Lexus, Mercedes Benz, and Porsche. These batches generally contain a high percentage of leather that is usable by Adventure. These manufacturers visually inspect the leather under close scrutiny. When some characteristic of the leather does not meet the stringent tolerance required for use by the luxury automobile manufacturers, the leather produced in that batch is put aside and subsequently auctioned outside the company.

These car manufacturers sell these rejects in the same way. A list is kept of purchasing agents who will buy leather with specific characteristics; these purchasing agents are emailed and informed when a batch of potential interest is available. If interested, each purchasing agent makes a sealed bid and the manufacturer sells the batch of leather to the winning bidder.

Over the past 5 years, Mr. Makins has bid on 305 previous batches of leather and has saved the winning bids, shown in Table 8.3. Mr. Makins has recently been informed of the availability of a batch of 300 yards of leather, identified by Porsche as lot MATS314Q.

The Porsche auction representative, Erica Johansson, always supplies an estimate of the yield of yards of good leather in each batch. It is in her best interest to supply a good estimate, because, in the long run, her ability to sell depends on providing her customers with at least as many units as she estimates. For the current batch, Ms. Johansson estimates the yield to be 90%. In the instances that Adventure won the bid, Mr. Makins has also recorded the number of yards of leather that was actually acceptable for use in production—that is, the actual yield of good leather.

Table 8.3 Auction data

Auction	Month	Bid quantity	Est. yield %	Bid	Actual yield
1	1	500	0.90	3793.50	
2	1	300	0.70	1787.10	214
3	1	300	0.90	2281.50	
4	1	500	0.80	3372.00	396
5	1	200	0.80	1376.00	
			.		
			.		
			.		
301	59	100	0.90	958.50	
302	60	300	0.70	2209.20	
303	60	200	0.70	1446.20	
304	60	300	0.90	2783.70	275
305	60	200	0.80	1678.40	

Case—cont'd

With the information from Porsche on the characteristics of lot MATS314Q, the production group has informed Mr. Makins that Adventure can use the item now. Adventure has received a contract to supply matching luggage to a sports team, and this order would require 265 yards of leather.

The cost for Adventure to manufacture the same leather by regular methods would be $1350 for setup plus a cost of $10 per yard required. Alternatively, Adventure's external cost for tested and guaranteed leather in quantities of 200 yards or less is $16 per yard. Adventure does not currently have this leather in inventory.

With this data, Mr. Makins is about to make his analysis and determine what to bid. As he looked over the data on the past bids, he remarked to his assistant, "It looks to me as if the other bidders are bidding about $10 to $11 per estimated good yard of leather. Thus, for a batch of 300 yards of leather with an estimated yield of 90%, I would guess the competitor's bid would be about $2835."

Simulation fit and significance: Chi-square and ANOVA

Are averages and proportions significantly different?

Chapter outline

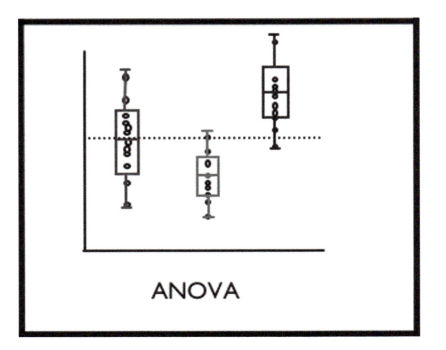

FIGURE 9.1

ANOVA: Are Group Averages Equal?

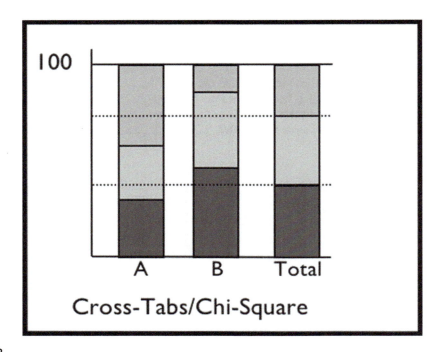

FIGURE 9.2

Chi-Square: Are Group Proportions Equal?

Introduction

Frequently, a decision maker will want to determine if a nonnumeric factor is important to a decision— that is, do the outcomes, and their associated probabilities, depend upon a factor? This question is answered by using either an *analysis of variance* (ANOVA) or *Chi-square* statistical test. Figures 9.1 and 9.2 illustrate the concepts of these two statistical tests. This chapter demonstrates the use of these two statistical tests and how the results are used in decision trees to make optimal managerial decisions.

9.1 Conditional probabilities—again

Conditional probability is a probability that depends upon the condition (state) of another factor. In the car rental example shown in Example 3.4, the probability of demand would depend upon many other factors, such as day of the week and time of year. As these factors have the potential to explain a portion of the variation in the outcome, demand in this situation, the factors will be referred to as *explanatory variables*. As a form of mathematical notation, X represents explanatory variables and Y represents the outcome variable. A handy mnemonic is:

$$X \text{ eXplains wh} Y \ Y \text{ varies } \ldots \text{ if you are lucky.}$$

With mathematical notation, conditional probability is expressed as $P(Y|X)$. The symbol "|" denotes the word *given*, and the expression is read: *The probability of Y given X*. Consider the car rental example: *The probability of demand depends upon the day of the week* can be written as $P(Demand|Day)$. More specifically, the probability that demand is 10 cars depends upon which day of the week: $P(Demand = 10|Day = Friday) = 2/20 = 10\%$. Thus, on a different day, the probability that demand is 10 cars could be different.

Statistical analysis is used to determine, *from data*, if, and how, various factors affect the probability. In other words, conditional probability is estimated using methods of statistical analysis. In the example of the car rentals, a statistical analysis would be performed to prove statistically that demand on Fridays is significantly different from demand on other days. Mathematically, statistical analysis answers this question:

$$P(Y \mid X) = P(Y)$$

If the answer is *no*, then condition X affects the probability of event Y. Conversely, if the probability of event Y is the same whether or not the condition X has occurred, then Y is not conditional upon X. Two other ways to express the same idea are as follows: (1) Y is not dependent upon X, and (2) Y is independent of X. In simple terms, does X influence Y . . . does X matter?

The most common types of statistical analyses used to determine and estimate conditional probability are illustrated in Fig. 9.3.

9.1.1 Examples of conditional probability estimation procedures

1. Do finance majors tend to make more money than other majors?
   X: Major → Group
   Y: Salary → Number
   Use *ANOVA*.

Statistical Procedures

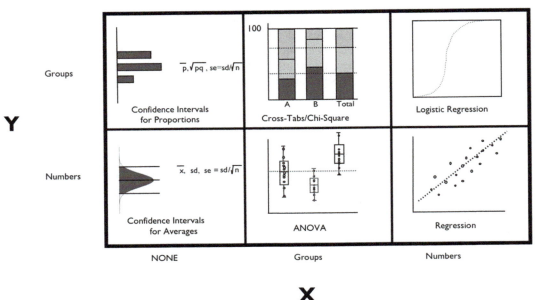

FIGURE 9.3

Basic Statistical Procedures

2. Do residents in one region tend to prefer one brand to another?
   X: Region → Group
   Y: Brand → Group
   Use ***Chi-square***.
3. Do students with more work experience tend to get higher-paying jobs?
   X: Months of Work Experience → Number
   Y: Salary → Number
   Use ***regression***.
4. Do companies with fewer assets tend to go bankrupt?
   X: Assets → Number
   Y: Bankruptcy → Group
   Use ***logistic regression***.

9.2 Conditional probability for groups

After considering the variation in outcomes (data), a natural question is *what is causing the outcomes to vary?* When the potential causes are ***discretely measured*** (nonnumeric), the data is often grouped according to the classes (***groups***) that generated the data. The question then becomes, *are the groups the same or different?* The focus of this chapter is situations in which the X (*eXplanatory*) variables are groups. If the outcomes are numeric, then an ANOVA is the statistical procedure that answers this question. If the outcomes are nonnumeric (groups), then a Chi-square answers this question.

Refer to the *statistical procedures* diagram in Fig. 9.4. The central portion of the figure is used when *X* is nonnumeric (group). If response (*Y*) is numeric, then use an ANOVA (the *bottom* of the center portion of Fig. 9.4) to determine whether the probabilities are conditional. If the *Y* is nonnumeric, then use a Chi-square (the *top* of the center portion of Fig. 9.4) to determine whether the probabilities are conditional.

9.2.1 Examples of ANOVA and Chi-square situations

Given nonnumeric (group) *X* and numeric (number) *Y*, ANOVA could be used in these situations in the various functional areas of business.

A marketing manager needs to determine which end-aisle display is more effective. Sales are sampled in 10 stores for each type of display.

X: Display Type → Group
Y: Sales → Number

A company must choose between three web designs. The number of click-throughs is measured as the three designs are randomly presented to website visitors.

X: Web Design → Group
Y: Click-Throughs → Number

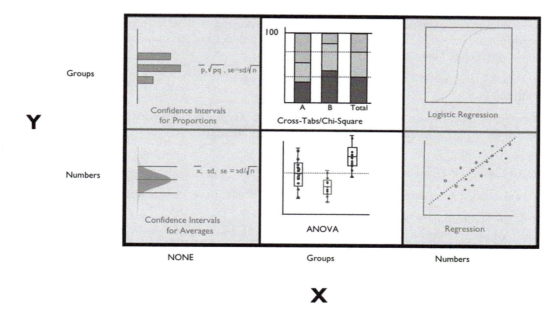

FIGURE 9.4

Basic Statistical Procedures When the *X* Variable Is Nonnumeric

A financial analyst must determine the difference in the rate of return between three industries (sectors): pharmaceuticals, medical instruments, and biotechnology.

X: Industry → Group
Y: Rate of Return → Number

A financial analyst must determine the difference in the rate of return between companies with, and without, long-term board members.

X: Long-Term → Group
Y: Rate of Return → Number

An operations plant manager must determine which of three process layouts to use. The hourly production volumes are simulated for the three layouts.

X: Process Layout → Group
Y: Production Volume → Number

A supply chain manager must decide which supplier to use. Three suppliers meet the technical and cost specifications. Lead times for each supplier vary and have been recorded.

X: Supplier → Group
Y: Lead Time → Number

Given nonnumeric (group) X and nonnumeric (group) Y, Chi-square could be used in the following situations.

A marketing manager needs to determine which packaging is more effective. Focus groups are shown different packaging for the marketing manager's product and the same packaging for the competition's product and then asked their brand preference.

X: Packaging → Group
Y: Brand Preference → Group

A company must choose between three magazine ad concepts. Focus groups from different regions are shown the different ad concepts, and their preferences are noted.

X: Region → Group
Y: Ad Concept Preference → Group

A bank analyst must determine if denying a loan applicant affects their retention.

X: Loan Application Acceptance → Group
Y: Retention → Group

A financial analyst for a bank must determine the risk of default of mortgages based upon regions within the bank's operations.

X: Region → Group
Y: Loan Status (Default) → Group

An operations plant manager must determine which machine to use for a particular process. The number of defective parts for each machine is measured during a trial period.

X: Machine $\rightarrow$ Group
Y: Defective $\rightarrow$ Group

A supplier must decide which method to use to deliver its product to a client. Three suppliers meet the technical and cost specifications. Whether or not the product reaches the client on time, early, or late varies and is recorded for each method.

X: Supplier $\rightarrow$ Group
Y: Lead Time $\rightarrow$ Group

9.3 Chi-square (χ^2): are the probability distributions the same?

A *Chi-square* (χ^2) test is used when both the *X* and the *Y* are groups (nonnumeric) and determines whether the proportions of different groups of data depend upon *X*. If so, then the proportions *are statistically significantly different*. These proportions are probability estimates for the groups within *Y*. Statistically speaking:

> *Null hypothesis*: Proportions of all groups *are* approximately *equal*: $P_{iA} \cong P_{iB}$, where *i* represents the different outcome groups (*Y*) within each group (e.g., *A* or *B*).
> (Note: The symbols $\cong$ and $\approx$ mean "approximately equal.")
> *Alternative hypothesis*: Proportions of all groups are *not identical*; at least one group is different (*statistically significantly different*): $P_{iA} \neq P_{iB}$

If the proportions are *not* statistically significantly *different*, then *not different* implies the proportions are approximately *the same*. Because the *X* variable is *not significant*, the data should not be separated by groups. This aggregation improves probability estimates by increasing the sample size.

Conversely, if the proportions *are* statistically significantly *different*, then the data should be separated by groups because the *X* variable *is significant*. Disaggregation improves probability estimates by conditioning probabilities of *Y* upon the *X* variable and reducing variability.

A *stacked bar chart* shows the proportions of the data for each group. The dotted lines are the overall (*Total*) proportions. These are probability measures for the outcomes dependent upon each group. Thus, if the two groups' (*A* and *B*) proportions align with the proportions of the Total, then the groups are not *statistically significantly different*. In the example in Fig. 9.5, the two groups' proportions are statistically significantly different.

Suppose there are two choices: *A* and *B*. Fig. 9.6 illustrates how the probability might be conditional upon the choices depending upon the Chi-square results.

9.3.1 Chi-square: actual frequencies versus expected frequencies

To test if the proportions of the groups are statistically significantly different, a table of *Actual* frequencies and a table of *Expected* frequencies must be computed. The term *Expected* means what frequencies you would guess (forecast) if the proportions for each group were equal to each other—and hence equal to the overall proportions. The Chi-square test then compares the frequencies in the Actual table versus those in the Expected table. One result of the Chi-square test is a *p-value*. If the *p*-value is small (usually ≤ 0.10), then the conclusion is that the proportions are statistically significantly different.

Expected = the frequencies if the proportions are *equal* for each group.

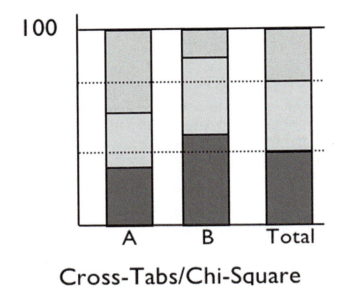

Cross-Tabs/Chi-Square

FIGURE 9.5

Stacked Bar Chart Comparing Two Distributions

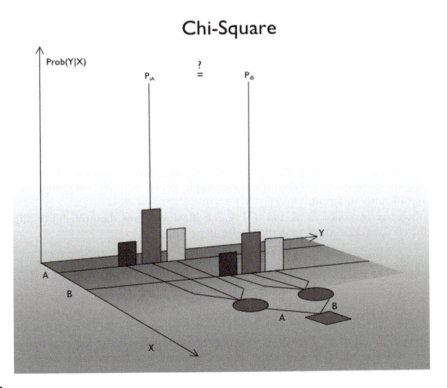

FIGURE 9.6

Decision Tree Utilizing a Chi-Square to Differentiate the Probabilities of the Two Choices

Table 9.1 Typical interpretations of p-values by range of p-value

p-Value range	Interpretation
0.001–0.01	X is highly significant: **Dist$_1$ ≠ Dist$_2$**
0.01–0.05	X is significant: **Dist$_1$ ≠ Dist$_2$**
0.05–0.10	X is marginally significant; depends heavily upon the context.
0.10–1.00	X is not significant: **Dist$_1$ ≈ Dist$_2$**

To test if the proportions are significantly different, statistical software is used to calculate the p-value for the Chi-square test. Reminder: A p-value is the probability of a type I error—that is, it is the probability of a false positive; the probability of claiming X is statistically significant when it is not. If the p-value is small (usually ≤ 0.05), then the conclusion is that the distributions (groups' proportions) are statistically significantly different. Typical interpretations of p-values are listed in Table 9.1.

Rather than thinking of these ranges as discrete levels, you should remember that since a p-value is also a continuous random variable, then there is a continuum for the interpretations. This continuum may be envisioned as shown in Fig. 9.7.

9.4 ANOVA: are the groups' averages the same?

In contrast to a Chi-square, an ANOVA compares the averages, rather than proportions, of two or more groups. An ANOVA determines whether the ***averages*** (means) of different groups of data depend upon a nonnumeric factor, X. If so, then it can be said that the means are *statistically significantly different*. Statistically speaking:

Null hypothesis: Averages of all groups are approximately equal: **Avg$_1$≈ Avg$_2$.**
Alternative hypothesis: Averages of all groups are not identical; at least one group is different (statistically significantly different): **Avg$_1$≠ Avg$_2$.**

If the averages are ***not*** statistically significantly ***different***, then *not different* implies the averages are approximately ***the same*** and the data should ***not*** be separated by groups because the X variable is ***not significant***. This aggregation has an advantage of improving probability estimates by increasing the sample size.

Conversely, if the averages ***are*** statistically significantly ***different***, then the data ***should be*** separated by groups because the X variable ***is significant***. This disaggregation improves probability estimates by reducing variability via conditional probabilities. This will be illustrated in Example 9.6.

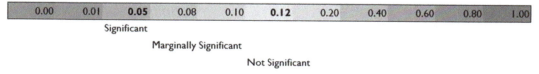

FIGURE 9.7

p-Value Continuum and Associated Interpretations

Example 9.1 Data fit: do hurricanes follow a Poisson distribution?

Records regarding storms in the Atlantic Basin are kept by the National Oceanic and Atmospheric Administration (NOAA), the National Weather Service, the National Hurricane Center, and other weather agencies. The data on the number of hurricanes since 1851 is given in Table 9.2. Test whether this data follows a Poisson distribution.

Table 9.2 Number of hurricanes since 1851 by year

Year	Hurricanes	Year	Hurricanes	Year	Hurricanes	Year	Hurricanes
1851	3	1901	6	1951	8	2001	9
1852	5	1902	3	1952	6	2002	4
1853	4	1903	7	1953	6	2003	7
1854	3	1904	4	1954	8	2004	9
1855	4	1905	1	1955	9	2005	15
1856	4	1906	6	1956	4	2006	5
1857	3	1907	0	1957	3	2007	6
1858	6	1908	6	1958	7	2008	8
1859	7	1909	6	1959	7	2009	3
1860	6	1910	3	1960	4	2010	12
1861	6	1911	3	1961	8	2011	7
1862	3	1912	4	1962	3	2012	10
1863	5	1913	4	1963	7	2013	2
1864	3	1914	0	1964	6	2014	6
1865	3	1915	5	1965	4	2015	4
1866	6	1916	10	1966	7	2016	7
1867	7	1917	2	1967	6	2017	10
1868	3	1918	4	1968	4	2018	8
1869	7	1919	2	1969	12	2019	6
1870	10	1920	4	1970	5	2020	14
1871	6	1921	5	1971	6		
1872	4	1922	3	1972	3		
1873	3	1923	4	1973	4		
1874	4	1924	5	1974	4		
1875	5	1925	1	1975	6		
1876	4	1926	8	1976	6		
1877	3	1927	4	1977	5		
1878	10	1928	4	1978	5		
1879	6	1929	3	1979	5		
1880	9	1930	2	1980	9		
1881	4	1931	3	1981	7		
1882	4	1932	6	1982	2		
1883	3	1933	11	1983	3		
1884	4	1934	7	1984	5		

Table 9.2 Number of hurricanes since 1851 by year—cont'd

Year	Hurricanes	Year	Hurricanes	Year	Hurricanes	Year	Hurricanes
1885	6	1935	5	1985	7		
1886	10	1936	7	1986	4		
1887	11	1937	4	1987	3		
1888	6	1938	4	1988	5		
1889	6	1939	3	1989	7		
1890	2	1940	6	1990	8		
1891	7	1941	4	1991	4		
1892	5	1942	4	1992	4		
1893	10	1943	5	1993	4		
1894	5	1944	8	1994	3		
1895	2	1945	5	1995	11		
1896	6	1946	3	1996	9		
1897	3	1947	5	1997	3		
1898	5	1948	6	1998	10		
1899	5	1949	7	1999	8		
1900	3	1950	11	2000	8		

https://www.aoml.noaa.gov/data-products/#hurricanedata

The empirical distribution was tabulated and the average number of hurricanes per year was computed: $936/170 = 5.51$. The average of 5.51 was then used to compute the Poisson probabilities (*pmf*). The graph in the spreadsheet in Fig. 9.8 shows the histogram for the empirical data distribution and the theoretical Poisson distribution. The probabilities (*pmf*) for each distribution are also shown side by side for comparison. The probabilities for each distribution were then multiplied by the sample size of 170 to create frequencies required for the Chi-square test. The Chi-square test is computed in Excel using the CHISQ.TEST function:

$$= CHISQ.TEST (actual\_range, expected\_range),$$

where *actual_range* is the empirical (sometimes called *observed*) data and *expected_range* is the basis for comparison. In this example, the *expected_range* is the range of frequencies from the Poisson distribution, and to test the fit of the empirical data, the *actual_range* is the range of frequencies from the data. In this manner, the *p*-value for the Chi-square test was computed to compare the empirical distribution with an average of 5.51 to the Poisson distribution with an average of 5.51. The empirical distribution and the Poisson are shown in the graph in Fig. 9.8 along with the appropriate *p*-value for the Chi-square test of fit.

The *p*-value resulting from the Chi-square test is **0.081**, which is in the range considered to be *marginally statistically significantly different* ($0.05 < p < 0.10$). Some areas of science would consider a *p*-value in this range to be *statistically significant*, and as such the significance would depend highly on the context. Thus, the Poisson might still not be considered to be a good fit for the 1851–2020 data. The Hurricane Research Division of the NOAA (http://www.aoml.noaa.gov/hrd/tcfaq/E11.html) uses the data since 1968 to compute

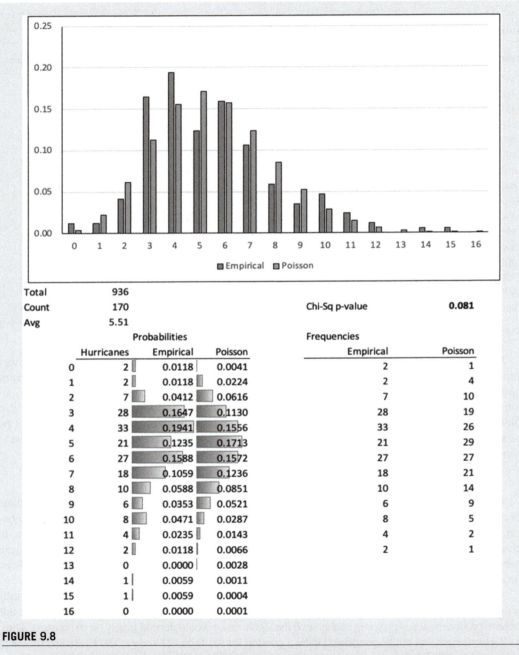

Total	936			
Count	170		Chi-Sq p-value	**0.081**
Avg	5.51			

		Probabilities			Frequencies	
	Hurricanes	Empirical	Poisson		Empirical	Poisson
0	2	0.0118	0.0041		2	1
1	2	0.0118	0.0224		2	4
2	7	0.0412	0.0616		7	10
3	28	0.1647	0.1130		28	19
4	33	0.1941	0.1556		33	26
5	21	0.1235	0.1713		21	29
6	27	0.1588	0.1572		27	27
7	18	0.1059	0.1236		18	21
8	10	0.0588	0.0851		10	14
9	6	0.0353	0.0521		6	9
10	8	0.0471	0.0287		8	5
11	4	0.0235	0.0143		4	2
12	2	0.0118	0.0066		2	1
13	0	0.0000	0.0028			
14	1	0.0059	0.0011			
15	1	0.0059	0.0004			
16	0	0.0000	0.0001			

FIGURE 9.8

Chi-Square Test for Goodness of Fit of 1851–2020 Hurricane Data With the Poisson Distribution $\lambda = 5.51$

the average annual number of hurricanes. The empirical distribution of the 341 hurricanes since 1968 (with an average of $341/53 = 6.43$) and the associated Poisson distribution (with an average of $\lambda = 6.43$) are shown in the graph in Fig. 9.9 along with the appropriate p-value for the Chi-square test of fit.

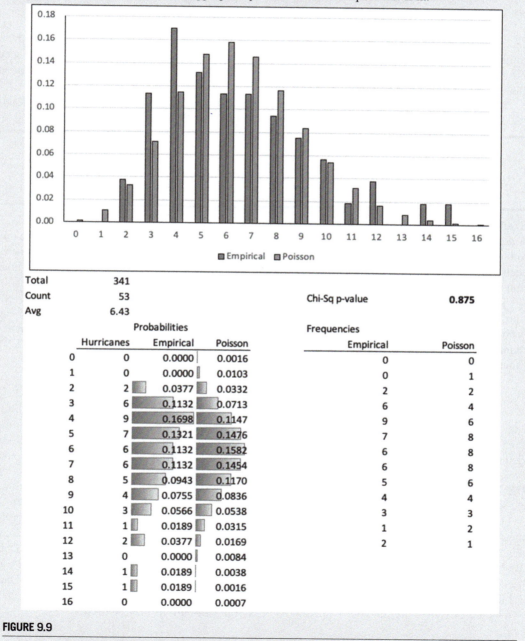

Total	341					Chi-Sq p-value			**0.875**
Count	53								
Avg	6.43								

		Probabilities				Frequencies	
Hurricanes		Empirical	Poisson			Empirical	Poisson
0	0	0.0000	0.0016			0	0
1	0	0.0000	0.0103			0	1
2	2	0.0377	0.0332			2	2
3	6	0.1132	0.0713			6	4
4	9	0.1698	0.1147			9	6
5	7	0.1321	0.1476			7	8
6	6	0.1132	0.1582			6	8
7	6	0.1132	0.1454			6	8
8	5	0.0943	0.1170			5	6
9	4	0.0755	0.0836			4	4
10	3	0.0566	0.0538			3	3
11	1	0.0189	0.0315			1	2
12	2	0.0377	0.0169			2	1
13	0	0.0000	0.0084				
14	1	0.0189	0.0038				
15	1	0.0189	0.0016				
16	0	0.0000	0.0007				

FIGURE 9.9

Chi-Square Test for Goodness of Fit of 1968–2020 Hurricane Data With the Poisson Distribution $\lambda = 6.43$

The *p*-value resulting from the Chi-square test is **0.875**, which is well beyond the range considered to be *not significantly different*. Thus, the empirical distribution of the 1968–2020 data is *not statistically significantly different* from the Poisson distribution with the same average, and the Poisson would be a good fit for the 1968–2020 data.

A manufacturer of propane has demand that is extremely sensitive to weather. In particular, people use propane to cook and power generators after hurricanes cause power outages. Thus, a simulation of demand for their product based upon hurricanes can use either the empirical data or assume a Poisson distribution. Much more analysis should be done to determine if the arrival rate is changing over time or is *stationary* (not changing).

Next, we will revisit Example 7.7 to determine how close the discrete normal approximation and Poisson distribution fit a binomial distribution for a set of specified parameters.

Example 9.2 Distribution fit: binomial, Poisson, normal

A delivery service has a fleet of 60 trucks. Each day, the probability of a truck being out of use due to factors such as breakdowns or maintenance is 10%. Thus, on average, 6 trucks are out of service each day and 54 trucks are available each day. Determine how well the discrete normal approximation and Poisson distributions fit the binomial distribution.

The graph in the spreadsheet shown in Fig. 9.10 shows the histogram for the binomial distribution. The probabilities (*pmf*) for each distribution are also shown side by side for comparison. The probabilities for each distribution were then multiplied by a sample size of 200 to create frequencies required for the Chi-square test. The Chi-square test is computed in Excel using the CHISQ.TEST function:

$$= CHISQ . TEST (actual\_range , expected\_range),$$

where *actual_range* is the observed data and *expected_range* is the basis for comparison. In this example, the *expected_range* is the range of frequencies from the binomial distribution ($F$24:$F$36), and to test the fit of the discrete normal approximation, the *actual_range* is the range of frequencies from the normal distribution (G24:G36). Similarly, to test the fit of the discrete Poisson distribution, the *actual_range* is the range of frequencies from the Poisson distribution (H24:H36), and the *expected_range* is still the range of frequencies from the binomial distribution ($F$24:$F$36). At a sample size of 200, both distributions fit the binomial distribution very well.

The *law of large numbers* dictates that as sample size (*n*) increases, probabilities converge to their true values. Thus, to test the significance of the differences in the three probability distributions, the sample size was increased and the *p*-values for the Chi-squares computed. A One-Way Data Table was used to calculate the corresponding *p*-values. Furthermore, the Goal Seek command was used to determine the samples sizes required to detect significant differences. The One-Way Data Table is shown in columns J, K, and L in Fig. 9.10. Thus, an analyst can determine the sample sizes at which the discrete normal approximation and Poisson distributions may be used.

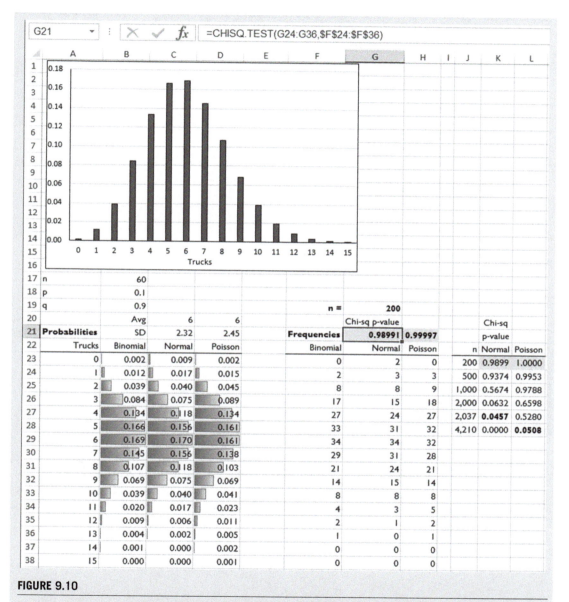

| | | | | | | G21 | | | f_x | =CHISQ.TEST(G24:G36,$F$24:$F$36) | | | | |

FIGURE 9.10

Chi-Square Test for Goodness of Fit Binomial With the Normal and Poisson Distributions

The next example demonstrates how a Chi-square is used to assess if a simulation distribution adheres to the prescribed distribution—that is, if the simulation is behaving as expected.

Example 9.3 Assessing simulation fit

Demand for a particular exclusive class of hotel rooms is Poisson with an average of two per week. Suppose the hotel has three such rooms. What is the probability that they will have to turn customers away—that is, what is the probability of shortage?

The graph of the *pmf* of the Poisson distribution with $\lambda = 2$ is shown in Fig. 9.11

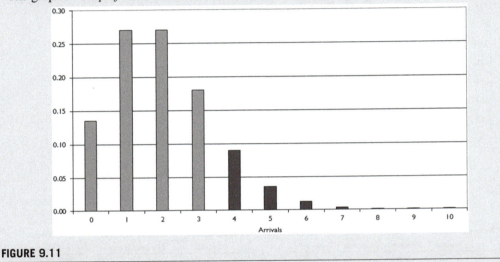

FIGURE 9.11

Poisson Distribution With $\lambda = 2$

In the spreadsheet shown in Fig. 9.12, the *p*-value of 0.6535 (located in cell N16) indicates that there is *no statistically significant difference* between the simulated demand and the Poisson distribution with an average (λ) of two per week. Thus, the random number generation mechanism successfully simulates a Poisson arrival process.

When a simulation is based upon an empirical distribution, such as the hurricane data, then a Chi-square test can be used in the same manner to test and validate the fit of the distribution of the simulation to the empirical distribution.

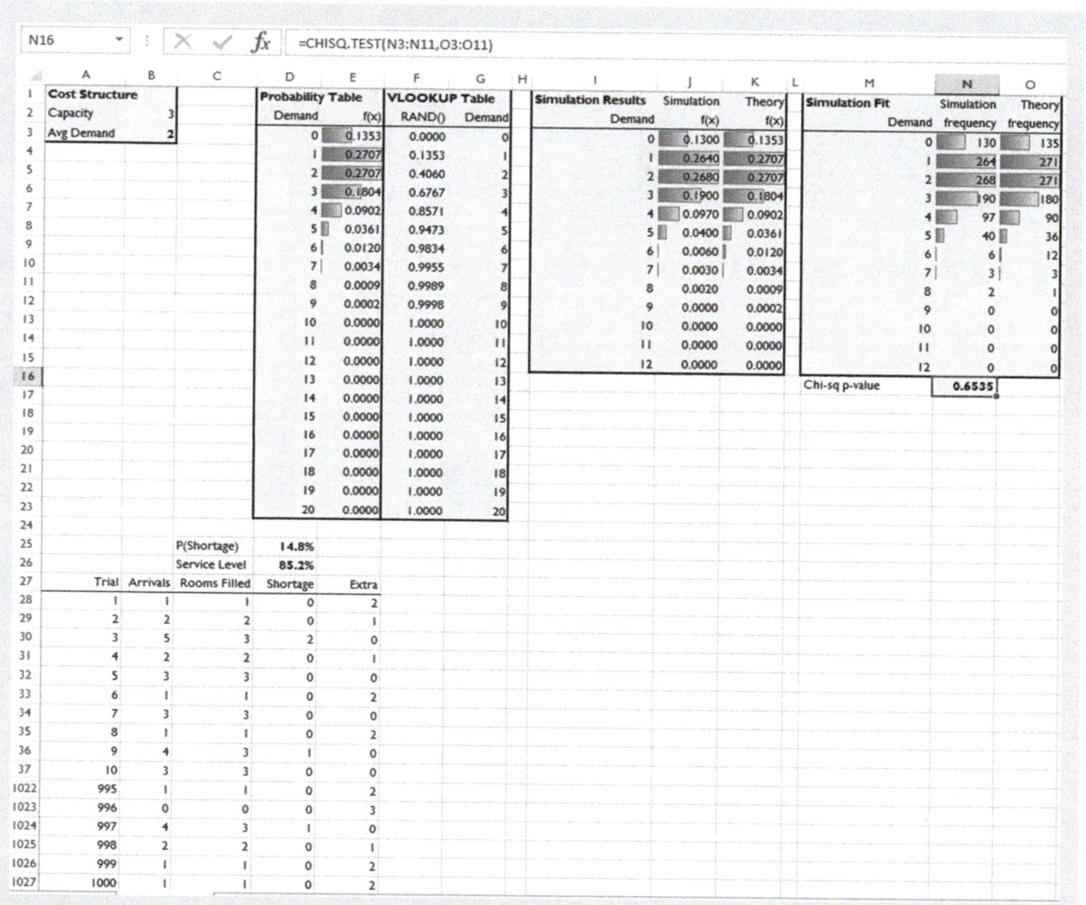

N16   =CHISQ.TEST(N3:N11,O3:O11)

Cost Structure

Cost Structure	
Capacity	3
Avg Demand	2

Probability Table

Demand	f(x)
0	0.1353
1	0.2707
2	0.2707
3	0.1804
4	0.0902
5	0.0361
6	0.0120
7	0.0034
8	0.0009
9	0.0002
10	0.0000
11	0.0000
12	0.0000
13	0.0000
14	0.0000
15	0.0000
16	0.0000
17	0.0000
18	0.0000
19	0.0000
20	0.0000

VLOOKUP Table

RAND()	Demand
0.0000	0
0.1353	1
0.4060	2
0.6767	3
0.8571	4
0.9473	5
0.9834	6
0.9955	7
0.9989	8
0.9998	9
1.0000	10
1.0000	11
1.0000	12
1.0000	13
1.0000	14
1.0000	15
1.0000	16
1.0000	17
1.0000	18
1.0000	19
1.0000	20

Simulation Results

Demand	Simulation f(x)	Theory f(x)
0	0.1300	0.1353
1	0.2640	0.2707
2	0.2680	0.2707
3	0.1900	0.1804
4	0.0970	0.0902
5	0.0400	0.0361
6	0.0060	0.0120
7	0.0030	0.0034
8	0.0020	0.0009
9	0.0000	0.0002
10	0.0000	0.0000
11	0.0000	0.0000
12	0.0000	0.0000

Simulation Fit

Demand	Simulation frequency	Theory frequency
0	130	135
1	264	271
2	268	271
3	190	180
4	97	90
5	40	36
6	6	12
7	3	3
8	2	1
9	0	0
10	0	0
11	0	0
12	0	0

Chi-sq p-value	0.6535

P(Shortage)	14.8%
Service Level	85.2%

Trial	Arrivals	Rooms Filled	Shortage	Extra
1	1	1	0	2
2	2	2	0	1
3	5	3	2	0
4	2	2	0	1
5	3	3	0	0
6	1	1	0	2
7	3	3	0	0
8	1	1	0	2
9	4	3	1	0
10	3	3	0	0
995	1	1	0	2
996	0	0	0	3
997	4	3	1	0
998	2	2	0	1
999	1	1	0	2
1000	1	1	0	2

FIGURE 9.12

Simulation of Poisson Arrivals With $\lambda = 2$ and the Chi-Square Test Validation of the Results

A Chi-square test of fit is also useful in data analysis to determine if a discrete factor, X, is statistically significant. Example 9.4 demonstrates how a Chi-square test is used to decide if a discrete factor, X, is statistically significant.

Example 9.4 Are groups' proportions significantly different? Advertising decision

A marketing analyst must decide between two different ads for a new consumer product. To test the effects of the two ads, two groups were each shown a different ad and asked if they would buy that product. Table 9.3 shows the cross tabulation (frequencies) of the Actual frequencies for the buyer behavior (buy or not buy) for each ad.

Table 9.3 Actual buyer behavior by advertisement type				
Actual	**Ad 1**	**Ad 2**	**Total**	**Overall %**
Buy	85	72	157	76.2
Not buy	17	32	49	23.8
Sample size	102	104	206	100.0

These results are shown in Fig. 9.13.

FIGURE 9.13

Stacked Bar Chart of Buyer Behavior by Advertisement

The Total percentages are the percentages we would expect if the two groups (Ad 1 and Ad 2) are the same (not significantly different). Thus, these percentages will be applied to each group's sample size to compute the table of Expected frequencies. For example, if we did not know the frequencies inside the table of Actual frequencies, we would forecast that 76.2% of the 102 Ad 1 viewers would be buyers,

$$\text{Expected Ad 1 Buyers} = 0.762 \times 102 = 77.7,$$

and the remainder would not be buyers,

$$\text{Expected Ad 1 Non - Buyers} = 0.238 \times 102 = 24.3.$$

Using the same overall proportions for the Ad 2 viewers:

$$\text{Expected Ad 2 Buyers} = 0.762 \times 104 = 79.3$$

Table 9.4 Expected buyer behavior by advertisement type

Expected	Ad 1	Ad 2	Total	Overall %
Buy	77.7	79.3	157	76.2
Not buy	24.3	24.7	49	23.8
Sample size	102.0	104.0	206	100.0

$$\text{Expected Ad 2 Non - Buyers} = 0.238 \times 104 = 24.7$$

This provides the Expected frequencies in Table 9.4.

Note that the Total, Overall %, and sample size are the same for both the Actual and Expected tables. The p-value resulting from the Chi-Square test is 0.017, less than 0.05. This indicates that the responses to the two ads are statistically significantly different (not approximately the same). Unfortunately, the Chi-square does not tell you *how* the groups are different—you must figure that out based on the context. In this example, Ad 1 is better because there are ***more Actual*** buyers than we would ***Expect***. Conversely, for Ad 2, there are ***fewer Actual*** buyers than we would ***Expect***. Thus, using Ad 1 is the appropriate decision.

A *boxplot* shows the min, max, median, and quartiles of the data; thus, 50% of the data is in the box. The dotted line is the overall average. In Fig. 9.14, the groups' averages are statistically significantly different.

Fig. 9.15 shows a three-dimensional view of three groups of numeric data with probability in the vertical dimension. If the groups are *not* statistically significantly *different*, then the normal curves are closely aligned. If the groups *are* statistically significantly *different*, then the normal curves are not closely aligned.

Fig. 9.16 shows ANOVA in a decision analysis context. Suppose there are two choices, *A* and *B*. The managerial question of the ANOVA in a decision analysis context is *will the choice of A or B affect the outcome?* Fig. 9.16 shows how the probability might be conditional upon the choices (*A* and *B*) and the ANOVA results.

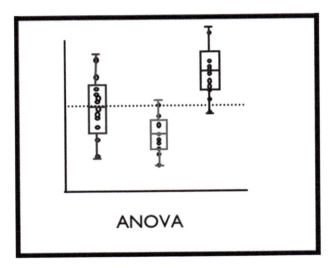

FIGURE 9.14

Boxplot Comparing the Averages of Three Groups

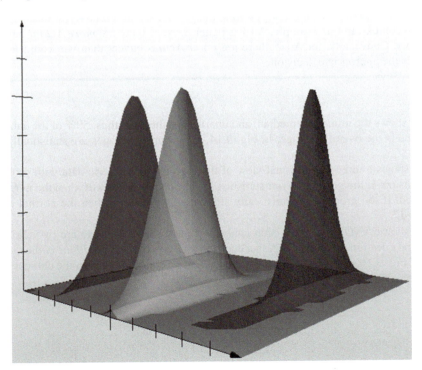

FIGURE 9.15

Three-Dimensional Representation of ANOVA

ANOVA

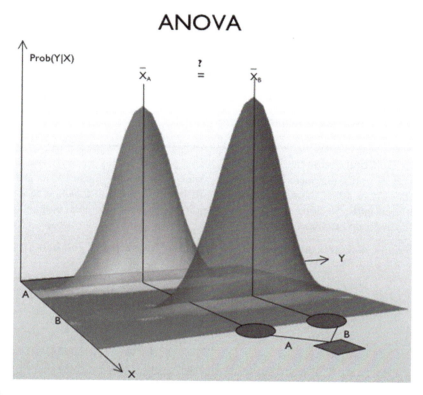

FIGURE 9.16

Decision Tree Utilizing an ANOVA to Differentiate the Probabilities of the Two Choices

9.4.1 Conducting an ANOVA: *p*-value *again*

To test if the averages are significantly different, statistical software is used to calculate an ANOVA table and compute a *p*-value. Recall that if the *p*-value is small (usually ≤ 0.05), then the conclusion is that the averages are statistically significantly different. Typical interpretations of *p*-values are listed in Table 9.5.

Table 9.5 Typical interpretations of *p*-values by range of *p*-value	
p-Value range	**Interpretation**
0.001–0.01	X is highly significant: $\text{Avg}_1 \neq \text{Avg}_2$
0.01–0.05	X is significant: $\text{Avg}_1 \neq \text{Avg}_2$
0.05–0.10	X is marginally significant; depends heavily upon the context
0.10–1.00	X is not significant: $\text{Avg}_1 \cong \text{Avg}_2$

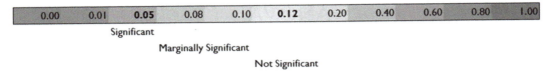

| 0.00 | 0.01 | **0.05** | 0.08 | 0.10 | **0.12** | 0.20 | 0.40 | 0.60 | 0.80 | 1.00 |

Significant

Marginally Significant

Not Significant

FIGURE 9.17

p-Value Continuum and Associated Interpretations

Example 9.5 Golf ball distance

A manufacturer of golf balls needs to determine which type of core to use for its golf balls. More specifically, does core affect the distance of the golf ball? A golf club attached to a machine was used to hit 30 golf balls, 10 of each core type. The distance (yards) for each ball and the summary statistics for each group are listed in Table 9.6.

Table 9.6 Sample distances and summary statistics for three types of golf ball

	Golf ball distance by core type		
	1	2	3
	251.2	263.2	269.7
	245.1	262.9	263.2
	248.0	265.0	277.5
	251.1	254.5	267.4
	265.5	264.3	270.5
	250.0	257.0	265.5
	253.9	262.8	270.7
	244.6	264.4	272.9
	254.6	260.6	275.6
	248.8	255.9	266.5
Avg	251.3	261.1	270.0
SD	6.0	3.9	4.5
SE	1.9	1.2	1.4
Lower 95% CI	247.0	258.3	266.7
Upper 95% CI	255.6	263.8	273.2

The graph in Fig. 9.18 is a variation of the boxplot using the statistics from Table 9.6. The shaded box surrounding each group's average represents the 95% confidence interval. The vertical dotted lines represent the range of the data. The ANOVA is determined by whether the average of a group is within the 95% confidence interval of another group's average.

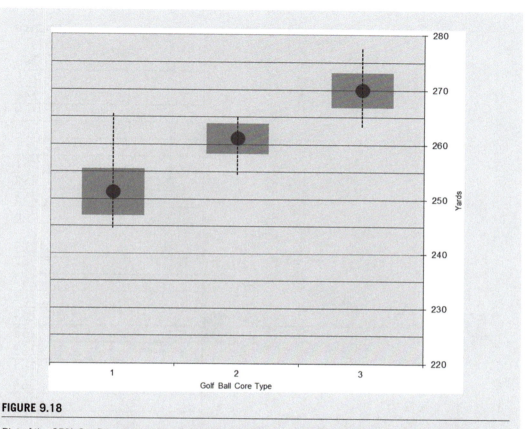

FIGURE 9.18

Plot of the 95% Confidence Intervals, Averages, Minimums, and Maximums of the Golf Ball Distance Data

The choice of which core to use can be illustrated by the decision tree shown in Fig. 9.19. The ANOVA helps to determine whether the groups have any effect—that is, whether the data should be separated by group or aggregated if the groups are not significantly different.

The results of the ANOVA are shown in Table 9.7.

Since the p-value is <0.05, the conclusion is that the type of core *does affect* the average distance and that group 3 is the best choice. Had the p-value been greater than **0.10**, the conclusion would be that the averages are *not* significantly different and that the type of core *does not affect* the *average distance* and any of the three cores could be chosen—or that the choice of core would have to be made based upon a different criterion, such as cost.

An r^2, indicated earlier by r^2, is known as the *coefficient of determination*. In general, the r^2 is a proportion of variation in the data that is explained by the statistical model. In this case, the type of core explains, or accounts for, 73% of the variation in the distance. The remaining variation (approximately 27%) could be due to other factors and randomness. In general, the r^2 is:

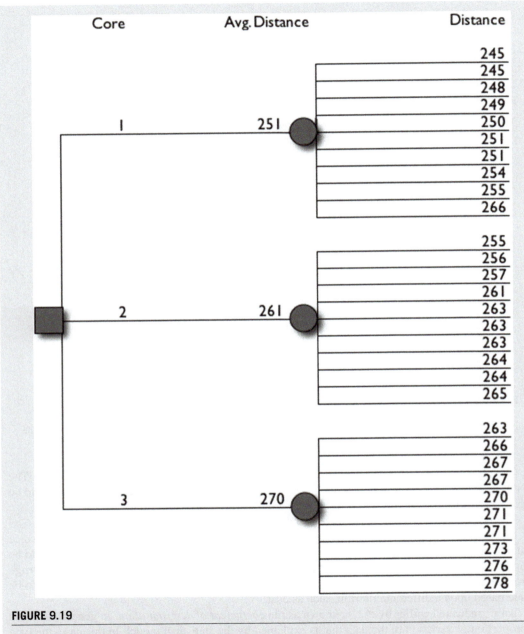

FIGURE 9.19

Decision Tree for the Golf Ball Distance Data

Table 9.7 ANOVA results for the average distances of three types of golf ball

ANOVA: single factor							
Summary							
Groups	Count	Sum	Average	Variance	Margin of error	Lower 95% CI	Upper 95% CI
1	10	2512.8	251.3	35.7	4.3	247.0	255.6
2	10	2610.6	261.1	14.9	2.8	258.3	263.8
3	10	2699.5	270.0	20.3	3.2	266.7	273.2

$r^2 = 73\%$

ANOVA

Source of variation	SS	Df	MS	F	p-Value	F crit	
Between groups	1744.165	2	872.082	36.886	0.000	3.354	
Within groups	638.345	27	23.642				
Total	2382.510	29					

Note: The margins of error, lower and upper 95% confidence intervals, and the r^2 were computed after the ANOVA was calculated using the ANOVA Analysis Tool in Excel.

$$r^2 = \text{Sum of squares model} / \text{Sum of squares total}$$

In the ANOVA output shown earlier, the r^2 is computed by:

$$r^2 = SS\ Between\ Groups\ /\ SS\ Total,$$

where SS is the *sum of squares*.

In a regression context, *sum of squares regression* and *sum of squares total* are often referred to by their initials: SSR and SST.

9.4.2 Why is it called analysis of VARIANCE if it compares averages?

A common question is *why is it called an Analysis of VARIANCE when it tests the groups' AVERAGES?* The reason is that whether the averages are significantly different depends not only on the spread between the averages but also on the spread of the data around each average—the *VARIANCE or STANDARD DEVIATION* of each group. Consider the graph in Fig. 9.20.

In the graph, the circle represents the average of each group. As before, the shaded rectangles around the averages are the 95% confidence intervals, indicating the likely range for other sample averages from the same groups. The vertical dashed lines indicate the range of the sample data for each group.

In this case, the averages have small variance (spread around each average). Consequently, the averages are relatively accurate measures of each group. Since we are "confident" about each group's

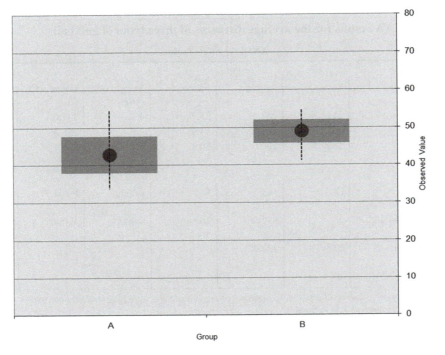

FIGURE 9.20

Plot of the 95% Confidence Intervals, Averages, Minimums, and Maximums for Two Groups That Are Statistically Significantly Different

average, we believe that the difference between the groups' averages *is* genuine—not a result of chance. Thus, the *p*-value is < 0.05 and the two averages ***are statistically significantly different***. See the ANOVA results in Table 9.8. Note that even though the lower 95% confidence interval of group B overlaps the upper 95% confidence interval of group A, the averages of the two groups are significantly different.

In contrast, consider the graph in Fig. 9.21.

The averages in this graph are the same as the averages in the previous graph (Table 9.8), but the averages each have a ***large*** variance (spread around each average). Thus, in contrast to the previous set of data, the averages are relatively ***inaccurate*** measures of each group. Since we are not "confident" about each group's average, we believe that the difference between the groups' averages is *not* genuine—they are merely a result of chance.

Thus, the *p*-value is > 0.10 and the two averages are not significantly different. See the ANOVA results in Table 9.9.

Thus, the ***variances*** (*standard deviations*) must be considered to determine if the averages are significantly different. That is why this procedure is called *analysis of VARIANCE*, or *ANOVA* for short.

Table 9.8 ANOVA results for two groups that are significantly different

ANOVA: single factor							
Summary							
Groups	Count	Sum	Average	Variance	Margin of error	Lower 95% CI	Upper 95% CI
1	10	428	42.8	46.9	6.8	37.9	47.7
2	10	489	48.9	18.6	4.3	45.9	52.0
$r^2 = 24\%$							
ANOVA							
Source of variation	Sum of square	Df	Mean square	F	p-Value	F crit	
Between groups	187.47	1	187.47	5.73	0.03	4.41	
Within groups	589.02	18	32.72				
Total	776.48	19					

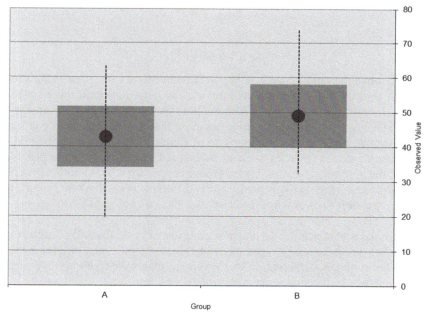

FIGURE 9.21

Plot of the 95% Confidence Intervals, Averages, Minimums, and Maximums for Two Groups That Are **Not** Statistically Significantly Different

9.4.3 An approximate comparison of more than two groups

A further addition to the standard ANOVA output shown earlier is the set of 95% confidence intervals for each group's average. These were computed as shown in Chapter 8.

Table 9.9 ANOVA results for two groups that are not significantly different

ANOVA: single factor							
Summary							
Groups	Count	Sum	Average	Variance	Margin of error	Lower 95% CI	Upper 95% CI
1	10	428	42.8	149.5	12.2	34.1	51.6
2	10	489	48.9	160.1	12.7	39.9	58.0
$r^2 = 6.3\%$							
ANOVA							
Source of variation		Sum of square	Df	Mean Square	F	p-Value	F crit
Between groups		187.47	1	187.47	1.24	0.29	4.41
Within groups		2786.29	18	154.79			
Total		2973.76	19				

$$sample\ average \pm t * se,$$

where *t* is used when the sample size is less than 30; otherwise, 1.96 (*z* for 95%) is used.

As an ANOVA tests if all the averages are equal, it can only indicate if there is a significant difference between the minimum and the maximum (the lowest and highest) averages—that is, the greatest difference between the groups. If there are more than two groups, then confidence intervals can be used to estimate whether or not groups are different. The confidence intervals indicate the range that other sample averages would likely be within had we gotten other samples for each group. In the example of the golf balls, because none of the averages are within another group's confidence interval, the three groups are most likely significantly different. Typically, *one group's average must be within another group's confidence interval* for the pair of groups to be *not* significantly different.

A common mistake is to conclude that a pair of groups are not significantly different when only the confidence intervals overlap. To repeat, a pair of groups are *not* significantly different when one group's average is inside the confidence interval of another group; otherwise (both averages are outside each other's confidence interval), the groups are significantly different.

As an example, the averages, standard deviations, and 95% confidence intervals are shown in Fig. 9.22 for six groups (each with $n = 30$). Furthermore, five ANOVAs were computed to compare each group, two through six, against the first group. The resulting *p*-values are also shown in Fig. 9.22. Some important comparisons to note:

$$Avg_1 = Avg_2\ Avg_1 \neq Avg_3\ Avg_1 = Avg_4$$

$$Avg_1 = Avg_4\ Avg_3 = Avg_4\ Avg_1 \neq Avg_3$$

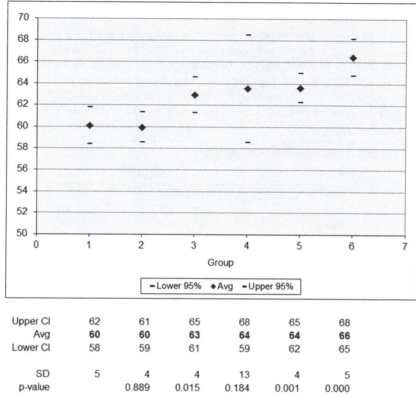

Upper CI	62	61	65	68	65	68
Avg	**60**	**60**	**63**	**64**	**64**	**66**
Lower CI	58	59	61	59	62	65
SD	5	4	4	13	4	5
p-value		0.889	0.015	0.184	0.001	0.000

FIGURE 9.22

Plot of the 95% Confidence Intervals and Averages for Six Groups With **p**-Values

$$Avg_3 = Avg_4 \quad Avg_4 = Avg_6 \quad Avg_3 \neq = Avg_6$$

These present an interesting contradiction to standard math . . . *how does that happen?*

9.4.4 What If groups are, or are not, significantly different?

As discussed earlier, the statistical significance provided by an ANOVA determines whether or not groups' data should be segregated or aggregated to estimate the probabilities in a decision tree. The following example demonstrates how and why the significance of group averages affects probabilities and decisions.

Example 9.6 How much to order?

A small chain of health-foods grocery stores must determine each month how much of each product to order. Ordering produce is particularly complicated due to the availability of various fruits and vegetables. There are three regional suppliers of mangoes. Due to the global supply of mangoes and an arrangement with a fruit wholesaler, the grocery chain cannot determine which supplier will have mangoes in any specific month. The mangoes typically cost the grocery store $3 per pound and sell for $5 per pound. Five years of demand (in pounds) and the supplier providing the mangoes is shown in Table 9.10.

Table 9.10 Demand for mangoes data by supplier

	Supplier		
	Arnos Grove	Bali Fruit	Canons Park
	650	650	599
	633	670	561
	631	755	599
	665	620	595
	672	618	568
	682	728	557
	677	643	533
	663	597	556
	623	644	581
	666	607	583
	694	646	575
	699	722	603
	684	735	614
	617	658	661
	642	588	548
	640	630	560
	628	683	600
	586	630	618
	645	680	
		647	
		609	
		676	
		666	
Avg	652.47	656.61	583.94
SD	29.35	45.18	30.71
N	19	23	18

What is your initial estimate for the probability of receiving mangoes from Arnos Grove? How many mangoes should the chain order if the probability of getting mangoes from Arnos Grove is 45%, from Bali Fruit is 45%, and from Canons Park is 10%?

Initially, it is of interest to determine whether the supplier has any influence upon demand—that is, do customers prefer one brand over other brands? Fig. 9.23 shows the groups' averages and the

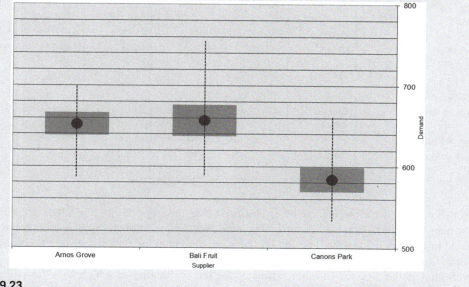

FIGURE 9.23

Plot of the 95% Confidence Intervals and Averages of Demand for Three Mango Suppliers

range of the groups' data. The circles represent the groups' averages, the shaded rectangles represent the 95% confidence intervals, and the vertical dashed lines show the range of the groups' data.

The ANOVA to determine the effects of supplier on demand is shown in Table 9.11.

The p-value < 0.000 indicates that there *is a* significant difference between at least two (the minimum and maximum) groups' averages. The subsequent 95% upper and lower confidence interval calculations indicate that the demand for Arnos Grove and Bali Fruit mangoes are not statistically significantly different, whereas demand for Canons Park mangoes is statistically significantly lower. Thus, demand for Arnos Grove and Bali Fruit mangoes can be aggregated (combined) and separated from Canons Park mangoes.

Table 9.11 ANOVA results for average demand of the three mango suppliers

ANOVA: single factor							
Summary							
Groups	Count	Sum	Average	Variance	SD	Lower 95% CI	Upper 95% CI
Arnos Grove	19	12,397	652.47	861.15	29.35	638.33	666.62
Bali Fruit	23	15,102	656.61	2,041.61	45.18	637.07	676.15
Canons Park	18	10,511	583.94	943.23	30.71	568.67	599.22
Overall			633.50				

$r^2 = 45.3\%$

ANOVA						
Source of variation	Sum of square	Df	Mean square	F	p-Value	F crit
Between groups	63,326	2	31,663	23.61	0.000	3.16
Within groups	76,451	57	1,341			
Total	139,777	59				

At this point, a decision tree can be established using the steps outlined in Chapter 2. The decision is how many pounds of mangoes to order. The random events are which supplier will provide the mangoes and how much demand will occur. The decision tree, with the forecasted supplier probabilities, is shown in Fig. 9.24.

Note that in the absence of other estimates for the probability of which supplier will supply the mangoes this month, a simple frequency method would provide the initial probability estimates. These estimates of the probabilities for each company of supplying mangoes are:

$$P\,(supplier = \text{Arnos Grove}) = \frac{19}{19+23+18} = \frac{19}{60} = 0.3166 \ldots \cong 31.67\,\%$$

$$P\,(supplier = \text{Bali Fruit}) = 23/\,(19+23+18) = 23/60 = 0.3833 \ldots \cong 38.33\,\%$$

$$P\,(supplier = \text{Canons Park}) = 18/\,(19+23+18) = 18/60 = 0.3000 = 30.00\,\%$$

A spreadsheet model based on the decision tree in Fig. 9.24 was used to create the table and graph shown in Fig. 9.25. Fig. 9.25 shows the pounds of mangoes to order and the resulting expected profit for each order quantity. The optimum amount to order is then determined from the table and graph.

Although the order quantities in Fig. 9.25 are in multiples of 5, the table and graph can be calculated and examined at a higher level of detail as needed, as shown in Fig. 9.26.

The next step of analysis would be to do a sensitivity analysis on the piece of information with the highest degree of uncertainty and leverage. What change in the probability of Canons Park being the supplier would it take to significantly change your result?

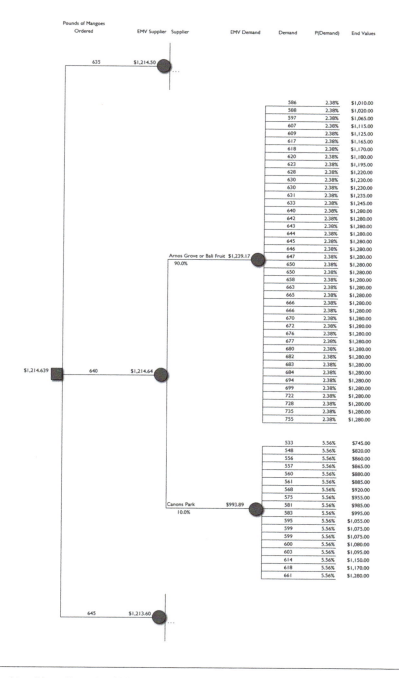

Pounds of Mangoes Ordered	EMV Supplier	Supplier	EMV Demand	Demand	P(Demand)	End Values
635	$1,214.50					
				586	2.38%	$1,010.00
				588	2.38%	$1,020.00
				597	2.38%	$1,065.00
				607	2.38%	$1,115.00
				609	2.38%	$1,125.00
				617	2.38%	$1,165.00
				618	2.38%	$1,170.00
				620	2.38%	$1,180.00
				623	2.38%	$1,195.00
				628	2.38%	$1,220.00
				630	2.38%	$1,230.00
				630	2.38%	$1,230.00
				631	2.38%	$1,235.00
				633	2.38%	$1,245.00
				640	2.38%	$1,280.00
				642	2.38%	$1,280.00
				643	2.38%	$1,280.00
				644	2.38%	$1,280.00
				645	2.38%	$1,280.00
				646	2.38%	$1,280.00
		Arnos Grove or Bali Fruit $1,239.17		647	2.38%	$1,280.00
		90.0%		650	2.38%	$1,280.00
				650	2.38%	$1,280.00
				658	2.38%	$1,280.00
				663	2.38%	$1,280.00
				665	2.38%	$1,280.00
				666	2.38%	$1,280.00
				666	2.38%	$1,280.00
				670	2.38%	$1,280.00
				672	2.38%	$1,280.00
				676	2.38%	$1,280.00
				677	2.38%	$1,280.00
				680	2.38%	$1,280.00
				682	2.38%	$1,280.00
				683	2.38%	$1,280.00
$1,214.639	640	$1,214.64		684	2.38%	$1,280.00
				694	2.38%	$1,280.00
				699	2.38%	$1,280.00
				722	2.38%	$1,280.00
				728	2.38%	$1,280.00
				735	2.38%	$1,280.00
				755	2.38%	$1,280.00
				533	5.56%	$745.00
				548	5.56%	$820.00
				556	5.56%	$860.00
				557	5.56%	$865.00
				560	5.56%	$880.00
				561	5.56%	$885.00
				568	5.56%	$920.00
				575	5.56%	$955.00
		Canons Park	$993.89	581	5.56%	$985.00
		10.0%		583	5.56%	$995.00
				595	5.56%	$1,055.00
				599	5.56%	$1,075.00
				599	5.56%	$1,075.00
				600	5.56%	$1,080.00
				603	5.56%	$1,095.00
				614	5.56%	$1,150.00
				618	5.56%	$1,170.00
				661	5.56%	$1,280.00
645	$1,213.60					

FIGURE 9.24

Decision Tree for How Many Pounds of Mangoes to Order With Uncertainty of Supplier and Demand

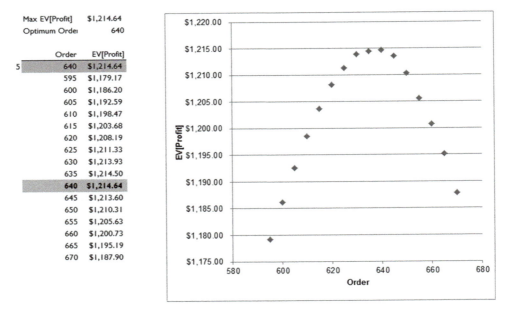

	Order	EV[Profit]
Max EV[Profit]		$1,214.64
Optimum Order		640
	Order	EV[Profit]
5	640	$1,214.64
	595	$1,179.17
	600	$1,186.20
	605	$1,192.59
	610	$1,198.47
	615	$1,203.68
	620	$1,208.19
	625	$1,211.33
	630	$1,213.93
	635	$1,214.50
	640	$1,214.64
	645	$1,213.60
	650	$1,210.31
	655	$1,205.63
	660	$1,200.73
	665	$1,195.19
	670	$1,187.90

FIGURE 9.25

Expected Profit Resulting From Incremental Order Quantities of Mangoes With Uncertainty of Supplier and Demand

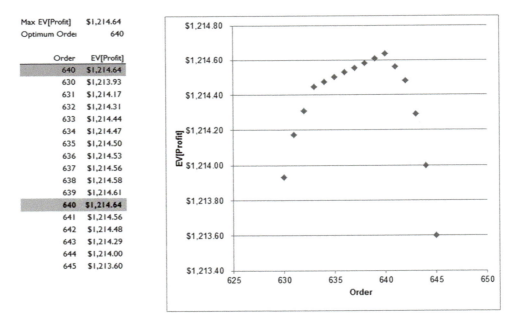

Order	EV[Profit]
Max EV[Profit] $1,214.64	
Optimum Order 640	
Order	EV[Profit]
640	$1,214.64
630	$1,213.93
631	$1,214.17
632	$1,214.31
633	$1,214.44
634	$1,214.47
635	$1,214.50
636	$1,214.53
637	$1,214.56
638	$1,214.58
639	$1,214.61
640	$1,214.64
641	$1,214.56
642	$1,214.48
643	$1,214.29
644	$1,214.00
645	$1,213.60

FIGURE 9.26

Expected Profit Resulting From Order Quantities of Mangoes From 630 to 645 Pounds

In examining the previous solution of ordering 640 units, the natural question that arises is this: *Is there a significant difference between ordering 639 and 640 . . . is the $0.03 a big deal?* Unfortunately, decision trees cannot answer this question because they do not provide a margin of error of what might happen—they do not provide a level of significance. As the next example will show, an ANOVA performed on a simulation can answer that question.

Example 9.7 Are simulation results significantly different?

A financial analyst is testing two different portfolio designs: one is a high-tech-focused portfolio, and the second is a utilities-focused portfolio. The analyst has run a simulation with 1000 trials of the rate of return for each strategy. The distributions for the trials and the summary statistics, along with the upper and lower 95% confidence intervals from the simulation results, are shown in Fig. 9.27.

Summary Statistics

	High-Tech	Utilities
Avg	7.94	7.93
SD	7.96	2.92
n	1,000	1,000
ME	0.49	0.18
Lower 95%	7.45	7.75
Upper 95%	8.43	8.12

Distribution

Return	High-Tech	Utilities
0	0.13	0.01
2	0.19	0.03
4	0.13	0.12
6	0.14	0.22
8	0.10	0.27
10	0.06	0.20
12	0.06	0.12
14	0.04	0.03
16	0.03	0.01
18	0.02	0.00
20	0.02	0.00
22	0.02	0.00
24	0.01	0.00
26	0.01	0.00
28	0.01	0.00

FIGURE 9.27

Distributions From Simulations of Rate of Returns for Two Portfolios

Notice that the average for *High-Tech* (7.94) is within the 95% confidence interval [7.75, 8.12] of *Utilities*, and vice versa. This fact indicates that the averages are not statistically significantly different—that is, $7.94 \cong 7.93$. This conclusion is supported by the *p*-value in the ANOVA results shown in Table 9.12.

Table 9.12 ANOVA results for average demand of the three mango suppliers

ANOVA: single factor							
Summary							
Groups	Count	Sum	Average	Variance	SD	Lower 95% CI	Upper 95% CI
High-tech	1000	7939.357	7.94	63.35	7.96	7.45	8.43
Utilities	1000	7934.863	7.93	8.5	2.92	7.75	8.12
$r^2 = 0.00\%$							
ANOVA							
Source of variation	Sum of square	df	Mean square	F	p-Value	F crit	
Between groups	0.010098	1	0.010098	0.000281	0.99	3.846	
Within groups	71,783.62	1998	353.92774				
Total	71,783.63	1999					

This indicates that the long-run performance of the portfolios is equivalent—but what about in the short run? Table 9.13 shows the results of the 1000 simulation trials in the form of the percentiles. Furthermore, Table 9.13 is a summary of the information shown in Fig. 9.28.

Table 9.13 Percentiles of rate of returns for the 1000 simulation trials of two portfolios

Percentile	High-tech	Utilities
0	0.01	−2.33
10	0.75	4.40
25	2.41	5.95
50	5.79	7.87
75	10.80	9.85
90	18.36	11.72
100	72.61	16.03

$P(Return_{Utilities} > Return_{High-Tech}) = 0.707$.

To comprehend the meaning of this, imagine each set of 1000 returns sorted smallest to largest, along with a 0,1 *indicator* variable to indicate if *Utilities* had a higher return than *High-Tech*, as shown in Fig. 9.28.

The 0.707 indicates that *Utilities* had a higher return than *High-Tech* in 707 of the 1000 trials—that is, there was approximately a 70% chance that the returns for the *Utilities*-focused portfolio would exceed those of the *High-Tech*-focused portfolio. A confidence interval for that probability can be calculated using the formula in Chapter 8.

SUM	▼	⋮	✕ ✓ $f\!x$	=(C8>B8)*1|

	A	B	C	D	E
1	rank	High-Tech	Utilities	0.707	
2	1	0.01	-2.33	0	
3	2	0.01	-1.59	0	
4	3	0.01	-0.77	0	
5	4	0.01	-0.71	0	
6	5	0.01	-0.67	0	
7	6	0.01	-0.28	0	
8	7	0.01	0.22	(C8>B8)*1	
9	8	0.02	0.48	1	
10	9	0.03	0.90	1	
11	10	0.03	1.29	1	
996	995	37.37	15.56	0	
997	996	37.86	15.62	0	
998	997	38.51	15.77	0	
999	998	46.74	15.86	0	
1000	999	54.28	15.92	0	
1001	1000	72.61	16.03	0	

FIGURE 9.28

Excerpt of 1000 Simulation Trials of Rate of Returns for Two Portfolios

Thus, although neither choice (decision) would be better than the other on average in the long run, the *Utilities*-focused portfolio has the **maximum likelihood** of the higher return. This demonstrates that there can be other objective functions rather than simply maximum expected value. Why do you think the averages are the same and yet *Utilities* has the higher probability of better performance?

9.5 ANOVA versus Chi-square: Likert scale

A *Likert scale* is a type of response scale in which responders specify their level of agreement to a statement typically in five points: (1) Strongly disagree, (2) Disagree, (3) Neither agree nor disagree, (4) Agree, and (5) Strongly agree. Marketing researchers tend to use an ANOVA for such scales. Unfortunately, although the ANOVA might tell you if the average rating is different, it does not necessarily indicate if the groups are actually the same. In other words, the groups could have the same average but still be significantly different.

How?

Example 9.8 Speaker ratings

You are trying to determine which audio speakers to buy. You have read the review of various speakers and narrowed your choice to three different models of speakers: A, B, and C.

Table 9.14 shows the ratings (1–5; 5 is the best) from online reviewers for each of the three models of speakers.

Table 9.14 Cross tabulation of speaker ratings by brand

Rating	A	B	C	Total
1	5	10	28	43
2	19	12	2	33
3	20	18	2	40
4	54	57	22	133
5	60	42	76	178
Sample size	158	139	130	427
Average	3.92	3.78	3.89	3.87

At first glance, the online ratings look about the same for all three models. More specifically, the ANOVA results in Tables 9.15 and 9.16 indicate *no* significant difference for either of the pairs of ratings.

Table 9.15 ANOVA results comparing brand *A* versus brand *B*

ANOVA: single factor						
Summary						
Groups	Count		Sum	Average	Variance	
A	158		619	3.92	1.27	
B	139		526	3.78	1.39	
ANOVA						
Source of variation	Sum of square	df	Mean square	F	p-Value	F crit
Between groups	1.3189	1	1.3189	0.9939	0.32	3.8732
Within groups	391.4556	295	1.3270			
Total	392.7744	296				

Table 9.16 ANOVA results comparing brand A versus brand C

ANOVA: single factor						
Summary						
Groups	Count		Sum	Average	Variance	
A	158		619	3.92	1.27	
C	130		506	3.89	2.61	
ANOVA						
Source of variation	Sum of square	df	Mean Square	F	p-Value	F crit
Between groups	0.0461	1	0.0461	0.0246	0.88	3.8732
Within groups	536.4227	286	1.8756			
Total	536.4688	287				

Table 9.17 shows the Actual and Expected frequencies that result in a p-value of 0.25 for the Chi-square test comparison of the distributions of ratings for speakers A and B. Table 9.18 shows the Actual and Expected frequencies that result in a p-value less than 0.001 for the Chi-square test comparison of the distributions of ratings for speakers A and C. These p-values indicate that the ratings of A and B are *not* statistically significantly different, but the ratings of A and C *are* significantly different. Comprehension question: Why are the Expected frequencies for brand A different when compared to brands B and C?

Table 9.17 Actual and Expected frequencies comparing brand A versus brand B

Actual					Expected			
Rating	A	B	Total		Rating	A	B	Total
1	5	10	15		1	8	7	15
2	19	12	31		2	16	15	31
3	20	18	38		3	20	18	38
4	54	57	111		4	59	52	111
5	60	42	102		5	54	48	102
Total	158	139	297			158	139	297

Table 9.18 Actual and Expected frequencies comparing brand A versus brand C

Actual					Expected			
Rating	A	C	Total		Rating	A	C	Total
1	5	28	33		1	18	15	33
2	19	2	21		2	12	9	21
3	20	2	22		3	12	10	22
4	54	22	76		4	42	34	76
5	60	76	136		5	75	61	136
Total	158	130	288			158	130	288

The two bar charts in Figs. 9.29 and 9.30 show the comparison of the distribution of ratings for brand A versus brand B and the comparison of the distribution of ratings for brand A versus brand C.

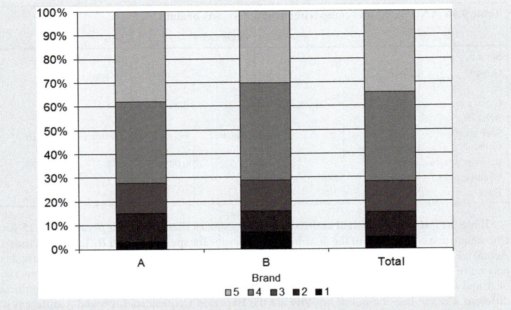

FIGURE 9.29

A Versus *B*: Chi-Square *p*-Value = 0.25

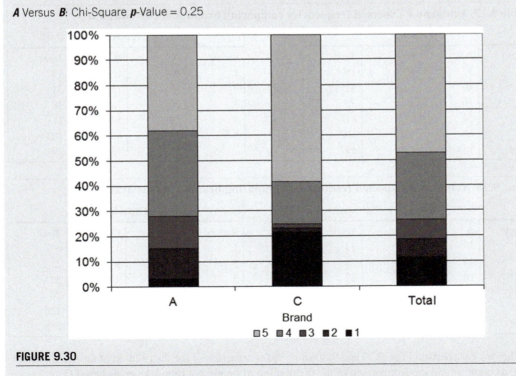

FIGURE 9.30

A Versus *C*: Chi-Square *p*-Value < 0.001

In contrast to the ANOVA results, the Chi-square results indicate that the ratings are significantly different for *A* and *C*; there are significantly more low ratings (1) and fewer high ratings (3–5) than would be *expected* if the ratings of the two speakers were approximately equal. Summarizing regarding the *C* speakers, the customers demonstrate either a strong like or dislike for the speakers, with few responses in the middle. In contrast, fewer customers rated speakers *A* and *B* as low as the segment that disliked *C*. Thus, to make your decision, you would have to determine if there was a consistent reason *C* speakers were rated so poorly and, if so, if that was an attribute of importance to you. As an example, suppose you read the reviews in which the raters assigned *C* speakers a **1** and found that these customers thought the speakers appeared too futuristic, but you like the way they look. Then, in effect, you could disregard the **1** ratings, thus having the effect of raising the average rating of *C* speakers—you could then choose those as being better than *A* or *B*.

This disparity between the ANOVA and Chi-square tests results from the unequal variances (*heteroscedasticity*) of *A* and *C*. This is why homoscedasticity (equal variances) is typically assumed for ANOVA and regression analysis.

In conclusion, although an ANOVA will detect a significant difference in averages (means), it will not necessarily tell you if the groups are significantly different in other aspects—such as distribution or spread (i.e., *variance*). Thus, it is important when using an ANOVA to consider the groups' variances. Furthermore, it is advisable to use a Chi-square when the response variable (*Y*) is genuinely a group (or even an ordinal variable) rather than an ANOVA.

Suppose every member of one group gave a product a rating of *3*. Meanwhile, in another group, half the respondents each gave the same product a rating of *1* and the other half of the respondents each gave ratings of *5*; both groups would average 3. Yet these two groups do not feel the same about the product.

To illustrate that the ANOVA is unable to detect this type of significant difference between the two groups, consider two groups: *A* and *B*. Each group was asked to respond on a five-point Likert scale for two questions.

Exercise Set 9: Statistical Tools: Chi-square and ANOVA

1. Construct a simulation to flip three coins.
    a. Construct a simulation to estimate the probability of each outcome.
    b. Compute the probability of each outcome.
    c. Compare (test) statistically the simulation probabilities (empirical) to the theoretical probabilities.
2. Create a simulation of flipping 100 pennies.
    a. Statistically test the significance of the distribution of the number of heads generated in the simulation versus a binomial distribution.
    b. Statistically test the significance of the distribution of the number of heads generated in the simulation versus a normal distribution.
3. As a marketing researcher in Florida, you must determine whether a particular ad campaign will be effective. After collecting a sample of 225 respondents, you want to determine whether the sample is valid—that is, if it accurately represents the target market. The sample frequencies from the respondents and the proportions of each group in the target market are shown in Table 9.19. What is your managerial conclusion?

Table 9.19 Age group sampling proportions and target proportions

Group	Sample frequency	Target proportions (%)
≤20	13	5
21–40	36	15
41–65	63	25
66–75	92	40
≥76	21	15
Total	225	100

4. A bank is reviewing the status of recent real estate mortgage applications for residential and commercial customers. Some applications have been accepted, some rejected, and some are pending while waiting for further information. The data is summarized in Table 9.20. What are your managerial conclusions?

Table 9.20 Mortgage status by loan segment

Mortgage status	Residential	Commercial
Accepted	78	57
Information requested	30	6
Rejected	44	13

5. One group of households was asked, on a five-point Likert scale, how satisfied they were with their new car, whereas another group was asked how dissatisfied they were. The results are summarized in Table 9.20. What are your managerial conclusions?

Table 9.20 Satisfaction response by form of question

	Question asked	
Response	"Satisfied"	"Dissatisfied"
Very satisfied	139	128
Somewhat satisfied	82	69
Neutral	15	15
Somewhat dissatisfied	12	20
Very dissatisfied	10	23

6. A brand manager wants to know if her brand's share is more strongly preferred in certain regions. Determine whether there are regional differences in brand preference based on the data in Table 9.21. What is the brand's market share?
7. The impact of the introduction of the Sarbanes–Oxley Act of 2002 on Small Firms is of interest to investment analysts and corporate strategists. A random sample of 112 companies' responses

Table 9.21 Brand purchase by region

	Northeast	Southeast	Midwest	West
Purchase the brand	47	52	43	49
Do not purchase brand	53	48	57	51

to the question "What is the impact of Sarbanes–Oxley upon your company?" is shown in Table 9.22. What is the managerial conclusion?

Table 9.22 Impact of the Sarbanes–Oxley Act by company size

	Small	Medium	Large
Little to no impact	17	13	6
Moderate to very major impact	13	41	22

8. A credit risk manager for a credit card company is interested in examining the payment behaviors of customers. Some customers have only one type of card, Visa or Mastercard, and some have both. The amount paid for each customer was classified as either paid in Full, Minimum, or somewhere in between (Middle). A summary of the data is shown in Table 9.23. What is the managerial conclusion?

Table 9.23 Contingency table of payment status by credit card company

	Visa	Mastercard	Both
Full	204	99	148
Middle	148	85	174
Minimum	55	37	81

9. A human resources benefits manager is trying to ascertain different employee preferences among health care plans. One plan (low dental/vision) has a low copay overall but has higher out-of-pocket costs for vision and dental. Another plan (high dental/vision) has higher copayments overall but lower out-of-pocket costs for vision and dental. Based on the data in Table 9.24, determine if there are significant differences in coverage preference based on salary level.

Table 9.24 Health care plan by compensation category

	Hourly	Salaried
Low dental/vision	89	64
High dental/vision	53	55

10. A FedEx contractor owns 50 trucks in a region. Twenty of the trucks are relatively new, and each of these trucks has a 5% chance of not being in service on any day. Ten trucks are older and only have a 50% chance of being in service on any day. Twenty trucks are much older and have a 90% chance of not being in service on any day.
    a. The contractor needs 40 trucks to deliver packages tomorrow. What is the probability that the contractor will have enough trucks?
    b. Test whether the distribution of the number of trucks in service to the distribution using the approximation from the aggregated binomial distribution.
    c. Is the number of trucks in service normally distributed? Why or why not?

11. A specific class of rooms at a resort hotel has a 5% rate of reservations in which the people do not show up (no shows). The hotel chain owns three similar hotels, two with 20 such rooms and the other with 30 rooms.
    a. Use theoretical probability to determine the probability distribution of demand if all 70 rooms are reserved.
    b. Create a simulation to determine the probability distribution of demand if all 70 rooms are reserved.
    c. Test whether the simulated distribution of the demand given 70 reservations is significantly different from the normal distribution using the approximation from the aggregated binomial distribution.

12. A study compared the effects of four 1-month point-of-purchase promotions on sales. The unit sales for five stores using all four promotions in different months is shown in Table 9.25. What is your decision based on this information?

Table 9.25 Sales by promotion and store

			Store		
Promotion	**1**	**2**	**3**	**4**	**5**
Free sample	77	86	80	88	84
On-pack gift	95	92	88	91	89
Cents-off	72	77	68	82	75
Refund by mail	80	84	79	70	82

13. Three advertisements have been tested, each one using a different random sample of consumers from the same city. Scores indicating the effectiveness of the advertising were analyzed, and the results are shown in Table 9.26.
    a. Use confidence intervals to determine if there are any significant differences between the averages.
    b. What is your managerial conclusion (decision) based on this summary data?
    c. Using the previous information and the ANOVA spreadsheet example, compute the ANOVA table and p-value.

Table 9.26 Advertising efficacy by advertisement

	Ad1	Ad2	Ad3
Sample size	101	97	105
Average	63.2	68.1	53.5
Standard deviation	7.9	11.3	9.2

14. A random sample of 50 households in one community has a sample average income of $44,600 with a standard deviation of $2200. Another random sample from a second (different) community has an average income of $43,800 with a standard deviation of $2800.

    a. Use two different confidence interval approaches to determine if these communities are similar on the basis of income.

    b. How and why would you run an ANOVA on the original data, and what would it look like?

15. An ad in the newspaper purports that consumers should expect to save money by shopping at Walmart. The results of a study of randomly selected items priced at Walmart and at Target are listed in Table 9.27.

Table 9.27 Item price by store

Obs	Product	Walmart ($)	Target ($)
1	Levi's jeans	41.65	41.99
2	Walking shoes	54.95	59.95
3	Dress shirt	26.95	24.99
4	Farberware pots & pans	39.97	44.99
5	Pod coffee maker	79.99	89.99
6	Chocolate meal replacement shake	6.50	4.79
7	Maxwell House coffee	6.59	6.25
8	Kolcraft baby stroller	87.90	69.99
9	Suave shampoo	2.94	2.99
10	Shaving cream	6.13	5.49
11	Schwinn bike	238.00	239.99
12	DVD player	70.00	79.99
13	*Friends* DVD	55.19	67.99
14	Headphones	39.99	39.99
15	Lego Friends house	56.00	59.00
16	Spalding NBA basketball	24.96	15.99

16. A marketing researcher must estimate the public response to proposed changes at the local airport; 66 respondents from Greensboro and Winston-Salem were asked to rate their feelings about the proposed changes on a five-point scale (1 = strongly opposed to the changes; 5 = strongly in favor of the changes). The data is given in Table 9.28.

    a. Which procedures can you use to analyze this data?

    b. What is your managerial conclusion regarding the proposed changes?

    c. What other marketing research would you conduct?

Table 9.28 Airport change survey response by city

Obs	City	Response	Obs	City	Response
1	Winston-Salem	3	20	Greensboro	5
2	Winston-Salem	4	21	Greensboro	5
3	Greensboro	3	22	Winston-Salem	4
4	Winston-Salem	4	23	Winston-Salem	2
5	Greensboro	4	24	Greensboro	5
6	Winston-Salem	5	25	Winston-Salem	3
7	Winston-Salem	3	26	Winston-Salem	3
8	Winston-Salem	4	27	Greensboro	4
9	Winston-Salem	4	28	Winston-Salem	3
10	Greensboro	4	29	Greensboro	3
11	Greensboro	5	30	Winston-Salem	3
12	Winston-Salem	4	31	Greensboro	5
13	Winston-Salem	4	32	Winston-Salem	4
14	Greensboro	5	33	Greensboro	5
15	Winston-Salem	4	34	Winston-Salem	3
16	Winston-Salem	5	35	Winston-Salem	5
17	Greensboro	4	36	Greensboro	4
18	Greensboro	2	37	Winston-Salem	4
19	Winston-Salem	3	38	Greensboro	4
39	Greensboro	2	53	Winston-Salem	5
40	Greensboro	1	54	Greensboro	3
41	Winston-Salem	4	55	Greensboro	5
42	Greensboro	4	56	Greensboro	1
43	Winston-Salem	2	57	Greensboro	5
44	Winston-Salem	4	58	Winston-Salem	5
45	Winston-Salem	3	59	Greensboro	5
46	Winston-Salem	4	60	Greensboro	4
47	Greensboro	3	61	Greensboro	4
48	Greensboro	1	62	Winston-Salem	2
49	Winston-Salem	3	63	Greensboro	5
50	Winston-Salem	4	64	Greensboro	2
51	Greensboro	2	65	Greensboro	5
52	Winston-Salem	4	66	Greensboro	5

17. A small chain of health-foods grocery stores must determine each month how much of each product to order. In particular, ordering produce is particularly complicated due to the availability of various fruits and vegetables. There are three regional suppliers of mangoes. Due to the global supply of mangoes and an arrangement with a fruit wholesaler, the grocery chain cannot determine which supplier will have mangoes in any particular month. The mangoes typically cost the grocery store $3 per pound, sell for $5 per pound, and have a cost of shortage (lost sales) of $0.45 per pound. Five years of demand (in pounds) and the supplier providing the mangoes is shown in Table 9.29. How many mangoes should the chain order if the probability of getting mangoes from Arnos Grove is 25%, from Bali Fruit is 15%, and from Canons Park is 60%?

Table 9.29 Demand by supplier

			Supplier		
Arnos Grove	**Bali Fruit**	**Canons Park**	**Arnos Grove**	**Bali Fruit**	**Canons Park**
650	650	599	684	735	614
633	670	561	617	658	661
631	755	599	642	588	548
665	620	595	640	630	560
672	618	568	628	683	600
682	728	557	586	630	618
677	643	533	645	680	
663	597	556		647	
623	644	581		609	
666	607	583		676	
694	646	575		666	
699	722	603			

18. Your firm purchases electronic components from three suppliers. You want to compare the quality of components from the three suppliers. Quality scores (ratings based on a scale from 0% to 100%) have been obtained for about 20 components from each supplier and are shown in Table 9.30. Determine the appropriate managerial conclusion regarding the quality of components from the three suppliers.

19. A music festival runs for three nights: Friday, Saturday, and Sunday. Friday night's performance is recorded, and CDs are made from this performance for sale on Saturday and Sunday nights. A marketing analyst for a jazz festival must decide how many CDs of the performance to order. Festival attendance depends on many factors. Based on data from the previous 12 years of the festival, the analyst expects a total attendance over the next 2 days of approximately 52,000 ± 6000.

Although there was no data available regarding the purchasing of CDs by the attendees, the analyst estimated that the proportion of attendees who would buy a CD was equally likely to be anywhere from 10% to 20%.

The local CD manufacturer sells the CDs in lot sizes of 1000 and quoted the following prices:

	Fixed costs
Production of master CD	$4200
Machine setup	$2800
Unit costs per CD	
Packaging	$2.00
Other manufacturing costs	$2.50

In addition, for each CD sold, the festival would have to pay $3.00 in royalties to the artists involved (royalties are paid when a CD is sold, not pressed). If they went ahead with the project, the festival would also incur $8000 in miscellaneous costs (for promotion, additional vendors, sound engineers, etc.).

Table 9.30 Quality score by supplier

Amalgamated	Bizparts	Consolidated
75	94	90
72	87	86
87	80	92
77	86	75
84	80	79
82	67	94
84	86	95
81	82	85
78	86	86
97	82	92
85	72	92
81	77	85
95	87	87
81	68	86
72	80	92
89	76	85
84	68	93
73	86	89
	74	83
	86	
	90	

The analyst currently plans to sell each CD for $18. After the festival, any unsold CDs will be destroyed.

20. The marketing managers of a consumer electronics company need to determine the effect of a competitor's television advertisements on the company's sales. Sales records for the last 120 weeks are shown in Table 9.31.
    a. Construct a contingency (frequency) table and a probability (relative frequency) table.
    b. Construct a probability tree.
    c. What is the probability that the competitor will advertise: $P(Comp.\ adv. = yes)$?
    d. Are sales significantly different when the completion advertises?
    e. Construct a decision tree for a decision the company might need to make.

Case

Carteret Dairy: milk production

It was Thursday, February 2, 2012, and Steve Horne had to decide how many gallons of milk should be produced by the Carteret Dairy Company for delivery the upcoming weekend to supply the following week starting Monday. Carteret was a regional dairy packager and wholesale firm that made a variety of products including milk, cheese,

Table 9.31 Sales and competitor advertising

Week	Sales	Competitor advertises	Week	Competitor advertises	Sales	Week	Competitor advertises	Sales
1	High	No	9	No	Low	17	No	Low
2	Low	No	10	Yes	Medium	18	Yes	High
3	Medium	Yes	11	Yes	High	19	Yes	Low
4	Low	No	12	No	Low	20	No	Low
5	Low	No	13	No	High	21	Yes	High
6	Medium	No	14	Yes	High	22	No	High
7	Low	No	15	Yes	High	23	Yes	High
8	Low	Yes	16	Yes	Low	24	No	High
25	High	No	57	No	High	89	Yes	High
26	High	Yes	58	Yes	Low	90	Yes	Medium
27	High	Yes	59	Yes	Low	91	No	Low
28	High	No	60	No	Low	92	No	Low
29	Low	No	61	Yes	Low	93	No	Medium
30	Low	Yes	62	No	Medium	94	No	Low
31	Low	Yes	63	Yes	Low	95	Yes	High
32	Medium	Yes	64	No	Low	96	No	Low
33	Low	Yes	65	Yes	Low	97	No	High
34	High	No	66	No	Medium	98	Yes	Low
35	High	Yes	67	Yes	Medium	99	Yes	Low
36	High	Yes	68	No	High	100	No	Low
37	Low	No	69	Yes	High	101	No	Medium
38	Medium	No	70	No	High	102	Yes	Low
39	Low	Yes	71	Yes	Medium	103	Yes	Low
40	Medium	Yes	72	Yes	High	104	Yes	Low
41	High	No	73	Yes	Low	105	No	High
42	Medium	No	74	No	Low	106	No	High
43	High	No	75	Yes	Medium	107	No	High
44	Medium	No	76	Yes	Low	108	Yes	Medium
45	Low	Yes	77	Yes	Low	109	Yes	Low
46	Low	Yes	78	No	High	110	Yes	Low

Continued

Table 9.31 Sales and competitor advertising—cont'd

Week	Competitor advertises	Sales	Week	Competitor advertises	Sales	Week	Competitor advertises	Sales
47	Yes	Medium	79	No	Medium	111	No	Low
48	No	Medium	80	Yes	Low	112	No	High
49	Yes	Low	81	No	High	113	Yes	Low
50	Yes	High	82	Yes	Low	114	No	High
51	No	High	83	No	Medium	115	Yes	High
52	Yes	Low	84	No	Medium	116	Yes	Low
53	Yes	Medium	85	No	Low	117	No	High
54	Yes	Medium	86	Yes	High	118	Yes	Low
55	Yes	Medium	87	Yes	High	119	Yes	Medium
56	No	Low	88	Yes	Low	120	No	High

yogurt, and milk. The milk that Mr. Horne was considering was sold through a group of company-owned "natural" stores in the region. The milk was a high-quality product; the marketing for it stressed its good taste and its "naturalness."

All milk had a short code life (the period that the health codes allowed between production and use), so it was not easy to avoid having to dump extra out-of-date product. Thus, Mr. Horne's problem was to try to meet demand without causing excessive wastage from such dumping.

Carteret had a regular production schedule, with each product (milk, cheese, ice cream, and yogurt) made on 1 or more days each week. Milk was produced every Friday during the winter. The operators of the stores placed orders for the product late in the day on Thursday for delivery on the weekend. Those deliveries used up only part of the Thursday production run; the remainder was put into cold storage in what was referred to as "the cold room." The store operators placed a second set of orders on Sunday morning for delivery on Monday. Any milk that had been produced on Thursday and was not needed for either the Friday or the Monday delivery was thrown away. If, however, the supply in the cold room was not sufficient to fill the orders for Monday delivery, a special overtime run was made on Sunday.

In trying to predict what demand would be during the following week, Mr. Horne knew that the orders from the stores closely matched the retail demand (the stores would not inventory such a perishable product). Moreover, he knew that the popular wisdom in the company linked sales levels of the various milk products very closely to the weather conditions. The people responsible for the storage cold room and for actually shipping the products tended to categorize various week's demands for milk products by the weekend weather, both because about half of the sales occurred over the weekends and because they felt that the weekend weather forecasts were the basis on which vacationers made their travel plans. Snowy weather was thought to greatly increase demand for milk (and other products). According to the accepted rule of thumb, sales on a snowy week would be 1½ times as high as those on a comparable nonsnowy week. Each Wednesday morning, the weather forecaster on the Weather Channel made a forecast of the week's potential for snow, and Mr. Horne had kept track of the forecasts, the actual weather conditions, and the orders from the store operators during the past 4 years (Table 9.32).

Table 9.32 Past demand and weather data

Year	Month	Week starting (Monday)	Forecast snow	Actual snow	Demand
1	12	52	0	1	1406
2	1	1	0	1	1406
2	1	2	0	0	1418
2	1	3	0	1	1470
2	1	4	0	1	1452
2	2	1	1	1	2373
2	2	2	1	0	2246
2	2	3	0	0	1478
2	2	4	0	0	1558
2	3	1	1	0	2492
2	3	2	0	0	1552
2	3	3	0	0	1502
2	3	4	0	0	1710
3	1	1	0	0	1500
3	1	2	0	0	1528
3	1	3	0	1	1399
3	1	4	0	0	1600
3	2	1	1	0	2267
3	2	2	0	0	1505

Continued

Table 9.32 Past demand and weather data—cont'd

Year	Month	Week starting (Monday)	Forecast snow	Actual snow	Demand
3	2	3	0	0	1577
3	2	4	0	0	1412
3	3	1	0	0	1493
3	3	2	0	0	1518
3	3	3	0	0	1391
3	3	4	0	0	1603
3	12	52	0	0	1736
4	1	1	0	0	1736
4	1	2	0	0	1427
4	1	3	0	0	1452
4	1	4	0	0	1428
4	2	1	0	0	1548
4	2	2	0	0	1416
4	2	3	0	0	1591
4	2	4	1	1	2301
4	3	1	0	0	1405
4	3	2	0	0	1519
4	3	3	0	0	1549
4	3	4	0	0	1268
5	1	1	0	0	1512
5	1	2	1	1	2346
5	1	3	1	1	2052
5	1	4	1	1	2015
5	2	1	0	0	1434
5	2	2	0	0	1493
5	2	3	0	1	1572
5	2	4	0	0	1521
5	3	1	0	0	1390
5	3	2	0	0	1515
5	3	3	0	0	1584
5	3	4	0	0	1394

The practice of the dairy was to meet demand and not to turn down requests for its products. Thus, the production department made a special run of milk if the Sunday orders were higher than the supply in the cold room at the time. Mr. Horne suspected that a policy of bending over backward to meet demand, without a thorough accounting for the costs (in overtime premiums, extra start-up and cleanup costs, and disruptions to the normal work schedule), was not necessarily wise, especially for perishable products like the milk mix. However, he did not think the policy would be changed in the immediate future unless he could make a strong argument for change.

Thus, for the time being, there would be an initial production run on Friday, then the orders would come in and the first shipments would be made on Saturday. If the Sunday orders were higher than the supply from the Friday run, another run would be made on Sunday. That run would involve setup costs of $2000 (as opposed to the $1200 setup costs for the regular run) and variable costs of $1.85 per gallon (as opposed to the $1.25 costs on the regularly scheduled run). The minimum possible batch size was 300 gallons. Above that amount, production could be increased in units of 100 gallons. Because production had to be in a batch of some multiple of 100 gallons (and could not be less than 300 gallons), even Sunday runs could not be matched exactly to demand, even though demand was known. If, for example, 450 extra gallons were needed, the Sunday run would have to be for 500 gallons. The excess production was not wasted, however; it was put into storage and became part of the next week's normal Saturday's supply.

At present, the storage cold room held no milk. Mr. Horne checked and found that the forecast was for an 80% chance of snow for the following week.

Regression

Do changes in values affect the average?

Chapter outline

Introduction to Business Analytics Using Simulation. https://doi.org/10.1016/B978-0-323-91717-9.00010-3

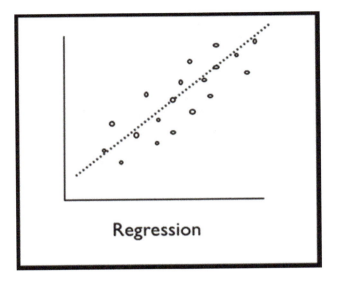

FIGURE 10.1

Scatterplot of a Simple Regression

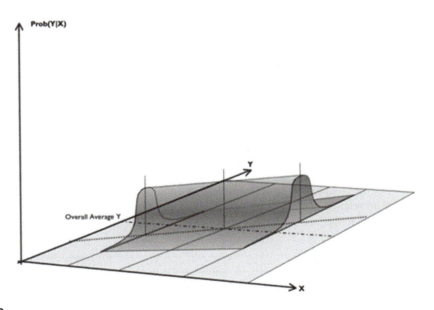

FIGURE 10.2

Three-Dimensional View of Regression

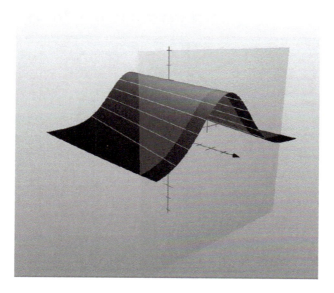

FIGURE 10.3

A Simple Regression With a Plane Intersecting at a Specified Value of X

Introduction .

Decision makers often must determine the numerical relationship between two numeric variables—the effect of numeric variables on another numeric variable. This line of inquiry is answered by using regression to ascertain the degree of correlation between numeric data. Regression is the core statistical procedure for predictive analytics. The use of regression in predictive and prescriptive analytical decision making is presented in this chapter. Methods of conducting regression tests and modeling are also explained and demonstrated.

10.1 Overview of regression

Regression is one of the most frequently used statistical methods and is used to predict a numeric response variable (Y) based on one or more numeric explanatory variables (X). Prediction is most straightforward when there is a straight-line relationship between a single explanatory variable (X) and the numeric response variable (Y). Regression is the appropriate statistical procedure when the explanatory variable (X) and the response variable (Y) are *both* numeric; refer to the *Statistical Procedures* diagram in Fig. 10.4.

Some examples of regression in this chapter include:

- How does cost increase as production increases?
- How could the performance of different size stores be compared?

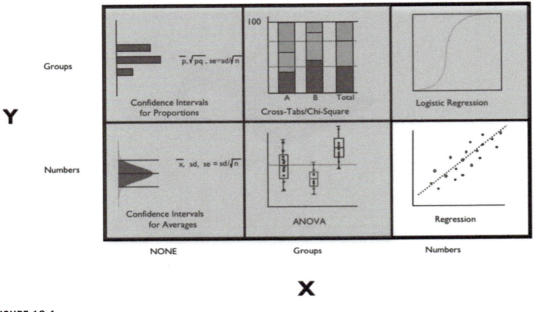

Statistical Procedures

FIGURE 10.4

Regression: Numeric *X* and Numeric *Y*

- What is the optimum amount of advertising?
- How could you estimate the appropriate selling price of a home?
- How could the delivery times for two different regions be compared?
- What is the comparative efficacy of two different types of advertising?

In general, regression answers the following question:

Does the average *Y* change as *X* changes?

In other words, is the average of *Y* conditional upon *X*? If so, then the distribution of *Y* depends upon the specific value of *X* as shown in Fig. 10.5.

10.1.1 Basic linear model

The phrase *simple linear regression* is used in the case of a single *X* variable. In such cases, regression is used to estimate the coefficients (β_0, β_1) for the line:

$$Y = \beta_0 + \beta_1 X,$$

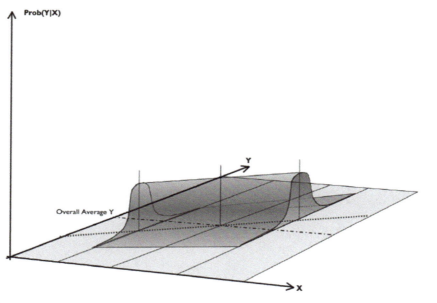

FIGURE 10.5

The Average Value of Y Depends Upon the Specific Value of X

where β_0 is the intercept and β_1 is the slope. The slope, β_1, expresses the relationship between X and Y and is the most important part of any regression. Fig. 10.6 shows the geometric definitions of slope (β_1) and intercept (β_0).

Regression provides estimates of the coefficients, β_0 and β_1, by calculating the coefficients that minimize the *sum of squared errors* (SSE). First, the estimated Y (denoted by $\hat{Y}$) is estimated by $\beta_0 + \beta_1 X$. In other words:

$$\hat{Y} = \beta_0 + \beta_1 X$$

The difference between the estimated Y ($\hat{Y}$) and the actual Y is called the *error* (or sometimes referred to as the *residual*):

$$e = Y - \hat{Y},$$

where e is the prediction (forecast) error.

By substitution, the squared errors are

$$e^2 = (Y - (\beta_0 + \beta_1 X))^2,$$

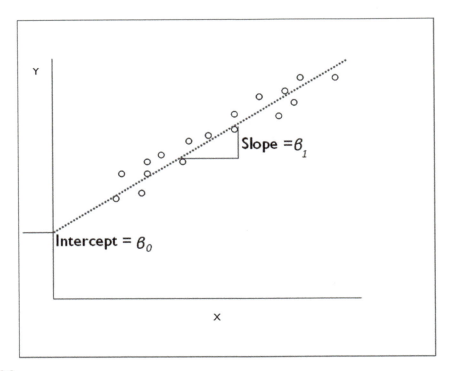

FIGURE 10.6

Slope (β_1) and Intercept (β_0) for a Scatterplot

and the SSE is

$$SSE = \sum (Y - (\beta_0 + \beta_1 X))^2.$$

Regression estimates the optimum coefficients, β_0 and β_1, by calculating the coefficients that minimize the SSE:

$$SSE_{Min} = \sum (Y - (\beta_0 + \beta_1 X))^2$$

Statistical software accomplishes this minimization using a matrix algebra solution to the calculus problem of calculating the coefficients β_0 and β_1 that minimize the SSE while also passing through the average X and average Y:

$$\bar{Y} = \beta_0 + \beta_1 \bar{X}$$

This type of regression is sometimes called *ordinary least squares*. The following example shows a managerial application of simple regression.

Example 10.1 Estimating costs

An operations manager is examining the costs of production for the previous year (Table 10.1). What can the manager learn from comparing these monthly production quantities and their associated costs?

Table 10.1 Manufacturing cost data

Month	Units Produced	Total Cost ($)	Estimated Total Cost ($)	Lower 95% ($)	Upper 95% ($)
January	30,000	450,000	501,800	409,122	594,478
February	14,000	300,000	273,026	180,348	365,704
March	12,000	150,000	244,429	151,751	337,107
April	25,000	440,000	430,308	337,630	522,986
May	10,000	180,000	215,832	123,154	308,510
June	11,000	240,000	230,130	137,453	322,808
July	20,000	350,000	358,816	266,138	451,494
August	18,000	400,000	330,219	237,541	422,897
September	17,000	360,000	315,921	223,243	408,599
October	16,000	320,000	301,622	208,944	394,300
November	27,000	490,000	458,904	366,227	551,582
December	34,000	540,000	558,993	466,315	651,671

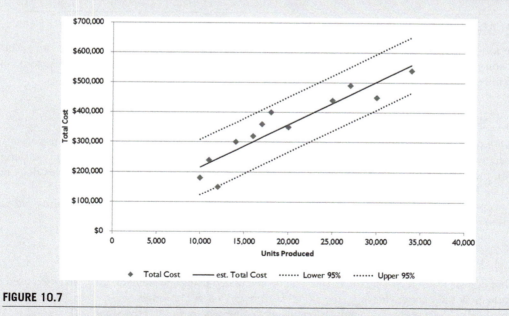

FIGURE 10.7

Scatterplot, Regression Line, and Approximate Confidence Interval for Cost Data

The regression will estimate the coefficients for the linear equation:

$$Total\ Cost = \beta_0 + \beta_1\ Units\ Produced$$

Regression output is shown in Table 10.2.

Table 10.2 Regression results for manufacturing cost data

$r^2 = 0.8609$				
Standard error of the estimate = 47,284.664				
Regression term	**Est. coefficient**	**Std error**	**t-Stat**	**Prob > $|t|$**
Constant	72,848.351	37,975.28	1.92	0.08404
Units produced	14.298	1.82	7.87	0.00001

The word *Constant* is another term for the *intercept* (β_0). The *Constant* (β_0) is 72,848.351, and the *slope* (β_1) is 14.30. Thus, the equation for the line, as estimated by regression, is:

$$Estimated\ Cost = 72,\ 848.35 + 14.30\ Units\ Produced$$

Once the regression equation has been estimated and validated, the equation must be interpreted. In this situation, the *Constant* (β_0) is 72,848.35 and is the fixed cost of production and the *slope* (β_1) of 14.30 is $14.30 per unit produced. Thus, in this setting, the slope is variable cost.

10.2 Measures of fit and significance

Before a regression equation can be interpreted and applied, it must be validated. There are several regression output statistics that facilitate the validation, interpretation, and subsequent usage of the regression equation.

10.2.1 Standard error of the slope: SE_{β_1}

The *standard error of the slope*, SE_{β_1}, is used to determine the accuracy of the slope. Most importantly, it is used to determine if the slope is equal to 0. If the slope is 0 (not statistically significantly different from 0), then the X and Y do not have relevant relationship. In other words, how Y varies does not depend on X, and X *is not significant* (*relevant*).

Conceptually, SE_{β_1} is the standard deviation of β_1. Thus, SE_{β_1} is how much the slope varies and can be used to determine the probability that the slope is nearly 0.

10.2.2 *t*-Stat

As in hypothesis testing, a t-statistic (t-stat) can be calculated using the standard error and then used to determine how far a parameter (e.g., the slope) is from any other test value.

Specifically, most regression analysis begins by testing whether or not the slope is 0.

$$0 = \beta_1 + t\ SE_{\beta_1}$$

Thus:

$$|t| = |\beta_1 / SE_{\beta_1}|$$

Using a threshold type I error of 5%, corresponding to a 95% confidence interval, generally if $|t| \geq$ 2, then we conclude that β_1 is *not* zero and that X *is* statistically significant. More precisely:

$$|t| < \mathbf{1.20} \rightarrow X \text{ is } not \text{ significant } (not \text{ correlated to } \mathbf{Y})$$

$$1.20 < |t| < 1.96 \rightarrow X \text{ is } \textbf{\textit{marginally}} \text{ significant}(\textbf{\textit{weakly}} \text{ correlated to } \mathbf{Y})$$

$$1.96 < |t| \rightarrow X \text{ is significant } (is \text{ correlated to } \mathbf{Y})$$

Similarly, the intercept has a corresponding *standard error of the intercept*, SE_{β_0}, which measures the variation in the intercept.

Note: Do not "drop the intercept" if it is not statistically significant. You are not dropping out that term—rather, you are forcing it to be exactly *0*, and that causes the estimate of the slope (β_1) to be incorrectly estimated, which causes β_1 to be wrong. Remember, because the slope is the relationship between the *X* and *Y* variables, the estimates of the slope are the most important part of a regression.

10.2.3 Standard error of the estimate

The *standard error of the estimate* (SEE) is approximately the standard deviation of the errors. As such, it is the standard deviation around the estimated $Y(\hat{y})$. The SEE is the standard deviation for the normal curve depicted in Fig. 10.8.

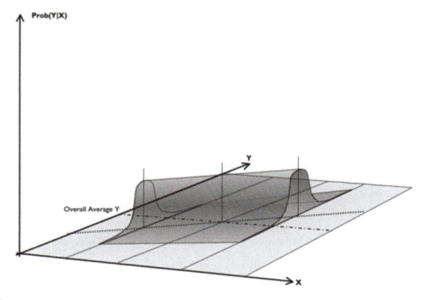

FIGURE 10.8

SEE Under the Assumption of Normally Distributed Errors

As such, you can see that regression is not simply the line through the data; rather, it is the normal probability distribution along the entire length of the regression line. Thus, the SEE can be used in decision trees to provide probabilities that are conditional upon the X variable. A useful statistic to measure regression accuracy is the *coefficient of variation (CV)*. The coefficient of variation is a relative measure of how large the SEE is relative to the average Y that you are trying to predict in percentage terms:

$$CV = SEE / \hat{Y}$$

10.2.4 Coefficient of determination: r^2

The most overused statistic in regression is the *coefficient of determination*, more commonly known as the *r-squared* (r^2). The r^2 is the proportion of variation in the data (Y) explained by the mathematical model. As in an *analysis of variance* (ANOVA), the r^2 is calculated as follows:

$$r^2 = SSM / SST = 1 - SSE / SST$$

where
  Sum of squares total:

$$SST = \sum (Y - \dot{Y})^2 = \text{Variation in the data} = \text{Difference between data and overall average}$$
$$\text{(naive estimate)}$$

Sum of squares model:

$$SSM = \sum (\dot{Y} - \dot{Y})^2 = \text{Variation accounted for by the model} = \text{Difference between the estimate}$$
$$\text{and average}$$

  SSE:

$$SSE = \sum (\dot{Y} - Y)^2 = \text{Variation not accounted for by the mode} = \text{Difference between the}$$
$$\text{estimate and data}$$

Regression minimizes SSE, the squared differences between the estimate and the data, thus making the regression line as close to the data (scatterplot) as possible by determining the line (slope and intercept) that strives to make the differences equal to 0.

Fig. 10.9 shows how the r^2 is the proportion of variation in the data (Y) explained by the model.

It is more important to have statistically significant terms than it is to maximize r^2.

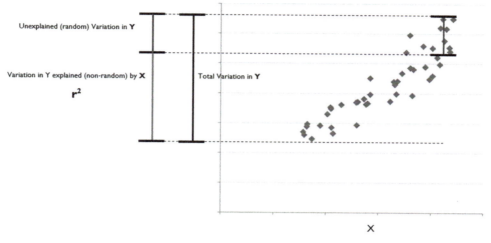

FIGURE 10.9

Conceptual Diagram of the Meaning of r^2

Example 10.2 Probability from regression

Based on a forecast for demand in the upcoming January, an operations manager needs to produce 28,000 units. The manager must estimate a budget that has a high probability of not being exceeded. What budget will provide the manager with a 90% chance of meeting (not exceeding) the budget?

The regression results from Example 10.1 are replicated in Table 10.3.

Table 10.3 Regression results for manufacturing cost data

		$r^2 = 0.8609$		
		Standard error of the estimate = 47,284.664		
Regression term	**Est. Coefficient**	**Std error**	**t-Stat**	**Prob > $\|t\|$**
Constant	72,848.351	37,975.28	1.92	0.08404
Units produced	14.298	1.82	7.87	0.00001

Given the regression output in Table 10.3 and production of 28,000 units, total costs are estimated using the regression coefficients:

$$Estimated\ Cost = 72{,}848.351 + 14.298\ (28{,}000) = \$473{,}192$$

Using $473,192 as the average and $SEE = \$47{,}284.66$ as the *standard deviation*:

$$Budget_{90\%} = \$473{,}192 + 1.28155\ (47{,}284.664) = \$533{,}790$$

Whether or not X is correlated to Y (statistically significant) must be proven statistically before a regression can be used to predict a value of Y, such as production costs. What happens when X is not correlated to Y is demonstrated in Example 10.3.

Continued

Example 10.2 Probability from regression—cont'd

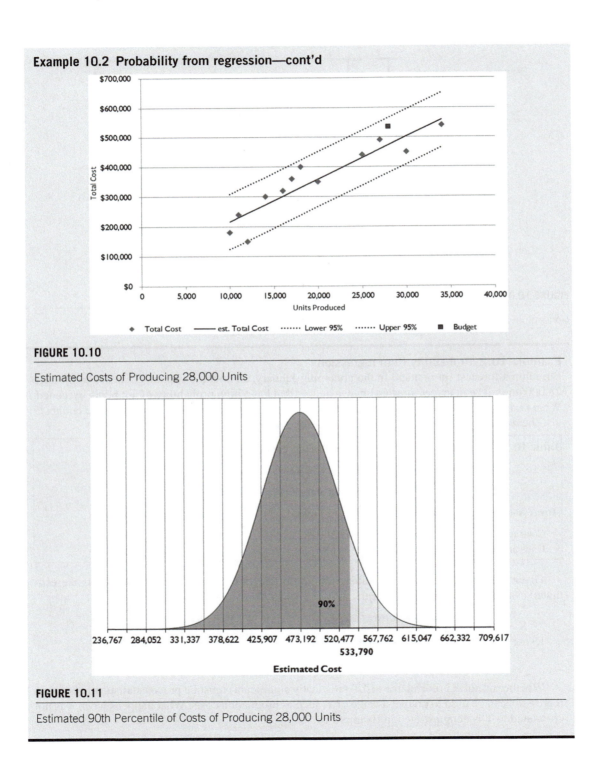

FIGURE 10.10

Estimated Costs of Producing 28,000 Units

FIGURE 10.11

Estimated 90th Percentile of Costs of Producing 28,000 Units

Example 10.3 Statistical significance

An airline marketing analyst must determine how changes in the price of a ticket for a specific flight influence the quantity of demand. Consider an airline ticket over the price range from $50 to $200 as shown in Table 10.4 and in Fig. 10.12.

Table 10.4 Airline ticket price–demand data	
Price ($)	**Demand**
50	100
60	140
70	99
80	96
90	99
100	112
110	108
120	105
130	119
140	120
150	107
160	125
170	91
180	111
190	95
200	115

The linear regression equation to be estimated is:

$$Demand = \beta_0 + \beta_1 Price$$

The regression results are shown in Table 10.5.

The *Constant* (β_0) is 110.088, and the *slope* (β_1) is −0.010. Thus, the equation for the line, as estimated by regression, is:

$$Estimated\ Demand = 110.088 - 0.010\ Price$$

Continued

Example 10.3 Statistical significance—cont'd

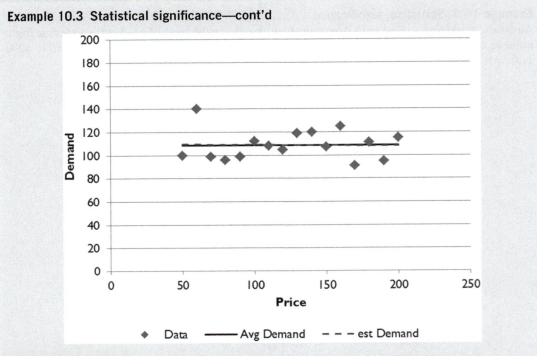

FIGURE 10.12

Scatterplot and Regression Line for Airline Ticket Price–Demand Data

Table 10.5 Regression results for airline ticket price–demand data				
$r^2 = 0.0013$				
Standard error of the estimate = 13.295				
Regression term	**Est. coefficient**	**Std error**	**t-Stat**	**Prob > $\lvert t \rvert$**
Constant	110.088	9.606	11.46	0.00000
Price	−0.010	0.072	−0.13	0.89483

But the standard error of the slope (SE_{β_1}) indicates that there is a significant probability that the true slope could be 0. The t-stat indicates that the slope is not statistically significantly different from 0. Thus, in this situation, *Price* is not statistically significant—that is, price has no significant effect on demand. As such, *Price* is not useful to predict demand and the unconditional empirical distribution of *Demand* should be used.

Example 10.4 Evaluating store performance

A regional manager of 15 retail stores must evaluate the financial performance of 15 stores in the region. Based on the data in Table 10.6, evaluate the performance of the stores.

Table 10.6 Store financial performance and square footage

Store	Square feet	Estimated contribution ($)	Contribution ($)	Lower 95% ($)	Upper 95% ($)
8	110,000	1,418,326	1,368,781	1,277,584	1,459,979
15	110,000	1,376,170	1,368,781	1,277,584	1,459,979
2	110,000	1,324,814	1,368,781	1,277,584	1,459,979
13	114,000	1,370,415	1,402,726	1,311,529	1,493,923
3	114,000	1,385,365	1,402,726	1,311,529	1,493,923
10	114,000	1,476,947	1,402,726	1,311,529	1,493,923
7	118,000	1,374,611	1,436,671	1,345,473	1,527,868
5	118,000	1,458,626	1,436,671	1,345,473	1,527,868
1	118,000	1,392,655	1,436,671	1,345,473	1,527,868
12	125,000	1,550,271	1,496,074	1,404,876	1,587,271
9	125,000	1,502,536	1,496,074	1,404,876	1,587,271
6	125,000	1,554,598	1,496,074	1,404,876	1,587,271
4	130,000	1,492,653	1,538,505	1,447,307	1,629,702
14	130,000	1,495,871	1,538,505	1,447,307	1,629,702
11	145,000	1,681,704	1,665,797	1,574,600	1,756,995

The linear regression equation to be estimated is:

$$Contribution = \beta_0 + \beta_1 \; Square \; Feet$$

Regression output:

The *Constant* (β_0) is 435,302.326, and the *slope* (β_1) is 8.486. Thus, the equation for the line, as estimated by regression, is:

$$Estimated \; Contribution = 435,302.326 + 8.486 \; Square \; Feet$$

Continued

Example 10.4 Evaluating store performance—cont'd

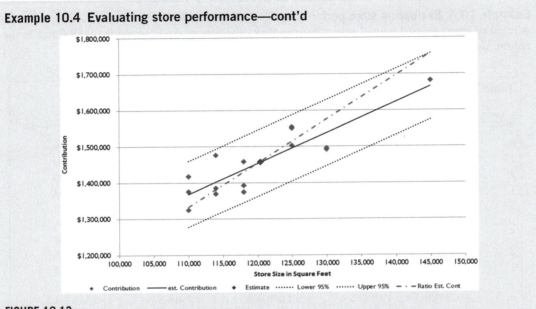

FIGURE 10.13

Scatterplot, Regression Line, and Ratio Analysis for Store Financial Performance

Table 10.7 Regression results for store financial performance and square footage				
$r^2 = 0.771$				
Standard error of the estimate = 46,529				
Regression term	**Est. coefficient**	**Std error**	**t-stat**	**Prob > |t|**
Constant	435,302.326	154,800.576	2.81	0.01469
Square feet	8.486	1.282	6.62	0.00002

In this situation, the *Constant* (β_0) is not equal to 0—thus, a ratio (or multiplier) alone is not a valid means of estimating the contribution. The *slope* (β_1) indicates that within the relevant range of the data, the contribution is about $8.50 per square foot.

Do not use RATIOS. Use REGRESSION!

10.3 Multiple regression

It is more common that many factors help explain the variation in the Y data. Regression with more than one X variable is called *multiple regression*. Consider the following general multiple linear regression equation with n explanatory (X) variables:

$$Y = \beta_0 + \beta_1 X_1 + \beta_2 X_2 \ldots + \beta_n X_n$$

Example 10.5 Multiple regression

A bank analyst must value a large number of home mortgage properties to make sure the total assets are sufficient to collateralize the portfolio of loans. The size of the property (in square feet), age of the property, and the price are listed in Table 10.8. The estimated price and approximate upper and lower 95% confidence limits resulting from the regression are also listed.

The linear regression equation to be estimated is:

$$\text{Price} = \beta_0 + \beta_1 \ \textit{Square Feet} + \beta_2 \ \textit{Age}$$

Table 10.8 Mortgage data

Square feet	Age	Price	Estimated price	Lower 95%	Upper 95%
1780	13	189,200	185,047	147,563	222,530
1479	30	202,400	190,393	152,910	227,876
1609	25	166,700	192,481	154,998	229,965
1702	32	222,100	213,833	176,350	251,317
2056	29	263,900	239,450	201,967	276,934
2262	31	223,300	261,390	223,906	298,873
2961	3	265,700	270,525	233,042	308,008
2246	39	288,600	274,997	237,514	312,481
2804	14	262,500	277,318	239,835	314,801
3088	3	318,900	281,736	244,252	319,219
2960	12	290,900	287,334	249,850	324,817
2702	32	300,700	302,108	264,625	339,592
3169	11	308,400	303,906	266,422	341,389
3433	9	328,600	323,456	285,972	360,939
3362	16	307,700	330,330	292,847	367,814
3441	13	303,900	331,672	294,188	369,155
3409	22	367,300	345,744	308,261	383,227
3540	24	368,400	361,063	323,580	398,546
4100	17	385,100	397,355	359,871	434,838
3792	36	390,000	405,838	368,355	443,321
4062	30	418,300	418,407	380,924	455,891
4242	35	460,100	443,684	406,201	481,168
4343	38	463,600	458,232	420,749	495,716

Continued

Example 10.5 Multiple regression—cont'd

Regression output is shown in Table 10.9.

As more X variables are added, the graphical interpretation of the data becomes more complex due to the higher dimensionality of the data. In this case, two Xs and a Y make a plane. Because it is often difficult to plot multidimensional data, it is useful to plot the actual Y value against the fitted (estimated) Y value ($\hat{y}$), as shown in Fig. 10.14.

Table 10.9 Regression results for house price, square footage, and age

	$r^2 = 0.950$			
	Standard error of the estimate = 19,124.186			
Regression term	**Est. coefficient**	**Std error**	**t-Stat**	**Prob > |t|**
Constant	3,510.12	16,787.78	0.21	0.8365
Square feet	88.28	4.66	18.95	<0.0001
Age	1,877.47	363.08	5.17	<0.0001

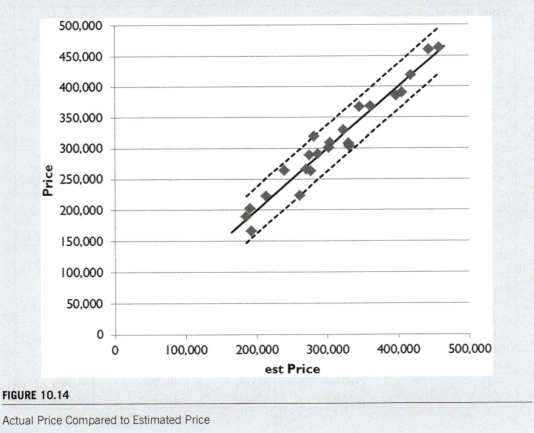

FIGURE 10.14

Actual Price Compared to Estimated Price

Example 10.5 Multiple regression—cont'd

$$\textit{Estimated } \text{Price} = 3510.12 + 88.28 \textit{ Square Feet} + 1877.47 \textit{ Age}$$

The t-stats indicate that β_0 is not statistically significantly different from 0 . . . yes, a house with no square footage and no age is worthless. Conversely, houses of the same age in this portfolio are worth about \$88.28 per square foot, and houses of the same size appreciate at about \$1877.47 each year.

One further point about the intercept: DO NOT "Drop the intercept out of the regression" . . . you are forcing the intercept to be 0 and incorrectly skewing the slopes.

10.4 Nonlinear regression: polynomials

Many numerical relationships are nonlinear. Consider your happiness (☺) versus the number of donuts consumed . . . that relationship probably is not linear. In some circumstances, regression can be used to estimate nonlinear relationships (functions).

10.4.1 Nonlinear models: polynomials

The simplest nonlinear relationship to estimate is that of a polynomial. Consider a parabola of the form:

$$\text{Price} = \beta_0 + \beta_1 X + \beta_2 X^2$$

Multiple regression can be used by simply adding an X^2 term. The next example uses a square to determine the nonlinear relationship between Y and X.

Example 10.6 Polynomial regression: optimum advertising
A marketing analyst must determine the optimum amount of advertising based upon data collected during a preliminary marketing research pricing experiment. In the experiment, different amounts of advertising expenditures were used in 18 similar markets (regions) and are listed in Table 10.10, along with the estimated sales using the regression equation.

The linear regression equation to be estimated is:

$$\textit{Sales} = \beta_0 + \beta_1 \textit{ Advertising} + \beta_2 \textit{ Advertising}^2$$

Regression output is shown in Table 10.11.
The scatterplot and estimated sales from the regression equation are shown in Fig. 10.15. Given the following regression equation,

$$\textit{Estimated Sales} = -74{,}679.875 + 31.490 \textit{ Advertising} - 0.000418 \textit{ Advertising}^2$$

Continued

Example 10.6 Polynomial regression: optimum advertising—cont'd

Table 10.10 Advertising data

Market	Advertising	Advertising^2	Sales	Estimated sales
1	43,000	1,849,000,000	460,000	506,517
2	11,000	121,000,000	250,000	221,129
3	50,000	2,500,000,000	460,000	454,836
4	53,000	2,809,000,000	410,000	420,147
5	12,000	144,000,000	260,000	243,005
6	18,000	324,000,000	380,000	356,705
7	27,000	729,000,000	500,000	470,827
8	25,000	625,000,000	410,000	451,319
9	37,000	1,369,000,000	540,000	518,213
10	34,000	1,156,000,000	500,000	512,775
11	14,000	196,000,000	220,000	284,249
12	47,000	2,209,000,000	500,000	482,001
13	30,000	900,000,000	540,000	493,821
14	16,000	256,000,000	270,000	322,149
15	10,000	100,000,000	230,000	198,417
16	20,000	400,000,000	380,000	387,918
17	17,000	289,000,000	340,000	339,845
18	40,000	1,600,000,000	530,000	516,127

Table 10.11 Regression results for polynomial (parabolic) fit of sales and advertising

$r^2 = 0.950$				
Standard error of the estimate = 19,124.186				
Regression term	**Est. coefficient**	**Std error**	**t-Stat**	**Prob > $|t|$**
Constant	−74,679.875	42481.218	−1.76	0.0991
Advertising	31.490	3.258	9.66	<0.0001
Advertising^2	−0.000418	0.00053	−7.94	<0.0001

the optimum amount of advertising can be determined either numerically or analytically with calculus:

$$dSales \,/\, dAdvertising = 31.490 - (2)\,0.000418\; Advertising^1 \equiv 0$$

Note that the $\equiv$ symbol means "set equal to":

$$Advertising_{opt} = 31.490 \,/\, (2)\,0.000418 = \$37,667$$

Example 10.6 Polynomial regression: optimum advertising—cont'd

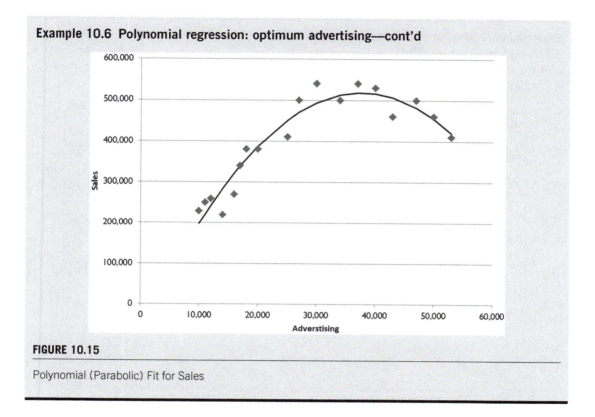

FIGURE 10.15

Polynomial (Parabolic) Fit for Sales

10.4.2 Nonlinear models: nonlinear (logarithmic) transformations

Exponential models of the general form,

$$Y = b \, e^{mX}$$

are often estimated by using the natural log (ln) of Y as the Y variable for the linear regression:

$$\ln(Y) = \beta_0 + \beta_1 X$$

Derivation:

$$Y = b e^{mX}$$
$$\ln(Y) = \ln\left(b \, e^{mX}\right)$$
$$\ln(Y) = \ln(b) + \ln\left(e^{mX}\right)$$
$$\ln(Y) = \ln(b) + mX$$

Since $\ln(b)$ and m are constants, linear regression can be used to estimate b and m:

$$\ln(Y) = \beta_0 + \beta_1 X$$

Example 10.7 Pricing and demand estimation

A pricing analyst for an airline must determine how changes in the price of a product influence the quantity of demand. Consider an airline ticket over the price range from $100 to $250 as shown in Table 10.12 and in the scatterplot in Fig. 10.16.

Table 10.12 Price and demand data

Price	Demand	ln(Demand)	Estimated ln(demand)	Estimated demand
100	65	4.174	4.152	63.6
125	54	3.989	3.941	51.5
150	41	3.714	3.731	41.7
175	30	3.401	3.520	33.8
200	27	3.296	3.309	27.4
225	24	3.178	3.099	22.2

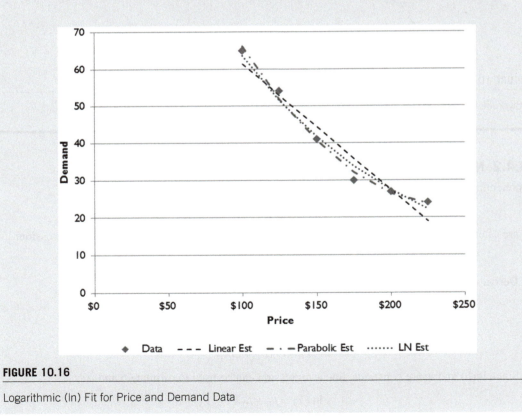

FIGURE 10.16

Logarithmic (ln) Fit for Price and Demand Data

Example 10.7 Pricing and demand estimation—cont'd

Table 10.13 Regression results for logarithmic (*ln*) fit of price and demand data				
$r^2 = 0.970$				
Standard error of the estimate = 0.0769				
Regression term	**Est. coefficient**	**Std error**	***t*-Stat**	**Prob > I *t* I**
Constant	4.9947	0.1236	40.42	<0.0001
Price	−0.00843	0.000735	−11.46	0.00033

The regression equation to be estimated is:

$$\ln(Demand) = \beta_0 + \beta_1 Price$$

Regression output is shown in Table 10.13.

In this context, the *slope* (β_1) estimates the price elasticity of demand. Thus, a \$1 change in price results in a negative 0.843% (roughly 1%) change in demand.

To estimate *Quantity* (demand):

$$Quantity = e^{\ln(Quantity)}$$

By using substitution:

$$Estimated\ Quantity = e^{(\beta_0 + \beta_1\ Price)}$$

$$Estimated\ Quantity = e^{(4.9947 - 0.00843\ Price)}$$

10.5 Indicator variables

Indicator, or *dummy*, variables are a method of using categorical (group) data in regression. Binary indicator variables take on two values: 1 and 0. These values are used to indicate if an observation is within a group (1) or outside a group (0). As an example, a dummy variable could be used to indicate if people are employed. The variable would be 1 if an individual is employed and would be 0 if the individual is unemployed. The choice of which group is the base (0) is arbitrary and thus cannot affect statistical significance. Indicator variables provide a method of incorporating ANOVA into regression when necessary.

Example 10.8 Indicator variable: two groups

An operations analyst for a package delivery company must compare the delivery times of two different service areas (regions). In this situation, the analyst has arbitrarily chosen region A as the 1 and B as the 0. Thus, B becomes the basis of the regression. Table 10.14 lists the delivery times by region and has the regions coded ($A = 1$; $B = 0$).

The linear regression equation to be estimated is:

$$Time = \beta_0 + \beta_1 \, Region \, A$$

Regression output is shown in Table 10.15.

$$Estimated \, Time = 39.165 + 15.885 \, Region \, A$$

Thus, to estimate the average delivery time for region B, use a value of **0** for the ***Region A*** indicator variable,

$$Estimated \, Time = 39.165 + 18.885 \, (0) = \mathbf{39.165} \, minutes \, (on \, average)$$

then use a value of **1** to estimate the average delivery time for region A,

$$Estimated \, Time = 39.165 + 18.885 \, (1) = \mathbf{58.050} \, minutes \, (on \, average).$$

Fig. 10.17 shows the data and estimated fit for the delivery times for both regions.

In managerial terms, delivery times in region B are about 20 minutes faster than in region A. A more specific answer would be the confidence interval for the β_1 coefficient: $18.885 \pm 1.96*3.933$ minutes.

When there are more than two groups, use more indicator variables. If there are n groups, then you need $n - 1$ indicator variables. As an example, if there are three regions, then you need two indicator variables. For reasons that will become apparent in the next example, it is a good practice to use the group with the ***minimum average*** as the base. Thus, use indicator variables for the groups that are not the minimum group. In this manner, the β_0 will be the minimum group's average and the other coefficients (β_i) will be relative to the minimum and thus positive.

Example 10.8 Indicator variable: two groups—cont'd

Table 10.14 Delivery times by region

Region	A	Time
A	1	27.7
A	1	62.3
A	1	65.0
A	1	43.3
A	1	42.0
A	1	79.6
A	1	66.2
A	1	39.8
A	1	75.8
A	1	69.9
A	1	72.6
A	1	65.7
A	1	55.4
A	1	55.8
A	1	58.3
A	1	43.7
A	1	58.4
A	1	63.4
B	0	28.5
B	0	37.4
B	0	36.5
B	0	54.6
B	0	54.1
B	0	43.3
B	0	49.5
B	0	31.6
B	0	30.3
B	0	41.3
B	0	61.9
B	0	27.4
B	0	39.6
B	0	38.4
B	0	26.7
B	0	42.5
B	0	34.4
B	0	29.8
B	0	28.0
B	0	47.5

Continued

Example 10.8 Indicator variable: two groups—cont'd

Table 10.15 Regression results for the region indicator variable and delivery time

Regression term	Est. coefficient	Std error	t-Stat	Prob $> |t|$
$r^2 = 0.39$				
Standard error of the estimate = 12.11				
Constant	39.165	2.7069	14.47	<0.00001
Region A	15.885	3.9331	4.80	0.00003

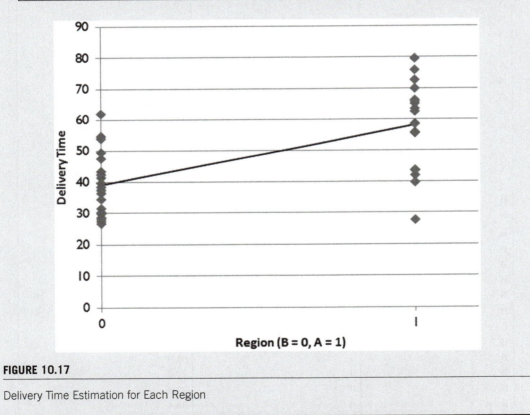

FIGURE 10.17

Delivery Time Estimation for Each Region

Example 10.9 Indicator variables: three groups

An operations analyst for a package delivery company must compare the delivery times of three different service areas (regions). To facilitate graphing of the data, the three regions were initially shown as $A = 1$, $B = 2$, $C = 3$. These group identifiers (*GroupID*) *cannot* be used as a meaningful regression variable! (Why not?) After examining the scatterplot (Figure 10.18), the analyst has determined that region B has the minimum (lowest) average and thus has chosen to use region B as the base and has created indicator variables for regions A and C. Thus, B becomes the basis of the regression.

Fig. 10.18 shows the data and estimated fit for the delivery times for both regions.

To demonstrate the importance of using the minimum group as the base, first consider the linear regression equation using region C as the base region:

$$Time = \beta_0 + \beta_1 Region\ A + \beta_2 Region\ B$$

Regression output is shown in Table 10.17.
The estimated regression equation is:

$$Estimated\ Time = 30.825 + 8.964\ Region\ A - 4.195\ Region\ B$$

Thus, to estimate the average delivery time for region C:

$$Estimated\ Time\ \overline{C} = 30.825 + 8.964\,(0) - 4.195\,(0) = \mathbf{30.8}\ minutes\ (on\ average)$$

But the t-stat for the β_1 term indicates that it is *not* statistically significant, indicating that the average delivery time in region A is not statistically significantly longer than the average delivery time in region C. If the β_1 term was statistically significant, then the average delivery time for region A could be estimated using:

$$Estimated\ Time\ \overline{A} = 30.825 + 8.964\,(1) - 4.195\,(0) = \mathbf{39.8}\ minutes\ (on\ average)$$

Similarly, the t-stat for the β_2 term indicates that it is *not* statistically significant and indicates that the average delivery time in region B is not statistically significantly longer than the average delivery time in region C. This result suggests that the three regions have similar average delivery times. Yet, as Chapter 8, it has not been proven whether $\overline{A} = \overline{B}\ or\ \overline{A} \neq \overline{B}$. If the β_2 term was statistically significant, then the average delivery time for region B could be estimated using:

$$Estimated\ Time\ \overline{B} = 30.825 + 8.964\,(0) - 4.195\,(1) = \mathbf{26.6}\ minutes\ (on\ average)$$

The next regression will instead use region B (the group with the smallest average) as the base group and will estimate the coefficients for the linear equation:

$$Time = \beta_0 + \beta_1\ Region\ A + \beta_2\ Region\ C$$

Regression output is shown in Table 10.18.
The estimated regression equation is:

$$Estimated\ Time = 26.630 + 13.159\ Region\ A + 4.195\ Region\ C$$

Continued

Example 10.9 Indicator variables: three groups—cont'd

Table 10.16 Delivery times by region

Group	GroupID	A	C	Time	Est. time
A	1	1	0	15.0	39.8
A	1	1	0	50.8	39.8
A	1	1	0	55.0	39.8
A	1	1	0	27.6	39.8
A	1	1	0	64.9	39.8
A	1	1	0	43.3	39.8
A	1	1	0	28.2	39.8
A	1	1	0	60.3	39.8
A	1	1	0	63.8	39.8
A	1	1	0	22.4	39.8
A	1	1	0	52.2	39.8
A	1	1	0	26.9	39.8
A	1	1	0	37.6	39.8
A	1	1	0	11.5	39.8
A	1	1	0	29.2	39.8
A	1	1	0	44.1	39.8
A	1	1	0	57.0	39.8
A	1	1	0	26.4	39.8
B	2	0	0	53.8	26.6
B	2	0	0	40.1	26.6
B	2	0	0	5.2	26.6
B	2	0	0	6.2	26.6
B	2	0	0	51.6	26.6
B	2	0	0	7.7	26.6
B	2	0	0	11.0	26.6
B	2	0	0	9.4	26.6
B	2	0	0	32.9	26.6
B	2	0	0	31.8	26.6
B	2	0	0	10.8	26.6
B	2	0	0	50.5	26.6
B	2	0	0	42.5	26.6
B	2	0	0	58.8	26.6
B	2	0	0	9.8	26.6
B	2	0	0	16.8	26.6
B	2	0	0	28.5	26.6
B	2	0	0	40.9	26.6
B	2	0	0	14.3	26.6
B	2	0	0	10.0	26.6
C	3	0	1	12.3	30.8

Example 10.9 Indicator variables: three groups—cont'd

Table 10.16 Delivery times by region—cont'd

Group	GroupID	A	C	Time	Est. time
C	3	0	1	52.4	30.8
C	3	0	1	22.8	30.8
C	3	0	1	24.1	30.8
C	3	0	1	20.4	30.8
C	3	0	1	19.9	30.8
C	3	0	1	25.7	30.8
C	3	0	1	23.5	30.8
C	3	0	1	18.4	30.8
C	3	0	1	50.4	30.8
C	3	0	1	22.2	30.8
C	3	0	1	24.8	30.8
C	3	0	1	50.7	30.8
C	3	0	1	53.3	30.8
C	3	0	1	45.7	30.8
C	3	0	1	26.6	30.8

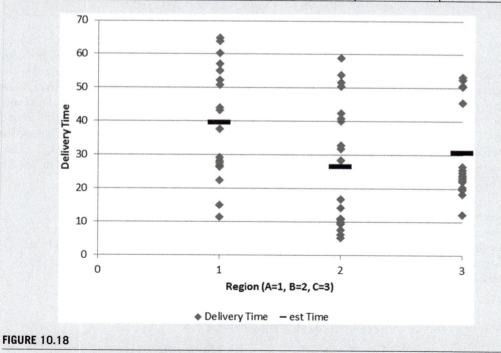

FIGURE 10.18

Delivery Time Estimation for Each Region

Continued

Example 10.9 Indicator variables: three groups—cont'd

Table 10.17 Regression results for region indicator variables and delivery time

$r^2 = 0.105$

Standard error of the estimate = 16.830

Regression term	Est. coefficient	Std error	t-Stat
Constant	30.825	4.208	7.326
Region A	8.964	5.783	1.550
Region B	−4.195	5.645	−0.743

Table 10.18 Regression results for region indicator variables and delivery time

$r^2 = 0.105$

Standard error of the estimate = 16.830

Regression term	Est. coefficient	Std error	t-Stat
Constant	26.630	3.763	7.076
Region A	13.159	5.468	2.407
Region C	4.195	5.645	0.743

Now choose the group with the lowest (the minimum) average, region **B**, as the base. Although the estimated average delivery times for each region are the same as they were from the previous regression, the t-stat for the β_1 term indicates that it *is* statistically significant, indicating that the average delivery time in region A *is* statistically significantly longer than the average delivery time in region B. Next, examine the t-stat for the β_2 term, which indicates that the term is not statistically significant. As earlier, the average 4.2-minute difference in delivery times between region B and region C is not statistically significant. This result requires that the data for groups B and C be pooled and then the regression be re-estimated. To do this, only one indicator variable is required: the variable for region A. This variable equals 1 for A and 0 for regions B and C (i.e., regions that are not A):

$$Time = \beta_0 + \beta_1 \ Region \ A$$

Regression output is shown in Table 10.19.

Now, although the r^2 and SEE are not quite as good as before, all of the regression terms are statistically significant. It is imperative that all of the regression terms be at least marginally statistically significant.

The estimated regression equation is:

$$Estimated \ Time = 28.494 + 11.294 \ Region \ A$$

Thus, to estimate the average delivery time for regions B or C:

$$Estimated \ Time \ \overline{BC} = 28.494 + 11.294 \ (0) \ = \textbf{28.5} \ minutes \ (on \ average)$$

Example 10.9 Indicator variables: three groups—cont'd

Table 10.19 Regression results for region indicator variables and delivery time

$r^2 = 0.095$

Standard error of the estimate = 16.76

Regression term	Est. coefficient	Std error	t-Stat
Constant	28.494	2.793	10.202
Region A	11.294	4.837	2.335

To estimate the average delivery time for region A:

$Estimated\ Time\ \overline{A} = 28.494 + 11.294\ (1) = 39.8$ minutes (on average) — the same as before

Thus, it takes a statistically significantly longer time to deliver in region A than in B or C. **It is more important to have statistically significant X terms than it is to maximize r^2.**

The purpose of indicator variables in multiple regression is not to supplant the ANOVA procedure, but rather to examine the effects of continuous X variables and different group X variables upon a numeric Y variable. When using a single X indicator variable and a single X continuous variable, the regression will estimate *two parallel* lines. Example 10.10 demonstrates the possible outcomes for groups with parallel lines. Subsequently, Example 10.11, presented later, will demonstrate the case when the groups' lines are not parallel.

Example 10.10 Nominal and continuous explanatory variables

A marketing analyst must determine how advertising expenditures and choice of ad influence the quantity of demand (sales) for a product. Ad$1, Ad$2, and Ad$3 represent three different hypothetical advertising expenditures. The data are listed in Table 10.20.

First, consider sales resulting from choice of ad type, A or B, as shown in Fig. 10.19.

The linear regression equation to be estimated is:

$$Sales = \beta_0 + \beta_1\ AdB$$

Regression output is shown in Table 10.21.

The *Constant* (β_0) is 50.463, the *slope* (β_1) is 55.421, and both are statistically significant. Thus, the equation, as estimated by regression, is:

$$Estimated\ Sales = 50.463 + 55.421\ AdB$$

In addition, without considering advertising expenditures, ad type B has nearly double the average sales of ad type A. Next, consider the effect of ad type (A or B) and advertising expenditures Ad1, shown in Fig. 10.20.

Continued

Example 10.10 Nominal and continuous explanatory variables—cont'd

Table 10.20 Advertising expenditures and sales

Ad	AdB	Ad$1	Ad$2	Ad$3	Sales
A	0	60	12	12	19.95
A	0	18	14	14	26.36
A	0	32	16	16	34.97
A	0	52	18	18	37.81
A	0	44	20	20	41.35
A	0	62	22	22	43.67
A	0	24	24	24	47.1
A	0	72	26	26	47.58
A	0	22	28	28	54.76
A	0	16	30	30	60.11
A	0	20	32	32	64.86
A	0	36	34	34	65.6
A	0	68	36	36	69.34
A	0	54	38	38	70.79
A	0	40	40	40	72.7
B	1	26	44	12	83.07
B	1	64	46	14	84.72
B	1	12	48	16	93.33
B	1	58	50	18	94.45
B	1	14	52	20	95.5
B	1	50	54	22	96.18
B	1	28	56	24	101.16
B	1	34	58	26	108.88
B	1	70	60	28	109.44
B	1	38	62	30	109.47
B	1	46	64	32	113.35
B	1	66	66	34	118.63
B	1	30	68	36	123.29
B	1	48	70	38	124.97
B	1	56	72	40	131.83

The regression estimates the coefficients for the linear equation:

$$Sales = \beta_0 + \beta_1\, AdB + \beta_2\, Ad\$1$$

This regression is only considering the variables separately (independently); as such, this type of regression is called *a main effects* regression model.

Regression output is shown in Table 10.22.

Example 10.10 Nominal and continuous explanatory variables—cont'd

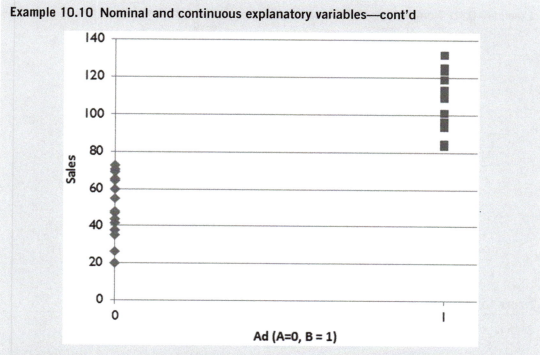

FIGURE 10.19

Sales by Ad Type

Table 10.21 Regression results for ad indicator variable and sales			
$r^2 = 0.768$			
Standard error of the estimate = 15.751			
Regression term	**Est. coefficient**	**Std error**	**t-Stat**
Constant	50.463	4.067	9.636
AdB	55.421	5.752	12.408

The equation for the pair of lines, as estimated by regression, is:

$$\text{Estimated Sales} = 46.868 + 55.305 \, AdB + 0.087 \, Ad\$1$$

But the t-stat for the β_1 term indicates that β_1 *is* statistically significant, implying that the average sales for ad type B *is* statistically significantly higher than the average sales for ad type A. Next, the t-stat for the β_2 term indicates that the term is *not* statistically significant. Thus, in this situation, the

Continued

Example 10.10 Nominal and continuous explanatory variables—cont'd

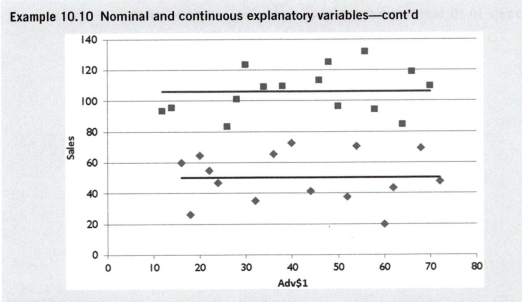

FIGURE 10.20

Sales by Ad Type and Ad Expenditures 1

Table 10.22 Regression results for advertising expenditures and sales			
$r^2 = 0.771$			
Standard error of the estimate = 15.954			
Regression term	**Est. coefficient**	**Std error**	**t-Stat**
Constant	46.868	7.801	6.008
AdB	55.305	5.829	9.487
Ad$1	0.087	0.160	0.543

Ad$1variable is not statistically significant. This means that this regression is not statistically valid, and the analyst should use the previous model with only the *AdB* variable.

The managerial interpretation is that although ad type *B* is significantly better than *A*, *Ad$1* expenditures do not affect sales. Thus, the manager would conclude to use the minimal amount of advertising dollars on *B* type ads.

Next, consider the data with the same *AdB* (X_1) and *Sales* (*Y*), and *Ad$2* ($X_2$) rather than *Ad$1*, as shown in Fig. 10.21.

Example 10.10 Nominal and continuous explanatory variables—cont'd

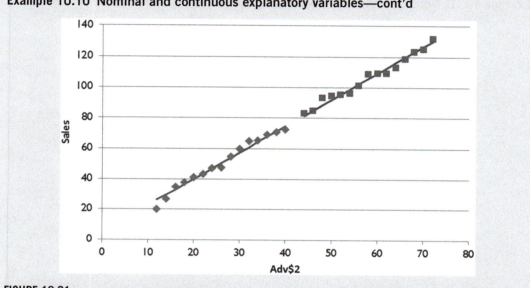

FIGURE 10.21

Sales by Ad Type and Ad Expenditures 2

Table 10.23 Regression results for advertising expenditures and sales			
$r^2 = 0.994$			
Standard error of the estimate = 2.532			
Regression term	**Est. coefficient**	**Std error**	**t-Stat**
Constant	5.250	1.537	3.415
AdB	−0.226	1.946	−0.116
Ad$2	1.739	0.054	32.500

The regression will estimate the coefficients for the linear equation:

$$Sales = \beta_0 + \beta_1\, AdB + \beta_2\, Ad\$2$$

Regression output is shown in Table 10.23.
The equation for the line, as estimated by regression, is:

$$Estimated\ Sales = 5.250 - 0.226\, AdB + 1.739\, Ad\$2$$

Now the t-stat for the β_1 term indicates that it is *not* statistically significant, indicating that ad type is *not* statistically significant. In contrast, the t-stat for the β_2 term indicates that the term *is* statistically significant. Thus, in this situation, the ad type variable is not statistically significant but

Continued

Example 10.10 Nominal and continuous explanatory variables—cont'd

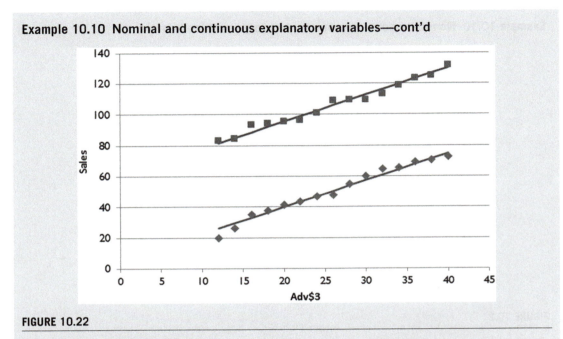

FIGURE 10.22

Sales by Ad Type and Ad Expenditures 3

the level of advertising, $Ad\$2$, is significant. This means that this regression should be re-estimated after removing the AdB variable and only using the $Ad\$2$ variable.

The managerial interpretation is that both ad types have the same efficacy—that is, expenditures do affect sales, but ad type does not. The broader interpretation is that the experimental design was flawed by spending different amounts of money on the two ad types and that a valid judgment regarding the two ad types cannot be determined based upon this information.

Next, consider the data with the same AdB (X_1) and $Sales$ (Y), but $Ad\$3$ (X_2) rather than $Ad\$2$, as shown in Fig. 10.22.

This experimental design is more appropriate than the previous example ($Ad\$2$) because the expenditures varied over the same range for both ads. The results were not biased by using significantly different amounts of advertising on the two types of ads. The regression will estimate the coefficients for the linear equation:

$$Sales = \beta_0 + \beta_1 \, AdB + \beta_2 \, Ad\$3$$

Regression output is shown in Table 10.24.

The equation for the line, as estimated by regression, is:

$$Estimated \; Sales = 5.250 + 55.421 \, AdB + 1.739 \, Ad\$3$$

Now the t-stat for the β_1 term indicates that β_1 is statistically significant, indicating that ad type is statistically significant. Similarly, the t-stat for the β_2 term indicates that the term is also

Example 10.10 Nominal and continuous explanatory variables—cont'd

Table 10.24 Regression results for advertising expenditures and sales

	$r^2 = 0.994$		
	Standard error of the estimate = 2.532		
Regression term	**Est. coefficient**	**Std error**	**t-Stat**
Constant	5.250	1.537	3.415
AdB	55.421	0.925	59.933
Ad$3	1.739	0.054	32.500

statistically significant. Thus, in this situation, the ad type variable is statistically significant and the level of advertising, *Ad*$3, is significant.

The managerial interpretation is that both ad types have the same additional dollar spent efficacy—that is, expenditures do affect sales *and* ad type does matter: ad **B** is more effective at all levels of advertising expenditures.

The next issue to be addressed is *what would happen if the dollar efficacy was different for each type of ad.* In other words, what happens when a dollar spent on one type of ad is not the same as a dollar spent on a different type of ad? For example, is a dollar spent on advertising on the radio the same as a dollar spent on advertising in a newspaper?

The TRUTH is the TRUTH, and nothing you do that is arbitrary will change the TRUTH.

The next section explains how to test for the condition when the slopes for each group could be different.

10.6 Interaction terms

Because groups can obviously have significantly different slopes, there is a need to estimate the difference between the slopes to determine if the slopes are indeed parallel. This is accomplished by using an *interaction* variable (or *interaction term*). An interaction term is simply the mathematical product of the continuous X variable and the indicator X variable. Remember, a model that does not include the *interaction* term is called a *main effects model*.

Let X be a continuous (numeric) explanatory variable and I be a categorical (group) *indicator* variable with two levels (a 0 or 1 indicator variable). Then,

$$Y = \beta_0 + \beta_1 X + \beta_2 I + \beta_3 XI$$

where XI is the product of X times I—that is, $XI = X \times I$.

Thus, the equation for the group with $I = 0$ is:

$$Y_0 = \beta_0 + \beta_1 X + \beta_2 0 + \beta_3 (X \times 0)$$

$$Y_0 = \beta_0 + \beta_1 X = \text{the simple regression for group 0}$$

The equation for the group with $I = 1$ is:

$$Y_1 = \beta_0 + \beta_1 X + \beta_2 1 + \beta_3 X \times 1$$
$$Y_1 = (\beta_0 + \beta_2) + (\beta_1 + \beta_3) X$$

Thus, the significance of the β_3 term determines if the slopes of the two groups are the same or not—that is, whether or not the two lines are parallel.

In some circumstances, it is desirable to determine at which value of X the two lines are equal—the intersection of the two lines. To find the point where the two lines intersect, set:

$$Y_0 = Y_1$$
$$\beta_0 + \beta_1 X = \beta_0 + \beta_1 X + \beta_2 + \beta_3 X$$

Subtracting $(\beta_0 + \beta_1 X)$ from both sides yields:

$$0 = \beta_2 + \beta_3 X$$

Solving for X:

$X = -\beta_2/\beta_3$ ... this is the value of X at which the two lines are equal: $Y_0 = Y_1$.

Example 10.11 Interaction term: slopes differ by group

An operations analyst is considering two processes, **A** and **B**, which manufacture the same type of product. The analyst must determine which process is the most cost effective. Production quantities and costs are listed by the process in Table 10.25 and are presented in Fig. 10.23.

The regression equation to be estimated is:

$$Sales = \beta_0 + \beta_1 \ Quantity + \beta_2 \ Process \ B + \beta_3 \ (Quantity \times Process \ B)$$

Regression output is shown in Table 10.26.

Because all of the t-stats are statistically significant, the regression equation is:

$$Estimated \ Cost = 1186.053 + 1.548 \ Quantity - 297.625 \ Process \ B + 2.499 \ (Quantity \times Process \ B)$$

To facilitate the managerial interpretation, first use the regression equation to estimate the costs for using process A (*Process B = 0*):

$$Cost_A = 1186.053 + 1.548 \ Quantity - 297.625 \ (0) + 2.499 \ (Quantity \times 0)$$
$$Cost_A = 1186.053 + 1.548 \ Quantity$$

As in Example 10.1, the fixed cost for process **A** is approximately $1186.05 and the variable cost is approximately $1.55.

Next, estimate the costs for using process B (*Process B = 1*):

$$Cost_B = 1186.053 + 1.548 \ Quantity - 297.625 \ (1) + 2.499 \ (Quantity \times 1)$$
$$Cost_B = 1186.053 - 297.625 + 1.548 \ Quantity + 2.499 \ Quantity$$

As β_2 and β_3 are statistically significant, the fixed costs of process B are approximately $300 less that the fixed costs of process A, and the variable costs of process B are about $2.50 higher than that of process A. The equation to estimate the costs of process B is:

$$Cost_B = 888.428 + 4.047 \ Quantity$$

Example 10.11 Interaction term: slopes differ by group—cont'd

Table 10.25 Production cost by process and quantity of units produced

Process	Quantity	Process B	Quantity × Process B	Cost	Estimated cost
A	50	0	0	1347.19	1263.44
A	50	0	0	1343.17	1263.44
A	50	0	0	1217.60	1263.44
A	100	0	0	1241.68	1340.83
A	100	0	0	1333.72	1340.83
A	100	0	0	1342.88	1340.83
A	150	0	0	1427.20	1418.22
A	150	0	0	1394.82	1418.22
A	150	0	0	1288.17	1418.22
A	200	0	0	1520.13	1495.61
A	200	0	0	1554.17	1495.61
A	200	0	0	1543.58	1495.61
B	50	1	50	1057.32	1090.77
B	50	1	50	1255.42	1090.77
B	50	1	50	1075.75	1090.77
B	100	1	100	1169.34	1293.12
B	100	1	100	1366.56	1293.12
B	100	1	100	1178.49	1293.12
B	150	1	150	1405.77	1495.47
B	150	1	150	1521.39	1495.47
B	150	1	150	1540.69	1495.47
B	200	1	200	1766.72	1697.81
B	200	1	200	1756.58	1697.81
B	200	1	200	1637.50	1697.81

Thus, due to the difference in the cost structures of the two processes, which process to use depends upon the production quantity.

The point at which the two lines are equal is the production point where the two costs are equal. As shown earlier, this point can be calculated by setting the two lines to be equal:

$$Cost_A \equiv Cost_B$$
$$1186.053 + 1.548 \, Quantity = 1186.053 + 1.548 \, Quantity - 297.625 \, (1) + 2.499 \, (Quantity \times 1)$$
$$0 = -297.625 + 2.499 \, Quantity$$
$$Quantity = 297.625 / 2.499 = 119.09$$

Thus, use process B for production quantities less than 120 and use process A for quantities of 120 or more.

Continued

Example 10.11 Interaction term: slopes differ by group—cont'd

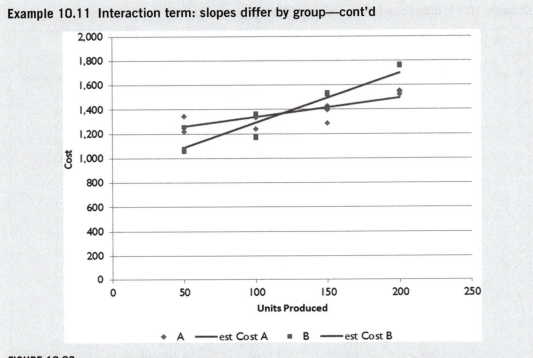

FIGURE 10.23

Production Cost by Process and Quantity of Units Produced

Table 10.26 Regression results for production cost by process and quantity of units produced

$r^2 = 0.768$			
Standard error of the estimate = 15.751			
Regression term	**Est. coefficient**	**Std error**	**t-Stat**
Constant	1186.053	57.910	20.481
Quantity	1.548	0.423	3.660
ProcessB	−297.625	81.897	−3.634
Quantity × ProcessB	2.499	0.598	4.179

10.7 Regression pitfalls

As regression is one of the most commonly used statistical procedures, it is also one of the most commonly *misused* statistical procedures. Here are some of the most common mistakes incurred when conducting regression analysis.

10.7.1 Nonlinearity

Obviously using *linear* regression on data that are inherently *nonlinear* is a mistake. Think carefully about what effect an additional unit of X might have on Y. What is the effect on your happiness (Y) of eating that next donut (number of donuts eaten = X)? You should always examine the scatterplot before using regression. The next example is strong proof of this concept.

Example 10.12 Anscombe's Quartet

Ansombe's Quartet is four pairs of data with amazing statistical properties. Look it up on the web! Ansombe's Quartet is listed in Table 10.27.

Table 10.27 Anscombe's Quartet

Set A		Set B		Set C		Set D	
X	y	x	y	x	y	x	y
10	8.04	10	9.14	10	7.46	8	6.58
8	6.95	8	8.14	8	6.77	8	5.76
13	7.58	13	8.74	13	12.74	8	7.71
9	8.81	9	8.77	9	7.11	8	8.84
11	8.33	11	9.26	11	7.81	8	8.47
14	9.96	14	8.1	14	8.84	8	7.04
6	7.24	6	6.13	6	6.08	8	5.25
4	4.26	4	3.1	4	5.39	8	5.56
12	10.84	12	9.13	12	8.15	8	7.91
7	4.82	7	7.26	7	6.42	8	6.89
5	5.68	5	4.74	5	5.73	19	12.50

Surprisingly, estimating the regression equation $Y = \beta_0 + \beta_1 X$ for each of the four data sets yields the *identical* regression output (Table 10.28).

For all four sets of data. the regression equation for the line is:

$$\text{Estimated } Y = 3.00 + 0.50\,X$$

Furthermore, the numerical diagnostics are not sufficient to distinguish between the four cases. Thus, it is obvious that plots of data are required to enable the analyst to judge whether *linear* regression is appropriate.

Example 10.12 Anscombe's Quartet—cont'd

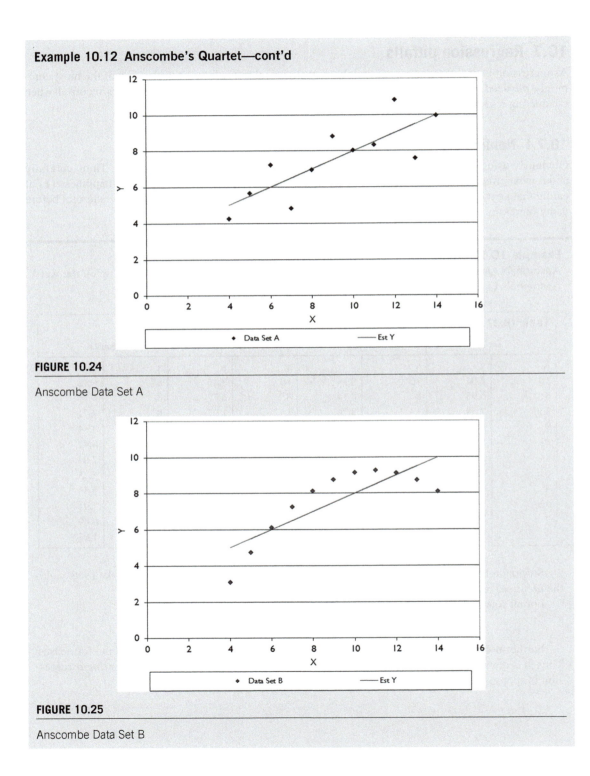

FIGURE 10.24

Anscombe Data Set A

FIGURE 10.25

Anscombe Data Set B

Example 10.12 Anscombe's Quartet—cont'd

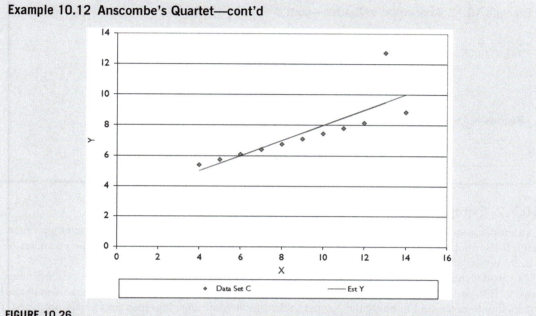

FIGURE 10.26

Anscombe Data Set C

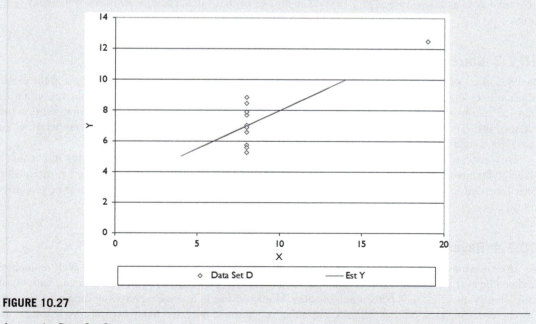

FIGURE 10.27

Anscombe Data Set D

Continued

Example 10.12 Anscombe's Quartet—cont'd

Table 10.28 Regression results for Anscombe's Quartet

	$r^2 = 0.678$		
	Standard Error of the Estimate = 1.24		
Regression Term	**Est. Coefficient**	**Std Error**	**t-Stat**
Constant	3.00	1.12	2.67
X	0.50	0.12	4.2

10.7.2 Extrapolation beyond the relevant range

Extrapolation beyond the relevant range is when values of Y are estimated beyond the range of the X data. If the unobserved data (data outside the range of the X data) is nonlinear, then the estimates of Y can be significantly outside the confidence interval of the estimated Y values.

Consider the production cost example (Example 10.1). The smallest amount previously produced was 10,000 units. An attempt to estimate costs below that production point might have significantly errors due to potential nonlinearities in cost in the production range less than previously produced. In other words, the line might curve outside the range of the data.

The exception to this caveat is time series forecasting (Chapter 11). In time series forecasting, the objective is to estimate values of Y beyond the range of the X data such as estimate of the next year's sales.

10.7.3 Correlation ≠ causality

Just because two variables demonstrate statistical correlation does not mean that changes in the X variable cause changes in the Y variable. Drownings are correlated to ice cream sales . . . that does not mean that ice cream sales should be prohibited. Obviously, there is a *lurking* variable, temperature, which causes both. The two variables, drownings and ice cream sales, are *associated* with temperature, and correlation then is not the appropriate term to describe their relationship.

This concept can be extremely deceptive. Consider the many cases in which sales might not be affected by advertising. There are many cases in which both sales and advertising have a positive slope over time that is caused by economic growth, and that changes in advertising might have no real effect on sales.

10.7.4 Reverse causality

As an extension, consider cases in which the direction of the X–Y relationship is not well understood and can be easily confused or manipulated. As an example, this happens when advertising budgets are consistently allocated as a percentage of sales. Managers might assume advertising increases are causing increases in sales, but the opposite might be true because the advertising budgets are being set as a percentage of sales prior to the advertising being spent to increase sales. Thus, the timing of the advertising and sales would be critical to study to determine the true effects of advertising on sales.

10.7.5 Omitted-variable bias

Omitted-variable bias is similar to situations with a lurking variable. Omitted-variable bias occurs when a model incorrectly leaves out one or more important causal X variables. The "bias" is created when the model compensates for the missing factor by over- or underestimating the effect of one of the other variables. The difference between omitted-variable bias and a lurking variable is that the lurking variable truly causes variables that are not causal (ice cream sales and drownings). However, the X variables estimated in an omitted-variable bias model still may actually belong in the model. Thus, the sales and advertising example is more of a case of potential omitted-variable bias than of lurking variables.

Two conditions must be true for omitted-variable bias to happen:

1. The omitted variable must be a determinant of the dependent variable—that is, its true regression coefficient is not zero.
2. The omitted variable must be correlated with one or more of the included independent variables.

Omitted-variable bias typically occurs when the analyst lacks sufficient contextual experience or knowledge to fully understand the factors involved that cause variation in Y. For example, if a statistician lacks business experience, they can easily assume that the increase in advertising caused the increase in sales, whereas an economist with an econometrics background will be more fully aware of other factors that can influence sales (changes in competitors' prices, prices of substitutes, etc.).

10.7.6 Serial correlation

Serial correlation occurs when the order of the observations is significant. This means that the sequencing of the data is important and can be easily tested by testing the statistical significance of the observation number as an X variable.

If the observation number is significant, then there is a sequencing variable that has been overlooked (omitted). Serial correlation is often present and desirable in time series data and will be discussed in Chapter 11.

10.7.7 Multicollinearity

Multicollinearity occurs when X variables are more correlated with each other than they are with the Y variable. In such cases, the number of X variables should be reduced by removing one of the highly correlated (redundant) X variables. Of the two highly correlated X variables, remove the X variable that is least correlated to the Y variable.

A typical method of examining the cross-correlations is to compute the correlation matrix to determine the strength of each of the variables' relationships with all other variables in the regression model.

Consider the example of $Y = profits$ with $X_1 = market\ share$ and $X_2 = number\ of\ employees$. If the two X variables are more correlated with each other than they are with the Y variable, then only one of the two variables should remain in the model.

10.7.8 Data mining

Although the current usage of the term *data mining* is associated with "big data," the original term is referred to as the possibility of falsely positive X variables (type I errors). Imagine 100 randomly generated X variables regressed against a randomly generated Y variable. One would expect there to be, on average, five X variables that appear significant (p-value ≤ 0.05). Thus, in "big data" analytics, without subject matter, contextual expertise, analysts can easily fall victim to false-positive conclusions of significant X variables.

10.7.9 Heteroscedasticity

Heteroscedasticity is unequal variance of the data along the regression line. Another way of thinking about this is when the spread of the dots is not constant. This means that the SEE is not valid for all values of X and that the regression estimates will not have consistent probability estimates.

Another important ramification of heteroscedasticity is that the estimate of the slope is not stable. In Fig. 10.28, imagine that the regression line has more flexibility (being more bendy or more wiggly) at the high end of X. The figure shows bivariate data that has equal variance—homoscedastic data.

Fig. 10.29 shows bivariate data that has unequal variance—heteroscedastic data.

A classic example of heteroscedasticity is income versus expenditure on meals. As one's income increases, the variability of food consumption will increase. By necessity, a poorer individual will

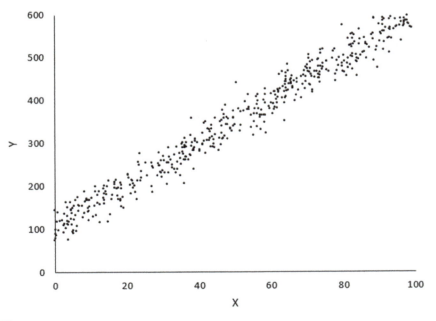

FIGURE 10.28

Homoscedastic Data

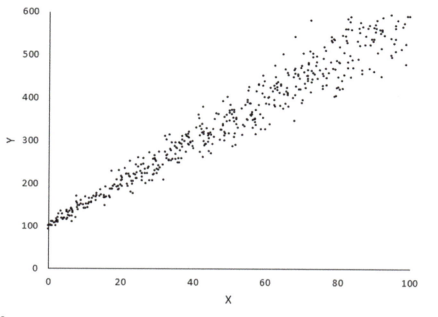

FIGURE 10.29

Data With Heteroscedasticity

spend a rather constant amount by always eating inexpensive food. Conversely, a wealthier person may buy inexpensive food and at other times eat expensive meals. Those with higher incomes display a greater variation in food expenditures.

10.8 Review of regression

To summarize, the typical sequence of regression analysis is:

1. Determine the specific questions you want the data to answer. Use an influence diagram to examine possible relationships to test.
2. Set up the data to answer the questions (determine X variables and the Y variable).
3. Run regression → get output.
4. Validate regression parameters and the equation using t-stats (or p-value).
5. Interpret regression to begin to answer questions.
6. Apply a regression equation to answer questions (plug X values into the equation). Possibly apply regression equation for decision analysis.

By extension, that sequence of analysis applies to other statistical methods (processes) such as Chi-square and ANOVA. Thus, the processes are substituted, or combined with, for *regression* in the sequence of analysis.

Table 10.29 summarizes various regression models.

Table 10.29 Examples of common regression models

Name	Form	Example
I. Simple Regression	$Y = \beta_0 + \beta_1 X$	$Cost = \beta_0 + \beta_1 Units\ Produced$
II. Multiple Regression	$Y = \beta_0 + \beta_1 X_1 + \beta_2 X_2$	$Sales = \beta_0 + \beta 1 Advertising + \beta_2 Promotion$
III. Polynomial Regression	$Y = \beta_0 + \beta_1 X + \beta_2 X^2$	$Sales = \beta_0 + \beta_1 Advertising + \beta_2 Advertising^2$
IV. Logarithmic Transform	$LNY = \beta_0 + \beta_1 X$	$LN(Sales) = \beta_0 + \beta_1 Price$
V. Indicator Variable	$Y = \beta_0 + \beta_1 I$	$Sales = \beta_0 + \beta 1 PromotionType$
VI. Interaction Term	$Y = \beta_0 + \beta_1 X_1 + \beta_2 I + \beta_3 X_1 I$	$Sales = \beta_0 + \beta_1 Advertising + \beta_2 AdType + \beta_3 Advertising * AdType$

Exercise Set 10: Regression

1. Consider the data shown in Table 10.30, representing ages in years and maintenance costs (in thousands of dollars per year) for five similar printing presses.

Table 10.30 Maintenance costs by age of machine

Age	Cost (thousands) per Year
2	6
5	13
9	23
3	5
8	22

   a. Create a scatterplot of the data. Describe the relationship.
   b. Find the correlation between age and maintenance cost. What is the managerial interpretation?
   c. Find the least-square regression equation. Is there a statistically significant relationship between the variables? If so, then what is the managerial interpretation of the regression coefficients?
   d. What would you expect the annual maintenance costs to be for a press that is 7 years old?
   e. What is the typical size for the prediction errors—that is, what is the distribution of the errors, and how does that affect the distribution of the predicted costs?
   f. How much of the variation in maintenance costs can be attributed to the age of the press?
2. A linear regression analysis has produced the following equation relating profits to hours of managerial time spent developing the past year's projects of a firm:

$$\text{Profits} = -\$957 + \$85 \times \text{Number of hours}$$

   a. What is the managerial interpretation of these regression coefficients?
   b. What is the break-even point?
   c. What is the managerial interpretation if the $r^2 = 0.25$ and the t-stat for the slope coefficient is 4.71?

3. A bakery makes specialty birthday cakes. Cost/production data is given in Table 10.31.

Table 10.31 Cost by quantity

Day	Quantity	Cost ($)
Monday	7	18
Tuesday	8	17
Wednesday	18	32
Thursday	3	16

   a. What is the managerial interpretation of the regression coefficients?
   b. What is your estimated cost for producing 10 units on Friday?
   c. What is the managerial interpretation of the r^2, t-stat, and the SSE?

4. One weekend when you reduced prices 5%, your store had sales of $58,000. The next weekend, with a 15% reduction, your sales were $92,000. The weekend after that, with a 17.5% reduction, sales were $95,000.

   a. Based on this information, what sales would you expect with a 10% price reduction?
   b. What sales would you expect with a 20% price reduction?
   c. Which estimate, sales at a 10% price reduction or sales at a 20% price reduction (if either), would you feel more confident about?

5. A regional manager of a chain of grocery stores is trying to evaluate the financial performance of 15 stores in her region. The square footage and contribution of each of the 15 stores is listed in Table 10.32.

Table 10.32 Contribution by size of store (in square feet)

Store	Square feet	Contribution ($)
6	90,000	1,311,938
4	90,000	1,256,787
7	90,000	1,292,572
8	94,000	1,373,949
14	94,000	1,358,616
5	94,000	1,372,179
12	98,000	1,431,077
1	98,000	1,434,016
15	98,000	1,386,794
10	105,000	1,536,215
3	105,000	1,523,173
2	105,000	1,442,114
13	110,000	1,482,266
9	110,000	1,499,960
11	125,000	1,739,878

   a. What is the estimated contribution for each store?
   b. Based upon the estimated contribution, what is the percentile contribution for each store?
   c. What is your estimated contribution for a store with 100,000 square feet?
   d. What is the optimum number of square feet for a store in this region to have?

6. A bank analyst is trying to determine the value of a portfolio of loans. Table 10.33 is a sample of loans that were defaulted upon and the corresponding amounts that were recovered.

Table 10.33 Loan and recovery amounts for loan loss write-offs

Obs	Loan amt ($)	Recovered ($)
1	20,933.77	17,656.31
2	21,435.00	13,215.29
3	39,642.88	22,358.55
4	25,854.28	14,632.61
5	36,036.33	24,259.47
6	17,411.68	12,296.61
7	27,664.94	18,157.64
8	41,203.60	26,038.61
9	42,235.97	32,511.71
10	15,718.57	13,515.49
11	32,899.38	21,996.69
12	38,529.11	27,951.04
13	33,151.75	21,454.17
14	36,008.05	29,796.37
15	28,474.48	19,842.13
16	26,071.32	18,550.96
17	41,631.81	24,860.13
18	20,313.85	16,452.15
19	28,479.59	22,556.20
20	33,443.76	19,857.93
21	16,498.78	14,817.15
22	15,921.67	13,026.47
23	27,969.95	18,337.10
24	41,767.75	31,001.21
25	18,956.30	14,555.44
26	44,197.48	32,537.04
27	42,536.35	28,892.08
28	43,552.72	27,688.15
29	32,222.69	18,649.82
30	36,454.16	19,621.92
31	21,099.48	14,211.14
32	38,860.89	24,483.44
33	40,303.38	27,594.38
34	43,639.48	27,066.56
35	35,237.94	26,863.88
36	40,234.40	22,982.80
37	33,624.74	22,063.67

Table 10.33 Loan and recovery amounts for loan loss write-offs—cont'd

Obs	Loan amt ($)	Recovered ($)
38	25,779.71	18,465.53
39	27,265.56	19,061.03
40	20,976.06	17,381.73
41	42,938.62	30,843.71
42	22,915.71	18,052.06
43	16,374.60	14,421.62
44	36,632.95	24,060.61
45	34,547.34	23,377.80

7. A foreign car manufacturer wanted to find leverage factors for marketing their upscale car model. The company hired a market research firm to carry out an analysis of factors that cause people to purchase models in the category under consideration. A questionnaire asked about the importance (on a scale from 0 to 100) of Prestige, Comfort, and Economy as well as an overall Appeal score (0–100) for the company's model. A regression was then computed with Overall Appeal as the dependent variable and Prestige, Comfort, and Economy as the independent variables. The regression results (LINEST) are shown in Table 10.34. What is the appropriate managerial conclusion based on this information?

Table 10.34 Regression results for automobile owners' survey

Economy	Comfort	Prestige	Constant
0.5139	0.3236	−0.1658	24.1421
0.1143	0.1228	0.1215	18.2244
0.4186	12.192	#NA	#NA

8. A bicycle shop is trying to determine the optimum price for a particular model of bike. The cost to the bike store for the bike is $225 per unit. Construct a decision tree and a simulation to determine the optimum price and quantity to order based on the five price–quantity pairs given in Table 10.35.

Table 10.35 Price–quantity pairs for the bicycle shop

Price ($)	Quantity
350	150
375	111
400	105
425	80
450	72

9. An analyst for Nationalized Airlines is trying to determine the optimum price for an 8:30 a.m. flight from Greensboro, North Carolina, to New York (LaGuardia) on Tuesday and Thursday of a specific week in October. Consider the variable cost to be negligible. (Why?) Construct a decision tree and a simulation to determine the optimum price and quantity to order based on the price–quantity pairs listed in Table 10.36.

Table 10.36 Price–quantity pairs for the airline flight

Price ($)	Quantity
100	65
125	54
150	41
175	30
200	27
225	24

10. Obtain the past 2 years of historical stock price data for S&P 500 (^GSPC), VFINX, Russell 2000 (^RUT), SPY, and DUK. Use the historical returns (daily percentage price change) to estimate the relative riskiness (BETA) of Duke Power versus the S&P 500. Do the same for the Russell 2000 (^RUT).
    a. Compare the returns of Vanguard's S&P 500 index mutual fund (VFINX) versus SPY.
    b. Construct a simulation to compare each stocks' returns with that of the S&P 500.

11. An ad in the newspaper purports that consumers should expect to save money by shopping at Walmart. The results of a study of randomly selected items priced at Walmart and at Target are listed in Table 10.37.

Table 10.37 Item price by store

Obs	Product	Walmart ($)	Target ($)
1	Levi's jeans	41.65	41.99
2	Walking shoes	54.95	59.95
3	Dress shirt	26.95	24.99
4	Farberware pots & pans	39.97	44.99
5	Pod coffee maker	79.99	89.99
6	Chocolate meal replacement shake	6.50	4.79
7	Maxwell House coffee	6.59	6.25
8	Kolcraft baby stroller	87.90	69.99
9	Suave shampoo	2.94	2.99
10	Shaving cream	6.13	5.49
11	Schwinn bike	238.00	239.99
12	DVD player	70.00	79.99
13	*Friends* DVD	55.19	67.99
14	Headphones	39.99	39.99
15	Lego Friends house	56.00	59.00
16	Spalding NBA basketball	24.96	15.99

12. Your firm purchases electronic components from three suppliers. You want to compare the quality of components from the three suppliers. Quality scores (ratings based on a scale from 0% to 100%) have been obtained for about 20 components from each supplier (shown in Table 10.38). Determine the appropriate managerial conclusion regarding the quality of components from the three suppliers.

Table 10.38 Component quality by supplier

Amalgamated	Bizparts	Consolidated
75	94	90
72	87	86
87	80	92
77	86	75
84	80	79
82	67	94
84	86	95
81	82	85
78	86	86
97	82	92
85	72	92
81	77	85
95	87	87
81	68	86
72	80	92
89	76	85
84	68	93
73	86	89
	74	83
	86	
	90	

13. An operations research analyst wants to determine the manufacturing times for producing various numbers of units using two different machines (A and B). Various production amounts (batch sizes) were produced on each machine. Production times were measured in minutes. The machine variable was coded as a 0 for machine A and a 1 for machine B. The results of a linear regression, *Time* $= \beta_0 + \beta_1$ *Units* $+ \beta_2$ *Machine* $+ \beta_3$ *Units*Machine*, are presented in Table 10.39.

Table 10.39 Regression results for production time, machine, and production quantity

		$r^2 = 0.998$		
		Standard error of the estimate = 12.344		
Regression term	**Est. coefficient**	**Std error**	**t-Stat**	**Prob > |t|**
Constant	190.858	8.729	21.866	<0.0001
Units	3.552	0.064	55.723	<0.0001
Machine	-194.146	12.344	-15.728	<0.0001
Units*Machine	1.474	0.090	16.349	<0.0001

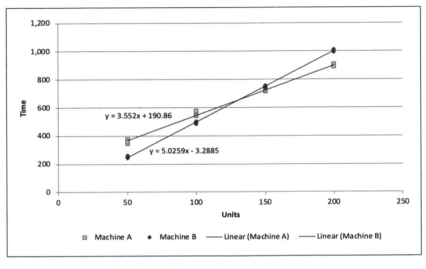

FIGURE 10.30

Graph of Production Time as a Function of Machine and Production Quantity

a. State the managerial interpretation for each of the regression coefficients.
b. Use the regression results to compute the expected time to produce 150 units on machine **B**.
c. Compute the number of units that both machines would take the same amount of time to produce.
d. State the appropriate managerial decision.
14. A marketing research analyst wants to compare the efficacy of advertising expenditures in two regions (**A** and **B**). *Advertising* and *Sales* were measured in thousands of dollars. Each region received the same levels of advertising expenditure ranging from $0 to $46,000. These data were recorded in thousands as the *Ad* data variable and are shown in Table 10.40. The *Region* variable was coded as a 0 for region **A** and a 1 for region **B**.
a. Compute the appropriate test statistic regarding advertising expenditures and region **B**.
b. State the managerial interpretation for each of the regression coefficients.
c. Compute the expected sales for region **B** if $25,000 was spent on advertising.
d. Compute the advertising amount that would cause both regions to have the same expected sales.
e. State the appropriate managerial decision.

Table 10.40 Sales by region and advertising expenditures

Region	Ad (thousands of dollars)	Sales (thousands of dollars)	Region	Ad (thousands of dollars)	Sales (thousands of dollars)
A	0	40.80	B	0	32.80
A	2	36.55	B	0	35.20
A	4	39.90	B	2	36.55
A	6	42.25	B	2	36.90
A	8	46.70	B	4	37.35
A	10	43.25	B	6	38.95
A	12	41.80	B	8	40.45
A	14	49.70	B	10	40.45
A	16	42.75	B	12	38.50
A	18	46.10	B	14	40.65
A	20	47.25	B	16	41.35
A	22	49.20	B	18	41.35
A	24	47.40	B	20	41.00
A	26	48.80	B	22	42.35
A	28	45.50	B	24	42.05
A	30	44.80	B	26	40.15
A	32	43.70	B	28	44.10
A	34	51.00	B	30	41.30
A	36	48.20	B	32	42.90
A	38	46.30	B	34	45.90
A	40	48.05	B	36	45.05
A	42	43.95	B	38	43.55
A	44	50.40	B	40	45.70
A	46	47.75	B	42	45.20
			B	44	48.20
			B	46	45.60

Cases

Triad Technology

Triad Technology Inc., a producer of digital equipment that specialized in supplying the automobile industry, had received an informal invitation to bid on the purchase of a batch of semiconductor devices from the Conchord Instrument Company. Ellen Barker, a purchasing agent for Triad Technology, was analyzing the question of how much Triad Technology should bid on the batch of 70,000 semiconductors.

Triad Technology needed 50,000 of these special semiconductors for use on a contract for controllers for the assembly lines of one of the automobile manufacturers. Triad Technology dealt very often with that auto company and was one of its regular suppliers of digital equipment. The auto company had a policy of maintaining multiple suppliers whenever possible, however, and thus had not awarded Triad Technology the contract for all of the controllers that were needed. Instead, it had contracted for half of the work with Triad Technology and for the other half

---

Case—cont'd

with NuWave Systems Inc., a nearby firm that was very much like Triad Technology in size, market, and capabilities. Ms. Barker knew that NuWave would also be bidding on the batch of semiconductors; she believed that NuWave and Triad Technology would be the only two bidders.

Requests to bid on components from Conchord were common; often Triad Technology bid in several batches in 1 month. Conchord did large amounts of defense contract work, and the specifications for components for use in building equipment for defense contracts were very tight—considerably stricter than the specs for components for commercial use. All of the semiconductor manufacturers rejected many of the components that came off their production lines; a manufacturer producing for military applications rejected a particularly high percentage of the units started. For example, on the semiconductor currently being offered by Conchord, if 10,000 good components were needed for military use, Conchord might start as many as 100,000 in production. Large numbers would be rejected at the various intermediate production steps, before reaching final testing. At the end of the production process, Conchord tested every component individually against the military specs; for 10,000 units meeting those specs, there would be several thousand units that had reached the final testing stage but were not suitable for the defense contracts. Conchord offered those rejects for bid to commercial users. The company knew that the rejects did not meet the military specs, but it did not know at all accurately how many of the units would meet the looser commercial specs. Conchord was able, however, to give a rough estimate of the fraction of a batch of rejects that would meet Triad Technology's commercial specs; its estimate on the current batch was 75% usable by Triad Technology.

The semiconductor industry and the industries that built equipment from semiconductors were changing rapidly. The technologies of these industries changed very often, and prices had been dropping rapidly. In addition, there were large numbers of similar, but not interchangeable, parts available. For these reasons, Conchord was always anxious to sell its components rapidly and to keep inventories low. For the same reasons, Triad Technology had a firm policy of not buying most parts for inventory; only the most commonly used parts would be held in inventory. The type of semiconductor then needed by Triad Technology was not likely to be required again in the near future, and so Ms. Barker knew that any semiconductors left over after the controllers had been built would be dumped.

If Conchord had not been offering the batch of rejects, Triad Technology would have bought the semiconductors from the regular supply of commercial-quality components at $0.16 a piece. Similarly, it would buy those regular commercial units if it bid on the rejects and lost the bid. These components would have been individually tested by the supplier against the commercial standard and verified as acceptable. The minimum order for the commercial-quality components was 30,000 units.

If Triad Technology did bid and win on the batch of military rejects, Triad Technology would test the 70,000 units as a normal part of the production process for the controllers. Ms. Barker was willing to assume that since the normal commercial units would also have to be tested in the same way, the testing of the rejects would not involve extra expense. However, there was always the possibility that the 70,000 rejects would not yield 50,000 good components. If not, Triad Technology could purchase somewhat higher commercial quality units in a small batch at $0.25 each; the minimum order was 2000 such units.

In thinking about the problem of how much Triad Technology should bid, Ms. Barker realized that the value of the batch of rejects was dependent on how many of the semiconductors were actually good. Moreover, she knew that because Conchord tested the components against the higher defense standard only, the estimate of the fraction meeting Triad Technology's commercial specs was rough. Conchord was quite frank about this fact; it told prospective bidders that its estimates were not precise and, moreover, that it suspected that the estimates which came from its testing procedures tended to give too high a figure for the fraction meeting commercial standards. Triad Technology had bid on many batches of rejects of similar but not identical products in the past year. (Semiconductor technology had not changed during that period.) Ms. Barker decided that the testing procedures for the different batches were very similar even though the semiconductors differed slightly. Consequently, she considered the data in Table 10.41 on the actual fractions good in batches that Triad Technology had won in the past year to be a good basis for inferences about the likely fractions good in the current batch.

Case—cont'd

Table 10.41 Fractions of good components

Conchord estimate	Actual	Batch size
0.60	0.59	80,000
0.65	0.39	65,000
0.60	0.50	75,000
0.80	0.94	60,000
0.75	0.58	50,000
0.50	0.55	50,000
0.70	0.50	80,000
0.60	0.67	70,000
0.70	0.58	75,000
0.50	0.47	80,000

In addition, Ms. Barker was concerned with what NuWave Systems would bid for the 70,000 rejects. She had collected information on the most recent 20 occasions on which Triad Technology and NuWave had bid on batches of units that were similar to the current semiconductors. The semiconductors involved had differed in some technical design details from one another and from the present 70,000 components. However, although the different batches would not have been interchangeable in use, Ms. Barker felt that the bidding processes in the different situations had been very similar. Moreover, the standard prices for the different components were the same. Thus, she was willing to base the current analysis on those 20 bids from the past year. Table 10.42 lists the information on the past bids, as well as the batch sizes and Conchord's estimates of the fractions of good components in the batches. Ms. Barker felt that NuWave had been bidding about $0.10 per estimated good unit, on average, but there was considerable variability in the actual bids. She also knew that Triad Technology's bidding procedure had not been entirely systematic in the past, and she hoped for the current bid to work out some more systematic procedures that Triad Technology could use in setting bids in the future.

Adventure Luggage 2

Adventure Luggage is a manufacturer of luggage and leather goods established in 1877 in Milwaukee, Wisconsin, by trunk maker Joseph S. Daventer, a Bavarian. In 1956, the company opened a manufacturing operation in Tennessee, and the company's headquarters and plant facilities followed in 1959. Adventure was bought by Brown-Forman Corporation before being acquired by Clarion Capital Partners (a private equity firm) in 2007.

Adventure luggage has been recognized as being of fine quality. The company is known for producing distinctive collections of luggage such as Wings and Tweed, which are associated with traditional American style.

Adventure uses leather in the production of many of its product lines. Due to design and style considerations, the specifications of the leather are, in fact, quite flexible, and it is common practice for the Adventure purchasing agent, Jim Makins, to search for good buys on batches of leather. Whenever he finds a potentially good buy, he obtains a sample of the leather from the seller and passes it on to the production group. The production group examines both the leather characteristics and the potential cost to determine whether that batch can be used without undue modification of the luggage line in which it will be used.

Quite frequently, Mr. Makins has been able to purchase batches of leather that have been classified as rejects by seat manufacturing divisions of luxury car manufacturers such as Acura, Audi, BMW, Lexus, Mercedes Benz, and Porsche. These batches generally contain a high percentage of leather that is usable by Adventure. These manufacturers visually inspect the leather under close scrutiny. When some characteristic of the leather does not meet the stringent tolerance required for use by the luxury automobile manufacturers, the leather produced in that batch is put aside and subsequently auctioned outside the company.

Case—cont'd

Table 10.42 Bidding history

Batch size	Est. good (%)	NuWave bid ($)	Triad Technology bid ($)
70,000	0.70	4300	4200
80,000	0.60	5000	5110
65,000	0.65	3930	4020
70,000	0.50	4340	4210
75,000	0.60	3690	3700
85,000	0.75	4320	4230
55,000	0.55	3980	3890
60,000	0.80	4730	4770
50,000	0.75	3650	3670
50,000	0.50	3860	3880
70,000	0.60	4250	4160
80,000	0.70	4380	4490
70,000	0.60	4420	4450
65,000	0.70	4220	4060
50,000	0.75	3340	3330
60,000	0.55	4480	4390
75,000	0.70	5630	5740
70,000	0.80	4490	4460
80,000	0.50	3990	4100
60,000	0.60	3800	3750

These car manufacturers all sell their rejects in the same way. A list is kept of purchasing agents who will buy leather with specific characteristics; these purchasing agents are emailed and informed when a batch of leather of potential interest is available. If interested, each purchasing agent makes a sealed bid and the manufacturer opens the bids sells the batch of leather to the winning bidder.

Over the past 5 years, Mr. Makins has bid on 305 previous batches of leather and has saved information regarding the winning bids (Table 10.43). For each of the 305 auctions Adventure has participated in over the previous 58 months, Mr. Makins has recorded the month, the size of the batch of leather being auctioned (Bid Quantity), the estimated percentage of leather in the batch that will be usable (Est. Yield %), and the winning total bid (Bid). In the instances that Adventure won the bid, Mr. Makins has recorded the number of yards of leather that was actually acceptable for use in production—that is, the actual yield (in yards) of good leather.

Mr. Makins has been informed recently of the availability of a batch of 300 yards of leather, identified by Porsche as lot MATS314Q. The auction representative, Erica Johansson, always supplies an estimate of the yield of yards of good leather in each batch. It is in her best interest to supply a good estimate, because in the long run, her ability to sell depends on providing her customers with at least as many units as she estimates. For the current batch, Ms. Johansson estimates the yield to be 90%.

With the information from Porsche on the characteristics of lot MATS314Q, the production group has informed Mr. Makins that Adventure can use the lot now. Adventure has received a contract to supply matching luggage to a sports team, and this order would require 265 yards of leather.

Case—cont'd

Table 10.43 Auction history

Auction	Month	Bid quantity	Est. yield %	Bid	Actual yield
1	1	500	0.90	3433.50	
2	1	300	0.70	1402.80	
3	1	300	0.70	1535.10	209
4	1	400	0.80	2070.40	
5	1	400	0.90	2584.80	332
6	1	400	0.80	1980.80	
7	1	300	0.70	875.70	
8	2	400	0.90	1825.20	
9	2	200	0.80	948.80	
10	2	100	0.90	638.10	
			.		
			.		
			.		
301	57	200	0.80	1217.60	
302	58	200	0.80	932.80	
303	58	400	0.90	2390.40	
304	58	400	0.70	1946.00	
305	58	500	0.80	2288.00	

The cost for Adventure to manufacture the same leather by regular methods would be $1350 for setup plus a cost of $10 per yard required. Alternatively, Adventure's external cost for tested and guaranteed leather in quantities of 200 yards or less is $16 per yard. Adventure does not currently have this leather in inventory.

With this information and the data listed in Table 10.43, Mr. Makins is about to make his analysis and determine what to bid. As he looked over the data on the past bids, he remarked to his assistant, "It looks to me as if the other bidders are bidding about $6 to $7 per estimated good yard of leather. Thus, for a batch of 300 yards leather with an estimated yield of 90%, I would guess the competitor's bid would be about $1755."

Hatteras Yachts advertising

Hatteras Yachts produced models that had been marketed for nearly four decades. Hatteras' marketing program had undergone little change for some time when a new product manager, Jack Rollins, assumed responsibility for the brand.

Background

The Cape Hatteras legends began on the barrier islands of the North Carolina shore where the frigid waters of the Labrador Current encounter the tropical Gulf Stream. The outcome is Diamond Shoals—home to some of the most turbulent waters in the Atlantic and some of the best sport fishing in the world.

In 1959 at Cape Hatteras, where nor'easters can blow almost as fiercely as hurricanes, Willis Slane envisioned building a boat that could conquer the waters of Diamond Shoals and surmount the Hatteras weather. It would not be an ordinary boat—no traditional wooden fishing boat could do this. This new boat would have to be rugged and robust to take the pounding of Hatteras waters. But most importantly, it would have to be a great sport-fishing boat—big enough to handle a group of avid fishermen and comfortable enough for family back at the dock.

Case—cont'd

Breaking with all tradition, Mr. Slane chose a new material—fiberglass—to build this yacht that launched an industry.

Hatteras produced its first sport-fishing yacht on March 22, 1960, in the town of High Point, North Carolina. Christened the *Knit Wits*, she was a 41-foot twin cabin sportfisherman with a 14-foot beam and a pair of 275-horsepower Lincoln V-8s. The response was enthusiastic, and the Hatteras legend was born. In a testament to the ruggedness that has become synonymous with Hatteras, the *Knit Wits* is still in service today after a fishing career that includes service in the Gulf of Mexico and Piñas Bay, Panama.

The market soon demanded bigger boats, and so the Hatteras sport-fishing fleet expanded—first to 50-foot boats and now up to 90-foot convertibles. Hatteras also began designing and producing a line of cruising yachts that now ranges from 63 to 100 feet in length.

In 1967, Hatteras added a second manufacturing facility in the coastal town of New Bern, North Carolina. Thirty years later, the original facility was closed, and all manufacturing was consolidated at the 95-acre waterfront site in New Bern, where operations remain today.

Mr. Rollins undertook a careful review of the brand's history and available marketing research information. There were several competing brands, four of which accounted for 60% of the market and were nationally distributed and supported by media advertising. Hatteras was an important but not dominant brand among the four, with a 15% share of market. No consumer promotion (financing, rebates, etc.) was used to any appreciable extent, and price cutting was negligible, but all four major brands were priced above the level of the remaining brands in the category, and all four advertised heavily.

After working on Hatteras for several months, Mr. Rollins became convinced that sales could be increased by repositioning the brand. The brand's advertising agency prepared and tested some new approaches in focus group interviews. The results were quite favorable.

Encouraged, Mr. Rollins authorized the agency to produce magazine advertisements representing two different advertising strategies: one emphasizing what was labeled a "sporty" appeal and the other a "technological" approach. Mr. Rollins planned a market test to determine which one to use in a national rollout at a later stage. Mr. Rollins was also uncertain about what level of advertising was needed to support the strategy change. After consulting with the marketing research manager, Mr. Rollins proposed that an advertising experiment be conducted to address the following issues:

1. Do the "sporty" and "technological" copy alternatives differ in their effectiveness?
2. What level of advertising should be used for Hatteras for the coming fiscal year?

Experimental Design

Two elements of the advertising campaign were to be systematically varied: copy and media spending. Two copy treatments ("sporty" and "technological") and three levels of advertising intensity were to be tested. Expressed in 6-month expenditures per 100 "prospects" (potential customers) in a geographical area, the levels to be tested were $3, $6, and $9. The company had divided the United States into two regions: region E consisted of states lying along the East Coast of the United States, and region W consisted of states lying along the West Coast of the United States. The two segments contained about equal numbers of total prospects. Twelve sales territories (out of a total of 75) were selected at random from the region designated as region E, and another 12 were selected from region W. The complete experimental design therefore provided 24 observations (2 regions × 2 copy types × 3 levels of media expenditure × 2 test territories).

Sales measurements were obtained based on sales information in each of the territories. The experiment was run for 6 months, a period known from prior investigations to be sufficient for the long-term response to advertising to become clear. Arrangements were made to monitor competitive advertising activity in each of the 24 test territories. Table 10.44 shows the experimental design and the resulting sales' units.

Case—cont'd

Table 10.44 Results of the Hatteras ad experiment

Region	Copy type	Hatteras ad ($)	Unit sales	Region	Ad
E	Sporty	3	26	1	1
E	Sporty	3	25	1	1
E	Sporty	6	31	1	1
E	Sporty	6	32	1	1
E	Sporty	9	36	1	1
E	Sporty	9	38	1	1
E	Technological	3	20	1	0
E	Technological	3	20	1	0
E	Technological	6	29	1	0
E	Technological	6	32	1	0
E	Technological	9	48	1	0
E	Technological	9	45	1	0
W	Sporty	3	24	0	1
W	Sporty	3	20	0	1
W	Sporty	6	35	0	1
W	Sporty	6	28	0	1
W	Sporty	9	34	0	1
W	Sporty	9	38	0	1
W	Technological	3	18	0	0
W	Technological	3	15	0	0
W	Technological	6	27	0	0
W	Technological	6	30	0	0
W	Technological	9	48	0	0
W	Technological	9	50	0	0

Forecasting

Time series data can be used to estimate probabilities.

Chapter outline

Introduction

Financial, marketing, and operations planning and decision making often begins with using predictive analytics to forecast cash flows, sales, demand, and other business metrics. The focus of this chapter is how to create, evaluate, and compare forecasts with regression. Specifically, forecasting the growth (trend) and seasonality components is demonstrated in detailed examples. Those two components are illustrated in Figures 11.1 and 11.2.

11.1 Overview of forecasting

Forecasting is the cornerstone of all financial, human resources, marketing, and operations planning. Managers require forecasting in a variety of decision-making settings as follows:

Production scheduling, inventory, and supply chain
Hiring, training, and staff scheduling

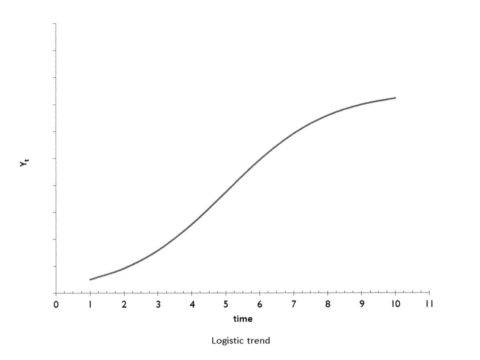

Logistic trend

FIGURE 11.1

Trend Component of a Time Series

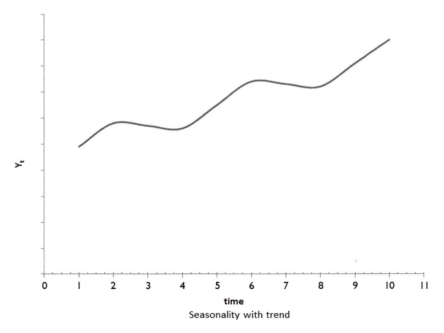

Seasonality with trend

FIGURE 11.2

Seasonality Component of a Time Series

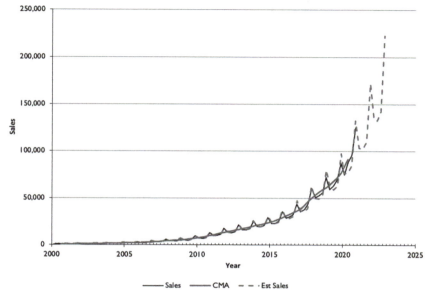

FIGURE 11.3

Trend and Seasonality Components of a Time Series

Advertising and promotional campaigns
Financial planning such as budgeting and estimating profit
Corporate strategy

Forecasts for such situations are made using *time series data*. A *time series* is data recorded sequentially over time. Some examples of time series data are as follows:

Units produced and units sold (demand)
Sales revenue
New hires
Store openings
Stock prices
Crude oil and gas prices
Housing starts
Unemployment

11.2 Measures of accuracy

Comparison of forecasting models' performance during and after the forecasting process is necessary to monitor and improve forecasting results. This process serves to measure how closely forecasts estimate the time series data. Measures of accuracy are often used in the development of forecasting models to assist in model selection—that is, these measures are often used to determine which forecasting model is best. There are many commonly used measures of the accuracy of forecasts based upon first computing the error (sometimes called the *residual*) associated with the forecast:

$$\text{Actual} = \text{Forecast} + \text{Error}$$

$$\text{Error} = \text{Actual} - \text{Forecast}$$

$$e_t = Y_t - \dot{Y}_t$$

$$\text{MAD} = \text{Mean Absolute Deviation} = \frac{\sum |e_t|}{n}$$

$$\text{MAPE} = \text{Mean Absolute Percentage Error} = \frac{\sum \frac{|e_t|}{Y_t}}{n}$$

$$\text{MSE} = \text{Mean Squared Error} = \frac{\sum e_t^2}{n}$$

$$\text{RMSE} = \text{Root Mean Squared Error} = (MSE)^{1/2}$$

$$\text{Mincer} - \text{Zarnowitz Regression}: \text{Actual} = \beta_0 + \beta_1 \text{Forecast}$$

$$\text{test}: \beta_0 = 0 \text{ and } \beta_1 = 1$$

then use the r^2 and standard error of the estimate (SEE)

Note that *MAD*, *MSE*, and *SEE* are in the same units as the data and thus provide a measure of how many units a forecast will typically vary from the actual outcome. *MAPE* and *coefficient of variance* (= *SEE/Average*) are measures of the percentage error that can be expected.

The **Mincer–Zarnowitz** regression tests the degree to which the *Actual* values are equal to the *Forecast* values. Ideally, the *Actual* is equal to the *Forecast*:

$$\text{Actual} = \text{Forecast}$$

$$\text{Actual} = 0 + 1 \text{ Forecast}$$

and thus the regression is

$$\text{Actual} = \beta_0 + \beta_1 \text{ Forecast}$$

$$Y_t = \beta_0 + \beta_1 \dot{Y}_t$$

with statistical tests of $\beta_0 = 0$ and $\beta_1 = 1$.

The r^2 and SEE from the Mincer–Zarnowitz regression are readily comparable to other forecasts regardless of whether the forecasts were constructed using regression.

In addition, note that the terms *estimated* and *forecasted* are used interchangeably.

Example 11.1 Evaluating Sales Forecasts
A sales representative has posted their forecast for next quarter's sales, and the regional manager must assess the accuracy of the forecast. Furthermore, a new analyst has started working for the regional manager and has a new method for forecasting sales. The sales data and the associated forecasts are shown in Fig. 11.4 and listed in Table 11.1. Which method, if either, is better?

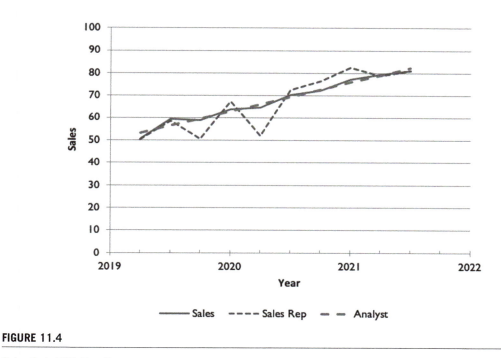

FIGURE 11.4

Sales Data With Two Forecasts

Fig. 11.5 shows the plot of the Forecasts *versus* the Actual Sales. The graph in Fig. 11.5 illustrates the basic principle of the Mincer–Zarnowitz regression: the *Forecast* should equal the *Actual*. For example, if a forecaster predicted sales of 80, then one would hope that the actual sales would be 80.

The Mincer–Zarnowitz regression results show how the forecasts fit the actual, as well as which forecast has the better accuracy.

Mincer–Zarnowitz regression equation to test the accuracy of the sales representative's forecast is:

$$Actual\ Sales = \beta_0 + \beta_1\ Sales\ Rep\ Forecast$$

Mincer–Zarnowitz regression results are shown in Table 11.2.

Table 11.1 Sales data with two forecasts (in $MM)

Year	Quarter	t	Actual sales	Sales rep	Analyst
				Forecasts	
2019	1	1	50.63	50.24	53.05
2019	2	2	59.27	58.41	56.31
2019	3	3	58.64	50.50	59.56
2019	4	4	63.78	67.34	62.82
2020	1	5	64.58	51.97	66.08
2020	2	6	70.44	72.66	69.34
2020	3	7	72.24	76.42	72.60
2020	4	8	77.21	82.34	75.85
2021	1	9	79.36	78.75	79.11
2021	2	10	80.94	81.06	82.37

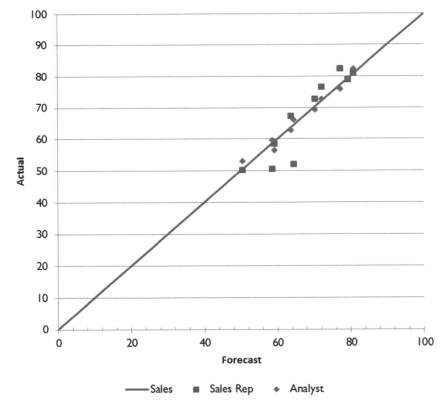

FIGURE 11.5

Scatterplot of Sales Versus Forecasts

Table 11.2 Mincer–Zarnowitz test of the sales representative's forecast accuracy			
$r^2 = 0.84$			
Standard error of the estimate = 4.23			
Regression Term	**Est. Coefficient**	**Std Error**	**t-Stat**
Constant	20.86	7.33	17.14
Sales Rep Forecast	0.70	0.11	2.79

Table 11.3 Mincer–Zarnowitz test of the analyst's forecast accuracy			
$r^2 = 0.97$			
Standard error of the estimate = 1.73			
Regression term	**Est. coefficient**	**Std error**	**t-Stat**
Constant	0.00	4.00	0.00
Analyst Forecast	1.00	0.06	0.00

Mincer–Zarnowitz regression equation is as follows:

$$Actual\ Sales = \beta_0 + \beta_1\ Analyst\ Forecast$$

Mincer–Zarnowitz regression results are shown in Table 11.3.

The r^2 and SEE from the Mincer–Zarnowitz regression are readily comparable to other forecasts regardless of whether or not the forecasts were constructed using regression. As the test is for $\beta_1 = 1$, the statistic for the test is:

$$t = |\beta_1 - 1| / SE_{\beta_1}$$

Note that $\beta_1 = 0.70 = 1$ and $\beta_0 = 20.86$ indicate a significantly biased forecast—a forecast that consistently and predictably mis-forecasts sales. In other words, you can forecast the sales representative's errors. If the sales representative's forecast was biased but more accurate than the analyst's forecast (higher r^2 and lower SEE), then the bias could be corrected using the Mincer–Zarnowitz regression equation. This new, unbiased forecast yields the same r^2 and SEE as reported in the Mincer–Zarnowitz regression.

11.3 Components of time series data

The four components of a time series of data are as follows:

1. The long-term ***trend*** indicates the annual growth, or decline, of the time series, typically as a straight line or an exponential curve. This is the backbone of the data and is useful in seeing the overall structure of the time series. Fig. 11.6 shows linear trend—data that grow by a constant amount. Fig. 11.7 shows exponential trend—data that grow by a constant percentage. Fig. 11.8 shows logistic trend—data that initially grow by a constant percentage and then have limited growth due to a finite population.

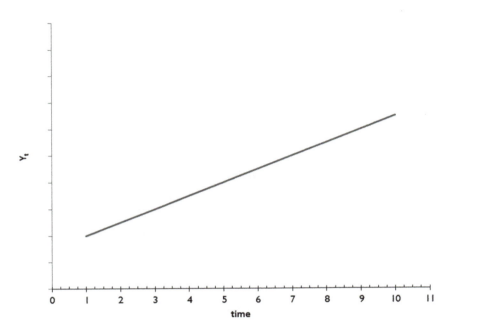

FIGURE 11.6

Linear Trend: $Y_t = \beta_0 + \beta_1 t$

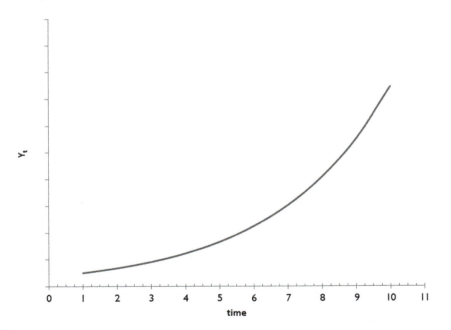

FIGURE 11.7

Exponential Trend: $Y_t = \beta_0 e^{\beta_1 t}$

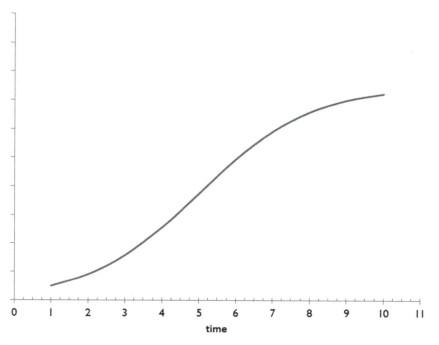

FIGURE 11.8

Logistic Trend: $Y_t = \dfrac{M}{1 + e^{-(\beta_0 + \beta_1 t)}}$

2. The **seasonal** component is a predictably repeating pattern within time periods. In addition to being within a year, seasonality can also be within a month, week, and day as well. For example, heating demands are high in the winter months, sales are high in December, and agricultural sales are high at harvest time. Each time period during the year can have a seasonal index, which indicates the percentage of how much higher or lower this particular time usually is as compared to the others. For example, with quarterly data there would be a seasonal index for each quarter, and an index of 1.235 for the fourth quarter indicates that sales are about 23.5% higher on average compared to an average quarter. An index of 0.921 for the second quarter indicates that sales for that quarter are typically 7.9% lower (since $1 - 0.921 = 0.079$) than an average quarter.

3. The medium-term **cyclic** component consists of the gradual ups and downs that do not repeat each year and so are excluded from the seasonal component. Since they are gradual, they are not random enough to be considered part of the independent random error (the irregular component). The cyclic variation is especially difficult to forecast beyond the immediate future, yet it can be very important, since basic business cycle phenomena (e.g., recessions) are considered to be part of the cyclic variation in economic performance.

4. The short-term, **random** irregular component represents the leftover, residual variation that cannot be explained. It is the effect of those one-time occurrences that happen randomly, rather than systematically, over time. The best that can be done with the irregular component is to summarize how large it is (e.g., using a standard deviation), to determine whether it changes over time, and to

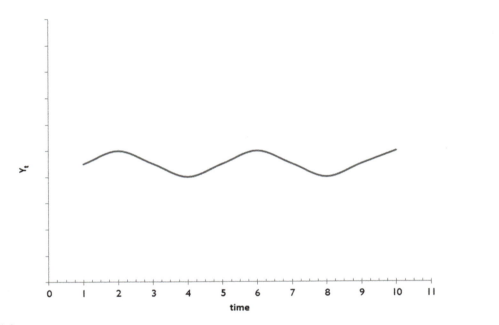

FIGURE 11.9

Seasonality

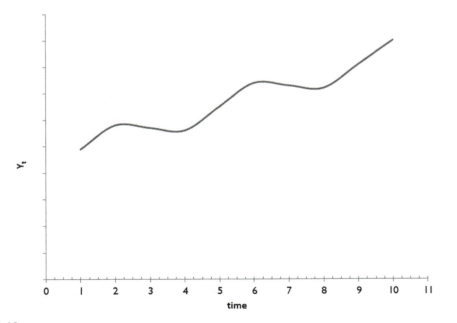

FIGURE 11.10

Seasonality With Trend

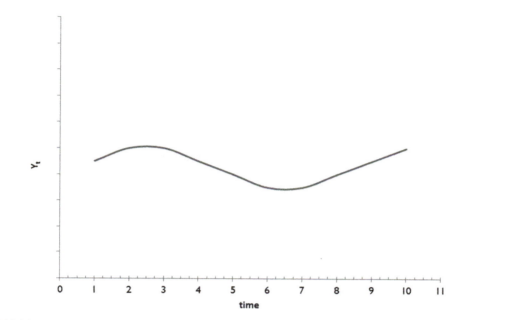

FIGURE 11.11

Cycle

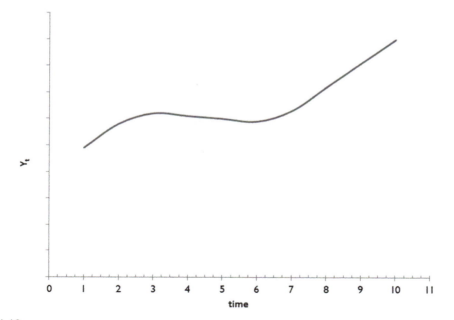

FIGURE 11.12

Cycle With Trend

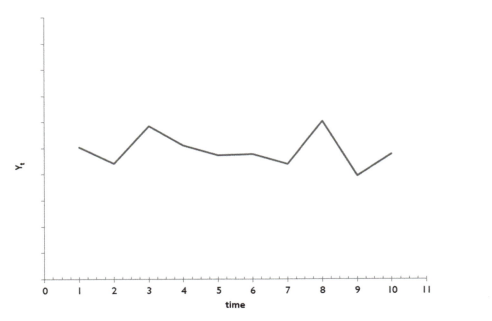

FIGURE 11.13

Random Variation

recognize that even in the best situation, a forecast can be no closer (on average) than the typical size of the random variation (as measured by the SEE).

11.4 Forecasting trend

Trend is the long-term growth, or decline, of the time series, typically a straight line or an exponential curve. This is the backbone of the data and is useful in estimating the growth in either a constant amount (linear) of growth or a constant percentage (exponential) of growth.

11.4.1 Linear trend

A trend with a ***constant amount*** is a linear trend and is computed using the following regression:

$$Y_t = \beta_0 + \beta_1 t$$

where t is an arbitrary unit of time and β_1 is the constant amount of growth. For annual time series, it is convenient to use the last two digits of the year as t.

11.4.2 Exponential trend

A trend with a ***constant percentage*** is an exponential trend and can be estimated using the following equation:

$$Y_t = \beta_0 e^{\beta_1 t}$$

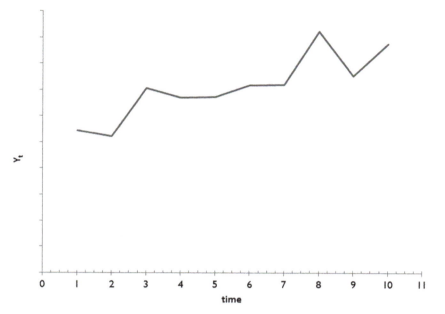

FIGURE 11.14

Random Variation With Trend

where β_1 is the annual percentage growth. This equation is not directly estimated using linear regression. Instead, the data is transformed into a linear form by taking logarithms (usually natural logs, *ln*) of Y_t and then regressing $\ln(Y_t)$ against t:

$$\ln(Y_t) = \beta_0 + \beta_1 t$$

Invert the equation to forecast in the original units: $Y_t = e^{\ln Y_t}$

$$Y_t = e^{\beta_0 + \beta_1 t}$$

The regression model for a linear trend:

$$Sales_t = \beta_0 + \beta_1 t$$

Example 11.2 Amazon annual sales

Amazon began as an online bookseller and now sells almost any item a customer could want. Amazon's annual sales can be used to study their rate of growth and to estimate the sustainability of such growth. Fig. 11.15 shows Amazon's annual sales (revenue in millions) from 2002 to 2020 along with a linear regression estimate of sales.

First, a regression of *Sales$_t$* versus t is calculated to estimate the fit of a linear trend. Table 11.4 lists Amazon's annual sales (revenue in millions) from 2000 to 2020 along with a linear regression estimate of sales. Just as k indicates units in thousands, MM is a common abbreviation for millions, Thus $MM indicates that the units are millions of dollars. The forecasts in gray are the time periods for which future sales were forecasted.

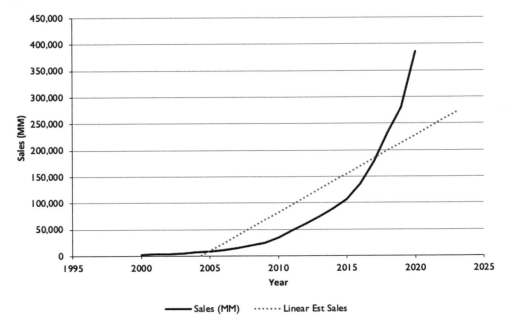

FIGURE 11.15

Amazon Annual Sales 2000–2020 With a Linear Trend

Table 11.4 Amazon sales with a linear forecast through 2023			
Year	t	Sales ($MM)	Linear est. sales
2000	0	2761.98	−63,688.37
2001	1	3122.43	−49,096.39
2002	2	3932.94	−34,504.41
2003	3	5263.70	−19,912.44
2004	4	6921.12	−5320.46
2005	5	8490.00	9271.51
2006	6	10,711.00	23,863.49
2007	7	14,835.00	38,455.46
2008	8	19,166.00	53,047.44
2009	9	24,509.00	67,639.41
2010	10	34,204.00	82,231.39
2011	11	48,077.00	96,823.36
2012	12	61,093.00	111,415.34
2013	13	74,452.00	126,007.32
2014	14	88,988.00	140,599.29
2015	15	107,006.00	155,191.27
2016	16	135,987.00	169,783.24
2017	17	177,866.00	184,375.22
2018	18	232,887.00	198,967.19
2019	19	280,522.00	213,559.17
2020	20	386,064.00	228,151.14
2021	21		242,743.12
2022	22		257,335.10
2023	23		271,927.07

Table 11.5 Linear regression results for amazon annual sales, 2000–2020

$r^2 = 0.7329$			
Standard error of the estimate = 56,081.50			
Regression term	**Est. coefficient**	**Std error**	**t-Stat**
Constant	−63,688.366	23,626.836	−2.70
t	14,591.976	2,021.037	7.22

Table 11.6 Amazon sales with an unbiased exponential forecast through 2023

Year	*t*	Sales (MM)	ln(Sales)	Estimated ln(Sales)	Sales forecast	Unbiased sales forecast
2000	0	2761.98	7.9237	7.8455	2554.16	4615.63
2001	1	3122.43	8.0464	8.0974	3286.05	5314.25
2002	2	3932.94	8.2771	8.3494	4227.66	6213.04
2003	3	5263.70	8.5686	8.6014	5439.10	7369.39
2004	4	6921.12	8.8423	8.8533	6997.67	8857.10
2005	5	8490.00	9.0466	9.1053	9002.85	10,771.10
2006	6	10,711.00	9.2790	9.3573	11,582.61	13,233.55
2007	7	14,835.00	9.6047	9.6092	14,901.60	16,401.63
2008	8	19,166.00	9.8609	9.8612	19,171.65	20,477.51
2009	9	24,509.00	10.1068	10.1132	24,665.28	25,721.34
2010	10	34,204.00	10.4401	10.3651	31,733.11	32,467.78
2011	11	48,077.00	10.7806	10.6171	40,826.21	41,147.41
2012	12	61,093.00	11.0202	10.8690	52,524.95	52,314.18
2013	13	74,452.00	11.2179	11.1210	67,575.95	66,680.79
2014	14	88,988.00	11.3963	11.3730	86,939.81	85,164.15
2015	15	107,006.00	11.5806	11.6249	111,852.37	108,943.90
2016	16	135,987.00	11.8203	11.8769	143,903.61	139,537.73
2017	17	177,866.00	12.0888	12.1289	185,139.13	178,898.21
2018	18	232,887.00	12.3583	12.3808	238,190.66	229,537.42
2019	19	280,522.00	12.5444	12.6328	306,444.09	294,687.27
2020	20	386,064.00	12.8638	12.8848	394,255.50	378,505.78
2021	21			13.1367	507,229.24	486,342.44
2022	22			13.3887	652,575.55	625,079.66
2023	23			13.6406	839,570.78	803,571.95

Next, a regression of ln(*Sales$_t$*) versus *t* is calculated to estimate the exponential trend model. Table 11.6 lists Amazon's annual sales (revenue in millions) from 2002 to 2020 along with the corrected (unbiased) estimate of sales using the logarithmic (*ln*) regression. The forecasts in gray are the time periods for which future sales were forecasted.

The regression model for an exponential trend:

$$\ln\left(Sales_t\right) = \beta_0 + \beta_1 t$$

Sales can then be forecasted using the following equation:

$$Forecasted\ Sales_t = e^{\beta_0 + \beta_1 t}$$

The coefficient $\beta_1 = 0.252$, for the time period t variable, indicates an average annual growth rate of 25.2% per year. Given that the variable used in the regression is a natural log (ln), the regression results shown are in natural logs rather than the original units and represent how well the transformed variable, $ln(Sales_t)$, is estimated. Thus, a Mincer–Zarnowitz regression should be used to measure the fit of the exponential model. The appropriate regression model is:

$$Sales_t = \beta_0 + \beta_1\ Forecasted\ Sales_t$$

The r^2 and SEE of the Mincer–Zarnowitz regression indicate that the exponential model is more accurate than the linear model. To test whether $\beta_1 = 1$, the appropriate t-stat for the β_1 term is:

$$t = |1 - 0.9545|/0.0107 = 4.27$$

That t-stat indicates that β_1 is *not* equal to 1. Thus, the forecasts are biased by being too high and need to be reduced by about 5% (=1–0.9545). This means that the forecasts have predictable errors and are biased. Because of the bias, the final forecast must be adjusted using the Mincer–Zarnowitz regression equation:

$$Unbiased\ Forecasted\ Salest = 2,177,619 + 0.9545\ Forecasted\ Sales_t$$

Table 11.7 Logarithmic regression results for Amazon annual sales, 2000–2020

	$r^2 = 0.9978$		
	Standard error of the estimate = 0.0745		
Regression term	**Est. coefficient**	**Std error**	**t-Stat**
Constant	7.845	0.0314	250.02
t	0.252	0.0027	03.87

Table 11.8 Mincer–Zarnowitz results for the exponential model of Amazon annual sales, 2000–2020

	$r^2 = 0.9976$		
	Standard error of the estimate = 5273.45		
Regression term	**Est. coefficient**	**Std error**	**t-Stat**
Constant	2177.619	1456.9788	1.49
Forecasted Sales_t	0.9545	0.0107	4.27

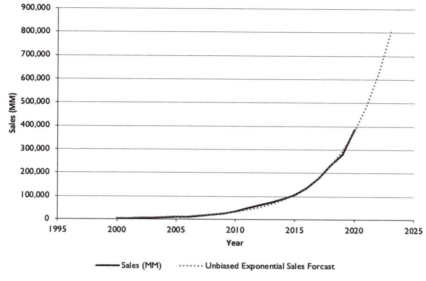

FIGURE 11.16

Amazon Annual Sales 2000–2020 With an Exponential Trend

11.4.3 Autoregression

A forecasting technique that takes advantage of the relationship of values (Y_t) to previous period values $(Y_{t-1}, Y_{t-2}, Y_{t-3}, \ldots, Y_{t-n})$ is called *autoregression*. In **autoregression**, the independent variables are time-lagged versions of the dependent variable. This means that we try to predict Y from Y from previous time periods. The independent variable can be lagged one, two, three, or more time periods. An autoregression model is typically denoted as an **AR(n)**, where n is the number of lags. For example, an AR(2) would be an autoregression model containing independent variables for two time periods:

$$Y_t = \beta_0 + \beta_1 Y_{t-1} + \beta_2 Y_{t-2} + n_t$$

A general AR(n) would be:

$$Y_t = \beta_0 + \beta_1 Y_{t-1} + \beta_2 Y_{t-2} + \ldots + \beta_n Y_{t-n} + n_t$$

An AR(1) is commonly used to measure trend. Consider the following AR(1) equation:

$$Y_t = 5 + 1.00\ Y_{t-1}$$

This equation could yield a time series of 5, 10, 15, 20, . . . , thus growing at a constant amount of 5 each period. Now consider the AR(1) equation:

$$Y_t = 0 + 1.05\ Y_{t-1}$$

This equation could yield a time series of 100.00, 105.00, 110.25, 115.7625, . . . , thus growing at a constant percentage of 5% each period. Finally, consider the AR(1) equation:

$$Y_t = 10 + 0.90_{Y_{t-1}}$$

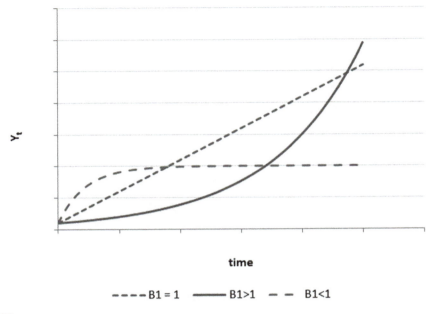

FIGURE 11.17

The Effects of $\beta_1 = 1$, $\beta_1 > 1$, and $\beta_1 < 1$ for an AR(1) Regression

This equation could yield a time series of 100, 100, 100, 100, . . . , therefore having a limited growth (a ceiling).

Fig. 11.17 shows examples for $\beta_1 = 1$, $\beta_1 > 1$, and $\beta_1 < 1$.

Thus, the growth of an AR(1) time series depends on whether $\beta_1 = 1$ and $\beta_0 = 0$. Thus, the AR(1) coefficients should be tested in a manner similar to the Mincer–Zarnowitz regression.

Example 11.3 AR(1) Amazon annual sales

Returning to Amazon's annual sales, estimate an AR(1) and the growth associated with sales.

Table 11.9 lists Amazon's annual sales (revenue in millions) from 2002 to 2015 along with the estimate of sales using the autoregression with a one-period lag: AR(1). The forecasts in gray are the time periods for which future sales were forecasted.

The autoregression model with a one-period lag (AR(1)):

$$Sales_t = \beta_0 + \beta_1 Sales_{t-1}$$

Thus, the AR(1) forecasting model is:

$$Forecasted\ Sales_t = -1,290.545 + 1.305\ Sales_{t-1}$$

Table 11.9 Amazon sales with an AR(1) forecast through 2023

Year	Sales $t-1$	Sales (MM)	AR(1) forecasted sales (MM)
2000		2761.98	
2001	2761.98	3122.43	2314.19
2002	3122.43	3932.94	2784.63
2003	3932.94	5263.70	3842.44
2004	5263.70	6921.12	5579.25
2005	6921.12	8490.00	7742.40
2006	8490.00	10,711.00	9789.98
2007	10,711.00	14,835.00	12,688.67
2008	14,835.00	19,166.00	18,071.01
2009	19,166.00	24,509.00	23,723.52
2010	24,509.00	34,204.00	30,696.81
2011	34,204.00	48,077.00	43,350.02
2012	48,077.00	61,093.00	61,456.05
2013	61,093.00	74,452.00	78,443.58
2014	74,452.00	88,988.00	95,878.78
2015	88,988.00	107,006.00	114,850.10
2016	107,006.00	135,987.00	138,365.88
2017	135,987.00	177,866.00	176,189.77
2018	177,866.00	232,887.00	230,847.19
2019	232,887.00	280,522.00	302,656.59
2020	280,522.00	386,064.00	364,826.32
2021	386,064.00		502,572.04
2022			654,629.84
2023			853,084.59

Table 11.10 Regression *r*esults for the AR(1) model of Amazon annual sales, 2000–2020

$r^2 = 0.9948$			
Standard error of the estimate = 7912.55			
Regression term	**Est. coefficient**	**Std error**	**t-Stat**
Constant	−1290.545	2312.981	−0.56
Forecasted Sales$_t$	1.305	0.022	13.73

Notice that after the last time period with data that the model input switches from the previous data to the previous forecast. In this example, the forecasting model for 2021 is:

$$Forecasted\ Sales_{2021} = -1290.545 + 1.305\ Sales_{2020}$$

$$Forecasted\ Sales_{2021} = -1290.545 + 1.305 * 386,064 = \mathbf{502{,}572.04}$$

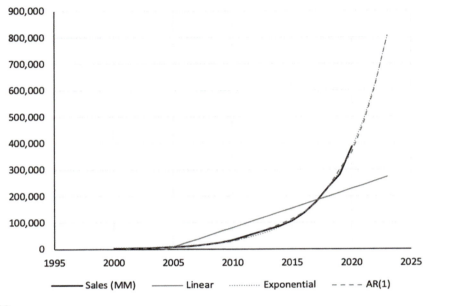

FIGURE 11.18

Amazon Annual Sales 2002–2020 With Linear Trend, Exponential Trend, and AR(1) Models

Then, because there is no data for 2021, the forecasting model for 2022 (and forward) is:

$$Forecasted\ Sales_{2022} = -1290.545 + 1.305\ Forecasted\ Sales_{2021}$$

$$Forecasted\ Sales_{2022} = -1290.545 + 1.305 * 502,572.04 = \mathbf{654,629.84}$$

The r^2 and SEE of the AR(1) model indicate that the AR(1) model is more accurate than either the linear trend or the exponential models. Examining the β_1 coefficient from the exponential model indicates that annual growth is approximately **25.2%**. In contrast, the significance of the β_0 and β_1 terms indicate that the annual growth rate is **30.5%** (= $1 - \beta_1$). To test whether $\beta_1 = 1$, the appropriate t-stat for the β_1 term is:

$$t = \frac{/1.305 - 1/}{0.022} = \mathbf{13.73}$$

Using a *time value of money* approach to estimate the rate of growth yields:

$$386{,}064 = 2761.98\ (1 + growth\ rate)^{20}$$

$$Growth\ rate = (386,064 / 2761.98)^{1/20} - 1 = \mathbf{29.7\%}$$

Fig. 11.18 compares the linear, exponential, and AR(1) trend models with the actual data.

Example 11.4 Housing Starts AR(2) autoregression

As an example, consider forecasting 2021–2023 Housing Starts from the following data by using data lagged by two time periods: an AR(2). The data listed in Table 11.11 show how the lags are created from the original time series, Y_t. The forecasts in gray are the time periods for which future Housing Starts were forecasted.

Table 11.11 Housing Starts 1990–2020 with AR(2) forecasts through 2023

Year	HStart$_t$ (thousands)	HStart$_{t-1}$	HStart$_{t-2}$	Est. HStarts$_t$
1990	14,438			
1991	12,105	14,438		
1992	14,417	12,105	14,438	11,279
1993	15,499	14,417	12,105	16,301
1994	17,352	15,499	14,417	16,382
1995	16,332	17,352	15,499	18,439
1996	17,624	16,332	17,352	15,674
1997	17,695	17,624	16,332	18,292
1998	19,454	17,695	17,624	17,537
1999	19,767	19,454	17,695	20,127
2000	18,880	19,767	19,454	19,423
2001	19,214	18,880	19,767	17,884
2002	20,523	19,214	18,880	18,977
2003	22,245	20,523	19,214	20,717
2004	23,394	22,245	20,523	22,426
2005	24,875	23,394	22,245	23,001
2006	21,743	24,875	23,394	24,456
2007	16,102	21,743	24,875	18,771
2008	10,800	16,102	21,743	12,401
2009	6648	10,800	16,102	8212
2010	7026	6648	10,800	5522
2011	7343	7026	6648	8857
2012	9405	7343	7026	9081
2013	11,138	9405	7343	11,961
2014	12,003	11,138	9405	13,185
2015	13,281	12,003	11,138	13,326
2016	14,125	13,281	12,003	14,666
2017	14,460	14,125	13,281	15,079
2018	14,968	14,460	14,125	15,019
2019	15,506	14,968	14,460	15,557
2020	16,759	15,506	14,968	16,025
2021		16,759	15,506	17,545
2022			16,759	17,889
2023				17,880

A regression model using annual Housing Starts from 1990 to 2020 as the dependent variable (Y_t) and one- and two-period lags of Housing Starts (Y_{t-1} and Y_{t-2}) as the independent (X) variables:

$$Housing\ Starts_t = \beta_0 + \beta_1\ Housing\ Starts_{t-1} + \beta_2 Housing\ Starts_{t-2}$$

Note that the regression analysis does not use data from the first 2 years because there are no values for the two lagged variables for those years.

The resulting autoregression model to estimate Housing Starts is:

$$Est.\ Housing\ Starts_t = 2754.8341 + 1.4996\ Housing\ Starts_{t-1} - 0.6669\ Housing\ Starts_{t-2}$$

The r^2 indicates that approximately 90% of the variation in Housing Starts can be explained by the previous 2 years of data and that a typical forecasting error will be about 3 million houses ($\cong 1.96 \times 1550.763 \times 1{,}000$). Note that both lagged variables are statistically significant ($|t| > 2.0$). Thus, this data has first- and second-order *autocorrelation*.

Table 11.12 Regression results for AR(2) model of annual Housing Starts, 2000–2020

$r^2 = 0.904$			
Standard error of the estimate = 1550.763			
Regression term	**Est. coefficient**	**Std error**	**t-Stat**
Constant	2754.8341	1008.9016	2.73
Housing Starts$_{t-1}$	1.4996	0.1403	10.69
Housing Starts$_{t-2}$	−0.6669	0.1401	−4.76

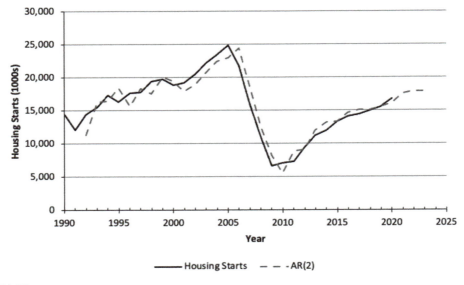

FIGURE 11.19

US Annual Housing Starts, 1990–2015, and the AR(2) Model

Autocorrelation means that the data is correlated to itself through time. Autocorrelation can be useful in locating seasonal or cyclical effects in time series data. For example, if data is given in monthly increments, then autoregression lagged by as much as 12 months can detect seasonality or quarterly effects.

11.5 Forecasting seasonality

Seasonality is a predictably repeating pattern within time periods. There are two standard methods of accounting for seasonality. The first is an additive method using regression with indicator variables and is the method used frequently in econometrics. The second method uses multiplicative seasonal indices and is more commonly used by businesses and the US Census Bureau and the Bureau of Labor and Statistics.

11.5.1 Additive seasonality using indicator variables

Indicator variables for months, or quarters, are used when the seasonal peaks and valleys are a consistent amount—that is, the peaks are the same height and not increasing over time. In the interest of detecting statistical significance, it is best to make the base quarter be the quarter with the *lowest* sales for the year. This will ensure positive signs for the seasonal variables' coefficients and detection of statistical significance. If you should happen not to make the base quarter the lowest sales quarter, then choose the quarter with the most negative seasonality regression coefficient as the base and recompute the regression.

Example 11.5 Amazon quarterly sales: additive seasonality
Most retailers experience significantly more sales in the fourth quarter each year than the other quarters of the year. Thus, most retailers' sales have significant seasonality in their monthly and quarterly data. Amazon experiences similar quarterly seasonality. Amazon's quarterly sales for 2000–2020 are listed in Table 11.13. Use quarterly indicator variables to forecast the next four quarters' sales.

First, create indicator variables for three of the four quarters. In the interest of detecting statistical significance, it is best to make the base quarter be the quarter with the lowest sales for the year. This will ensure positive signs for the seasonal variables' coefficients and detection of statistical significance. For Amazon, the first quarter of each year has the lowest sales and was used as the base quarter.

Based on the AR(1) model of annual trend, the one-period lag of sales, $Sales_{t-1}$, was included in the model to measure trend. The regression model was computed using the data in Table 11.13 without the first row of the data due to the lagged term.

The AR(1) model with additive seasonality:

$$Sales_t = \beta_0 + \beta_1 Sales_{t-1} + \beta_2 Q_2 + \beta_3 Q_3 + \beta_4 Q_4$$

Table 11.13 Amazon quarterly sales, 2000–2020, with one-period lag and indicator variables						
Year	Quarter	Sales (MM)	Sales $t-1$	Q2	Q3	Q4
2000	1	573.89		0	0	0
2000	2	577.88	573.89	1	0	0
2000	3	637.86	577.88	0	1	0
2000	4	972.36	637.86	0	0	1
2001	1	700.36	972.36	0	0	0
2001	2	667.63	700.36	1	0	0
2001	3	639.28	667.63	0	1	0
2001	4	1115.17	639.28	0	0	1
2002	1	847.42	1115.17	0	0	0
2002	2	805.61	847.42	1	0	0
2002	3	851.30	805.61	0	1	0
2002	4	1428.61	851.30	0	0	1
2003	1	1083.56	1428.61	0	0	0
2003	2	1099.91	1083.56	1	0	0
2003	3	1134.46	1099.91	0	1	0
2003	4	1945.77	1134.46	0	0	1
2004	1	1530.35	1945.77	0	0	0
2004	2	1387.34	1530.35	1	0	0
2004	3	1462.48	1387.34	0	1	0
2004	4	2540.96	1462.48	0	0	1
2005	1	1902.00	2540.96	0	0	0
2005	2	1753.00	1902.00	1	0	0
2005	3	1858.00	1753.00	0	1	0
2005	4	2977.00	1858.00	0	0	1
2006	1	2279.00	2977.00	0	0	0
2006	2	2139.00	2279.00	1	0	0
2006	3	2307.00	2139.00	0	1	0
2006	4	3986.00	2307.00	0	0	1
2007	1	3015.00	3986.00	0	0	0
2007	2	2886.00	3015.00	1	0	0
2007	3	3262.00	2886.00	0	1	0
2007	4	5672.00	3262.00	0	0	1
2008	1	4135.00	5672.00	0	0	0
2008	2	4063.00	4135.00	1	0	0
2008	3	4264.00	4063.00	0	1	0
2008	4	6704.00	4264.00	0	0	1
2009	1	4889.00	6704.00	0	0	0
2009	2	4651.00	4889.00	1	0	0
2009	3	5449.00	4651.00	0	1	0
2009	4	9520.00	5449.00	0	0	1
2010	1	7131.00	9520.00	0	0	0
2010	2	6566.00	7131.00	1	0	0
2010	3	7560.00	6566.00	0	1	0

Table 11.13 Amazon quarterly sales, 2000–2020, with one-period lag and indicator variables—cont'd

Year	Quarter	Sales (MM)	Sales *t*–1	Q2	Q3	Q4
2010	4	12,947.00	7560.00	0	0	1
2011	1	9857.00	12,947.00	0	0	0
2011	2	9913.00	9857.00	1	0	0
2011	3	10,876.00	9913.00	0	1	0
2011	4	17,431.00	10,876.00	0	0	1
2012	1	13,185.00	17,431.00	0	0	0
2012	2	12,834.00	13,185.00	1	0	0
2012	3	13,806.00	12,834.00	0	1	0
2012	4	21,268.00	13,806.00	0	0	1
2013	1	16,070.00	21,268.00	0	0	0
2013	2	15,704.00	16,070.00	1	0	0
2013	3	17,092.00	15,704.00	0	1	0
2013	4	25,586.00	17,092.00	0	0	1
2014	1	19,741.00	25,586.00	0	0	0
2014	2	19,340.00	19,741.00	1	0	0
2014	3	20,579.00	19,340.00	0	1	0
2014	4	29,328.00	20,579.00	0	0	1
2015	1	22,717.00	29,328.00	0	0	0
2015	2	23,185.00	22,717.00	1	0	0
2015	3	25,358.00	23,185.00	0	1	0
2015	4	35,746.00	25,358.00	0	0	1
2016	1	29,128.00	35,746.00	0	0	0
2016	2	30,404.00	29,128.00	1	0	0
2016	3	32,714.00	30,404.00	0	1	0
2016	4	43,741.00	32,714.00	0	0	1
2017	1	35,714.00	43,741.00	0	0	0
2017	2	37,955.00	35,714.00	1	0	0
2017	3	43,744.00	37,955.00	0	1	0
2017	4	60,453.00	43,744.00	0	0	1
2018	1	51,042.00	60,453.00	0	0	0
2018	2	52,886.00	51,042.00	1	0	0
2018	3	56,576.00	52,886.00	0	1	0
2018	4	72,383.00	56,576.00	0	0	1
2019	1	59,700.00	72,383.00	0	0	0
2019	2	63,404.00	59,700.00	1	0	0
2019	3	69,981.00	63,404.00	0	1	0
2019	4	87,437.00	69,981.00	0	0	1
2020	1	75,452.00	87,437.00	0	0	0
2020	2	88,912.00	75,452.00	1	0	0
2020	3	96,145.00	88,912.00	0	1	0
2020	4	125,555.00	96,145.00	0	0	1

Table 11.14 Regression results for the AR(1) model of Amazon annual sales, 2000–2020

	$r^2 = 0.977$		
	Standard error of the estimate = 4192.437		
Regression term	**Est. coefficient**	**Std error**	**t-Stat**
Constant	–6060.396	1029.892	–5.88
Sales$_{t-1}$	1.086	0.019	56.44
Q_2	5555.440	1313.393	4.23
Q_3	6172.720	1312.158	4.70
Q_4	11,613.244	1310.658	8.86

Because the indicator variables measure the group averages, the comparisons used in comparing groups in an analysis of variance (ANOVA; Chapter 9) can be used to compare the seasons. The regression results indicate that quarters 2, 3, and 4 are statistically significantly different from quarter 1 (the base quarter). The standard errors also indicate that sales for quarters 2 and 3 are statistically significantly higher than quarter 1, and they are significantly lower than quarter 4:

$$6172.720 + 2\,(1312.158) < 11,613.244 \text{ or } (11,613.244 - 6172.720)\,/\,1312.158 > 2$$

Furthermore, the standard errors indicate that quarters 2 and 3 are *not* statistically significantly different from each other:

$$5555.440 + 2\,(1313.393) > 6172.720 \text{ or } (6172.720 - 5555.440)\,/\,1313.393 < 2$$

Examine the graph of the additive seasonality forecast in Fig. 11.20 and note the forecasts for quarter 4. The model consistently overestimates sales during the time periods from 2000 to 2010 and then underestimates sales during the time periods from 2016 through 2020. This type of predictable error indicates the need for a proportionate seasonal model rather than an additive model.

11.5.2 Ratio-to-moving-average method (X-11, X-12)

The *ratio-to-moving-average* (RTMA) method is a decomposition forecasting method with proportionate (percentage) seasonality and is the foundation of the US Census Bureau's X-12 seasonal adjustment method. Here is an overview of the RTMA method:

1. A *centered moving average* (CMA) is used to eliminate the *seasonal* effects by averaging over the entire year. This reduces the random component and produces a combination of trend and cyclic components.
2. Dividing the data by the smoothed moving-average series provides the RTMA, which includes both *seasonal* and *random* components. Grouping by time of year and then averaging within groups determines the *seasonal index* for each time of year. The *seasonally adjusted values* are then computed by dividing each series value by the appropriate *seasonal index* for its time of year.
3. Depending on the characteristics of the time series data, either the *CMA* or the *seasonally adjusted* series is used to estimate the long-term trend over time. This trend has no seasonal variation and leads to a seasonally adjusted forecast.

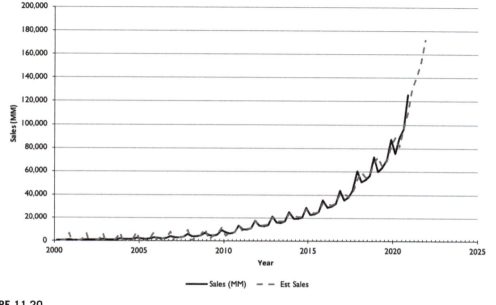

FIGURE 11.20

Amazon Quarterly Sales, 2000–2020, With the Additive Seasonality Model

4. Forecasting is done by *seasonalizing* the trend. Forecasts that reflect both the long-term trend and the seasonal behavior are computed by using the predicted values from the trend model for future time periods and then multiplying by the appropriate seasonal index.

5. To measure the forecasting accuracy (r^2, *SEE*), regress the actual data (Y) against the forecast (X) using the Mincer–Zarnowitz regression:

$$Actual = \beta_0 + \beta_1 \ Forecast$$

Test for bias and accuracy using the Mincer–Zarnowitz regression and testing for $\beta_0 = 0$ and $\beta_1 = 1$, as previously demonstrated.

The advantages of the RTMA method are ease of computation, interpretation, and accuracy. Example 11.6 demonstrates these attributes.

Example 11.6 Amazon quarterly sales: RTMA

The graph of Amazon's fourth-quarter sales in Fig. 11.20 reveals that fourth-quarter sales get larger as the volume of sales get larger. This indicates that the seasonality is proportionate to sales rather than a constant amount above, or below, sales. This indicates the need for ***multiplicative***, rather than *additive*, seasonal indices.

Continued

The first step is to compute the CMA. Given that there is an even number of quarters per year, the year cannot be centered at the date corresponding to the 2.5 period. To remedy this, a weighted average of five quarters is used:

$$CMA_t = (\tfrac{1}{2} Sales_{t-2} + Sales_{t-1} + Sales_t + Sales_{t+1} + \tfrac{1}{2} Sales_{t+2})/4$$

thus providing a four-period CMA. An easier way to accomplish this in Excel is:

$$= AVERAGE\,(Sales_{t-2} : Sales_{t+2},\ Sales_{t-1} : Sales_{t+1})$$

This formula will have eight terms and weight the $Sales_{t-2}$ and $Sales_{t+2}$ terms each once and the $Sales_{t-1}$, $Sales_t$, $Sales_{t+1}$ twice.
For example:

$$CMA_{2000\,:\,3} = ((573.89 + 577.88 + 637.86 + 972.36 + 700.36) + (577.88 + 637.86 + 972.36))/8 = 706.30$$

Table 11.15 Amazon quarterly sales, 2000–2020, with a four-period CMA

Year	Quarter	Sales$_t$ ($MM)	CMA
2000	1	573.89	
2000	2	577.88	
2000	3	637.86	**706.30**
2000	4	972.36	733.33
2001	1	700.36	744.73
2001	2	667.63	762.76
2001	3	639.28	798.99
2001	4	1115.17	834.62
2002	1	847.42	878.37
2002	2	805.61	944.05
2002	3	851.30	1012.75
2002	4	1428.61	1079.06
.	.	.	.
.	.	.	.
.	.	.	.
2020	1	75,452.00	79,729.11
2020	2	88,912.00	101,481.97
2020	3	96,145.00	
2020	4	125,555.00	

This calculation is shown in **bold** in Table 11.15.
The next step is to compute the RTMA by dividing the actual sales by the CMA:

$$RTMA_t = Sales_t\,/\,CMA_t$$

The RTMA indicates the percentage above (>1) or below (<1) expected sales for that specific period.

Table 11.16 Amazon quarterly sales, 2000–2020, with CMA and RTMA				
Year	**Quarter**	**Sales, ($MM)**	**CMA**	**RTMA**
2000	1	573.89		
2000	2	577.88		
2000	3	637.86	706.30	0.903
2000	4	972.36	733.33	1.326
2001	1	700.36	744.73	0.940
2001	2	667.63	762.76	0.875
2001	3	639.28	798.99	0.800
2001	4	1115.17	834.62	1.336
2002	1	847.42	878.37	0.965
2002	2	805.61	944.05	0.853
2002	3	851.30	1012.75	0.841
2002	4	1428.61	1079.06	1.324
.	.	.	.	.
.	.	.	.	.
.	.	.	.	.
2020	1	75,452.00	79,729.11	0.901
2020	2	88,912.00	101,481.97	0.969
2020	3	96,145.00		
2020	4	125,555.00		

For example, $RTMA_{2000:3} = 637.86/706.3 \cong 0.90$ indicates that the third-quarter sales for 2000 were about 90% of what would be expected if there were no seasonality—that is, about 10% less than a typical quarter (if such a thing existed). Similarly, the RTMA for the fourth quarter of 2000 indicates that that quarter's sales were about 33% (= 1.326 – 1) higher than a typical (average) quarter. Table 11.16 shows the RTMA column added to Table 11.15.

The next step is to compute the **seasonal indices** (often indicated by the Greek symbol Φ) by averaging the RTMAs for each set of seasons (e.g., quarters). In other words, to compute the seasonal index for quarter 1, calculate the average of all quarter 1 RTMAs. The seasonal index indicates the percentage above (>1) or below (<1) expected sales in general for that period. For example, consider an index of 0.88 for quarter 1. Such an index indicates that quarter 1 has 88% as much sales as an average quarter—that is, quarter 1 has 12% less sales than an average quarter.

Furthermore, because seasonal indices must average 1.00, quarterly indices must sum to 4. If they do not sum to 4, then they must be adjusted accordingly. The average RTMAs for the Amazon data sum to 3.988, so they are adjusted (inflated) to sum to 4 by multiplying each average RTMA by 4/3.988.

Quarter	Avg RTMA	Index
1	0.944	0.946
2	0.874	0.876
3	0.880	0.882
4	1.291	1.295
SUM	**3.988**	**4.000**

Table 11.17 Regression results for the AR(1) model of CMA			
$r^2 = 0.9995$			
Standard error of the estimate = 506.190			
Regression term	**Est. coefficient**	**Std error**	***t*-Stat**
Constant	−64.912	74.537	−0.871
CMA_{t-1}	1.0677	0.00267	25.316

These seasonal indices indicate that quarter 2 is the worst quarter and quarter 4 has about 34.6% higher sales than an average quarter. These indices also indicate that quarters 2 and 3 are nearly the same. Furthermore, quarter 4 accounts for about 33.75% (= 1.346/4) of annual sales.

The next step is to use the **seasonal indices** to compute the **seasonally adjusted sales** (*Sales SA*) by dividing sales by the season index: $Sales_t / \Phi_q$. Seasonally adjusted sales contain all the variation in the data except for seasonality. This time series is often used as the *Y* variable for regression analysis to determine the effects of other variables, such as price, promotion, interest rate, housing starts, and leading economic indicators, on sales.

For the Amazon data, this step will be omitted because there are no exogenous variables to be considered at this time. Instead, the CMA will be forecasted to estimate trend. For this example, an AR(1) for the CMA will be used as the regression model:

$$Estimated\ CMA_t = \beta_0 + \beta_1 CMA_{t-1}$$

Note that the r^2 and *SEE* measure the fit of the **estimated** CMA to the **actual** CMA, not the fit of the **estimated** CMA to sales. Also note that the β_1 term is tested for $\beta_1 = 1$ rather than 0 to determine whether there is statistically significant quarterly percentage growth as opposed to linear growth. At this point, the CMA can be estimated using the AR(1) regression equation:

$$CMA_t = -54.912 + 1.0677\ CMA_{t-1}$$

As shown in the AR(1) trend example, it is very important that when forecasting beyond the available CMA_t, the estimated CMA_t is substituted for the CMA_t:

$$Estimated\ CMA_t = \beta_0 + \beta_1\ Estimated\ CMA_{t-1}$$

This happens in the fourth quarter of 2020 for this time frame (from 2000 Q1 to 2020 Q4) of Amazon data.

Table 11.18 shows how sales are subsequently forecasted by multiplying the estimated CMA by the appropriate seasonal index.

Finally, the Mincer–Zarnowitz regression is computed to evaluate the accuracy for the forecasting model:

$$Sales_t = \beta_0 + \beta_1\ Forecasted\ Sales_t$$

These results indicate an excellent fit. But $\beta_1 = 1$ must be tested to determine if the forecast is biased.

$$|t| = (1 - 0.9772)\ /\ 0.01177 = 1.936$$

Table 11.18 Amazon quarterly sales, 2000–2020, with forecasted sales

Year	Quarter	Sales, ($MM)	CMA	RTMA	Index	Est. CMA	Sales forecast
2000	1	573.889			0.946		
2000	2	577.876			0.876		
2000	3	637.858	706.304	0.903	0.882	689.19	892.63
2000	4	972.360	733.331	1.326	1.295	718.05	679.53
2001	1	700.356	744.728	0.940	0.946	730.21	639.77
2001	2	667.625	762.757	0.875	0.876	749.46	661.27
2001	3	639.281	798.992	0.800	0.882	788.15	1020.80
2001	4	1115.171	834.622	1.336	1.295	826.19	781.87
2002	1	847.422	878.372	0.965	0.946	872.90	764.78
2002	2	805.605	944.054	0.853	0.876	943.03	832.06
2002	3	851.299	1012.751	0.841	0.882	1016.37	1316.39
2002	4	1428.610	1079.057	1.324	1.295		
.	.	.	.	.	.	.	.
.	.	.	.	.	.	.	.
2020	1	75,452.00	83,716.00	0.901	0.946	82,420.24	77,998.76
2020	2	88,912.00	91,751.25	0.969	0.876	89,316.34	78,253.25
2020	3	96,145.00			0.882	97,895.35	86,375.55
2020	4	125,555.00			1.295	104,455.23	135,288.78
2021	1				0.946	111,459.04	105,479.76
2021	2				0.876	118,936.81	104,204.81
2021	3				0.882	126,920.62	111,985.28
2021	4				1.295	135,444.71	175,425.85
2022	1				0.946	144,545.64	136,791.40
2022	2				0.876	154,262.45	135,154.87
2022	3				0.882	164,636.82	145,263.25
2022	4				1.295	175,713.25	227,581.04
2023	1				0.946	187,539.25	177,478.60
2023	2				0.876	200,165.53	175,372.21
2023	3				0.882	213,646.27	188,505.53
2023	4				1.295	228,039.28	295,352.89

Table 11.19 Mincer–Zarnowitz results for the RTMA model of Amazon annual sales, 2000–2020

Regression term	Est. coefficient	Std error	t-Stat
\multicolumn{4}{c}{$r^2 = 0.989$}			
\multicolumn{4}{c}{Standard error of the estimate = 2877.023}			
Constant	431.1134	406.6908	1.060
Forecasted Sales$_t$	0.9772	0.01177	1.936

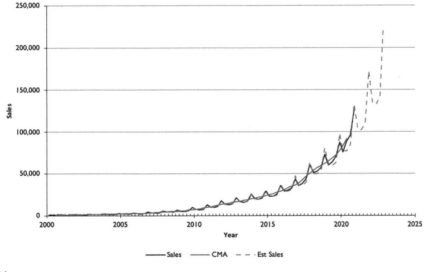

FIGURE 11.21

Amazon Quarterly Sales, 2000–2020, and the Unbiased Multiplicative Seasonality Model

This *t*-stat indicates that the forecasts have predictable errors that are marginally statistically significant and are slightly biased. Thus, the final forecast must be adjusted using the Mincer–Zarnowitz regression equation:

$$Unbiased\ Forecasted\ Sales_t = 431.1134 + 0.9772\ Forecasted\ Sales_t$$

A comparison of the r^2 and SEE from the Mincer–Zarnowitz regression to the r^2 and SEE of the seasonal indicator variable (additive) method show that the RTMA method performed better in this situation. This is because Amazon's seasonality is proportional to the level of sales. Fig. 11.21 shows the graph of actual sales and the unbiased forecast. The fit is excellent.

11.5.3 Summary of the ratio-to-moving-average method

1. Find the **CMA** for each quarter by averaging over the year to smooth out the seasonal effect	$CMA \text{ for } Q3 = \dfrac{(0.5 * Q1) + Q2 + Q3 + Q4 + (0.5 * Q1_2)}{4}$
2. Calculate the **RTMA** to isolate the seasonal effect	$RTMA = \dfrac{Actual\ Sales}{CMA}$
3. Calculate the **Seasonal Index** (ϕ) to provide a relative performance measure of sales across each season	
a. Compare ϕ to RTMA to evaluate performance of each quarter	ϕ = Average RTMAs for each quarter (i.e., all Q1s, all Q2s)
4. Calculate **Seasonally Adjusted Sales** (**SA**), a.k.a. "Deseasonalized Sales," to show what you would expect without any seasonal impact	
a. In other words, removing the seasonal bias	$\dfrac{Actual\ Sales}{\phi}$
5. Estimate the **CMA**; an AR(1) is often a good start	=LINEST(A2:A45,A1:A44,1,1) *Remember to use CTL + Shift + Enter
6. Use the regression equation to find the **Estimated CMA**	
a. Use previous quarter sales to estimate what sales will be in the following quarter	Estimated $CMA_t = \beta_0 + \beta_1 * CMA_{t-1}$ *Remember to use the CMA from the previous quarter (e.g., Estimated $CMA_{Q2} = \beta_0 + \beta_1 * CMA_{Q1}$)
7. Find **Forecasted Sales** by multiplying seasonality times the **Estimated CMA**	$Forecast_t = $ Estimated $CMA_t *$ Seasonal Index
8. Run regression of **Actual Sales** to **Forecasted Sales**	
a. Tests and corrects for biases in the forecasting process b. r^2 indicates how much trend and seasonality account for variation in the data	$Actual_t = \beta_0 + \beta_1\ Forecast_t$
9. Calculate **Upper** and **Lower Confidence Intervals** using regression equation from #8	Upper 95% $= Forecast_t + (1.96 * SEE)$ Lower 95% $= Forecast_t - (1.96 * SEE)$

11.6 Aggregating sales

Quarterly (or monthly) forecasts can be aggregated to provide annual forecasts. The Mincer–Zarnowitz regression can then be used to measure the aggregated forecast's accuracy. Similarly, there are occasions in which disaggregating the annual forecasts can provide accurate quarterly (or monthly) forecasts.

Example 11.7 Aggregating quarterly sales: Amazon annual sales

Aggregate (total) each years' sales and then use the Mincer–Zarnowitz regression to assess Amazon's annual sales.

First, aggregate *Sales* and *Forecasted Sales*, for each year by summing each variable by year as shown in Table 11.20. For example, the forecast for 2021 is the sum of the four quarterly forecasts within 2021:

Continued

$$Sales_{2021} = Unbiased\ Forecasted\ Sales_{2021:1} + Unbiased\ Forecasted\ Sales_{2021:2} +$$
$$Unbiased\ Forecasted\ Sales_{2021:3} + Unbiased\ Forecasted\ Sales_{2021:4}$$

The forecasts in gray are the time periods for which sales were forecasted.
Then calculate the Mincer–Zarnowitz regression:

$$Sales_t = \beta_0 + \beta_1\ SalestForecast$$

Table 11.20 Amazon annual sales, 2001–2020, with forecasted sales = sum of quarterly sales

Year	Sales ($MM)	Est. sales	Unbiased est. sales
2001	3122.43	4657.39	2609.35
2002	3932.94	5335.32	3304.45
2003	5263.70	6594.07	4595.07
2004	6921.12	8249.20	6292.12
2005	8490.00	9946.90	8032.81
2006	10,711.00	11,964.67	10,101.67
2007	14,835.00	15,705.24	13,936.97
2008	19,166.00	20,478.21	18,830.79
2009	24,509.00	25,257.36	23,730.97
2010	34,204.00	34,595.32	33,305.39
2011	48,077.00	47,935.22	46,983.10
2012	61,093.00	62,014.41	61,418.81
2013	74,452.00	75,678.81	75,429.24
2014	88,988.00	90,900.30	91,036.17
2015	107,006.00	108,206.96	108,781.09
2016	135,987.00	136,195.28	137,478.15
2017	177,866.00	174,851.21	177,112.96
2018	232,887.00	232,391.77	236,110.60
2019	280,522.00	281,782.48	286,752.03
2020	386,064.00	371,026.03	378,255.48
2021		487,488.65	497,667.26
2022		631,816.75	645,650.16
2023		819,360.54	837,943.08

Table 11.21 Regression results for Amazon annual sales, 2000–2020, with forecasted sales = sum of quarterly sales

$r^2 = 0.9994$			
Standard error of the estimate = 2656.074			
Regression term	**Est. coefficient**	**Std error**	**t-Stat**
Constant	–2165.980	778.896	–2.78
Forecasted Sales$_t$	1.025	0.006	4.33

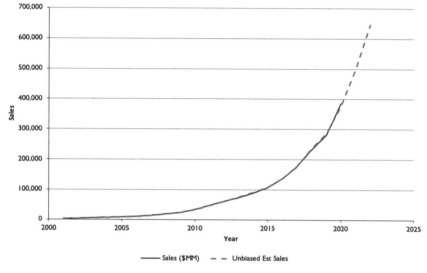

FIGURE 11.22

Amazon Annual Sales, 2000–2020, and the Aggregate Forecast Model

Table 11.22 Comparison of Amazon annual sales forecasts		
Trend model	r^2	**SEE**
Linear	0.7329	56,081.50
Exponential	0.9976	5273.45
AR(1)	0.9948	7912.55
RTMA$_{aggregate}$	0.9994	256.07

These results indicate an excellent fit, but the sales forecasts are biased—that is, they contain predictable errors.

The aggregated sales (*Sales$_t$*) and aggregated sales forecast are shown in Fig. 11.22.

The *t*-stats indicate that the forecasts have predictable errors that are statistically significant and are biased. Thus, the final forecast must be adjusted using the Mincer–Zarnowitz regression equation:

$$Unbiased\ Forecasted\ Sales_t = -2165.980 + 1.025\ Forecasted\ Sales_t$$

To return to the initial idea of the chapter, the comparison of different forecasting methods and model selection, compare the r^2 and SEE for the unbiased linear, exponential, AR(1), and RTMA aggregated models shown in Table 11.22.

Note the improvement in the SEE. That is the general aim of forecasting—to continually minimize the variation in the errors.

11.7 Review of forecasting with regression

Table 11.23 summarizes various regression forecasting models.

Table 11.23 Examples of common regression forecasting models

Name	Form	Example
I. Simple Trend Model	$Y_t = f(t)$	$Y_t = \beta_0 + \beta_1 t$
II. Autoregression AR(n)	$Y_t = f(Y_{t-1}, Y_{t-2} ..., Y_{t-n})$	$Y_t = \beta_0 + \beta_1 Y_{t-1} + ... + \beta_n Y_{t-n}$
III. Structural	$Y_t = f(X_{1t}, X_{2t}, ..., X_{nt})$	$Y_t = \beta_0 + \beta_1 X_{1t} + ... + \beta_n X_{nt}$
IV. Vector Autoregression (VAR)	$Y_t = f(Y_{t-1}, X_{1t-1}, X_{2t-1}, ..., X_{nt-1})$	$Y_t = \beta_{0y} + \beta_{1y} Y_{t-1} + \beta_{2y} X_{1t-1} + ... + \beta_{ny} X_{n-1t-1}$
	$X_{1t} = f(Y_{t-1}, X_{1t-1}, X_{2t-1}, ..., X_{nt-1})$	$X_{1t} = \beta_{0X1} + \beta_{1X1} Y_{t-1} + \beta_{2X1} X_{1t-1} + ... + \beta_{nX1} X_{n-1t-1}$
	$X_{nt} = f(Y_{t-1}, X_{1t-1}, X_{2t-1}, ..., X_{nt-1})$	$X_{nt} = \beta_{0Xn} + \beta_{1Xn} Y_{t-1} + \beta_{2Xn} X_{1t-1} + ... + \beta_{nXn} X_{n-1t-1}$

Exercise Set 11: Forecasting

1. A company that sells tanks of propane for grilling is in the middle of their quarterly budgeting process. The past 10 quarters of budgeted and actual expenditures (in $MM) for each quarter are listed in Table 11.24.

Table 11.24 Ten quarters of budgeted and actual expenditures

Year	Quarter	Budget ($MM)	Actual ($MM)
2019	1	41.50	47.09
2019	2	50.62	58.54
2019	3	49.59	56.72
2019	4	53.92	62.77
2020	1	61.75	68.90
2020	2	60.90	69.69
2020	3	59.50	67.31
2020	4	64.34	74.67
2021	1	64.75	75.11
2021	2	69.88	78.40

    a. Forecast the upcoming expenditures.
    b. Evaluate the previous expenditures.
    c. Evaluate the upcoming expenditures.
    d. Compute the likelihood that expenditures will exceed $80,000,000 for the next quarter.
2. Use the quarterly sales data in Table 11.25 to forecast the next year's sales.
3. Obtain entertainment per US consumer unit:

Table 11.25 Fifteen quarters of sales		
Year	Quarter	Sales ($MM)
2018	1	438
2018	2	432
2018	3	591
2018	4	475
2019	1	459
2019	2	506
2019	3	736
2019	4	542
2019	1	676
2019	2	645
2019	3	1084
2019	4	819
2021	1	710
2021	2	817
2021	3	1073

a. Forecast entertainment per consumer unit for the next 3 years.
b. What other data could you use to improve the forecasts?
c. List several situations in which you could use these results in decision analysis frameworks.
4. Find US retail sales (US Census Bureau website) for the previous 10 years (including this year). Forecast retail sales for the next 12 months.
5. Find US Housing Starts (US Census Bureau website), and forecast Housing Starts for the next 12 months.
6. Obtain the most recent quarterly revenue (in billions) for PepsiCo, and append it to the data in Table 11.26.
  a. Forecast annual sales for the next 3 years.
  b. Forecast quarterly sales for the next 3 years.
  c. What other data could you use to improve sales forecasts?
  d. List several managerial situations in which you could use these results in decision analysis frameworks.
7. Obtain the most recent Ford auto sales (in billions) data, and append it to the data in Table 11.27.
  a. Forecast annual sales for the next 3 years.
  b. Forecast quarterly sales for the next 3 years.
  c. What other data could you use to improve sales forecasts?
  d. List several managerial situations in which you could use these results in decision analysis frameworks.

Table 11.26 PepsiCo quarterly revenue (in billions)

Year	Q1	Q2	Q3	Q4
2000	4.191	7.000	6.421	7.867
2001	4.700	5.865	5.981	6.966
2002	5.311	6.119	6.300	7.382
2003	5.530	6.538	6.830	8.073
2004	6.131	7.070	7.257	8.803
2005	6.585	7.697	8.184	10.096
2006	6.719	8.714	9.134	10.570
2007	7.350	9.607	10.171	12.346
2008	8.333	10.945	11.244	12.729
2009	8.263	10.592	11.080	13.297
2010	9.368	14.801	15.514	18.155
2011	11.937	16.827	17.582	20.158
2012	12.428	16.458	16.652	19.954
2013	12.581	16.807	16.909	20.118
2014	12.623	16.894	17.218	19.948
2015	12.217	15.923	16.331	18.585
2016	11.862	15.395	16.027	19.515
2017	12.049	15.710	16.240	19.526
2018	12.562	16.090	16.485	19.524
2019	12.884	16.449	17.188	20.640
2020	13.881	15.945	18.091	22.455

Table 11.27 Ford quarterly auto sales (in billions)

Year	Q1	Q2	Q3	Q4
2000	42.904	44.499	40.055	42.600
2001	42.446	41.860	35.737	40.711
2002	39.461	42.207	39.338	41.580
2003	40.815	40.491	36.973	46.059
2004	44.723	42.873	39.121	44.929
2005	45.136	44.548	40.510	46.641
2006	40.789	41.878	37.095	40.303
2007	43.005	44.242	41.078	42.247
2008	43.292	41.102	31.746	27.444
2009	24.390	26.810	30.272	34.811
2010	31.566	35.067	29.893	32.428
2011	33.114	35.527	33.047	33.917
2012	32.445	33.211	32.172	35.731
2013	35.649	37.923	35.775	37.570
2014	35.876	37.411	34.920	35.870
2015	33.900	37.263	38.144	40.251
2016	37.718	39.485	35.943	38.654
2017	39.146	39.853	36.451	41.326
2018	41.959	38.920	37.666	41.793
2019	40.342	38.853	36.990	39.715
2020	34.320	19.371	37.501	35.952

Cases

Joseph, Patterson, and Thomas

Margaret Jones was involved in a new project in her second year with the management consulting firm of Joseph, Patterson, and Thomas (JPT). It was a common project in which she was expected to make some money-saving recommendations and then find the follow-on project to produce next month's billable days.

The client was an organization of magazine publishers that had become aware of the large amounts of money being wasted printing copies that were not sold. Industry practice had been always to print and deliver to newsstands more magazines than would be needed. The practice ensured that every customer requesting a copy at the newsstand could have one, thereby keeping numbers high for both newsstand circulation and advertising revenues. It also produced a phenomenal number of unsold copies. JPT was hired to investigate this practice and make some recommendations for improved procedures.

Unsold magazines were generally worthless when the next issue hit the newsstand. Ms. Jones decided to begin by looking at one magazine, *Traditional Home*. She knew *Traditional Home* magazine sold for $4.95 at the newsstand, but she only had an estimate of the variable costs to produce the magazine ($1.70), as well as the price to the wholesaler ($2.20) and the price from the wholesaler to the newsstand operator ($3.50). There was no risk to the retailer or the wholesaler because they could return for full price any magazines not sold.

Another related issue was the establishment of an annual rate base. This was the number of copies of *Traditional Home* that were guaranteed to sell each month and was used to determine the advertising rates. If they did not meet the base value, they would refund an amount proportional to the shortage. If they exceeded the base, they were not able to go back and collect more advertising revenues. This value was set each year for the entire year.

Ms. Jones thought saving money on production would be assured, provided she could find a way to forecast each issue's sales. She started on this task by obtaining data on total circulation of *Traditional Home* over the past 8½ years from the Publisher's Statement to the Audit Bureau of Circulation.

Ms. Jones pondered how time patterns in past sales might help her predict the sales of a future issue. *Traditional Home* was not a magazine that she read, but she had seen it while waiting for the dentist, and her aunt had it in her house. She knew that the December issue greatly increased newsstand sales because of its holiday recipes and gift-giving ideas. The January issue always seemed to be low because people evidently felt like they had overspent and overeaten during the holidays and were trying to cut back. Changes in the interest of purchasers and the content of the magazine were also important forces that could gradually move the sales up or down over time. Table 11.28 lists the circulation of *Traditional Home* for the previous 9 years.

Just as Jones was going to dive into the calculations, a representative from *Traditional Home* magazine called and said they had just been given the opportunity to raise their advertising rate base from its current level of 4.87 million copies. The representative was concerned about setting the rate too low, in which case there would be considerable lost revenues, and setting the rate too high, in which case there would be considerable refunds to advertisers. The rate base was used as follows.

Advertising revenue equaled $1*the rate base, but there was a contingent penalty. If circulation was less than the rate base, they must make up the advertising in an amount equal to $1.25 in value for every impression they were off.

The new rate base talked about was 5.1 million, and again the decision rested upon a forecast of circulation. Ms. Jones knew that she would quickly have to find the best method of forecasting based on the data she had. Then she would test the method the next year.

Tuscany Kitchens

Swain Food Products (SFP) markets a variety of pastas under the brand name Tuscany Kitchens. These pastas come in many sizes and shapes but are all made from the same ingredients. The Tuscany Kitchens pasta is an established brand, and although its sales are not large, it is a consistently profitable item. Susan Franklin has just joined SFP as the brand manager, and the pasta product was assigned to her. Her first task is to prepare a sales forecast and a budget for promotion and advertising for the next year. She collected the historical data shown in Table 11.29. The data included sales of the pasta and the expenditures for promotion and advertising over the past 24 quarters, all in thousands of dollars. Also included is an index of general economic conditions in the pasta market area. High values of the index indicate good economic times.

Table 11.28 Monthly circulation for _Traditional Home_ (in millions)

Month	Year 1	Year 2	Year 3	Year 4	Year 5	Year 6	Year 7	Year 8	Year 9
January		5.023173	5.350502	5.073651	5.335737	5.198585	5.023818	5.133963	5.159840
February		5.333352	5.371371	5.553245	5.618540	5.501741	5.099829	5.180897	5.274075
March		5.224234	5.327700	5.439363	5.604606	5.329592	5.253739	5.161222	5.179002
April		5.079207	5.269993	5.363948	5.343116	5.322838	5.138210	5.174238	5.269295
May		5.167277	5.240438	5.367404	5.294990	5.178815	5.251664	5.047775	5.005048
June		5.006445	5.273266	5.316957	5.327995	5.247590	5.450869	5.152063	5.166569
July	5.264165	5.150974	5.439920	5.412745	5.177176	5.194827	5.022522	5.001222	5.068848
August	5.313127	5.180346	5.378584	5.387779	5.290109	5.118408	5.206132	5.232314	5.007388
September	5.117969	5.223467	5.329516	5.439224	5.449099	5.291564	5.042725	5.235207	5.265191
October	5.098771	5.153303	5.292129	5.341392	5.344570	5.047946	5.096277	5.009584	5.046595
November	5.187708	5.247109	5.378127	5.396853	5.334053	5.105056	5.067717	5.352370	5.300978
December	5.645295	5.789798	5.736465	5.961612	5.763516	5.448542	5.508198	5.498755	5.526153

Table 11.29 Tuscany Kitchens pasta sales data (in thousands)				
Quarter	Sales ($)	Promotion ($)	Advertising ($)	Index
1	2775.96	85.80	165.00	100
2	2236.25	122.10	198.00	102
3	2192.03	0.00	247.50	104
4	3232.68	0.00	313.50	104
5	3294.06	0.00	214.50	104
6	3869.91	174.90	115.50	100
7	2129.82	117.15	66.00	98
8	2011.19	21.45	33.00	96
9	2137.91	0.00	33.00	98
10	2051.28	46.20	165.00	103
11	3318.15	249.15	165.00	105
12	3381.02	275.55	181.50	107
13	2664.09	217.80	33.00	107
14	1252.68	23.10	181.50	107
15	1810.22	0.00	33.00	108
16	1695.38	0.00	16.50	105
17	2386.23	0.00	247.50	103
18	2832.39	75.90	264.00	108
19	2225.85	97.35	0.00	110
20	1349.87	0.00	82.50	112
21	2382.60	95.70	49.50	113
22	3449.82	207.90	297.00	112
23	3561.86	232.65	198.00	113
24	1885.46	62.70	214.50	114

Note: The sales/quarterly sales of Tuscany Kitchens pasta, promotion/funds spent on promotion activities in the quarter, advertising/funds spent on advertising during the quarter, and index/economic index of general economic conditions in the Tuscany Kitchens market area were calculated by the SFP economic research department.

Tuscany Kitchens pasta is sold through food brokers in Atlanta, Chicago, New York, Seattle, and San Francisco. Advertising expenditures are directed at the consumer in magazines such as *Southern Living* and *Cooking Light* and in newspapers. Promotion expenditures, however, are directed at the food broker or store manager. These consist of special deals such as getting a fifth case free if four are purchased, short-term increases in broker commissions, or sales contests among broker salespeople (with prizes like trips to Hawaii).

Ms. Franklin was quite puzzled by the great variability in the sales of pasta from quarter to quarter, and at the great variations in past expenditures for promotion and advertising. On inquiry, the sales vice president explained that there was a general policy that the company should either promote or advertise in each quarter but not both. However, there had been a long-standing dispute in the company about the relative effectiveness of promotion and advertising on pasta sales. Ms. Franklin's predecessors had tried various strategies, but no one had been able to determine what had or had not been successful. Some skeptics felt that both promotion and advertising expenditures were wasted, since neither seemed to affect sales. Others felt that promotion was effective, but the effect was merely to reduce future sales. In other words, they felt that brokers and store managers bought heavily during promotion periods and then did not order in subsequent periods until inventories were back to normal. The effect of advertising was equally confusing since sales seemed to vary greatly even during periods when advertising was relatively constant. For example, in the last two quarters in the data shown in Table 11.29 (quarters 23 and 24), advertising had been about the same ($198,000 and $214,500, respectively), but sales were $3,561,860 in one quarter and $1,885,460 in the other.

If this was not confusing enough, the economist in the economic analysis department insisted that pasta was a countercyclical product, meaning that it sold better in bad times than in good. His theory was that pasta was a less expensive meal than other meals, and people ate more of it during tough times. Furthermore, he felt that there was a seasonal pattern in sales, with more being sold during colder months than in the summer.

Oat Loops

Kenny Herbert, general sales manager of the Breakfast Foods Division of Harmony Foods Inc., was having difficulty in forecasting the sales of Oat Loops. Oat Loops was a ready-to-eat breakfast cereal with an important share of the market. It was also the major product in those company plants where it was manufactured. Mr. Herbert was responsible for the sales forecasts from which production schedules were prepared.

In recent months, actual Oat Loops sales had varied from 50% to 200% of his forecast. Most of his difficulty in preparing forecasts arose from the great variability in historical sales; that variability can easily be seen in Table 11.30. Since sales were debited on the day of shipment, Table 11.30 presents unit shipments as well as sales.

Manufacturing problems

Accuracy in production forecasts was essential for the health of the entire business. The individual plant managers received these forecast schedules and certified their ability to meet them. Acceptance of a schedule by a plant manager represented a "promise" to deliver; crews and machines were assigned, materials ordered, and storage space allocated to meet the schedule.

Schedule changes were expensive. On the one hand, the lead time on raw material orders was several weeks, so ordering too little caused shortages that were expensive in lost production time and disappointed customers. On the other hand, after schedule reductions, the raw material could not be used as fast as it arrived. Storage space was short, so some of the material had to be left on the truck, railroad car, or barge in which it had been shipped. The resultant tie-up of these vehicles was extremely expensive in demurrage charges. Demurrage charges are assessments made by a carrier against a consignee for delays in unloading (or the initiation of unloading) of a transport vehicle. Typically, there is an allowance of 1 free hour in excess of normal unloading time for trucks. Rail cars and barges have typical allowances of 3 days and 1 day, respectively, including unloading time.

Even more important than the storage problem was the problem of efficient workforce utilization. Production schedules were kept tight to avoid unnecessary costs. Overtime was avoided because it was expensive and interfered with

Table 11.30 Sales of Oat Loops (standard cases)

Month	Year 1	Year 2	Year 3	Year 4
January	425,075	629,404	655,748	455,136
February	315,305	263,467	270,483	247,570
March	432,101	468,612	429,480	732,005
April	357,191	313,221	260,458	357,107
May	347,874	444,404	528,210	453,156
June	435,529	386,986	379,856	320,103
July	299,403	414,314	472,058	451,779
August	296,505	253,493	254,516	249,482
September	426,701	484,365	551,354	744,583
October	329,722	305,989	335,826	421,186
November	281,783	315,407	320,408	397,367
December	166,391	182,784	276,901	269,096

weekend maintenance. The labor force was highly skilled and difficult to increase in the short run. Layoffs, however, were avoided to preserve the skills of the crew. This job security resulted in a high level of employee morale and was an important part of the company's labor policy. Thus, the production manager had to try to make production schedules efficient for a constant-sized work force and to use as little overtime as possible.

Advertising expenditures

Accuracy in production forecasts was essential for the health of the entire business. Most of the advertising dollars for Oat Loops were spent on children's network shows broadcast on Saturday morning, a time for which was purchased up to a year in advance. This time was relatively expensive, costing $280,000 for a half-minute commercial, but it was the opinion of all the brand managers in the Breakfast Food Division that these network programs delivered the best value for each advertising dollar spent. This opinion was based upon cost per million messages delivered, viewer-recall scores, and measures of audience composition.

It was the policy of Harmony Foods, as at many companies, to budget advertising expenditures at a fixed amount per unit sold. Each year monthly budgets for advertising were established based on forecast sales. Brand managers tended to contract for time on network programs to the limit of their budget allowance. When shipments ran high, however, brand managers tended to increase advertising expenditures to the level warranted by the actual sales. In such circumstances, they would seek contracts for time from other brand managers who were shipping below budget. Failing this, they would seek network time through the agencies, or if such time were unavailable, they would seek spot advertising as close to prime program time as possible. Thus, unplanned advertising expenditures could result in the use of time that gave lower value per advertising dollar spent than did the best network time.

Budgets and controls

The errors in forecasts were also the subject of complaints from the controller of the Breakfast Foods Division. Each brand prepared a budget based on forecasted shipments. This budget "promised" a contribution to division overhead and profits. Long-term dividend policy and corporate expansion plans were based in part on these forecasts. Regular quarterly increases in earnings over prior years had resulted in a high price–earnings ratio for the company. Since the market value of the common stock was a chief interest of the owners, profit planning was an important part of the management control system.

The discretionary "overspending" on advertising noted earlier tended to amplify the problems of profit planning. These expenditures did not have budgetary approval, and until a new "budget base" (sales forecast) for the fiscal year was approved at all levels, such overspending was merely borrowing ahead on the current fiscal year. The controller's office charged only the budgeted advertising to sales in each quarter and carried the excess over, since it was unauthorized. This procedure resulted in spurious accounting profits in those quarters with sales in excess of forecast, with counterbalancing reductions in profit in subsequent quarters.

The extent to which profits could be affected by deferred advertising expenditures had been demonstrated in the past fiscal year. Oat Loops, along with several other brands, had overspent extensively in the early quarters; as a result, divisional earnings for the fourth quarter were more than $2 million below corporate expectations. The divisional manager, as well as his sales manager, brand managers, and controller, had felt very uncomfortable in the meetings and conferences that had been held because of this shortage of reported profits. The extra profits reported in earlier quarters had offset shortages of other divisions, but in the final quarter there had been no division to offset the Breakfast Foods shortage.

Brand manager

Marlon Carson, the brand manager for Oat Loops, prepared his brand's "budget base," or set of monthly, quarterly, and annual forecasts that governed monthly advertising and promotional expenditures. These forecasts, along with forecasts from the division's other brand managers, were submitted to Mr. Herbert for his approval. This approval was necessary because, in a given month, the sales force could support the promotions of only a limited number of brands. Once approved, the brand managers' forecasts served as the basis of the "official" forecasts made by Mr. Herbert.

The use of the brand managers' forecasts as the basis for the sales manager's official forecasts (and thus, the basis for production scheduling) required mutual confidence and understanding. From the sales manager came information on Harmony Food's (and the competitors') activity and pricing at the store level. From the brand manager came knowledge of market trends for his brand and its competitors. The brand manager also kept records of all available market research reports on his and similar brands and was aware of any package design and product formulations under development.

As brand manager, Mr. Carson knew that the responsibility for improving the reliability of sales forecasts for Oat Loops rested with him. After talking to analysts in the market research, systems analysis, and business analytics departments, he concluded that better forecasts were possible, and Maura Haas of the business analytics department offered to work with him on the project. Mr. Carson received enthusiastic support for his planned undertaking from both the sales manager and the controller. Although such projects were outside the normal scope of a brand manager's duties, Mr. Carson recognized the opportunity to find a solution to his forecasting problem that would have company-wide application.

Factors Affecting Sales

Mr. Carson and Ms. Haas discussed at great length the factors that influenced sales. A 12-month moving average of the data in Table 11.30 indicated a long-term rising trend in sales. This trend confirmed the A.C. Nielsen store audit, which reported a small but steady rise in market share for Oat Loops, plus a steady rise for the commodity group to which Oat Loops belonged.

In addition to trend, Mr. Carson felt that seasonal factors might be important. In November and December, sales slowed down as inventory levels among stores and jobbers were drawn down for year-end inventories. Summer sales were often low because of plant shutdowns and sales vacations. There were fewer selling days in February. Salespersons often started new fiscal years with a burst of energy to get in a good quota position for the rest of the year.

Nonmedia promotions, which represented about 25% of the advertising budget for Oat Loops, were considered to have a very strong influence on sales. Such promotions were of two main types. Promotions targeted directly at the consumer were called *consumer packs*, so named because the consumer was reimbursed in some way for each package of Oat Loops that was purchased. Promotions that sought to increase sales by increasing the degree to which the brand was "pushed" by dealers were called *dealer allowances*, so called because allowances were made to dealers to compensate them for expenditures incurred in promoting Oat Loops. Consumer packs and dealer allowances were offered two or three times per year during different canvass periods. (A sales canvass period is the time required for salespersons to make a complete round of all customers in their assigned areas. Harmony Foods scheduled 10 (5-week) canvass periods each year. The remaining 2 weeks, one at midsummer and one at year-end, were for holidays and vacations.)

Consumer packs

Consumer packs usually took the form of a $0.50-per-package reduction in the price paid by the consumer. The offer could also take the form of a coupon, an enclosed premium, or a mail-in offer, but based on the results of consumer-panel tests of all such offers, Carson was confident that each of these forms was roughly equivalent to the $0.25 price reduction in its return to the brand. Consequently, he decided to group all forms of consumer packs together.

Consumer packs, along with supporting advertising material and special cartons, were produced ahead of the assigned canvass period for shipment throughout the 5-week period. Any packs not shipped within this period would be allocated among salespersons for shipment in periods in which no consumer promotion was officially scheduled. From a study of historical data covering a number of consumer packs, Ms. Haas found that approximately 35% of a consumer-pack offering moved out during the first week, 25% during the second week, 15% during the third week, and approximately 10% during each of the fourth and last weeks of the canvass periods. Approximately 5% was shipped after the promotional period was over (Table 11.31). Since they saw no reason for this historical pattern to change, Ms. Haas and Mr. Carson were confident that they could predict, with quite reasonable accuracy, the monthly consumer-pack shipments that would result from a given promotion undertaken in the future.

The impact of consumer packs on total shipments was, of course, favorable in the month in which the consumer packs were actually shipped, but since the consumer ate Oat Loops at a more or less constant rate over time, Mr. Carson was convinced that part of this increase in total shipments was the result of inventory buildups on the part of jobbers, stores, and consumers. Thus, it seemed reasonable to expect that consumer packs might have a negative impact on total shipments as these excess inventories were depleted in the first and possibly the second month after the packs were shipped.

Dealer allowances

Sales seemed even more sensitive to allowances offered to dealers for cooperative promotional efforts. These allowances were provided to participating dealers via a $1 to $2 per case discount on their purchases during the canvass period of the allowance.

The total expenditure for dealer allowances during a given promotional canvass period was budgeted in advance. As with consumer packs, any "unspent" allowances would be allocated to salespersons for disbursement after the

Table 11.31 Consumer packs (standard shipping cases)[a]

Month	Year 1	Year 2	Year 3	Year 4	Year 5
January	0	75,253	548,704	544,807	299,781
February	0	15,036	52,819	43,704	21,218
March	0	134,440	2793	5740	157
April	0	119,740	27,749	9614	12,961
May	15,012	135,590	21,887	1507	333,529
June	62,337	189,636	1110	13,620	178,105
July	4022	9308	436	101,179	315,564
August	3130	41,099	1407	80,309	80,206
September	422	9391	376,650	335,768	5940
October	0	942	122,906	91,710	36,819
November	5	1818	15,138	9856	234,562
December	220	672	5532	107,172	71,881

[a]One case contains 24 packs.

Table 11.32 Dealer allowances (in dollars)

Month	Year 1	Year 2	Year 3	Year 4	Year 5
January	198,388	228,866	0	332,356	16,266
February	76,148	127,198	157,598	268,412	11,734
March	78,820	129,976	351,812	275,780	225,172
April	123,032	133,684	99,232	75,040	250,452
May	167,858	79,252	239,440	290,400	0
June	163,156	215,006	228,586	217,540	0
July	131,642	194,258	354,740	180,572	23,052
August	244,338	112,808	22,690	48,922	46,126
September	16,964	521,152	14,040	15,186	243,496
October	112,014	487,046	55,760	75,162	188,278
November	152,002	150,946	133,600	146,522	188,278
December	176,436	38,074	177,152	81,394	276,268

promotional period was over. The actual weekly expenditures resulting from these allowances were found to follow approximately the same pattern as was found for the shipment of consumer packs, and consequently Mr. Carson felt that the monthly expenditures resulting from any given schedule of future dealer allowances could also be predicted with reasonable accuracy.

Promotional efforts by dealers took the form of "giant spectacular end-of-aisle displays," newspaper ads, coupons, or fliers, among others. The extent to which such efforts could affect sales is illustrated by the fact that an end-of-aisle display located near a cash register could give an average of 5 weeks' business in a single weekend. As with special packs, however, Mr. Carson believed that much of the resulting sales increase was attributable to inventory buildups, and therefore he expected reactions to these buildups as late as 2 months after the initial sales increase. Actual expenditures made for dealer allowances over the past 5 years are shown in Table 11.32.

Conclusion

Mr. Carson and Ms. Haas felt that they had identified, to the best of their ability, the most important factors affecting sales. They knew that competitive advertising and price moves were important but unpredictable, and they wished to restrict their model to those variables that could be measured or predicted in advance.

Ms. Haas agreed to formulate the model, construct the data, and write an explanation of how the solution of the model could be used to evaluate promotion strategies, as well as to forecast sales and shipments. Mr. Carson and Ms. Haas would then join in planning a presentation to divisional managers.

Alexander Hotel room forecasting

"A hotel room is a perishable good. If it is vacant for one night, the revenue is lost forever." Anne Williams was commenting on the issue of capacity utilization in the hotel business. "On the other hand, the customer is king with us. We go to great pains to avoid telling a customer with a reservation at the front desk that we don't have a room for him in the hotel."

As reservation manager of the Alexander Hotel, Ms. Williams faced this trade-off constantly. To complicate the matter, customers often booked reservations and then failed to show, or canceled reservations just before their expected arrival. In addition, some guests stayed over in the hotel extra days beyond their original reservation and others checked out early. A key aspect of dealing with the capacity management problem was having a good forecast of how many rooms would be needed on any future date. It was Ms. Williams's responsibility to prepare a forecast on Tuesday afternoon of the number of rooms that would be occupied each day of the next week (Saturday through Friday). This forecast was used by almost every department within the hotel for a variety of purposes; now she needed the forecast for a decision in her own department.

The Alexander Hotel

The Alexander Hotel was a large downtown business hotel with 1877 rooms and abundant meeting space for groups and conventions. Management of the Alexander Hotel regularly reported occupancy and revenue performance.

Hotel managers were rewarded for their ability to meet targets for occupancy and revenue. Ms. Williams could not remember a time when the targets went down, but she had seen them go up in the 2 years since she took the job as reservation manager. The hotel managers were continuously comparing forecasts of performance against these targets. In addition to overseeing the reservations office with eight reservationists, Ms. Williams prepared the week-ahead forecast and presented it on Tuesday afternoon to other department managers in the hotel. The forecast was used to schedule, for example, daily work assignments for housekeeping personnel, the clerks at the front desk, restaurant personnel, and others. It also played a role in purchasing, revenue, and cost planning.

Overbooking

Currently, however, Ms. Williams needed her forecast to know how to treat an opportunity that was developing for next Saturday. It was Tuesday, August 18, and Ms. William's forecasts were due by mid-afternoon for Saturday, August 23, through Friday, August 29. Although 1839 rooms were reserved already for Saturday, Ms. Williams had just received a request from a tour company for as many as 60 more rooms for that night. The tour company would take any number of rooms less than 60 that Ms. Williams would provide, but no more than 60. Normally, Ms. Williams would be ecstatic about such a request: selling out the house for a business hotel on a Saturday would be a real coup. The request, in its entirety, put reservations above the capacity of the hotel. Weekend nights produced a lot of "no-show" reservations. Thus, a reservation on the books Tuesday was not the same as the "head in the bed" on Saturday. "Chances are good we still wouldn't have a full house on Saturday," Ms. Williams thought out loud. "But if everybody came and someone was denied a room due to overbooking, I would certainly hear about it, and maybe the management would also!"

Ms. Williams considered the trade-off between a vacant room and denying a customer a room. The contribution margin from a room was about $90 since the low variable costs arose primarily from cleaning the room and check-in/check-out. However, if a guest with a reservation was denied a room at the Alexander Hotel, the front desk would find a comparable room somewhere in the city, transport the guest there, and provide some gratuity, such as a fruit basket, in consideration for the inconvenience. If the customer were a Marquis cardholder (a frequent guest staying more than 45 nights a year in the hotel), he or she would receive $200 cash plus the next two stays at the Alexander Hotel free. Ms. Williams was not sure how to put a cost figure on a denied room; in her judgment, it should be valued, goodwill and all, at about twice the contribution figure.

Table 11.33 First 3 weeks of demand data

Week	DOW indicator	Demand	Tuesday bookings	Pickup ratio	DOW index
1	1	1470	1512	0.972	0.868
	2	870	864	1.007	0.918
	3	986	827	1.192	0.977
	4	1247	952	1.310	1.021
	5	1109	740	1.499	1.067
	6	1197	908	1.318	1.104
	7	1500	1311	1.144	1.045
2	1	1854	2034	0.912	0.868
	2	1489	1584	0.940	0.918
	3	1792	1682	1.065	0.977
	4	1708	1684	1.014	1.021
	5	1787	1600	1.117	1.067
	6	1314	1077	1.220	1.104
	7	1136	956	1.188	1.045
3	1	1537	1455	1.056	0.868
	2	1132	1001	1.131	0.918
	3	1368	1131	1.210	0.977
	4	1488	1151	1.293	1.021
	5	1392	942	1.478	1.067
	6	1321	884	1.494	1.104
	7	1469	1315	1.117	1.045

Note: The full data set contains 98 weeks of demand data.

Forecasting

Ms. Williams focused on getting a good forecast for Saturday, August 20, and making a decision on whether to accept the additional reservations for that day. She had historical data on demand for rooms in the hotel; Table 11.33 shows 3 weeks of demand for the dates starting with Saturday, May 21. (Additional weeks are contained in the accompanying spreadsheet; thus, Saturday, August 20, was the beginning of week 14 in this database.) "Demand" figures (third column) included the number of turned-down requests for a reservation on a night when the hotel had stopped taking reservations because of capacity plus the number of rooms actually occupied that night. Also included in Table 11.33 is the number of rooms booked (fourth column) as of the Tuesday morning of the week prior to each date. (Note that this Tuesday precedes a date by a number of days that depends on the date's day of week. It is 4 days ahead of a Saturday date, 7 days ahead of a Tuesday, and 10 days ahead of a Friday. Also note that on a Tuesday morning, actual demand is known for Monday night but not for Tuesday night.)

Ms. Williams had calculated pickup ratios for each date where actual demand was known in Table 11.33 (fifth column). Between a Tuesday 1 week ahead and any date, new reservations were added, reservations were canceled, some reservations were extended to more nights, some were shortened, and some resulted in no shows. The net effect was a final demand that might be larger than Tuesday bookings (a pickup ratio > 1.0) or smaller than Tuesday bookings (a pickup ratio < 1.0). Ms. Williams looked at her forecasting task as one of predicting the pickup ratio. With a good forecast of pickup ratio, she could simply multiply by Tuesday bookings to obtain a forecast of demand.

From her earliest experience in a hotel, Ms. Williams was aware that the day of the week (DOW; DOW indicator: 1 = Saturday, 2 = Sunday, 3 = Monday, 4 = Tuesday, 5 = Wednesday, 6 = Thursday, 7 = Friday) made a lot of difference in demand for rooms; her recent experience in reservations suggested that it was key in forecasting pickup ratios. Downtown business hotels, like Alexander Hotel, tended to be busiest in the middle of the workweek (Tuesday, Wednesday, Thursday) and light on the weekends. Using the data in her spreadsheet, she had calculated a DOW index (shown in the sixth column of Table 11.33) for the pickup ratio during each DOW based upon each week's average. Thus, for example, the average pickup ratio for Saturday is about 86.8% of the average pickup ratio for all DOWs. Her plan was to adjust the data for this DOW effect by dividing each pickup ratio by this factor. This adjustment would take out the DOW effect and put the pickup ratios on the same footing. Then she could use the stream of adjusted pickup ratios to forecast Saturday's adjusted pickup ratio. To do this, she needed to think about how to level out the peaks and valleys of demand, which she thought from experience could not be forecasted. Once she had this forecast of adjusted pickup ratio, then she could multiply it by the Saturday DOW index to get back to an unadjusted pickup ratio. "Let's get on with it," she said to herself. "I need to get an answer back on that request for 60 reservations."

Thomas' Department Store

Thomas' Department Store, located in Wilmington, North Carolina, suffered heavy damage when Hurricane Alex struck in early August. The store was closed for 5 months (August through December). During this time, the department store lost a significant portion of sales. The management believed that because of back-to-school sales and holiday sales, the store could have lost as much as half a year's revenue. Furthermore, other stores reported higher than average sales after the storm as residents replaced damaged clothing and furnishings.

In anticipation of a settlement with the insurance company, Thomas' needs a reliable estimate of the amount of lost sales during the time the store was closed. Two key issues must be resolved: (1) the amount of sales Thomas' would have made if the hurricane had not struck and (2) whether Thomas' is entitled to any compensation for excess sales due to increased business activity after the storm. More than $8 billion in federal disaster relief and insurance money came into the county, resulting in increased sales at department stores and numerous other businesses.

Table 11.34 gives Thomas' sales data for the 47 months preceding the storm. Table 11.35 reports total sales for the 47 months preceding the storm for all department stores in the county, as well as the total sales in the county for the 5 months Thomas' was closed.

To perform a viable settlement valuation, the insurance company has access to the same sales information and is unlikely to get the same valuation as Thomas'. If the insurance company's valuation of lost sales is not satisfactory, there

Table 11.34 Thomas' Department Store sales (in millions)

Month	Year 1	Year 2	Year 3	Year 4	Year 5
January		1.45	2.31	2.31	2.56
February		1.80	1.89	1.99	2.28
March		2.03	2.02	2.42	2.69
April		1.99	2.23	2.45	2.48
May		2.32	2.39	2.57	2.73
June		2.20	2.14	2.42	2.37
July		2.13	2.27	2.40	2.31
August		2.43	2.21	2.50	
September	1.71	1.90	1.89	2.09	
October	1.90	2.13	2.29	2.54	
November	2.74	2.56	2.83	2.97	
December	4.20	4.16	4.04	4.35	

Table 11.35 County-Wide Department Store Sales (in millions)

Month	Year 1	Year 2	Year 3	Year 4	Year 5
January		46.80	46.80	43.80	48.00
February		48.00	48.60	45.60	51.60
March		60.00	59.40	57.60	57.60
April		57.60	58.20	53.40	58.20
May		61.80	60.60	56.40	60.00
June		58.20	55.20	52.80	57.00
July		56.40	51.00	54.00	57.60
August		63.00	58.80	60.60	61.80
September	55.80	57.60	49.80	47.40	69.00
October	56.40	53.40	54.60	54.60	75.00
November	71.40	71.40	65.40	67.80	85.20
December	117.60	114.00	102.00	100.20	121.80

is an opportunity to take the settlement valuation to arbitration. The first step of the arbitration process is a summary judgment in which the arbitrator will decide whether to hear the case. It will cost Thomas' $18,000 in fees to prepare for summary judgment, and Thomas' estimates that there is 90% chance that the arbitrator will decide to hear the case and a 10% chance that the case will be dismissed. If the case is dismissed, it is likely that the insurance company's valuation will have to be accepted. If the case is heard, Thomas' best guess is that there is about a two out of three chance that Thomas' value will be accepted. The arbitration hearing will cost an additional $50,000 in lawyer fees.

Constrained linear optimization

12

There are always limitations . . .

True optimization is the revolutionary contribution of modern research to decision processes.
—**George Dantzig (Developer of the Simplex Algorithm)**

Chapter outline

Introduction

Prescriptive analytics are used to decide, based upon the predictive models, the best (optimum) decisions to make. Fig. 12.1 shows the typical stages of business analytics. Note that decision making provides the managerial direction and actions of the prescriptive analytics stage.

Many decision-making situations are subject to limited resources. These limitations include deadlines (limited time), budgets (limited financial resources), raw materials, advertising time and space, and employee capacity. Limitations such as these are expressed mathematically using equations known as **constraints**. Decisions that are subject to such limitations are known as **constrained optimization** problems and form a core segment of prescriptive analytics. When the constraints and the equation used to compute the managerial objective are linear, the decision problem is a **constrained linear optimization** problem.

FIGURE 12.1

Stages of Business Analytics

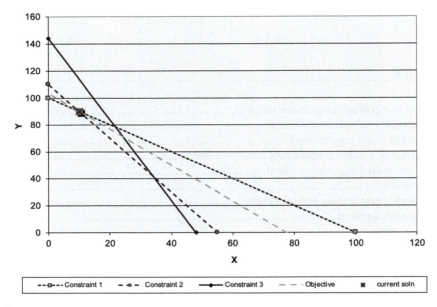

FIGURE 12.2

Graph of the Linear Constrained Optimization Problem

12.1 Overview of constrained linear optimization

One method of solving constrained linear optimization problems is *linear programming*. In this context, the term *programming* is not used to describe a set of computer instructions. Instead, it is an outdated word formerly used by mathematicians to describe the process of setting up and solving a mathematical problem. Linear programming is a process used to optimize (maximize or minimize) a linear objective function comprised of decision variables (algebraic unknowns) subject to a set of linear constraint equations. As an example from business, linear programming is used by airlines to determine the optimum prices and routes to maximize profit subject to limited aircraft availability.

To begin studying linear programming, consider a situation with two numeric decisions (*X* and *Y*), a linear objective, and three constraints. Such a problem is depicted graphically in Fig. 12.2.

Note that the optimum solution occurs at the point of the intersection of two constraints. Further notice that the slope of the objective is between the slopes of those two constraints. This example will be explained further in Example 12.2. For now, it is sufficient to note that there are two decisions (X and Y), a linear objective, and three linear constraints.

12.1.1 Linearity rules

A review of linear equations is a useful point to begin setting up and solving linear programming models. Recall that the elementary equation for a line is:

$$Y = mX + b,$$

where m is the slope of the line and b is the intercept. In linear programming, the lines are arranged in the form:

$$C_1 X + C_2 Y = C_3,$$

in which C_1, C_2, and C_3 are constants. In this form, it is easier to see the limiting quantity is C_3. In most of the constraints, the equality (=) is replaced by an inequality ($\leq$ or $\geq$). To enter the constraints into Excel, it is necessary to arrange all constraints in this manner: *variables on the left side of the equation and a constant on the right side of the equation*. From this form, the slope $= C_1/C_2$ and the intercept $= C_3/C_2$.

A summary of linearity:

All variables are "first power": For example, $X^1 = X$ only; no X^2, $X*Y$, or X/Y

Put variables on the "left-hand side": Use algebra to get all the variables on the *left* side of the constraint equation. For example:

$$3Y = 5X + 42$$

should be rearranged to be

$$-5X + 3Y = 42.$$

Constant on the "right-hand side": Once all the variables are on the left side of the constraint equation, there should be a single constant on the right-hand side. For example:

$$3Y = 5X$$

should be rearranged to be

$$-5X + 3Y = 0.$$

12.2 Components of linear programming

It is important to define the terminology used in linear programming to have a language that specifically addresses various ideas and concepts of linear programming. Setting up a linear programming problem is referred to as *formulating* the model. When formulating linear programming models, it is useful to consider a linear programming model as composed of three parts:

I. *Decision variables*: The algebraic variables (unknowns) that will be determined by Excel's *Solver* optimization software (i.e., the *Answer* once the Solver has determined the optimum solution).

II. *Objective function*: The equation that calculates the goal (objective) of the problem: usually either maximize profit or minimize cost.

   Objective function coefficient: A value (number) in the objective function that is multiplied times a decision variable. An example would be a contribution margin in a maximize profit problem.

   Objective function value: The number calculated by the objective function, such as the profit (for a maximization problem) or the cost (for a minimization problem). Excel refers to this as the *target cell*.

III. *Constraints*: Equations (usually inequalities) that represent limitations imposed on possible solutions to the problem. An example is a budget constraint that would establish a limit on the amount of funding available.

   Right-Hand Side: A number (constant), rather than a variable, on the right-hand side (on the *right*, as opposed to the *left*, side of the inequality sign) of a constraint. For example, in a budget constraint with a budget (limit) of $150,000, the $150,000 would be the right-hand side because it should be to the right of the inequality sign ($\leq$).

A mathematical example is shown in Example 12.1 to demonstrate and explain how a linear programming model is formulated and solved.

Example 12.1 The mathematical linear programming model

Consider an algebra system consisting of three variables: X, Y, and Z. The mathematical task is to find the values of X, Y, and Z that will maximize the following equation:

$$5X + 3Y + 7Z$$

Thus, X, Y, and Z are the *decision variables*, and the preceding equation is the *objective function*. The **5** in the *objective function* is a *coefficient* (for the X variable) in the *objective function*. The mathematical result of the equation is called the *objective function value*. For example, if $X = 1$, $Y = 2$, and $Z = 3$, then the objective function value is **27**:

$$5(1) + 3(2) + 7(3) = 27$$

Obviously, if there were no constraints, then infinity (∞) for X, Y, and Z would maximize the objective function. Thus, constraints are needed to limit the solution. The following linear inequalities provide the *constraints* that create a boundary for the problem:

$$X + Y + Z \leq 100$$

$$2X + 3Y \leq 40$$

$$Y + 5Z \leq 35$$

$$X \geq 0$$

$$Y \geq 0$$

$$Z \geq 0$$

The last three constraints are referred to as the nonnegativity constraints. All of the decision variables in a linear programming model are required to be greater than or equal to zero.

How to enter this linear programming model into Excel and solve it will be shown in Example 12.2 in the next section.

12.3 General layout of a linear programming model in Excel

There are many ways to set up optimization models in Excel depending upon the problem. For this book, one method can be used for all forms of linear programming models, regardless of the setting. Fig. 12.3 shows the general schematic layout for linear programming (constrained linear optimization) problems in Excel.

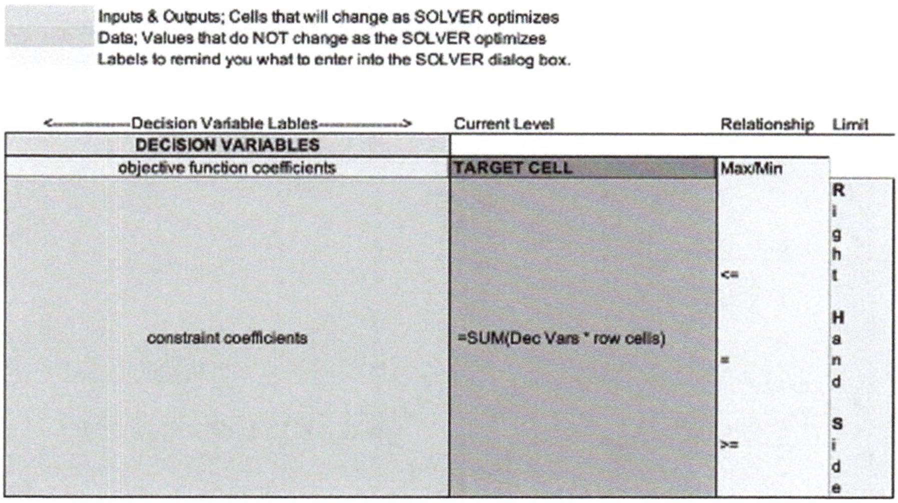

FIGURE 12.3

General Layout of a Linear Programming Model in Excel

Example 12.2 Excel Solver: mathematical linear programming model
The mathematical formulation shown in Example 12.1 is summarized:

$$\text{Maximize } 5X + 3Y + 7Z$$

Subject to:

$$X + Y + Z \leq 100$$

$$2X + 3Y \leq 40$$

$$Y + 5Z \leq 35$$

$$2X - Z \geq 10$$

$$X, Y, Z \geq 0$$

Before Excel's optimization add-in, **Solver**, can be used, the coefficients for the objective function and constraints, and their corresponding right-hand side constants, must be entered. Note that in constraints, such as $2X + 3Y \leq 40$, that the coefficient for variables that are not present in the equation (e.g., Z) is **zero**. Note that Excel treats empty cells as zero. The SUM function is used for the objective function and the constraints to calculate the results of different combinations of values for the decision variables. Fig. 12.4 shows how the mathematical model is entered into Excel prior to using the Solver.

SUM		× ✓	f_x	=SUM($B$13:$D$13*B14:D14)			
	A	B	C	D	E	F	G
1	**Example 1: Formulation and Solution of Linear Programming Model**						
2							
3			Maximize 5X + 3Y + 7Z				
4			subject to:				
5							
6			X + Y + Z	<=100			
7			2X + 3Y	<= 40			
8			Y + 5Z	<= 35			
9			2X - Z	>= 10			
10			X, Y, Z	>=0			
11							RHS
12		X	Y	Z	current level	relationship	limit
13							
14		5	3	7	=SUM($B$13:$D$13*B14:D14)		
15		1	1	1	0	<=	100
16		2	3		0	<=	40
17			1	5	0	<=	35
18		2		-1	0	>=	10

FIGURE 12.4

Excel Layout to Use the Solver to Optimize a Linear Programming Model

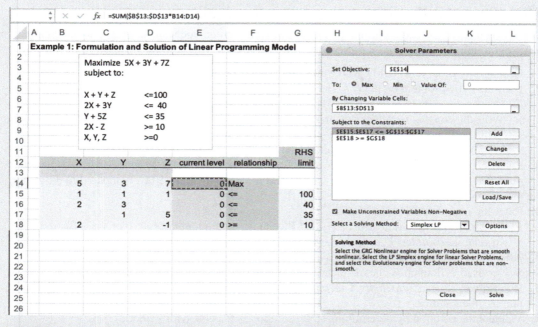

FIGURE 12.5

Excel Solver Dialog Box Input to Optimize a Linear Programming Model

X	Y	Z	current level	relationship	RHS limit
20	0	7			
5	3	7	149	Max	
1	1	1	27	<=	100
2	3		40	<=	40
	1	5	35	<=	35
2		-1	33	>=	10

FIGURE 12.6

Excel Solution to Optimize a Linear Programming Model

Fig. 12.5 shows how the mathematical model is entered into the Solver after being entered into an Excel spreadsheet.

Fig. 12.6 shows the solution to the mathematical model resulting from the Solver.

12.4 Steps for the linear programming modeling

The following steps broadly outline the process of formulating, entering, solving, and analyzing a linear programming model:

1. Read the problem thoroughly. Make notes regarding the various factors.
2. Formulate the problem on paper.
   - Draw a diagram (e.g., a network), if possible, to visualize the situation.
   - Write the **decision variables** (*X*'s, the unknowns). Be sure to state the units of the decision variables.
   - Write the **objective function** (the goal) → max or min.
   - Write the **constraints** (the equations that limit the solution).
3. Enter the problem into Excel → enter the coefficients and use the SUM function to compute the *objective function value* and *current level* for each constraint that will be compared to the *right-hand side* constants.
4. Enter the parameters into Solver.
   - Select *Min* or *Max* objective, *SimplexLP* solution method, nonnegativity (*X*'s ≥ 0), and constraints' *current level* versus the *right-hand side limit.*
5. After solving, use Save As to make a copy in which the problem is set up but has not had the Solver used → Backup is cheap—heart failure is not!
6. Run Solver, choose **Sensitivity Analysis Report** and then Save As again to make a backup copy that has the solution.
7. Validate the solution by determining if the solution is feasible (if it works).
8. Interpret Sensitivity Analysis.

An application of these steps is demonstrated in Example 12.3. This example also provides a general conceptual explanation of how linear programming determines the optimum solution.

Example 12.3 Production mix problem: graphical method

An automobile plant makes two models of car: Model X and Model Y. Both models of car are produced using the same production facility. The facility has two 8-hour shifts per day and can produce any mix of output, as long as the total hours per day are no more than 16 hours per day. Because there are multiple production lines at the facility, three Model X cars or nine Model Y cars can be produced per hour. The cars contain computer processors (chips) that are presently in short supply; the plant can obtain at most 110 processors per day. One Model X requires two processors, whereas a Model Y only requires one processor. Cars leave the facility on car carrier trucks. There are 10 trucks per day available, and each truck can hold 10 cars.

The plant manager has calculated that at current prices, the contribution from each Model X is $16,000, and it is $12,000 for Model Y. There appears to be no difficulty in selling the entire output of the plant, no matter what production mix is selected. How much of each kind of model should be produced?

First, the problem will be formulated. There are two decision variables, *X* and *Y*, where *X* is the number of Model X cars to produce in a day and *Y* is the number of Model Y cars to produce in a day. The objective function is:

$$\text{Maximize Contribution per day} = 16,000X + 12,000Y$$

The first constraint is the limited production time available each day. Because there are two 8-hour shifts per day, there are 16 total hours of production available each day. Using the factor-label method helps write the constraint:

$$\frac{1\,hour}{3\,ModelXcars}\ X \text{ cars per day} + \frac{1\,hour}{9\,ModelYcars}\ Y \text{ cars per day} \leq 16 \text{ hours per day}$$

This constraint is simplified to:

$$1/3\,X + 1/9\,Y \leq 16$$

Constructing the constraint representing the limited availability of computer processors (chips) is also facilitated using the factor-label method:

$$\frac{2\,chips}{1\,ModelXcar}\ X \text{ cars per day} + \frac{1\,chip}{1\,ModelYcar}\ Y \text{ cars per day} \leq 110 \text{ chips per day}$$

This constraint is simplified to:

$$2X + Y \leq 110$$

Using the factor-label method helps compute the trucking capacity: 10 trucks per day times 10 cars per truck equals 100 cars per day. This is then used to construct the trucking capacity constraint:

$$X \text{ cars/day} + Y \text{ cars/day} \leq 100 \text{ cars/day}$$

This constraint is simplified to:

$$X + Y \leq 100$$

The required nonnegativity constraints are:

$$X \geq 0 \text{ and } Y \geq 0$$

Next, a graph of the problem is constructed. The *X* nonnegativity constraint ($X \geq 0$) is represented by the positive space to the right of the *Y axis*, and the *Y* nonnegativity constraint ($Y \geq 0$) is represented by the positive space above the *X axis*. Thus, the upper-right quadrant represents the initial set of possible answers before the other constraints are imposed. The set of possible answers is called the *feasible region*. Fig. 12.7 shows the graphical representation of the initial restrictions imposed by the nonnegativity constraints. Note that initially there are *zero* cars produced, and thus the *current solution* is initialized at the origin.

Adding the trucking constraint ($X + Y \leq 100$) reduces the feasible region to the space bounded by the *X axis* ($Y \geq 0$), the *Y -axis* ($X \geq 0$), and the trucking constraint. Note that the absolute value of the slope (denoted by |slope|) for the trucking constraint is $1/1 = \mathbf{1.00}$. Fig. 12.8 shows the graphical representation of the feasible region after the trucking constrain has been added.

Adding the computer processor constraint ($2X + Y \leq 110$) reduces the feasible region to the space bounded by the *X axis* ($Y \geq 0$), the *Y axis* ($X \geq 0$), the trucking constraint, and the computer processor constraint. Note that the |slope| for the computer chip constraint is $2/1 = \mathbf{2.00}$. Fig. 12.9 shows the graphical representation of the feasible region after the trucking constraint has been added.

Adding the production constraint ($1/3\,X + 1/9\,Y \leq 16$) reduces the feasible region to the space bounded by the *X axis* ($Y \geq 0$), the *Y axis* ($X \geq 0$), the trucking constraint, the computer processor constraint, and the production constraint. Note that the |slope| for the production constraint is $(1/3)/(1/9) = 0.33333/0.11111 = \mathbf{3.00}$. Fig. 12.10 shows the graphical representation of the feasible region after the production constraint has been added. Note that the optimum solution will be along the boundary of the feasible region.

Continued

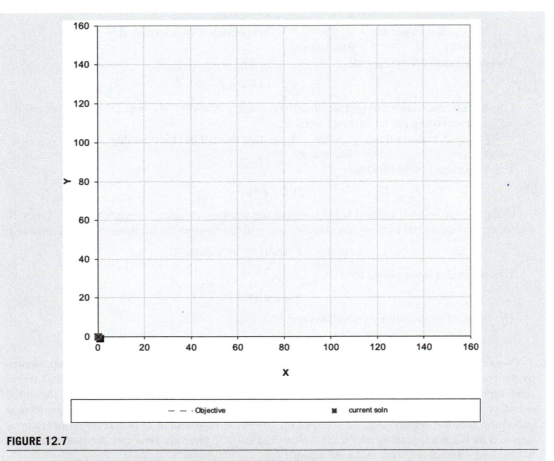

FIGURE 12.7

Initial Feasible Region Created by the Nonnegativity Constraints

The initial solution is making 0 Model X cars and 0 Model Y cars and is illustrated by the point indicated at the origin (0, 0) in Fig. 12.10. To maximize contribution, cars must be produced, and the solution will move away from the origin toward the upper right portion of the graph. The exact direction is determined by the |slope| of the objective function. Consider a nonoptimal production solution of making 20 Model X cars and 40 Model Y cars. This nonoptimum solution lies in the interior of the feasible region as shown in Fig. 12.11. This is not optimum because there are resources remaining for the production of more cars that would increase contribution.

As the Solver attempts to maximize the objective function, it will continue to move away from the origin (0, 0) toward the upper-right portion of the graph until the solution reaches the boundary of the feasible region and cannot proceed any further. This will occur at the point at which the |slope| of the objective function is between two constraints' |slope|. In this case, the |slope| of the objective function is 16,000/12,000 = 1.33 . . . . That places its |slope| between the |slope| of the trucking con-

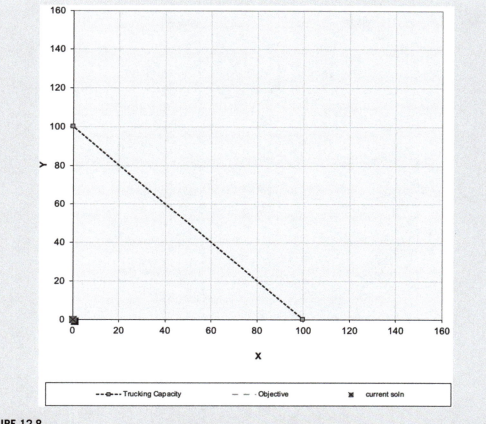

FIGURE 12.8

Feasible Region After Adding the Trucking Constraint

straint and the |slope| of the computer processor constraint: 1.00 < 1.33 < 2.00. Thus, the optimum solution occurs at the intersection of those two constraints; that point is their simultaneous solution (10, 90), as is shown in Fig. 12.12.

To solve this problem using the Solver in Excel, this problem would be entered as shown in Fig. 12.13. The slope computations are not required. They are shown to help explain how the Solver uses the slopes to compute the optimum solution.

After entering the information into Excel as shown in Fig. 12.13, the required information would be entered into the Solver dialog as shown in Fig. 12.14. That would yield the optimum solution of **10** Model X cars per day and **90** Model Y cars per day.

Continued

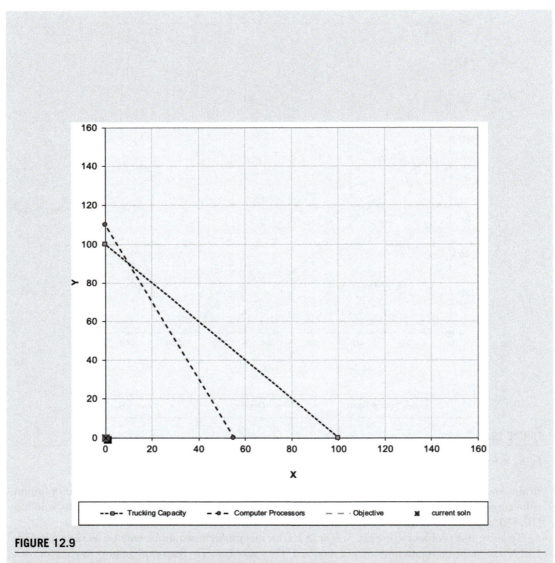

FIGURE 12.9

Feasible Region After Adding the Computer Processor Constraint

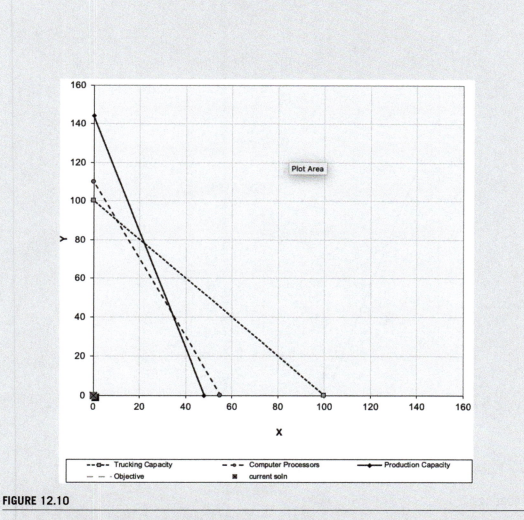

FIGURE 12.10

Feasible Region After Adding the Production Constraint

Continued

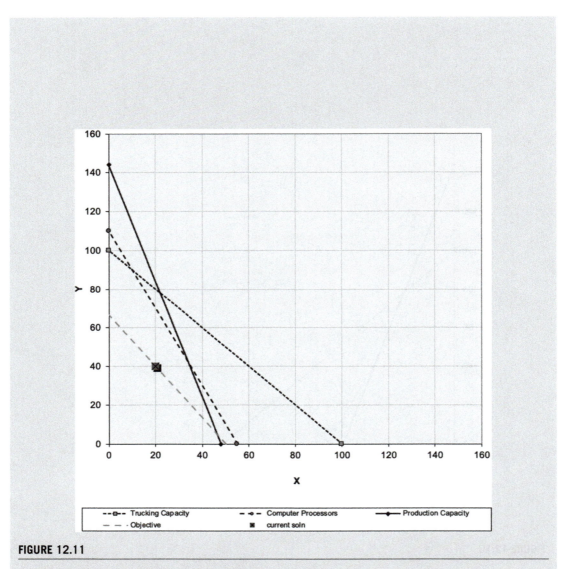

FIGURE 12.11

Nonoptimum Solution of 20 Model X and 40 Model Y Cars

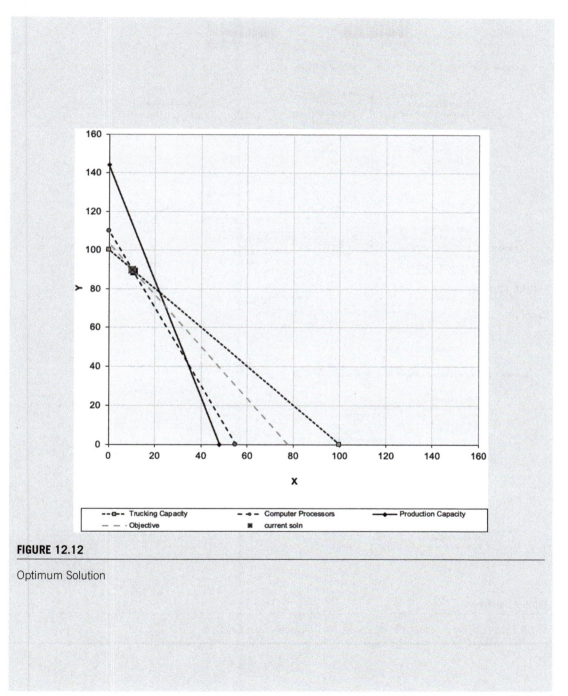

FIGURE 12.12

Optimum Solution

Continued

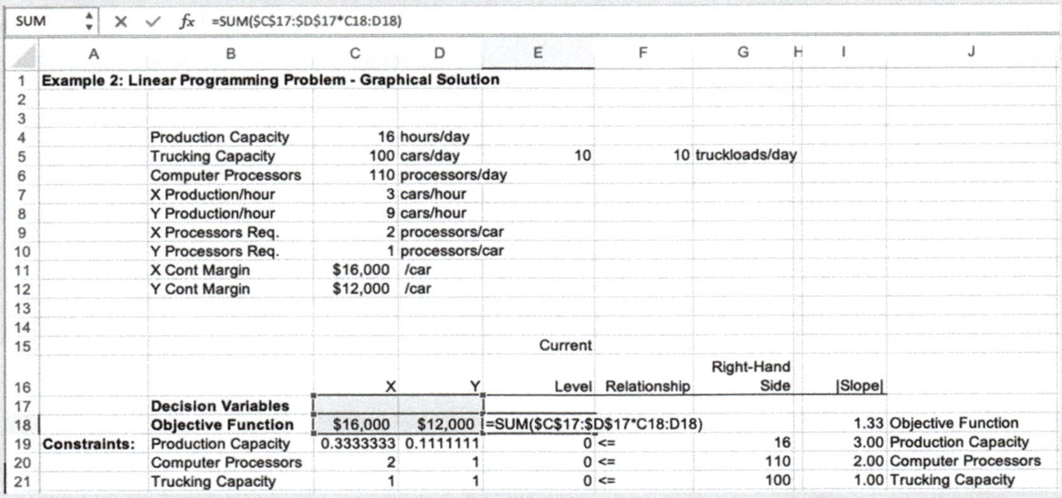

SUM | fx =SUM($C$17:$D$17*C18:D18)

	A	B	C	D	E	F	G	H	I	J
1	**Example 2: Linear Programming Problem - Graphical Solution**									
2										
3										
4		Production Capacity	16	hours/day						
5		Trucking Capacity	100	cars/day	10	10	truckloads/day			
6		Computer Processors	110	processors/day						
7		X Production/hour	3	cars/hour						
8		Y Production/hour	9	cars/hour						
9		X Processors Req.	2	processors/car						
10		Y Processors Req.	1	processors/car						
11		X Cont Margin	$16,000	/car						
12		Y Cont Margin	$12,000	/car						
13										
14										
15					Current					
16			X	Y	Level	Relationship	Right-Hand Side		|Slope|	
17		**Decision Variables**								
18		**Objective Function**	$16,000	$12,000	=SUM($C$17:$D$17*C18:D18)				1.33	Objective Function
19	**Constraints:**	Production Capacity	0.3333333	0.1111111	0	<=	16		3.00	Production Capacity
20		Computer Processors	2	1	0	<=	110		2.00	Computer Processors
21		Trucking Capacity	1	1	0	<=	100		1.00	Trucking Capacity

FIGURE 12.13

Excel Layout to Use the Solver for the Production Mix Example

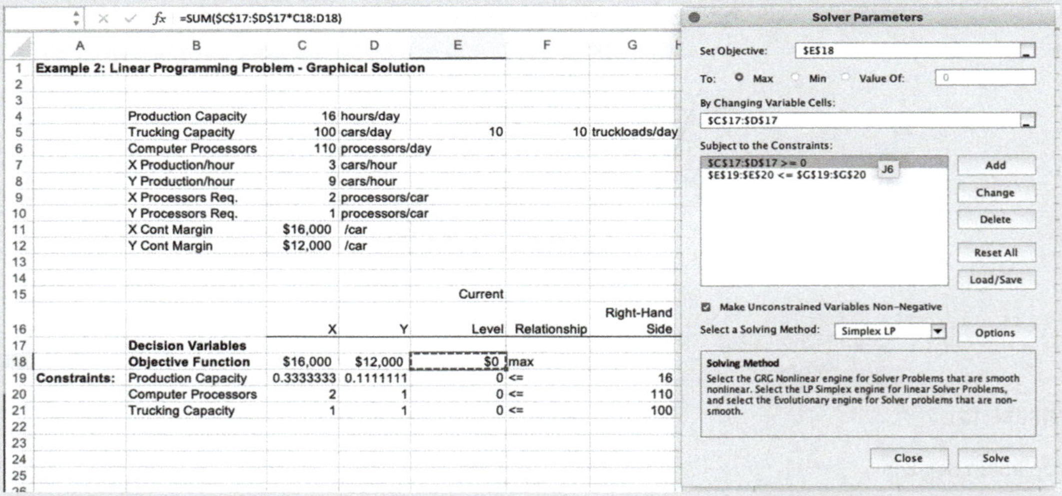

fx =SUM($C$17:$D$17*C18:D18)

	A	B	C	D	E	F	G
1	**Example 2: Linear Programming Problem - Graphical Solution**						
2							
3							
4		Production Capacity	16	hours/day			
5		Trucking Capacity	100	cars/day	10	10	truckloads/day
6		Computer Processors	110	processors/day			
7		X Production/hour	3	cars/hour			
8		Y Production/hour	9	cars/hour			
9		X Processors Req.	2	processors/car			
10		Y Processors Req.	1	processors/car			
11		X Cont Margin	$16,000	/car			
12		Y Cont Margin	$12,000	/car			
13							
14							
15					Current		
16			X	Y	Level	Relationship	Right-Hand Side
17		**Decision Variables**					
18		**Objective Function**	$16,000	$12,000	$0	max	
19	**Constraints:**	Production Capacity	0.3333333	0.1111111	0	<=	16
20		Computer Processors	2	1	0	<=	110
21		Trucking Capacity	1	1	0	<=	100
22							
23							
24							
25							

FIGURE 12.14

Excel Solver Dialog Box Input to Optimize the Production Mix Example

12.5 Network models

Network models are a common type of linear programming model. Network models have patterns of flow in a connected system. These flows might involve material, products, people, money, or time. Some business applications include retail supply chain and distribution, especially online retail distribution, airlines routing and scheduling, production line design, production scheduling, military logistics, and financial modeling of investments and cash flows. The latter is particularly useful for start-up companies.

A major benefit of network models is that they can be depicted in a network diagram to help formulate and solve the linear programming model. In a network diagram, the flows are typically represented by arrows and indicate decision variables, and the constraints are nodes that connect arrows. Example 12.4 provides an example of a simplified supply chain/distribution network.

Example 12.4 The transportation network model

An online retail store ships its excess seasonal inventory from two warehouses, one in Albuquerque and the other in Baltimore, to three outlet stores in Charlotte, Denver, and Evanston. It is estimated that Albuquerque will have an excess of 145 units, whereas Baltimore has an excess of 275 units. Furthermore, it is estimated that demand in the Charlotte outlet will be 135, demand in Denver will be 88, and demand in Evanston is estimated to be 176. The shipping costs ($/unit) are shown in Table 12.1.

Table 12.1 Shipping costs

	Albuquerque	Baltimore
Charlotte	4.15	1.85
Denver	2.25	4.65
Evanston	3.50	3.50

First, begin creating the network diagram by drawing a circle on the left side of the diagram for each warehouse. These circles are called *nodes* and indicate where the flows originate. In general, a circle from which flows begin are called a *source*.

Next, nodes are drawn on the right side of the diagram for each outlet (destination). These nodes indicate where the flows terminate (end) and are called *sinks*. Typically, each node represents a constraint in the formulation of the linear programming model.

The sources and sinks are connected by arrows that represent the amounts of units that flow from the warehouses (sources) to the outlets (sinks). These arrows represent the decision variables in the linear programming model. For this example, the decision variables are named for their starting and ending nodes. For example, is the decision variable *AC* is the number of units to ship *from* Albuquerque *to* Charlotte. Because each combination of source and sink is available, there are six (2 sources * 3 sinks) decision variables. Fig. 12.15 shows the network diagram for this model along with the appropriate capacity (supply) and demand for each node.

Continued

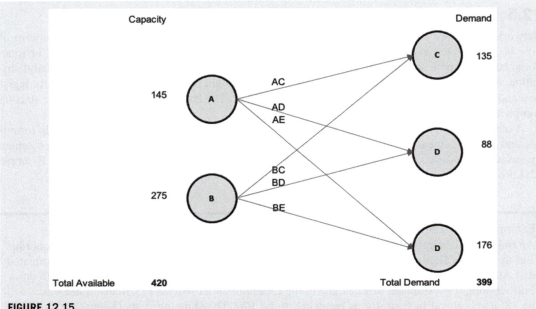

Capacity

Demand

145   A

275   B

C   135

D   88

D   176

AC

AD
AE

BC
BD

BE

Total Available   420

Total Demand   399

FIGURE 12.15

Network Diagram for the Example Transportation Model

The network diagram can now be used to formulate the linear programming transportation network model. As noted earlier, there are six decision variables (represented by the six arrows in the network diagram) that are the amounts to be shipped from the two warehouses (**A** and **B**) to the three outlet stores (**C**, **D**, and **E**):

$$AC, AD, AE, BC, BD, \text{ and } BE$$

The objective is to minimize total shipping cost. The objective function is:

$$\text{Min total shipping cost} = 4.15AC + 2.25AD + 3.50AE + 1.85BC + 4.65BD + 3.50BE$$

The five nodes indicate that there are at least five constraints. The first two constraints are the warehouses' capacities. It is often useful to express constraints using words before writing them as equations.

$$\text{Warehouse Shipments Out} \leq \text{Warehouse Inventory}$$

For Albuquerque:

$$\text{Amount shipped from Albuquerque} \leq \text{Albuquerque Capacity}$$

Expressing this as a constraint:

$$AC + AD + AE \leq 145$$

This means that the amount shipped cannot exceed the amount available. Briefly stated, what goes out must be less than what is in: out ≤ in.

Similarly, the constraint for Baltimore's node is:

$$BC + BD + BE \leq 275$$

Next, the constraints for each outlet store can be expressed in words as follows:

Warehouse Shipments In ≥ Outlet Store Demand

For Charlotte:

Amount shipped to Charlotte ≥ Charlotte Demand

Expressing this as a constraint:

$$AC + BC \geq 135$$

Similarly, the constraint for Denver is

$$AD + BD \geq 88,$$

and the constraint for Evanston is

$$AE + BE \geq 176.$$

The greater than or equal to inequality (≥) is appropriate for this model because the minimization of the objective function will not allow there to be excess units shipped, as that would cause higher costs. The use of inequalities, rather than equalities, is encouraged to facilitate the Solver's ability to solve the model by reducing the restrictions on the solution as much as possible. Models with too many equalities are often too constrained ("too tight") for the Solver to readily compute the solution.

Fig. 12.16 shows the linear programming transportation network model set up and entered into Excel. The Solver dialog box, with the appropriate information entered, is also shown.

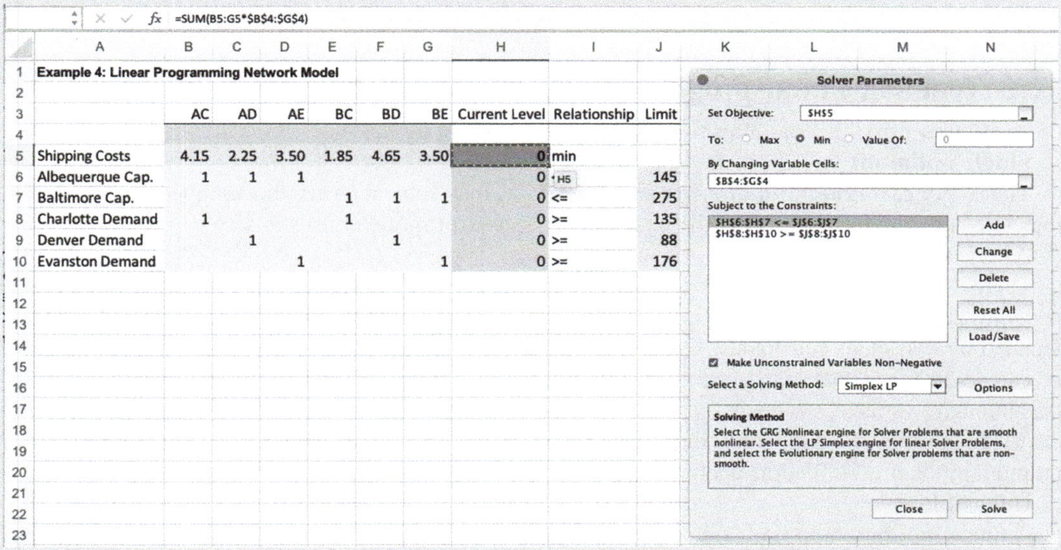

FIGURE 12.16

The Transportation Model in Excel

Continued

| SUM | | X | ✓ | f_x | =SUM(B5:G5*$B$4:$G$4) | | | | | | |

	A	B	C	D	E	F	G	H	I	J
1	**Example 4: Linear Programming Network Model**									
2										
3		AC	AD	AE	BC	BD	BE	Current Level	Relationship	Limit
4		0	88	57	135	0	119			
5	Shipping Costs	4.15	2.25	3.50	1.85	4.65	3.50	$B$4:$G$4	min	
6	Albequerque Cap.	1	1	1				145	<=	145
7	Baltimore Cap.				1	1	1	254	<=	275
8	Charlotte Demand	1			1			135	>=	135
9	Denver Demand		1			1		88	>=	88
10	Evanston Demand			1			1	176	>=	176

FIGURE 12.17

The Optimum Solution Transportation Model in Excel

The optimum solution is shown in Fig. 12.17. Notice that neither Albuquerque nor Baltimore shipped more than their capacities. Also note that Baltimore still has units remaining and that no outlet store received more than was demanded.

12.6 Types of linear programming end conditions

There are four possible outcomes for a linear programming model.

Single optimum

There is *one, singular, unique, optimum solution*. In graphical terms, this unique point is where the objective function has stopped at the intersection of two, or more, constraints.

Alternate optima

There is *more than one optimum solution*. In graphical terms, this is a set of points, typically a line segment or plane segment, where the objective function has stopped along a line segment of a constraint that is bounded by two other constraints. Excel does not directly indicate *alternate optima*; such a condition is indicated when the value of a decision variable is 0 (zero) and the *reduced cost is also zero*. This indicates that although a variable was not in solution, it could be introduced into the solution at no penalty to the objective function value. In other words, the variable is 0 and not used, but it could be used without changing the optimum profit or cost. Finding alternate optima is further explained and demonstrated in Example 12.5.

Infeasible

A linear programming problem may become *impossible* to solve due to conflicting, mutually exclusive constraints. This type of problem is referred to as *infeasible*. This typically occurs when an inequality is incorrect (pointing the wrong way). For example, the constraints X<6 and X>12 would create an *infeasible* model. Problems may also become infeasible by making the constraints equal to (=) their right-hand sides rather than ≤ or ≥. Such a set of constraints are said to be "too tight." As mentioned earlier, try to make the constraints no more restricted than necessary. Another possibility is that the right-hand side constant may be calculated incorrectly or in the wrong units.

Unbounded

In contrast to an *infeasible* problem, a linear programming problem may become impossible to solve due to there being **no limitations** being provided by the constraints. This type of problem is referred to as **unbounded**. In such a case, Excel runs until the maximum number of iterations is reached. This typically occurs when an inequality is incorrect (pointing the wrong way). For example, max profit with a constraint of X>12 could be unbounded when the constraint should have been X<12. Problems may also become unbounded by having the wrong objective: max rather than min, or vice versa.

12.7 Sensitivity analysis terms

Given the uncertainty of much of the information analysts use to build decision models, it is important to explore how changes in the information used to build the model can impact the decisions resulting from the model. As an example, consider a financial analyst constructing a model to determine an optimum financial portfolio. The model is built using information and assumptions that are uncertain. Exploring these uncertainties is known as *sensitivity analysis*.

Mathematically, sensitivity analysis is the process of exploring the effects of changes in model inputs on the results of the model. Often, some of the most valuable managerial decision-making information comes more from the sensitivity analysis than the optimum solution itself. Fortunately, the linear programming optimization algorithm, called the *simplex method*, provides a rudimentary sensitivity analysis. The sensitivity analysis report provided by the simplex method notes the effects of changes to the initial values of the objective function coefficients and the constraints' right-hand sides.

It is necessary to introduce critical terms prior to learning about the sensitivity analysis report that results from the solution of a linear programming model.

In solution

The variables that are nonzero and constraints that are equal to their right-hand sides (*binding*) have been solved for are said to be *in solution*.

Qualitative solution

The term **same qualitative solution** refers to not changing which variables and constraints are in solution. A solution is qualitatively different when a variable that was previously zero (*out of solution*) becomes part of the solution (in solution) by becoming nonzero.

Allowable increase/decrease

The amount that a right-hand side or objective function coefficient can be increased/decreased, without qualitatively changing the solution.

Shadow price

The change in the objective function value that results from a one-unit change in the right-hand side. The *shadow price* is valid over the range determined by the *allowable increase/decrease*.

Reduced cost

The change in the objective function value (a penalty) that results from forcing one unit of a nonoptimal variable into the solution (i.e., forcing a variable that was equal to 0 to be 1).

Example 12.5 presents a linear programming problem that is readily solved by inspection so that changes to the solution can be easily determined. This facilitates the explanation and understanding of sensitivity analysis concepts.

Example 12.5 Sensitivity analysis: allocation problem

The State Safety Council must allocate its national budget for the next fiscal year. Irrevocable decisions have already been made concerning various "program areas" and their total funding. For example, a total of $110,000,000 has been budgeted to the missions of prevention of automobile fatalities and reduction of property damage. However, detailed allocation decisions must be made concerning specific projects designed to contribute to the program missions. In the case of automobile fatality prevention and reduction of property damage, Table 12.2 contains the projects recommended by council analysts, together with appropriate data. The decision makers of the council must make the budget allocation (project choice and magnitude) decisions.

In response to a question concerning which of the two missions is more important, they replied: "That's a tough question! On one hand, human life is sacred and cannot be purchased for any amount of money. On the other hand, if there are two competing ways to save the same number of lives, we should naturally prefer the project that also results in the lower amount of property damage." When asked specifically what "trade-off" between lives saved and property damage would make them indifferent, they said: "That's really a tough question! However, we are aware that a certain government agency has, for internal resource allocation purposes, an implicit dollar value for a human life saved of $3,000,000 (we think another agency also uses this number in making decisions about building additional safety into their equipment)."

The setup for this problem in Excel is shown in Fig. 12.18.

The sensitivity report for this linear program (LP) is shown in Fig. 12.19.

Recall that the sensitivity analysis report notes the effects of changes to the initial values of the objective function coefficients and the constraints' right-hand sides. For the most part, the validity of the effects is limited to the qualitative solution given in the optimum solution. In other words, a fundamental concept is that the sensitivity report states *how much the initial data can change without changing the qualitative solution*. Therefore, prior to interpreting the sensitivity analysis report, it is important to note that the variables and constraints currently in solution are the variables *SB*, *HD*, and *DD* and the constraints regarding the *Budget*, and the limits for *AD*, *SB*, and *DD*. Thus, those are the four variables and four constraints that are in solution.

	Project	Upper limit of project expenditure (in millions)	Expected fatalities prevented per million expended (in millions)	Expected reduction in property damage per million expended (in millions)
1.	Seat belt advertising	80	33	0
2.	Research in improved highway design	20	25	20
3.	Research in improved automobile design	75	15	30
4.	Dollars spent lobbying for tougher "drunk driving" laws	100	27	10

Table 12.2 Project allocation data

	B10		× ✓	fx	=F2*B1+G2				
	A	B	C	D	E	F	G	H

	A	B	C	D	E	F	G	H
1	One Life	$3			Limit	Fatalities Prevented	Property Reduction	
2		1 Seat belt advertising			$80	33	$0	
3		2 Research in improved highway design			$20	25	20	
4		3 Research in improved automobile design			$75	15	30	
5		4 Dollars spent lobbying for tougher "drunk driving" laws			$100	27	10	
6								
7								
8		SB	HD	AD	DD	Current Value	Relationship	Limit
9		80	20	0	10			
10	Benefit	$99	$95	$75	$91	$10,730	Max	
11	Budget	1	1	1	1	$110	<=	$110
12	SB	1				$80	<=	$80
13	HD		1			$20	<=	$20
14	AD			1		$0	<=	$75
15	DD				1	$10	<=	$100

FIGURE 12.18

The Optimum Solution Transportation Model in Excel

Variable Cells

Cell	Name	Final Value	Reduced Cost	Objective Coefficient	Allowable Increase	Allowable Decrease
$B$9	SB	80	0	99	1E+30	8
$C$9	HD	20	0	95	1E+30	4
$D$9	AD	0	-16	75	16	1E+30
$E$9	DD	10	0	91	4	16

Constraints

Cell	Name	Final Value	Shadow Price	Constraint R.H. Side	Allowable Increase	Allowable Decrease
$F$11	Budget Current Value	$110.00	91	110	90	10
$F$12	SB Current Value	$80.00	8	80	10	80
$F$13	HD Current Value	$20.00	4	20	10	20
$F$14	AD Current Value	$0.00	0	75	1E+30	75
$F$15	DD Current Value	$10.00	0	100	1E+30	90

FIGURE 12.19

Optimum Solution and Sensitivity Report From Excel's Solver

Continued

The top portion of the report concerns what happens when the objective function coefficients are changed. It is very important to remember that the sensitivity report information is only true when considering each change independently—that is, only changing one thing at a time.

First, notice that the solutions for each of the decision variables are listed in the Final Value column. The current values of the objective function coefficients for each decision variable are listed in the Objective Coefficient column.

Next, note the *reduced cost* for *AD* is −16. As such, $16,000,000 is the penalty to the objective function value if one unit ($1,000,000) of *AD* is forced into solution. In other words, if you were forced to spend a single unit of *AD*, then the value being maximized would be changed by the amount of the reduced cost: −16 (in millions). This penalty would be incurred because the one unit spent on *AD* would gain 75 but would come at the expense of 95 due to the unit less from *DD*, creating a net change in the objective function value of +75−91 = −16.

Proceeding to the Allowable Increase column, *1E+30* is Excel's method of expressing infinity (∞). The value for the allowable increase for *SB* and *HD* occurs because it is possible to increase their benefits (objective function coefficients) infinitely, and such changes would not alter the solution. Similarly, the benefit of *AD* (objective function coefficients) could be reduced infinitely, and such changes would not alter the qualitative solution. In other words, making the best choices better, or the worst choice worse, will not alter the qualitative solution.

A similar symmetry of *AD*'s allowable increase of 16 and *DD*'s allowable decrease of 16 exists due to *AD*'s reduced cost of −16. Increasing the objective function coefficient of *AD* by 16 would create a qualitatively different solution by allowing *AD* to enter the optimum solution set. The same is true if the objective function coefficient of *DD* is decreased by 16.

The allowable decreases for *SB* and *HD* are due to the fact that their entire allocations could be reallocated to *DD* if their objective function coefficients were reduced to that of *DD*. Thus, if either *SB* or *HD* were to have their objective function coefficients reduced to 91, because *DD* has the capacity to fully absorb the $80,000,000 of *SB* or the $20,000,000 of *HD*, a qualitatively different solution (with either *SB* or *HD* out of solution) would be created. Likewise, if the objective function coefficient for *DD* was increased by 4, to 95, then *DD* would be able to fully absorb the allocation of *HD* and a qualitatively different solution (with *HD* out of solution) would be created.

The bottom portion of the sensitivity report presents what happens when the values of *the right-hand sides are* changed. Each constraint has a line of information in this portion of the sensitivity report. Just as the Objective Coefficient column in the top portion of the report listed the data given (the objective function coefficients), the Constraint R.H. Side column lists the data initially given for each constraint.

To begin the interpretation of this portion of the sensitivity report, first notice that the Final Value column lists the *current level* for each of the constraints. It is easier to interpret the sensitivity analysis report for constraints with a *final value* **not equal** to Constraint R.H. Side—those constraints are *not binding*; they have not reached their limitations. Because those constraints have not reached their limits (right-hand sides), then increasing the right-hand sides will not affect the solutions. Therefore, the allowable increase for each constraint that is nonbinding (*slack*) is infinity (∞).

The **shadow price** is the effect on the objective function value if the right-hand side is increased by one unit. Furthermore, decreasing the right-hand side by one unit will change the objective function value by the shadow price in the opposite direction. In other words, if the shadow price is positive, then decreasing the right-hand side by one unit will *reduce* the objective function value by the shadow price. The shadow price effect is true for each unit that the right-hand side is changed as long as the change is within the *allowable increase* and *allowable decrease*. In other words, the shadow price is valid as long as the change to the right-hand side is not more than the allowable increase or allowable decrease.

Thus, a constraint that is *nonbinding* (final value is not equal to the constraint right-hand side) will have a shadow price of zero (0). Note that neither *AD* nor *DD* reached their limits (constraint right-hand side), and thus they each have an allowable increase of infinity (represented by 1E+30) and a shadow price of 0.

For the constraint on *AD*, the allowable decrease of **75** means that decreasing the original limit of 75 to 0 will not change the qualitative solution, and it will not change which variables and constraints are in solution.

Next, examine the sensitivity analysis report for the *Budget* constraint. If the constraint right-hand side were to increase by one unit ($1,000,000), then the objective function value would increase by the shadow price of 91 due to the allocation of the additional unit to the *DD* variable. Because the *DD* constraint has **90** unused units remaining (100 – 10), the *Budget* constraint could be increased by 90 and the *DD* project could utilize 90 additional units at a benefit of 91 per each additional unit. After that 90, the *DD* project limit constraint would become binding and would enter solution. This is the same reasoning that applies to the allowable decreased of 90 for the *DD* limit constraint.

Conversely, the objective function value would decrease by 91 for each of the 10 units the *DD* project would lose if the *Budget* constraint were reduced by 10. After that 10, a different qualitative solution (*DD* would be out of solution) would be reached.

The sensitivity analysis for the *SB* and *HD* constraints follows similar logic. The shadow price of **8** for the *SB* limit constraint is due to the reallocation to *SB* from *DD* that would occur if the constraint right-hand side of 80 were to increase by one unit. That reallocation would produce in a gain of 99 but at the loss of the 91, resulting in a net gain of **8** (99–91). The same applies to the shadow price of **4** (95 – 91) for the *HD* limit constraint. The shadow prices for those two constraints are valid as long as any funding is available to *SB* or HD. That is why the allowable decreases are equal to the project limits for those two constraints. The allowable increase of **10** for each of those two constraints results from the reallocation of the 10 units from *DD* to one of those two projects.

Alternate optima occur when there are multiple optimal solutions. To demonstrate this condition, the objective function coefficient for *AD* (*auto design*) is changed from **75** to **91**—the same as that of *DD*. Thus, *AD* could become in solution at no penalty. Fig. 12.20 shows the sensitivity report *after changing the objective function coefficient for auto design to 91.*

The existence of *alternate optima* is identifiable by the **reduced cost = 0** that is associated with the **final Value = 0** for the *DD* decision variable (highlighted in Fig. 12.20). In this model, the specific alternate optima are also identified by the *allowable increase* and *allowable decrease* = 0.

Continued

Variable Cells

Cell	Name	Final Value	Reduced Cost	Objective Coefficient	Allowable Increase	Allowable Decrease
$B$9	SB	80	0	99	1E+30	8
$C$9	HD	20	0	95	1E+30	4
$D$9	AD	10	0	91	4	0
$E$9	DD	0	0	91	0	1E+30

Constraints

Cell	Name	Final Value	Shadow Price	Constraint R.H. Side	Allowable Increase	Allowable Decrease
$F$11	Budget Current Value	$110.00	91	110	65	10
$F$12	SB Current Value	$80.00	8	80	10	65
$F$13	HD Current Value	$20.00	4	20	10	20
$F$14	AD Current Value	$10.00	0	75	1E+30	65
$F$15	DD Current Value	$0.00	0	100	1E+30	100

FIGURE 12.20

Example of the Alternate Optima Solution and Sensitivity Report From Excel's Solver

12.8 Excel Solver messages

Some of the common messages that can result from Excel's Solver are as follows:

Solver found a solution. All constraints and optimality conditions are satisfied.

Solver has converged to the current solution. All constraints are satisfied.

These messages indicate that although Excel has found what it appears to be a solution, there may be a better solution. To direct Excel to look for a better solution, reduce the Convergence setting using the Solver Options dialog box.

Solver cannot improve the current solution.

This message indicates that Excel has calculated a rough, appropriate solution, but there may be a better solution. To direct Excel to look for a better solution, adjust the Precision setting to a smaller value using the Solver Options dialog box.

Solver could not find a feasible solution.

This message probably indicates that your optimization modeling problem has no answer. Alternatively, this error message may suggest that you have incorrectly described the objective function or, perhaps more likely, one or more of the constraints' inequalities are incorrect.

The linearity conditions required by this LP Solver are not satisfied.

Conditions for assume linear model are not satisfied.

These messages indicate that you selected the *Simplex LP* solving method, but Excel, after reviewing the calculation results, concludes that your model is not linear. Check your constraints, and rewrite them if necessary. Remember: constant times variable (cX) on the left and constant on the right-hand side.

The Objective Cell values do not converge.
The Set Target Cell values do not converge.

These messages indicate that the objective function continues to increase or decrease even though all the constraints are already satisfied. In other words, with each iteration, Excel gets a better objective function value but does not appear any closer to a final objective function value. If you encounter this error, review your objective function (be sure you have the correct objective: max or min) and constraints (you might have omitted one or more constraints), and make sure that you have correctly described the optimization problem.

Stop chosen when the maximum time limit was reached.

This message indicates that Excel ran out of time. You can attempt to retry solving the solution using a larger Max Time setting. To specify a larger Max Time value, use the Solver Options dialog box.

Stop chosen when the maximum iteration limit was reached.

This message indicated that Excel ran out of iterations. You can attempt to retry solving the solution using a larger Iterations setting. To specify a larger Iterations value, use the Solver Options dialog box.

Solver encountered an error value in a target or constraint cell.

This message indicates that one of your formulas results in an error value or that you have incorrectly specified an integer or binary constraint. To address the Solver problem, you need to fix the incorrect formula.

There is not enough memory available to solve the problem.

This message, as you would suspect, indicates that Excel does not have enough memory to successfully run Solver. To free up memory, try closing open documents and any other open programs.

Exercise Set 12: Constrained Linear Optimization

1. Formulate and solve the allocation model presented in Example 12.5 (Safety Council budget). Derive and explain the numbers in the sensitivity analysis.

2. We want to select an advertising strategy to reach two types of customers: those in families with annual incomes over $40,000 and those in families with annual incomes under $40,000. We feel that people in the first group will purchase twice as much of our product as people in the second, and our goal is to maximize purchases. We may advertise either on TV or in a magazine; one unit of TV advertising costs $20,000 and reaches approximately 20,000 people in the first group and 80,000 in the second. One unit of magazine advertising costs $12,000 and reaches 60,000 people in the first group and 30,000 in the second. We require that at least 6 units of TV advertising are used and that no more than 12 units of magazine advertising be used for policy reasons. The advertising budget is $180,000. Solve this problem graphically.

3. An insulation plant makes two types of insulation called *type B* and *type R*. Both types of insulation are produced using the same machine. The machine can produce any mix of output, as long as the total weight is no more than 70 tons per day. Insulation leaves the plant in trucks; the loading facilities can handle up to 30 trucks per day. One truckload of type B insulation weighs 1.4 tons; one truckload of type R weighs 2.8 tons. Each truck can carry type B insulation, type R insulation, or any mixture thereof. The insulation contains a flame-retarding agent that is presently in short supply; the plant can obtain at most 65 canisters of the agent per day. One truckload of (finished) type B insulation requires an input of three canisters of the agent, but one truckload of type R insulation requires only one canister.

The plant manager has calculated that at current prices, the contribution from each truck-load of type B is $950 and $1200 for type R. There appears to be no difficulty in selling the entire output of the plant, no matter what production mix is selected. How much of each kind of insulation should be produced?

4. An electronics manufacturer is planning next month's shipments for a specific product from its three manufacturing plants to its four stores and is seeking an optimum production and shipping plan. Each plant has a monthly capacity with associated variable costs (VC) of manufacturing that product in that plant as shown in Table 12.3. Each store has a demand forecast and selling price for the product as shown in Table 12.4. The shipping costs ($/unit) are shown in Table 12.5. Draw the network diagram and then formulate and solve this as a linear programming problem. Interpret the sensitivity analysis.

5. Acme Coffee Company blends coffee beans from four sources (Brazil, Colombia, Ecuador, and Peru) to make the coffee it sells to retailers. Coffee from each source has a unique combination of aroma and strength. Those two attributes are measured using specific chemical analyses. The company is going to produce a coffee blend with an aroma of at least 78 and a strength of at least 16 and not more than 22. The company is going to produce 5 million pounds of this blend that meet these requirements. Due to previous purchasing agreements, there are limitations on the

Table 12.3 Plant production capacities and variable costs

Plant	Capacity	VC
Austin	14,000	$45.35
Boston	9000	$52.26
Charlotte	12,500	$55.62

Table 12.4 Store demand and selling price

Store	Demand	Price
Dallas	7500	$72.00
Eugene	12,000	$72.00
Fort Wayne	9000	$76.00
Gainesville	9000	$74.00

Table 12.5 Per-unit shipping costs

Plant	Store				
	Dallas	Eugene	Fort Wayne	Gainesville	
Austin	3.10	6.45	1.78	6.25	
Boston	4.29	2.52	5.80	2.25	
Charlotte	1.98	3.60	4.25	2.80	

availability of coffee from each source. Table 12.6 provides the information regarding the aroma, strength, cost, and availability of coffee from each source.
Formulate and solve this as a linear programming problem. Interpret the sensitivity analysis.

6. A loan company is planning its operations for the next year. The company makes five types of loans, listed in the following, together with the annual return (in percentage) to the company. Legal requirements and company policy place the following limits on the amounts of the various types of loans. Signature loans cannot exceed 10% of the total amount of loans. The amount of signature and furniture loans together cannot exceed 20% of the total amount of loans. First mortgages must be at least 40% of the total mortgages and at least 20% of the total amount of loans. Second mortgages may not exceed 25% of the total amount of loans. The company wants to maximize the revenue from loan interest, subject to the preceding restrictions. The firm can lend a maximum of $1.5 million. The rate of return of each type of loan is shown in Table 12.7.

7. The director of maintenance services for an airline was trying to decide how many new mechanics to hire and train over the next 6 months. The requirements in number of mechanic-hours needed are given in Table 12.8.

Table 12.6 Coffee data for each source				
Source	Aroma	Strength	Cost per Pound	Available (millions of pounds)
Brazil	75	15	$0.50	1.50
Colombia	60	20	$0.62	1.20
Ecuador	70	25	$0.65	1.80
Peru	85	18	$0.70	2.50

Table 12.7 Annual return for each type of loan	
Type of loan	Annual return (%)
Signature	15
Furniture	12
Automobile	9
Second home mortgage	10
First home mortgage	7

Table 12.8 Monthly Labor Demand	
Month	Hours Needed
January	8000
February	7000
March	8000
April	10,000
May	9000
June	12,000

The problem was complicated by two factors. First, it took 1 month to train mechanics before they could be used. Hence, hiring had to be done a month before the need arose. Second, training of new mechanics required the time of already trained mechanics. It took approximately 100 hours of regular mechanic time for each trainee during the month training period. In other words, the number of hours available for flight service by regular mechanics was cut by 100 hours for each trainee. The director of maintenance was not worried about January because there were 60 mechanics available. Past records showed that a mechanic would not work more than 150 hours in any month. This meant that the director had a maximum of 9000 hours available for January, 1000 in excess of needs. Mechanics were not laid off in such cases; each merely worked fewer hours.

Company records also showed that 10% of the mechanics quit their jobs for various reasons. The cost to the airlines for a regular mechanic was $4250 per month for salary and fringe benefits, regardless of how many hours were worked. The cost of a trainee was $2050 per month for salary and fringe benefits.

Cases

Unimog Motorworks

At Unimog Motorworks' monthly planning meeting in July, the company's president expressed dissatisfaction with Unimog's financial performance during the 6-month period from January to June. "I know we are operating at capacity in some of our production lines," he remarked to Unimog's controller and sales and production managers. "But surely we can do something to improve our financial position. Maybe we should change our product mix. We don't seem to be making a profit on our Model U01 truck. Why don't we just stop making it altogether? Maybe we should purchase engines from an outside supplier, relieving the capacity problem in our engine assembly department. Why don't the three of you get together, consider the different options, and come up with a recommendation?"

Unimog manufactured two specialized models of trucks, Model U01 and Model U02, in a single plant in Stoughton, Wisconsin. Manufacturing operations were grouped into four departments: engine assembly, metal stamping, Model U01 assembly, and Model U02 assembly. Capacity in each department was expressed in manufacturing machine-hours available (net of maintenance downtime). Machine-hours available, in conjunction with machine-hours required for each truck model in each department, determined Unimog's production decisions. For example, the company's engine assembly capacity was sufficient to assemble engines for either 4000 Model U01 trucks per month (4000 machine-hours available ÷ 1 machine-hour required per truck) or 2000 Model U02 trucks per month (4000 machine-hours available ÷ 2 machine-hours per truck), if devoted fully to either model. Of course, Unimog could also assemble engines for both models. For example, if 1000 Model U01 trucks were produced, sufficient engine assembly capacity was available for 1500 Model U02 trucks ([4000 − 1000 * 1.0] / 2.0). Data on the machine-hour requirements for each truck model in each department and the monthly machine-hour availability in the departments are given in Table 12.9. The company could sell as many trucks as it could produce.

Table 12.9 Machine-hours: requirements and availability

Department	Machine-hours required per truck		Total machine-hours available per month
	Model U01	Model U02	
Engine assembly	1.0	2.0	4000
Metal stamping	2.0	2.0	6000
Model U01 assembly	2.0	–	5000
Model U02 assembly	–	3.0	4500

Unimog's production schedule for the first 6 months had resulted in a monthly output of 1000 Model U01 trucks and 1500 Model U02 trucks. As this level of production, Model U02 assembly and engine assembly were operating at capacity. However, metal stamping and Model U01 assembly were operating at only 83.3% and 40% of capacity, respectively. Table 12.10 gives standard costs at this level of production; Table 12.11 gives details on overhead costs.

A meeting of the controller, sales manager, and production manager was arranged to discuss production decisions. "I have been studying the figures for standard costs for the two truck models," the sales manager began. "Why don't we just stop making Model U01 trucks? As I see it, we are losing $1205 for each Model U01 truck we sell." One Model U01 truck sold for $60,000, and one Model U02 truck sold for $59,500.

The controller objected. "The real problem is that we are trying to absorb the entire fixed overhead of Model U01 assembly over only 1000 trucks. We would be better off increasing production of Model U01 trucks and cutting back, if necessary, on Model U02 production."

The production manager entered the discussion. "There is a way to increase Model U01 production without cutting back on Model U02 production," he said. "We can relieve the capacity problem in engine assembly by purchasing Model

Table 12.10 Standard product costs

		Model 101	Model 102
Direct materials		$36,000.00	$30,000.00
Direct labor			
	Engine assembly	$1800.00	$3600.00
	Metal stamping	$1200.00	$900.00
	Final assembly	$3000.00	$2250.00
Overhead[a]			
	Engine assembly	$3787.50	$7275.00
	Metal stamping	$5220.00	$4620.00
	Final assembly	$9300.00	$5250.00
	Total	$60,307.50	$53,895.00

[a]Based on a monthly production rate of 1000 Model U01 trucks and 1500 Model U02 trucks.

Table 12.11 Overhead budget

Department	Total overhead per month (millions)	Fixed overhead per month[a] (millions)	Variable overhead per month[b] (millions)	Variable overhead units	
				Model 101	Model 102
Engine assembly	14.70	2.55	12.15	$3150.00	$6000.00
Metal stamping	12.15	4.05	8.10	$3600.00	$3000.00
Model 101 assembly	9.30	4.05	5.25	$5250.00	
Model 102 assembly	7.88	2.25	5.63		$3750.00
Total	44.03	12.90	31.13	$12,000.00	$12,750.00

[a]Based on a monthly production rate of 1000 Model U01 trucks and 1500 Model U02 trucks.
[b]Fixed overhead was distributed to the two truck models in proportion to the degree of capacity utilization.

U01 or Model U02 engines from an outside supplier. If we pursue this alternative, I suggest we furnish the necessary materials and engine components and reimburse the supplier for labor and overhead."

Chatham Shipping

The Chatham Company was one of the country's leading manufacturers and distributors of a line of packaged goods that it sold nationally under the trade name of American Products. The company operated three factories from which it shipped to five regional warehouses.

Demand for American Products last year was 3,200,000 "equivalent" cases, distributed according to the five sales regions as shown in Table 12.12.

Annual production capacity in each of the three plants is listed in Table 12.13.

Estimated freight costs per case from each of the factories to each distribution center are given in Table 12.14. Although not all shipments were routed through regional warehouses, on average the freight cost on direct shipments to outlets was quite close to the cost that would have been incurred if the shipment had been routed through the servicing warehouse.

Chatham followed a philosophy of decentralized management. Top executives favored this approach for several reasons. First, by enriching the experience of subordinate managers, it provided better training for ultimate top management responsibility. Second, it insured that, insofar as possible, operating decisions were made by those persons most familiar with the detailed circumstances that would determine the success or failure of the decisions. Under the decentralized approach, subordinate managers were held responsible for the profitability of operations under their control. Consistent

Table 12.12 Demand forecast by sales region

Sales region	Demand forecast (100,000 cases)
Atlanta	5
Los Angeles	4
Dallas	4
Chicago	11
New York	8
Total	32

Table 12.13 Production capacities by plant

Plant	Production capacity (100,000 cases)
Denver	12
Memphis	7
Santa Fe	15
Total	34

Table 12.14 Schedule of freight rates (dollars per case)

Factory	Regional warehouse				
	Atlanta	Los Angeles	Dallas	Chicago	New York
Denver	6.65	7.35	5.60	1.05	7.00
Memphis	2.45	12.60	9.80	5.60	2.10
Santa Fe	6.30	12.60	11.20	4.90	5.95

with the policy of decentralization, each of the five regional warehouses was under the direct supervision of a regional sales manager. The warehouses were not assigned to a particular plant for servicing, as demand shifts made a certain amount of flexibility necessary. Rather, the regional sales manager or a delegate subordinate decided upon which plant to place an order. The price paid by the warehouse was $66.25 per case FOB the plant. This price was set to recover costs plus a reasonable return on investment for the manufacturing division (variable costs of manufacture were quite similar in the three plants). Since the regional warehouse was required to absorb the freight costs, it was expected that the regional sales managers would place their orders so as to minimize their own freight costs and hence those of the company as a whole.

Over a period of time, this procedure had led to increasing amounts of organizational friction, and some officials of Chatham were beginning to question whether the procedure was even achieving the objective minimizing freight costs. Because Santa Fe was not the least expensive plant for any of the regional warehouses, it was never deliberately selected as a source by a regional sales manager. Rather, the managers would initially order from Denver or Memphis, whichever was closer. Since these plants had inadequate capacity to meet all sales demands, it was then necessary for the plant managers to reject some orders. No consistent procedure was followed in determining which orders would be accepted, but it was largely a matter of "first-come, first-served." The regional managers whose orders were rejected were then usually forced to take them to Santa Fe, typically at a considerable increase in freight cost. This aspect of the situation resulted in much grumbling by the regional managers.

Moreover, since the orders placed with Santa Fe were not placed there in a conscious effort to minimize freight costs, there appeared to be a strong possibility that the resulting overall shipping program was not optimal. For this reason, some executives felt that the practice of leaving shipping decisions to the decentralized judgments of regional managers should be discontinued. They proposed instead that all orders be routed through a central office that could then determine an optimal shipping program from an overall company point of view. The actual quantities shipped over each possible route last year are given in Table 12.15. Total shipping costs that year were about $15,925,000.

Other executives were concerned about the effect such a proposal would have on the general effectiveness of decentralized management. They also observed that one result of the proposal would be to saddle the regional sales managers with freight costs over which they could exercise no control.

Hanover Compressors

Emma Wood, general manager of the compressor manufacturing department of Hanover Industrial Company, quickly spotted the reports that she had been waiting for in the pile of mail that had accumulated during her trip to a West Coast industrial equipment trade show. A sales forecast and a cost tabulation for a proposed new, light-weight compressor provided her with the information she needed to ascertain whether or not to introduce it, what volume to produce, and what price to charge.

Hanover was a major supplier of automatic industrial paint systems (used for painting newly manufactured goods like agricultural machinery, metal furniture, and appliances) and related industrial equipment. The compressor department manufactured a standard compressor for use in the company's paint systems and for a wide variety of other purposes as well. Ms. Wood was recently promoted to her present position in recognition of her strong technical and managerial capabilities. The company employed almost 1200 persons and had more than $200 million in sales.

The sales forecast, shown in Table 12.16, from the marketing department for the new product looked promising. The numbers seemed to indicate an upper price limit of $7500 to $8000 and a maximum demand of approximately 30 units per week. Although the lower weight and size made the new compressor attractive for certain applications, it was less rugged than the standard unit. It also required customers with standard units to carry another set of spare parts.

Table 12.15 Shipping program in the previous year (100,000 cases)

Factory	Regional warehouse					
	Atlanta	**Los Angeles**	**Dallas**	**Chicago**	**New York**	**Total**
Denver	0	1	2	9	0	12
Memphis	3	0	0	2	2	7
Santa Fe	2	3	2	0	6	13
Total	5	4	4	11	8	32

Table 12.16 Sales forecast for the light-weight compressor

Price	Units per week
$5500	31
$6000	30
$6500	28
$7000	24
$7500	17
$8000	10

Table 12.17 Light weight compressor per unit cost estimate

Direct labor	$1250	(wages and benefits)
Material	1463	
Other direct charges	137	(power, materials handling, etc.)
Depreciation	1406	
Other mfg. overheads	152	
Cost of goods sold	$4408	
Sales	1102	(25% of COGS)
General & administrative	441	(10% of COGS)
Total cost per unit	$5951	

The cost figures for the new product that had been prepared by the production engineering department were higher than Ms. Wood had anticipated. The cost figures are shown in Table 12.17. This was of some concern to her since the compressor department was operating at full capacity, and the new unit therefore would have to generate a higher return than the standard product to justify displacement.

Standard compressors
The compressor plant, capable of producing four standard compressors per day, operated two shifts for 6 days weekly. (The union contract restricted Hanover from running a third shift. This time, however, could be used for routine maintenance and special repairs.) Ten of the 24 units produced each week were required as a component for the automatic paint systems sold by the company. The remaining units were sold on the open market through industrial distributors to meet whatever demand there might be for this common product. The 50 direct labor employees averaged $20 per hour in wages and benefits during the normal week. They received time-and-one-half on Saturday and double-time on Sunday. The plant was closed on Sunday because the higher labor costs resulted in an operating loss for each unit produced. Table 12.18 presents the standard model compressor profit and loss, and Table 12.19 presents the estimated weekly compressor department profit.

Light-weight compressors
Because of its design, the new compressor could be manufactured on Hanover's new numerical control machinery instead of the older equipment used to make the standard unit. As a result, each unit required only 62.5 hours of direct labor as compared to the 100 hours for the standard model. The cost savings in labor and materials were partly offset by the higher depreciation charges resulting from the use of more expensive machinery. The company had added certain features to the machinery center to accommodate the manufacturing process for the new compressor. The extra hardware and hoists already installed had cost $417,000. Additional jigs, sensors, and software were expected to add another $218,000 to this total. Both of these amounts had been taken into account in calculating the depreciation charge for the new compressors.

Table 12.18 Standard model compressor profit and loss

	Weekdays	Saturday	Sunday
Price	$10,000		
Direct labor	$2000	$3000	$4000
Material	$3244	$3244	$3244
Other direct charges	$156	$156	$156
Depreciation	$497	$497	$497
Other mfg. overheads	$177	$177	$177
Cost of goods sold	$6074	$7074	$8074
Sales	$1519	$1769	$2019
General & administrative	$607	$707	$807
total cost per unit	$8200	$9550	$10,900
Profit per unit	$1800	$450	($900)
Return on sales	18%	4.5%	Negative

Table 12.19 Compressor department profit (weekly)

Monday–Friday	20 units x $1800 =	$36,000
Saturday	4 units x $450 =	$1800
Sunday	None	0
Department profits per week		$37,800

As Ms. Wood prepared to analyze the numbers, she was relieved to see that despite the high costs for the new compressor, it could still generate a higher profit than the standard unit. With that bit of encouragement, she set out to calculate the price and volume for the new compressor that would result in the best financial return. Because of practical difficulties in changing purchasing orders, production scheduling, and price lists, Hanover had a policy of limiting any changes in manufacturing and marketing plans to twice a year. Revisions were normally made in November and May. Exceptions could be made but were embarrassing to the managers making such requests.

Leisure Air

Revenue management involves managing the short-term demand for a fixed perishable inventory to maximize the revenue potential for an organization. The methodology, originally developed for American Airlines, was first used to determine how many airline flight seats to sell at an early reservation discount fare and how many airline flight seats to sell at a full fare. By making the optimal decision for the number of discount-fare seats and the number of full-fare seats on each flight, the airline is able to increase its average number of passengers per flight and maximize the total revenue generated by the combined sale of discount-fare and full-fare seats. Today, all major airlines use some form of revenue management.

Given the success of revenue management in the airline industry, it was not long before other industries began using revenue management. Modern systems have been expanded to include pricing strategies, overbooking policies, short-term supply decisions, and the management of nonperishable assets. Application areas now include hotels, apartment rentals, car rentals, cruise lines, and golf courses.

The development of a revenue management system can be expensive and time consuming, but the potential payoffs can be substantial. For instance, the revenue management system used at American Airlines generates nearly $1 billion in annual incremental revenue. To illustrate the fundamentals of revenue management, consider a revenue management plan for Leisure Air, a regional airline that provides service for Pittsburgh, Newark, Charlotte, Hilton Head, and Orlando.

Leisure Air has two Boeing 737 airplanes: one based in Pittsburgh and the other in Newark. Both airplanes have a coach section with a 132-seat capacity. Each morning, the Pittsburgh-based plane flies to Orlando with a stopover in

Table 12.20 Fare and demand data for origin-destination-itinerary fares

ODIF	Origin	Destination	Fare class	ODIF code	Fare ($)	Forecasted demand
1	Pittsburgh	Charlotte	Q	PCQ	178	33
2	Pittsburgh	Hilton Head	Q	PHQ	268	44
3	Pittsburgh	Orlando	Q	POQ	228	45
4	Pittsburgh	Charlotte	Y	PCY	380	16
5	Pittsburgh	Hilton Head	Y	PHY	456	6
6	Pittsburgh	Orlando	Y	POY	560	11
7	Newark	Charlotte	Q	NCQ	199	26
8	Newark	Hilton Head	Q	NHQ	249	56
9	Newark	Orlando	Q	NOQ	349	39
10	Newark	Charlotte	Y	NCY	385	15
11	Newark	Hilton Head	Y	NHY	444	7
12	Newark	Orlando	Y	NOY	580	9
13	Charlotte	Hilton Head	Q	CHQ	179	64
14	Charlotte	Hilton Head	Y	CHY	380	8
15	Charlotte	Orlando	Q	COQ	224	46
16	Charlotte	Orlando	Y	COY	582	10

Charlotte, and the Newark-based plane flies to Hilton Head, also with a stopover in Charlotte. At the end of the day, both planes return to their home bases. To keep the size of the problem reasonable, consider only the Pittsburgh–Charlotte, Charlotte–Orlando, Newark–Charlotte, and Charlotte–Hilton Head flight legs for the morning flights.

Leisure Air uses two fare classes: a discount-fare Q class and a full-fare Y class. Reservations using the discount-fare Q class must be made 14 days in advance and must include a Saturday night stay in the destination city. Reservations using the full-fare Y class may be made anytime, with no penalty for changing the reservations at a later date. To determine the itinerary and fare alternatives that Leisure Air can offer its customers, we must consider not only the origin and the destination of each flight but also the fare class. For instance, possible products include Pittsburgh to Charlotte using Q class, Newark to Orlando using Q class, Charlotte to Hilton Head using Y class, and so on. Each product is referred to as an origin-destination-itinerary fare (ODIF). For May 5, Leisure Air established fares and developed forecasts of customer demand for each of 16 ODIFs. These data are shown in Table 12.20.

Suppose that on April 8, a customer calls the Leisure Air reservation office and requests a Q class seat on the May 5 flight from Pittsburgh to Hilton Head. Should Leisure Air accept the reservation? The difficulty in making this decision is that even though Leisure Air may have seats available, the company may not want to accept this reservation at the Q class fare of $268, especially if it is possible to sell the same reservation later at the Y class fare of $456. Thus, determining how many Q and Y class seats to make available are important decisions that Leisure Air must make to operate its reservation system.

Hamilton Wireless

Hamilton Wireless is a medium-sized producer of wireless network products for industry. The company currently operates two plants: one in Clemmons, North Carolina, and one in Danville, Virginia. Hamilton's sales force is primarily paid by salary but also receives modest commissions.

The Clemmons Plant

Due to its rural location and favorable union contract, labor costs at the Clemmons plant are relatively low. The plant has also been recently renovated. Hamilton currently operates the Clemmons plant at full capacity, making three kinds of wireless network devices: *Express*, *Extra*, and *Extreme*. All products occupy competitive positions in the market such

Table 12.21 Clemmons plant production rates and availability

| Machine | Hours required per CU of production | | | Hours available per month |
	Express	Extra	Extreme	
Molder	0.1	0.2	0.4	7180
Stamper	0.1	0.2	0.1	6220
Packager		0.3	0.2	5240
Contribution/cu	$10.50	$22.00	$12.00	

Table 12.22 Monthly demand estimates for high-speed wireless device

Price (per cu)	Demand (cu/month)
$200	1600
$225	1300
$250	1000
$300	600

that Hamilton's output volume has no significant effect on the market price, and the company has little difficulty selling its entire output. Production is measured in "hundred units," abbreviated as "cu." The principal limitations on production at Clemmons are the availabilities of time on three types of machines: molder, stamper, and packager. Table 12.21 shows the total available hours per month for each kind of machine and the number of hours required to make a cu of each type of device. Table 12.21 also shows the contribution attributable to a cu of each of the three kinds of device, as calculated by Hamilton's operations department.

To cover general, administrative, and production development costs, Hamilton charges product lines produced at Clemmons an overhead allocation equal to 30% of direct factory cost.

The Danville plant

The Danville plant has higher labor costs than the Clemmons plant and has older equipment. Therefore, Hamilton operates the Danville plant well below capacity. Danville's current production is limited to older products, which Clemmons is not set up to make. Because factory-related overhead, such as insurance, must be spread over less production volume, the overhead percentage charged at Danville is 35% of factory cost, which is slightly higher than the rate at Clemmons. However, depreciation charges at Danville are lower due to the older equipment.

A new product line: high-speed wireless

Hamilton's engineering group has recently patented a new process for making a high-speed wireless device, a specialty product that Hamilton has not produced previously. Management feels that the new product should give Hamilton a large cost advantage over the smaller firms that are now making such wireless products and should enable it to become the dominant US producer for at least the next 3 years.

Due to the relatively small and specialized market for the high-speed wireless device, demand for the new product is expected to vary significantly depending on the price Hamilton sets. Based on recent fluctuations in the market, Hamilton's marketing group has estimated the monthly demand for the new device at four different price levels, as shown in Table 12.22. Hamilton will use its existing sales staff to market the new wire. It has already been decided that Hamilton's salespeople will be paid a commission of $7.50 per cu of high-speed wireless devices sold.

Two options

Hamilton will have to invest in special equipment if it wishes to produce the high-speed wireless device. Management has decided that if Hamilton is to make the new wireless device, it will initially produce it at only one plant. One option would

Table 12.23 Total cost estimates for the high-speed wireless device

Costs	Clemmons	Danville
Materials	$45.00	$45.00
Direct Labor	$23.00	$39.00
Maintenance and power[a]	$7.50	$9.00
Depreciation	$8.23	$2.57
Factory cost	$83.73	$95.57
Sales[b]	$20.93	$23.89
G&A[c]	$25.12	$33.45
Total	$129.78	$152.91

[a]"Maintenance" includes all repair and maintenance expenses to maintain machinery in full working condition. Hamilton typically replaces machines only for reasons of obsolescence. Maintenance and power expenses can be avoided by turning machinery off when not in use.
[b]Sales expenses are recovered by charging 25% of factory cost, regardless of the commission structure for a particular product.
[c]Thirty percent of factory cost at the Clemmons plant; 35% of the factory cost at the Danville plant.

be to make the device at the Danville plant, which would require roughly an investment of $650,000 in improvements and new equipment. The production process for the high-speed wireless device would make use of stamper equipment previously installed at Danville, but because of the spare capacity situation, this would not interfere with existing operations there.

Another option was to make the new wireless device at Clemmons, using Clemmons's existing stampers. Stamping one cu of the high-speed wireless device was estimated to take 0.7 hours of machine time. No use would be made of existing molding or packaging machines. Because of the Clemmons plant's better condition, setting it up to make the new wire would cost only $500,000.

Total cost estimates for making the new device at each plant are shown in Table 12.23. The new product would not require any additional supervisory staff.

Summary of simulation

A1.1 Overview of the simulation process

1. Identify the problem—what decisions are to be made?
2. What factors are given (data)?
3. Which factors are uncertain (random)? What distribution does each factor look like? For example, is it normal, uniform, historical?
4. What is the timing/precedence of events? Draw a decision tree if necessary!
5. How is "success" measured; how is the best policy going to be measured?
6. Construct one trial—based on a given policy. Proceed from left to right for each event in the correct time order.
7. Once you have one trial correct, repeat the trials a sufficient number of times (usually at least 100 trials) to create a single run that will give you a good idea of how the system is operating. The number of trials required depends on the complexity of the situation. Generally speaking, if the average of the set of trials is not stable, then more trials are needed. More trials are typically required if the situation has the following:
    a. Several random variables
    b. Several decisions
    c. Large variance in a random variable
8. Create several runs of your trials to determine the optimal policy. Data tables in Excel are a good method to use one set of trials to create several runs. For example, a set of 10 runs is 10 sets of trials.

Table A1.1 Summary of Properties of Common Probability Distributions *(cont.)*

A1.2 Review of probability distributions

Table A1.1 Summary of Properties of Common Probability Distributions

Distribution Continuous/discrete (c/d)	Description	$f(x)$	Mean & SD	Distribution
1. **TRIANGULAR** c	Subjective estimate from minimum, maximum, and most likely	n.a.	$(a + b + c)/3$ $((a^2 + b^2 + c^2 - ab - ac - bc)/6)^{.5}$	
2. **QUARTILE** c	Subjective estimate based on Median, Min, Max, and Quartiles	n.a.	n.a.	
3. **EMPIRICAL** c/d (Historical)	Collected data that does not fit a known distribution	$F(x) = \frac{\#x \leq X}{n}$	$\overline{X}$ sd	
4. **UNIFORM** c/d	No information—all events are equally likely	$1/(b - a)$ $1/(b - a + 1)$	$(a + b)/2$ $(b - a)/\sqrt{12}$	
5. **BINOMIAL** d	Two events—number of successes → proportion	$\frac{n!}{x!(n-x)!} p^x q^{(n-x)}$	np $\sqrt{np(1 - p)}$	
6. **POISSON** d	Number of events (occurrences) in a given amount of time	$\frac{e^{-\lambda} \lambda^x}{x!}$	λ(events/time) $\sqrt{\lambda}$	
7. **EXPONENTIAL** c	Time between events (occurrences)—frequently service/processing time	$\lambda e^{-\lambda x}$	$1/\lambda$(events/time) $1/\lambda$	
8. **NORMAL** c	Symmetric about mean—one "bump"— distribution of sums and averages	$\frac{1}{\sigma\sqrt{2\pi}} e^{-\frac{1}{2}\left(\frac{x-\mu}{\sigma}\right)}$	$\overline{x} = \mu$ sd $= \sigma$	

A1.3 Methods to simulate probability distributions

The methods to generate random numbers in Excel are divided into two categories:

1. Single formula
2. Using a corresponding table of probabilities, cumulative probabilities, and outcomes.

Some distributions, such as the uniform distribution, can be generated by either method. Examples of some commonly used probability distributions and their corresponding methods of generation are shown next according to whether they are generated by a single formula or with a corresponding table of cumulative probabilities.

A1.3.1 Random numbers by the single formula method

A1.3.1.1 Uniform

Parameters, with example values:

$$\text{LOWERBOUND} = 1$$
$$\text{UPPERBOUND} = 6$$

Discrete example:

$$= \text{TRUNC(RAND( ) * (UPPERBOUND} - \text{LOWERBOUND} + 1) + \text{LOWERBOUND})$$

Continuous example:

$$= \text{LOWERBOUND} + \text{RAND( ) * (UPPERBOUND} - \text{LOWERBOUND})$$

A1.3.1.2 Binomial

Parameter, with example value:

$$\text{Probability, } p, \text{ of "yes"} = 60\%$$

Example:

$$= \text{IF(RAND( )} < 0.60, \text{"Yes", "No")}$$

or, for (1 = yes, 0 = no):

$$= \text{(RAND ( )} < 0.60) * 1$$

A1.3.1.3 Triangular

Parameters, with example values:

> $min:a = 20$
> $most\ likely:c = 40$
> $max:b = 50$
> $range: (b - a) = 30$
> $range1: (c - a) = 20$
> $range2: (b - c) = 10$
> $F(c): (c - a)/(b - a) = 0.67$

Example:

rand# = 0.309

= IF $(rand\# < F(c)$, min + $(range * range1 * rand\#)^{0.5}$, max − $(range * range2 * (1 − rand\#))^{\wedge 0.5})$

or

= IF $(rand\# < F(most\ likely)$, min + $range1 * RAND()^{\wedge 0.5}$, max − $range2 * RAND()^{\wedge 0.5})$

A1.3.1.4 Normal

Parameters, with example values:

$$MEAN = 50$$
$$SD = 3$$

Example:

$$52.37 = MEAN + NORM.S.INV(RAND(\ )) * SD$$

Alternate versions:

$$52.37 = NORM.INV(RAND(\ ), MEAN, SD)$$
$$48.66 = MEAN + SD * SQRT(−2 * LN(RAND(\ ))) * COS(2 * PI(\ ) * RAND(\ ))$$

A1.3.1.5 Exponential

Parameter, with example value:

$$1/mean = MU = 4$$

Example:

$$= −LN(RAND(\ )) / MU$$

A1.3.2 Random numbers by method

A1.3.2.1 Poisson

Parameters, with example values:

$$LAMBDA = 4$$
$$rand\# = 0.63228 \quad \text{(this is cell C47 in the example)}$$

Example: = VLOOKUP(C47, POISSONTABLE, 2)

	Prob($A \le X$)	X	
	0.00000	0	(this is cell H64)
= POISSON(H64,LAMBDA,1) →	0.01832	1	
	0.09158	2	
	0.23810	3	
	0.43347	4	
	0.62884	5	
	0.78513	6	
	0.88933	7	

	0.94887	8	
	0.97864	9	
	0.99187	10	
	0.99716	11	
	0.99908	12	
	0.99973	13	
You will need to	0.99992	14	
continue the table further	0.99998	15	
for larger lambdas	1.00000	15	

A1.3.2.2 Empirical

(from data sorted smallest to largest)

    Example: $N = 20$

                 = VLOOKUP(RAND( ), PROBTABLE,

	Prob$(A \leq X)$	X (data)
	0.000	6
$= (Obs - 1)/N \rightarrow$	0.050	6
	0.100	7
	0.150	7
	0.200	7
	0.250	7
	0.300	7
	0.350	7
	0.400	8
	0.450	8
	0.500	8
	0.550	8
	0.600	8
	0.650	8
	0.700	9
	0.750	9
	0.800	9
	0.850	9
	0.900	10
	0.950	10
	1.000	10 (not a data point)

      From a set of data already in the format of a distribution:

                 = VLOOKUP(RAND( )), PROBTABLE2, 2),

where PROBTABLE2 is the last two columns in the following table:

Value (X)	Freq(X)	Prob($A = X$) (%)	Prob($A < X$)	X
6	2	10.00	0.00	6
7	6	30.00	0.10	7
8	6	30.00	0.40	8
9	4	20.00	0.70	9
10	2	10.00	0.90	10
TOTAL =	20		1.00	10

A1.3.2.3 Quartiles
Given the MEDIAN, MIN, MAX, and QUARTILES

$$\text{rand\#} = 0.115$$
$$= \text{VLOOKUP(rand\#, QTABLE, 3)} * \text{rand\#} + \text{VLOOKUP(rand\#, QTABLE, 4)},$$

where QTABLE is the following table:

Quartile (%)	Value	Slope	Intercept
0	150	120	150
25	180	80	160
50	200	40	180
75	210	120	120
100	240	120	120

$Slope = (Value_2 - Value_1)/(Quartile_2 - Quartile_1) = \Delta Y/\Delta X$
$Intercept = Value - Slope*(Quartile) = Y - Slope(X)$

Statistical tables

A2.1 Normal distribution

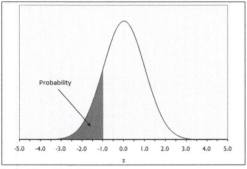

Standard Normal Probabilities

z	0.00	0.01	0.02	0.03	0.04	0.05	0.06	0.07	0.08	0.09
-3.5	0.00023	0.00022	0.00022	0.00021	0.00020	0.00019	0.00019	0.00018	0.00017	0.00017
-3.4	0.00034	0.00032	0.00031	0.00030	0.00029	0.00028	0.00027	0.00026	0.00025	0.00024
-3.3	0.00048	0.00047	0.00045	0.00043	0.00042	0.00040	0.00039	0.00038	0.00036	0.00035
-3.2	0.00069	0.00066	0.00064	0.00062	0.00060	0.00058	0.00056	0.00054	0.00052	0.00050
-3.1	0.00097	0.00094	0.00090	0.00087	0.00084	0.00082	0.00079	0.00076	0.00074	0.00071
-3.0	0.00135	0.00131	0.00126	0.00122	0.00118	0.00114	0.00111	0.00107	0.00104	0.00100
-2.9	0.00187	0.00181	0.00175	0.00169	0.00164	0.00159	0.00154	0.00149	0.00144	0.00139
-2.8	0.00256	0.00248	0.00240	0.00233	0.00226	0.00219	0.00212	0.00205	0.00199	0.00193
-2.7	0.00347	0.00336	0.00326	0.00317	0.00307	0.00298	0.00289	0.00280	0.00272	0.00264
-2.6	0.00466	0.00453	0.00440	0.00427	0.00415	0.00402	0.00391	0.00379	0.00368	0.00357
-2.5	0.00621	0.00604	0.00587	0.00570	0.00554	0.00539	0.00523	0.00508	0.00494	0.00480
-2.4	0.00820	0.00798	0.00776	0.00755	0.00734	0.00714	0.00695	0.00676	0.00657	0.00639
-2.3	0.01072	0.01044	0.01017	0.00990	0.00964	0.00939	0.00914	0.00889	0.00866	0.00842
-2.2	0.01390	0.01355	0.01321	0.01287	0.01255	0.01222	0.01191	0.01160	0.01130	0.01101
-2.1	0.01786	0.01743	0.01700	0.01659	0.01618	0.01578	0.01539	0.01500	0.01463	0.01426
-2.0	0.02275	0.02222	0.02169	0.02118	0.02068	0.02018	0.01970	0.01923	0.01876	0.01831
-1.9	0.02872	0.02807	0.02743	0.02680	0.02619	0.02559	0.02500	0.02442	0.02385	0.02330
-1.8	0.03593	0.03515	0.03438	0.03362	0.03288	0.03216	0.03144	0.03074	0.03005	0.02938
-1.7	0.04457	0.04363	0.04272	0.04182	0.04093	0.04006	0.03920	0.03836	0.03754	0.03673
-1.6	0.05480	0.05370	0.05262	0.05155	0.05050	0.04947	0.04846	0.04746	0.04648	0.04551
-1.5	0.06681	0.06552	0.06426	0.06301	0.06178	0.06057	0.05938	0.05821	0.05705	0.05592
-1.4	0.08076	0.07927	0.07780	0.07636	0.07493	0.07353	0.07215	0.07078	0.06944	0.06811
-1.3	0.09680	0.09510	0.09342	0.09176	0.09012	0.08851	0.08691	0.08534	0.08379	0.08226
-1.2	0.11507	0.11314	0.11123	0.10935	0.10749	0.10565	0.10383	0.10204	0.10027	0.09853
-1.1	0.13567	0.13350	0.13136	0.12924	0.12714	0.12507	0.12302	0.12100	0.11900	0.11702
-1.0	0.15866	0.15625	0.15386	0.15151	0.14917	0.14686	0.14457	0.14231	0.14007	0.13786
-0.9	0.18406	0.18141	0.17879	0.17619	0.17361	0.17106	0.16853	0.16602	0.16354	0.16109
-0.8	0.21186	0.20897	0.20611	0.20327	0.20045	0.19766	0.19489	0.19215	0.18943	0.18673
-0.7	0.24196	0.23885	0.23576	0.23270	0.22965	0.22663	0.22363	0.22065	0.21770	0.21476
-0.6	0.27425	0.27093	0.26763	0.26435	0.26109	0.25785	0.25463	0.25143	0.24825	0.24510
-0.5	0.30854	0.30503	0.30153	0.29806	0.29460	0.29116	0.28774	0.28434	0.28096	0.27760
-0.4	0.34458	0.34090	0.33724	0.33360	0.32997	0.32636	0.32276	0.31918	0.31561	0.31207
-0.3	0.38209	0.37828	0.37448	0.37070	0.36693	0.36317	0.35942	0.35569	0.35197	0.34827
-0.2	0.42074	0.41683	0.41294	0.40905	0.40517	0.40129	0.39743	0.39358	0.38974	0.38591
-0.1	0.46017	0.45620	0.45224	0.44828	0.44433	0.44038	0.43644	0.43251	0.42858	0.42465
0.0	0.50000	0.49601	0.49202	0.48803	0.48405	0.48006	0.47608	0.47210	0.46812	0.46414

FIGURE A2.1

Normal Distribution, $z \leq 0$

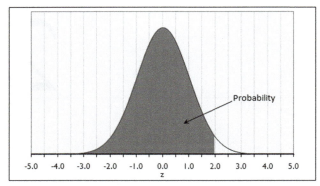

Standard Normal Probabilities

z	0.00	0.01	0.02	0.03	0.04	0.05	0.06	0.07	0.08	0.09
0.0	0.50000	0.50399	0.50798	0.51197	0.51595	0.51994	0.52392	0.52790	0.53188	0.53586
0.1	0.53983	0.54380	0.54776	0.55172	0.55567	0.55962	0.56356	0.56749	0.57142	0.57535
0.2	0.57926	0.58317	0.58706	0.59095	0.59483	0.59871	0.60257	0.60642	0.61026	0.61409
0.3	0.61791	0.62172	0.62552	0.62930	0.63307	0.63683	0.64058	0.64431	0.64803	0.65173
0.4	0.65542	0.65910	0.66276	0.66640	0.67003	0.67364	0.67724	0.68082	0.68439	0.68793
0.5	0.69146	0.69497	0.69847	0.70194	0.70540	0.70884	0.71226	0.71566	0.71904	0.72240
0.6	0.72575	0.72907	0.73237	0.73565	0.73891	0.74215	0.74537	0.74857	0.75175	0.75490
0.7	0.75804	0.76115	0.76424	0.76730	0.77035	0.77337	0.77637	0.77935	0.78230	0.78524
0.8	0.78814	0.79103	0.79389	0.79673	0.79955	0.80234	0.80511	0.80785	0.81057	0.81327
0.9	0.81594	0.81859	0.82121	0.82381	0.82639	0.82894	0.83147	0.83398	0.83646	0.83891
1.0	0.84134	0.84375	0.84614	0.84849	0.85083	0.85314	0.85543	0.85769	0.85993	0.86214
1.1	0.86433	0.86650	0.86864	0.87076	0.87286	0.87493	0.87698	0.87900	0.88100	0.88298
1.2	0.88493	0.88686	0.88877	0.89065	0.89251	0.89435	0.89617	0.89796	0.89973	0.90147
1.3	0.90320	0.90490	0.90658	0.90824	0.90988	0.91149	0.91309	0.91466	0.91621	0.91774
1.4	0.91924	0.92073	0.92220	0.92364	0.92507	0.92647	0.92785	0.92922	0.93056	0.93189
1.5	0.93319	0.93448	0.93574	0.93699	0.93822	0.93943	0.94062	0.94179	0.94295	0.94408
1.6	0.94520	0.94630	0.94738	0.94845	0.94950	0.95053	0.95154	0.95254	0.95352	0.95449
1.7	0.95543	0.95637	0.95728	0.95818	0.95907	0.95994	0.96080	0.96164	0.96246	0.96327
1.8	0.96407	0.96485	0.96562	0.96638	0.96712	0.96784	0.96856	0.96926	0.96995	0.97062
1.9	0.97128	0.97193	0.97257	0.97320	0.97381	0.97441	0.97500	0.97558	0.97615	0.97670
2.0	0.97725	0.97778	0.97831	0.97882	0.97932	0.97982	0.98030	0.98077	0.98124	0.98169
2.1	0.98214	0.98257	0.98300	0.98341	0.98382	0.98422	0.98461	0.98500	0.98537	0.98574
2.2	0.98610	0.98645	0.98679	0.98713	0.98745	0.98778	0.98809	0.98840	0.98870	0.98899
2.3	0.98928	0.98956	0.98983	0.99010	0.99036	0.99061	0.99086	0.99111	0.99134	0.99158
2.4	0.99180	0.99202	0.99224	0.99245	0.99266	0.99286	0.99305	0.99324	0.99343	0.99361
2.5	0.99379	0.99396	0.99413	0.99430	0.99446	0.99461	0.99477	0.99492	0.99506	0.99520
2.6	0.99534	0.99547	0.99560	0.99573	0.99585	0.99598	0.99609	0.99621	0.99632	0.99643
2.7	0.99653	0.99664	0.99674	0.99683	0.99693	0.99702	0.99711	0.99720	0.99728	0.99736
2.8	0.99744	0.99752	0.99760	0.99767	0.99774	0.99781	0.99788	0.99795	0.99801	0.99807
2.9	0.99813	0.99819	0.99825	0.99831	0.99836	0.99841	0.99846	0.99851	0.99856	0.99861
3.0	0.99865	0.99869	0.99874	0.99878	0.99882	0.99886	0.99889	0.99893	0.99896	0.99900
3.1	0.99903	0.99906	0.99910	0.99913	0.99916	0.99918	0.99921	0.99924	0.99926	0.99929
3.2	0.99931	0.99934	0.99936	0.99938	0.99940	0.99942	0.99944	0.99946	0.99948	0.99950
3.3	0.99952	0.99953	0.99955	0.99957	0.99958	0.99960	0.99961	0.99962	0.99964	0.99965
3.4	0.99966	0.99968	0.99969	0.99970	0.99971	0.99972	0.99973	0.99974	0.99975	0.99976
3.5	0.99977	0.99978	0.99978	0.99979	0.99980	0.99981	0.99981	0.99981	0.99982	0.99983	0.99983

FIGURE A2.2

Normal Distribution, $z \geq 0$